REFLECTIONS
OF A STATESMAN

Also published:
COLLECTED POEMS

REFLECTIONS OF A STATESMAN

The Writings and Speeches of
ENOCH POWELL

Selected by Rex Collings

BELLEW PUBLISHING
London

First published in Great Britain in 1991 by
Bellew Publishing Company Ltd
7 Southampton Place, London WC1A 2DR

Collection copyright © Enoch Powell 1991

ISBN 0 947792 88 0

Designed by Bob Vickers

Phototypeset by Intype Ltd, London

Printed and bound in Great Britain by
Billing & Sons Ltd, Worcester

CONTENTS

ACKNOWLEDGEMENTS

Grateful acknowledgement is made to the following for permission to reprint the material in this book:

The *BBC* for kind permission to reproduce 'Panorama', an Interview with Anne Brown, 'Sue Lawley's Desert Island Discussions', 'The Great Debate', 'The Great Prayer', 'Whitehall and Beyond', 'The Parliamentarians', 'Jewel in the Constitution?', 'Disraeli's One Nation', 'Churchill and the War', 'Any Questions', and 'Race and Immigration'.

The *Trinity Review* for 'Politicians and Other Artists'.

Radio Clyde for the article 'Towards 2000'.

To *Times Newspapers Limited* for the following: 'Losing the peace' *Sunday Times*, 6 November 1983; 'A Life in the day of . . .', *Sunday Times Magazine*, 11 May 1986; 'Not necessarily so', *The Times*, 4 March 1972; 'Why Washington has its own plans for the Falklands', *The Times*, 29 June 1982; 'Dancing to the Washington tune', *The Times*, 17 September 1983; 'What Commonwealth?' *The Times*, 26 January 1984; 'End this fiction', *The Times*, 17 July 1986; 'Rab Butler: the man who saw his prize snatched away', *The Times*, 10 March 1982; 'But parsimony spoilt all chances of a sentimental goodbye', *The Times*, 8 July 1960.

To *The Times Supplements Limited* for 'Pommy Professor' which first appeared in *The Times Educational Supplement* and 'Social Services' which first appeared in *The Times Health Supplement*.

'On Translation' reproduced from a speech given at The Third Annual Folio Literary Dinner & Debate, 1987.

To the *Spectator* for the articles 'How Macmillan Deceived the Queen', 'Superwhig?' 'Harold Wilson', 'No Answers Blowing in the Wind', 'The Archetypal Demagogue', 'Office Before Honour', 'Envy', 'Giving Away the Rod' and 'The Causes of Suez'.

The extracts from 'Face the Press' are reproduced by permission of *Tyne Tees Television*.

To the *Birmingham Post* for the article 'Influences that Shape Party Programmes'.

The article 'Sovereignty' is reproduced from *Freedom and Stability in World Economy* published by Croom Helm Methuen, London, 1976.

To the *British Medical Journal* for the article 'Human Rights' which was first published in the *Journal of Medical Ethics*, 1977.

Whilst all reasonable attempts have been made to contact the relevant copyright holders, the Publishers would be happy to hear from those they have been unable to trace, and due acknowledgement will be made in future editions.

EDITOR'S NOTE

'I see seven archbishops, which one shall I paint?' The portraitist's cry of frustration could be echoed by any biographer or, indeed, by the selector who seeks by choice of the subject's own words to present a true and recognisable portrait of their originator. Selection implies both rejection and suppression; even were this volume twice or thrice its size the picture presented would tend to be a caricature, too much emphasis perhaps on the Ulster Warrior, too little on the Parliament Man; and what has happened to the Romantic Poet, Housman's follower, where is the admirer of the Hunting Grocer, where the eager Wagnerite frequently waiting in the anterooms of Valhalla? The image in the glass is distorted but not unrecognisable, for the glass, like one of those fairground mirrors, distorts the reflection; it is not so much that the lookers are expected to 'agree to a short armistice with truth'* but rather that they should accept that not all seven archbishops can be present.

Except in the case of Powell the Parliamentarian the material is presented under broad subject headings. In the matter of the speeches made in Parliament it was thought that these should be together, for they show the man in the forum of which above all others he was master.

Rex Collings

---

* No, not Lord (Sir Robert) Armstrong but Byron: *Don Juan*, Canto III, Stanza 88

FOREWORD

I am indebted to Rex Collings and to his publisher for having done for me what I could not possibly have done for myself – so much so, that I can forgive them for having used in the title the term 'statesman', which I have always eschewed as a niminy-piminy equivalent for the straightforward, honest word 'politician'. 'Politics' has been my profession for close on fifty years, and I am not ashamed of having learnt that profession where alone it can be learnt, in the hard school of practice.

In the governance of a nation the darker and less avowable aspects of human nature have, and always have had, to be managed as they present themselves both in those who are governed and in those who do the governing. Without that management, government would be impracticable; and those folk are either ignorant or insincere who affect to avert their gaze from human nature in that context.

It has been my good fortune to find the means in my political life of doing what I wanted most to do. That was to discourse, in speech or writing, to my fellow citizens about the future, the past and the present of their country, and from time to time to catch and hold their attention. I did it in my own way and in my own language. The vicissitudes, however, of my political life enabled me, for most of the time, to choose my topics and to voice my reflections without taking into account the reactions of the Whips' Office or the repercussions upon any prospect of ministerial or other reward.

There is no particular merit about that. If an act of choice was involved, it was a choice implicit already in my own personality. I do not deny that I would like to have been Secretary of State for Defence or Chancellor of the Exchequer; but that would have been at the price of renouncing the freedom to speak my mind on matters which seemed to me to be of transcendent interest and importance and on which my own conclusions were out of line with commonly accepted views, conclusions and conventions. To decline to pay that price was a renunciation which proved to be congenial; but to avow this casts no aspersion on colleagues whose choice was different. The balance and vitality of a political system such as Britain has evolved depends upon those who form its centre of gravity as much as upon those who operate on its periphery.

There have been two subjects upon which I exercised my liberty of self-expression most audibly. One was the tardiness and consequently the incompleteness with which Britain after the Second World War provided itself with a modern law of citizenship and reformed the ancient feudal law which classified the huge populations of countries already self-governing as 'British subjects' with the right of entry and abode in the United Kingdom. I could, and perhaps I should, have done more to awaken by fellow citizens to the consequences, as yet unexhausted, of indulging in their daydream of a British Empire which had transformed itself into a Commonwealth equally glorious and powerful.

On the second subject I had the opportunity, which I took to the utmost of my power, to warn my fellow countrymen against surrendering to the European Community their historic right to make their laws, impose their taxes and settle their policies through their representatives in their own parliament. I am not aware of any occasion when I avoidably failed to denounce that surrender. I have never since regretted that I kept myself clear of responsibility for it when I gave up an English seat in Parliament in 1974. It would have been worth any sacrifice to continue to warn and advise against the loss of a free nation's liberties. In the event I was given the bonus of an unexpected extension of my parliamentary life by thirteen years during which I helped to represent the majority in Northern Ireland who, despite all that the United Kingdom had surrendered, still steadfastly voted to remain part of it and of its Parliament.

However, I set out to express my thanks to the makers of this book. Anybody who speaks and writes for fifty years leaves behind him an appalling trail of verbiage. Some there are, including some in politics, who conscientiously preserve and classify all that debris. I have a confession to make. I have been intolerably careless with my debris. Admittedly, I tucked it away, not complete but as chance permitted, and stored it in fireproof safes. It was by no means all political; for I am not all political myself. I was decoyed in the course of essay-writing or reviewing or lecturing into the pursuit of special interests, such as the history of the churches of England, and the results accumulated with the rest of the archive, buried and, as far as the author was concerned, forgotten.

It is, I know, a deplorable story of indifference, and it forms the occasion for an even graver confession. I must be in some way different from my contemporaries, by whose autobiographies and memoirs I am incessantly bombarded; but the very idea of sitting down to write such a book fills me with a sensation that I can only compare to nausea. The stomach turns over at the mere contemplation of setting out to plough through one's past documentation and then digesting it into a kind of spurious history: 'at this point, I made a speech, in which I said the following . . .'; or 'invited by the *Daily Telegraph* to intervene in this controversy, I wrote . . .'

In this predicament, still feeling guiltily ignorant or oblivious of what lurked in my safes, there came to my rescue someone who would actually sift through all the stuff for the first time and arrange it, as he did so, to form a kind of pattern which would not be of my devising; and behind him was discernible the figure of a publisher sufficiently courageous, or perhaps imaginative, to identify a public which would be inquisitive enough to be interested in the earlier stages or the unsuspected vagaries of a tale that is told. So there I am, saved, rescued: there is, after all, no duty incumbent upon me to relive all those events, with their lights and shadows, twists and turns. I can, without qualm of conscience, uncover a past over which the tombstone of oblivion had been laid. I do not even have to claim to have been right or wrong. Others may note with quizzical amusement how in the meantime old controversies have surfaced again, with much the same arguments and the same conundrums. Did I hear somebody murmur something just then about 'fixed' or 'floating' rates of exchange?

Above all, I have been preserved from the gross presumption of appearing to know what others ought to find interesting in thoughts and words now beyond the reach of influencing or being influenced. The supreme benefit which such a book as this confers upon its principal character is to restore to him the unity of his personality. That is something which a simple collection of speeches cannot do. There they stare back at him, the separate personal reactions to specific and changing situations: the speaker remains fragmented. That somebody reading what had been said or written found in it sufficient unity and consistency to be arranged to create a book, restores faith in one's continuing identity, and very often reveals an underlying continuity of which sight had been lost and which it had seemed too presumptuous to assume. There must after all be a person there, living, feeling, teaching in obedience to an internal imperative.

There are, I believe, philosophers who claim that memory is the only valid evidence of a person's identity through time. If 'I' can remember what 'I' felt and said and did at a past moment, that must surely be the same 'I' who is here and now. The experience happened to me before. It happened when my late friend John Wood in 1965 threaded speeches of mine on to his string and created *A Nation Not Afraid*, which became a precedent for *Freedom and Reality* (1969) and *Still to Decide* (1972), a precedent which Richard Ritchie to my repeated astonishment successfully followed in subsequent years. Those books have been for me a reassurance and a compendium of evidence.

Rex Collings has stood off at a somewhat greater distance and thereby, it seems to me, perceived more of the landscape. For the first time, he insisted on overstepping the boundaries of politics and tracing some of my excursions outside them. That too is a reintegrating experience. Perhaps, after all, my reflections upon the replacement of a Saxon chancel by a Norman apse draw upon the same source as my appeals to my fellow citizens to defend the inheritance which their fathers fashioned in the last thousand years.

J. Enoch Powell,
London,
August 1991

PART ONE

POWELL THE MAN

INNER CHARACTER

POWELL: I'm not one of those who thinks of his childhood as an unhappy time. Home, entirely happy. If I could remake it and reconstruct it I wouldn't know what to do to have made it better.

'Panorama', 2 December 1968

ANNE BROWN: How would you like to be remembered?
POWELL: I should like to have been killed in the war.

BBC Radio, 13 April 1986

'PANORAMA'

BBC TV, 2 December 1968

POWELL: It's like watching a nation busily engaged in heaping up its own funeral pyre.

(*music*)

ROBIN DAY: Good evening. The Right Honourable John Enoch Powell – is he a racialist or a realist? Is he facing facts or inflaming prejudices? Well, those were the questions we raised after his Eastbourne speech. Tonight, we return to the subject, with a profile of this ex-Professor of Greek who has become the most reported and the most discussed politician in this country. What kind of a man is Enoch Powell? And what is Powellism? Tonight's programme includes answers to these questions from Mr Powell himself. And on the question, 'how much support does he have?', you'll see the significant results of an opinion poll specially commissioned among white and coloured people in Britain. 'Panorama' looks at Powell and Powellism, Robert MacNeil reporting:

ENOCH POWELL: The discrimination and the deprivation, the sense of alarm and the resentment lie not with the immigrant population, but with those among whom they have come and are still coming. This is why, to enact legislation of the kind before Parliament at this moment is to risk throwing a match on to gunpowder.

EDWARD HEATH: I told Mr Powell that he could not remain a member of the Shadow Cabinet because of the inflammatory nature of his speech at Birmingham. I considered that this was likely to make racial relations more difficult.

MACNEIL: A storm of political passion swept Britain after Enoch Powell's emotional April speech. He claimed to be surprised by the reaction.

SIR GERALD NABARRO: . . . that we ought to stop all immigration into this country and if any immigrant wants to go back home, then we would help subsidise him to go back home. So that's all Enoch Powell has said.

FIRST MAN: What Enoch Powell said was right . . . (*hear hear*) There's enough of 'em. We can't take no more . . . (*men shouting*)

SECOND MAN: If this society is not going to accept us and if they are going to reject us and if they are going to hate us, we'll have to fend for ourselves by organising ourselves. If I am hit I will have to hit back. (*shouting*)

MACNEIL: What kind of a man would raise an issue others considered too dangerous to touch?

POWELL: I'm not one of those who thinks of his childhood as an unhappy time. Home, entirely happy. If I could remake it and reconstruct it I wouldn't know what to do to have made it better.

MACNEIL: Home was in Stetchford, a suburb of Birmingham. He was born John Enoch in 1912 and spent his early years in a semi-detached Victorian house. He liked being a city boy and couldn't understand how people lived in the country. His parents were both schoolteachers, his father an elementary school headmaster. Mrs Powell devoted herself to their only child.

POWELL: My father was, as it were, a warm presence and another boy around the place. But my childhood is very much my mother. I wrote in the introduction to one of my books, I referred to my mother as my first Greek teacher as she was also my first teacher and I suppose some of my earliest recollections are of my mother putting up the alphabet round the kitchen wall so that I could learn it and my saying the most elementary lessons to her standing on a chair in the kitchen while she worked at the stove or the sink. And, from the very beginning right up to the sixth at grammar school she took a part in my learning, encouraging me and helping me and very much working with me.

MACNEIL: Her efforts guided a brilliant mind into great powers of concentration. He won a scholarship to Birmingham's famous King Edward's Grammar School.

POWELL: I remember when I was transferred and moved across from one desk to another in big school where we all assembled in the morning and was greeted somewhat quizzically by the classical form that I'd joined. I remember informing them that after two terms I would be top of the form. I was.

REV PROFESSOR C. F. EVANS: He was in the back row of the sixth form when I was in the front row; he'd come streaking up from the lower forms at a tremendous pace and, although he was two years younger, he had already arrived in the back row of the sixth form and those of us in the front row, of a rather powerful sixth form, though I was the most undistinguished member of it, were I think, at least I was, pretty frightened. I think he was a very formidable scholar even in classics even at that age. And he was really unlike, I think, any other schoolboy one had known. He was austere. One seldom, if ever, saw him standing up against a wall with his hands in his pockets just talking. He didn't play games, though I gather he had quite a capacity for gymnasium. He was either at his books or if not he was walking purposefully from A to B with a goal in mind with either his books under his arm or his clarinet, pale, head rather forward, shoulders slightly stooped. He was very . . . quite a phenomenon.

MACNEIL: Over one Christmas holiday, he learned two years of Greek to catch up. In 1930 he swept the school's classics prizes and gained his scholarship to Cambridge, but not without some inner struggle.

POWELL: This was how one got on and up. One was certainly not saying, well if I go to Cambridge I can get a degree in so-and-so and then I can have a career as a this or a that. That wasn't it at all. It was much more that here is an opportunity, an opportunity to rise, I'm sorry the word must seem so crude but that I'm sure is how I saw it – get on has too much of a connotation of economic connotations, get on would understate it but perhaps rise is the best I can do to describe it. Of course there had been a conflict. I was very musical as a younger boy and at fifteen or sixteen I was very seriously anxious to make music a career and it was only at sixteen, I think, that I took the decision, one of these essential concentration decisions which one, I think, sees throughout that if it was going to be Cambridge, well Cambridge it had got to be and I put my clarinet away for the last time, I've never looked at a sheet of music since, though music heard remained very important to me throughout the . . . my pre-war life, that was put behind me, but still it was not for career; it was, as it were, well if this is the way up, so be it.

MACNEIL: At Trinity College, he immersed himself in Greek and worshipped the poet, A. E. Housman, who was lecturing then. Powell won enough scholarships to have a surplus of money. He took the university scholarship and emerged with all the top prizes in classics as a Fellow at twenty-two. But an obsession not to dissipate his mental energies or himself kept him a lonely, Spartan figure.

REV PROFESSOR C. F. EVANS: I went to ask him to tea as one used to ask freshmen from the old school and climbed up the stairs of these garret rooms at Trinity and knocked on the door and Powell said 'Come in' and I opened the door and I think I'm right in saying that it was, you know, in the middle of November, and very cold, the room was quite bare except for the College furniture, as I remember it there was no fire, there were no pictures, Powell was sitting in his overcoat with a rug across his knees and the whole of the table was . . . he was surrounded by eighteenth-century folios and I said: 'Hello Powell, would you like to come to tea?' and he said, 'No', and I'd never met this response before and so to recover my wits I walked over to his mantelpiece and leant on it and took

out a cigarette and he said, 'Would you mind not smoking.' And
so I left.

POWELL: I saw my life when I went up to Cambridge, and I saw it far
too much, as I realise in retrospect, as a simple condition of the
prize-scholarship-winning knowledge-eating process of the working
side of my school life. I literally worked from half-past five in the
morning until half-past nine at night behind a sported oak except
when I went out to lectures. This was not because I disliked my
fellows, that's not the point at all. It was that I didn't know there
was anything else to do and since I wasn't thrown into a social
environment in which I worked as I always have done and always
have done since, have swum and swum happily, I didn't get into
the water. But it is true that the social life of a College was a social
life completely unfamiliar to me. Even the sheer mechanics of it,
of how to tie a bow-tie, were unknown to me and I had no environment which would, as it were, tell me how to tie the bow-tie.

MACNEIL: Even today, when forced by an active political life to be
gregarious, Powell still seems austere. People find he has no small-
talk. If he thinks a remark foolish, he says so. He has never smoked
and only recently graduated from an occasional glass of sherry to
an appreciation of wines. He does not mix with other MPs in the
smoking rooms of the Commons. (*background*)

RT HON RAY GUNTER MP: He does lead a very austere life and he doesn't
mix. As far as I know he is rarely in company as most MPs are at
some time or another, either with their colleagues, their friends,
sometimes with their political enemies and . . . but you don't see
him in that sense and he is, his very nature is I think puritanical
and puritans have always been a bit funny to live with as you know,
speaking as one who was brought up in that faith, that they have
always been awkward people to live with because they don't understand the weaknesses of other people so much.

MACNEIL: Today, the cold gaze from his unblinking green eyes often
hides a passionate life-hungry personality. At Cambridge, he
longed to break out of the confining atmosphere. He made several
attempts to join the Diplomatic Service but accepted a Fellowship
as Fate's gift.

POWELL: If I can take off the shelf being a Fellow of Trinity, very
well then I will, so be it. But there remained all the feelings which
have predisposed me to look for a diplomatic career, to look for,
not a diplomatic career specially, but something, for God's sake,
outside. So the question of a classical career never really existed
in my mind. Indeed, I would have had a positive horror of it and
I can remember to this day the sense of . . . well suffocation would
hardly be too strong a word . . . which I used to feel as an under-

graduate when I went under the great gate at Trinity. One felt . . . I felt that I was going out of the world into something enclosed, that all my instincts were to get out of what was enclosed into the world. (*background, army*)

MACNEIL: He really found fulfilment in the army. After Cambridge, he spent two years in Australia as Professor of Greek at Sydney University. When war broke out, he enlisted in the Royal Warwickshire Regiment as a private. Peacetime soldiering, like this training today, would not interest Powell but enlistment in 1939 meant release from the fear that Britain would go under without fighting. (*army training*)

POWELL: I wrote a poem in which I described people joining up at the outbreak of the war, like bridegrooms going to meet their bride. That's how it was to me. The thing expected for so many years. The thing which one had feared wouldn't happen but would, instead, be replaced by disgrace and humiliation. It had happened. The chance had come at last. As I once described it, I felt I could hear the German divisions marching across Europe and I could hear this drumming coming through the earth and it was coming up again in Australia where no one else could hear it. And then the interludes between this. Germany itself, in the winter of '38/'39, no, this was a blessed explosion of relief if you like.

MACNEIL: Powell rose swiftly. He worked in Army Intelligence in the Middle East and India and was a Brigadier by 1944. Even senior officers sometimes found his manner and intelligence intimidating. Powell found contentment. (*army drilling*)

POWELL: I loved it. I took to it like a duck to water. I enjoyed best of all being a private soldier. It's the nicest thing there is to be. It seemed to me such a congenial environment, but the whole institution of the army, the framework of discipline, the exactitude of rank, the precision of duty was something almost restful and attractive to me and I took great pride in smartness at drill. One always remembers I suppose the compliments that have . . . some absurd compliments one remembers. One of them that I remember, I shall remember all my days, was my Platoon Sergeant saying to the company commander that I was the smartest soldier in the company. I take that as a very, very great compliment.

BURROWS: Most Staff Officers practically all wore a bush shirt and slacks but not Enoch Powell. It was quite a sight in the Headquarters, you could see Enoch always, even in the sort of hottest day in Delhi with a tie and collar, regimental insignia and a Sam Browne belt, walking through the corridors with a great determination, going from one office to another and back again, and I've

never seen him in the Headquarters without his Sam Browne belt
while on duty and his tunic and his tie.

POWELL: I can remember the day in June, it was the day the monsoon
broke in Delhi in June 1944, when I suddenly said to myself:
You're going to survive. There'll be a time when you won't be in
uniform, painful though it may be, you've got to face it. True,
Japan is not yet defeated but the chances are mounting that there
will be a lifetime for you and a lifetime, not as a soldier, and I
opened the door, as it were, this was the opening of the door from
one mental room to another and there was the answer. Of course
you'll go into politics, in England. (*students*)

MACNEIL: Politics for Powell has meant almost continuous controversy
and since he spoke out on immigration last April, controversy has
meant public turmoil and violence.

POWELL: Thank you ladies and gentlemen . . . for your intelligent
reception and for your demonstration of the academic principles
of . . . (*inaudible over background*)

MACNEIL: It should not have been surprising that Enoch Powell would
be the politician with the temerity to lift the stone on race that
others would not touch for fear of what's seen beneath. He brought
into politics the same single-minded dedication to a chosen task
he'd shown as a scholar.

POWELL: . . . we can give and receive reason. Thank you.

MACNEIL: Powell also brought into politics an indifference to opposition and a thick skin for political hostility. Powell has represented Wolverhampton South West for eighteen years. He is a conscientious MP. It is essentially a working-class constituency and his
majority has steadily increased. Powell was one of the bright young
men hired by R. A. Butler to modernise Tory philosophy after
1945. His colleagues were Heath, Maudling, Macleod. But he's
often been out of step with them. Powell has a propensity for
splitting off, for not compromising, exhibiting a prickly personality
in politics. He is a loner, a maverick figure. Extreme political
stands provoking extreme ractions have been the essence of Powellism. He has resigned from office once, been dismissed once and
refused three times to serve. He risked his career in 1958 when he
resigned with Thorneycroft as Financial Secretary in Macmillan's
Government. Powell opposed an increase in Government expenditure.

POWELL: . . . whenever an earthquake – whenever a landslide happens, it always starts with a pebble moving. But it doesn't start
because of a pebble, or over a pebble; nor do the minutiae – if
you like – of the monetary debate . . . should they conceal the real
divergence between Macmillan and Thorneycroft – in '57/'58, which

had been dramatised and spelt out in British political experience since then, and against which only now is the Conservative Party more and more reacting.

MACNEIL: In 1963 there was another dramatic illustration. Macmillan, ill and retired, recommended that the Queen choose Lord Home to succeed him. Powell and others wanted 'Rab' Butler. There were ten days of suspense while top people manoeuvred behind the scenes. Before Home accepted the Queen's commission Powell had refused to serve with him. Powell's refusal with Macleod was a bombshell that might have wrecked his career.

POWELL: . . . on Friday he was deciding whether to accept that commission. The only way in which a member of the Cabinet could influence the outcome was by telling the enquirer – in this case, Lord Home, what would be his answer to a then hypothetical question – namely: If I accept the Queen's commission and ask you to serve under me, will you? Now – the answer which you give to that question when it is still hypothetical – is the only power that as a Cabinet Minister you have, at that moment when you are almost part of an electoral college, as it were.

And my answer, because I believed that the right answer was Rab Butler – my answer had to be: No. Otherwise I was not exercising my vote; I was not influencing the mind of Alec Home in deciding whether or not to accept the Queen's commission. So when, on Saturday, having accepted the Queen's commission, he asked me again the same question, I said to him, looking him in the eye as I am looking at you now – I said: Well, I don't expect, Alec, you expect me to give you a different answer on Saturday from the one I gave you on Friday. I'd have to go home and turn all the mirrors round.

GUNTER: I don't think that he is what I think R. A. Butler once described him as, a natural resigner. But let us get one thing clear about Mr Powell: he is a man of very great principles . . . and very great honesty. And I have the feeling that there is too much of the streak of the puritan about him, that he does not possess this gift that politicians must have, of compromising themselves sometimes, and adjusting and adapting themselves to the will and the desires and the policies of those whom he has to discuss these matters with. So in that sense he is a man of principle. He takes wrong attitudes, but they are taken seriously, therefore it is perhaps not unnatural that a man of that sort would find it so difficult to compromise and therefore he perhaps does resign more easily than most politicians.

HON NICHOLAS RIDLEY: His purity is very great and I think he is probably an awkward colleague in any administration because if he is not resigning he is probably threatening to resign – not that I was in any government with him. But I think this is true and I think it is because he has got this tremendously strong logical idea of what he wants this country to do and any deviation from this goal is to him anathema. And anything which he doesn't think is likely to move in this direction is something which he must resist by every means at his disposal. And all this confirms what I am saying – that he is a character of big size, and big-sized people find it awfully difficult to serve – they can only lead. And whether his leadership would turn inwards or outwards, I don't know. As I said earlier, I think he is a very enigmatic character; but I think this explains his inability to stay for long in one position and under one political leadership. And I think also to some extent it explains his desire always to be in the wilderness – to be alone.

MACNEIL: The paradox is that Powell is not always in the wilderness. Returning to the Macmillan Government as Minister of Health was philosophically, if not politically, compromising his principles.

POWELL: Life goes on. One make's one's point. One makes one's point firmly and dramatically; but life goes on and government goes on and Parliament goes on. You remain a Member of it. And one cannot be a non-juror – to put it in the terms of British history – for ever. And so it was natural and not, I think, seen by anyone as a contradiction that one should resume a place, which eventually became a Cabinet place, in a Macmillan administration.

(Party political broadcast, May 1963)

MACNEIL: It was ironic that the keenest critic of Government spending should take one of the highest-spending Ministries; but Powell was regarded as a very efficient administrator of the Health Service he fundamentally opposed and, for such a noted opponent of Government economic planning, he showed a remarkable enthusiasm for that exercise in his own Ministry.

(Powell interview on film)

Today Powell's dramatic solutions to economic problems have made him the darling of constituency Conservatives; as the apostle of the free market, the keeper of the Tory faith in free enterprise, he is a much sought-after speaker.

Recently Powell unveiled his own Budget, or nostrum for Britain's economic ills. It was characteristically extreme, abolishing a host of Government activities, like housing subsidies and institutions like the Prices and Incomes Board. Anything which means Government interference with the free market – the nationalised industries would all be sold.

He further endears himself to constituency Tories, tired of milk-

and-water Conservatism, with a pungent vocabulary that arouses their patriotism and nationalism.

POWELL: . . . Why are the British hag-ridden and bullied from year to year? Bullied and badgered and despised and impoverished for the sake of their blessed balance of payments, when the thing would do itself if people would let it.

(*applause and singing of national anthem*)

MACNEIL: It is race that has swung the full machinery of publicity on to Powell. Nearly all his public appearances attract hostile demonstrators. All his speeches are reported. When he spoke again on immigration in November, newspapers gave the full text of the speech. Powell insists that he is merely raising an issue which worries his constituents, and which other politicians have suppressed; but hammering race in speeches mainly outside Parliament creates suspicion that Powell is not just satisfying his own constituency but courting a national one.

(*rowdy meeting*)

Students like these at Bath university have been his most vociferous and demonstrative critics.

POWELL: . . . No. The important thing is this – if this is, as I argue it is bound to do under present policies, going to increase two-, three-, fourfold in size during the rest of this century, then it will so alter the character of great areas of this country that that alteration will be found intolerable and unacceptable by the people of this country at large; and that therefore it is in the interests of all concerned to do what is necessary to ensure that at any rate it is stabilised at about the present size. At about the present size. As I said in my speech at Eastbourne, we can live with it, and the slow mercy of the years will gradually enable even this unparalleled introduction into the population of this country – and it is, numerically and in other respects, unparalleled in a thousand years – to be absorbed.

MACNEIL: By stressing only the intolerable future, don't you run the danger of encouraging people who find the present intolerable to bring their frustrations out into the open and feel them respectable in a way that they didn't before?

POWELL: No – the opposite, for the danger lies not in intolerance even at the present. My own constituents – I am proud of them. The tolerance which they have shown over these fifteen years in the great changes which have come about which they have not wanted. No. The danger lies in their fear of what the future holds; and if they found that nobody was prepared to look at what they see coming, nobody was allowed to talk about what they fear, nobody was allowed even to discuss what seems to them an imminent and overwhelming prospect – that is where the danger will be. No. I'm a safety valve – the greatest safety valve this country has got in this matter.

GUNTER: I have heard this argument that he is a safety valve and all he is doing is allowing all their puff to come out and that sort of thing. Well – it all depends which way you look at it. This is a very very serious human problem. Before you start playing about with safety valves you've got to be quite sure what are the consequences of your action, what emotions they do let out, and how many bad people, really bad people, will take advantage to exploit a situation which he says he's used as a safety valve. We knew it was bad. We were doing our best to come to terms with it.

MACNEIL: You see no danger that in raising the question in the terms that you've raised it, that you cause some white people to harass those Commonwealth immigrants they otherwise felt constrained to . . .

POWELL: No; much more likely the other way. If they feel that this, their lives are not being ignored, that this is not being swept under the carpet, as the phrase is. If they feel that their problem is seen and understood by Members of Parliament and by those who write and by those who speak, then they are much more likely to say: 'Then, indeed, there is no need for us to take the law into our own hands. There is no need for us to think of methods which cannot be misunderstood and make noises that can't be not heard.' No, the . . . to speak about what one's constituents see and fear if one believes it to be, as I do, a well-founded prospect and fear, is to serve the cause of harmony inside this country, now and even more in the future.

GUNTER: I think that he has brought to the surface . . . allowed to surface the . . . some of the worst instincts of our people . . . that the problem was there and they had to live under the stresses and the strains of this multi-racial community in certain areas. I think he has exacerbated feelings to a great degree there. I get hundreds of letters now about Mr Powell from people that I don't believe have ever met a coloured immigrant – so much agreeing with him . . . and telling that these black so-and-sos ought to be sent home, and all the rest of it.

MACNEIL: Let's leave aside the evidence you present and go instead to the action you advocate; and the one action which has attracted most attention is the idea of creating a Ministry to repatriate . . .

POWELL: A Ministry or some other authority . . .

MACNEIL: . . . or some other authority – yes . . . to repatriate. What evidence do you have beyond the cursory newspaper's survey that you quote in your speech that any substantial number of coloured immigrants really want to go back?

POWELL: Well – you have been good enough to say that you've read my speech. You will be aware that in the latter part of that speech I produced evidence of many different kinds to show that at present the immigrant population was not rooted in this country . . . that it still belonged to the communities back home, both west and east, and this is again the difficulty of getting across the facts to people who are unacquainted with it and who think of the immigrants preponderantly in terms of individuals, who've taken an individual decision to pack their suitcases and go and find a new life and a new home. For the vast majority it is nothing like that. For the vast majority it has literally been transportation within a community setting across the globe into – it happens to have been Britain. It might have been anywhere else. So . . . I instance that as one other fact about the phenomenon which is material to the question of repatriation.

GUNTER: . . . which sounds very nice on a sheet of foolscap; but how you are going to do it on a voluntary basis I don't know and neither does Mr Powell know, because many of the immigrants who are here, who have been here for many years . . . comparatively a number of years anyhow . . . they have in a sense got bedded down in our economy. They have wage rates, they have standards of living that are impossible for them to achieve if they went home. And therefore the number who would voluntarily go home, I should imagine, would not be the answer to Mr Powell's problem. It would be a trickle. The only temptation to them, I suppose, would be the sun. But the sun is no adequate substitute for a full tummy, you know.

MACNEIL: To measure the reaction to Powell's repatriation proposal and to his other views on immigration, Panorama commissioned two special polls last week. They investigated the opinions of coloured immigrants and of white Englishmen. These are the results:

Coloured immigrants were asked whether they would like to return to their country of origin if they received financial help. A startling thirty-eight per cent said: Yes. Forty-three per cent said: No. Eight per cent said Britain was their country of origin.

Coloured immigrants were asked if they would favour further controls on immigration or not. A surprising forty-seven per cent (nearly half) said: Yes. Thirty per cent said: No.

These figures tend to support what Mr Powell has been saying about immigrants' attitudes. The research firm cautioned, however, that difficulties in polling immigrants might mean that findings were not completely representative of their views, but that the broad conclusions were reliable.

In a national sample white Englishmen over twenty-one were

asked whether they agreed with Powell's proposal for a large-scale plan for voluntary repatriation of immigrants. Seventy-four per cent said: Yes. Were they in favour of compulsory repatriation – that is deportation? Fifty-five per cent said: No. Thirty-five per cent said: Yes. Should there be further controls on immigration? Eighty-two per cent: Yes. Should wives and children be stopped from joining immigrants already here? Fifty-nine per cent: No. Is Powell's campaign making relations between races better or worse. Fifty-nine per cent: Worse. Twenty-four per cent said it made no difference. Eleven per cent: Better.

Liberal opinion, especially among the student left, depicts Powell as a racist with fascist views on preserving the purity of the English race. Certainly, Powell is moved by a great reverence for Englishness and English institutions. Not least is the Church of England, to which he has turned devoutly after a youth of intellectual atheism. A sentimental affection for the English landscape warms his published verse. A favourite recreation is exploring old churches, lecturing his wife and daughters on their merits.

Powell strongly denies any racial prejudice. The important political question is whether he is exploiting mass prejudices for political ends, in particular, to oust Edward Heath as Tory leader.

Powell has made one overt bid for the job – the great surprise of the 1965 leadership election was when Powell suddenly challenged Heath and Maudling. Powell got only fifteen votes to 150 for Heath and 133 for Maudling. But he had established his long-term intention, and an identity as a politician of leadership stature. Heath could not avoid giving him a Shadow Cabinet post and his dismissal after the April speech has angered many Powell supporters.

Conservative MP Nicholas Ridley is a friend of Powell's and was his sponsor in the leadership election. He thinks Heath could not bring Powell into the Shadow Cabinet.

RIDLEY: . . . but I would say that it is totally unrealistic. You couldn't have expected Mendès-France to bring de Gaulle back into his Cabinet. Enoch is far too far out on a limb for it to be realistic to suggest that he could serve in a Shadow Cabinet with the present leadership and I don't think he would expect it for one moment. He's long since passed the point where that is possible and I don't see a possibility of marrying these two points of view in the next year or two. Eventually – things may be different, but at the present time, it doesn't mix – it doesn't work.

GUNTER: I don't think that Mr Powell has a very great future in the field of politics. If you are thinking on the lines that many people think, that he really is aspiring to the leadership of the Conservative

Party, that his real object is to displace Mr Heath, possibly in a time of crisis, to take over the reins of the Conservative Party, I would doubt it very much. You have to look at the background of the Conservative Party for one thing. They on the whole are not given to extremists in positions of authority. Their whole history has been one of compromise; that is why they have always remained alive . . . that they have adapted and adjusted themselves to current circumstances. And I would doubt very much whether Mr Powell would have that understanding of the leadership of men to . . . to be the leader of the Conservative Party.

I also feel that the Conservative Party are now in such a mood that it would . . . they could only think of Mr Powell as a major disaster for them. He has aroused so much hostility, not only with the leadership, but also with the rank and file of the Conservative Party. Many of them have sympathy with his point of view – nevertheless they feel that he has done the Conservative Party a great disservice. So – what I am trying to say, in effect, is that Mr Powell has no – sort of – roots of power there. He has no group that can be identified with him . . . who would aid him in his path to power – if that be what he wants.

MACNEIL: Are you seeking the leadership of the Conservative Party?

POWELL: No. There is no vacancy.

MACNEIL: You did stand for it the last time there was a vacancy.

POWELL: . . . yes. There was a vacancy – yes.

MACNEIL: Is it inconceivable that if the situation arose again you would not stand for it again?

POWELL: Now, that is one of those hypothetical questions which politicians – even much less experienced than me – would be foolish to ask. Are you asking me whether if there were a vacancy in ten, fifteen or twenty years' time, I knowing nothing of the then circumstances or of my then circumstances, should now tell you what I would then do? That's clearly absurd. You can't mean that.

MACNEIL: I'm asking you whether you would like to be the leader of the Conservative Party.

POWELL: Most prominent politicians in a party nurture the hope that they might be the people to lead their party and through their party, their country. Men would not go into politics unless that possibility – not the goal – that is a different matter – but that possibility, was in their minds. What sort of men would they be? If they started by saying: No, that is not what I am interested in at all. But it is quite different to say: That is my aim – in the sense that if it didn't happen – and it's much more a matter of chance than of any other cause – that if that didn't happen I would say: Oh dear, I have failed. It is not an aim in that sense; if one is to be sane and happy, one must realise that the gifts of fortune cannot be a man's aim in life.

MACNEIL: But he doesn't refuse them if they fall to him?

POWELL: No. That would be ungrateful – wouldn't it?

MACNEIL: Politicians are waiting for Powell's next move, to reveal how actively he is seeking the leadership. But much depends on others. If Heath loses the next election, Powell's chances will be greatly increased. If Heath wins they will be much diminished.

Powell's motive in raising the race question is open to debate. He argues that the issue chose him but raising it in the emotional terms he does lays him open to the charge of demagoguery.

Many politicians feel Powell's behaviour gives him an extremist image, a man outside the main stream of British politics.

RIDLEY: He may be – he could be a sort of de Gaulle figure. On the other hand he could be a sort of Mosley figure. If he is accepted at any time and things become much worse and he is sort of called for in ten years' time from the wilderness to come and save us as de Gaulle was, then that would be a possible interpretation, because just like de Gaulle, he is saying that everything we are doing is out of context and out of scale and is wrong and we must have a new approach to what is in our national interests.

But it could be that he is leaning in a direction which will make him in the end hysterical, which will make him lose touch with reality and the gentleness of the Englishman as a political voter and he'll become an extremist who ends up in the same sort of humiliated position as Oswald Mosley is in now.

'POLITICIANS AND OTHER ARTISTS'

An Interview with Enoch Powell by
John Goodbody and Robert Silver, *Trinity Review*,
Summer 1977

GOODBODY: In May 1974 you said, 'I'm impelled by some inner necessity. Religion isn't a matter of intellectual proof, it's more analogous to music or art. Man is a creature who has lost instinct – but not entirely – and gained reason – but not entirely. There are many mansions of truth.' I'd like to know whether politics should be conducted as far as possible on intellectual grounds.

POWELL: I assume that we would all of us claim to use intellect and logic where intellect and logic are applicable – for instance, in making our own way from the end to the means. Very often, I'm sure, people assume that they are using intellect and logic when in fact they are working from presumptions, from starting-points which, when confronted with them, they would agree were not demonstrable or derivable by logic. So in politics, the ends, in my view, are not logically or even intellectually based on agreed premises. They are things given – given, no doubt, differently to different groups, to different people – but still given. From those objects one makes deductions as to methods, actions, consequences and the rest, which deductions are more likely to be wholesome if they are rational. There is no advantage in an irrational deduction.

GOODBODY: You said two years ago that 'an act of abandon for a cause, total abandon for a cause is something that accompanies me through life, the notion of it'. What is your cause at the moment?

POWELL: The sovereign independence of the United Kingdom, which I regard as an object overriding all others in its importance and justifying all manner of political risks and loss thought to be necessary.

SILVER: Do you think that there could come a time when it would be more desirable to merge sovereignty or power with other countries?

POWELL: I don't know. There won't come such a time for me, but there are other people who now feel differently and the proportion of other people who feel differently might well change. That doesn't help me: I feel as I feel. It's no use saying to a man who is obeying the call of his country and joining Kitchener's army, 'Don't you think that in fifty years' time your children and grand-children might be disinclined to obey the call of country?'

SILVER: The fact that public opinion might have changed on an issue would never affect your private feelings?

POWELL: We're talking about my activity as a politician; we're not talking about my private feelings. All feelings are private, of course; but some are kept private and others are not. The essence of politics is that it's about feelings that are not kept private. A politician is in this respect not like a poet. You can imagine – you can just imagine – a poet or another artist (though with great difficulty) who said, 'This is beautiful to me, but I doubt whether there is anybody else alive today who would think it beautiful.' But a politician who said, 'This seems right to me, but I very much doubt whether there's anybody else to whom it seems right,' would be a contradiction in terms. He must believe in the possibility. Indeed, his own conviction will to him be inseparable from the belief that others share it or would share it, if it were presented to them as it presents itself to him. However, I'm not sure that I haven't exaggerated the difference in this respect between a poli-tician and other artists. Clearly a musician, although he may prac-tise dissonance, only practises it in the belief that he can bring some hearers to understand what he means and what he feels in the dissonance. He would not do so if it were his conviction that no other human being was capable of attaching to the dissonance the significance that he attaches to it. You may educate your audi-ence, but the very act of educating your audience, or, in political terms, leading your people, implies the belief that they are predis-posed to share, or have the basic conditions of sharing, your insight and your convictions. You may be wrong, you may be right; but that's a different matter.

SILVER: Do you think that there are times when a democratic politician should advocate something to which he's personally indifferent in order to ventilate a widely-held public desire or feeling?

POWELL: Yes. As you have expressed it, my answer to that must be yes. Let me take a specific example. There are a large number of matters on which I believe in regard to Northern Ireland I am expressing the wishes and the feeling of those who elected me. But I have no doubt there are other matters to which they attach importance but to which, for the life of me, I can't attach import-ance. It would be very wrong of me therefore to suppress them just because I was personally indifferent to them. Of course, if I thought them harmful, if I thought they were asking for things which were either counter-productive from their own point of view or inherently harmful, it would be my duty to persuade them of that. But you said 'indifferent'; and if you say 'indifferent', then my answer must be yes, because a representative cannot be so selective that he will only represent his constituents on those matters on which he himself feels strongly.

SILVER: And he should when he's talking about those questions on which he's personally indifferent express them as strongly as his constituents or those people who voted for him feel?

POWELL: Clearly one is a more effective advocate if one is not indifferent. But it constantly happens that one raises matters and pursues them, believing them to be a rational point of view though they concern objects or subjects to which one is personally indifferent.

GOODBODY: Do you find this conflict difficult?

POWELL: I don't think there is any conflict there. Obviously, over the whole range of matters which a member puts forward or helps to put forward on behalf of his constituents or his party, there will be a big range between those in which he feels strongly involved and those in which he feels hardly involved at all. For example, I can imagine that as Member of Parliament for Wolverhampton I would have participated in the debate on fisheries in the EEC. But I clearly participate in it differently now, representing one of the principal fishing constituencies in the UK. There are a number of matters, from small to big, where one recognises that one's constituents have perfectly harmless and legitimate interests which one doesn't share oneself but which are properly brought to expression through political channels. They may call for legislation, amendment of the law, and so on; but there's no problem there. Naturally I would say if I had a colleague who was more interested, 'look, would you take the lead in this? I'll give you any support I can,' because he'd be likely to make a better job of it.

GOODBODY: Some people have observed the paradox that the logic of your arguments in public speaking is conveyed with a powerful emotion. Do you regard this in fact as a paradox? If so, do you think that this is necessary as a practising politician?

POWELL: The emotion applies to the word convey and not to the word logic?

GOODBODY: That's right.

POWELL: It applies to the language and not to the content. Let's go back to what I said earlier. All the time a politician is trying to find whether there will be an echo. He's trying to discover whether things as they seem to him are seen similarly by others or whether he's living in a private world – which, as I've said, is uninhabitable for a politician. So he's always looking for reaction, audience reaction, though in a very different sense from an artist or a lecturer;

for if the ends of politics are beyond intellect and logic, then, while
one may be advocating causes, consequences and means in relation
to ends as accurately and logically as one can, one is all the time
concerned with ascertaining whether the action which reason would
indicate is sustained by a shared will, a shared aim. Thus the
language in which political argument is framed is the language best
designed to elicit the existence or non-existence of sympathy.

SILVER: Would I be correct if I described you as a Tory?

POWELL: If we do some defining. Some people use 'Tory' as a four-
letter word, and therefore handy for 'Conservative'. Others use it
in a specific sense; but the specific senses tend to vary. I'm a
Church-and-Queen Tory. Indeed I've been defining a sort of Toryism in saying that the most important things for men in political
society are not ascertainable a priori and largely not within their
control, that the validity of institutions, laws and so on cannot be
judged from first principles, but depend upon the given data of a
human society, that a human society is not an artificial construction
but something that we can control or alter with less assurance than
we can control or alter the form of a plant or the nature of a strain
of wheat, and that the factors given by nature, the instinctual
factors, are overwhelmingly important.

SILVER: Do you think that Toryism as a political theory can be so
constructed as to provide the correct response to each specific issue
that comes up, in your case from Ulster to immigration to capital
punishment to the Common Market, or is it rather simply a temperament, an outlook which describes a sort of human character?

POWELL: It's a view but not a system, and a point of view can be
consistent within the limits of the material to which it is applied.
You mentioned, I notice, capital punishment. It seems to me that
all the other subjects that you mentioned could be brought within
a single view, and that you could reasonably assume that a man,
who took a given view of society, would be likely to arrive at a
similar view on all those other subjects. Now this might also be
true of capital punishment; but it happens not to be so in my case,
so far as I'm conscious of being actuated by the intersection of two
beliefs: first, that it cannot be shown that capital punishment is a
deterrent to murder; and secondly that, other things being equal,
it is a desirable object to avoid violence being inflicted by members
of a society on one another. This is ultimately a social point of
view; but I can't consider any of these matters out of the context
of a society. I do not know of human beings existing outside society,
nor can I give any meaning to the propositions about such things
as capital punishment in abstraction from a society. However, I
don't approach this question either from the point of view of

religion or from the point of an overriding principle but from a consideration of practical or demonstrable effects. Let me reverse this, and say that if I were convinced by the evidence that the existence of capital punishment resulted in a much lower incidence of murder than I believe I would be in favour of it.

GOODBODY: May I leave politics? As a classicist do you believe that your subject provides the best training for the mind and, if so, why?

POWELL: I am dubious about this expression, 'training of the mind'. It seems to me the sort of phrase which one should use in carefully controlled scientific discourse but not otherwise, because it imports a great many assumptions and calls for great exactitude before one handles it. Training in the use of language is important for the purpose of thinking. It's also important for the purpose of action, collective action. As a training in the use of language as an instrument of thought and action, I believe a classical education to be unrivalled in Western Europe – I wouldn't state that of China or Siberia or Patagonia. However, though I would certainly assert that I wouldn't rest my case upon it, though I count myself extremely fortunate to have received a classical education, even to the extent of regarding those not so fortunate as scarcely to be recognised as educated at all. I would rest it much more upon the fact that Greek and Roman literature and history are, in a sense which I shall define, 'classical'. The sense in which I will define it 'classical' is that recurrent human experience is lived through, expressed and reflected upon with an intensity and a completeness which makes it unnecessary for that task to be made again. A classical scholar is equipped with the pre-digestion of a great range of human experience, political and also non-political, so that amongst non-classicists he is rather like a man who knows the times-table, compared with people who don't know it and who, when they want to multiply eight by nine have to work it out for the first time. The classical scholar already knows that eight times nine are seventy-two because that's in the *Antigone*, as it were.

I wrote an article recently in *The Spectator* in which I described a certain type of conflict as 'Sophoclean'. I was there referring to the analysis in the *Antigone* of the clash between two equally binding duties from different spheres and using it as a shorthand sign which denotes for everyone with knowledge that this thing has been lived through, has been worked out once for all, has achieved 'classic' expression. So when you say Sophoclean you not merely use a sort of index or label but avail yourself of all this predigestion. It does not come to you, as if for the first time in human history, that there can be this sort of conflict. You were brought up to

know that such a conflict exists and that it makes tragedy and
that it is expressible in terms of the fate of Antigone and Creon.
Otherwise you might feel that this had occurred for the first time.
I often felt that Nye Bevan illustrated the effects of lack of education in general but specifically of classical education when one
constantly saw that extraordinarily able and sensitive man fighting
his way might-and-main to conclusions which were waiting for him
all the time. It's like watching a man having to discover the calculus
or the propositions of Euclid all over again. He *could* do it; but
why have to?

SILVER: Do you have any regrets about any of the language that you
used in your first well-known public speeches about immigration?

POWELL: I've been asked this so many times that I give the same
answer automatically. I would have wished to make two alterations
in the text, as issued, of the speech I made in Birmingham on 20
April 1968. The first is that I would have wished to insert, as old-
fashioned printers used to do, quotation marks in front of every
paragraph of the quotation which I used instead of only at the
beginning and the end. Secondly, I would not have deleted the
Latin of the quotation from Virgil, which I did because it might
appear pendantic to include it in a hand-out, though I did in fact
use it when I spoke. One never knows the relationship between
cause and effect; but it did result in an extraordinary number of
misquotations. I am hesitant about using that word, since all quotation is by definition misquotation, and all representation is by
definition misrepresentation, because no representation is complete
and no quotation is complete. Even if you quote all I say, you still
haven't quoted the context. I'm not just playing with words – this
is a very serious limiting fact of all communication, but particularly
of political communication. However, allowing myself to use the
word 'misquotation', a great many misquotations would have been
avoided by those two simple typographical differences. That's the
answer I've always given to that question; and it's a good principle,
having once settled upon an answer, to go on giving it.

SILVER: You have no regrets about the use of the word 'piccaninny'?

POWELL: I didn't use it. It was in quotes, you see. So you've made
my point.

*(Enoch Powell was an undergraduate of Trinity from 1930–3, and a fellow
from 1934–8.)*

'TOWARDS 2000'

Radio Clyde, 1977

They call this programme 'Platform'. Well, I'm not entirely unaccustomed to platform speaking, but in the studio you can't speak as you would on a platform, or at least you should not, and so I am going to speak to you, whoever you are, just as if you were in the room with me and they say what the programme is about is Britain in the year 2000.

Well now, in the year 2000, if I am still alive, I shall be eighty-eight. Well I suppose I might be around but, what is certain, is that I can't be certain, and as you get older, although it is not true to say that you think less about the future, in some ways you think a lot more about the future than when you were younger. You think about the future as somewhere you won't be. The young man thinks about the future and his part in it, but when you are no longer young you are thinking about the future without yourself and the world in which you see yourself is the world of the past. So I am going to do, first, what I never could do on a public platform and that is talk a bit about myself because this is the person who is looking forward to a Britain where he won't be.

Most of my life's been taken up, one way or another, with the past because I was a classical scholar and I was a classical historian and I suppose it was a natural bent that led me to that rather than other forms of study and attainment. So I have always been used to living in four dimensions: the three dimensions of space and the fourth dimension of the past. I cannot see either the present or the future except in terms of the past and, as a classical scholar a quite long past, within which history has so often repeated itself. There is one possible advantage in this, and that is one is immunised against the error of supposing that everything is happening for the first time. Indeed, I am not sure that isn't one of the main causes of human mistakes, that people think that they are in a situation that men have never had to cope with before. Well, I won't say there are never such situations but they are rarer than people suppose.

So the early background is a preoccupation with mankind and men and their thoughts but at a distance of time. The second major thing that has occupied my life is this nation, Britain, my nation, because from well before the war, certainly from 1935, I was convinced that there was going to be a second world war and I was determined that I was going to be in it from day one. I wasn't actually, it took me a few weeks because I was in Australia when it broke out, but what happened to me, more than anything else, what mattered to me, more than anything that could happen to me personally was the outcome of that war that was to come for the existence of the nation.

And so for four years before the war and for the seven years that I was in uniform my whole life was dominated by the self-preservation against the threat of destruction from outside, of this thing, which was infinitely more important than anything else, the nation. Though, I admit I saw the nation in the framework of the British Empire. I had the misfortune to be born in an age when what we now see largely to have been the myth of the British Empire was at its height and I suppose I shall go to the grave with the idea at the back of my mind somehow that all over the oceans of the world there are those grey battleships which are invincible and the wireless message sent out from the Admiralty with switch them to wherever they are needed. I know it's not true but that is a background that you can never escape from, if it is the background of your childhood. So, as we came out of the war it was Britain and the Empire that was what mattered to me and I had to go through a long process of discovering that within the comparatively temporary phenomena of the British Empire, on which the sun never set, the flag that waved over all the continents, within that there was the nation itself, the nation in these islands, the nation, as I came more and more to see, which was represented in its central institution of Parliament and in 1950 I came to Parliament. I took to it as a duck takes to water. I never wanted any other environment to live or work in. Everything else that I have done ever since over these twenty-seven years has been subordinate to the House of Commons and so the nation is that which has given meaning to my life, purpose to my life, something that one lived for, has over the last quarter of a century been focused in the House of Commons. To which, except for an interval of eight months, I have belonged, where I have almost literally lived, certainly worked, eaten, drunk and occasionally slept.

And that brings me straight into the recent past and one of the good things that's happened in the last four months that the House of Commons, which I have thought was torpid, if not dead, bestirred itself and killed the Devolution Bill. Now I don't rejoice over that because I presume to prejudge whether Scotland can still be, is still to be included in the British nation or not, for a nation is what it thinks it is and nobody else can tell it, nobody else can decide this for it. But the thing from which the House of Commons drew back and drew back with, I believe, immensely important and so hopeful consequences, was to fudge the whole thing up and to say, well you know does it really matter, is there such an important thing as a nation represented in a sovereign House of Commons that we cannot have it both ways, coming and going. Can't we let the Scots say that they are a nation and that they can have a Parliament and that the Parliament can live side by side with the Parliament of the United Kingdom. It would not make any difference and so a Bill was put in front of the House of Commons that said just that.

It said, well the Scots as a nation can have anything they like, they can have a Parliament, but it won't make any difference to the United Kingdom, but it was nonsense and, God be praised, the House of Commons said it was nonsense and threw it out. Oh, we did it in our own way, we didn't do it by voting against the second reading or anything drastic like that but we did it in our way, saying we must be allowed to talk about this for ever because this is nonsense and we must talk it out. Now that was very important. I am sure it did no harm to Scotland, whatever Scotland's particular destiny is and whether it has a particular destiny, as no destiny is to be had through fudging but I am also sure it was very good for the House of Commons and I believe it will be good for the nation because it brought back into that place a self-consciousness of what it has been, of the voice of a nation, of a proud and sovereign nation, and through Parliament it could bring that sense back to the British people as a whole.

Now I sit in the House of Commons for the last two and a half years and, not as a Conservative from my own native West Midlands but as an Ulster Unionist. And how did I get there? Well, I got there partly for a reason I will come back to presently and a very big reason indeed and a reason which I believe is going to be fought out and decided in the future, has to be, but the immediate reason why, on finding myself no longer in the House of Commons in 1974 for reasons which I shall come back to in a moment, people in Northern Ireland asked me if I would go there and those who had been my Northern Ireland colleagues said would I come and help them and why I could and did was that right from 1969 when the present phase of violence began in Northern Ireland I didn't believe any of the conventional presentations of what was going on.

That this was something to do with Civil Rights and the electoral register and gerrymandering or that it was something to do with the difference between people who believe in Transubstantiation at the Mass or the Lord's Supper on Sunday evening or even that it was something to do with the economics and deprivation and bad housing conditions and all the rest of it. It was perfectly clear to me that this was about a nation. About whether you belonged or didn't belong or how badly you wanted to belong or how important you thought it was and that of the population a very good majority, by no means all of them Roman Catholics, felt that they belonged to the same nation as I felt I belonged to, felt that it was just as important to them and as worth, if necessary, fighting for, as I thought and still thought and so I found myself all through those years trying to bring that simple fact out. Once again the simple fact that you can't have it both ways, you can't fudge this thing, you can't say: Oh well let's find something which pretends that somehow the North East part of Ireland and the people who live there can be part of a Republic and they can also be part of the United Kingdom because don't you know it all doesn't matter. It's all out of date, it's quite unimportant, this sort of stuff. In a way, Northern Ireland in its tragic fashion has been living protest against the notion that you can treat nationhood lightly. That you can pretend it out of existence. It is not that sort of thing, it is a thing by which people live and die and for which, therefore, if necessary, they will live and die.

And so in Northern Ireland what is being settled is whether this nation, of which Northern Ireland is a part, has the will to defend itself, even against those who say that it should not be a nation. And so this brings me now to what is, I think, the great question, the great question which involves the very existence of Britain as a nation. And I use Britain, I hope I may, as a brief term for the United Kingdom of Great Britain and Northern Ireland, which is, admittedly, an inconvenient expression and we are unfortunate indeed in that the name, correct official name, of our nation is so clumsy but we know what we mean, we mean Britain.

Whether Britain is to be a nation, is to go on being a nation, is going to govern itself, is going to decide so far as humanly it can what its future is going to be, or whether it has given all that up or is prepared to give all that up in order to become a province in a new state.

That is what belonging to the European Economic Community is about. It is about the ultimate. It is To Be or Not To Be. It is about whether this nation is to be independent and self-governed as Iceland is independent and self-governed or Zambia is independent and self-governed. Just as much as the United States or the Soviet Union. Or whether our idea of our future is to be a province and a small minority province incidentally, in a state comprising the greater part of Western Europe and perhaps more than that as well.

Now there was a time when it could be argued that the European Economic Community was about free trade. I toyed with that idea myself fifteen years ago and there was a time when it could be argued if Britain with its worldwide connections and its stubborn parliamentary traditions of independence became part of it well then they could see to it that all that nonsense about creating a new state didn't happen.

That one had the advantages, with which I am a passionate believer, in free trade but that wasn't so, I believe ever and it certainly isn't so now and if we needed any proof it is the fact that our Government is, well let us say it is committed to this country, returning to a Parliament of the European Economic Community directly elected representatives. That is to say people carrying the sovereign will of the electors, just as we do in what used to be the sovereign House of Commons. And remember that four or five years ago to my consternation and I think still incredulity that House of Commons passed a Bill in which it said that a power outside this country could impose taxes, make laws, decide policies and call our Government to account over the heads of the House of Commons.

Well, you can't have a more far-reaching abnegation of everything that this parliamentary independent nation has been. So we are being asked, so we are told shall be asked, to put the seal upon that renunciation and sign and seal the document which says we are just a province like Middlesex and Renfrewshire, send representatives to a sovereign Parliament which makes laws for all of them. We shall send representatives to a sovereign Parliament, in which, like Renfrewshire and Middlesex, we shall be in a minority, which will – and who shall say 'nay'.

After all it will have a sovereign representative Parliament, being the Government of this new state. Now since the House of Commons roused itself from its torpor and said no to sharing its sovereignty with any institution like itself inside this United Kingdom, I regain my faith that the House of Commons in the name of the British people is going to say no to sharing its sovereignty, no that's an understatement, to finally resigning its sovereignty to a body created, if you like, in its own image but in a giant brockenspectre of an image in a continental state, that it's going to recall what it renounced, though it had no right to renounce it, for you can't renounce what is the vested property of a free people, what it purported to renounce back in 1972 when we went into the EEC. So my life is bound up and I can't help my image of the future being bound up with this struggle to regain the independence, the legislative sovereign independence, to regain what Iceland has still got, forgive me rubbing it in, but to regain in it the sense that the members of a nation, in my belief, cannot achieve what they are capable of when their own nation is engaged in denying its own existence.

So I am going to switch to an area in which, you might say all this had little to do. Some of the contemporary economic messes or delusions or nightmare fantasies with which the people of this country are hag-ridden today and from which I'd like to see them set free.

There's this business about the Britain that doesn't pay its way in the world.

Poor old Britain, the sick man of Europe, that has to be helped along with scraps thrown to it by other nations and crutches provided by international organisations. Well I'd hate the lot of it even if it was true but, if possible, I hate it all the more because it isn't true. It is not true that Britain cannot pay its way as they say in the world, it is not even true that it does not pay its way. All this mumbo-jumbo about our huge deficit on the balance of payments. I know this can become boring and I'm going to try not to bore you but I have to put what is economically stated in economic terms. All it is about really is a desire by other countries to rig the exchange range of sterling.

After all, what business is it of anybody else whether for reasons that seem good to ourselves we so handle our own currency that it exchanges one for one with the dollar. That is our business and if we like to run it that way I resent people coming round and saying you can't do that there. You must fix the exchange rate of your currency at an untrue point, at a point therefore at which you appear to have a huge deficit in your trade with the rest of the world, which we then, very generously, will counterbalance for you by lending you a lot of our own paper so that you can sell it again in exchange for your paper and force the exchange rate up to an unreal figure.

Now this, I admit, sounds very technical stuff, the stuff that a few gentlemen in top hats in the City of London spend their time managing but it's not really. All this is about whether we are an independent nation or not, whether we will go our own way or not, whether we will say to the rest of the world, look we will trade with you, we will trade with you on the going terms, we will borrow and lend on the going terms but we are not going to be framed within these institutions, the International Monetary Fund and all the rest of them, International Energy Authority which is going to fix the price of Scottish oil by the way, over our heads presumably, not in the market but over our heads. All these prison houses that we have built round ourselves, no, which we have allowed others to build round us, until they come to us and say you're a pretty miserable specimen aren't you, skulking there in the corner of your cell, you're no good at all, you're not fit to be an independent nation. These are gossamer bonds, these are like cobwebs – as strong as you think they are. If you think it is steel then of course you can't snap it but the moment you have seen that it is hallucination you can snap out of it, and we cocoon ourselves in this cobweb, woven round us by so many false comparisons between ourselves and the outside world.

How angry it makes me to be told that Britain does not grow like other nations. Well they say the figures show that Japan grows 10, 15, 20 per cent to our 2 per cent or 0 per cent. All I can say if this is growing, what I see and understand of the way that the Japanese live, well give me nil growth.

The things that this country's great in are things the majority of which you can't measure on these statistics. And I resent those who, well it's their choice let them have their own choice, go for the things that can be measured in quantity, turning round and saying to us, because we went through, 100 years ago, the stage of economic development that they are going through, turning round to us and saying you are lagging behind. You must imitate us if you wish to catch up with us.

I do not believe there is any catching up to be done but I do believe that we shall lose that in which we were great unless we are prepared to be true to ourselves and we cannot be true to ourselves unless we are both free and self-governed. And then the same people, they are often the same people, will say . . . we are still talking about the year 2000 aren't we?

Because these are the people who in the year 2000 want to see a great West European State, a sort of Empire, mustn't talk about Empire nowadays, but the only great West European state that we have had to do with over our long history as an offshore group of islands has been European Empires. So perhaps it is not inappropriate to remind ourselves that what we are talking about is a great West European Empire, the great West European Empire that I do not want to see come about and if it does come about I do not want to see Britain as part of it.

I don't want to dream an old man's dream of Britain being a part of it in the year 2000 . . . but these same people whose vision that is, they come and say but we are too weak to defend ourselves, to defend ourselves as a nation, we have got to be swept up into some great third force. It gives me the willies this idea of a third force, because the people of these islands, because they are the people of these islands, have always been opposed to the creation of great forces in the world. They have been the people who have helped to bring the great forces of this world crumbling into the dust, the apparently invincible forces.

Goodness I am talking as if I was on a platform. I am sorry, I didn't mean to do it. One does get rhetorical you know. This talk about giant forces, it's really a bit of rhetoric so one must forgive when one is dissecting it for one falls into a rhetorical habit. But when these great forces have come into existence we have sought a balance between them and it has proved that there was something in our position, perhaps something in us ourselves which enabled us to be the deciding element in that balance over and over again – and what has it been. What it has been has been that our island position, our island nature, as well as nationhood has given us the strength, moral and physical disproportionate to our numbers and to our wealth and to our resources just as in a continental nation it was the discipline of Prussia which gave it, a small poor country, the position and a power, not perhaps very happily used, but still a power disproportionate to its size, so those characteristics, very different, which have created and cradled this nation have given us our special power. I believe that that is not essentially changed.

I believe that we, and only we, can throw it away by ceasing to recognise ourselves for what we are. And I see us as in danger of doing that in this preoccupation with somehow being part of a third big thing. For what is this third big thing to be? We are told it is to be something like the Soviet Union only counterbalancing it as it were. Well my first observation is I don't want to be at all like the Soviet Union and I don't want to be part of anything which would counterbalance the Soviet Union.

I don't even want to be part of something like the United States for the United States is almost as different from the United Kingdom as is the Union of Soviet Socialist Republics. And this third force, this other thing, what would it be, it would be a great continental land mass and what would its defences be, what would its armageddon be, what would its battle be? It would be the great continental land battle.

Well, thank God our ultimate existence has never rested not even in 1940, no, not even in 1914–18, and by the way I'm a Landsdowne man. . . . I believe, Lord . . . perhaps you've forgotten who Lord Landsdowne was. Lord Landsdowne was the last of the Whigs, so they say. Well as a Tory that's not necessarily a commendation to me but he had the heart of the matter in 1917. He said in 1917: Look it's perfectly obvious now that the Central Powers can't win and it's perfectly obvious to them. Well let's draw the conclusion and let's make peace before we have destroyed everything because the war's decided. Let's be civilised, let's be like rational human beings and recognise the conclusion which has already been arrived at. But they had to go on, they had to go on for another year, another year or more of total destruction, though they hadn't invented the words unconditional surrender or I think not. As a matter of fact I was a Landsdowne man in World War II, in uniform as a soldier and if there were ten wars in my lifetime to come I want to be in the army in every one of them.

But as I was saying I was a Landsdowne man in the sense that in 1943 I wished, I argued that we should draw the same conclusion. It was perfectly clear by then that the Central Powers of World War II couldn't win. Let them settle scores with their unsuccessful regimes, let them deal with the dictators that had brought them to that pass, but no need to carry on the chess game to the point of sweeping all the pieces off the board and smashing the board up as well into the bargain. But apparently we had to go on.

Still I suppose this was a digression but happily at no time have we ever been subject, this nation, to arbitrament of the land battle and we were not subject to it just by the skin of our teeth in 1940 and in 1940 we were the third force, and we were the balancing factor and we were able in the old phrase to save Europe by our example and ourselves by our exertions, not because we were better men, braver men, more resolute men that the men of other nations but just because we were the nation that we are, situated as we are. Now that capability is still there.

True the North Atlantic Alliance makes sense in the present circumstances but the North Atlantic Alliance for us is a grouping within which we should preserve before all else our characteristic strength, which is our power as an island Atlantic nation to control the sea space and the air space above and around us.

So over all the years that I have been in Parliament and especially in the years when, and I thought it a privilege, and it was one I wanted and one I valued when I had it, to be the spokesman of the opposition of matters of defence . . . through all those years I have argued that first and foremost for Britain there should come this concentration, an overwhelming concentration on what it is to be a maritime nation.

That the whole shape of our outlook upon defence, the whole shape of our forces, the whole shape of our preparation for an unforeseeable war, for wars there will be. . . . I will say a word about the Bomb in a minute . . . but that that whole shape should be a shape appropriate to the nation that we are.

And that our army therefore and I say again I'm an army man, I love the British army, I loved every minute of my army service, I rejoiced in it. But that our army should be the army that is appropriate to a maritime nation. An army therefore that is no longer a colonial army, an imperial army, a garrison army, nor an army which is a component in a continental land battle army, though we need to understand the thinking, the philosophy, the technology and so on of the continental land battle. But in this sense a citizen army, namely, an army which will be ready when the continental phase, the land phase of the self-defence of a continental nation comes along in its due place in the struggle for existence and survival.

So I want to see the Britain of the future capable of the ultimate self-defence of what this nation is. And that ultimate capability is a maritime capability . . . sea, air, surface, under the surface . . . but that above all, though retaining the will to arm expressed inevitably by an army which is an essential part of being a nation and being an independent nation.

But I promised that I would say a word about the nuclear theology, for, by jove, it is a pretty abstruse theology in some of its ranges and it belongs in this picture because it has been used these many years. It has been used these thirty years since the war as a means of beating down, beating into the ground our belief that there is such a thing any longer as a nation, that nations exist unless they be these fantasm, dinosaur nations. Well when the Spartans were at Thermopylae, the pass which they held against the invading Persian hordes, someone came to them and told them in order to frighten them that when the Persians let off their arrows it darkened the sky and you could not see the sun. Well, said the Spartans, in that case we shall have to fight in the dark.

I believe that this is a good metaphor for the only practical effect of the advent of the nuclear capability. It is a sort of roof, a very lofty roof, erected over the nations of mankind, under the shadow of which, if you like, in the darkness of it, if that isn't too dramatic, they will still fight, not for extermination but for the mastery of one over the other. For the imposition of one's system upon another. For all the things for which nations sought to preserve their freedom or to impose their will upon others. So I don't believe that nations and nationhood and all that goes with it has been rendered obsolete or can be rendered obsolete by mankind having theoretically the capability to perform the ultimate insanity. So I want to see, under that stratospheric roof that has been erected, I want to see in the year 2000 as in the year 1900 and the year 1600, a nation that in its own element is ready to defend as a nation its freedom, its right to govern itself.

So I'd best, at the end, come home and look at the way we govern ourselves, a look at our society, what is amiss in it and what we perhaps wrongly tell ourselves is amiss and here I cannot help mentioning, I literally cannot help mentioning it, I only wish I could have done and perhaps it wouldn't have been my fate to do so if it hadn't been my fate to represent in Parliament over nearly twenty-five years a town in the West Midlands to which this reason to fear the future came sooner than it came to most parts of the nation.

But the essence of a nation is that it is in this sense homogeneous, that it accepts a single sovereignty, it accepts a single system, yes, but above all that every part of it thinks that the whole is more important than the parts. That all its parts however diverse, all its elements for all their differences and their separate prides, in the last resort, though they might strive to pretend otherwise would let all that go for the sake of the existence and the survival and the well-being of the whole to which they belong, the nation to which they belong.

Inside a nation, you cannot contain elements which are foreign to it in the sense that they cannot share that devotion to the whole as against the parts. Of course if such elements are very small then the challenge which they pose to the integrity of the nation is correspondingly small.

Now it is my misfortune that I foresaw sooner than most that there is portended by what exists today, that there is portended an England in which up to one-third of some of the main cities, including inner London, will be inhabited by those who, for no fault of their own, I make this no complaint, it is in the nature of things, do not, and I believe, will not, because I believe they cannot, have the same relationship to the nation, that relationship of part to the whole, to which all, in the last resort must be sacrificed, as the rest.

I repeat, that this is not a guess, that this is not one of those extrapolations, I think they call them, whereby you take hold of a line on the graph which is going in a certain direction, put a ruler on it and draw its projection with a pencil until it goes off the graph at a horrifyingly high or low point. No, this prospect around the beginning of the next millennium, the year 2000 that one is talking about, this projection of cities one-third, the word is coloured, but colour is just a convenient word or an index, one-third inhabited by populations as strange to the rest as if those populations were still living in Asia, or Africa, or the West Indies.

That prospect is already constituted by the composition, age, structure and so on of the population as it is today.

Therefore, that constitutes a question mark over the future of the nation, which I have not been able to repress in my own mind and no more than one can withhold the sight of danger from my, once fellow, human beings, have I been able to keep silent. I suppose it is implanted upon us by instinct, just as it is implanted in other animals by instinct, that the one who sees the danger or thinks he sees it, raises a white tail or utters a particular cry.

So it is instinctive that a member of a society, especially a member belonging to that specialist function of the society, whose business it is to speak for, about the future of that society, should utter the cry of alarm, should try to define what it is that he sees so that if others see it then they can be warned, warned one hopes in time.

Now that is all I'm going to say about that particular subject, but, by leaving it there, I don't mean to imply that I don't regard it as capable of negating and neutralising everything else. If I thought otherwise I would not have been able, and I would not have been prepared to sacrifice, in order to do so, all that it is necessary to sacrifice, by those who think they see and therefore think they must draw attention to this question mark over the future.

And so let me come back to other aspects of our society. And I am coming back largely to where I started because I am coming back to where I live, I come back to the House of Commons. My belief in what we call democracy, by a Greek word – we don't have it, fortunately, in the Greek form, which was a very unmanageable form of it – what we call democracy, but the form we classify as democratic, but which is really parliamentary self-government and what's that?

That is the self-government of a nation which talks itself through to its decisions. Which talks itself through to reconciling, but not compromising, differences of opinion. Which talks itself through to those adjustments, often painful, which changes in the environment of the outside world, changes which affect industry, which affect the class structure, which affect the way we live, which affect the place, the numbers in which we work, which affect British Leyland. We are a nation which has learnt, which has indeed formed itself, which has become conscious of itself in the process of learning to live by talking its way through, but not talking anyhow.

Not talking on the street corner, not talking in great crowds, not talking at one another and not talking in pulpits but talking to the Government in a particular place and in a particular way and under particular conventions. And talking to a Government which is part of a club, talking to a Government, even the most mighty, are in that club, exactly equal to all the rest. Just as liable to be laughed at, just as liable to be shouted down and who only count for one when they walk through a rather peculiar door and are counted in a rather peculiar way. But that place is where the talking of the nation is brought to a focus and in that place we have to try to make sense to one another. We have each to try to convince one another that though they may not agree with us, we have a rational motivation and a motivation which we can ultimately reconcile with the same standards as those with which they too, our opponents, must reconcile their arguments and their objects. Now that to me is the meaning of democracy which has formed our nation and which ultimately makes this a nation worth preserving, worth retaining its freedom, worth living for and worth dying for. And so I want to see, I hope there will be when I am no longer there, a House of Commons, extraordinarily like this one.

Because this one, you know, is extraordinarily like the House of Commons of Pitt and Burke, extraordinarily like the House of Commons of Cromwell and Hyde, Clarendon, the rest, those who formed this nation and made it self-conscious.

But in the last resort we shall go out as individuals when the time for us comes, and when that moment comes, I still believe that out beyond the year 2000 there will be that other nation, that other citizenship by which our nation has also been formed, to which from this place we shall go hence.

'THE IMPERFECT DREAM: A RETURN PASSAGE TO INDIA'

The Times, 7 May 1983

I never read *A Passage to India* until last year, at a great distance therefore of time and circumstance from the years either of its composition or of the huge popularity which it enjoyed immediately after its publication in 1924.

Forster was in India for five months in 1912–13 and for nine months in 1921, mainly in the United Provinces (Uttar Pradesh) and Bihar, and in the State of Dewas Senior. I ought, before addressing myself to an assessment of Forster's book, to lay my own credentials on the table.

I was in India as an officer (British service, General Staff, Lieutenant-Colonel to Brigadier) for two years and a half, from August 1943 to February 1946. It was at my own desire (as often happens in the British Army in wartime) that I went east after two years' service in the Middle East and North Africa Commands. I wanted to get into the war against Japan as soon as the crisis of the war with Germany was past, with a view, as I used to put it, to 'getting to Singapore before the Americans'. In the summer of 1943 I jumped into Wingate's taxi in Cairo to beg a place in the Chindits, but he was killed before I cashed the cheque. In the end I persuaded General Cawthorn, a 16th Punjabi, the Director of Military Intelligence (India), to take me on his staff to organise joint service intelligence.

I saw this as just a stepping-stone to the Far East; but by the time Lord Mountbatten in 1944 moved South-East Asia Command HQ from Delhi to Kandy (Sri Lanka), I had fallen hopelessly and helplessly in love with India, and I refused a transfer to Mountbatten's staff. If in 1946 there had been a foreseeable future in the Indian Army, I would have opted to 'leave my bones there'. There was not, and I came home. General Cawthorn, who became almost a second father to me, continued in senior military and civil capacities to serve the successor state of Pakistan. He never lost his faith in India or Pakistan. He had watched with pleasure and approval the growth of my Indian absorption.

The love affair started on my first night in India, which I passed in my valise on a platform at Delhi railway station. With the sights, the sounds and the odours I drew in a new intimation. For the next two years and a half I studied, enquired and read voraciously about India. It was in Delhi that for the first time in my life I began to take an interest in buildings. I became an amateur of Islamic architecture, travelling in search of the more celebrated examples by train and bicycle – above all by bicycle, the ideal form of Indian locomotion.

On short leaves my bearer and I put our bicycles in the luggage van and might have been filmed in silhouette cycling in single file along a *bund* somewhere in the U. P. or Gujerat. He was a tall, solemn Poonchi, whom I remember on the day I left India for home bursting into tears which trickled slowly down his long henna-dyed beard. It was not the only sad leave-taking that day. The other was from my Urdu teacher, a man of Panipat, himself a poet and nephew of one of the greatest Urdu poets, Hali. He had not only taken me through my interpretership but we had worked together at the prosody and scansion of Urdu poetry, he reflectively chewing betel from his silver pan-box as I read aloud.

No man can see India in ten or twenty times as long as I was there. But I was fortunate, though huge areas remained blank on my map, to cross and re-cross the sub-continent from Rawalpindi to Akyab in Burma, from Karachi to Dacca, from Madras to Darjeeling; and not the least rewarding months were those when I wrote – all but single-handed – the report of the Committee on the Post-War Indian Army, the army that was to be torn in two, to whose last commander-in-chief, Auchinleck, I gave my own copy thirty years later. But I must discipline myself, and not run on, adding memory to memory from the torrent of pictures that come tumbling out at the summons of an Indian word or an Indian event. Still, the nature of my own Indian experience is strictly relevant to the impression left upon me by *A Passage to India*.

That impression was initially one of repugnance at a representation so patently and grossly distorted. N. C. Chaudhuri was near the mark when he associated the book with 'the growth of that mood which enabled the British people to leave India with an almost Pilate-like gesture of washing their hands of a disagreeable affair'. Even taking into account the fact that most of the book was written during the aftermath of the massacre in the Jallianwala Bagh, Amritsar, the book reads like a deliberate caricature, as biased and as ill-informed as the deliverances of that proverbial fun-figure, Paget MP, who spent 'twenty-one days in India' before writing his authoritative accounts.

To me it simply rang false that the National Anthem 'was the Anthem of the Army of Occupation: it reminded every member of the Club that he or she was British and in exile'; or that an English woman 'who had been a nurse in a native state' said that a dying

Indian 'can go where he likes as long as he doesn't come near me, they give me the creeps'; or that a city magistrate would say, 'I am out here to work, mind, to hold this wretched country by force'; or that the lieutenant-governor of a province, because 'exempted by a long career in the Secretariat from personal contact with the peoples of India' was therefore 'able to speak of them urbanely and deplore racial prejudice'; or that the same city magistrate would write, 'the longer one lives here, the more certain one gets that everything hangs together; my personal opinion is, it's the Jews'.

My second thoughts began when I discovered that Forster had nevertheless perceived, and, as far as it can be done at all, described, that sense of hallucination which pervades India. 'Nothing in India is identifiable, the mere asking of a question causes it to disappear or to merge in something else.' As I once heard it remarked of the rope-trick, 'it is essentially Indian, because no such trick ever existed'. The English in India, for all their doing and striving, became part of that hallucination. The Raj itself (without intending the pun) was a mirage, a dream which British and Indians dreamed together and which individuals will still dream again when they meet, long, long after other dreams and other hallucinations have succeeded it. Leave out Forster's pasteboard figures of fun, and his physical descriptions of scenes and cities evoke the dream as they only could if someone who also felt it had written them.

The Indians in the book are nearer reality that the Europeans. It was, after all, Forster's tutorship of a young Indian Muslim, and his affection for him, which booked the passage, and it was to princely India and to Muslim Indian society – admittedly through the medium of western education and the English language – that he was introduced. The Indian hero of the book, Dr Aziz, is well drawn, with his endearing self-knowledge of the limitations and embarrassments felt by those like himself in confrontation and comparison with the Englishman. Very significantly, Forster fathered upon Aziz a shrewd observation: 'Aziz liked soldiers – they either accepted or swore at you, which was preferable to the hauteur of the Englishman.'

I found the hint pregnant. In fact the army, British or Indian, and soldiers in general, are totally absent from the *Passage*. If Pierre Loti's India was *Les Indes sans les Anglais*, Forster's India is India without the army. I much question if the attempt to depict or understand India under the Raj with that enormous omission is not foredoomed. It would in any event go far to account for the incompatibility of Forster's India with mine.

Unlike any other native army of the European colonial powers, the Indian Army was quite deliberately and self-consciously Indian: its language was Urdu, its European officers were on an extraordinarily low cadre – a system derived from the so-called irregular units of the Punjab, not from the East India Company's regiments – and success, promotion and opportunity lay for them through deep and thorough knowledge of the people and the country. Whoever else may have mistaken the army for an 'Army of Occupation', the army itself did not. I write as one who was hardly ever out of uniform in India wherever he travelled, often alone, and whose encounter with India began less than a year after the 'rebellion' of 1942.

The word I constantly recur to when I attempt to describe the atmosphere up to a mere fifteen months of the sudden (and cata-strophic) British withdrawal in 1947 is 'inevitability'. Whatever the politicians were saying and the papers were writing, the British seemed – seemed, I say, for all is hallucination – a natural part of the scene. The moon rose, the cow walked through the village, the British magistrate or officer went about his duties, as if from time immemorial. In fact, in parts of Bihar within the present century the British were called 'the Muslims', so natural was their identification with the dynasties of the past.

Dr Aziz and the officer played a chukka of polo together, 'the fire of good fellowship in their eyes'; but Forster could not leave it so. 'Nationality had returned, but before it could *exert its poison* [my italics] they parted, saluting each other. "If only they were all like that", each thought.' I wonder what Forster's *Passage* would have been like if – unimaginably – he had served there in a British line regiment and then, after that initiatory year, in an Indian unit.

Fielding, the English schoolmaster, is in his way as overdrawn and caricatured as the other European figures, though he is still a recognisable type and I could put two or three names and faces to it; but Fielding is the subject of another pregnant hint which perhaps complements the hint about Aziz liking soldiers. 'He had discovered that it is possible to keep in with Indians and Englishmen, but that he who would keep in with Englishwomen must drop the Indians. The two wouldn't combine.' This is well-trodden ground: ' "Do kindly tell us who these ladies are," asked Mrs Moore. "You're superior to them anyway. Don't forget that. You're superior to everyone in India except one or two of the Ranis, and they're on an equality." '

Two great causes enforced the situation described in Fielding's aphorism. In the first place, the totally different social conventions governing the life of Indian women, Muslim and to a lesser degree Hindu, raised between them and European women (and therefore European mixed society) a barrier to which no obstacle between European and Indian men was in any way comaparable.

Only outside the bounds of mixed society – in the camp, on tour, or when, as in wartime, medicine or missionary work, performing analogous roles to men – would the European woman ever be in India other than a stranger at a distance in a strange land. This factor was intensified by the other. Soon after the middle of the nineteenth century, when improved conditions of communication and living made it possible and therefore unavoidable, the English family, civilian and to a lesser degree military, straddled uneasily and often unhappily the poles apart of Britain and India.

To this degree there is a core of truth beneath the crudity and bias with which, for all its literary skill, the plot of *A Passage to India* is woven. The dream that the British and the Indians dreamed together for so long, a dream unique in human history in its strangeness and its improbability, was bound to break one day. Even India, the land of hallucinations, could not preserve it for ever from its contradictions. This the wisest of the British in India had seen and known all along, though some of us, under the influence of our love affair, dared to believe otherwise. Yet the dream was always imperfect; it was a dream that only the men would ever dream.

Taken from the summer edition of the Folio Society quarterly magazine

INTERVIEW WITH ANNE BROWN

BBC Radio, 13 April 1986

BROWN: Enoch Powell is one of the most enigmatic and controversial figures in British politics. He's respected as a brilliant intellectual and parliamentarian, but he's probably best known for his outspoken views on immigration which got him the sack from Ted Heath's Shadow Cabinet in 1968. Six years later he parted company with the Conservatives altogether over the Common Market issue and became an Ulster Unionist. Most recently he's been campaigning vigorously against the Anglo-Irish Agreement. But Enoch Powell wasn't always a politician – he was thirty-seven when he entered Parliament. Before that he'd been a Professor of Greek and served as a Brigadier in India during the war . . . Enoch Powell, what did you want to be when you were a small boy?

POWELL: I could read reasonably at the age of three . . . and I imagined that I would be a scholar.

BROWN: Your mother was a teacher by profession. How much do you think that influenced her approach to your learning?

POWELL: My mother and father were both teachers, elementary-school teachers and my father once said to me that if I were not a teacher, it would be contrary to the laws of biology . . . and I suppose looking back over my misspent political life, perhaps I have been teaching after all . . . but that is the essence of what I have been doing. I have a natural instinct myself for teaching and I find myself at home in that environment, but maybe my er early environment contributed to that . . . mind you, I'm dubious about environment having so big a share in what we are. I think what we are is overwhelmingly congenital . . . that our fate is more or less settled when that individual comes into the world.

BROWN: But I mean, if you were this academic child . . . my image of the academic children that I knew when I was young was that they tended to be outside the mainstream – they didn't have so many friends – people were a bit jealous of them.

POWELL: I never had any sense of separation because of the clarity and power of my own mind. I never regarded it as a basis for a sense of superiority to other people.

BROWN: Did you have a nickname at school?

POWELL: Scowelly Powelly!

BROWN: How on earth did you . . .

POWELL: I had a bad habit of frowning! . . .

BROWN: Maybe this was because you were thinking deeply when . . .

POWELL: Maybe, but I think it's . . . it's just a facial habit.

BROWN: How did you get on with the other boys?

POWELL: I've always been happy in a collective environment . . . I've always been happy with a group of people . . . if er my memories of my undergraduate life are not so happy, they are simply because I had not learned by the time I went to Cambridge to take part in that sort of collective existence . . . but I learned afterwards.

BROWN: Why did you not, though, take advantage of the environment of Cambridge as so many people did . . . ?

POWELL: I didn't know how to do it . . . I thought that I had to go on working.

BROWN: And you went on working very hard . . .

POWELL: So I got up at half-past five in the morning and I worked right through and I didn't know what else there was to do . . . it's true . . . I was terribly wrapped up in what I was doing . . . when I got up at half-past five it was to write my translation of Herodotus into Bible English, so, I wasn't doing this under any sense of constraint, or duress, it was just that I didn't know what else there was to do.

BROWN: Did you hide behind it perhaps, were you very shy?

POWELL: I wasn't shy . . . I was uneducated socially. I felt suffocated in Cambridge. They offered me, or there would have been available to me a Fellowship under Title F which would have secured me a lasting Research Fellowship at Cambridge . . . but the whole idea of that oppressed me . . . so from the time I was twenty-three, I put in for professorships . . . nothing less was worth having . . . in Red Brick . . . and all went well until they discovered I was only twenty-three or twenty-four when their ardour cooled . . . but Sydney's ardour didn't cool . . . I was twenty-four at the time and they appointed me so I accepted it.

BROWN: You were an arrogant young intellectual, weren't you?

POWELL: Well, I am intellectually arrogant . . . this is one of the things about me, I'm afraid . . . that I have a conviction in my own capability of being right when everybody else is wrong. I have a savage reliance on the working of my own intellect, which renders me impervious to intellectual isolation.

BROWN: Has it ever failed you, your arrogance?

POWELL: Once . . . I got to learn how it worked . . . my brain has never let me down. I have never set it a problem with the solution to which it has declared itself unable to cope. But I have to leave it alone . . . I have to be patient with it . . . and yet I have learned to know that if I send something down there . . . the machine will grind on it and I shall be provided with my answer to it . . . it will come up sometimes quite belatedly, but it comes up out of a machine . . . it's like that . . .

BROWN: You see, I would say that that happens to everyone . . . but it's not necessarily the intellect that we attribute it to. I would very often say it's a gut reaction at the end of the day that makes the decision . . . that you feed the information in and from somewhere very deep down, the answer emerges.

POWELL: My gut reaction is much quicker than my intellectual combination. Outburst is a word which is often used in reporting my actions and sayings. Nothing could be less true. I never say anything I haven't intended to say. I never say it when I haven't intended to say it . . . I never say what I haven't intended to say. The last thing I seek to do is to see myself as inherently different from my fellow beings . . . I don't. I'm a herd animal . . .

BROWN: You've always been fond of institutions . . . I mean you seem to go from one institution to another.

POWELL: I love my school . . . I honour my school. I love my College and I am proud of my College . . . and I am proud of my regiment . . . but the sense of being shoulder to shoulder with other human beings is very powerful for me.

BROWN: What is it . . . ?

POWELL: And of conformity if you like . . .

BROWN: Well, yes is it that?

POWELL: I'm a great conformist and this shows in politics . . . this shows in the House of Commons. Perhaps this is what, if anything has, has given me a place in the House of Commons. Conformity and precedent are modes of living in which I rejoice.

BROWN: Is there a sort of safety in being within the confines of an institution?

POWELL: Not that I am conscious of . . . though you're probably right . . . because no one is intellectually freer than when he is outwardly conforming. I am fortunate to be a member of the Church of England which, provided I conform . . . allows me to think what I think.

BROWN: But in your teens and early thirties, you were an atheist . . . and yet you've embraced the Church of England later on. How did that come about?

POWELL: One night I was coming back to my lodgings in Wolverhampton from the station and I passed St Peter's Church and the bells were ringing for Evensong . . . and I turned right and went in. I was quite ashamed of myself and I sat right by the door in a dark corner because I didn't know what I was doing . . . and I opened a prayer book and I thought to myself . . . 'This is wonderful' . . . and I came again and again and again . . . and I realised a necessity upon me which I couldn't refuse.

BROWN: But I can't imagine that the intellectual didn't question the reasons and question again the atheism that you had felt.

POWELL: The intellect still works . . . but it doesn't fight any longer with the rest of the personality which worships.

BROWN: So we're back to the gut reaction, to the emotional man.

POWELL: A human being is not primarily an intellectual machine.

BROWN: Yes, you've often said you're an emotional man . . .

POWELL: I'm quixotic . . .

BROWN: . . . and that you have to hide your emotions, you have to fight to keep them down . . .

POWELL: I suppose that everybody who is conscious of his emotions has to control them.

BROWN: You wrote poetry in those days at Cambridge and you continued to write poetry. What subjects did you write about?

POWELL: I wrote lyric poetry. I wrote lyric poetry first about the pangs of growing old and my goodness how old you grow when you become twenty-three after being twenty-two. And then, as the war cast its shadow at any rate over me . . . I wrote poetry about the coming war.

BROWN: But how did poetry exorcise those feelings . . . why . . . why through that particular medium?

POWELL: If you're a poet, you say what most needs to be said in poetry.

BROWN: And whom do you say it for? Do you say it for yourself, or do you say it . . .

POWELL: Oh, no, no, no, no. All artists do what they do for somebody else. To write poetry which nobody will read is inconceivable. I can't write an autobiography . . . and never shall. There's something which sickens me about turning in on oneself and saying today I did this and that's what I had for breakfast and those were my wise thoughts and I put them down in this diary and now I close it and lock it up. Like music, poetry is something which you say to other people in the conviction that they will feel the same if they hear those words . . . thus arranged and thus ordered . . . and I suppose in politics, that's what I have been doing. I have been saying to people . . . this is how I feel . . . you surely must feel the same.

BROWN: You had this foreboding of war . . . perhaps it was more than that because you travelled in Europe and you saw what was happening in Europe. I always think of it as a time when there was a heightened sense of living perhaps . . . particularly for the young. Did you feel that . . . that time perhaps was not going to be very long?

POWELL: Well, I didn't . . . but this was the rare exception. It was, I think, only those of us who had an insight into what was happening on the continent of Europe who were seized with this conviction of doom and I was convinced that my intention to volunteer immediately war came meant that I would not survive, so I lived until the middle 1940s a life which I assumed to be shortly to be terminated. But in 1944, it began to look less like that and there was one day when it suddenly struck me. It was the day the monsoon came and I went out on the verandah as one does in the monsoon and stood and got wet just for the joy of it . . . and I said to myself . . . you're going to survive the war . . . there'll be a life after the war, what will you do? . . . I'll go in to the House of Commons, I said. Now, why did I say that? For the wrong reason . . . for the mistaken reason . . . for the reason which turned out wrong. I was deeply bound up with India and I felt that a connection Britain had with India was a profound and lasting connection . . . but that it could be destroyed if the wrong decisions were taken in the House of Commons. I was quite mistaken about this . . . but that was what I thought and it was therefore from India, as it were, that I went into the House of Commons.

BROWN: Having felt this sense of foreboding and then realising you were going to survive the war . . . were you disappointed in any way that you had managed to survive the war and that you hadn't actually been involved in any major battle?

POWELL: Well, all soldiers who come home alive carry a sort of shame with them to the grave. 'Why wasn't I taken? Why was I left?' I'm sure that every man who's served in war and survives, has that in his mind.

BROWN: You wrote some poems about this . . .

POWELL: Yes, I tried to say this . . . er . . . rather metaphorically . . . in one poem I put it more directly, the poem that I wrote about the Battle of Alamein.

> I dreamt that I saw with waking eyes
> Scenes so often in imagination wrought
> The flame-wall in the night at Alamein,
> Before the attack.
>
> And I was glad and thought,
> My sorrow and despair was, after all,

Some evil dream.
It still is not too late. . . .

My friends who passed before me through
Through that wall not lost,
Nor I forever separate from them
Condemned to live. . . .

I break tonight as they did
Through the fire
Knowing and known shall pass
Into their sight. . . .

But then I awoke and recollection came
That I forever and alone
Remain on this side
Of the separating flame.

That's the guilt of the soldier who survives.

BROWN: I can see from your tears now that those feelings are still with you, very strong. What was it like for you . . . coming back to England with your strong conviction to go into politics and that guilt, probably a changed man from the time you went into the war?

POWELL: Because something was released in me. Because a lifetime lay ahead. I saw women for the first time. I saw a whole life ahead for the first time . . . and that change was terrific. So there was, I suppose, a second crisis which had to be passed through, of initiation, into the full life . . . and I tried to break into it prematurely and I have left some record of that too.

BROWN: This is a poem which you wrote after you'd met your wife? . . . is that right?

POWELL: No, it's not about my wife . . .

I dreamt that on the mountain crest
That in the sheep-cropped grass we lay.
The words that ever at my breast
Leap and are striving to be spoken,
Suddenly I began to say.

Yet, words not those I purposed
From lips and heart impassioned broke
But as it seemed to me, I said,

'Therefore, with all Archangels, I,
All Angels in Heaven's company
Thy glorious name do magnify
Thee praising and for evermore saying . . .

And from your mouth,
Reply not such that I waited for
In whispered tones mysterious came
But, 'Holy thou of Hosts, the Lord
Full of thy Glory Earth and Sky,
Glory to Thee oh God most high.'

You ceased.
The wind that through the sward with
With steady breathing passion swept
From flower and grass and heather
Amen to that strange sacrament.
And silent, as it seemed, we wept. . . .

And that had to be buried . . . buried on the same mountain . . . so there.

BROWN: What did you learn from women, once you'd discovered them? How different do you think women are from men?

POWELL: You learn that they have the other half of the universe, that they command the other half of the potentialities of human nature, which is why the whole notion of equality in the sense of doing the same thing is so absurd. We are respectively programmed, each to do things that the other cannot do.

BROWN: But, are there not also areas where we can do the same thing but in different ways . . . bring our own . . .

POWELL: In different ways . . . we do it together.

BROWN: And what about women in society . . . I mean, with your views on the male and the female personalities being different and one having one half of the world and the other having the other . . . if you can . . .

POWELL: Well, we tried the experiment and we are still trying it socially and politically – of using women to do the jobs for which men are programmed. As long as we don't push that experiment too far, I think we shall gropingly find the bounds of the potentialities of the two sexes . . . I think through women attempting to do these things, we shall be more conscious of how these things are best done and how the specialisation, the programming of the two sexes is destined to be applied in society, in human society.

BROWN: How would you push the balance too far?

POWELL: I suppose you can destroy your society by casting people into roles which they do not belong in. The fear that man has the power to destroy himself is one of the main motivating forces in politics. We are an animal which very specially is capable of committing suicide and we are capable of committing collective as well as individual suicide. We don't know how . . .

BROWN: I mean, having a woman Prime Minister . . . is that pushing it near . . .

POWELL: Or having . . . er . . . women soldiers and women commanding regiments. I think there is an ultimate incompatibility between the nature of a woman and the organisation and enjoying of killing, which is something which is known to the male sex.

BROWN: OK, if we're restricted to politics, women in politics . . . do you see women having a role in politics . . . they're in there . . . some of them are in there, but . . . are they rightfully in there?

POWELL: They're in there, and very uncomfortable they are there.

BROWN: Why is that? I wonder if that's because the men make them feel uncomfortable?

POWELL: They're uncomfortable because they've found themselves in the sixth form of a boy's school . . . and they've found themselves amongst a very dramatic expression of collectivity. The collective sense of the House of Commons is something very male. I'll give you an example of what I mean . . . One of the ways in which a male survives in a collective environment is by making a fool of himself . . . by deliberately inducing the other members of the herd to laugh at him. No woman does that without self-destruction. A woman is not programmed to make herself look ridiculous. Many men are . . . and any man can use that as one of his instruments of collaboration with his fellow men. I find life very funny. I find that humour and finding life funny gets me through difficult periods and that my tendency in emergency is to joke.

BROWN: Have you found much to laugh at in your political career?

POWELL: Oh a lot, yes, I laugh all the time.

BROWN: What sort of occasions did you resort to laughter? I mean I'm sure you do in the day to day . . .

POWELL: The drollery of pushing the thing . . . to seeing the absurdities which are implicit in it overcome one at the most liberating moment.

BROWN: But, you can't just say that that's the way it is, and because that's the way men behave in the House of Commons, it is right and therefore women shouldn't be in there . . .

POWELL: Well, there's a very strong argument for saying that, because that's how it is, that's how it's right . . . after all, things are because they have survived that way. There is an inherent presumption in favour of how it has come to be, isn't there?

BROWN: But we're evolving all the time, and society has changed . . .

POWELL: But are we evolving all the time? You're making a very big assumption there. Is *homo sapiens* still evolving?

BROWN: But it seems to me, the alternative is to say that *homo sapiens* is standing still and society is standing still . . . we may not be evolving for the better, but surely we are changing? The very fact that the role of women has changed . . .

POWELL: I don't think human nature changes. But these are conjectures . . . I admit . . . everybody discriminates between all his fellow human beings. We differentiate between one and the other and we react to one another differently and we behave to one another differently. I discriminate between my wife and other women. I discriminate between women and men. I can't help it, I do.

BROWN: But why did you discriminate between coloured immigrants coming into this country and other immigrants coming into this country?

POWELL: Because they discriminate between themselves and us . . . they see themselves as we see themselves and they cannot help but see themselves and it is not their fault that they see themselves as essentially different . . . as not belonging.

BROWN: Are you not simply voicing a gut reaction?

POWELL: Yes, but we've agreed on the dominant importance in human affairs of gut reaction, haven't we? It's not possible for someone who sees a danger which he believed threatens the very existence of what he belongs to and not utter a cry . . . and if his cries aren't heard, he goes on crying . . . no doubt we're programmed to do that too.

BROWN: It was a dangerous cry, though, and it got you the sack in '68. How did you react then, when you were sacked?

POWELL: It had happened.

BROWN: Is there something about being an outsider which attracts you?

POWELL: No, it doesn't attract me at all . . . but I can survive in that environment . . . but it doesn't attract me . . . because everything is achieved collectively, everything is achieved by persuading others, by carrying others with you . . . so by definition, isolation is failure.

BROWN: Do you see yourself as having failed, because you did have a vision, you hoped when you entered politics that one day you might be a Prime Minister.

POWELL: Only in the sense that, no doubt, everybody who goes into the law wants to become Lord Chief Justice, for all I know . . . but it would be a caricature to say that one says that I want to become Prime Minister. I think there have been such people, but I don't think they've been either happy or successful.

BROWN: But supposing you had become Prime Minister, what would you have liked to see . . . ?

POWELL: Oh, if I had become Prime Minister, that could only have happened as a result of the acceptance by the Conservative Party and the electorate of what I am and what I stood for – so it's a circular question.

BROWN: And how would you sum yourself up? What sort of a person are you?

POWELL: Others will form their pictures of what I am and what I was.

BROWN: How would you like to be remembered?

POWELL: I should like to have been killed in the war.

'THEORY AND PRACTICE'

from *Philosophy and Politics*, Cambridge, 1990

I intend, here, in reflecting on my life to see if, by taking what appear to me in retrospect to be three critical points of vantage from which to describe my situation, my intentions and the thought, if any, which lay behind them, I can be of service.

I start in February, 1946. I am still wearing the King's uniform, which I have worn for the previous six and a half years, and I have just returned to England after an absence of nearly five years, of which the last two and half have been spent in India. Having reconciled myself more or less reluctantly to the uncovenanted bonus of a probable normal length of life, I have already asked myself what I intend to do with it; and that other self, which stands there on the doorstep when you open the door, like an unwanted caller, has given me the answer: 'You are going into politics.' But why? A negative reason first: I never meant to go back to a university, for I felt that I would be smothered there and eaten alive. But why politics? I had not only no sympathy, but deep hostility during the 1930s towards the Conservative Governments of the United Kingdom, which I regarded as having been purblind to the situation in which the United Kingdom found itself and having pushed to the extremity of danger the safety and survival of . . . and I would undoubtedly have followed the preposition 'of' at that time with the words 'the British Empire', for, in 1939 it was in fact the British Commonwealth and Empire, which, in a somewhat ragged fashion, did at last and belatedly go to war, and I had participated in my own way in the success with which that structure, if it *was* a structure, had defended itself and, if it survived, had survived. As I mentioned, the last two and a half years had been in India, the centre in many ways, emotionally, organisationally, and strategically, of that conglomeration, and it seemed to me, that the way things were going there pointed to dissolution. There is a saying (I hope I attribute it correctly to Burke, and I hope I locate it correctly in the trial of Warren Hastings) to the effect that 'the keys of India are not in Calcutta, they are not in Delhi, they are on the dispatch box in the House of Commons'. I certainly believed, wrongly, that the necessary willpower and the necessary decisions were still located there in 1946, and I wished, in this uncovenanted extension of my life, to take a hand in the governance of India. The route was to be the route to that key – through Parliament and via the despatch box.

So, I had answered my own question with the reply: 'You are going into politics,' and within twenty-four hours of landing at Brize Norton – and on landing at Brize Norton I remember weeping when I saw green fields – I looked up 'C' in the telephone directory, 'C' for 'Conservative', for 'Conservative Central Office'. Now, why, having already indicated my total antipathy to the Conservative Party and successive Conservative Governments as I had known them before 1939? Because I supposed that, if there was to be a vehicle and a framework for what I imagined I would be doing, it had to be the Conservative Party. I was born a Tory. Define: a Tory is a person who regards authority as immanent in institutions. I had always been, as far back as I could remember in my existence, a respecter of institutions, a respecter of monarchy, a respecter of the deposit of history, a respecter of everything in which authority was capable of being embodied, and that must surely be what the Conservative Party was about, the Conservative Party as the party of the maintenance of acknowledged prescriptive authority. (I would not at that stage have yet been using the term 'prescriptive' as readily as I was to train myself afterwards to use it.) There was something else; it would be a party which did not believe in always starting afresh over and over again, it would be a non-innovatory party, a party which chimed in, therefore, with my own prejudices and nature. Anyhow, 'C' it was in the London telephone directory. Within a fortnight I was already on the speakers' panel; I was already (it was much easier in those days) on the candidates' list; and I was already employed in the Conservative Parliamentary Secretariat, which did its best to supply information to the sorely depleted Opposition Front Bench of 1946.

Pitchforked into an array of internal politics, pitchforked into parliamentary politics as they were in the 1940s, I set about the business of getting myself a seat, which I did not achieve until the end of 1948 after something like twenty rebuffs from other constituencies before Wolverhampton South-West. They were years in which I read voraciously in political history, in constitutional history. (Some of the results found their way into a book on the House of Lords in the Middle Ages which was published in 1968). And I began to practise my trade.

Before long, I was overtaken by the events of 1947 and the acceptance by the Conservative Party in Parliament of the inevitability of the separation of India from the rest of the British Empire and Commonwealth. So, the basis on which my decision had been taken no longer existed. I was bereft of the ground on which I thought I was treading when I walked into Conservative Central Office in

March 1946. But I was not entirely, by then, unprepared for handling this shock, a shock so severe that I remember spending the whole of one night walking the streets of London trying to come to terms with it. Being an aspirant for the House of Commons, I had begun to familiarise myself with the nature of that extraordinary assembly and its central position in the politics and governance of my own country, a subject on which, before that, I had been woefully ignorant and unreflective; and I was feeling my way towards understanding the axiom of government subject to parliamentary representation, namely that such government cannot logically extend over populations which cannot be there represented. It was the old proposition of the American Colonies (by which I was later to understand that my own country had been haunted for the best part of two centuries), to which I was already addressing myself and which I had begun to grasp sufficiently to perceive dimly the contradictory nature, as the earliest of the British in India had understood it, of British rule in India, the responsibility of the representative of Wolverhampton South-West for the governance of a population which could never be represented in the Parliament of the United Kingdom.

Something else was also happening during these years in which the ground fell away from under my feet. As an officer of the Conservative Parliamentary Secretariat, I had the advantage of attending, in the official box, the sittings of the House of Commons (in those days, of course, in the House of Lords, since the Commons Chamber had not yet been rebuilt). I found an immensely strong affinity in myself with this institution, an affinity which was to strengthen and to live with me all the days of my life until I was finally bereft of it in 1987. Thus a motivation not initially parliamentary was replaced by a self-sufficient motive, that of becoming and being and remaining a member of that institution.

I want to stress, because I think it gets understressed where the motivation of politicians is discussed, the self-sufficient nature of this motivation. At every stage, from 1947 to 1987, to be and to remain a member of the House of Commons was the overriding and undiscussable motivation of my life as a politician. The attempt to make myself a Member of Parliament, to get there, involved me in talking – first of all at a by-election in the West Yorkshire coalfield in 1947, and thereafter where I could persuade them to listen – to my fellow countrymen in public meetings. So I had to explore, as one not unaccustomed to addressing audiences, though of a different character, the presumptions upon which I addressed my fellow citizens in political meetings. Though I had not yet formulated it as I was later to do, I have no doubt that I was already conscious of the great assumption of the politician addressing his fellow countrymen, namely the identity of introspection, the identity of insight, the suppressed major premise of the syllogism. A politician talks to his fellow men, exhorts his fellow men, instructs his fellow men, upon a common basis which he assumes to exist between him and them, the basis of a common insight, a common self-recognition. He would be bereft of his power to persuade if he could not assume a common dimension, a common background, rarely spelled out but always present in his course of argument. In short, I assumed that my fellow countrymen felt and thought as I did about their own country. It is, stated naked like that, perhaps a startling proposition. Yet I feel sure it underlies most political discourse – the assumption of addressing those who are peers not only in the sense that, of course, by their vote collectively they hold the power to give you what you want or to withhold it, but peers in the sense that they can be addressed upon the basis of common unstated assumptions. That is the major premise from which, by the application of explicit minor premises, all conclusions are drawn in political discourse.

So, here was I in the late 1940s, addressing my fellow countrymen on the assumption that the country I lived in, the country in whose successful self-defence I had participated for six or seven years, was also the country in which they lived and about which they felt and thought in the same way that I did. On that basis, I sought and obtained a narrow majority in Wolverhampton South-West in 1950 and began to address another assembly, also an assembly of peers, but in a rather different sense, though still an assembly of peers with this in common: the validity (and it is a most remarkable proposition if you step away from it) of decisions arrived at in that place by a majority is upheld by all who participate. It is the link between that place and those outside who constitute it – the assumption that law is made and authority is exercised by means of a certain procedure gone through in that place and decisions arrived at in that place, however debatably and however narrowly. I had become aware, in other words, of debate, I had discovered that debate in the House of Commons was congenial. It had something in common with the kind of discourse with which I was already familiar; it was a discourse in which peers have to be persuaded. Parliamentary debate is special in this respect: it is debate carried on in the foreknowledge of the end result, but it is debate which nevertheless is carried on for the purpose of affecting the mind and point of view of those addressed upon the assumption of a common basis which they all share, namely, the function and authority of that place, the manner in which it goes about its own business and the validity of the results.

It was an environment so attractive, an environment so congenial to me that I remember distinctly the sensation which I had on each of the three occasions when I refused government office. (By the way, for the record, this well-known 'resigner' resigned only once in all his political career, and that in a junior capacity, though he did in fact decline office three times.) I remember on each occasion the sensation when I re-entered the House of Commons after notifying my decision. It was like coming home to one's mother. It was as though I said, 'I am back again; I am back where I belong, I have not gone away, I am back.'

This congenial nature of the House of Commons, though I believe it was established early, continued to strengthen and deepen its hold on me during the whole of the time that I was a member. If I am asked, as I sometimes am in sixth forms, about the motivation of a politician, I tell them 'his real motive is that he wants to remain what he is because he enjoys it, the only justification you will find for doing anything in your life'. I am not sure this is always understood by sixth forms, nor always well received by those who instruct sixth forms; but at any rate that is the offering which I have to make.

So, here was I by the middle 1950s, with the original grounds on which I had decided to make my life in politics immensely remote, immensely obsolete, but hooked upon a way of life, an all-embracing way of life and one which utilised all my available faculties. It is a paradox all right, but it is a paradox which, when he gets his scalpel out, Professor Skidelsky may even succeed in finding instructive.

I want now to move on from my first point of vantage (which you remember was in February 1946) and come nearer to modern times with October 1963. In October 1963, Iain Macleod and I, having declined to accept office under Lord Home, were out of office. One's life as a politician, especially as a junior politician, is lived in the presence of what the Romans called the *cursus honorum*, it is lived in the presence of a gradation of achievement, not a gradation of achievement which your essential Member of Parliament would admit to, but a gradation of achievement which is pressed upon them from many quarters. Of course, office is very amusing. It is an amusing exercise of the intellect to take part in the machinery of government and apply one's analytical talents to the content of administration, not to mention legislation. I will not seriously attempt to disclaim having enjoyed office – in the Ministry of Housing and Local Government for just over a year, in the Treasury in 1957 and curiously enough as Minister of Health for three and a quarter years from 1960 to 1963, the longest period I think that anybody was Minister of Health in that meaning of the term. Now all that was over – over for an unforeseeable period. It was as if a spring in my mind snapped back into action. I had lived through years in which the Government to which I belonged had been engaged in the business of attempting to create governmental control over essential prices, including the price of labour. It was the age of Franco-Macmillanite planning, it was the age (the early age) of prices and incomes policy. I had found this profoundly repugnant, repugnant because it jarred with another Tory prejudice, the Tory prejudice that, upon the whole, things are wiser than people, that institutions are wiser than their members and that a nation is wiser than those who comprise it at any specific moment. The notion that there could be vested in ascertainable individuals in government wisdom sufficient to lay out and dispose the effort and resources of society as they expressed themselves in prices was to me deeply repugnant. Now in 1963 I was able to articulate and to explore this prejudice.

I had to reconcile it, of course, with the rest of my political framework, the intellectual framework within which I had been living for fifteen or sixteen years. I found no great difficulty in doing that to my own satisfaction. (One's own satisfaction is the criterion by which one judges intellectual achievement.) To my own satisfaction, I reached the conclusion that the price mechanism is one of the means by which a society takes certain collective decisions in a manner not necessarily ideal, but a manner which is manageable and acceptable and broadly speaking regarded as workable, a mechanism which cannot safely or wisely be replaced by conscious formulation and by compulsion.

So there started a period in which I was formulating to my fellow countrymen the doctrine of the market and following that doctrine as far as it would go in all directions.

I found myself engaging in a fundamental critique of the whole theory of trade unions, since this was the use of coercion in order to produce a different price for an article from that which would otherwise be placed upon it by supply and demand. Thus I found myself drawn into all that intense argument, which was to run on for another twenty years, on the legal basis of the trade unions. I found myself exploring the theory of nationalised industry. I found myself (conveniently) embattled against the Labour Government of the years 1964–70 and taking my part in providing language for a Conservative Party which received its majority in the 1970 election as offering propositions recognisably identifiable with what in those days was called 'Selsdon Man'. (The conference held in those early days of 1970 to decide the attitude of the Conservative Party towards prices and incomes policy was held at Selsdon Park.)

I had in fact done a major intellectual job upon my relationship with my political environment and upon my relationship with the public at large and with my own constituents. I had taken them all through it with me and they had found sufficient interest in it to bring me larger audiences during the 1960s than any other politician in or out of government was attracting. It was evidently something they were prepared to examine and on which they were prepared to find some commonality of understanding. Or was I mistaken about that? At any rate, I had re-established and refined the assumed identity of introspection upon which I had always felt that my business as a public man and a representative was to be conducted.

Now I am going to skip over 1968 – 1968 was not really very important as I will explain in a moment – and move on to my third vantage point, in July 1972. In July 1972, having fought in the country, on the continent and in the House of Commons the battle against the European Communities Bill and lost – lost only because a guillotine motion was carried with the aid of Liberal votes, but still lost – I had to face the inconceivable. The inconceivable was that, without a wave of public and national resentment, the House of Commons had solemnly and deliberately voted away its historic and essential powers and functions, the unique right to tax, the accepted right to legislate and the undoubted right to call the policies of government to account, the power to demand that the House's confidence should be enjoyed by whoever governed the United Kingdom. All this was part of the universe in which I had lived since the war. The pillars had been removed, but 'earth's foundation stayed' and I had to cope with this shattering event. I drafted a letter, to be sent to the Chancellor of the Exchequer on the last day of that session, applying for appointment to the Chiltern Hundreds, for I did not see how it was possible to continue to belong to a body which had disembowelled itself and disavowed its essential nature. However, it so happened that by 1972 another feature in my intellectual scenery had established itself, another element in my understanding of that common introspection which I presumed. A nation which could support that House of Commons, a nation which could be governed in this way 'godly and quietly', was a nation of such a character that it would accept as law, and as morally binding upon it, what was decided by an elective body, provided always that elective body could periodically be remoulded by it. ('It' is a collective expression which, like all collective expressions, contains an undue admixture of metaphor. But where would we be without metaphor? We would not be talking at all.) The concept, therefore, of a nation which talked and could be talked to and was governable as this nation was governable, depended upon this characteristic – that its members would so identify themselves with one another that the non-existence of a Conservative vote in County Durham or the non-existence of a Labour vote in Hampshire would not render Durham or Hampshire ungovernable as part of the United Kingdom by Labour or Conservative Governments. I looked for a word and I did not find a satisfactory word. The only word which I found for working purposes was 'homogeneous', homogeneous in that defined sense, politically homogeneous, capable of perceiving the totality of the nation in such a way as to submit to the will of the totality, given that the totality's will could be altered, influenced and manipulated through the nation's parliamentary institutions. This underlying characteristic of homogeneity was defied by the underlying assumptions of what the nation had done in 1972. There was no such homogeneity between this nation and the other nations of the European Economic Community so long as they were nations at all – if the term 'nation' could be employed in the same way, and the natural assumption was that it *could* be employed in the same way.

Meanwhile, there had been a 'little local difficulty' over the homogeneity of the population of the United Kingdom, the question whether changes in that population did not threaten the eventual survival of political homogeneity. Were there limits of tolerance beyond which homogeneity could not be sacrificed without the whole system, the whole assumption becoming untenable? It was because I had become identified with that question that after 1968 I enjoyed a freedom of expression pretty well unique in the politics of my time – the freedom of a man who does not want anything that those in power can give. There is nothing virtuous about this, because he knows he is not anyhow going to get what he wants: still, he has got the freedom. Such was the freedom, which, after 1968, I enjoyed. I had deployed it in the attempt to convince the nation that in 1972 with the European Communities Act it had done something impossible for it, something which it could not possibly have meant to do. There, I think, lies the significance for me of this third vantage point to which I have asked you to accompany me. At that point I was saying to myself: 'It is true there is this common introspection which I have assumed all along and without which I cannot live and exist as a politician. Therefore they cannot possibly have meant what they have done. Therefore, if I can bring home to them, if events bring home to them, that they did what they did not mean, they will reject it.' In that framework, I have lived my life (I suppose, to an extent, though politically dead, I am still living) to this day, appealing to what must be the implication of a common introspection. The term 'common introspection' is one which I would like to leave as part of my submission. I have seen it used, and this is entirely congenial to me, as part of a definition, indeed perhaps the essential definition, of a nation as those between whom there is a commonality of introspection. At least it comes near to what I am attempting by my unsatisfactory adjective 'homogeneous'.

A politician's life is much more dependent upon faith than it is dependent upon knowledge and belief. For persistence (which is the same as survival) there has to be a continued faith in the assumptions upon which a political lifetime has been founded. I do not think that I am probably so very different from other politicians – except maybe in being a little more self-analytical – when I say that assumed commonality of introspection between themselves and those whom they represent and those whom they govern lies at the heart of their ability to function and to stay alive.

'Give Richard leave to live till Richard die.' I have been accustomed since June 1987 to refer to myself as a dead man. I have got a sympathy now for the dead that I never had before, when I go through a cemetery, I say to myself, 'I know just how they are feeling! They are not there.' The experience that has made me a 'no-man' since June 1987 was that I had no constituency. It was not being no longer a member of the House of Commons, not being debarred from the institution, from the club; it was having no ground on which to stand that convinced me that I had been shot through the head and was living thereafter a kind of ghostly sort of existence. Perhaps it paid me back for the story that I used – I am sure, with tiresome iteration – to tell my constituents in Wolverhampton and also in South Down, the story of the mythological giant, Antaeus, who could only be overcome if you could lift him off the ground and keep his feet off it for a sufficient length of time. His is the very image of a politician.

OFF DUTY

In the summer months, which for the Powell family tend to run from February to November, we are enthusiastic ramblers and picknickers.

'A Life in the Day of Enoch Powell'
Sunday Times Magazine, 11 May 1986

'RIDDLE OF A KING'S TOMB ALTERED INTO A SUBJECT'S'

Express and Star, 24 September 1965

When Richard's II's first consort, Anne of Bohemia, died in June 1394, his grief knew no bounds.

He decided that, unlike any previous king and queen of England, they should both be buried in the same tomb, and that on it their gilded effigies should lie (in the words of the contract with the coppersmiths) 'crowned, side by side and clasping their right hands and holding sceptres in their left hands'.

The tomb was to be in the Chapel of Edward the Confessor in Westminster Abbey. As the space there was already full, room was made by removing a tomb on the south-west, which probably contained the bodies of Hugh and Mary Bohun, children of an Earl of Hereford and grandchildren of Edward I.

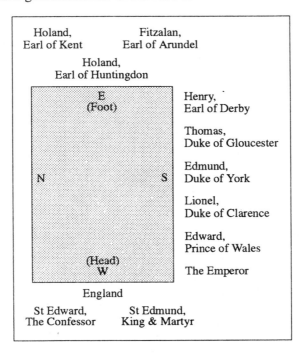

Into the space thus made the body of Anne was lowered at a funeral of unexampled splendour, when the famous quarrel took place between the king and the Earl of Arundel.

The contracts for making the tomb and effigies, in accordance with sealed plans, were let in 1395; and the work was to be completed in two years. In his last will, dated April 1399, the king enjoined that he should be buried with Anne in his tomb, then evidently already complete. The final payments for it appear in the 'Issue Rolls', early in 1399.

Anne's death caused all previous arrangements for Richard's own interment to be abandoned; but it happens that the tomb that had been prepared for him previously, and which was superseded by the splendid double tomb in Westminster Abbey, still exists, though hitherto unrecognised as such, in the parish church of King's Langley, Hertfordshire.

It is a chest tomb, designed to stand free in a chancel or chapel, with the head of the effigy to the west, so as to face the altar, and the feet to the east.

There are three shields with coats of arms in relief in quatrefoils on the two short sides, and seven on one of the long sides; but the moulding on base and top runs round all four sides, so that seven shields must have existed, or at least been intended, on the fourth side also.

These, and the original top, have disappeared. The surviving shields are shown on the diagram above.

There is only one person for whom a tomb could have been made which bore at its head the undifferenced arms of England, flanked by the two royal saints. That person is a king of England.

There is only one king of England on whose tomb these particular arms could be placed. That king is Richard II.

Apart from his grandfather, Edward III, only he bore these arms of England – England and France ancient, quarterly. Only he affected the company of the two royal English saints, Edmund and the Confessor, who, together with John the Baptist, present him to the Virgin and Child on the Wilton diptych.

Only he could have placed the Emperor of Germany (Charles IV, father of his beloved wife, Anne of Bohemia) in the place of honour above all the sons of Edward III.

At his feet were his connections through his mother, the 'Fair Maid of Kent' – his half-brothers, the Earls of Kent and Huntingdon, and the Earl of Kent's father-in-law, the Earl of Arundel.

In the sequence of Edward III's sons on the south or right side of the tomb, the third place must have been occupied by John 'of Gaunt', Duke of Lancaster. As to the missing left-hand side, there was no lack of other relatives who could have occupied it – the Mortimers, for instance, and the Veres.

What happened to this tomb after it became redundant in 1394? The arms now on the centre shield of the long side are those of Isabel, wife of Edmund 'of Langley', Duke of York (York impaling Castile and Leon).

The next entry in the St Albans chronicle, after that which records the death of Anne of Bohemia, runs as follows: 'The same year died the Duchess of York . . . she was buried by the King's command at his manor of Langley in the Friars' church.'

In fact, Isabel of Castile had died over a year before in December 1392, but the annalist's mistake is intelligible if the final interment only took place after the death of Anne.

Richard not only commanded her to be interred at Langley. He also allowed his uncle to convert for the purpose the tomb in which he himself had been destined to lie in the chancel of the Dominican Friars' church at King's Langley.

It was only in the previous century or so that predecessors of his had been buried at Westminster. But Edward II was at Gloucester, and before that John was at Worcester, Stephen at Faversham, the earlier Angevins at Fontevrault, Henry I at Reading and Rufus at Winchester. Why not Richard in the favourite rural resort of his family?

Conversion of the tomb for its new purpose was easy. It would be moved from the centre of the chancel into a canopied recess on the north side, thus rendering superfluous the seven shields on the left side of the tomb, which was now flush against the wall; and the centre shield on the south side, which now became the front, was changed, so as to replace Lancaster's arms by Isabel's.

This was an easy operation; for all the shields are separately carved and affixed. The three tell-tale royal shields at the west end were now partly or wholly concealed, and so were the Holand arms at the east end – though, as it turned out, this would not have mattered, because the Duke of York himself, at a later date unknown, married a Holand as his second wife.

> Instead of the effigy, a slab, with an inset brass of Isabel and no doubt an inscription, was made to cover the tomb. A king's tomb had been altered into a subject's.

In August 1402, the Duke of York also died, and in accordance with his will of November 1400, was buried in this tomb 'at Langley, by my well-beloved erstwhile partner Isabel, on whom God have mercy'.

Meanwhile, in February, 1400, the body of Richard II, after being brought south from Pontefract, where the deposed monarch had mysteriously died, received the last rites in St Paul's Cathedral.

> It was then, by Henry IV's command, conveyed the same night – to King's Langley! There it was buried privately at dawn by the Abbots of Waltham and St Albans and the Bishop of Chester in the place, but not in the tomb, originally destined to receive it.

It is inconceivable that Henry IV pitched by accident on the very place for disposal of his deposed predecessor that contained a tomb which could only have been made for him.

Fourteen years later, as an act of expiation, Richard's body was exhumed by Henry V and brought from King's Langley to be buried with great pomp in Westminster Abbey in the marble tomb, with the gilded effigies, which contained the bones of Anne of Bohemia.

After the Reformation the church of the Dominican Friars at King's Langley fell into ruins; and apparently in Elizabeth I's reign, the tomb of Isabel and Edmund was brought down the hill to the parish church and placed against the north wall of the chancel.

As it also abutted on the east wall, the Holand shields were moved round from the east end to cover the exposed part of the north side. The cover, robbed of its brass, was put on one side and replaced by a cut-down altar top.

Finally, in 1877, the tomb was moved to the east end of the north aisle and re-erected in the position of an altar, with its long sides facing east and west, and the Holand shields back in their proper place.

Above it is an heraldic stained glass window to which Queen Victoria subscribed. The old cover, with its matrix of a female figure, stands a few feet away.

On the occasion of the removal, the tomb was found to contain the jumbled bones of a man and a woman, who, so far as their ages could be ascertained, might have been Edmund and Isabel. There was also, mysteriously, the body sheathed in lead of a woman aged under thirty.

'MY TWO FAVOURITE BOOKS'

From *Books and Bookmen*, 1986

My two favourite books as a boy were an ill-assorted pair – *The Harmsworth Encyclopedia* and Richard Jefferies' *Bevis*. The *Encyclopedia* was one of those which came out in parts, and my great-grandfather had bought the bindings and given it to his granddaughter, my mother. It displayed to me an illimitable vista over the ocean of knowledge, and many of its illustrated entries remain indelible memories.

Richard Jefferies captured magically the combination of practicality with pretence which every boy likes to find in his adventures. It was the tragic author's love-child, an epic fit in its own way to stand on the same shelf with *Don Quixote*.

'BUT PARSIMONY SPOILT ALL CHANCE OF A SENTIMENTAL GOODBYE

The Times, 8 July 1960

It was the last building left. Everything else on that side of the street had been demolished – by war damage, by slum clearance, and now to make way for one of the great new thoroughfares which were rapidly removing all the known landmarks from the city where I was born and went to school.

It was a second-hand bookshop, one of half a dozen which the street had once boasted. As a schoolboy I used to make my way along it once or twice a month in the lunch-hour, to rummage in the penny boxes and scan the sixpenny shelves. This particular shop, it was commonly agreed among us of the classical sixth, had an exceptionally good penny box in those days, and more than one leather-bound volume out of it stands on my shelves to this day.

There is something special for a schoolboy – and perhaps not only for a schoolboy – about a second-hand book picked up really cheap. It tends to get read and studied with more than ordinary loving care, and I am sure that a disproportionate share of my classical knowledge when I left school had come not out of the prescribed textbooks, but out of the second-hand bargains which I bought and studied 'on the side'.

And now here was the old shop about to disappear. The big notice 'Clearance Sale' in the window was a superfluous indication of its impending fate. 'For old times' sake,' I thought to myself, 'for the sake of all the pleasure and good learning I have had out of that shop's penny box, I'll go in and buy one last book there; for assuredly the next time I happen to pass through the city this way it will be too late, and the old place will have gone for ever. So it was with feelings of affection and a romantic sense of leavetaking that I stepped inside to perform this act of piety.

I began to work my way round the shelves. What an immensely depressing as well as fascinating place a second-hand bookshop is. The mind becomes overwhelmed with all the labours, ambitions, hopes, and aspirations that are entombed in the dust there.

If a man writes books himself the sense of doom is doubly oppressive. Here in this cemetery are all his predecessors, despised and unregarded: who dare hope that his own fate will be better than theirs? The pity of it all; all the love and toil that go even into one short book, and then of a certainty come to this. The second-hand bookshop is the author's *memento mori*, a skull-and-crossbones more terrifying than any other kind of reminder that art, as well as life, is nearly always short.

To this familiar sense of depression was added here the poignancy of farewell to a boyhood scene. However, I persevered and had soon marked down a number of things which it would be nice to buy. But now I was assailed by another emotion which I find as inseparable from a visit to a second-hand bookshop as that melancholy I have just described.

This other emotion is parsimony, or, not to put too fine a point upon it, plain downright meanness. I have only to open the cover of a book which might reasonably cost fifteen shillings and see it marked at ten, to be overcome by a grudging miserly spirit which says to me: 'You oughtn't even to pay five shillings for that.'

Well, here for instance was Timberland's *Proceedings of the House of Lords* from 1660 to 1742. It had been marked down and down, and now was 'ten shillings the set'. Two volumes were missing, but still it was cheap at ten shillings and I decided I would like it.

I approached an apathetic-looking youngish woman in a green overall – everybody in second-hand bookshops seems to have an apathetic look – and asked her how much she wanted for it. Without replying she retreated to an inner sanctum to which I followed her. It contained a boy of about eight playing what looked like snakes-and-ladders with a grey-haired woman, who fixed me at once with a steely eye:

The woman in green: 'How much is the Timberland?'

She: 'Ten shillings.'

Myself: 'It's a pity two volumes are missing: it spoils the set.'

She: 'Those two have always been missing, but I can sell them as odd volumes. Boys come in who will give a shilling just to have a book of that sort.'

Myself: 'Then suppose I give you six shillings for the lot?'

She: 'All right.' (To the woman in green) 'Wrap them up.'

Before she could do so, however, I dived into the outer shop again and came back with three other things which my eye had fallen on: a 1662 history of the Rebellion (nice to have in Restoration centenary year), a *Lincolnshire Poll Book* of 1854 and an 1832 *Guide* to the first reformed Parliament. The marked prices came to £1.

I put them down beside the still unwrapped Timberland, and said: 'I'll give you fifteen shillings for the lot.' The books were handed to the grey-haired woman, and she looked them over: 'All right,' she said, 'I'll take fifteen shillings for the three.' 'I meant fifteen shillings altogether,' I replied. She fixed me with the steely gaze again: 'What, with the Timberland? No, I can get more than that in the trade.'

We glared at one another. I had meant, when I went in the shop, to tell them why I had come, and that I used to come there as a schoolboy, and that I still had the books I bought there thirty-five years ago, and to ask where they were going, and wish them well, and to bid and be bidden goodbye like an old and honoured friend. All that was impossible now. My heart had turned to flint. If the pious pilgrim was to receive treatment like this, the shop might keep its books and they might be demolished with it, for all I cared.

We glared at one another. 'Very well,' I said, 'just wrap up the Timberland.' The elderly woman tossed my six shillings into an open money-box and went on playing snakes-and-ladders with the boy. The woman in green wrapped up the six volumes with the minimum of string and paper. As for me, I tucked them under my arm, strode briskly to the door, and closed it behind me for ever.

'Strange,' I thought as I hurried along the fast-changing street of the second-hand bookshops, to get my train back to London: 'the place doesn't seem to know me any more.'

'DIRTY WORK AT THE OLYMPICS'

Daily Telegraph, 31 January 1976

To modern man the ancient Greeks present a paradox, a paradox such as neither the Romans nor any other of the peoples of the ancient world present.

We read their prose and their poetry, and our understanding and response are total. Intuitively we know, when we relish a line of Homer or shudder at a chorus of Aeschylus, that we are feeling what the poet felt and hearing what he meant us to hear. The immediacy is overwhelming. Even our own flesh and blood, Chaucer and Shakespeare and Milton, are no more present to us than these men whose words miraculously leap the gulf between two worlds and travel with the speed of light across 2,500 years.

Yet the next instant they can recede into inaccessible distance and strangeness: their world, their ways, their values, their lives reveal themselves as so weirdly different. This never happens with the Romans. We would not be surprised to meet them if they came alive again: we should expect them to be as knowable and predictable as the Americans or the Germans, tiresome or unimaginative or imposing, but quite decidedly a part and parcel of our own world. Not so the Greeks, which is what Nietzsche meant when he called them wonderful savages. That is what they were: immensely primitive and immensely civilised, both in the same instant.

The Olympic Games, for instance. We have such things in our modern world, which, by a kind of pun, we have christened with the name of one of the most incomprehensible Greek institutions; but there is no more in common than the name.

From the earliest time that we hear from them, the Greeks honoured or propitiated the deities or the souls of the departed by racing and wrestling, racing on foot or in horse chariots, wrestling and fighting 'with no holds barred'. So far as we know, no other branch of the Indo-German peoples preserved or acquired this primitive, compulsive addiction, far back steppe-wards though it must reach in their history.

They themselves recognised it as one of the most striking marks of the impassable gulf between themselves and the remainder of humanity (whom they called 'barbarians'). The games, athletic competitions, the gymnasium, the *agon* (or contest) and its prizes – these were the hallmarks, from the beginning to the very end, of being Greek.

Because the games were uniquely Greek, therefore they were a bond of recognisable union – not political, of course – between Greeks, who could all compete in them by virtue simply of being Greek. They were, in a word, Panhellenic. By an ironical inversion, the modern Olympic games, which aspire to be *inter*national and to surmount national differences and distances, are named after an institution which was essentially exclusive and nationalist, not to say racialist.

For reasons we do not know, the games held in honour of Olympian Zeus at a not very important shrine in a not very important state in the north-west of the Peloponnese had secured as early as the eighth century before Christ a nation-wide pre-eminence, which remained unchallenged until Christianity put an end to these pagan practices altogether, more than a thousand years later. Throughout the Greek cities there were games, old and new, of which any Greek could go the rounds. Indeed, there was a major cycle of four such games, the Olympic and three others, which was recognised as the 'first division', and offered the chance to be a *periodonikes* or 'peripatetic victor'. But in its strictness and the pristine purity of its rules and in the reputation which rendered its simple wreath a sufficient prize, Olympia was always unrivalled.

We can now* read all that can be put together from its millennial existence; and the more we know, the more incommensurable the Greek games become with modern games, 'Olympic' or not. They were, and they remained, a religious act: the rules, the disciplines and the 'truce' which enabled competitors and spectators to traverse Greece even in time of war to take part in them were designed to prevent the deity from being offended or his shrine from being desecrated. It was nothing to do with peace or peace-making.

They were essentially unsporting and unsportsmanlike. The game did not matter; all that mattered was victory. There were no 'runners-up' but a victory, even if gained by a punished foul, even if an uncontested walk-over, was a victory as good as any other. They were dangerous and brutal; and the most sublime poetic glorification, by Theban Pindar, of victory in the games included emphasis on the gratification of inflicting shame upon one's defeated opponent. It is

---

The Olympic Games: the First Thousand Years by M. I. Finley and H. W. Pleket, Chatto and Windus

no accident that the first and most famous contest in Greek literature, the chariot race in the funeral games in the *Iliad*, was won by cheating.

In the chariot races, which carried the supreme prestige, it was the owner who gained the glory of the victory and not the charioteer; and the glory, for which aristocrats and rulers competed and which they commemorated on monuments and coins, was the glory of the superabundant wealth which had been lavished upon the purchase of teams or horses and the hiring of skilful jockeys.

The Greeks were an intensely competitive people. The pathology of envy, with which all human societies have to devise means to cope, was highly developed among them. In every aspect of their social life it reveals itself in a preoccupation with being 'best'. On the morrow of their heroic victory over the Persian invaders, the Greeks had to take a vote to decide who should be declared the best, and must needs resort to trickery in settling it. On top of this the Athenians institutionalised envy by the system of ostracism, which enabled them to remove their 'best' into exile. One is tempted to conjecture that, just as Aristotle diagnosed the tragic drama – also, incidentally a matter of annual competition – as the means of 'purging' emotions of their intolerable intensity, so the agonistic or envious side of the Greek nature was provided with an outlet through the formalised triumphs and defeats of the sacred games.

Like the elderly American tourist who, being pressed to describe Europe, finally declared, 'It's not like Hoboken,' we can at least say of Olympia – the real Olympia, that is – that: 'It's not like Munich or Toronto.'

'THRILL OF THE CHASE'

Observer, 28 March 1976

I always hoped that such a book* would be written, and now it has been.

There is nothing in the world like English fox-hunting. That is not the observation of an intolerant ignorance that every sport, however improbably, has its own lore and its own lure. It is an observation as much about England as about fox-hunting. When you have followed fox-hunting through two and a half centuries of English social and economic history you can start again and follow it through the subtle ramifications of English psychology.

At the end you will have learnt a great deal about England and the English, and still be no nearer to understanding why it is that, however late a man comes to fox-hunting, however shockingly he rides, however rarely his ears catch 'the sweet cry of hounds', all his life he is sure it would have been a poorer thing for him without fox-hunting.

Is it the miraculous combination of the special aptitudes of three animals – or four, if you count the human being? Is it the marriage of a purpose with that ardour and excitement which only the horse can give to man? 'There is a sting in it, riding a good horse and jumping the big black fences, that once felt, can never be forgotten' – a good quotation, that, for which I am grateful.

It is these, but also it is the genius of the English for institutionalising, half in earnest, half in irony, the smallest and the largest things in life. After all's said, Jorrocks has the last word with his famous 'image of war, with none of the guilt and five and twenty per cent of the danger' – a deeper analysis and a more instructive analogy than perhaps even its author was aware.

An Oxford professor of history who rides to hounds ('When I hears a man's a fox-hunter, I loves him at once') has actually done what so many of us just wondered about – unpicked and examined the separate strands which a unique process wove together to make the history of English fox-hunting. It is a story with many twists and turns and crises when the devotees of fox-hunting were sure it would soon be over and done with.

English Fox Hunting by Raymond Carr, Weidenfeld

Fox-hunting, as we recognise it, was specialised out of earlier forms of the chase by the concurrence of three separate but interacting factors: the improvement of the performance of the English hound by the infusion of the faster French blood; the improvement of the performance of the English riding horse by the infusion of the Arab strain; and finally the transformation of the English countryside into one vast steeplechase course by the enclosures.

This preference of the once despised vermin ('the uneatable') to the exclusion of all alternative quarry (pursuit of which became mere 'puss-hunting' or – worse – 'riot') made possible, together with the almost consciously co-operative cunning of the fox, that marvellous compound equation on which fox-hunting depends – that the hound is slower than the fox but has more endurance, or, as Jorrocks put it anthropomorphically, 'the 'orse loves the 'ounds and the 'ounds loves the fox'. The finishing touch was applied by the collapse of arable agriculture at the end of the 1870s which, with the switch to pasture, produced the great fields (in both the literal and the hunting sense) of the Midland shires.

Meanwhile the tenant-farming and the landed wealth of the generation on either side of 1800 had given place to industrial wealth and, later, to owner-farming; but the railways, which were to have been the death of fox-hunting, only broadened its accessibility and swelled the numbers and the classes who followed it. Then again, when the fox-hunting men who survived came back from the First World War with Siegfried Sassoon, they found smallholdings, and wire (barbed what's worse), and estates broken up, and pastures ploughed, and above all the stinking motor car – which also was to have been the death of fox-hunting.

Nothing of the kind: the cars pulled the trailers, the girls 'did' the horses, the clubs took the wire down in autumn and put it back in spring, and still a new, more motley – dare I say, more democratic? – generation in larger numbers than ever followed the fox on horseback across English landscapes. Even its 'last enemy', the antis in Parliament, have so far 'not prevailed against it'.

All which, and much more, is to be found at large between Mr Carr's covers (spelt 'coverts'?). All fox-hunters will disagree with him somewhere. This one, for instance, happens to think that he greatly underestimates the role of the military, especially the cavalry regiments. And I gave a great whoo-oop! when I caught the professor failing to recognise an excellent parody of Tennyson's 'Break, break, break' and dismissing it as 'bad verse'. But a good day was never spoilt by a little mishap; and this run was a veritable Billesdon-Coplow.

'A LIFE IN THE DAY OF ENOCH POWELL'

Sunday Times Magazine, 11 May 1986

The trouble with most magazine features, including this one, is that they are concerned with trivialities.

Why it should matter at what time the subject gets up each morning, I don't know. However, I wake at 7 a.m. and start the day on a flask of tea prepared the night before.

I stay in bed until 8 a.m. reading *The Times*, and only glance at items in other papers to which my wife may happen to draw my attention. Being by training a slow and careful reader I prefer to read one newspaper thoroughly rather than skim many.

I have the traditional British breakfast and give thanks for a voracious appetite and good digestion, both of which I consider the indispensable basis of mental activity. By around 9 a.m., I'm at work with my part-time secretary who comes to my London home in the mornings. But of course most of my day will usually be spent at the House of Commons, a considerable part of it in the chamber, which is the prime source of information. Writing – the writing of reviews, essays, articles, books – belongs to the afternoon and evening hours, and, like most of my work for the past thirty-five years, is done at a table in the House of Commons library, where I find the most congenial atmosphere for work.

I've noticed a curious thing about writing a speech. (Nowadays in order to be reported you have to write in advance; journalism has become idle, especially with the new technology.) The curious thing is that the more elaborately a part of the speech is worked on, the more natural it sounds. On the other hand, if a whole slab has written itself, run off the end of the pen, it always sounds wooden when it is delivered.

I lunch heartily. I remember a text my mother used to quote to me as a very small child before I understood its meaning or context: 'Eat what is set before you asking no questions.' That is what I tend to do – not that I am not discriminating enough to know the difference between good food and bad, between French food and English.

Pressure of work holds no terror for me. I can unwind any time. I am blessed with the ability to sleep soundly. Whatever may be causing anxiety, I can go to sleep at night. If you sleep soundly and keep the Sabbath, you can work very hard.

The House of Commons is my other home. Do I have many friends there? Well we are all supposed to be either honourable friends or honourable gentlemen and one category tends to merge into the other. It is doubtful whether there are such things as friends in politics in the same sense as friends outside.

Indeed it would be awkward – it would be making oneself a hostage to fortune – and even dangerous, to form a deep friendship in politics. Some of the deep friendships in politics have gone tragically astray.

As for enemies – enemies in the sense of hating a person, not being able to bear the sight of him – that's very rare indeed. I could name, but I won't, one or two figures in parliamentary life in the past thirty-five years to whom I would apply that description, but no more than one or two.

I have been asked what I think of the calibre of today's politicians, but I can't tell. I have changed and therefore I cannot measure any of the changes around me. People think they can measure change during their lifetime. They are deluding themselves. They cannot differentiate between the change in themselves and the changes in their environment so as to be able to measure the one against the other.

At home I have always been what's called a handyman. When the family was growing up, the house had to be fitted and refitted and I was often busy with carpentry. I am still not beyond putting up a nest of shelves.

Fox-hunting ended for me some years ago, when I came off for the second time in a run and my daughter stood over me and said: 'Daddy you go home now, and you don't come out again.' I realised she was right. If you hunt regularly and ride every day you can hunt in your eighties; but to hunt occasionally is simply asking for trouble when you are no longer young.

I keep the Sabbath; it is very important to me. Keeping the Sabbath means not doing on Sunday what I do on the other days of the week. If I don't go to church at least once on Sunday, I've missed something and I know I've missed it – like missing a meal. Otherwise Sunday is a day when from midnight to midnight one tries to forget the work of the week. It is quite incredible how far off Saturday seems on Monday morning if you have kept the Sabbath.

Do I pray? Yes in public worship, and yes in what I suppose is ejaculatory prayer. It can happen when I know I have to speak in the House of Commons. There is a convenient responsory in the Prayer Book: 'Lord, open thou my lips; and my mouth shall show forth thy praise.'

In the summer months, which for the Powell family tend to run from February to November, we are enthusiastic ramblers and picnickers. We always have been, since before the children were born. We have two daughters and two grandchildren. Like most grandfathers I'm delighted to be one. I've always enjoyed very small children; I find them irresistible.

There are no pets in the house now. The children used to keep hamsters, but one was glad when the hamster era was over, especially as one hamster ate the whole back off a mackintosh of mine.

We spend our holidays in France. Where? One province after another. It's a country we enjoy very much. Why should one go anywhere but France?

I hardly listen to music although I enjoy reading. Most of it is historical, political and biographical. The more I read the more I kick myself that I do not read more. No time spent reading history is misspent for a politician.

Reading is something that gets itself done in the gaps in life. That's why I like reviewing; it forces me to read books which I otherwise would decide I haven't got time for. It's difficult to sit down and read a book simply for the sake of reading. This is not the sort of life in which one goes over to an armchair, opens a book and just reads for an hour.

I find being in my seventies not so much enjoyable as surprising. You've no idea how strange the world becomes as you get older. One discovers all kinds of questions, doubts, unexplored regions. It's a constant opening of doors, almost a bursting of doors.

The notion young people have that the old are settled, staid and comfortable, because nothing shakes them, is quite mistaken. One is much more likely to question things. One ceases to take anything for granted. Everything on which your gaze lights can conceal a puzzle. Wonderment, I find, is a response which grows more powerful with the years. Perhaps in this respect, as in so many others, I am a lucky man.

ENOCH POWELL'S EIGHT RECORDS, BOOK AND LUXURY

From *Sue Lawley's Desert Island Discussions*, 1990

'Entry of the Gods into Valhalla' from *Rheingold* (Wagner)
'Siegmund's Spring Song' from *Die Walküre* (Wagner)
'Siegfried's Forging Song' from *Siegfried* (Wagner)
'Renunciation of Siegfried' from *Twilight of the Gods* (Wagner)
Symphony No. 6, 'Pastoral' (Beethoven)
Symphony No. 9, 'Choral' (Beethoven)
Prisoners' Chorus from *Fidelio* (Beethoven)
'In Native Worth and Honour Clad' from *The Creation* (Haydn)

Book: the *Old Testament* (in Hebrew) and the *New Testament* (in Greek)

Luxury: A fish smoker

SUE LAWLEY: 'Can you remember the moment when you realised you were not going to die?'

ENOCH POWELL: 'Yes, it's very vivid. It was a moment in 1944. I was in India and it was the night that a monsoon broke, and I did what everybody else does on the night that the monsoon breaks – I walked out from under the verandah, and stood in the rain and got soaked. And I suddenly said to myself, "What are you going to do then? – the chances now are that you will survive, so what are you going to do? There will be a life, a world after the war. What are you going to do?" And it happened to me as I think it happens to most people when what externally seems to be a major decision is taken: you don't actually take the decision, the decision was there. It's like hearing a knock on the door – you open the door and there's somebody standing on the doorstep, and what was standing on the doorstep was, "You will go into politics".'

SUE LAWLEY: 'Why do you say that you would like to have been killed in the war?'

ENOCH POWELL: 'I think this is something commonly felt by those who served but from whom life was not demanded in the war.'

SUE LAWLEY: 'But was that not very hurtful to your family?'

ENOCH POWELL: 'I'm not conscious that my daughters were terribly shocked.'

SUE LAWLEY: 'And your wife?'

ENOCH POWELL: 'My wife, I think, tended to take it personally. But wives do, don't they?'

'GÖTTERDÄMMERUNG'

BBC Radio, 14 November 1990

One of the moments of climax in European thought and literature takes place on the banks of the Rhine in *The Twilight of the Gods*. It takes place when Siegfried, having been at first minded to return the Ring of the Nibelung to the Rhinemaidens at their request, changes his mind and thrusts it back on to his finger again when the Rhinemaidens try to frighten him by warning him of the curse which it carries. He will not do for fear, in order to save his life, what he would have done for love. He seals his choice and his own fate in the ritual, immortal, gesture of throwing backwards over his head a clod of earth with the words

> Body and life,
> Thus fling I them
> Far from me.

The restoration of the Ring and the untying of the knot in which Wotan had involved himself and his world order by the contradiction between two duties – to keep his word to the Giants and to do justice to the Rhinemaidens – stirs, as so much in late Wagner does, echoes of Christianity. God's son, begotten to free men from sin, accomplishes the task by voluntarily giving up his life when he could have saved it.

Tantalisingly – and the complex texture of the Ring *is* tantalising – the natural analogy fails to hold good. It is to be the destruction of Wotan's world order itself, effaced by fire and water, which puts right the ancient wrong and ends the cosmic drama of the Ring. If there is a self-immolation in *The Twilight of the Gods* it is Brünnhilde's self-destructive ride on to Siegfried's funeral pyre. But where would that fit in? Surely it is no more than a striking statement of the destruction of Wotan's world and the failure of Wotan's attempt to escape from his dilemma while remaining in power.

We need not, however, be distracted by the absence or defectiveness of any logical scheme from being thrilled by the grandeur of Siegfried's renunciation, his refusal, like T. S. Eliot's archbishop, to do 'the right thing for the wrong reason'. Wagner was deeply preoccupied with renunciation. It has its own particular motif running through *The Ring* – we heard it, for instance, when in *Siegfried*, Wotan came to terms at last with having begotten *Ein Sohn der freier ist als ich*, 'A son who is freer than I'. The preoccupation is linked with that fascination which Buddhism held for Wagner, with its promise of redemption from suffering through the achievement of total indifference.

Siegfried, of course, does not fully understand or intend the consequences of his action. But who among us does? That aspect of the redemptive process – redemption through folly – was to dominate Wagner's last music drama, *Parsifal*, already taking shape in his mind as he concluded composition of *The Ring of the Nibelung*. Amfortas, caught like Wotan in the toils of his own sinful past, can be rescued only by *der reine Tor*, 'the pure-hearted fool', who gains understanding through his own suffering. Parsifal, who mistook the witch Kundry for his mother (as Siegfried had thought that Brünnhilde must be *his* mother), managed to gain the insight while retaining the innocence.

It is not at all Christian really. Though Nietzsche accused Wagner of having in his old age 'collapsed, helpless and broken, at the foot of the Cross', neither *The Ring of the Nibelung* nor *Parsifal* is Christian, for all the weird resonances. Perhaps that is what makes Wagner's music drama so integral a part of Europe's heritage.

That inheritance is both Christian and humanist. The greatest act of which man is capable – and capable because he *is* man – is to choose death instead of life. In that decision humanity acknowledges the saving, immortality-conferring power of sacrifice which Christianity is all about.

MAN OF LETTERS

So the early background is a preoccupation with mankind and men and their thoughts but at a distance of time.

'Towards 2000', Radio Clyde, 1977

Nobody will ever persuade me that the author of the sonnets and plays was the man William Shakespeare, baptised and buried in Stratford-upon-Avon.

'Shakespeare's Sonnets', BBC Publications 1983

'GREEK IN THE UNIVERSITY'

Inaugural Lecture, Sydney University, 7 May 1938

Mr Chancellor, Your Excellency, ladies and gentlemen: let me say at once that in delivering an inaugural address before you as your new Professor of Greek, I feel that it would be improper for me to fight on the defensive, or to take the line of justifying the existence of my own branch of university studies. If I did so, I should be preaching to the converted. The only university in Australasia which maintains a chair of Greek must be sufficiently satisfied already of the value of Greek studies. Its appreciation of Greek scholarship has been demonstrated again and again, though never more strikingly than when England's best Greek scholar during the second half of the last century, Charles Badham, found in this, his adoptive country, the honour and opportunities which his native country had denied to him.

For these reasons, I say, I do not feel called upon to stand before you like a prisoner in the dock, to defend a profession which you have already approved. Nevertheless, having been obliged during the past weeks to restrict my discourses in another part of this building to such necessary but pedestrian subjects as the uses of the Greek optative in indirect speech or the exceptions to Porson's law of the final cretic, I welcome this opportunity to take a somewhat wider ambit and indulge in a little amateur theorising: and I am going to ask your patience while I attempt to analyse the motives of Greek scholarship.

I will begin appropriately enough by a *diaeresis*, or subdivision of my subject in the Aristotelian manner. For there are really two separate questions involved: one, why people should wish to know Greek at all, and the other, why, granted that, they should further make it a branch of university teaching. For there are many branches of knowledge offering far more opportunities for research than Greek scholarship, which never have claimed, and never could claim, to engage for three years the attention of pass-degree students at a university.

The first question presents little difficulty. A certain inquisitiveness natural to the human mind has from immemorial time not rested content with the acquisition of knowledge which could be turned to practical account in life. It has blazed a trail and brought order out of chaos in every direction which it saw, whether inquiring into the intervals and composition of the stars, or the life-history of viruses, or, lastly, into the many aspects of its own self. A great proportion of this curiosity has always been devoted to the human past, to the attempt to reconstruct that vast jigsaw puzzle of which infinitely more pieces are lost than remain, or can ever be rediscovered.

There are good reasons why the period of human existence called classical antiquity, and of that period the classical age of Greece, should be a favourite part of this jigsaw puzzle. The evidence, literary and archaeological, for classical Greece is ample enough to hold out some hope of a probable reconstruction, while still fragmentary enough to add a peculiar zest to the interpretation of it and the search for fresh scraps. Greece is not a closed book like Etruria or Mexico. More than this, there is the possibility of attaining to a real inward comprehension of things Greek. For the Greeks are in race and language ultimately akin to the nations of Western Europe; culture, as we understand it, is connected by a direct line of descent with Greek civilisation; and many of the canons of thought and taste which we accept as given are in fact the creation of the Greeks. There may be no more known or discoverable about classical Greece than about classical China; but it concerns us more closely. Indeed, in a sense, it belongs to us and we are of it.

But I must turn at once to the more difficult part of my thesis, and attempt to show, not why Greek should be *learnt*, but why it should be *taught*. I believe – and I should be very unsuited to sit in the chair with which you have honoured me if I did not believe – that a leaven of classical students, and in particular of Greek students, is needed to leaven the lump of every university, and that at the present time we have not got enough of this leaven either here or elsewhere. On what grounds can I base this claim?

When a young man comes to the university at seventeen or eighteen years of age, his character, both intellectual and moral, is no longer pliable. It is already all but fixed. And for this reason university teaching has a certain tragic quality which school teaching has not; for the university, from one point of view, is a hospital in which nearly all the cases are incurable. You must therefore not expect me to argue that learning Greek up here will make a youth a jot more intelligent or a jot more honest, either. Not Greek, or any other subject, can do that for him now. The benefits which I believe that Greek is able to confer are very much slighter and more superficial, but not necessarily for that reason unimportant. For civilisation itself is a superficiality.

One of these benefits can be the cultivation of good taste. Ours is an age when the engines for the diffusion of bad taste possess great force. With rare exceptions, the cinema, the newspaper and the wireless tend powerfully to promote vulgarity. By day and by night in our cities the eye and the ear are continually assaulted by objects of bad taste. And the need of counteracting these influences is not at its least among a nation like the Australian, which has no tradition to fall back upon, and none of the sobering and steadying influences of a 'past at its doors'. Now, Greek scholarship in all its activities demands the constant exercise of taste.

In their passage through two and a half millennia, Greek texts have reached us, not in their pristine condition, but admixed with the dross of interpolation and corruption. Their purification has been the labour of innumerable scholars (and others) since, and even before, the Renaissance. Yet the humblest pass-degree student who has to read a book of Sophocles or Plato is still confronted on every other page with open questions. Many of these, especially those where authenticity or interpolation is at issue, are in the last resort questions of taste; and every reader has to form for himself an idea of the standards of the age and author under consideration, and then judge the particular passages in the light of these.

I once heard Housman, when referring in a lecture to a certain corrupt epithet in Lucretius, remark that 'a modern poet, I suppose, might write such a phrase as that and fancy that it was good, but Lucretius could never have done so'. The words echo in my mind today; and whenever I have achieved a daring adjective in a poem, 'and fancy that it is good', my conscience asks me whether Lucretius and Housman would have thought the same or not. That illustrates exactly what I mean by the cultivation of taste; and the textual study of a Greek author, especially a Greek poet, ought to mean the continual formation and application of such aesthetic judgements.

But why especially *Greek*? We have to read *Latin* to matriculate in Arts; will not that do just as well? The answer is, that Latin scholarship can indeed be made to perform the same functions as Greek, but neither so readily nor so well. To begin with, in studying Latin literature we are in a sense only studying Greek literature at one remove. It is hardly possible to mention a branch of literature in Latin which is not modelled upon a Greek original. Nor, again, did the Romans, either in the plastic arts or in literature, at any time possess the instinctive good taste and self-restraint which distinguished the classical Greeks. The Romans knew and confessed this themselves. I do not deny, therefore, that much is to be learnt about style from Virgil, Horace and Seneca, or that without a knowledge of them much in modern literature cannot fully be understood; but I do affirm that as models for the formation of literary taste and judgement they are far inferior to their Greek prototypes, Homer, Alcaeus and Euripides.

The qualities of taste and discrimination are trained and strengthened by the exercise of Greek composition, the translation into Greek of passages of English prose and verse. I add 'verse'; because now that the honours courses here are being reconstituted and extended, I hope it will be possible to introduce before very long the writing of Greek iambics for which English scholarship has ever been distinguished, and which was the indispensable training-ground and gymnasium of all our great verbal scholars – how indispensable will be realised when I say that in the department of conjectural emendation, that supreme test of taste and scholarship, Germany, for all her industry and acumen, has always been astonishingly deficient, and that this deficiency is widely, and probably with truth, attributed to the neglect in that country of *Hinübersetzung*, or translation *into* the ancient languages.

The object of translating English into Greek is not mainly linguistic training, as in the case of translation into a living tongue. The main value of the exercise is to stimulate observation of style by personal experience of the problems and difficulties. A student may read through a book of Plato without any sense of the profound difference between philosophical and historical prose-writing or of the peculiar exemplification in Plato of that indefinable Attic quality which the Romans called *urbanitas* and the Greeks ἀστειότης. Set him now to translate into Greek a piece of Hume or Jeremy Bentham, and you send him back to his Plato in a very different frame of mind. He is now obliged to observe every turn of expression, to choose his vocabulary with an eye to Plato's; and he begins to appreciate the unapproachable skill with which his model has been executed.

This, then, is the main object in view. But there is a subsidiary one, by no means unimportant, that is very relevant to my present purpose. No one can deny, I am afraid, that a good deal of present-day English writing is very shoddy stuff. This shoddy stuff we are obliged to absorb month in, month out from newspapers, novels, textbooks, and, in short, to use Carlyle's phrase, from all 'that mighty froth-ocean which we call literature'. Inevitably, after a diet like this, we ourselves produce shoddy writing in turn, and so the evil goes on. Immediately, however, the attempt is made to translate shoddy English into Greek, the shoddiness of it becomes apparent: it simply 'will not go'. Before it can be rendered, it must be rewritten into logical and tasteful English; and after a number of experiences of this kind the student begins to recognise the characteristic marks of bad writing, such as otiose epithets and the straining after variety without difference; and he is bound eventually to imbibe a permanent distaste for them, which tends to purify and strengthen his own thought and writing.

I have dwelt at some length upon the object of translation *into* Greek, in order to combat the very prevalent opinion that, because we can never hope to write classical Greek in the sense that we can learn to write good modern German, therefore the attempt is not worth making. It is true that Richard Porson himself, when already a ripe scholar, declared that he would compose no more, because, said he, 'he preferred reading good Greek to writing bad'. I often feel the same myself, though not perhaps altogether disinterestedly, when faced with the task of producing a 'fair copy'. But Porson would not have denied that the unrivalled observation of tragic metres and diction on which his fame chiefly rests had been greatly aided and stimulated by the effort to compose, and that though the exercise cannot itself make good poets or good prose-writers, it does promote discrimination and taste by forcing upon the student a clearer conception of what good poetry and good prose *are* than he would gain from reading alone.

I must now invite you to recall for a moment the process by which the Greek classics, unlike those of any other literature, have come down to us through two thousand five hundred years; for with the nature of that process of transmission the educative value of Greek scholarship is in many ways bound up. The story of that transmission, which is almost the story of culture itself, is as fascinating as any episode in human history. And it has had two results for Greek scholarship. Every student of a Greek author, if he is properly taught, must exercise his critical faculty continually upon the text which the editions and manuscripts offer him; and in order to do that intelligently he must have present to his mind's eye the cultural history of all those ages of transmission. In other words, he must cultivate not only an independent and critical judgement, but a historical sense.

We do not live in a world where independent judgement is a superfluity or healthy scepticism a disadvantage. Day by day the newspapers of all allegiances present their readers with the statement, in almost so many words, that black is white; and only too many of those readers are thoughtless or trusting enough to accept the perilous falsehood as truth. Year after year political parties secure a return to power by promising the electorate that they will do what any one of those electors, with a few minutes of clear and dispassionate reflection, could perceive to be either impossible or disadvantageous. Stranger still, the world has recently been treated for nearly a decade to the unusual spectacle of a great empire deliberately taking every possible step to secure its own destruction, because its citizens were so obsessed by prejudice, or incapable of thinking for themselves, as never to perform the few logical steps necessary for proving that they would shortly be involved in a *guerre à outrance*, which could be neither averted nor escaped. In a world like this there seems to be some need for the same injunction which every conscientious teacher of Greek at a university will repeatedly address to his students in the words of the comic poet Epicharmus, νᾶφε καὶ μέμναὅ ἀπιστεῖν, 'keep a clear head and don't believe what you are told' – not even what you are told by me, unless independently it commends itself to your reason.

In reading the works of Goethe, or even of Dante, a student has hardly at all to concern himself with the integrity of what is offered to him. He may safely take that for granted; for there are countrymen of Goethe and of Dante alive and available who can instantly detect a false locution and to whom, in their native tongue, a textual absurdity will be nakedly apparent, to say nothing of the fact that Dante's work was printed less than two centuries after he wrote it, and that Goethe marked the proofs of his. A student of a Greek text, of Sophocles, for example, is very differently situated. No necromantic art is known which can summon the shade of a classical Greek to say whether a given piece of grammar was possible in his day or not. Nor dare the student rely upon the supposed authority – *authority* is a word which I should like to delete from his vocabulary altogether – of even the most respectable editors. The most celebrated editor of Sophocles, to use the same example again, whose work is in the hands of almost every student and who for half a century enjoyed the adulation of his countrymen, and even of others, is a man prepared, whenever it suits his prejudices, to bamboozle the reader deliberately by any variety of false argument of dishonest trick which occurs to him. Add to all this that two thousand years elapsed between the composition of the plays of Sophocles and their first appearance in print; and that, as a consequence of this interval of manuscript transmission and the destruction century after century of the best copies, anyone who has learnt Greek soundly and has the courage of his opinions is bound to confess that at the most conservative estimate one line in every four of Sophocles contains an error more or less serious.

Compelled thus to sail between the Scylla of utter scepticism and the Charybdis of faith in authority, the student of a Greek text will, unless his teachers make it their business to throw dust in his eyes, learn the exercise of unceasing vigilance, vigilance against the attempts of a corrupt manuscript tradition to palm off upon him nonsense for sense and gibberish for grammar, under the decent cloak of a dead language, and vigilance against the attempts of scholars to persuade him that just that nonsense is sense and just that gibberish grammar, because they are afraid of being thought rash and destructive critics if they speak their minds.

It is in the nature of things that only an infinitesimal proportion of those who study Greek can ever attain a sufficient knowledge of the language to be able to pronounce upon the state of a given Greek text, still less to see where corruption, if it exists, lies and what was the original which has been obscured. The true Greek textual critic – for that is another way of describing the same things – is so excessively rare a bird that Trinity College itself has hardly produced more than half a dozen of them in three centuries. Certainly I cannot hope to see an epiphany here in my time. But this I am prepared to assert: that it is possible for any pass-student to take away from a course in Greek, not only some insight into the process of reasoning by which sound judgements about a text may be arrived at, but in general a disposition to treat statements on their own merits and not on those of the authorities from whom they emanate, an eye sharpened to detect special pleading, false argumentation and hocus-pocus, and a healthy freedom from the prevalent though often entirely subconscious superstition that the printed word and the established opinion have some mysterious and inherent claim to be believed.

I alluded just now to the value of Greek studies as giving an insight into the history of culture as a whole. This is to my mind of paramount importance. It is no uncommon thing to find highly educated men, men engaged perhaps in teaching not only scientific but even humanistic subjects, who have the most grotesque conceptions of the history of Western culture, conceptions which no one could entertain after even a superficial course of Greek study; and remember, I mean only Greek literary study, without any special concentration upon history. Consider, to use our old example, the student of a play of Sophocles. He cannot intelligently read his author without being made aware of all the major vicissitudes of Greek literature from the time of Sophocles to our own.

How comes it that the plays produced annually for competitions at the great Athenian festivals during the fifth century B.C. were preserved at all? The succeeding century, already poorer in talent, already looking back to the fifth century as to a classical age, brought back on to its stage the plays of the other dramatists, and canonised for all time the triumvirate, Aeschylus, Sophocles and Euripides, to the exclusion of any rivals they may in their own day have had. A law was even passed which aimed at keeping the original texts pure by imposing penalties for the interpolation of lines by actors, or, as we should now call it, 'gagging'. But it is a far cry from the local stage of little Athens to fame throughout the Mediterranean world. To understand the transition it is necessary to appreciate the ecumenical consequences of the conquests of Alexander, which made Greek the *lingua franca* of the then world and so secured diffusion and permanence to its literature. In particular, the city of Alexander's foundation, Alexandria, became, with its great library, the university of the world for six centuries, where Greek literature was collected, catalogued, studied, commented on.

Why then have we only seven plays out of the scores which Sophocles wrote and which were to be had in the library at Alexandria? The answer is another chapter in the history of culture. The Greek classics come to us not direct from Alexandria, but indirectly, via Byzantium; and not only did an enormous amount of epitomising and consequent loss attend the transition from Alexandria to Byzantium, but the Byzantines had tastes in literature very different from our own and dictated by the predominantly rhetorical character of their education and culture. In lyric poetry they were not interested: accordingly we have today only a few fragments of Sappho and Alcaeus. In tragedy they looked for rhetoric: accordingly we have nineteen plays of Euripides, the most rhetorical of the tragedians, but only seven each of Sophocles and Aeschylus. Now comes another question: Byzantium was Christian, at times fanatically so, and for three centuries, after the compulsory closing of the University of Athens on the ground that it was a seat of pagan culture, the classics were hardly read, and in consequence hardly copied, at all. How is it that we are so fortunate as to possess any Greek classics?

This inquiry leads to the discovery that there was at Byzantium in the ninth century a revival of learning less well-known but not less important for us than the celebrated one in Western Europe in the fifteenth century; for it saved the Greek classics in the nick of time, though not before much had been lost of them even since the fall of Alexandria to the Arabs. After the ninth century a tradition of scholarship and of interest in the classics persisted and was not again broken. The outward and visible sign of this renaissance was the minuscule hand, not the least of humanity's achievements; and it so happens that the earliest of the manuscripts of Sophocles is a monument of this very era.

For fear of wearying you, I will not complete the story in full, but only allude to the Turkish conquests and their connection with the revival of learning, to the invention and spread of the printing-press, and to all the ups and downs of culture and learning in the various polite nations of Europe from the fifteenth century to the present which are reflected in the tradition of such an author as Sophocles, and which force themselves upon the student's attention. Had I chosen Homer as my example instead of Sophocles, there would have been something to say of the early history of writing, as well as of the elaborate Homeric scholarship of Aristarchus and his school two thousand years ago. On the other hand, I might equally well have cited the fascinating story of Aristotle's text, which incidentally involves some knowledge of what the Arabs have, and what they have not, contributed to Western culture.

But I have laboured thus at length this matter of the history of culture as an inevitable complement of Greek studies, because upon it, before all else, rests the claim of Greek to be *the* education *par excellence* of the cultured man. And a sound and broad understanding of the history, and consequently of the nature, of our culture itself, is the best antidote to that barbarism of a present without a past of which I find many thinking people in this continent afraid. Borrowing and utilising an idea of the Newnham scholar Jane Harrison, I would offer as the ideal university education, apart entirely from any vocational considerations, the following curriculum of study: Latin, and some one modern Romance language, preferably perhaps Italian; Greek, and the modern language of that country which stands in the same relation to Byzantium as we of the West of Europe do to Rome, namely, Russian, which unhappily is not yet a subject on our syllabus here. Nourished from seventeen to twenty-one upon this fare, our ideal student would be in a position to become a man of true culture and a good European, a *'guter Europäer'* in the sense in which Nietzsche coined that term. But I am straying into the realms of fancy. Enough if I have exploded the misconception of Greek studies as the specialised knowledge of a remote and tiny field.

My predecessor in the chair which I have the honour to occupy* was a distinguished exponent of the art, the archaeology and the topography of Greece. He would not have left thus one-sided this attempt to estimate the benefits derivable from Greek studies, but could have told you also the educational value of the tangible relics of Greek civilisation. But every scholar has his own penchant, and mine has resulted, I am afraid, in my over-stressing the literary and critical side of Greek studies. Nevertheless, I want to say, with all the emphasis I can, that the benefits of Greek studies which I have discussed are not the benefits of specialisation. They are advantages to a greater or less degree within the reach of every pass-degree student here in Sydney, and which to the best of my ability I shall endeavour to secure to all my pupils.

With the possible exception of papyrology, there is no branch of classical research which either now or at any conceivable future time can be carried on effectively at Sydney. There is no reason why

---

* William John Woodhouse, Professor of Greek in the University of Sydney 1901 to 1937.

our library should not provide an adequate working implement for students and their teachers; but there are sufficient reasons why it can never be made an instrument of research in the classics. Photography has scarcely alleviated at all the insuperable difficulties in any serious textual work presented by our distance from the great manuscript collections of the world. As for research in art, archaeology and topography, which in most of the European countries can to a varying degree be prosecuted at home, we are altogether shut out from it. But you will remember that I began by drawing a line of separation between research in Greek and the teaching of Greek; and the impracticability of the former does not affect the fruitfulness of the latter. There is no essential reason why a Sydney undergraduate should not derive as much educational benefit from a course in Greek as his contemporary at Cambridge or Oxford. If this is not so at present, then it is the business of every teacher of Greek in this state, from myself downwards, to bring it about; for the object is an attainable one.

'POMMY PROFESSOR'

The Times Educational Supplement, 28 February
1964

Twenty-five years, a world war and two careers away – the remoteness
seems immense. But sharp and vivid, as if the Australian sunlight
were on them, the telescope of memory picks up the outline and
some of the detail.

A young 'pommy' professor, very young, appointed 'sight unseen'
from a Cambridge fellowship to the chair of Greek at Sydney, arrives
by the first flying-boat to come through with passengers to Singapore,
then on by Qantas de Havilland to Sydney – fourteen days from
Southampton, not counting stops for engine-trouble.

His world was expanding with explosive speed. Still scribbling
poetry, emending Arrian, racing through d'Annunzio and Nietzsche,
he projected himself, as though he had never lived before, into a
whole new continent, with the university as a base camp.

There are brief periods in a man's life when he feels that by a kind
of intuition he is privileged to sense the contemporary presences of
a past age. I have been lucky: it has happened to me three times. As
a recruit in the Royal Warwicks at the beginning of the war I thought
I saw and felt the old 'mercenary' army of the Peninsula just before
it disappeared for ever. I was in India in time to touch the hem of
the British Raj, which can be described to no one who has not
experienced it. In Sydney, as only the third successor of Charles
Badham, who became the university's professor of Greek in 1866 –
it was founded in 1850 – I sensed the spirit of the early colonial
university, something equally unknown in Oxbridge and to Redbrick,
a defiant assertion of the culture of the old world in a harsh and, by
nature, unfriendly environment.

It was this tang of defiance, still perceptible in the air, which gave
life inside and outside the university its peculiar exhilaration. The
department of Greek was not large. It had consisted hitherto only of
the professor himself, though a lecturer and a part-time lecturer were
soon added. Beginners' classes might range up to thirty and forty;
but the entry of honours students was in the region of ten or a dozen.

The small size of classes, however, made it possible to convert
lectures into informal encounters between students and professor.
Going was heavy at first. There was suspicion that the Englishman

was leg-pulling, 'trying it on' and perhaps, one never knew, intending not to play the game, come examination time.

Then suddenly the atmosphere altered, and we experimented together. One method we all enjoyed was to put up a Greek text which contained a corruption and then, picking on one student, not always of the brightest, take him on from one deduction to another, always asking questions but never answering them, until he produced the emendation which restored the sense and explained the error. The class waited for the ritual conclusion: 'Ladies and gentlemen, you will all, I am sure, wish me to congratulate Bloggs on a most brilliant discovery. I should in,ite him to publish it in a learned journal without delay but for the fact that he has been anticipated by Porson' (or whatever other famous scholar it might be).

If the detail of Greek scholarship was to be made a school for severe and disciplined reasoning, Greek civilisation was to be made a challenge to uncritical acceptance of modern conventions, moral and social. They were different, fearfully different, these Greeks, whose voices we could still hear and (at a pinch) understand. What had we in the vast, sprawling suburbs of Sydney with the gardens and the poinsettias and jacarandas, that would deserve their envy rather than their contempt?

By now, indeed, the university's defiance was directed more against the suburb than the bush. The suburb ran out into the bush; but the student belonged to the paved roads. When a Greek class went uninstructed one Monday morning because the professor had been 'bushed' and had to spend the night in a cave by a gumstick fire, more were surprised by the taste for exploration than by the getting lost. A suburban society living in the lee of Asia lacked the continuous dialogue with Europe to keep it at the stretch: its danger was complacency and a kind of cultural solipsism. To be brought face to face with the Greeks had to be a shock.

Missionary journeys took me over New South Wales in term-time and round the continent in vacation. Unless there were unintentional omissions, every school where Greek was taught, or ever had been taught, was visited. In a little over a year I had made friends on their home ground with all my classical colleagues in the other five universities – there are two more now. I recall each of them framed in a vignette of some Australian scene: Perth against the desert sunsets from the end platform of the overland train across the Nullarbor; Hobart in delicious orchard valleys, the trees ringed with heaps of apples: Brisbane's lights seen from the neighbouring hills, as splendid a vision as Hongkong or any other in the world: Melbourne in the long avenues of autumn trees; at Adelaide I remember my colleague

FitzGerald's volumes of aboriginal vocabularies, compiled year after year on journeys into the interior.

Always the meeting of minds, whether on teaching Homer or editing Greek tragedy, was heightened and given a kind of never-never quality by the strange un-European sense of distance and discovery.

I suppose I must have encountered those who questioned or denied that Greece and Greek were relevant to education in Australia. If so, I am afraid I have forgotten them. What I remember is how many people, of how many sorts, were ready to help – from the university itself, in the person of the Vice-Chancellor, Sir Robert Wallace, to the Department of Education, whose Minister and Director saw more than a little of me, or the Australian Broadcasting Corporation which gave me my own regular half-hour to talk about 'antiquity in the news'. Two remarkable but very different men I will name, neither alive today. One was an expatriate Ulsterman, 'Sammy' Angus, professor of theology in the Presbyterian college and central figure in a recent and notorious 'heresy trial'. The other was Richard Windeyer, KC, celebrated at the criminal bar of New South Wales, an Australian of the fifth generation. From these two, beyond all the host of others, I received the best of what remains with me to this day from those few months of crowded experience a quarter of a century ago.

One last picture of all is cast on the screen: evening at Darwin, huge hermit crabs on the beach, the gaunt deserted canning factory of Vesteys, the 'digger' hat and bayonet of a sentry. The aircraft which took off a few minutes after was flying towards the war.

'THE LOVE OF HONOUR'

From *Shakespeare*, BBC Publications,
London, 1965

All the other political passions derive from ambition, and are subservient to it. It is a poor, inexpressive Latin word, 'Ambition', which literally means 'canvassing', most fit in a Roman mouth ('Did this in Caesar seem ambitious?') and suggesting the external action of soliciting and acquiring office. Far better is the Greek word 'Philotimia', 'love of honour', implying something passionate, something directed inward, which feeds upon the idea of an abstract state or attribute, 'honour'.

This is the 'honour' which Falstaff catechised and found wanting. ('Tis insensible then? Yea, to the dead. But will it not live with the living? No. Why? Detraction will not suffer it. Therefore I'll have none of it – honour is a mere scutcheon.') This is the 'honour' of which the passionate love drives to destruction characters so diverse as Richard of Gloucester, Gaius Marcius Coriolanus, and the Thane of Glamis. It is difficult to find this 'honour' in Wolsey's injunction to Cromwell in *Henry VIII*:

> Say, Wolsey that once trod the ways of glory
> And sounded all the depths and shoals of honour
> Found thee a way, out of this wreck, to rise in.
> Mark but my fall and that which ruined me.
> Cromwell, I charge thee, fling away ambition.
> By that sin fell the angels; how can man then,
> The image of his maker, hope to win by it?

It is a famous passage. But so shallow and moralising is the treatment of 'ambition', even in the mouth of a broken politician, that one doubts if the lines can really be by Shakespeare. The ambition which consumes his great political characters is not a 'sin', nor something they could 'fling away', nor would if they could. If it 'ruins' them, it does so from causes wholly internal to their nature, not the fancy of a Henry for an Anne Boleyn or the mislaying of a paper.

Envy, pride, hatred – these may be sins, but they may flow outward from an inward passion not for place or power in themselves but for these things as symbols and evidences of honour.

In Coriolanus, indeed, place and power themselves are indifferent.

The essential narcissism of ambition is clearest in him. It is self-worship which makes him an easy prey to the Roman tribunes and to the Volscian Aufidius. 'There is a world elsewhere,' he says, as he quits Rome; but for him there is no external ladder or framework to ambition: the Roman consulship is not the crown – of England, or even of Scotland.

In Macbeth we witness the passion apparently taking possession of a man from the outside and transforming him. In reality it was rooted from the beginning in his nature. When the witches utter their prophecy, Banquo notices Macbeth 'start'; we hear the note in the words 'no more to be Cawdor'; it is blown fortissimo in 'the greatest is behind'; and with the phrase 'happy prologue to the swelling act of the imperial theme' the certainty is absolute. But Lady Macbeth knew all this before she married him:

> Wouldst thou have that
> Which thou esteem'st the ornament of life
> And live a coward in thine own esteem?

After Duncan's murder, it is still the inward passion, now enflamed with envy, which determines Macbeth upon Banquo's death: the motive is less precaution against being unmasked by Banquo than fury that Banquo should be acclaimed the forerunner of future kings:

> If 't be so
> For Banquo's issue have I fil'd my mind,
> Put rancours in the vessel of my peace
> Only for them; and mine eternal jewel
> Given to the common enemy of man
> To make them kings, the seed of Banquo kings.

But Fleance escapes, the object of the passion still eludes pursuit, and hatred and recklessness take possession of the owner:

> I am in blood
> Stepped in so far, that should I wade no more,
> Returning were as tedious as go o'er;

And so on to the final defiance:

> Blow wind, come wrack;
> At least we'll die with harness on our back.

There is a large formal parallelism between Macbeth and the Richard III of twelve or thirteen years earlier. In both ambition, at the zenith, turns on itself like a scorpion plunging its sting into its own body. 'The sere, the yellow leaf' of Macbeth is Richard's 'prosperity begins to mellow, and drop into the rotten mouth of death!' Both men emerge into triumphant human defiance from all the supernatural apparatus of witches, prophecies, and ghosts: 'hang out our banners on the outward walls' – that is Macbeth; 'a thousand hearts are great within my bosom; advance our standards, set upon our foes' – that is Richard III. His all but last words 'Slave, I have set my life upon a cast, and I will stand the hazard of the die' might as well have been spoken by the Scottish as by the English king.

But the very savagery of Macbeth disturbs the anatomy of ambition, which is far more intimately and lovingly explored in Richard, a civilised prince, who might have been Machiavelli's father.

We do this anatomy less than justice by the common habit of treating the play of *Richard III* in isolation. The character of Richard is drawn deliberately and consistently from his first youthful appearance in *Henry VI*, Part III, which he enters carrying the Duke of Somerset's head, to be greeted by his father: 'Richard hath best deserved of all my sons'. Then follows the Yorkist council at Sandal. The first words are Richard's to Edward: 'Brother, though I be younger, give me leave'. They might stand as the epitome of ambition's inward consciousness that it has a right and a power which override seniority, authority, law, and morality itself. ('I have no brother, I am like no brother . . . I am myself alone.')

Richard persuades his father to break the recent oath to Henry, and take up arms:

> And father, do but think
> How sweet a thing it is to wear a crown,
> Within whose circuit is Elysium,
> And all that poets feign of bliss and joy.

The only pleasure and purpose of life, its only fulfilment, is the getting – the getting much more than the keeping – of the mystical thing, sovereignty, like a kind of blasphemous Holy Grail. There is nothing else in life: in the first instants of success a new precipice to climb has to be erected. Hence, when the House of York has prevailed and 'the winter of our discontent' been 'made glorious summer by this sun of York' Richard has 'no delight to pass away the time'. Hence on his own throne, his immediate question:

> Shall we wear these glories for a day
> Or shall they last and we rejoice in them?

But indeed ambition knows not how to possess in quiet: the disruption of Richard's character and purpose from the moment of his crowning are as true to ambition as all that went before. When all rivals have once been outstripped, even the salt of hatred which ambition sprinkles so liberally on its food – 'down, down to Hell, and say I sent thee thither' – is found to have lost its savour. Richard is bored, and of his boredom comes the carelessness and loss of judgement. Macbeth's words could have been his: 'I 'gin to be a-weary of the sun, and wish the estate of the world were now undone'.

To pull down, upon its own head, the structure, which it spent its life and lost its soul to rear and to dominate, is the only ending which can suit ambition. But the world, which sees nothing of all this, will simply announce:

The bloody dog is dead.

'SENTIMENTAL JOURNEY'

From *A Second* Listener *Anthology*,
BBC Publications, London, 1970

> On fine evenings I was wont to carry-forth my supper (breadcrumb boiled in milk), and eat it out-of-doors. On the coping of the Orchard-wall, which I could reach by climbing, or still more easily if Father Andreas would set-up the pruning-ladder, my porringer was placed: there, many a sunset, have I, looking at the distant western Mountains, consumed, not without relish, my evening meal. Those hues of gold and azure, that hush of World's expectation as Day died, were still a Hebrew Speech for me; nevertheless I was looking at the fair illuminated Letters, and had an eye for their gilding.

From those words of *Sartor Resartus*, where Thomas Carlyle describes the boyhood of his imaginary German scholar and philosopher, I set out upon a sentimental journey. I remember, as sharply as Keats recalled first looking into Chapman's Homer, the moment – it must have been in 1927 – when I opened my first German book. Here was the language I had dreamt of but never knew existed: sharp, hard, strict but with words which were romance in themselves, words in which poetry and music vibrated together. The opening of this new world was followed not long after by another initiation: I discovered Carlyle. So there had been someone else who thrilled to German as I did and could express in English – and in what English! – all that I felt about my newfound spiritual home.

> 'I have read in most Public Libraries,' says he, 'including those of Constantinople and Samarcand: in most Colleges, except the Chinese Mandarin ones, I have studied, or seen that there was no studying. Unknown Languages have I oftenest gathered from their natural repertory, the Air, by my organ of Hearing; Statistics, Geographics, Topographics came, through the Eye, almost of their own accord. The ways of Man, how he seeks food, and warmth, and protection for himself, in most regions, are ocularly known to me. Like the great Hadrian, I meted-out much of the terraqueous Globe with a pair of Compasses that belonged to myself only.'

There was the unique and authentic flavour of that German scholarship which I was soon learning to worship in the footnotes to the classics and the New Testament – the Wilamowitzes and the Tischendorfs.

We hear of Entepfuhl standing 'in trustful derangement' among the woody slopes; the paternal Orchard flanking it as extreme outpost from below; the little Kuhbach gushing kindly by, among beech-rows through river after river, into the Donau, into the Black Sea, into the Atmosphere and Universe, and how 'the brave old Linden', stretching like a parasol of 20 ells in radius, over-topping all other rows and clumps, towered-up from the central Agora and Campus Martius of the Village, like its Sacred Tree; and how the old men sat talking under its shadow, and the wearied labourers reclined, and the unwearied children sported, and the young men and maidens often danced to flute-music. 'Glorious summer twilights,' cries Teufelsdröckh, 'when the Sun, like a proud Conqueror and Imperial Taskmaster, turned his back, with his gold-purple emblazonry, and all his fireclad body-guard (of Prismatic Colours); and the tired brick-makers of this clay Earth might steal a little frolic, and those few meek Stars would not tell of them!'

The description of Entepfuhl into which Carlyle had transfigured his own little village of Ecclefechan seemed to catch and hold all the romance of the old Germany, pre-Bismarck, pre-Hohenzollern, peaceful, earnest, humorous, Düreresque: those who have known or imagined it from afar still cannot keep from tears when they hear the sound of it. There was an even deeper note of philosophy and poetry which echoed through Carlyle from a higher source – Goethe himself, whom Carlyle sought from time to time to render.

Nevertheless, I were but a vain dreamer to say, that even then my felicity was perfect. I had, once for all, come down from Heaven into the Earth. Among the rainbow colours that glowed on my horizon, lay even in childhood a dark ring of Care, as yet no thicker than a thread, and often quite overshone; yet always it reappeared, nay ever waxing broader and broader; till in after-years it almost over-shadowed my whole canopy and threatened to engulf me in final night. It was the ring of Necessity whereby we are all begirt; happy he for whom a kind heavenly S n brightens it into a ring of Duty, and plays round it with beautiful prismatic diffractions; yet ever, as basis and as bourne for our whole being, it is there.

To the source, then, one must go, and find in Goethe's life-work the scholar, the lover, the man of the world, all suffused with that restless insatiable yearning which is the authentic mark of Faustian man, *homo Faustianus*. Another new world, a new era of experience, began with the magical words of the 'Prologue in Heaven'.

GABRIEL: Swift, unimaginably swift
The glory of the earth rolls round,
And scenes of heavenly radiance shift
To fearfulness of night profound;
By floods of sea in foaming forces
Cliffs at their shuddering base are churned,
And flung in planetary courses
The seas and cliffs are ever turned.

MICHAEL: And storms contend in angry fuming
From sea to land, from land to sea,
A chain of raging force assuming,
In their tempestuous majesty.
The flame of brilliant devastation
Now lights the thunderbolt his way;
But angels, Lord, in adoration,
Hail the sweet progress of thy day.
THE THREE: New strength have angels at the sight,
Amazed at thy infinitude,
And splendid as in primal light
Are all thy mighty works renewed.

On the very next page was the different magic of the opening scene on earth. Faust, in the high Gothic chamber, among the alembics and the parchments but seething with unsatisfied ambition and a thirst for the beauty of the living world, spoke a language that was instantly recognised in the Cambridge garret where I switched back and forth between Greek lexicography or textual criticism and dashing down stanzas of lyric poetry. To learn and to teach, to learn and to teach – somehow one must break out of the circle. And so, for month after month, in odd hours on journeys and in the intervals of other work, I fought my way through the lifelong wanderings of that impossible and, in the literal sense, incomprehensible work, to emerge at last upon the plateau of the supreme declaration.

FAUST: A swamp along the mountain's flank
Makes all my previous gains contaminate;
My deeds, if I could drain this sink,
Would culminate as well as terminate:
To open to the millions living space,
Not danger-proof but free to run their race.
Green fields and fruitful; men and cattle hiving
Upon this newest earth at once and thriving,
Settled at once beneath this sheltering hill
Heaped by the masses' brave and busy skill.
With such a heavenly land behind this hedge,
The sea beyond may bluster to its edge
And, as it gnaws to swamp the work of masons,
To stop the gap one common impulse hastens.
Aye! Wedded to this concept like a wife,
I find this wisdom's final form:
He only earns his freedom and his life
Who takes them every day by storm.
And so a man, beset by dangers here,
As child, man, old man, spends his manly year.
Oh to see such activity,

Treading free ground with people that are free!
Then could I bid the passing moment:
'Linger a while, thou art so fair!'
The traces of my earthly days can never
Sink in the aeons unaware.
And I, who feel ahead such heights of bliss,
At last enjoy my highest moment – this.

I've several times already tried to describe that marriage of logical statement and intellectual precision with the ardour and infinitude of Romantic poetry which haunted me like a passion in all things German. To its reflected expression in Carlyle and its native expression in Goethe, I recognised the counterpart in Beethoven. A single phrase of Beethoven, the great discord of the Ninth Symphony – let along the structure of the movement – conveys this illusion to the hearer, of receiving at one and the same time a perfectly logical and precise communication which might be translated straight into Latin, and an instant revelation of the indescribable depths of the universe. I choose deliberately the discord of the Ninth Symphony; for the illusion which Beethoven conveys of a reconciliation between the rational and the cosmic, between logic and instinct, is, ultimately, an illusion – a veil, a bridge over the chasm of discord which from time to time he permits us to see.

Like some traveller who, in the moonlit clearing of a forest, comes upon another human being pursuing the same journey, I fell in at this point along my road with a certain young scholar of my own age. A classic too, and another precociously appointed university professor.

Here it is necessary to raise ourselves with a daring bound into a metaphysics of Art. I repeat, therefore, my former proposition, that it is only as an aesthetic phenomenon that existence and the world appear justified: and in this sense it is precisely the function of tragic myth to convince us that even the Ugly and Discordant is an artistic game which the will, in the eternal fullness of its joy, plays with itself. But this not easily comprehensible proto-phenomenon of Dionysian Art becomes, in a direct way, singularly intelligible, and is immediately apprehended in the wonderful significance of musical dissonance: just as in general it is music alone, placed in contrast to the world, which can give us an idea as to what is meant by the justification of the world as an aesthetic phenomenon. The joy that the tragic myth excites has the same origin as the joyful sensation of dissonance in music. The Dionysian, with its primitive joy experienced in pain itself, is the common source of music and tragic myth.

Is it not possible that, by calling to our aid the musical relation of dissonance, the difficult problem of tragic effect may have meanwhile been materially facilitated? For we now understand what it means to wish to view tragedy and at the same time to have a longing beyond the viewing:

a frame of mind, which, as regards the artistically employed dissonance, we should simply have to characterise by saying that we desire to hear and at the same time have a longing beyond the hearing.

The young Friedrich Nietzsche was destined to be my companion through every published scrap of his writing from the opening bars of *The Birth of Tragedy* right on into the ultimate explosion into insanity of *Ecce Homo*. The journey ran parallel in the years from 1933 to 1939 with the collapse of the Germany of Beethoven and Goethe, the enthronement of Satan upon its ruins, and the launching of war in Europe. Meanwhile one dived in and out of the mighty river of German nineteenth-century philosophy – itself, despite the often less than sensuous language clothing it, as much poetry as pure reason. In particular, for one torn between myth and reality, poetry and prose, Schopenhauer was unavoidable. His *World as Will and Imagination* was consumed in half-hour stretches day by day on Sydney tramcars that clanged their way through the hot Australian sunlight.

Will is the thing-in-itself, the inner content, the essence of the world. Life, the visible world, the phenomenon, is only the mirror of the will. There-fore life accompanies the will as inseparably as the shadow accompanies the body; and if will exists, so will life, the world, exist. Life is, therefore, assured to the will to live, and so long as we are filled with the will to live we need have no fear for our existence, even in the presence of death. It is true we see the individual come into being and pass away; but the individual is only phenomenal, exists only for the knowledge which is bound to the principle of sufficient reason. Certainly, for this kind of knowledge, the individual receives his life as a gift, rises out of nothing, then suffers the loss of this gift through death, and returns again to nothing. But we desire to consider life philosophically, i.e. according to its Ideas, and in this sphere we shall find that neither the will, the thing-in-itself in all phenomena, nor the subject of knowing, that which perceives all phenomena, is affected at all by birth or by death.

It was precisely the same sentiment that led the Greeks and Romans to adorn their costly sarcophagi, just as we see them now, with feasts, dances, marriages, the chase, fights of wild beasts, bacchanalians, etc; thus with representations of the full ardour of life, which they place before us not only in such revels and sports, but also in sensual groups, and even go so far as to represent the sexual intercourse of satyrs and goats. Clearly the aim was to point in the most impressive manner away from the death of the mourned individual to the immortal life of nature, and thus to indicate, though without abstract knowledge, that the whole of nature is the phenomenon and also the fulfilment of the will to live. The form of this phenomenon is time, space and causality, and by means of these individuation, which carries with it that the individual must come into being and pass away. But this no more affects the will to live, of whose manifestation the individual is, as it were, only a particular example or specimen, than the death of an individual injures the whole of nature.

But to return to Nietzsche and *The Birth of Tragedy from the Spirit of Music*, he and I had both drunk to intoxication at the fountain where those spirits which Goethe and Beethoven had known, however painfully, to banish underground, burst into the open in a torrent of self-confidence and power. As Nietzsche himself was later to say, 'Faust and Gretchen had died out and been replaced by Siegfried and Brünnhilde.' But, at first, all had been hope.

> Let no one believe that the German spirit has for ever lost its mythical home when it still understands so obviously the voices of the birds which tell of that home. Some day it will find itself awake in all the morning freshness of a deep sleep: then it will slay the dragons, destroy the malignant dwarfs, and waken Brünnhilde – and Wotan's spear itself will be unable to obstruct its course!

Siegfried's was the voice of boundless confidence in the unaided intellect and the unaided inspiration which breaks with whatever would limit or constrain it. In the forging of the sword in *Siegfried* every rule of experience is broken and every artificial aid is rejected. The hero knows that he must reduce to scrap the sword which broke in his father's hand, in order to remake it as his own. Faust, who realised that 'he only earns his freedom and his life who takes them every day by storm', is speaking, or rather singing, in a heightened excitement through the mouth of Siegfried. Every decisive element in the making of the unconquerable sword is a defiance of what went before. 'What the master could not, how could the pupil if he should for ever obey?'

But Siegfried's was also the voice which proclaimed one of the great moral discoveries of humanity: that it is better to die than to live in fear. The moment when Siegfried, about to restore the ring to the Rhinemaidens, thrusts it back again upon his finger because, once he knows that the curse attaches to it, his act would be tainted with fear, from which he can only regain freedom by deliberately incurring the curse, is one of the supreme moments in literature – the pagan counterpart of the Crucifixion itself.

To overcome fear by deliberately incurring the inevitable destruction, to take up arms against a sea of troubles and by opposing end them – it was a mood which matched the accelerating plunge into the abyss in the later thirties. But could the act of atonement be performed by the fool who had never learnt to be afraid? To Nietzsche it seemed that one step more and all was marsh. The fool who knew no fear reappeared in *Parsifal* as the fool who knew no suffering. The road was a blind alley which led nowhere. It was the fate of

Nietzsche to spend the rest of his life striving to exorcise the forces which Wagner had called from the vasty deep and which he learnt to hate and dread.

> I am fond of clearing the air. It is even part of my ambition to be considered as essentially a despiser of Germans. I expressed my suspicions of the German character even at the age of six-and-twenty. To my mind the Germans are impossible. When I try to think of the kind of man who is opposed to me in all my instincts, my mental image takes the form of a German. The first thing I ask myself when I begin analysing a man, is, whether he has a feeling for distance in him; whether he sees rank, gradation everwhere between man and man; whether he makes distinctions: for this is what constitutes a gentleman. A man lowers himself by frequenting the society of Germans: the German places everyone on an equal footing. With the exception of my intercourse with one or two artists, and above all with Richard Wagner, I cannot say that I have spent one pleasant hour with Germans. Suppose, for one moment, that the profoundest spirit of all ages were to appear among Germans, then one of the saviours of the Capitol would be sure to arise and declare that his own ugly soul was just as great. I can no longer abide this race with which a man is always in bad compa ìy, which has no idea of nuances and which has not *esprit* in its feet, and cannot even walk withal! In short, the Germans have no feet at all, they simply have legs. The Germans have not the faintest idea of how vulgar they are; but this in itself is the acme of vulgarity – they are not even ashamed of being merely Germans. They will have their say in everything, they regard themselves as fit to decide all questions; I even fear that they have decided about me. My whole life is essentially a proof of this remark. In vain have I sought among them for a sign of tact and delicacy towards myself. Among Jews I did indeed find it, but not among Germans.

The Nietzsche who wandered in the Forest of the Ring and taught the youth of Switzerland from a professorial chair had long ago turned into Nietzsche-Zarathustra.

> But Zarathustra remained still and the body fell quite close to him, badly injured and broken but not yet dead. After a while, consciousness returned to the shattered man and he saw Zarathustra kneeling beside him.
> 'What are you doing?' he asked at length. 'I've known for a long time that the Devil would trip me up. Now he's dragging me to Hell: are you trying to prevent him?'
> 'On my honour, friend,' answered Zarathustra, 'all you have spoken of does not exist: there is no Devil and no Hell. Your soul will be dead even before your body: therefore fear nothing any more.'
> The man looked up mistrustfully. 'If you are speaking the truth,' he said, 'then I leave nothing when I leave life. I am not much more than an animal which has been taught to dance by blows and starvation.'
> 'Not so,' said Zarathustra. 'You have made danger your calling; there

is nothing in that to despise. Now you perish through your calling: so I will bury you with my own hands.'

Alas, poor Zarathustra: to have turned sexton and be doomed to dig the grave, if only in premonition, of a whole civilisation. And so it ends with the thoughts which flit between the strokes of midnight.

One
O man, give heed.
Two
What says the midnight deep?
Three
I slept, I slept.
Four
And woke from dream profound.
Five
Deep is the world,
Six
And deeper than the day had known.
Seven
Deep is its woe;
Eight
Its joy yet deeper than its grief.
Nine
Perish, says woe;
Ten
But all joy wills eternity,
Eleven
Wills deep eternity.
Twelve

'THE LANGUAGE OF POLITICS'

from *The State of the Language*, California, 1980

To sit down to write about 'the English of politics now' is to be appalled by the difficulty of finding any objective instruments which would prevent description from being mere whimsy or subjective guesswork.

It is possible certainly to identify a priori some of the influences which might have made the English of politics in 1980 different from what it was in 1880 – different, that is to say, in ways additional to those in which all or any English of 1980 is different from the English of 1880. Even at the outset, however, unanswerable queries arise. How, for instance, are the standard differences, so to speak, to be distinguished from those specific to political English? Where does one go to find an analysis of the vocabulary gained and lost, the constructions invented and abandoned, the meanings altered, the changes in sentence form and structure which occurred during the century? Even if such an analysis were procurable, it would have to be founded upon a comprehensive survey of all kinds and purposes of speech, including that of politics.

To press the same point further by posing one particular case, it is surely to be assumed that the extensions of the franchise between 1880 and 1980 must have tended to replace the sort of diction addressed by educated gentlemen to others of the same background by language calculated to be attractive and intelligible to mass audiences of widely diverse attainments and knowledge. One might go further and point to the near elimination from the education of the average Englishman of two great formative influences, acquaintance with at least the Latin classics and knowledge of the King James Bible, from which it would follow that both the conscious and the unconscious echo of those originals must have almost disappeared. These general and harmlessly uncontentious observations having been made, however, how is it possible to disentangle the consequent changes which are specific from those which are general? How far would the disappearance of latinity and Jacobean English from political harangues be due to the change in the electorate rather than to changes in education and religion generally?

The mere reference to 'political harangues' opens up another vista of incurable uncertainty: where does political English begin and end?

Is it restricted to speech in Parliament or does it include speech at political public meetings and on the hustings? Is it restricted to that used by politicians themselves or does it include leading articles in *The Times* and the *Daily Express* when they are on political topics? I could point to numerous influences which in my opinion might have altered parliamentary English – the increasing demand for brevity in speeches, the alteration in the class composition of the two houses, the increasing professionalism attempted or pretended by politicians themselves, even the altered racial composition of the House of Commons through the disappearance of the Irish component – but I have no reason to suppose that these have affected political English outside Parliament. In short, what sorts of changes are common to all forms of political speech without being also common to English speech in general?

Fresh embarrassments present themselves at every turn. Changes in fashion, in scientific knowledge, in popular prejudices are almost bound to produce their effects upon vocabulary and diction; and because politics is peculiarly a realm where what is fashionable holds sway, these changes will often be luxuriantly exemplified in political speech. Yet it would be a falsification to present as characteristic of political English something which is only the impress of current modes of thought and expression. There is a particular degeneration of speech, which has flourished during the last ten or fifteen years, consisting in periphrases formed with the word *situation*. Thus a war becomes 'a war situation', two rival mobs are not fighting but 'in a conflict situation', a firm losing money has 'moved into a loss situation', partly due perhaps to having been '*involved*' (a related periphrastic word) 'in strike situations'. I have little doubt that the quite pathological popularity of this periphrasis, which has wreaked havoc in political English, derives from the current popularity of the environmentalist theory of human behaviour: people are supposed to behave as they do because of the situations in which they find themselves, and to be the creatures, not to say the victims, of their circumstances.

Finally – to make an end of the tedious accumulation of difficulties – about *which* politician's English are we talking? In every respect – vocabulary, syntax, sentence structure, rhetoric – one politician probably differs more from another politician than all politicians collectively, if we could make a composite photograph, differ from non-politicians collectively. Ernest Bevin seldom finished a sentence, though *Hansard* finished a good many for him. Michael Foot on the other hand has rarely left a sentence unfinished. Which, if either of them, represents the English of politics now?

I am not arguing that it is impossible to record and characterize the English of politics now in a strict sense of the terms. What I am saying is that to do so in any objective or scientific manner would require a massive processing of material which only a computer could cope with. No doubt some university which is better endowed with computer time than with fruitful subjects for research will set a team to work on first establishing a record of standard English today, by way of control and then comparing it with a balanced sample of political English. Not having a computer or a university to hand and suspecting that, if I had, I would not employ them in that way, I propose to do something infinitely more modest and grossly arbitrary. I am going to take four speeches made in the House of Commons, seventy and ninety years ago, and two made there in the last thirty years. In the past and in the present samples I shall include one speech by an acknowledged outstanding orator on a great occasion, and one, albeit on an important occasion, by a speaker whom no one ever accused of being an orator. I intend to examine them closely to see what, if anything, comes out of so limited and random a sample. The four are Gladstone introducing the first Irish Home Rule Bill in 1886; Campbell-Bannerman speaking to the Address on becoming Prime Minister in 1906; Aneurin Bevan moving the Second Reading of the National Health Service Bill in 1946; and Edward Heath concluding the debate of principle in 1971 on British entry into the European Economic Community. It is convenient to attempt to characterise first the contemporary specimens, and then to treat the earlier ones as a 'control'.

Though introducing a measure of great comprehensiveness and complexity Aneurin Bevan did so in much under 9,000 words, including brief responses to a few brief interruptions; he got them off in seventy-three minutes, which, at 123 words a minute, is fast by oratorical standards – I personally find it safe with a platform speech to assume an average of no more than a hundred. Yet Bevan was evidently sensitive to the length of his speech and twice apologised for it. The average length of a sentence was eighteen words and of a word 4.9 letters. As to vocabulary, *situation*, though not yet sociological, had made its appearance: 'the actual situation as it exists' (tautology and trite at that); 'one of the tragedies of the situation'; 'it will not affect the existing situation'. So had the verb *involved*, which in later years was to become, not least in Edward Heath's mouth, the prince of periphrases, against much the same background as *situation*; 'a person ought to be able to receive medical help without being involved in financial anx :ty' – where the words *being involved in* could be omitted altogether. There is also one sociological *ism*: 'defend the very small hospital on the ground of its *localism*'.

A good deal of verbal attrition is noticeable, from the over-frequent intensive *very* to such terms as *carry out* ('carrying out all these principles and services'), *quite frankly*, 'the best *solution of the difficulty*', or the overuse of *field* (another sociologism?): 'consultations have taken place over a very wide field', 'they cover a very wide field indeed', 'when we come to the general practitioners, we are of course in an entirely different field'. This attrition sometimes descends to slovenly colloquialism: 'the whole thing is the wrong way round'; the voluntary hospitals 'came along' (i.e. arose); 'problems that it was up against'; 'to go along for a consultation'.

Bevan had his own personal favourite words, *priority, frivolously, instrument*, and *fructify* (the last no doubt from Gladstone). But the most striking feature of his diction is the number of expressions, especially metaphorical, which are slightly misused through insensitivity to their exact or etymological meaning: *denigrate* in the sense of 'depreciate'; *repulsion* instead of 'revulsion'; '*repugnant* to a civilised community for hospitals to have to rely upon private charity'; '*communal* interests' instead of 'common' or 'general'; 'achieve reasonable and *efficient* homogeneity'; 'the health services are to be *articulated* to the health centre'; 'endowments *waived* by Scottish Acts' (in the sense of 'diverted'); 'an *elastic resilient* service' (which? not both?); 'this is a *field* in which *idiosyncrasies* are *prevalent*', meaning that individual preferences vary.

I noted only one quotation (implicit): 'the *vaulting ambitions* of those in charge' – and that, without particular point – and several slightly off-beam metaphors: 'hope before long to build up a high tradition'; 'a young man gets a load of debt around his neck'; 'I am astonished that such a charge should lie in the mouth of any Member' (meaning simply 'be made by'); 'freedom of movement inside a budget'. However, it would be churlish not to end with a splendid Bevanism, which illustrates his way of using metaphor with ironic humour: 'I would rather be kept alive in the efficient if cold altruism of a large hospital than expire in a gush of warm sympathy in a small one.'

Edward Heath's wind-up of the debate on British entry into the European Community was compressed by the convention of the house into the last half-hour before the vote – 4,000 words at 136 a minute. The average length of a sentence was nearly twenty-three words, and of a word 4.4 letters.

The most marked feature of the language is the quantity of metaphor eroded to the point of cliché: 'to set this against a world *canvas*'; 'move along the *path* to real unity'; 'the position *facing* the western world'; 'fit into the *framework* of European unity'; 'should any of the apprehensions . . . materialise, then the *machinery* exists to deal with them'. Perhaps the bureaucratic clichés '*play* an increasing *part*; and '*vitally* affect the *balance* of forces' (though mixed) are no longer metaphors at all; but the only live metaphor in the speech was 'no one is sitting there waiting to have an amicable cup of tea with the leader of the Opposition'.

There is a profusion of situational periphrases: 'in the *situation* which I have described, the United States is bound to *find itself involved* more and more with the large economic powers'; 'new institutions have been invented to meet the realities of the new *situation*'; 'the position in Europe today is that . . . the *situation* has been transformed by China'. The interesting periphrastic verbs are *dealing with* and *handle*, which I suggest are not merely characteristic of Edward Heath personally but denote the modern view of politics as a sort of engineering. 'When it comes to *dealing with* the major economic powers in creating what has now to be a changed policy'; 'we must see how these *problems* can best be *handled* by Britain'; 'these matters are being *handled* the whole time'; 'we differ on how best this can be *handled*'; 'the necessary and appropriate means for *dealing with* the problems of its members'. More prominent than *problem* as a non-word is *question*: 'the *questions* of larger firms, technology, capital investment and rate of growth are of immense importance' – so they may be, if only we were asked them; 'what is important is the *question* of being in the best possible position to influence economic decisions', where *the question of being* merely means 'to be'.

Of single vocables the most significantly prominent is *world*. 'A *world* canvas' has already been quoted; 'the *world* was watching New York . . . tonight the *world* is watching Westminster'; 'the balance of forces in the *modern world*'; 'the position facing the *western world* today'; 'on the *world* scene against which we must set this debate'; 'an outward-looking aspect towards *the developing world*; our influence in Europe and the *world*'; those parts of the *world* which still lie in the shadow of want'; 'many millions of people right across the *world* will rejoice'. The significance is not of course purely verbal – that the abstraction *world* has been talked into a part of speech – but that its prevalence marks the extent to which external systems of thought and values have come to dominate political action.

Quotations or conscious allusions do not occur at all in the speech; and the one slightly allusive term turns out to be a malapropism: 'by some strange *permutation of history* in this very short span all these changes have come together', where *permutation* is used, in defiance of etymology, in the sense of 'coincidence' or 'conjuncture'.

Turning back almost ninety years to Gladstone's introduction of the first Home Rule Bill on 8 April 1886, it is hard not to be overwhelmed by the sheer magnificence of an oration of over 19,000 words, pronounced (so far as the Official Report goes) without interruption at a speed of under 100 words a minute in nearly three and a half hours. 'I sometimes thought,' he wrote in his diary, 'it could never end.' Nevertheless some objective contrasts can be identified which may be typical rather than Gladstonian. The average length of words is lower – as low as 4.3 – but the length of average sentence is high, at thirty words, covering an enormous range, modulated on a wavelike pattern, from ninety words or more to half a dozen. A characteristic *diminuendo* is the following sequence: 40, 37, 14, 22, 27, 9, 7; or again 86, 47, 23, 17, 6. In sentence construction the prevalence of the rhetorical trick of anaphora is impressive. It takes the form both of iteration ('it must be *different, differently* maintained and maintained with a *different* spirit, courage and consistency' – a marvellous sentence, with its balancing triplets, and subtle use of assonance) and of repeating the beginning of a sentence after a parenthetical self-interruption.

Despite its rhetoric, the speech has an intimacy like that of chamber music, the intimacy of a speaker playing with an audience he knows and who know him: 'it may not seem much to say, but wait for what is coming' (note the effect of the monosyllables). A fully political use is made of circumlocution: 'we have arrived at a point where it is necessary that we should take a careful and searching survey of our position' – a modern 'situation'-monger need not blush too deeply after reading that. Metaphor is modest, and mingles the trite ('look this problem in the face') with the noble: 'stripping law of its foreign garb and investing it with a domestic character', where a consciousness of the etymology of *invest* is necessary to full enjoyment. Equally rare, perhaps surprisingly so, is quotation or allusion: in the first half of the gigantic speech I have noted one only: 'There is the head and fruit of our offending', and even that both misquotes and, in its context, misapplies *Othello* 1.3.81.

The vocabulary is less impregnated with the language of contemporary political notions than would have been expected – unless indeed the modern reader is tone-deaf to them. The word *world* already noted as a myth word today, was colourless and literal then ('that manufacturing industry which overshadows the whole world') while *empire* – shimmering between UK and British Empire – was already irrationally emotive ('this great, noble and world-wide empire'). If there is an overworked adverb, it is probably *infinitely*; but there is a remarkable absence of cheap emphasis. Even high Victorian sentiment and self-righteousness have to be looked for with a lantern before a few mild specimens can be turned up: 'advanced in the career of liberal principles and actions'; 'our ineffectual and spurious coercion is morally worn out'.

I confess that when I came to Campbell-Bannerman's Prime Ministerial speech, the last of my four chosen specimens, I was dismayed; for it turned out to be a speech presenting no apprehensible characteristics of vocabulary, diction or construction whatever. But the dice must be allowed to lie where they fall: it is as well to be reminded that political speech can – at least could – be perfectly colourless in the mouth of a practitioner who by then had had nearly forty years in the collar.

The statistical count is unremarkable: average sentence length almost twenty-eight words, substantial but behind Gladstone; average word length 4.6 letters. The only quotation or allusion in the whole speech was simply a continuation of the use which the preceding speaker, Joseph Chamberlain, had made of a passage from Sydney Smith. At most a certain tendency to pleonasm, not unpleasant if a trifle pompous, can be detected: 'he shrinks *in some measure* from a *public* appearance in the House' is really absurd, since a Member – especially a Foreign Secretary (as here) – either does or does not appear in the house, and if he does is bound to do so publicly. Orotund, too, is a certain fondness for not leaving a noun without an adjective: 'extraordinary circumstances', 'strenuous observations', 'lamentable circumstances', 'perfect amity', Metaphor is well worn, too worn: 'temperance is the keystone, or the cornerstone, of the edifice of the prosperity of this country'; 'the late Government wished to have a pistol in their hands in order to terrify foreign nations'; 'last session there was no disclosure: we knocked at every door that we could find'.

When all is done, one is forced to admit that the attempt to find anything specifically political in the selected specimens has ended in a negative. Whether 'ancient' or 'modern', whether great oratory or run-of-the-mill discourse, the English remains undifferentiated, the English of the day, such as would have been spoken by contemporaries, or by the speakers themselves, on any other subject or in any other walk of life. Politics on one side, the changes are less over the course of ninety years than would probably have been expected. There is now a certain tendency to greater brevity, a certain increased susceptibility to the infection of cliché; but it would be hard to argue that the change is from the speech of more educated to that of less educated men, or from the expectations of a smaller audience of gentlemen to those of a wider audience of plebeians. The language in short has remained remarkably standard: in terms of a century, in the mouth of politicians, English now is hardly to be distinguished from English then.

INTRODUCTION

to *Mr Romford's Hounds* by Robert Smith Surtees, 1982

After Surtees ceased to be compulsory reading aloud to the family on holiday evenings, a gap of many years intervened before the old favourites were taken up again. The first sensation, which persisted and raised many questions, was that of the sheer speed at which Surtees' readers find themselves carried along. It is a sensation like that produced by a smart run on a determined horse, who is a bit of a puller and means to enjoy himself at least as much as his rider does. After a while the inexhaustible tirelessness of this mount persuades the rider that he is not really 'up' but is enjoying hunting from the train.

The sensation would not be so surprising if it were produced only by the brilliant descriptions of actual hunts. The pace, of course, does slacken a little here and there, but always quickens again immediately afterwards. It is a 'spanker' from start to finish. Like views of the countryside from horseback, the often lengthy and painstakingly detailed descriptions of people and places do not diminish the sensation of pace. In this respect they are quite different from the descriptive passages in other novelists, which the writers, one feels, have deliberately settled down to pen at leisure. However much one enjoys Surtees' recurrent types of individuals and scenes, one never treats the descriptions as other than integral: they are never 'skippable'; they are features of the run itself.

One characteristic of Surtees' writing which either causes, or is at any rate connected with, this fox-hunting pace of his is his knack of making the doings of all his characters seem to be first person, though, in grammatical terms, there is hardly any first person writing. The manner in which the characters assess their situation, deliberate and strike a balance between conflicting motives – motives mostly which they would not avow or perhaps not be aware of – helps to create this illusion of first person. 'If it had but stood at Allington Banks or Greenhope, he thought it would have been the most convenient residence a Master of Hounds could possibly have had, might have reached every cover in the country without lying out, that lying out being a terrible bugbear to Mr Facey, on account both of the expense and the irregular habits of Chowey and Swig. However, Mr Romford consoled himself by thinking that his Lordship would be very sly if he got any rent out of him.'

The passage happens to illustrate also the use of a loose and sometimes syntactically rather careless sentence-structure, which helps to internalise the descriptions of behaviour, despite the deliberate distance at which the narrator keeps himself from his characters. Or does he?

That question mark raises another of the qualities which make Surtees irresistible to his devotees. It is his sheer undisguised enjoyment of just everything that comes along. This enjoyment radiates from the writing, whatever the subject, sordid or roguish, comical or commonplace. It is enjoyment like that of one of those days (surely everybody has them?) when, from the moment of setting foot outside one's door, everything suddenly seems novel or humorous or simply pleasurable. It is a mood not limited by place or season; it arrives unexpected and unsought, like a gift of grace. Surtees has that kind of delight in every feature of the scene which he creates, rascality and roughriding, cowardice, dishonesty, folly, meanness, no less than courage, generosity and frankness, all become the material of sheer enjoyment.

It must be admitted that the rogues and cads and fools greatly outnumber their opposites in Surtees' pages. In fact one is as hard put to it as Diogenes with his lantern in Athens to find an honest man in Surtees' novels. When you do find him, he is, not by chance, likely to be a Geordie like Surtees himself. The immortal James Pigg of *Handley Cross* and Independent Jimmy of *Facey Romford* were both 'Northumbrians'. Yet Surtees is not writing as a *censor morum* or with a detectable moral purpose, like a Hogarth or a Dickens. With few exceptions, he does not find humanity attractive; but still he enjoys the contemplation of it, and chooses to write books about rotters. Nor does he palliate the rotters; if any complaint is to be made against the characterisation of those great heroes, Soapey Sponge and Facey Romford, it is that Surtees lays on with a trowel their disreputable and despicable traits.

They are allowed one redeeming quality only; but it is that quality which makes them heroes, albeit hopelessly flawed heroes. It is their passion for fox-hunting, matched with courageous and skilful horsemanship. 'Tell me a man's a fox-hunter,' asserted Jorrocks, 'and I loves 'im at once.' The more loathsome and unattractive the rest of the make-up of Soapey or Facey, the more brightly this one quality shows and the more it distinguishes them from the common herd of equally dubious or contemptible snobs, climbers, tricksters, impostors, with whom both the stage and the stalls are packed. Those are not fox-hunters, or at best they are indifferent fox-hunters or pretended fox-hunters. Surtees' apotheosis of fox-hunting consists precisely in placing the souls of his great fox-hunters in such an otherwise contemptible setting. If even they could be sanctified by fox-hunting, how wondrous must be the might of that matchless way of life!

It is not quite the same with the heroines. Surtees has a weakness for handsome women, and Lucy Glitters is allowed some soft endearing touches ('And Lucy thought of the time when another sportsman, Mr Sponge, placed a well-worn brush in her hat, and sighed'). Surtees understands that no woman can quite enter heart and soul into the rational indescribability of fox-hunting – any more than into the irrational indescribability of the House of Commons. It is by their horsemanship rather than their love of fox-hunting *per se* that his heroines are redeemed: they ride impossible screws over impracticable fences, and they look pretty while doing so. ('Facey had no idea that Lucy was such a fine horsewoman, not knowing she had been in a circus before she took to the stage.')

Lucy Glitters is the main character who links the two best novels and the two greatest character creations of Surtees – Sponge and Romford. A period of eleven years separated their publication and presumably their composition. Though *Handley Cross* (1843) laid the foundation of Surtees' readership – it was thought advisable to describe him on later title pages as 'the author of *Handley Cross*' – and though the character of Mr Jorrocks, introduced into subsequent novels, like *Hillingdon Hall* (1845), much as Shakespeare's Falstaff was spread forward from 1 *Henry IV*, has become part of the English heritage, there was still something deficient as long as fox-hunting was apotheosized in the person of a loveable, if less than hard-riding, bourgeois.

To me Surtees' novels of the 1840s are immature compared with the heroic rascality of *Sponge* (1853) and *Romford* (1864). Surtees was himself conscious of the sharp change in gear which he had made and acknowledged it, probably ironically, in that absurd Preface to *Sponge* where it is excused as a device to 'put the rising generation on their guard against specious, promiscuous acquaintance and train them to the noble sport of hunting to the exclusion of its mercenary, illegitimate offshoots'. The two books show clear signs of having been conceived from the start as a pair, rather than that *Mr Romford's Hounds* latched as an afterthought on to *Sponge's Sporting Tour*. In the interval Surtees attempted, in *Ask Mamma* (1858) and *Plain or Ringlets?* (1860), those society themes which played subordinate parts in the fox-hunting novels proper, but Surtees' heart was not in them, and fortunately for us he lived just long enough to complete the companion piece to *Sponge*.

Like Auberon Waugh in his introduction to *Sponge*, I personally have always thought *Facey Romford* the cream of Surtees. We enjoy it, no doubt, the more for the memorable illustrations by Leech and Browne, but what on earth was the matter with Thomas Seccombe, the assistant editor of the *Dictionary of National Biography*, when he asserted in his entry for Surtees that 'without the original illustrations' the work [*Facey Romford*] 'has very little interest'? Anyhow, users of this reprint can enjoy both.

'ON TRANSLATION'

Folio Society Literary Dinner and Debate, 1987

My lords, ladies and gentlemen: I am here to invite you to agree to the proposition that even the best translations are not versions, but perversions, of the original. When I was served with this motion to move, I thought that it was due to someone in the Folio Society who had an unnatural affection for assonance. Fortunately, at an early stage of these proceedings, I was informed that this was a quotation from St Jerome.

None the less, I do beseech you not to take the word 'perversion' in any pejorative sense, as though translations were necessarily inherently inferior to the original. Rather, I ask you to agree with me in the proposition that in translation there is no such thing as *equivalence* – no such thing as 'transportation' from one language into another, even though the end-result of attempting it may be, and sometimes has been, something greater than the original starting-point.

I stand here in the quality of a culprit turned prosecutor. In 1948, the Oxford University Press published a translation of *The History of Herodotus* into 'biblical English' – if you please! – which I commenced as an undergraduate in my first year at Trinity in 1930, and finally accomplished and polished after the Second World War.

It was a most extraordinary undertaking. The idea was that *The History*, being our first surviving specimen of Greek prose, and the style of Herodotus being delusively simple, the easiest way to convey some sense of these qualities of Herodotus was (quite deliberately), instead of resorting to the fustian of earlier translators, to use strictly and in regimented fashion the English of the King James Bible.

It was, of course, a perversion. It was a perversion because there could be no real parity between the text of Herodotus and those resonances and associations which the language of the King James version has awakened in English minds for three and a half centuries. So, as is appropriate at the beginning of a service, I here confess my faults.

The essence of my case (the case which I hope will win acceptance with you), is that in any work of literary art there is an integral coherence between the language and the content, which is, of necessity, lost when the language is changed. Each language has its peculiar-

ities of sound; its peculiarities of expression; its native peculiarities
of association; and these enter into the very texture of whatever is
written or sung in that language. The attempt to detach the *language*
from the content of what is being *said* is a hopeless attempt because
language was initially of the essence.

And how different the great languages are in this respect! Musi-
cally, there are differences between German, Italian and French –
each having their own type of music which has been used by their
masters of both poetry and prose. It is impossible to disassociate the
'music' of each language from the 'words'.

Then there are several modes of thought. Write Latin, and you
think with a particular kind of logic and severity. Write German,
and, if you write German well, you *become* half German yourself.
Write French, and you enter into a unique inheritance of pride and
self-confidence. Whatever is said, written or poetised in any of these
languages, is inseparably coloured by the *nature* of those languages.

The notion that you can take it with you from Virgil into English
or from Goethe into English or from Hugo into English is inherently
impossible. You will have left the best behind you as you accomplish
your journey.

There is something more which should be said about these impossi-
bilities. We *say* – and it is arguable that we *think* – only what we are
able to say. The manner in which we speak – the capabilities and
possibilities of our language determine what we are able to say and
probably what we are to think. Now, languages differ fundamentally
in the capability of what you can say in them. A language like Welsh
is *designed* for poetry, but is a difficult one for prose because of its
lack of a relative pronoun. This is totally different from Greek which
resembles German in its facility for creating and expressing abstractions – it is a language of philosophy.

Yet, bearing all these difficulties in mind, it has to be admitted that
the consequences of translation are often constructive and sometimes
creative. It is one of the secrets of our human condition that error is
often the source of truth and mistakes often the means of learning.

'Thou shalt love thy neighbour as thyself.' An immensely significant
statement – a statement which is a translation from Greek, but from
Greek which is a translation from Hebrew. Now it happens that the
Hebrew conjunction is so vague that this can only be (I was going to
say translated – but shrank from the very word!) transported as
meaning merely 'like you'. The Hebrew doesn't have to say whether
'you' is nominative or accusative. It doesn't have to say either, 'like
you are' or 'like you love yourself. But Greek *does* have to. And the
Greeks plumped for the accusative: 'Love your neighbour', therefore,
'as you love yourself.' So a new command had come into existence,

a command of importance, depth and beauty; *but* was it what the original (if Hebrew was the original) meant to say? *Almost certainly not.* Thus, the difference between the two languages brought about not a translation, but the *creation* of a new thing.

What I am asking you to accept is that translation at its best is always the creation of something different, something new, something fine – something of importance for the future. For a translation is directed to those to whom the original was not spoken or written: to a different age, a different generation, to men in societies with different thoughts, different assumptions. And the translation has to absorb something of those assumptions, of those thoughts.

The word *Kamoka* mystically transformed into the translated command is a little miracle, setting out as a translation, but ending up as something new in its own right, something which men will not willingly give up.

This goes on happening. Homer's Greek is the commemoration of a lost civilisation, jewelled, literary speech addressed to a society and a hierarchy which had almost disappeared before the poems came to be composed. Pope converted it – triumphantly, as Flaxman bore witness – into Augustan thought, Augustan English. There emerged something new, something of which men say, 'It was not here in times past.' – not a *version* but a *creation*.

I have used Hebrew already, and I end my appeal to you with a verse from the Hebrew. One of the possessions of the English people (thanks to a German musician!) is the thought lodged in so many millions of minds in this phrase: 'I know that my Redeemer liveth' – a statement of endless importance and indelible impression. Yet the words upon which the supreme assertion of the physical resurrection depends are nowhere to be found in the original! Consult your Bible and you will confirm that this is so. The verse, for the translators, simply had to be about the resurrection. So a statement of faith in the physical resurrection was created out of what was not there. This was not straightforward transfer from the *Book of Job*; it *was* something new, a *creation*.

What I ask you to agree then, is that a translation is not a transportation of the same thing unaltered from one language into another. It is a creation, a creation of that which is not only new but wonderful and imperishable. I trust that you will so accept the meaning of the motion and in that sense will join me in approving it.

INTRODUCTION

to *Phineas Finn* by Anthony Trollope, 1989

Phineas Finn was finished in May 1867 and began to appear from October 1867 onwards in the *St Paul's Magazine*, of which Trollope became editor, having resigned in September, before retirement age and without pension, from his lifelong employment in the Post Office.

The year 1867 was a year of considerable political turmoil. John Russell (Earl Russell since 1861), who became Prime Minister on Lord Palmerston's death in October 1865, had resigned in June 1866, following a defeat – not, as implied in the novel, over the issue of the ballot – on his Government's Reform Bill. Lord Derby took office, with Disraeli leading in the Commons. They 'dished' the Whigs, and in the session of 1867 carried their own Reform Bill. So dissolution did not come until 1868, when Disraeli, who succeeded as leader on Derby's retirement in February 1868, was heavily defeated at an election largely fought on the issue of disestablishment of the Church of Ireland.

The novel was thus written when the end of the Parliament elected in 1865 was thought more imminent than it turned out to be. Trollope himself had undertaken in 1867 to stand for election in an Essex county seat, which under the Conservative Reform Bill disappeared. He was abroad in the United States on a Government mission when dissolution took place in 1868, but was adopted at short notice as Liberal candidate for the Yorkshire borough of Beverley, which with great distaste and discomfort he actually fought, coming bottom of the poll. The seat itself was in fact abolished following that election owing to the corrupt practices of the successful candidate.

For the purposes of the novel, Trollope took liberties with the political events of 1865–7. The election of 1865 was that at which his hero found himself unexpectedly elected for the Irish borough of Loughshane, though it did not directly instal 'Mildmay' (Lord Russell) in office. The subsequent election when Phineas Finn was returned for the English 'pocket borough' of Loughton was the one which never happened, in the spring of 1867.

Trollope himself regarded the novel very highly: '*Phineas Finn*,' he wrote in his *Autobiography*, 'I certainly think was successful from first to last.' It is described as a political novel – Trollope's own significantly different term is 'semi-political tale' – but it is not a political novel in the sense that, for example, Disraeli's Young England trilogy were political novels, a book written as a means of saying something political that was consumingly important to the author. There is a devastating admission to this effect by Trollope himself:

> I was conscious that I could not make a tale pleasing chiefly, or perhaps in any part, by politics. If I write politics for my own sake, I must put in love and intrigue, social incidents, with perhaps a dash of sport, for the benefit of my readers. In this way I think I made my political hero interesting. It was certainly a blunder to take him from Ireland – into which I was led by the circumstance that I created the scheme of the book during a visit to Ireland. There was nothing to be gained by the peculiarity, and there was an added difficulty in obtaining sympathy and affection for a politician belonging to a nationality whose politics are not respected in England. But in spite of this *Phineas* succeeded. It was not a brilliant success – because men and women not conversant with political matters could not care much for a hero who spent so much of his time either in the House of Commons or in the public office. But the men who would have lived with Phineas Finn read the book, and the women who would have lived with Lady Laura Standish read it also. As this was what I had intended, I was contented. It is all fairly good except the ending – as to which till I got to it I made no provision. As I fully intended to bring my hero again into the world, I was wrong to marry him to a simple pretty Irish girl, who could only be felt as an encumbrance on such return.

Could there be more innocently revealing candour – It was a blunder to take him from Ireland? Here is Trollope writing his 'semi-political' novel, within twelve months of a general election fought upon Irish issues which was to open an era lasting fifty years when Ireland would tear the British Parliament apart and turn politics and party in Britain upside down; and the author of a political novel makes the 'blunder' of taking his hero from Ireland, and a Roman Catholic, to boot. Of all that political volcano that was threatening eruption, Trollope had nothing to say, gave evidence of having no notion.

Trollope was a perfectly recognizable type: the person who has preconceived self-satisfied political notions, with not a suspicion of the depth, the passion and the complexity of politics. He would have been a predictable and perfectly typical Social Democrat voter in 1987. The artless confession is in his own words of self-righteous complacency:

> I have always thought that to sit in the British Parliament should be the highest object of ambition to every educated Englishman. I do not by this mean to suggest that every educated Englisman should set before himself a seat in Parliament as a probable or even a possible career; but that the man in Parliament has reached a higher position than the man out – that to serve one's country *without pay* is the grandest work that a man can

> do – that, of all studies *the study of politics is the one in which a man may make himself most useful to his fellow-creatures* – and that of all lives, public political lives are capable of the highest efforts.
>
> Writing now at an age beyond sixty, I can say that *my political feelings and convictions have never undergone any change.* They are now what they became when I first began to have political feelings and convictions. Nor do I find in myself any tendency to modify them as I have found generally in men as they grow old. I consider myself to be an advanced, but still a conservative Liberal, which I regard not only as a possible but as a rational and consistent phase of political existence. I can, I believe, in a very few words, make known my political theory; and as I am anxious that any who know aught of me should know that, I will endeavour to do so.

The passage, which I have not been able to refrain from occasionally italicising, is the prelude to several pages of the sort of platitudes with which any plain citizen will, if given the chance, bore a real live politician to distraction.

The fact is that Trollope's interest and talent lay altogether elsewhere. He has the novelist's capacity for absorbing and describing the scenes and moods of walks of life other than his own. There is a Zolaesque conscientiousness in the way he set about finding out what the House of Commons was like:

> As I could not take my seat on those benches where I might possibly have been shone upon by the Speaker's eye, I had humbly to crave his permission for a seat in the gallery, so that I might thus become conversant with the ways and doings of the House in which some of my scenes were to be placed. The Speaker was very gracious, and gave me a running order for, I think, a couple of months. It was enough, at any rate, to enable me often to be very tired – and, as I have been assured by members, to talk of the proceedings almost as well as though Fortune had enabled me to fall asleep within the House itself.

The experience was sufficient to enable Trollope to identify and describe with his tolerantly humorous and slightly acidulated cynicism the sensations and motivations of politicians in Parliament, in and out of office – even daring on one occasion to produce a mock-up of discussion in Cabinet. The descriptions of the manner in which Members of Parliament behave towards one another, of the hopes and fears which agitate the breasts of parliamentary aspirants, of the conventional insincerities of parliamentary intercourse and the physical sensations of the Chamber itself are remarkably well done; but not done in a way which, if Trollope had himself entered the House, would have endeared him to his colleagues or presaged a happy and contented life for him on the green benches. This is confirmed by the anguish he was to experience at Beverley, when he briefly – indeed, very briefly – had to live the life of a parliamentary candidate. Unlike the hunting-field, it was not an arena in which the novelist could be both a humorously detached observer and an enthusiastic participant.

However, it was the surface manifestations and not the deep underflowing currents which interested Trollope. His business – and how superbly he knew how to go about it! – was to present characters in social landscapes, from the hunting-field to the lawyer's chamber or the lodginghouse-keeper's bedroom. With inimitably gentle fluency he presented them as they behaved under the pressure of the events of human, and specifically English, social life. His study was individual character and not society itself, of which the forms, the wave movements and the dynamic laws are the stuff of politics.

As regularly with Trollope, the study is the study of a weak character. Phineas Finn is a weak character not as, for instance, Coningsby is Disraeli's novel of that name is a weak character. because he is made subordinate to the function of conveying the author's political philosophy and political programme. He is a weak character because Trollope wanted a character weak but amiable and fundamentally not dishonest, in order to subject it to a series of social pressures in a political environment and then view it through the refracting medium of certain more manly characters – mostly female! Trollope did not, as his readers often do, groan to himself: 'if only the chap had some real spunk in him – half the spunk, say, of Lady Laura Standish!' He needed Phineas to have no spunk.

As with many successful artists, it is not absolutely clear that Trollope was without illusions about what he was really doing. It is all very well for him to write:

> By no amount of description or asseveration could I succeed in making the reader understand how much these characters [the immediate reference is to Plantagenet Palliser and his wife, Lady Glencora] with their belongings have been to me in my latter life; or how frequently I have used them for the expression of my political and social convictions. They have been as real to me as free trade was to Mr Cobden, or the dominion of a party to Mr Disraeli; and as I have not been able to speak from the benches of the House of Commons, or to thunder from platforms, or to be efficacious as a lecturer, they have served me as safety-valves by which to deliver my soul.

By no stretch of the imagination is the depiction of Phineas Finn MP a compensation for inability to speak in the Commons, to 'thunder from platforms' or to deliver 'efficacious' lectures – the very adjective is a give-away! The characters of the Palliser novels do nothing of the sort; but the fact that Trollope imagined they did and told himself that that was his motive in creating them is revealing. The novelist who wanted (but not badly enough) to be in Parliament was salving his regret by telling himself he had produced a surrogate. Fortunately the delusion did not disable him from doing what he did well and discerning what the artist's eye which he did possess was constituted to discern.

The proof of Trollope's true disinterest in politics is in the denouement of the novel itself. On the surface, the hero sacrifices a promising career in order to vote against the Government in which he has attained the rank of an Under-Secretary, and in the event to defeat it on the issue of tenant-right in Ireland. But how did Phineas Finn come to be so committed to Irish tenant-right as to incur political suicide for the sake of it? Not because he had all along interested himself in Irish land law and rural conditions, made speeches on the subject and identified himself with it. Not at all. He strikes up a friendship with a senior but independent-minded Cabinet Minister, whom he admires. To his immense gratification, he accompanies his distinguished friend on a tour of Ireland, which redounds to Finn's local reputation. In the course of the tour the Minister, who knows exactly what he is about, launches a campaign for tenant-right in Ireland, and Finn in a fit a loyalty and enthusiasm commits himself to it in the intoxication of a public meeting. That is not the story of even a semi-political hero nor the plot of an author who is even semi-serious about politics.

The contraption is a piece of stage machinery to enable Trollope to perform his real business as an artist. The political scene, the parliamentary scene, is wallpaper. What fascinates Trollope is the way men and women in a certain social milieu behave under the pressures of amatory emotion. With an intensity and determination akin to that of a research scientist he limits his field of vision, selects his experimental materials and constructs a series of tests to which he will subject them. It is when Trollope is about this business that his enthusiasm infects the reader and the speed and pitch of the writing rise to match it. Great though the distance in style and conventions may be, the nearest fellow researchers to Trollope are the dramatists who re-explored and re-exploited the subjects of Greek tragedy. Racine in French and Alfieri in Italian used Phaedra or Medea for their psychological investigations, in a kindred spirit to that in which Trollope created for his purposes a Lady Laura Standish, a Madame Goesler, a Violet Effingham and a Mary Flood Jones.

I do not think it accidental that my examples are all women. It was the behaviour of the female personality under laboratory-controlled conditions that was Trollope's chosen study. His men were only the indispensable reagents: painstakingly though Trollope worked upon them, what reader would not confess that a perfunctoriness, an artificiality, an unsatisfactoriness even, which the females vivisected and displayed never convey, hang about all Trollope's masculine characters – about the Duke of Omnium, about Plantagenet Palliser, about Mr Kennedy, nay about Phineas Finn himself?

Trollope was a specialist, indeed, a relatively narrow specialist. The fact is masked for us by his huge productivity and the deceptive apparent facility of his writing. There is a significant passage, describing Finn's resignation speech, where Trollope says that Finn 'had learned the task of turning his thoughts quickly into language while standing with a crowd of listeners around him – *as a practised writer does when seated in his chair*'. What is not certain with Trollope, as with many artists, is whether he could himself have defined the content and the self-imposed limits of his work. The artist can be unconscious or in ignorance of what others see that he is doing.

'SHAKESPEARE'S SONNETS'

BBC Publications, London, 1983

Why is that one of the most hauntingly beautiful couplets in English, those first two lines of the thirtieth of Shakespeare's sonnets? Part of the secret – but only part – is not difficult to guess. The lines are saturated with a magical alliteration: the dominant s-sound in the words 'sessions', 'sweet', 'silent', 'summon' is faintly echoed in the endings of 'remembrance', 'things' and 'past'. Long before English poetry adopted rhyme, it lived with alliteration, and the English ear has somehow never forgotten that older pleasure. The spell of alliteration not only hovers over our poetry: it is mingled in our prose, and many a moving passage, especially in English oratory, proves upon examination to be indebted to a choice of words that was dictated by the desire for alliteration.

But this purely sensual pleasure of the repeated s-sounds in Shakespeare's couplet is heightened by a pleasure which is intellectual: the unexpected use of legal imagery. Those three words, 'sessions', 'summon' and 'remembrance', belong originally to law books and the jargon of the courts. But you do not need to know that. Even the hearer who is unconscious of the allusions experiences nevertheless the emotional impact of honeyed words conveying legal imagery.

The rest of the sonnet is not equal to its opening. How could it be? But only another poet will know what happened – how the revelation of those opening lines burst upon the author in complete isolation and how they were carried around in his brain for days, perhaps weeks or months, until the rest of the poem could be fitted to them. Nearly every short poem contains, hidden but still detectable, the germinal phrase or thought which caused it to be written. The business of hammering out the framework for it can be a grim and painful one, and nowhere more so than in a sonnet, with its rigorous and demanding shape.

The poet knew the thought with which his poem had to conclude, and we watch him forging his way towards it from the triumphant commencement, like a determined swimmer buffeted by the waves and gradually tiring. The first two lines, still sustained by the s-alliteration and by a new w-alliteration, 'with', 'woes', 'wail', 'waste', bear up splendidly. Even more alliterations – 'drown', 'death' and 'dateless', 'moan' and 'many' – follow and they bring along the essential preparatory word, 'friends'; for it is, we must understand, the poet's *friends* who throng from the past to his 'sessions of sweet silent thought'. But the going is unmistakably heavy. Emotion will have nothing more to say until the conclusion is reached, and the void has to be filled up with conscientious ornament and a forced metaphor about paying bills.

Then comes at last what we were waiting for: 'But if the while I think on thee, dear friend, All losses are restored and sorrows end.' It is quiet, satisfactory and sufficient – but no more than that.

Why then did the poet insist on using a verse form which committed him to the constraints of three rhyming quatrains and a concluding couplet with its inevitably staccato effect and epigrammatic about-turn? I do not think we in this age can answer that question completely; for we can never experience again the jubilation of our Elizabethan forefathers when they discovered that whatever the Italians could do, they could do better – or at least as well – in their own language. But in every age and tongue there is a need which only the struggle with a restrictive form can fulfil: 'Dancing in fetters', Nietzsche once called it. It is the need to give compulsive power to an emotion or a fantasy by confining it in a strict form, like steam compressed in a cylinder.

So is it a great poem? Yes, for the sake of the marvellous jewel in its forehead 'men would not willingly let it die'. But an imperfect poem? Yes, perhaps a careless or a youthful poem. And that lands us in the question what the sonnets are, which in turn is a bit of the greater question, who or what 'Shakespeare' was.

The collection of sonnets is more like an exercise book or a portfolio of pieces than a deliberate act of poetic self-revelation. In 1598 a hack called Francis Meares was writing about Shakespeare's 'sugared sonnets among his private friends'. We only possess the sonnets at all because of a mysteriously pirated edition of them which came out in 1609; and 1609 happens to be the last year when anything new under the name of 'Shakespeare' was published until the folio of 1623 brought to light sixteen hitherto unpublished plays.

Did the poet of the sonnets and the author of the plays ever intend us to have them? I do not know; but this confession I will make. Nobody will ever persuade me that the author of the sonnets and plays was the man William Shakespeare, baptised and buried in Stratford-upon-Avon.

'FURTHER THOUGHTS: GRAMMAR AND SYNTAX'

from *The State of the Language*, California, 1990

In 1989, we celebrated – some of us – in the Church of England the fifth centenary of the birth of Thomas Cranmer, to whom, no doubt rightly but without absolutely cogent evidence, is attributed the principal hand in the language of the Book of Common Prayer. The current form of that Book is that authorised in 1662 after the restoration of the monarchy; but substantially the text is that of the Elizabethan Book of 1558, which, after the Roman Catholic interlude under Mary (1553–1558), reverted to the Edwardian Book of 1552, a slightly more Protestant edition of 'Cranmer's' original English Prayer Book of 1548.

The struggle now going on in England to preserve the traditional sixteenth-century text against supersession by the twentieth-century 'Alternative Service Book' is part of a wider contemporary struggle within English education. Government and the political parties have awoken with horror to the inroads made into schooling by two combined influences: the view of education as a universal right rather than the privilege of an élite; and the rising proportion in the school population – it was already 8 per cent nationally by 1985 – of what are gingerly called 'ethnic minorities'. Under the present Government an endeavour is being made to stem those inroads through central prescription of curriculum and standards.

In that prescription there is a notable preoccupation with the English language, and in particular with reviving the grammatical study and analysis of it. What those at the centre know, but dare not say, is that the great disaster has been the loss of Latin as an obligatory element in school education. From Cranmer's time until the very recent past, English was a language written by those who knew Latin, who self-consciously analysed it as they wrote, and who understood and exploited the resources of an essentially Latin syntax for the enrichment and enlargement of human thought and expression. This was something made possible by the widespread knowledge of Latin, despite the fundamental linguistic difference between English which is lightly inflected and Latin which is strongly inflected.

Written – and spoken – English is rapidly becoming today the

tongue of those who do *not* know Latin. We are for instance losing
– as transatlantic English has already lost – the expressive resource
of the difference in English (uniquely among European languages)
between the aorist (*I saw*) and the perfect (*I have seen*). 'What is
your judgement of George Eliot as a writer of English? I ask because
I have just reread *The Mill on the Floss*.' As likely as not, the wording
today would be: 'I just reread *The Mill on the Floss*,' spoken without
the least consciousness – grammatical consciousness – of what has
been sacrificed by degrading the perfect *have read* into the aorist
read. The result is English impoverished because it is English ungram-
matical.

Another powerful asset of English – including (what is by no means
irrelevant to ordinary speech and writing) a rhetorical asset – is the
peculiarly flexible English relative pronoun. How brilliantly Cranmer
exploited this and how ruthlessly his revisers have dispensed with it
is strikingly illustrated by the prayer of consecration in the Holy
Communion (' commonly called the Mass', 1548), which in Common
Prayer consists of one continuous vast sentence, made possible by
the relative pronoun: 'Almighty God, our heavenly father, *who* of
thy tender mercy . . . *who* made there by his one oblation . . . HEAR
US and GRANT . . . *who* in the same night that he was betrayed . . .
Amen.' Quite deliberately the revisers have destroyed this architectural structure and replaced it with a series of separate independent
sentences, in the belief presumably that English speakers and hearers
no longer understand and appreciate relative pronouns – have, in
other words, become de-Latinized and linguistically uneducated.
Only draughtsmen who were themselves in that condition could have
dared in the *Te Deum* to replace the correct English equivalent 'we
praise thee, O God' with the horrific mistranslation 'You are God,
and we praise you'.

Much of the discussion on the changes in a language tends to
concentrate upon vocabulary. My contention is that a language,
especially one like English, which can legitimately make a verb out
of any noun from anywhere in the world, can cope with no end of
damage to its vocabulary. What it cannot survive is assault upon its
structure – its grammar and its syntax. That after all is the process
which barbarised classical Greek into modern Greek and the process
(though it turned out to be wonderfully fruitful) which debased Latin
into the Romance languages. The protection for the structure of
English, which it is doubtful can now be restored even by the edict
of a more reactionary Government than Britain is likely to elect, is
a cultural elite which has absorbed its English while being educated
in Latin grammar and the Latin classics.

And yet that ship is still no farther off than hull down on the horizon. When the Jewish refugee professors of Classical Philology turned up in England in the 1930s what astonished them most was the linguistic standard of public-school boys who not only translated unseen passages which (as one of them put it to me) 'I should have been lynched for setting to doctoral candidates', but – what is far more to the point – translated superb examples of their own English tongue into passable Latin and Greek prose and verse. For that no substitute will be found.

MAN OF GOD

POWELL: I can be censured as a Christian. I don't like applying the term to myself: it's a presumption always to apply to oneself.

TREVOR HUDDLESTON: I don't think so at all, you are a Christian, you are a baptised member of the Church. You may be a bad Christian, but you are a Christian; that's a fact of life, you can't help that.

'The Great Debate', BBC TV, 9 September 1969

'QUICUNQUE VULT'

from *Sermons from Great St Mary's*, 1968

The Prayer Book commands that at Christmas, Easter, Whitsun and no fewer than ten other feast days there shall be said or sung at Morning Prayer, instead of the Apostles' Creed, a confession of our Christian faith 'commonly called the Creed of Saint Athanasius'. Though the number of prescribed occasions was not at first so large, this injunction has been part of our law from the very first English Prayer Book.

The Creed in question is also, and better, known by its first two words in Latin, *quicunque vult*, 'whosoever will (be saved)'. Its origin is extremely obscure. What is certain about it is that it can have had nothing to do with St Athanasius, but is an entirely Western Creed; it is now thought to have originated in Spain or northern Italy in the fifth century.

The most famous phrases of the Creed, in the definition of the Trinity ('not three incomprehensibles but one incomprehensible'), are familiar to countless people who have no idea of their source, and they have been the subject of innumerable allusions and parodies. But the keynote of the Creed is the fiercely absolute assertion at the outset: 'which (Catholic faith) except everyone do keep whole and undefiled, without doubt he shall perish everlastingly'. The same solemn assertion is repeated in respect of each of the two halves into which the Creed divides – the doctrine of the Trinity ('he that will be saved must thus think of the Trinity') and the doctrine of the Incarnation ('it is necessary to everlasting salvation that he believe rightly the incarnation of our Lord Jesus Christ'). It ends on the same note: 'This is the Catholic faith, which except a man believe faithfully he cannot be saved.'

This is what essentially differentiates the Athanasian Creed from the more familiar Apostles' and Nicene Creeds. They define the content of the faith, and refer explicitly to the means of salvation. This alone asserts the faith to be indispensable to salvation.

It is this no doubt which makes the Athanasian Creed unpopular; for unpopular it is, and the injunction that it be read is perhaps (what Shakespeare did *not* mean by) 'more honoured in the breach than the observance'. We find it grotesque that eternal damnation should be attached to ignorance of, not to mention disbelief in, a definition of the Trinity and the Incarnation, especially so detailed and so difficult a definition. In any case, eternal damnation itself, to 'perish everlastingly'. has long been quite out of fashion, something regarded in the light of a period piece, wax flowers under glass, and reminiscent of Victorian Sunday afternoons or black-coated preachers in Welsh chapels. So people think, if they do not actually say: 'Let's skip those pages – they're quite out of date' – or 'spent', as the parliamentary lawyers would put it.

The proposition I wish to put to you is that the bath water frequently and all but unthinkingly jettisoned contains a very large and important baby – if not more than one! It is unusual to discover that when we suppose ourselves to have risen superior to what generations of our predecessors found overwhelmingly significant and self-evident, we are in reality describing our own impoverishment of imagination or of vision. The generations of men who found nothing impossible, on the contrary found something inescapably compelling, in the central assertion of the Athanasian Creed were not unthinking fools in the grip of vulgar superstition, nor were they, with few exceptions, bloodthirsty bigots, intent on forging subtle instruments of dissension and oppression. If their words appear to us to present them in that light, it may be that we have not troubled to translate; for their mental furniture was as different from ours as their language. It may however also be that we are afraid to face what they were able to look upon fearlessly.

Let me then attempt a very rough and approximate translation. It might run somewhat as follows: 'The thoughts we hold about ourselves and our fellows and about our relation to the universe are overwhelmingly important, so important as to make the whole difference between true success in life and failure, between utter happiness and utter misery. Just any thoughts at our own option will not do; they must be thoughts of a particular nature, if they are to have this result. Being each of us unique and bound in by time, our failure, if we fail, cannot be made good, the tape cannot be run back, erased or edited. Once for all, it makes our eternity.'

My paraphrase, I know, is terribly free; but one obstacle to comprehension, at least, it seeks to remove. It shows the problematic assertion about faith, salvation and damnation as not a threat but a statement. We are wrong if we read the assertion as a threat of punishment, as if it were that anyone failing to get a hundred per cent in this examination paper will be taken out and shot. Assuming a tyrant God to be in the writers' minds and filling in the picture with weighing-scales and demons from the later mediaeval dooms, we interpret the words accordingly. I suggest we should be over-shooting the mark much less far in the other direction if we treat the words as the statement of an equation: 'to hold the Catholic faith *equals* salvation; to be possessed by a true view of the Deity as expressed in the doctrines of the Trinity and the Incarnation *is* the life everlasting.'

It is the overtones of judicial punishment, which we have to make an effort to banish from our mental ear, that also render the expressions of time so grotesque and repulsive. We read the words 'everlasting' and 'everlastingly' as if they were the term of a sentence of penal servitude and get them mixed up subconsciously with notions about 'making the punishment fit the crime' or 'getting greater uniformity of sentences in the magistrates' courts'. Heard as a judicial sentence on an offender, the disproportion between an eternity of punishment and a defect or error of belief in the brief span of human life strikes us as ludicrous, not to say unjust. Restated as a proposition not merely of cause and effect, automatic, inevitable, impersonal, but even of actual equivalence, the assertion loses its repellent quality, and we are set free to consider what it is really telling us.

It seems to me that the Creed confronts us with three facts which we are extremely reluctant to recognise, and to which the prevalent mood of our age and society renders us particularly allergic.

The first fact is that Christianity is an intellectual religion. Some religions are not: their demands can be fulfilled, and their promises obtained, by actions divorced from thoughts. Christianity, on the other hand, is a faith which makes demands upon people's minds, and relates its promises to the results of mental activity. You do not have to rely on the Athanasian Creed to verify this. It is stated with frightening directness in one of the sentences cited before the Burial Service; 'He that believeth on me, though he were dead, yet shall he live, and he that liveth and believeth on me shall never die.' So far as the connection between belief and salvation is concerned, the Athanasian Creed goes not a whit beyond that. Christianity is about the content of a human mind.

From this follows the second fact which we are desperately anxious to avoid seeing, namely, the possibility, indeed the probability, the prevalence, of failure. If success, life, salvation – use which term you will – depends on a content of the mind, then those incapable for any reason of the requisite mental activity, or of entertaining the essential propositions, must fail, or die, or be damned, according to the terminology chosen. Ignorance, incapacity, perversity, the sheer human propensity to error are sufficient to ensure a high failure rate.

This again is not something invented for the purpose of the Athanasian Creed. Over and over again the Christ of the Gospels asserts that his salvation will not be for all, not even for the majority, that 'few are chosen'. We need not involve ourselves here in the theology of election and predestination, to admit that failure – the possibility, probability, prevalence of failure – is asserted by Christianity as a corollary of its assertion that success consists in a mental state.

Throughout two thousand years one expedient after another has been tried in the attempt to modify or avoid this corollary: they range from certain interpretations of infant baptism to the retrospective conversion of Socrates and Virgil to Christianity. But for no generation perhaps has it been so difficult to face this hard saying as our own place and time, with its shibboleth of 'equality of opportunity' and its idolisation of 'fair shares'. In a sugary, romantic, cosy religion, suitable to match the Welfare State, there would not only be equality of opportunity to be saved, but an insurance scheme thrown in, to ensure that nobody missed salvation just through being born in the wrong place at the wrong time, and not happening to entertain the necessary belief, or being incapable of doing so. It would be a religion in which every story had a happy ending, here or hereafter. There may be, and no doubt are, such religions; but Christianity is not one of them. Christianity is not for us unless we are able to face the fact that failure exists.

What is more, and this is the third fact, which the Athanasian Creed will not allow us to evade, failure can be final, absolute and irrevocable. The Creed expresses this by means of the time metaphor – 'everlasting salvation', 'he shall perish everlastingly' – that being a convenient, effective and even indispensable way to convey finality. But this assertion of the finality of the success or failure of the individual human soul, the finality (to use the forensic metaphor) of the judgment, is not an invention of the catechists and the creed-writers. The teaching of Christ in the Gospels is saturated with it. This life, and above all the nature of a man's belief and disbelief in this life, determine once for all what he is to all eternity. It is this awful sense of finality which has endowed with urgency and earnestness not only the Christianity of the early Churches, with their expectation of an imminent second coming, but all Christianity down the ages.

Once more, men have sought means to cushion and shield themselves against having to meet this truth face to face. The comfortable doctrines of Purgatory and intercession for the dead attract because they offer some escape from the intolerable finality of judgment on the human life completed. Yet that finality is already implicit in the basic assertion of Christianity that salvation is about belief. Whether or not Macbeth so meant it, the connection is marvellously expressed in that –

> But here, upon this bank and shoal of time,
> We'd jump the life to come; but in these cases
> We still have judgment here.

Indeed we do; for that judgment runs concurrently with the mental act, a judgment continuously pronounced as life itself proceeds.

By this insight the hours of human life, which at most moments seem to us so brief and mean, are endowed with the awe of eternity. This individual unique atom of self-consciousness subtends the whole universe of space and time.

It is an uncomfortable conviction to live with, a conviction which imposes solemn, almost insupportable responsibility. But here we stand already on the threshold of the *content* of that catholic faith, 'which except a man keep whole and undefiled without doubt he shall perish everlastingly'. Tonight I have remained outside that threshold, not purposing more than to suggest that the context and outer framework in which the Athanasian Creed expounds the catholic faith, so far from being obsolete or repugnant, is there to remind us of certain truths which we dare not forget or blur about the nature of that faith itself.

'THE GREAT DEBATE'
BBC TV, 9 September 1969

ENOCH POWELL: I cannot understand how, unless my motives can be identified as evil, I can be censured as a Christian. I don't like applying the term to myself; it's a presumption always to apply to oneself.

TREVOR HUDDLESTON: I don't think so at all, you are a Christian; you are a baptised member of the Church. You may be a bad Christian, but you are a Christian; that's a fact of life, you can't help that. The point I want to make: there are two points I want to make really. I don't regard this as a secular issue, I regard this as a profoundly religious issue, because it affects man where he is as man, and this is the only view I can take of it. Like yourself, I am a person who has had experience over many years, mine being in Africa and yours being in England, of human situations. If the Christian faith has got nothing to say to human situations, it is not the faith to me. I am just not interested in a religion which is not concerned with man where he is, and if man where he is is subject to the consequences of racialism in any form, that is to say, if man's dignity on both sides of the colour line is lowered by racialism then I have got to protest . . .

POWELL: Yes, I agree with every word you said . . .

HUDDLESTON: Let me just finish. So I think it isn't fair to say that these are deductions. The Institute of Race Relations has carried out an enormous, thorough survey.

POWELL: Which is now three years out of date, and the great part of which I can logically destroy.

HUDDLESTON: Well I would like to see you do it; I am not saying it is impossible to do so, but there are certain facts which are conclusive I would say; and one of those facts is that a very large proportion of those who have come into the country in the last ten or fifteen years are part of this country, that their increase is going to be within this country. I know West Indian families who regard themselves as wholly absolutely English; the children will support, so to speak, an English Test Team against the West Indian one because they are so English.

POWELL: But you see, Bishop, we are merely opposing secular observations to one another; and then when you are gratified with the conclusions that you arrive at, you dignify them as the consequence of Christian belief.

HUDDLESTON: Not at all.

POWELL: This is what you are doing. We differ upon facts, upon deductions, and upon estimates of the future. Now what I cannot understand, thought I am willing to do if possible, is why your deductions are specifically Christian and mine are not.

HUDDLESTON: Simply because my deductions flow from the Christian Gospel I would maintain, and I . . . you have got to prove that they don't.

POWELL: But the Christian Gospel tells you nothing either about the position in the United Kingdom today, or about the prospects of the position in the United Kingdom twenty years hence, or about the manner in which people are likely to act in those circumstances twenty years or so ahead.

HUDDLESTON: No, the Christian Gospel tells me a great deal about man where he is; whether it's the United Kingdom, or the United States or the Republic of Tanzania is totally immaterial. And if man where he is is concerned, the Christian Gospel is concerned. How do you interpret such parables as the Parable of the Good Samaritan? What is this telling us about man?

POWELL: Well, I'll take the dilemma which the Parable of the Good Samaritan presents us with. The lawyer asked, 'Who is my neighbour?' and he was given an answer: 'Your neighbour is everyone, the whole of the world.' I cannot apply this. My neighbour, as a politician, that is to say, those for whom I am responsible, is not the whole of the world. So I am confronted with a religion which, as it seems to me deliberately and by its very essence, denies certain profound characteristics of actual human life; it seems to me to be its nature.

HUDDLESTON: This is the gulf between us, this is the total gulf between us. You have said that the Parable of the Good Samaritan simply says this, tells us our neighbour is everyone; it certainly tells us that, but it specifically says the Samaritan, the enemy of the Jewish people at that stage of their history, the man who could not be thought of as a neighbour because of his religious and cultural differences, this is the man who is to show, who shows love, to the other; this is the man, in this particular situation, this particular historical situation. Now, has this not got anything to say to you about the attitude of the white race to the black race, in its local situation? It's got nothing to say to you about that?

POWELL: It says to me that in Christianity there is neither black nor white, bond nor free; but in the world in which I live there *is* black and white, bond and free; there are nations, who lift up their hands against other nations; and I cannot as a politician assume that that which will happen as the Kingdom comes, is happening or has happened. If I do that, then I shall inflict harm upon those for whom I am most responsible.

HUDDLESTON: Well then, what does your Christian faith mean, in terms of everyday living? If it has nothing to say to you about these situations at all; but it's only concerned with the Kingdom which is to come?

POWELL: What I have been trying to say throughout, Bishop, is that I find it insuperably difficult to draw deductions from my Christian religion, as to the choices which would lie open to me in my political life. I can draw deductions as to what should be my frame of mind, I know – not always, but often enough – when I, in my attitude of mind, offend against what is my Christian duty; that I know. But I cannot find enlightenment or guidance as between two alternative policies and courses of action.

HUDDLESTON: The Christians all through history have in fact found precisely this enlightenment, I mean the initiative – well let's take this example – the initiative of the abolition of the slave trade, was the Christian initiative; it wasn't the initiative of the established Church, but it was a Christian initiative; and would you say that this, so to speak, is just irrelevant, is some little quirk of history?

POWELL: And yet from Christianity one could not deduce – and the ancient world did not deduce – the unacceptability of the institution of slavery. Of course in the eighteenth and nineteenth century, both the phenomena of slavery as it was then practised, and the changing attitude of society, and not only Christian society, made slavery intolerable; but that doesn't seem to me to be a deduction from the teaching of Christianity. Otherwise it would have been a deduction in the Roman world.

HUDDLESTON: I don't think it would have at all.

POWELL: What was stated in the Roman world is that bond and free have been abolished in Christ, not that the institution of slavery is abolished by Christ.

HUDDLESTON: No, but there is room for development in the Christian Church and certainly I would say, that this is the principle that has been operative through the Christian century. However, what I really feel divides us, is that I believe in a social Gospel and you don't.

POWELL: Well, you can make that mean anything . . .

HUDDLESTON: Well what I want it to mean, let me try and say. I believe that it is essential for the Christian, and especially for the leaders of the Christian Church, to concern themselves with political, economic and social issues wherever they are, because it is within this environment that man lives, and because the Christian Gospel is concerned with man where he is.

POWELL: Yes indeed, you can not help concerning yourself, but what I do not believe you can do is legitimately draw a deduction from Christianity which on many of the issues which we have been discussing – given the judgements, the facts and the judgements, as granted – will point to one course of action rather than another.

HUDDLESTON: Well, supposing the result of a racist speech is to make hundreds, perhaps millions of Christians in the new African and Asian countries lose their faith in the integrity of the Christian Gospel, is that not our concern?

POWELL: Well, we've been over this. You pose a situation; but then, the assumption is (unless we are questioning motives, which we have agreed not to do) that that speech, the impact of it, and the proposals which it contained, were believed to be necessary to avert a probable or foreseeable evil. Once one has granted that, then we're back again, as we said before, with a choice of disadvantages, and I, with specific responsibilities as a politician, cannot be in doubt, it seems to me, where my duties there – not my Christian duties, but my duty in my function in society – must lie.

HUDDLESTON: But your Christian duty ought to be the same as your duty in society, this is what I cannot understand with regard to your attitude. You are a Christian. I cannot simply know how you can separate the two.

POWELL: I can see that a Christian can have duties in society, but many of these duties don't seem to me to be derivable – as for example many of my duties as a politician don't seem to me to be derivable – from the essential teachings of Christianity, which seem to me, characteristically and essentially, both to be absolutes and to be in deliberate and direct conflict with human reality and human experience.

HUDDLESTON: I agree, there is plenty of conflict between the Christian faith and the social order in which the Christian Church operates; there is plenty of conflict.

POWELL: It seems to me it must be absolute conflict.

HUDDLESTON: No, I would disagree with that totally. There is a great area of conflict, there is a great area within the whole Christian ambit, within which men can disagree, but there is one fundamental principle on which the whole of our faith rests, and that as I said at the beginning is the fact – not the idea, but the fact – that God became man, took flesh and therefore gave to man, where he is, a dignity which can not be taken from him, and it is when that dignity is imperilled, that the Church must speak and act.

POWELL: Yes, and I can't dissent from what you have just said; but it seems to me (and this I think is my last word) that what we have been doing, Bishop, is analysing our respective functions in society. These functions overlap: you cannot be all priest, you are bound to be citizen and a politician as well; I cannot be all politician, I have presumably to be Christian, and many other things as well. But the emphasis of our respective functions, and our purpose in society, seems to me distinct, and I feel that it is that distinction, which is so easy for either of us to leap over, which we have been analysing this evening.

'NOT NECESSARILY SO'

The Times, 4 March 1972

A clergyman of my acquaintance, a most excellent clergyman, recently sent me his parish letter for Lent. I was struck by one sentence in it, all the more because the writer happens to be an outspoken opponent of the uncritical enlistment of Christianity in the cause of trendy fashions – aid, race, concern, pollution and the rest. The sentence was this: 'Our Saviour reminds us in the parable of Dives that neglect and indifference towards those that need our help who come within our scope is a dreadful sin deserving rightly God's wrath.'

So it is commonly supposed: but so it can only be supposed by either not reading the story – it is, by the way, not a parable – or altering it mentally as we read. Let us take it calmly. There was once a rich man who had a splendid time. There was also a destitute person who had a rotten time. When they died the rich man went to hell fire and the beggar went to 'Abraham's bosom', the Jewish heaven.

The first thing to notice is not that the rich man went to hell, but that the beggar went to heaven. There is no suggestion whatever that he had done anything to deserve it, or even that he belonged to the ranks of the 'deserving poor'. We are not, for instance, told that he was blind, or crippled or otherwise unfortunate. As far as we know, he never did a hand's turn in his life or ever tried to. Misery, not merit, was his sole passport to Paradise.

Conversely, there is not the slightest suggestion that the rich man did anything wrong. It is we, not the Scripture who blame him for not bringing Lazarus inside and giving him three good meals a day for the rest of his life. If that had been the moral of the story, it would have had to stop with the rich man going to hell, and have nothing at all about the destination of Lazarus. As it was, however, Lazarus could count himself exceedingly fortunate to have escaped the attentions of the charitably disposed. If he had been 'comforted' in this world, there would have been no Abraham's bosom for him in the next.

It may be objected, 'But then what is all that about Moses and the prophets?' Let us look at it more closely. The rich man's grotesque request in hell that Lazarus should make the incredible journey from heaven, and for no more important or enduring a purpose than to put a drop of water on his tongue, has been rejected with Abraham's assertion that the great gulf between heaven and hell is impassable in either direction. And the story has been rounded off with Abraham's conclusive observation: 'You had your good time, and Lazarus had his bad time, during your lives; now he is comforted and you are tormented.'

Thereupon follows something quite different – another part of the story, or another story – namely, the request that Lazarus be sent from the dead to the rich man's surviving five brothers, in order to 'bear witness' to them and so avoid their finding themselves in hell likewise. If the story had had the supposed moral, the urgent message to get across to the brothers would have been to build or endow a hospital, or at least a rehabilitation centre, with the minimum delay, and that at all costs there must be no repetition of scandals like the Lazarus case.

There is no hint that this was to be the point of the mission, and in fact Abraham retorts in quite general terms: 'They have Moses (i.e. the law) and the prophets; let them hear them.' Lazarus had nothing to add to the law and the prophets. Indeed, there is nothing to indicate that Lazarus ever bothered his head with the law and the prophets any more than the rich family had evidently done.

The point of the dialogue becomes clear only when the rich man persists that his brothers will 'repent' or 'be converted' if someone comes to them from the dead. This give Abraham the opportunity, to which this part of the story has evidently been working up, to reply that those who will not hear the law and the prophets will not 'be persuaded' by a resurrection.

Abraham was to be proved right, and yet only partially right, by the central event of the Gospels, the death and resurrection of Christ, which the world apparently ignored. But there was another and more disturbing confirmation. In St John we find the deeply moving narrative of how Jesus actually did bring someone back from the dead. His name (surely not by chance?) was Lazarus – the only other place where that name appears in the New Testament.

This Lazarus, described in the story of his resurrection as the 'friend' of Jesus and brother of Martha and Mary, plays no other part whatsoever in the Gospels: he exists only to be raised from the dead. The pithy dictum of Abraham in Luke inspired in John a marvellous piece of imaginative and poetic writing: a man (he might be the Lazarus of the old story) actually did return from the dead, and still no one 'believed'. That passage was John's prelude to Calvary itself.

So the social gospel, warning us not to be indifferent towards those who need our help, has dissolved as we looked at it. In its place have made their appearance two strange, uncomfortable and uncompromising assertions.

One tells us that the rich are punished for having been rich, and the wretched rewarded for having been wretched. As Lord Melbourne might have said: 'There is no damned merit about it.' If there is a moral, that is it. The other assertion is that the impossible happened before our eyes, and it left us all no different from before – all, or perhaps nearly all, of us.

No wonder people are afraid to read the Bible.

'BEYOND IMMIGRATION'

Frontier, February 1973

RICHARD COHEN: What do you mean by race?

ENOCH POWELL: It is a term with which I have never operated. If you read my speeches and writings with a microscope, you will find no reference, except perhaps occasionally a reference to what other people have said, to the concept of race. On the contrary, I have said that I do not know what race means. For example, I do not know whether a Welshman and an Englishman are of the same race or of different races. It seems to me a term which does not belong to my profession of politics.

COHEN: But many see the word 'race' as central to any discussion on immigration and many people involved in immigration policy-making think it important to define the word. Can't you say what understanding you have of the word?

POWELL: I have difficulty in finding any satisfactory meaning to it. The Race Relations Act of 1968 is so drawn up that it covers not only race, but many other differences – for example, 'national origins' – and therefore it doesn't have to define race. For the purposes of that Act my question: 'Are a Welshman and an Englishman of the same race?' doesn't arise, and I cannot be compelled to define a term which I do not use and which only other people use.

COHEN: I'm not compelling you to do so. I'm saying that it would be interesting to know how far you had got in your own mind in thinking about the question.

POWELL: I have said that I have not applied myself to a term which, if it has any significance, must be a term in disciplines, such as anthropology or physiology, which I do not practise and which I do not regard as relevant to my business as a politician.

COHEN: If, then, I were to ask you if you believed in the separation of races, would that question make sense to you?

POWELL: No, it wouldn't, because I must be told whether there is a separation of races in the United Kingdom, and then I would be back to the same impasse. Of course I know how this word comes into parlance. It comes from the United States, where 'race' is used to distinguish Negro from non-Negro; but this is clearly a specialised and American acceptance of the term. The importation of American vocabulary into the discussion of circumstances in the United Kingdom is dangerous and misleading – and not because it's the United Kingdom; I'm sure it would be equally dangerous and misleading if it were imported into a discussion of affairs in Soviet Russia.

COHEN: I do find it strange that, with so many people talking about race – one thinks of reactions to General Amin's recent speeches, for instance – you do not think it vital to have a working idea at least of how other people use the term, even if you had no satisfactory definition yourself.

POWELL: I don't have to concern myself with what General Amin means by whatever word of his is translated (if it is translated), into the English word 'race', any more than I have to concern myself with it if people are expelled from Soviet Russia or from Nazi Germany. I must ask: What are the ideas which either actually caused this event or were alleged to be the reason for it?

COHEN: But isn't it part of the job of being a politician to understand other politicians, even other foreign politicians, especially where it influences your own duties and responsibilities?

POWELL: I very much doubt whether a foreign policy based on an attempt to understand the policies of others – though we would have to say, at what level of understanding and in what sense of understanding – would be more successful than one which dealt with the objective phenomena, irrespective of motive. If a foreign country is going to levy war upon us, I'm not sure if it is not a distraction to apply one's mind to the reasons for this – which might be very remote and deep, and of which they themselves may not be conscious.

From that we can draw this point: what I regard as the errors of immigration policy are not errors imposed upon us from outside or which are a reaction to events elsewhere in the world. They are of our own making, and explicable and resolvable on arguments and sentiments local and domestic to the United Kingdom. Clearly I'm not excluding some external effect upon those opinions or sentiments. Still, that does not prevent me from maintaining, as I have consistently done, that this is our own affair in every possible sense of the term.

COHEN: One of your biographers, T. E. Utley, has said that you believe in the inevitability of conflict between nations and men and, in certain fields, in the possible fruitfulness of such conflict. Would you agree with this?

POWELL: Conflicts don't take place between races; they take place between social organisations. These may be tribes, or nations, which are in turn terms of some difficulty of definition, but at least are social or political terms, not biological terms. Certainly, the term 'nation' is a political term; and it is between nations that war takes place. War is a political event.

COHEN: I want to move on to your understanding of another important word, 'community'. It seems to me that there are two crucially opposed conceptions of the word. In one a community is something organised, and defines itself in relation to those outside it whom it regards as alien. The second idea of community would contain these elements, but has the important difference in that it sees a community as open-ended. Despite geographical, political, social, economic or religious barriers, there is a desire to overcome them and grow outwards into a larger community. What does the word mean to you?

POWELL: Community is a very general expression, which means 'having something in common', and its nature will differ according to what is had in common. 'Community', in the *political* sense with which I am concerned, must imply having something political in common. For example, if a local authority is concerned with a community, what that community has in common is being under one local administration. The national community has in common an exclusive government and sovereignty. 'Community' in itself is an empty expression – a file on which no papers have yet been placed. The Church is clearly a community, having in common a belief; but there can be communities within the Church which have in common more narrowly defined beliefs.

COHEN: This is getting away from the most interesting question about community, whether you regard it as a closed thing or open-ended.

POWELL: It depends on what the things in common are. If what you have in common politically is the same government, then to wish that government to be extended to, or imposed on, others must be judged according to the circumstances, but doesn't seem to me inherently or self-evidently good. On the other hand, the good tidings which Christians have in common seem, of their nature, to demand to be communicated, to be made common to still more people. So it must depend on what you put on your file; we get into trouble if we operate with 'container' expressions and not with the contents.

COHEN: It's very difficult to define what one's talking about here–

POWELL: Perhaps this is the difficulty of having been a classical scholar – one tends not to take seriously anything which cannot be translated into Latin.

COHEN: Precision can be a virtue, but it can also be a limitation. I would have thought that you can go beyond saying 'Well, what is the content of the "community"?' to some idea of what community is.

POWELL: I don't think there can be community in general any more than there can be equality in general. Community is just an abstraction, which only derives significance from the context which is given to it.

COHEN: Haven't Christians some joint responsibility in matters of immigration?

POWELL: Immigration policy, which is what I talk about, is concerned with the movement of persons from one jurisdiction to another, a political matter, of which Christianity knows nothing and on which it can shed no more light than upon the chemical properties of substances and gases.

Those who talk about a 'Christian duty' – or, to be less precise and therefore fairer, those who say that there can be a 'Christian point of view' – on whether or not citizens of the United Kingdom and colonies should be admitted to the United Kingdom have no justification for maintaining any control at all over movement across frontiers.

COHEN: It sounds as if you're saying that there is no such thing as Christian ethics.

POWELL: There is nothing in Christian ethics which enables us, having recognised the existence of nations, to decide what policy a particular nation should follow in admitting or not admitting those who do not belong to it, or in distinguishing among those external to it between some as belonging and others as not belonging. These are concepts of which Christianity knows nothing.

COHEN: What would you say, then, are the concerns of Christian ethics? What kinds of questions do you think Christianity can concern itself with, in the ethical realm?

POWELL: I'm not sure that you know what you mean by the ethical realm. You are talking to me as a politician, who is faced with certain political decisions.

COHEN: I am talking to you as a Christian who happens to be a politician. Shouldn't it be that way round?

POWELL: Well, both a Christian and a politician. But the content of my political action is not derivable from my Christianity, any more than would be the content of my behaviour as a research chemist or as a banker. True, there are certain states of mind denied to me by Christianity, which as a Christian I recognise to be sinful; and if I am active as a politician while in those states of mind then I am failing as a Christian, just as I would be if I were active as a banker or a research chemist in such states of mind.

COHEN: Doesn't Christianity affect your conduct in any way?

POWELL: I hope it does, but I couldn't tell you how.

COHEN: What then does Christ mean to you?

POWELL: Isn't that a very unfair question – to ask a man to summarise in a sentence what his own faith in its most summary form expresses in the clauses of a creed?

To ask the question 'what does Christ mean to you?' and expect an answer suitable to form part of such a discussion as we are having, seems to me grotesquely contradictory of what I understand by Christianity.

COHEN: Can you expand on that? It seems to be an important question, not an unfair one. It is obviously one to which one can only get a partial answer; but that is understood.

POWELL: Week by week I hear and participate in the liturgy of the Holy Communion. Week by week different elements and meanings and connections present themselves to me. I am conscious that, as I do so, the same thing is happening not only to those around me but to infinite multitudes throughout the world. But suddenly to say to any of these – catching him, as it were, as he came through the church door – 'What does Christ mean to you?', is to ask a question to which he could perhaps only reply, as someone else once did, by saying 'Come and see'. That's my first attempt to rationalise my shocked reaction to your question. I am deeply aware of a dilemma and a contradiction (which I believe to be a deliberate and central contradiction) between Christianity and human life. There is a standing, continuing, inevitable conflict between the living of all personal lives and belonging to that other community we were talking about earlier, the 'blessed company of all faithful people'. I don't believe that this is one of those dilemmas which are resolvable. There are a great many dilemmas in human life which are not resolvable. Well, Christianity brings into people's lives a dilemma which wasn't there before, and holds it in front of them all the time, like the crucifix held before the eyes of a dying man.

COHEN: Do you conceive the possibility that there could be a conflict between political expediency and Christian belief?

If so, have you ever found yourself as a politician making a compromise with your Christian beliefs? And would not that place you in spiritual danger?

POWELL: The word 'expediency' begs this question, because it implies falsity of word or deed; but in practice the political decisions are not between known truth and falsehood, or evident right and wrong. I cannot see that a decision between SET and VAT, or EFTA and EEC, whichever way taken, could conflict with Christian belief.

The answer to the second part of your question: No doubt, I sin day by day – in thought, word and deed – and that is presumably spiritual danger. I am tempted, and do not always withstand the temptation, to hate, to curse, to do mischief: but that has nothing to do with the policies which one espouses or opposes.

COHEN: There are many compassionate and intelligent people, often with their hands on the reins of power, certainly people of great influence, who abhor what you have to say. Many Christians could be included in that number. Don't you feel you could do more to make such people understand you, and your views?

For instance, they might feel that they would be the more ready to understand and agree with you if you troubled to look at the word 'race' and explain what it meant to you.

POWELL: Oh yes, I understand that I'm intended to fall into a trap; but I'm not going to. That was a trap laid for my unwary feet; but my feet are wary. I'm talking about politics; I'm talking about nations; I'm talking about passage across frontiers and the policy which should govern it; and I am not going to be trapped into talking about race when I don't mean race.

COHEN: But what of those who say, 'He doesn't do enough to convince us of his good faith, he doesn't do enough to show that he loves people, or what he means by love: he doesn't show us that he cares for people, whatever their skin, or wherever they belong'?

POWELL: Well, they must form their own opinions on that; but if a man were to set out to conform his actions and his words in order to prove to people that he loved his fellow men, then, if he wasn't a humbug, he would be a fool.

I have certain political objects, I have certain political intentions – it's my profession – and I decide how these are most likely to be attained. Now, there will also be those, whatever one is talking about, the floating pound, or the money supply, who will always be unconvinced for various reasons. I do everything I can, whenever people enquire, to provide them with the accurate text of what I have said. I answer fair questions which are put to me as accurately as I can. But nothing could be more foolish than, as it were, to set up a department for dealing with misunderstanding. This is one of the beginners' mistakes in politics. Misunderstandings are removed, not by direct attempts to remove them, but by everybody going on living.

COHEN: What would you have to be shown for you to change your views on immigration control? What would have to come about?

POWELL: How can you ask me that question? If you asked me what would have to come about for me to change my views on capitalism, or the market process, or the floating pound, what answer could I give you? I don't see how those questions are of a different kind.

COHEN: It may need a change in human nature to bring such a change about. But what kind of change? What part of human nature?

POWELL: This is almost like asking a man what changes he would require in order to make two and two make five instead of four – it's not quite the same, but it strikes me as the same sort of question. It isn't as though one could pull out the fuse and then say, 'Now all the lighting in the house is out.' The nature of citizenship, of the nation as a political community, like the nature of money and price, is such that there is no single phenomenon by which the whole is controlled. I can of course conceive contexts in which one could say, 'Well, if we can deal with that, then the whole matter might change'; but I don't think the question of a nation's control over its frontiers is of that kind.

'THE GREAT PRAYER'
BBC Radio, 1 May 1981

The brief prayer which goes under the name of the Lord's Prayer is one of the strangest and most paradoxical documents in the world. It is a prayer which is used from one end of Christendom to the other and from one extreme of the spectrum of Christianity to the opposite. Children learn to say it as soon as they can form words at all, and still in their old age its words return as an ejaculation to their lips. It is used on all occasions and in all companies, religious and profane, ecclesiastical and secular. It is the one prayer which comes nearest to being universal in the Western world and throughout the rest of the globe wherever Christianity has found a hold.

From all this it might be supposed that its contents would be plain and simple, presenting no problems or obstacles to understanding or acceptance. In fact its text is of so great an obscurity as to have evoked whole libraries of commentary and to have resisted the assaults of intellect and scholarship through the ages. This much at least the student discerns about it through all the difficulties. It came originally from a context which has been lost and can hardly now be reconstructed; and the meaning of every part of it has changed beyond recognition on the way.

The discovery is at first bewildering; but after a while it prompts an insight which illuminates one of the secrets of Christianity itself. The prayer could not have become the universal prayer of Christianity and a great part of mankind if its nature and history had been different. Its very obscurity is the quality which made it adaptable to all kinds of conditions of men in every sort of situation through two thousand years. Because it no longer has its original context, therefore it can fit every context. Because it no longer has its original meaning, therefore it can fit every meaning. Plain and perspicuous language has its uses; but the heart often speaks best in words that are mysterious and numinous. Nobody, I think, however casually or indifferently the prayer passes his lips, remains totally untouched by a certain sensation of the unknown. For us who speak English, there is an added magic; for it comes to us echoing the language and cadences of our forefathers.

The prayer is found in the first gospel, as one of the assorted items of precept and admonition assembled together in the collection known traditionally as 'the Sermon on the Mount', with large parts of which it shares the characteristic of baffling obscurity. It is very brief, and Luke in his book made it briefer still; the other two gospel-writers did not include it at all. Let us look at it first as it stands in Matthew.

It consists, like all prayers, of two parts; one, the name and qualities of the deity addressed; and two, the actual petitions. Owing to differences of thought and language between Hebrew and the language in which our gospel is written, Greek, the three qualities of the deity addressed – our Heavenly father – have come to us as if they were themselves petitions: 'holy be thy name, let thy Kingdom come, let thy will be done', with the logically grotesque result, to which only habitual usage has rendered us insensible, that we request the holy and omnipotent one to sanctify himself and to get on and do what he intends to do.

By a curious change the original sense of the invocation is preserved, or at least is proffered, by the formula, known as the doxology, with which the recitation of the prayer is habitually concluded: 'for thine is the kingdom, the power and the glory, for ever and ever'. These words, which might serve as a paraphrase of the first three clauses of the prayer, are not found in the very oldest manuscripts of Matthew, though their addition is certainly of great antiquity. They come from King David's prayer as recorded in 1 Chronicles 29.

The actual petitions are four only: 1. Give us our bread; 2. Cancel our debts; 3. Do not take us into testing; 4. Save us from the evil.

All four are highly remarkable. The bread for which we ask is described by a Greek word which does not exist but which, if it did exist, could not mean 'daily'. Nobody knows what it does or could mean, though oceans of ink have been spilt upon it. What is inconceivable is that the original word would have been unique and unintelligible or that it would have been translated by a unique and unintelligible Greek word. We are therefore in the presence of a corruption, and a corruption which must have occurred in the Greek and became hallowed by usage, since Luke did not venture to alter or replace it.

However, some meaning had to be attributed to it, and two such meanings – 'today's' and 'daily' – are preserved in Matthew and Luke respectively. Their chance insertion side by side with it proved endlessly important; for they provided the pivot upon which a request which originally had nothing to do with the continuing life of this world could turn into a homely prayer for daily use. What bread it was for which the prayer originally asked we will for a moment not enquire, until we have looked at the petitions which follow. The next is: 'cancel our debts', and it is accompanied by the statement 'as' –

or 'because' (the two are the same in Hebrew – 'we have cancelled (them) to our debtors'.

There is no doubt this time about the stark reality of either the meaning or the translation. Those who make the petition have already cancelled all debts owed to them – in modern terms, they have no financial assets, not even currency notes ('I promise to pay the bearer on demand'). They have stripped themselves of all worldly contractual links, and in that condition they ask God not to exact from them the debt which they owe him but cannot pay. The perfect commentary – if not from the same source, from the same circle – is in the parable of the unmerciful creditor, later on in the gospel. The austere significance of the petition is already modified by Luke: 'forgive us our sins'; for 'we too give remission to all our debtors'. He has replaced the part, 'we have cancelled', with the present, 'we remit' – a continuing, habitual attitude. He has, too, substituted 'sins' for 'debts' as between men and God, thus no doubt providing a correct interpretation but destroying the logic and symmetry; for he knew that only God can forgive sins and dared not continue 'as we too forgive sins'. It was left to a later age to make use of explanatory words which follow the prayer in Matthew and substitute: 'forgive us our trespasses, as we forgive those that trespass against us'.

The second petition, then, in its original form, is the prayer of those who have left the world behind them in the imminent expectation of another to come. It is to that coming that the remaining petitions refer; for the coming of the kingdom is heralded by the almost intolerable testing of the chosen and the all but complete triumph of the Evil. The petitioners, trembling on that threshold, ask to be spared the ultimate test and to be saved in the great day from 'the evil thereof'.

So, what is the bread that they ask to be given? Once asked, the question must be answered, however fearsome the answer. To those who are chosen to share in the kingdom established on the great day, bread will indeed be given. A group of sayings, which follows shortly after the prayer in the collection, describes how they will be fed by their Heavenly father – and clothed moreover, more magnificently than Solomon himself; for a large part of the contents of the Sermon on the Mount are eschatological, that is to say, concerned with preparation for the last judgment and the kingdom, and, as we have seen, the prayer itself is an eschatological prayer, the words of a group who, believing themselves to be chosen for survival, prepare by the sincerity of their lives and the purity of their observance for an event that cannot be long delayed.

It was a doctrine which, from the brief notices we have about him, we know that John the Baptist shared with the Jesus of the gospels;

and there is a curious fact which may bear upon this about the setting in which Luke places the prayer. In Matthew the prayer has no preface; but Luke has provided it with an introduction; for he felt the so-called sermon was too long and broke up the second half and fitted the items in wherever he could find suitable places in his narrative. This is how he introduced the prayer: 'And it happened that when he was somewhere praying one of his disciples said unto him: 'Teach us a prayer, as John taught his disciples'. And he said to them, 'When you pray, say . . .' The words, 'as John taught his disciples', are haunting. Was the prayer that we call the Lord's Prayer the prayer of John the Baptist? That we can scarcely know. What we can know, and with reasonable assurance, is what was meant by it by those who used it originally. We may also suppose, from the paucity of the petitions and the curious order in which they appear, that the prayer of which this formed part was originally longer. What we have is a fragment.

Our study has brought us face to face with the full paradox of the Lord's Prayer. A partially corrupt and possibly incomplete eschatological prayer, framed in obscure circumstances in Palestine under the influence of expectations which were not historically fulfilled, became the supreme general-purpose prayer of the Church and of Christendom for two millennia, and is daily on the lips of millions upon millions of human beings. When launched upon its future course in the earliest form of the gospel, it was already cut adrift from its original context and barely comprehensible. From then onwards its use formed its meaning: it weathered with time and became encrusted with the deposit of the passing generations.

In the course of this process every sentence, almost every word, has been transmuted, as though by alchemy, into something different. The descriptions of the deity's glory, kingdom and power, which had become petitions, took on a tentative, hesitant, almost fearful tone as if God's name might *not* be sacred, as if his kingdom might *not* come, as if his will might somehow *not* prevail on earth as it no doubt does in heaven. Thus the three petitions become an anxious looking forward to a distant future, something projected beyond the immediate vision and expectation of the worshipper, who, if he does not actually by a kind of co-operation promote and hasten the desired outcome, at least expresses the fervent, if uncertain, hope of seeing it 'in the land of the living'.

Journeying across the intervening desert, the Christian – actually that word is an anachronism, for the prayer is not a Christian, but a pre-Christian prayer, there being nothing specifically Christian in it – asks for sustenance day by day. The bread may be envisaged as the mundane necessities of life which the creator provides; or it may be felt as supernatural, as in Dante's marvellous paraphrase in the *Divine Comedy:*

> This day to us our daily manna give,
> Without the which, across this desert drear,
> He backward goes who most strives to progress.

The messianic feast has become our 'daily bread', whether on the altar or upon the table.

Day by day, too, the worshipper strives to be merciful to his fellow man and thus to earn God's mercy, not so much in a final act of judgment as continually and repeatedly. He sins and is forgiven and will sin again, knowing, as he asks forgiveness, that the need for it will continue all his life-long.

Like the messianic banquet, those tremendous eschatological shapes, the testing time and the day of evil, have taken under the influence of repetition and this-worldliness, the homely forms of ever-present temptation and ever-lurking evil. The need of the worshipper and the succour of the deity have ceased to be instantaneous and final. They have become the accompaniment of daily life. Armageddon has been tamed into the encounters of Everyman's existence. The key word is Everyman; for indeed the Lord's Prayer is the prayer of the few which, by an inscrutable destiny, became the prayer of Everyman.

'THE LANGUAGE OF THE PRAYER BOOK' (1983)

The Salisbury Review, Winter 1984

It was the sound of church bells and the language of the Book of Common Prayer, heard almost thirty-four years ago now across the Aleian plain of atheism, which recalled me home, gently yet imperiously, to the Church. I have needed therefore no prompting or persuasion to take my place in defending against its powerful and determined opponents the liturgy of the Church of England as by law established in 1558 and 1662. And as a ranker in the army of the Book of Common Prayer, I am singularly fortunate and happy to be called to address you this morning.

I want to share with my fellows here in the same cause an anxiety which repeatedly assails me. It is the anxiety that we are given to understating our cause, or, to be more precise, founding it upon grounds less exalted and less substantial than those which are capable of sustaining it. In decisive engagements it is the main forces that must be committed. This it often seems to me we are reluctant or afraid to do. Why, can perhaps be explained, and is, in due course, worth examining; but explanation is not justification. It is easy to extol the Book of Common Prayer linguistically and literarily. Its superiority in beauty of language and power of diction over the alternatives in the field against it is all too effortlessly demonstrated. The consequence is that we often seem to rest content with that demonstration, as if the argument were thereby ended – at least, for all with ears to hear and emotions to be stirred. We drift thus into the easy option of conservationism: here is a thing of beauty, we say, a fair inheritance, so let us preserve it. The argument is all right so far as it goes; but it goes scarcely any distance.

The efficacy of the Book of Common Prayer consists in its being archaic and in its being prescriptive. Such is the thesis I put forward; and I assert further that on no lesser grounds ought the cause of the Book of Common Prayer to be rested.

When the liturgy in English replaced the Latin liturgy, it replaced a language that not only was no longer spoken but had not been a live tongue even in its native land for over a thousand years. It was, in most senses of the word, a dead language, but a dead language which was hieratic, the language of prescribed ritual and customary worship. It was not for the most part particularly good or beautiful Latin – Cicero would have found it excruciating – but it had been used immemorially and the Western Church had known no other. Those words in that language, and no other words in any other language, were efficacious.

To replace them with English words, even with the august, rhetorical and inspired English of the Prayer Book, was a violently revolutionary event. It was revolutionary in what it destroyed; it was revolutionary in its professed object. How severe that revolution was, we Anglicans can form some mild notion today when we contemplate the devastation which the Roman Church has been busy inflicting upon itself in recent years. The assumption which underlay, and underlies, the revolution is that words used in worship can be, and ought to be, 'understanded of the people'. But ought they? And can they? Not unlike music, worship and ritual say things and do things which cannot be stated in plain language and which are destroyed or trivialised or caricatured in the attempt so to state them. It is of the essence of worship and rite that their language has overtones which defy analysis or paraphrase.

I must resort here to a term which cannot be fended off. The language of worship and rite is in itself *sacramental;* that is to say, it is more than, and different from, its natural sense. The converse is also true – that sacramental acts depend upon sacramental language: supercharged action and the supercharged words which accompany it are mutually dependent, inseparable aspects of one and the same event.

The humiliating and baffling fact about supercharged language is that we cannot voluntarily and intentionally construct it: it is, like so many of the other capabilities which make human life sustainable, 'begotten, not made'. There is only one process known whereby it arises, and that process is – call it archaism, call it obsolescence if you please – that it has continued to be used until it has become detached from its original meaning, context and associations, that it has lived over from one world to another. That occurs easily and obviously when an actual language, which has been otherwise disused, survives in religious use, as Latin did in the Western Church until the vandals put an end to it. But the process can also occur, though less violently and visibly, when an earlier form of a still spoken language is preserved in a religious context; and this process is exemplified by the Book of Common Prayer. By one of those happy combinations of circumstance in English history which half persuade us that our nation is specially favoured by Providence, the Book of Common Prayer was preserved intact through more than four centuries while the passage of time subtly imparted to it the super-charge of archaism and familiarity which it could not possess at the outset but which make it a uniquely English vehicle of religious and ritual expression. Cranmer did not put the supercharge there – he could not – it grew there of its own accord, which makes its existence the more difficult and embarrassing to acknowledge.

One reason why this happy outcome was possible was the fact that the Book of Common Prayer, being a statutory document embodying a compromise, was peculiarly entrenched. I do not want however to come yet to the subject of authority. Another contributory cause was the intense conservatism of the Church of England in that long stretch of time – 250 years – between the Restoration of the monarchy and the religious ferments of the early nineteenth century. By the time the depths were stirred by the Evangelicals and the Tractarians, the Book of Common Prayer had already completed its transmutation into a hieratic tongue, as sacramental in its own way as the Latin in the Tridentine rite.

I am going to offer a small specific example of the sacramental nature of liturgical language: it will serve as a transition to the next, and the most difficult, suggestion which I have to offer. Nobody, surely, can be unaware that something is made to happen by the opening words of the *Sanctus:* 'Holy, holy, holy, Lord God of Hosts'. In modern English 'Lord God of hosts' is effectively inexplicable. The origin of the words can indeed be elucidated, not without some difficulty, from the Biblical Hebrew; but that elucidation does not contain the secret. Significantly, the Roman Missal embalmed the Hebrew word itself, *dominus deus Sabaoth;* but the Book of Common Prayer has achieved the same result of power and mystery by a literal translation of the Hebrew feminine plural which is no more to be 'understanded of the people' than the original would be. The Alternative Service Book, rite A, offers us, as usual, a piece of bathos: 'God of power and might'!

The reason why I selected that particular, rather minuscule case is that it illustrates a surprising and even alarming characteristic which is apparently normal if not essential to religious and ritual language – unintelligibility. Greatly presuming, I venture to designate this as 'the nonsense factor'. It was in the course of textcritical studies of the synoptic Gospels that I found myself forced to admit that frequently error creates truth and absurdity creates beauty. It is almost a matter of rule that when a Gospel phrase or thought has passed into the lips and hearts of men and been recognised by them as conveying by the splendour of its imagery an otherwise inaccessible truth, it turns out to be the product of deep-seated corruption which has altered whatever was the original sense into undeniable nonsense.

I am not talking here about archaic expressions open to misunderstanding, such as the 'evil communications' which 'corrupt good manners' or 'spiritual wickedness in high places'. I am talking about real nonsense, such as the famous 'lilies of the field which toil not neither do they spin', or 'entering in at the strait gate' when self-evidently entry (as opposed to exit) by the 'wide gate' will get you to exactly the same place, or 'the faith no larger than a mustard seed' which 'moves mountains', or 'if thy right eye offend thee, pluck it out', or 'moth and rust doth corrupt'.

In all such places it would be possible, with varying degrees of assurance, to substitute a text and a translation which eliminated the illogicality and often cast a new and penetrating light upon the passages which were thus brought into closer relevance. The result would also be total devastation – a spirit would escape from the bottle and evaporate. It is not so much that the verbal magic is invulnerable to difficulties of sense, construction and logic. The suspicion is hard to resist that those difficulties actually play a creative and perhaps indispensable role. An irrational element is part and parcel of the supercharge of religious and ritual language.

Like those treading the foothills of a high mountain range, we are here in the presence of huge, daunting and ill-defined possibilities, such as the question to what extent the truth, the power and the success of the Gospel itself were dependent upon the contradictions and unintelligibilities which successive stages of its verbal and credal evolution deposited. On all that, however, I hasten to turn my back, in order to descend to the relative safety of the plain, observing only that much, though not the whole, of the case for the Book of Common Prayer applies equally to the Authorised or 'King James' Bible. The known and acknowledged defects of its underlying original and of the translation are not corrigible; but the penalty which attaches to the attempt to remove them is the loss of the precious essence itself.

It is possible to champion the Authorised Version and those earlier versions embalmed in the lectionary of the Book of Common Prayer without being ignorant or obscurantist – and without being fundamentalist either. The fundamentalists, nevertheless, are right in their instinct that 'one step, and all were marsh' beyond the arbitrary safety of 1611. Those who have seen most deeply into what lies behind and beneath the *textus receptus* and the Authorised Version are most aware how endlessly insecure is the advance of the scholar and the historian into the unknown.

Reference to the Authorised Version has brought me, by something more than a pun, to another indispensable attribute of religious and ritual language – authority. When words are to do something, to bring something into existence which was not there before, they must be the *right* words, their secret lies in their rightness: out of all the possible selections and combinations, one only is efficacious. Not for nothing do we pray, in the BCP of course, that bishops and curates may 'rightly and duly administer thy holy sacraments' – 'rightly and duly' *rite et debite*, the condition of success in all collective religious action.

Until the synodical revolution of the Worship and Doctrine Measure 1974, the language of the Book of Common Prayer was distinguished by being uniquely authoritative, established and fixed by the Crown in Parliament, the supreme source of authority in this realm. This authoritative fixity of the wording not only, as I have mentioned already, 'held the ring' (as it were) during the long period of supercharging while what was new became archaic. It also liberated meaning; for if words and formulae are fixed, change must express itself in interpretation. The Tractarians were doubly right when they acclaimed the Book of Common Prayer as the proof of the catholicism of the Anglican Church: right because the words and formulae, being themselves impregnable, were susceptible of an interpretation which bridged the gulf of the Reformation; and right because the essential mark of catholicism, uniformity imposed by universal authority, was placed upon it by the untrammelled *imperium* of the English nation state. Without the authoritative fixity of its liturgy, the unique comprehensiveness and broad-mindedness of the Church of England would not have been possible. For where formulation can be altered, differences of interpretation cannot be tolerated: that is the logic which the long fissiparous history of the dissenting sects has demonstrated ad nauseam. The freedom of the Anglican to say 'I conform because it is commanded' is not unworthy to stand beside the freedom of Tertullian to say 'it is certain because it is impossible'.

The cause of the Book of Common Prayer is not a literary or an aesthetic cause: it is a religious cause. It lies athwart the religious dilemma of our society, a society not emancipated from the necessities, including the religious necessities, of all human societies, but a society where the intellectual and emotional scaffolding of religious observance has been dismantled, not least by the very caste which is specialised in society for sustaining, commending and interpreting it. The deliberate attack upon the Book of Common Prayer which the last decade has witnessed is a conscious and integral part of that dismantling process – inevitably so, because the Anglican Church and its liturgical heritage survive, almost alone since the ravaging of the Roman Church, as living evidence of essential elements in religious experience and expression. I suspect that we who maintain the Book of Common Prayer are fighting in a wider warfare than we can know.

'THE CHURCH OF ENGLAND AND PARLIAMENT'

from *The Synod*, 1986

All questions which concern the Church of England, as do questions on the General Synod and its relations with Parliament, presuppose an answer to the question: what is the Church of England? That is to say, what is its essential characteristic, without which it would be something different in kind? I must, therefore, before I write about the General Synod and Parliament, make clear my own answer to that question. The Church of England is that Church of which the Supreme Governor on earth is the Crown of England. This description applies to no other Church, or part of the Church, and it applies to the Church of England irrespective of all other characteristics and of doctrine. Its essential nature is thus not doctrinal but political.

The Church of England may be in communion with other Churches, implying mutual recognition of the validity of each other's orders and sacraments. This does not make those other Churches part of the Church of England. The doctrines and liturgy of the Church of England are shared by other Churches throughout the world which were planted by it or derived from it; but the Anglican Communion, as the totality of those Churches is called, is not the Church of England, although the latter and its members are often described and often describe themselves as *Anglican*.

This relationship of the Anglican Communion with the Church of England is at least potentially at odds with the latter's essential characteristic. The Anglican Communion, being episcopal, has always voluntarily recognised the Primate of All England as its president or chief prelate; and Archbishops of Canterbury, including the present one, have tended to pay great regard to, and derive much satisfaction from, this worldwide position, travelling about the continents like Paul VI and John Paul II, almost as if they were popes themselves.

Not one of the other Churches in the Anglican Communion is governed by the supreme lay or secular authority in its own territory. They are self-governing or synodical churches, as have become, for instance, the Church in Wales and the Church of Ireland, since the English Crown renounced the supreme government of the church in those territories. The Archbishop and the General Synod of the

Church of England are thus unique among the prelates and synods of the Anglican Communion, in that they are, by the essential nature of the Church of England, respectively appointed by the Crown and subordinate to the governorship of the Crown. Membership, not to say leadership, of the Anglican Communion is thus apt to predispose the prelates and the General Synod to be impatient and intolerant of that very royal supremacy which is essential to the definition of the Church of England. If all other Anglican prelates are elected, they think, why not they? If all other Anglican synods are sovereign in doctrine and in church government, why not the General Synod?

The Crown of England which became Supreme Governor of the Church of England in the sixteenth century had not yet placed almost its whole prerogative in commission with Parliament. This constitutional development has had the consequence that the Crown which is Supreme Governor of the church is a crown that acts on the advice of Ministers and legislates with the advice and consent of Parliament. It is a parliamentary crown, and the Church of England is accordingly a parliamentary church, not because Parliament represents the Church of England or is representative of the members of the Church of England, but because the supreme authority in this realm is the Crown in Parliament.

What is unique about the Church of England is not so much that its Supreme Governor is royal as that its supreme authority is lay or secular. In that respect the Church of England resembles the fourth-century conciliar church, whose catholicity – we English call it *uniformity* – was guaranteed by its subordination to the Imperial authority. It is a characteristic which the western church lost with the fall of the Roman Empire but which England regained by the assertion of complete sovereign independence in its own territory.

For the Church of England is territorial. It is of necessity the Church *in* England which the Crown governs. That preposition *in* is significant and fruitful. *Ecclesia anglicana* before the Reformation meant the Church in England, that is, the part of the Church which subsisted in England. It was over that Church in England that the Crown became Supreme Governor. Logically its governorship extended no farther than the outer limits of its territorial sovereignty. Equally logically it applied to everybody within that territory, whence, despite the rise and toleration of other churches and of irreligion, the Church of England is still the Church of every resident in every parish throughout England: he may not claim it, but if he does his claim is upheld by the law. It is the Church of all the English, of all in England, precisely because, and only because, the supreme authority in it is the supreme secular authority. No other Church in the Anglican Communion can occupy the same position in its own country.

Of course the counterpart of the inclusiveness of the Church of England is its geographical exclusiveness: only an Englishman – strictly speaking, only an inhabitant of England – can be Church of England – others may be Anglicans, if they see fit.

The automatic and permanent consequence of the royal supremacy was, and is, that the legislature of the Church of England is no other than Parliament. Whatever legislative power the Convocations of Canterbury and York possessed in the Middle Ages, they surrendered it in May 1532, and the surrender was confirmed in 1534 by the Act for the Submission of the Clergy. The royal supremacy over the Church in England was established by the Crown in Parliament. The instrument that Henry VIII used for doing so was the omnicompetence of Parliament, and thenceforward the law ecclesiastical no less than the law temporal would be made in England by Parliament. The foundation deeds of the Church in England, the *Ecclesia anglicana*, by custom translated *Church of England*, are Acts of the so-called Reformation Parliament 1529–36. Repealed under Philip and Mary, they were reinstated by the Act of Supremacy of 1559. The Book of Common Prayer and the Articles were given legal force by statutes of 1559 and 1571 respectively.

After making the canons of 1604, which, not having been enacted by Parliament, did not have the force of law, the Convocations atrophied and eventually, between 1717 and 1850, were non-existent altogether. They were revived in the second half of the last century as forums of clerical debate, but they could of course have no legislative function.

By the time of the First World War, however, the assumption became prevalent that a body of law basically almost four centuries old was going to require amendment and extension. Meanwhile Parliament and Government had ceased, by virtue of religious toleration, to be identifiable with the Church of England, so that neither the preparation or initiation of legislation appeared to be appropriate functions for government nor the detailed debate and scrutiny of legislative proposals appropriate functions for the two Houses of Parliament. Those functions would have to be performed, therefore, it was argued, by some other body or bodies which *were* identifiable with the Church.

The solution of the problem adopted in 1919 was to create a new body by adding to the upper (episcopal) and lower (clerical) houses of Convocation a third element which should be lay and elective, and to enable measures duly sent forward to Parliament from that body to be given the force of law by the Crown in Parliament through a summary procedure. Profound and difficult issues of principle were raised or rather, implicitly, burked by the Church of England (Powers) Act 1919, which embodied that solution.

Devolution of legislative authority by the Houses of Parliament subject to a simple affirmative or negative vote has always been a ticklish matter. It is true that statutes have conferred upon Ministers of the Crown powers to make subordinate legislation, where the regulations or orders are themselves unamendable and are affirmed or negatived as they stand by the two Houses. These powers however are exercised by those responsible to Parliament, which can and sometimes does compel them either to withdraw and alter the proposed legislation or to drop it altogether.

If anyone should object that on joining the European Economic Community in 1972 Parliament did in fact pass to an external body, for the first time in at least four centuries, the right to legislate over its head, I would caution him against deducing from this *gran rifiuto* that Parliament will easily submit to a similar renunciation in any other direction. It remains a fearsome thing, from which powerful Ministers, like monarchs before them, have shrunk, to say to the House of Commons: 'This you must pass, and pass unaltered.'

One disagreeable consequence of legislation put forward to Parliament for its approval by another body is that Parliament is thereby deprived of the opportunity to exert its most fruitful legislative activity on behalf of the subject, namely, to question and examine in detail each and every separate provision and formulation.

These fundamental drawbacks of delegated legislation are enhanced rather than lessened by the procedure used in relation to measures which the General Synod passes and submits to Parliament for approval. They are, before submission to either House, considered by a statutory joint select committee of both Houses, which is empowered to take evidence, including evidence offered on behalf of the General Synod, and is known as the Ecclesiastical Committee. The Committee lays before each House a report of any evidence taken and its opinion whether or not the measure is 'expedient'.

In the House of Commons measures of the General Synod are proposed for approval by the Second Church Commissioner, a Member who is a Government appointee but not a member of the Government, and no responsibility for them is formally taken by the Government. Nevertheless it is the almost invariable custom for a government to support such measures by putting through the division lobbies, if necessary, what is known as the 'payroll vote', that is, Ministers and such hangers-on as have their bread buttered on the Government side. The consequence is that in effect the Government passed General Synod measures without taking responsibility for them.* True, the Ecclesiastical Committee will have reported to both Houses as to a measure's 'expediency, especially in its relation to the constitutional rights of all Her Majesty's subjects'; but despite the generality of the term 'expediency' and the vagueness of 'constitutional rights', it has interpreted its terms of reference narrowly, on the basis of a philosophy which excludes considerations of policy and principle on such grounds as are discussed in this chapter and might be brought forward in debate in either House. Very rarely does the Committee induce the Synod, through the latter's Legislative Committee, to withdraw a proposed measure with a view to submitting it again in a modified form.

There is thus an ultimate incompatibility between the legislative supremacy of Parliament and the legislative functions of the General Synod under the Church of England Assembly Act, 1919. This always existed potentially from the start. It would become impractical and intractable if there were, for instance, on the part of the General Synod a presumption that Parliament is bound to approve measures of the Synod if declared 'expedient' by the Ecclesiastical Committee – which is tantamount to telling the House of Commons to function as a rubber stamp. For any body to accept the obligation so to function is to acknowledge that it is not sovereign. The presumption would therefore be in itself a repudiation of the royal supremacy and thus of the essential nature of the Church of England.

There are two distinct grounds on which that presumption could be argued. One is that the General Synod, inasmuch as it is duly representative of the Church of England, is alone entitled to take decisions about its government, worship and doctrine, irrespective of whether they require to be given effect by changing the law of England. The second ground is that Parliament is not of itself a fit authority to legislate for the Church of England. I will examine both these contentions on their own terms, although each is incompatible inherently with the continued existence of what I believe the Church of England to be.

The legislative authority of the Crown in Parliament has always been bound up with the idea of representation, i.e. with assent validly given on behalf of a larger body, such as the electorate, through a smaller body of persons duly elected for the purpose in a particular way defined by custom and precedent, and not otherwise. Hence the enactment of all legislation 'by and with the advice and consent of . . .

---

* In recent years the case which caused most offence was the passage of the Worship and Doctrine Measure, 1974 by the 'payroll vote' against the manifest sense of the debate. The exception which proved the rule was the defeat of the Appointment of Bishops Measure on 15 July 1984 because of the Government's decision, which I elicited at the commencement of the debate, to stand aside.

the Commons in this present Parliament assembled'. There is no other representation than this by the advice and consent of which the law can be made or changed on any subject. The local by-laws proposed by elected councils have to be enacted by Parliament; trades union law is not made by representatives (elected or not) of trades unionists, nor is commercial law by representatives (elected or not) of merchants or manufacturers. In short, election carries of itself no implication of legislative capacity: law purporting to be made by any wholly or partly elected body other than Parliament would be as horrid a tyranny as law made by individual caprice.

The Church Assembly acquired no claim to legislative competence by the fact that two of its three components comprised persons appointed to that component by a process of election, even though the elective representation of the clergy was different in kind in an important respect from the elective representation of the laity by the third component. The clergy, cathedral and diocesan, are a precisely definable and identifiable body of persons, and directly or indirectly all those persons take, or are entitled to take, part in the electoral process, a process, incidentally, which has been accepted as valid by those concerned over an extremely long, though not unbroken, period of time.

In the case of the laity, it is not only the electoral process itself – a process of cumulative indirect election through a hierarchy of electoral colleges – which has not been hallowed by habit and custom. The underlying electorate itself is open to question.

The electoral process is as follows. The annual parish meetings elect triennially the representatives of the respective parishes to form the House of Laity of the deanery synods. These Houses in turn elect the House of Laity of the diocesan synods. It is the Houses of Laity of the deanery synods which, when a General Synod is to be elected, choose the representatives who shall go from each diocese to the House of Laity of the General Synod.

There are three counts at least on which any claim to representative authority on the part of the House of Laity of the General Synod is open to question. First, there is the feature of indirect, collegiate election itself. The members of the House of Laity might, in some subtle sense, be held responsible to their diocesan synods for the action they take and the votes which they cast. What is certain is that they cannot be responsible through the diocesan and deanery synods to the underlying electorate, the membership of the annual parish meetings, who have been electing persons to sit in a deanery synod to deal with matters within the scope of that synod and not to take on their behalf the sort of decisions which the General Synod takes.

This flaw is closely linked with another, namely, that the parish elections which – albeit indirectly through the deanery synods – create the diocesan synods are not taking place with the General Synod in view or at a time when a new General Synod is to be elected. There is, so to speak, no such thing as a General Synod general election. Yet a general election is of the essence of the representative claim of the body elected. The underlying electorate at large is not able to mandate its representatives on the issues with which the new General Synod is expected to deal. Individual members of the parish meeting are in no position to bind a candidate to vote, in circumstances which do not as yet exist, for a deanery candidate for the diocesan synod which will send representatives to the General Synod, so that these latter will vote one way rather than another on questions which are not before the electors who attend the annual meeting.

The most fundamental defect however lies in the nature of the underlying electorate itself: the persons on the parish electoral rolls. I will not make much of the attendance at parish meetings, nor enquire what percentage turn-out they represent of those whose names are on the rolls, though I suspect that the percentage would by any political standards be derisory. I ask rather: who are these people who are on the electoral rolls? They are qualified by habitual attendance at public worship during the previous six months. I concede that parish priests generally make an effort to ensure that as many as possible of such persons as are known to him do get on to the roll. But are those persons, in the necessary sense, the people – the *laos* – of the Church of England? The contrary would indeed follow automatically from my earlier proposition that the Church of England is the right and possession of all the people of England, both those who do and those who do not avail themselves of it, so that all the people of England are, as such, potentially members of the Church of England in a sense in which they can not be potentially members of the Roman or any other Church. But that is not what I am arguing here. I am here making the more limited claim that those whose worship and attendance are occasional, who are not even annually communicant, but who look to the Church of England to hallow the great events of their lives, are also entitled to be regarded as its laity and to be included in its representation. If so, the electorate which underlies the indirect, pyramidal election of the House of Laity of the General Synod is too narrow and partial to sustain a claim by that body to represent the Church of England for the purpose of consenting to changes in its law.

We have at this point come close to the nature of the other ground for the General Synod's claim to legislate for the Church of England, namely, that Parliament, and in particular the House of Commons, is not a fit authority to speak, or therefore to legislate, for the Church of England.

Let it first be reiterated that Parliament legislated, and legislates still, for the Church of England not as being representative of it but because the Crown, the Church's Supreme Governor, makes all law through Parliament and only through Parliament. It is as a representation of the whole realm that Parliament advises and consents on legislation. In so doing, it makes law for many parts or elements or interests in the nation of which it would not claim to be representative. It is doing that all the time, though most instructive is the fact that the law in Scotland and Wales and (albeit by a different procedure) Northern Ireland is made, where different from that of England, by the whole Parliament and the whole House of Commons – not, for instance, just by the Scottish peers and the MPs from Scotland alone. It is as much a function of the whole Parliament to legislate for the Church of England as to legislate for Wales.

Of course that is not the whole story. The House of Commons, believe it or not, is a highly reasonable body and proceeds in a commonsensical way to respect the views and wishes of those of its Members which it regards as particularly concerned or particularly knowledgeable. English constituency members do not generally orate upon Scottish affairs, taking it that the Scottish members are most involved in them and probably know more about them. If, indeed, an issue of general policy or of party division arises, the Government and its opponents will use their whips and there will be a full turnout, if not in the Chamber, at any rate in the division lobbies. For the rest, however, Parliament, being a very English institution, tends to lean towards the English principle of 'live-and-let-live'.

The House of Commons has not since the eighteenth century been exclusively Church of England. Religious surveys of its membership are not popular, but a recent estimate of a recent House of Commons produced a breakdown* in which the largest single denomination was, nominally at least, Church of England. Moreover, England, to which since Irish and Welsh disestablishment the Church of England has been territorially confined, returns out of the total of 650 members 523 who might be said to have a specifically constituency connection with the Church of England. The House of Commons is on these facts still a body in which many members would regard the Church of England's business as of concern to them, personally or as constituency representatives. Nor should it be supposed that Dissenters, Roman Catholics, Jews and those avowedly without personal religion

* Of 334 members of the October 1974 House of Commons who answered an enquiry on their religious belief, 203 reported 'Church of England' (*Cassell's Parliamentary Directory*)

are necessarily without interest in, or concern for, the Church of which the Sovereign is the Supreme Governor. Their contributions to debates on Church of England measures have sometimes been notable. There is thus nothing in the character or composition of Parliament or the House of Commons which makes grotesque in practice its constitutionally logical function as the legislator for the Church.

If, of course, it were to be demanded of Parliament that it should renounce that function – a renunciation, be it noted, which could only be simultaneous with the Crown's renunciation of the supreme government of the Church of England and consequently (on the definition here adopted) with the ending of the Church of England itself – Parliament would not resist. Admittedly Parliament in renouncing or transferring power is apt to be embarrassingly inquisitive about the status and bona fides of the recipient; and it is not at all certain that it would regard the General Synod as sufficiently in the image of Parliament to be entrusted with the powers which Parliament was renouncing.

However, it is necessary to be clear about what is the meaning of the word *demand* in this context. It means a demand from those whom Parliament represents which it cannot prudently refuse. Demands in that sense have been made and conceded before now – to Roman Catholics for enfranchisement and to Dissenters for civil recognition. It is the sort of demand for the detection of which the House of Commons is bred as a hound is bred to scent a fox. When English members are besieged in their 'surgeries', and threatened through their postbags with loss of votes and seats, if they persist in legislating for the Church of England, then, and only then, will they know that there is a 'demand'.

Bishops and functionaries of the General Synod are apt to be startled when they discover that Members of Parliament who concern themselves with the Church of England and with its legislation are almost invariably extremely conservative, not to say reactionary, quite irrespective of their party allegiance or their individual line of thinking on other matters. This ought to be a salutary observation. It ought to give food for thought if those whose business, nay, whose very existence, is bound up in keeping in touch with the grass roots in their constituencies, detecting 'the way the wind blows' and trimming their sails to it, turn out, where the Church of England, its law and worship and doctrine are concerned, to be totally unreconstructed and quite horribly allergic to what is fashionable or *avant garde* in the General Synod. It would be unwise to deduce that members are ignorant or unthinking. Are they not perhaps all too representative? Could it be Church House and not St Stephen's that is out of touch?

If Parliament remains the supreme legislature of the Church of England, it not merely will not but can not rubber stamp all and any measures submitted to it by the General Synod. There are those who believe that this proposition poses for the Synod a dilemma between confrontation with Parliament, leading to formal termination of the royal supremacy, or acquiescence in a subordinate and essentially advisory status, with no 'inherent authority of its own' (an expression used in the General Synod by the Bishop of Kensington). Quite apart from any question whether the confrontation would enjoy sufficient support among the Church's members and the public in general for it to succeed, I believe that, like most such stark dilemmas, this one is unreal.

Parliament is past master in the art of living with insoluble dilemmas: that is part of the political genius which has enabled the English people to create and maintain a parliamentary monarchy. Parliament, and the House of Commons in particular, has not the remotest intention of concerning itself, aye or no, with the over-whelming majority of changes in the law which the General Synod, using its far from over-hasty procedures, may find in the course of the years to be 'expedient' (blessed word). We have enough on our legislative plate not to want all that to be ladled on to it for the full treatment. On the other hand, there are some changes in the law of the Church of England which Parliament, and particularly what George II called 'that damned House of Commons', will not pass. What is necessary is that degree of mutual understanding between the two bodies which will ensure that both of them respect these facts. How is that common comprehension, that 'getting inside each other's mind', to be sufficiently achieved to avert collision?

The statutory machinery of the interlocking Legislative and Ecclesiastical Committees will not do the job. It is too formal and, without offence, too unpolitical. What is wanted must be both informal and political. Those who guide the General Synod must not be too proud to try to understand what makes Parliament 'tick' in ways that to them are disconcerting and disappointing. It would be worth the effort, and it would be welcomed in Westminster, where, if we hate anything, we hate *faits accomplis* and are practised in deftly avoiding them. That is why I have no intention of using this chapter to set down specific proposals in black and white. There are precedents; and there are people of sufficient goodwill in Parliament and the General Synod to find a way of using them.

There is a third party to all this, however, and this chapter would be incomplete if it were left out. The Crown is not only the Crown in Parliament: it is also the Crown in Council – the executive. The two must chime together. A recent leading article under the title 'Is

Confrontation Coming'* referred to 'the illusion that since the passing of the Worship and Doctrine Measure and the setting up of the Crown Appointments Commission the Church has the substance, if not the appearance, of power'. The collocation of the two items in that sentence is apt and significant. The executive functioning of the Crown on advice is no less integral to its governorship of the Church of England than is its legislative functioning by the advice and consent of Parliament. There is no doubt what the advice in question is. It is the collective advice, tendered on their behalf by the Prime Minister, of ministers who command the confidence of the House of Commons. On no other advice is the executive authority of the Crown exercised in this country, and on no other advice *can* it be exercised. So long therefore as the Church of England is governed on earth by the Crown of England, the Crown's executive acts as governor of the Church must be on the advice of ministers.

Such acts indisputably include the appointment of the prelates, no less than secular government includes appointments to the lay offices in the state. This logic in no way depends upon, or, still less, is invalidated by, the fact that diocesan bishops – since 1848 *certain* diocesan bishops only – have places in Parliament, the House of Lords, as a consequence of the feudal rights which were owed to the Crown by their predecessors in respect of the temporalities of their sees – in other words, as barons. If the prelatical office were confined to possession of the spiritualities, to the possession and exercise of episcopal functions in relation to the Church, appointment to that office by the Crown on the advice of ministers would be no less implicit in the royal supremacy. Indeed, one of the achievements of the Henrician Reformation settlement was the final and logical termination which, so far as England was concerned, it brought to the ancient and, in papal terms, insoluble investiture controversy by recombining temporal and ecclesiastical sovereignty.

It is now nine years since an event occurred more blatantly incompatible with the essential character of the Church of England than any claim to effective power of legislation which might be advanced or implied on behalf of the General Synod. In June 1976 Prime Minister Callaghan announced a proposal that in future the Crown would not be advised to appoint to a bishopric any person who was not one of two or more nominated for that purpose by a body described as 'set up by the Church'. If anyone doubts that this proposal, if it had any effect at all, would amount to annulment of the royal supremacy, let it be considered what would be the consequences

---

* *English Churchman* (10/17 May 1985).

of a comparable restriction in any other field of the advice on which the Crown is constitutionally obliged to act.

The proposals were announced in a written answer to the then Leader of the Opposition and purported to be 'supported by the leaders of the main Opposition parties'. Staggeringly, no debate or discussion of them whatsoever has taken place from that day to this in either House of Parliament. Nevertheless they have been treated as having come into effect as a result of a favourable vote in the subsequent session of the General Synod. With breathtaking effrontery Prime Minister Callaghan stated that 'arrangements on these lines would not in themselves involve legislation'. Despite the weasel words 'in themselves', a more insultingly preposterous assertion could not have been advanced.

It amounted to asserting that the royal supremacy in the Church of England, though by law established, can be repudiated and rendered invalid by a simple statement on the part of the Prime Minister and other politicians that in tendering advice to the Crown on the appointment of bishops in the Church they would limit themselves to persons nominated by an unspecified body in an unspecified manner, so that in effect they themselves are not responsible for that advice. That the law of the land can be thus changed by prime ministerial declaration, because other party leaders and the General Synod give assent to it, is not a proposition which anyone concerned for the rights and liberties guaranteed to the people of this country by Parliament could for an instant accept.

It would in my opinion be erroneous to deduce from the mere silence of Parliament for the last eight years on the subject of the so-called concordat of 1976 that this will remain unbroken, and that the executive and legislative supremacy of the Crown in the Church of England can be evacuated of all reality by a series of wheezes which, in the words of Prime Minister Callaghan's Written Answer, will 'settle this issue in a satisfactory way for the foreseeable future'. If what the Answer called 'the Church' – which turns out to mean the pyramidal elective process embodied in the constitution of the General Synod – intends to 'have, and be seen to have, a greater say in the process of choosing its leaders', the removal of responsibility from ministers answerable to Parliament cannot be effected within a Church of England still by law established under the royal supremacy.

A church which 'chooses its leaders', like a church which 'makes its own laws', will not long remain the church which is the common right and possession of all the people of England. Whether the representatives of the people of England are prepared to see that possession and right removed from them, we have yet to learn. It would, however, in the matter of appointments as in that of legislation, be misunderstanding the attitude of Parliament to suppose that it wishes ministerial responsibility for advising the Crown on the executive exercise of the royal prerogative to be used in any way to the offence or scandal of the people of the Church of England.

The prominence of references to the Bishop of Durham in the debate of 15 July 1984, which ended in the House of Commons rejecting the Appointment of Bishops Measure, was neither adventitious nor a sign of levity. What the House was in effect saying was this: episcopal appointments made by the Crown on prime ministerial advice may from time to time have been open to criticism but we see no merit or advantage to the Church of England in destroying lay supremacy in order that something called 'the Church' can make appointments by which the Church itself is divided and scandalised.

Parliament knows very well that royal patronage exercised on political advice will often pass over the saintliest and the wisest. So will any other system of preferment to institutional office. What Parliament also knows, however, is that there is no substitute for the sanction of visible and personal political responsibility if the institution is to be a national, not a sectional possession.

'A NATIONAL CHURCH' (1981)

from *The Incorruptible Church*, Gothic House, London, 1987

In a recent article on Poland an American diplomat of wide experience wrote: 'The Poles are and have always been the most intensely and proudly nationalist people of Eastern Europe. The Roman Catholic Church has been, throughout centuries, the most enduring and venerable guardian of Poland's national conscience. It has always been a national church.' It is to those last words, 'a national church', that I would direct attention.

There is, at first hearing, a paradox in this. Whatever else can be said about the Roman Catholic Church, it is not 'national'. It claims by its very title to be the opposite of national – namely, universal. Yet here before our eyes that Church is in Poland the 'national' Church. What can that mean? At the most superficial level it may be said that the Roman or Western alignment of the Poles marks them off from the Orthodox or Eastern alignment of their eternal enemies, the Russians. Maybe, too, more recently it marked them off from the Lutheran Protestantism of their westward enemies, the Prussians. But these antitheses would not suffice to make the Roman Church their 'national' Church, though without them it might not have been possible. Something else was necessary; and this was that the Roman Church should be perceived as Polish, as the exclusive and characteristic possession of the Polish nation. So the question still remains, how a universal church, subject to a non-Polish authority centred far outside Poland, has been, and still manifestly is, so perceived.

For all its paradox, the Polish experience is not unique. Long before the period when conventional historians allows us to identify nations in Europe, the Church in many countries already had strongly marked national traits. Perhaps the Celtic Church, distinctive though it was, cannot be thus classified; but there was certainly a Gallican Church and an Anglican Church before the Reformation was dreamt of.

We have been reminded, in the course of the discussion which followed the election of the new Bishop of London, that in the twelfth century the king was as insistent as any modern Prime Minister upon his right to nominate bishops; and in the Middle Ages the *Ecclesia anglicana*, untranslatable except as 'Church of England', was an accepted political as well as ecclesiastical reality. Clearly the Church, the universal, catholic church, could also be a national church.

In feudal thinking loyalty was indivisible: the bishop who received the temporalities of his see as faithful liege man of his lord the king could not receive the spiritualities either, except by the appointment and permission of that same lord. To attempt to conceive two loyalties was to tear asunder two aspects of the person, to separate (as it were) body and soul. Significantly, when the papacy attempted to resist the king's claim, it found it could only do so by itself claiming to be his temporal overlord.

The logic goes beyond the limits of feudalism. The attempt to divide the loyalties of the community between the secular sphere and the religious has always ended by either nationalising the church or secularising the nation. In the modern Western world, the latter conclusion has been that most commonly drawn: the new Western states, from the French and American revolutions onwards, have been secular – they limited their claim on the loyalty of their citizens to the material aspects only of the human personality and of society.

In this respect our own nation is among the exceptions, having so far refused to admit that the nation is exclusively secular, and in consequence still possessing a national church. The nature of that national church is unique, because the historical experience of our nation is unique. Unlike all the other nations of Europe we have retained our prescriptive monarchy; and unlike them, and through the agency of that monarchy, we have transformed a common feudal institution which elsewhere died out, into the supreme self-expression of the nation, Parliament.

When we say, as we must say when we are accurate, that our sovereign is the Crown in Parliament, that is no cold and empty formula: it unites the double focus of our loyalties, our personal loyalty to the personal monarch, destined by descent and consecrated by God, and our political loyalty to the institutionalised expression of the will of a free people, by the advice and consent of which she reigns.

It was thus not accidental but logical, that when England divested itself of the last vestiges of external dependence, it was the monarch who became on earth the supreme head, and later governor of the church and that the monarch exercised that spiritual authority through Parliament, of which Henry VIII asserted: 'We are nowhere so high in our estate royal as in this our high court of parliament'. The imperial power, or *imperium*, which had once conferred universality – in Greek, catholicity – upon the Church in the ancient world, by enacting and authorising uniformity, was replaced in England by the Crown in Parliament, which likewise enacted and authorised uniformity. By virtue of that fact the Anglican Church, the *Ecclesia anglicana*, to this day continues the catholic church of this land.

While the sovereign cannot be otherwise than the governor of that church, it is a common but dangerous error to suppose that its nature is altered by the fact that Parliament is no longer composed exclusively of Anglicans, or by the fact that the uniformity of the Church is now accompanied by toleration of other forms of Christian worship, whether forms based upon the appeal to individual judgement or forms based upon continued acknowledgement of the external authority of Rome. I would go further and say, with hope though not entirely with conviction, that the nature of the Church of England has not – at least has not yet – been altered by the delegation of legislative initiative and subordinate legislative powers to the Church Assembly and its present-day successor, the General Synod.

This brings me directly to the remarkable event of historic importance for the Church of England. On 8 April 1981 each House of Parliament by substantial majorities decided to initiate legislation to strengthen the entrenchment of the Book of Common Prayer in the worship and doctrine of the Anglican Church* – an entrenchment which the measure passed in 1974 had been claimed to embody, but which, in the opinion of the majority voting, had proved to be inadequate in practice. In this action Parliament – and by no means all who voted were Anglicans – was renewing its essential function in regard to the Church of England in two respects: it was intervening to protect uniformity, and it was speaking in its capacity as the representation of the people.

Too much stress, in discussing this event, has been laid upon the literary and linguistic excellences of the Prayer Book. It was not an Act for the Preservation of Pure English upon which Parliament was embarking when the two Houses fired the double volley across the bows of the bishops and clergy of the established church. Parliament is the guardian of that Prayer Book which embodies forms of worship and expressions of faith that are broad, generous and deep enough to embrace the wide spectrum which a national church must comprehend. It is the Act of Uniformity – in other words, it is Parliament and the Prayer Book – which prevent the Anglican Church from ever becoming one sect among many – I almost said, one trend among many – and which keep it the Church of all the English, the Church of the nation, the Church to which in the great moments of individual and national existence the overwhelming majority of this people turn

*Lord Cranbourne's Bill did not make progress after leave to introduce but was the springboard for discussions which resulted in the unfulfilled pledge of the Archbishop of Canterbury to ensure that the Book of Common Prayer was taught in all Church of England theological colleges

or return, in birth, in marriage, in death, in peace, in war, in victory. It is Parliament and the Prayer Book which are the guarantee of the nation's church against schism and take-over. A national church, because it *is* national, cannot be immune from movements which question or threaten the nation. In the last generation that threat has not, as in the past, taken the form of overt violence, internal or external; it has been the more subtle and imperceptible yet deadly threat of simple denial that the nation exists at all, coupled with what might be taken for general public indifference to the whole question. A generation which has seen the courts of this realm subordinated to external courts and its legislature subordinated to external legislative institutions, and which has heard the absorption of the United Kingdom into a larger political entity openly advocated and approved, is a generation in which a national church must expect to be the object of scepticism and attack. It is under attack from within by those who would be prepared to sacrifice or compromise the Royal Supremacy which is its essential foundation; it is under attack from outside by those who declare that a national church no longer commands the understanding, let alone support, of the people at large.

The picture is a mirror image of the attack upon the nation in its temporal aspect: the ascendancy in high places of those who deny its validity, and the prevalence among the public of what looks like bored indifference.

For my own part, I believe that appearances are delusive, and that underneath it all the national instinct and identity continue to exist: she '*is not dead, but sleepeth*'.* That is an assertion which only the future can prove – or disprove: meanwhile it remains in the realm of faith, the sort of faith upon which we all of us act, that in heart and mind, feelings and hopes, one's fellow countrymen cannot after all be other than like oneself.

*Mt. 9: 24

PART TWO

POWELL THE PARLIAMENTARIAN

SPEECHES AND STRUCTURE

The House of Commons is my home.

'A Life in the Day of Enoch Powell',
Sunday Times Magazine, 11 May 1986

MAIDEN SPEECH

16 March 1950

Mr J. Enoch Powell (Wolverhampton, South-West): There is no need for me to pretend those feelings of awe and hesitation which assail any hon. Member who rises to address this House for the first time, but I trust I shall receive the indulgence which is usually accorded to one undergoing that ordeal. I wish to address myself to the same problem as the hon. Member for Coventry, East (Mr Crossman), but to address remarks to it expressed rather in the form of manpower than, as he did, in that of finance.

To anyone who reads the White Paper on Defence, the one outstanding feature is the staggering burden in terms of manpower which this country is called upon to shoulder. How great that burden is may be seen by a simple comparison with pre-war commitments. Our Defence Forces are today approximately double the size they were in 1938, but it is an underestimate to say that our burden has only doubled, for the difference between our pre-war manpower in defence and our present manpower is filled by the National Service man, or conscript. The expenditure of manpower in the form of conscript service is the least efficient and the most dislocating to the national economy of any use of manpower. Therefore, it is fair to say that in so far as we have been obliged to double our burdens by taking upon ourselves the burden of conscription, that burden has more than doubled and any hon. Member in any part of the House must seriously address himself to the question whether that burden can be borne in its present weight and otherwise in what way it can be diminished.

In examining that, I wish to address myself particularly to the Army. There is good reason for doing so. The Minister of Defence concentrated attention on the Army requirement in manpower when dealing with this aspect of the question, and in any case two-thirds of our conscripted manpower are called for by the Army, so that if we focus our minds upon those causes which have doubled our commitments in respect of the Army, we may find some indication of the direction in which relief is to be sought.

Upon a rough comparison, we may say that we had serving with the Colours in the Army in 1938 200,000 men – actually the figure was slightly lower. The figure at which the Government aim by April, 1951 – which is a figure, one gathers from the White Paper, they do not expect will thereafter diminish, or at any rate will not rapidly diminish – is approximately 350,000. We have a contrast between a pre-war Army of 200,000 and a post-war 1951 Army of 350,000. It is not, however, correct to assume that the commitments which our Army is meeting have increased in that ratio, because the 150,000 or 160,000 conscripts serving in the Army are not doing the work of 160,000 Regulars.

Approximately one-third of the service of a National Service man is not of practical utility because he is undergoing his initial training. There is the question of transport to his overseas station and transport back, and so forth. Besides that, we have an extra demand upon our Regular Forces for the training of the National Service man. I think it more than fair to say that the 150,000 or 160,000 conscripts in the Army are fulfilling the demand of approximately 100,000 Regulars, so that in broad terms the change which has taken place is an increase in our commitments of the order of some 200,000 to 300,000.

Before analysing the reasons for that increase, may I point out that it is upon the commitment for troops with the Colours that we must fasten our attention. The Minister of Defence was right in saying that there are two grounds on which the case for a conscript force rests – the meeting of current commitments and the formation of a Reserve. But no one will assert that if our current commitments could be met with Regular troops, we could not find more effective methods, more successful and economical methods, than the present system of National Service for forming the Reserve forces which we need.

We therefore have to ask what are these additional commitments which have enforced upon us the requirement of an Army of the equivalent of 300,000 as against 200,000 before the war. If we examine the distribution of our Army now and in 1938, we shall perhaps be surprised that the number of troops abroad, outside Europe, is no larger today – in fact it is rather smaller – than it was in 1938; but we should be very wrong to jump to the conclusion that therefore there had been no increase in our extra-European commitment, for one simple reason. My right hon. Friend the Member for Woodford (Mr Churchill) pointed out that in those 90,000 British troops who were outside Europe in 1938 were included the 55,000 British component of the Indian Army. Those 55,000 men were not merely, not even mainly, fulfilling an Indian commitment. They were a strategic reserve for the whole of the Middle and Far East and also, if need were – and on two occasions this was realised in fact – for Europe itself.

Therefore, if we now find ourselves obliged to station outside Europe as many men as before the war, that means that we have an increased commitment of the order of 50,000 men for the Middle and Far East, and have at the same time lost the mass of manoeuvre, the strategic reserve of our British and Indian component of the lost Indian Army. So we find in these facts the first great change which has come over our position. It is a change which follows from the loss of the Indian Army and the intensification of the threat to the Middle and Far East.

The remainder is attributable to the greater threat in Europe, which may be measured in numerical terms, perhaps, by comparing the small forces of occupation present in Germany five years after the First World War with the 70,000 or 80,000 stationed in Germany today. So we find that these two great changes, the loss of the Indian Army coupled with the increased threat to the Middle and Far East, and on the other hand the increased threat in Europe, are the reasons which entail upon us far more than anything else this doubling of our manpower commitment for defence.

Is there any escape? As the hon. Member for Coventry, East, asked in other terms, must we continue to stagger under this burden until it weighs us down and breaks us, or is there some escape? I suggest that there are two directions in which we could look. The first has already been suggested in my analysis of the causes of our difficulties. We have lost the greatest non-European army which the world has ever seen, an Army which made possible, as did no other institution in the world, the active and affectionate co-operation of European and non-European. I do not intend to go into the reasons for or justification of that event, but it is lost.

If we are an Empire defending the Empire, we must draw far more than we do on the vast reserves of Colonial manpower which exist within the Empire. The virtues which enabled British officers and British administrators to create the Indian Army are not dead. The virtues which made the Indian Army so great an instrument, although some of them are perhaps peculiar to the martial races of India, are paralleled in other parts of the world. Not only is it not impossible, it is imperative that we should create from the other parts of His Majesty's Dominions a replacement for that which we have lost.

Thinking in these terms, one is shocked to see from the Army Estimates that in the last twelve months there has been a decrease of 15,000 in the Colonial manpower serving with the Colours outside Europe, and an increase in the British manpower. Surely we are moving in the wrong direction. It is not to the point to say that this is also a question of finance. After all, Nepal does not pay for the Gurkhas but we are very fortunate indeed to be able to supplement our British manpower with the assistance of Nepalese manpower. Exactly the same argument applies to the manpower which can be afforded by our Malayan or our great African territories.

That is the first direction in which we ought to look – the replacement of the Indian Army. The demand that we shall do so rests ultimately upon the conception that what we are defending, His Majesty's Dominions as a whole throughout the world, are in reality a whole, and that the manpower of those Dominions has a right and a duty to come to their defence. I do not think that we are applying that principle to the maintenance of the European forces which defend His Majesty's Dominions. It is far from my mind to criticise or appear to criticise the Governments of the Dominions, but it is the fact that the populations of Australia,

New Zealand and Canada together amount to between one-third and one-half of the population of the United Kingdom, whereas the proportion of their manpower which is engaged in the tasks of defence is less than one-eighth of our manpower.

If what we are defending is indeed a unity – and the Tory Party at all events asserts that it is a unity – the duty of this defence is equally incumbent upon what we call the Dominions and upon the United Kingdom. We require, instead of mere consultation, mere machinery of co-operation, usually left somewhat vague, a real recognition of a truly joint responsibility amongst all His Majesty's Governments for the defence of His Majesty's Dominions. I am well aware that such a demand raises far-reaching political implications. I am not afraid of those implications, indeed I desire them, for I am certain that unless we summon to the defence of this worldwide Empire all its resources, be they European or non-European, we shall fall under the load which we are attempting to bear.

ROYAL TITLES BILL

3 March 1953

Mr J. Enoch Powell (Wolverhampton, South-West): My right hon. and gallant Friend the Member for Kelvingrove (Lieut.-Colonel Elliot) referred to the embarrassment which the House had felt in dealing with this Bill. I confess that I feel more than my own share of embarrassment in rising to agree with those hon. Members who have opposed it. But there my agreement with them ceases, because the objection to this Bill relates to the central fact of what it does and what, when it is passed, will be done by virtue of the Prerogative.

My right hon. and learned Friend the Home Secretary said in his speech that this Bill departed in a substantial point from the Statute of Westminster. I think that it was a matter of perhaps more importance than he devoted to it. When the Statute of Westminster gave statutory recognition to the legislative independence of the Parliaments of the Empire it recognised in its Preamble two voluntary limitations upon that independence. Those two limitations were that any alteration either in the succession or in the title of the Crown would be made, if at all, only by the agreement of all concerned.

It is important that the House should have the words of that Preamble in its mind. '. . . it would be in accord,' said the Preamble,

> with the established constitutional position of all the members of the Commonwealth in relation to one another that any alteration in the law touching the Succession to the Throne or the Royal Style and Titles shall hereafter require the assent as well of the Parliaments of all the Dominions as of the Parliament of the United Kingdom . . .

Mr Glenvil Hall (Colne Valley): Surely the hon. Member has read the Bill. The second paragraph of its Preamble makes it quite clear that agreement has been reached.

Mr Powell: If the right hon. Gentleman had listened to me for a little longer there would have been hardly any need for that shallow intervention.

The Statute of Westminster preserved what were then considered to be the two essential unities – the unity of the person of the Monarch, by maintaining that the succession, if changed, should be changed simultaneously and in the same way – and the unity of the identity of the Monarch by maintaining that the title, if changed at all, should be changed simultaneously and in the same way. The second of those two unities, the unity of title, is deliberately departed from by the agreement which this Bill implements. Agreement there has indeed been; but that agreement is only an agreement to differ.

It is a consequence of that agreement to differ that, whereas in the only previous case since the Statute of Westminster where the Royal Style has been altered, that alteration was specified and written into the Statute which made it, the alteration has here been left unspecified both as regards time and as regards nature. Therefore, to see what alteration is proposed in virtue of this Bill, we have to look to the White Paper.

The new style for the United Kingdom which is foreshadowed in the White Paper is not quite the first attempt at a new style which has been made. Over a year ago, on 7 February, when Her present Majesty was proclaimed, she was proclaimed by an unknown style and title and one which at that time had no statutory basis. It is not quite the same title as is proposed in the present White Paper. I am not quibbling over whether the use of a title in a proclamation requires statutory authority or not. I would only remark in passing, however, that it is remarkable that we should have this necessity for Commonwealth agreement and for legislation by the Parliaments if upon that solemn moment of her accession the Queen could be proclaimed by a title unknown to the law. I notice that the other Dominions proclaimed her by her existing style.

Mr Gordon Walker: No.

Mr Powell: With only an addition, following that style, equivalent to the asseverance of loyalty which followed our own expression of the title in the Proclamation. I think that the right hon. Gentleman will find that that was the case if he makes the comparison.

When we come to the proposed new style for the United Kingdom, I find in it three major changes, all of which seem to me to be evil. One has been very clearly and correctly pointed out by the right hon. Gentleman the Member for Smethwick. It is that in this title, for the first time, will be recognised a principle hitherto never admitted in this country, namely, the divisibility of the crown.

The second feature of the new title is the suppression of the word 'British', both from before the words 'Realms and Territories' where it is replaced by the words 'her other' and from before the word 'Commonwealth', which, in the Statute of Westminster, is described as the

'British Commonwealth of Nations'.

The third major change is that we have a new expression and concept – the 'Head of the Commonwealth'. I shall deal with these three major changes in order.

The term 'Realms', which is to appear in the new title, is an emphatic statement that Her Majesty is the Queen of a considerable number of separate kingdoms. Hitherto, that has not been this country's acceptance of the term. For example, in introducing the corresponding Royal and Parliamentary Titles Bill in 1927, the then predecessor of my right hon. and learned Friend said:

> . . . the word "Realm" is constituted an alternative expression for the "Dominions of the Crown" '
> (*Official Report*, 9 March 1927; Vol. 203, *c.* 1265).

That had come to be the case by a well-recognised historical process. If you look back at the Act of Succession, Mr Speaker, you will find a reference there, in respect of England, to the Imperial Crown of this Realm and France and Ireland. By the process of events the claim to the throne of France was dropped and by the successive Acts of Union the three Kingdoms of England, Ireland and Scotland, each with their separate historical origins, were merged into one. There was one realm, over which was the Imperial Crown of the United Kingdom of Great Britain and Ireland and the territories thereto belonging.

Mr Gordon Walker: Henry VIII also referred to the Imperial Crown, meaning of this kingdom alone.

Mr Powell: I am not dealing with the word 'Imperial'. Of course, Henry VIII was referring to England; but when he used the word 'empire' he meant it in the medieval sense and was proclaiming the independence of this country from the Holy Roman Empire. But that is a by-way.

Within this unity of the realm achieved by the Acts of Union there grew up the British Empire; and the unity of that Empire was equivalent to the unity of that realm. It was a unit because it had one Sovereign. There was one Sovereign; one realm. In the course of constitutional development, indeed, the Sovereign began to govern different parts of that realm upon the advice of different Ministers; but that in itself did not constitute a division of the realm. On the contrary, despite the fact that he or she ruled his or her Dominions on the advice of different Ministers, the unity of the whole was essentially preserved by the unity of the Crown and the one Kingdom.

That unity we are now formally and deliberately giving up, and we are substituting what is, in effect, a fortuitous aggregation of a number of separate entities. I have not deliberately exaggerated by using the word 'fortuitous'. Here we find these different entities defining the identity of their Sovereign differently. By recognising the division of the realm into separate realms, are we not opening the way for that other remaining unity – the last unity of all – that of the person, to go the way of the rest?

Mr Godfrey Nicholson (Farnham): My hon. Friend may recollect that when the Dominion of Canada was set up there was a proposal that it should be called the Kingdom of Canada. If that is the case his claim that this diversity of realms is an innovation falls to the ground.

Mr Powell: I did not say it was an innovation; I said it is an innovation in the view of this country. Hitherto, in the United Kingdom, the view has never been held that there were separate kingdoms. It has been held that there was one single realm.

Incidentally, I notice that I am not alone in my repugnance to this change. Unless the proceedings in the Australian Parliament have been misreported, the same feeling was alive in Australia. In *The Times* of 19 February the Australian Prime Minister is reported as saying:

> He had strongly opposed the suggestion that the Queen should be named Queen of Australia without first mention of the United Kingdom, because this would tend to work against unity.

The report goes on:

> It was unnecessary anyway, as the Queen was, under strict law, Australia's Queen, because Australia had never made an Act of secession.

As I read those words they bear witness to the same sense of repugnance to the recognition of a division of the realm.

I come now to the second major alteration which will be made by the eventual use of the Royal Prerogative – the suppression of the word 'British' from the description both of Her Majesty's territories outside the United Kingdom and of the Commonwealth. Incidentally, and as a minor by-product, this suppression of our nationality has resulted in what is really nonsense. Strictly speaking, to describe the Queen as Queen of the United Kingdom and 'Her other Realms and Territories' is meaningless.

We describe a Monarch by designating the territory of which he is Monarch. To say that he is Monarch of a certain territory and his other realms and territories is as good as to say that he is king of his kingdom. We have perpetrated a solecism in the title we are proposing to attach to our Sovereign and we have done so out of what might almost be called an abject desire to eliminate the expression 'British'. The same desire has been felt – though not by any means throughout the British Commonwealth – to eliminate this word before the term 'Commonwealth'. I noticed that the Leader of the Opposition in Australia also said that: 'He thought the time had come to change the description of the Commonwealth in the Statute of Westminster as the "British Commonwealth of Nations" into the "British Commonwealth".'

Why is it, then, that we are so anxious, in the description of our own Monarch, in a title for use in this country, to eliminate any reference to the seat, the focus and the origin of this vast aggregation of territories? Why is it that this 'teeming womb of royal Kings', as Shakespeare called it, wishes now to be anonymous?

When we come to the following part of the title we find the reason. The history of the term 'Head of the Commonwealth' is not a difficult one to trace. I hope I may be forgiven if I do so very briefly. The British Nationality Act, 1948, removed the status of 'subject of the King' as the basis of British nationality, and substituted for allegiance to the Crown the concept of a number – I think it was nine – of separate citizenships combined together by statute. The British Nationality Act, 1948, thus brought about an immense constitutional revolution, an entire alteration of the basis of our subjecthood and nationality, and since the fact of allegiance to the Crown was the uniting element of the whole Empire and Commonwealth it brought about a cor-

responding revolution in the nature of the unity of Her Majesty's dominions.

The consequence of that Act immediately followed. If the British dominions were not those territories which acknowledged the Queen, but were an aggregation of separate countries enumerated in a statute, it might be possible not only to add or to subtract, but for any of those territories to throw off their allegiance without any consequential result; and that was, in fact, what happened.

In the following year, India declared its intention to renounce its allegiance to the Crown and become a republic. Because of that change in the whole basis of unity of this great entity, that intention did not involve the consequences which would have followed as little as a year before. The declaration of the Prime Minister, of 28 April 1949, included the following passage:

The Government of India have declared and affirmed India's desire to continue with her full membership of the Commonwealth of Nations and her acceptance of the King as the symbol of the free association of those independent member nations and as such the Head of the Commonwealth.

It was accordingly enacted by the India (Consequential Provision) Act, 1949, that the law of this country should continue to apply to India as it would have done if India had not renounced its allegiance to the Crown. The result of that is, as we have found in a queer way in the only definition of the term 'Commonwealth' on the Statute Book – it occurs in one of the sections of the Finance Bill, 1950, because a Member of the then Opposition put down an Amendment to draw attention to the omission – that the Commonwealth consists of 'Her Majesty's dominions and India'.

The status of India resulting from these changes and declarations is an ungraspable one in law or in fact. The Indian Government say that they recognise the Queen as the head of the Commonwealth. Well, I recognise the right hon. Member for Walthamstow, West (Mr Attlee) as Leader of the Opposition, but that does not make me a Member of Her Majesty's Opposition.

Mr Frederick Messer (Tottenham): Thank God.

Mr Powell: I see, Mr Speaker, that any serious remarks on this subject must be addressed to hon. Members on this side of the House.

When we endeavour to ascertain into what relationship with Her Majesty's dominions this recognition of the Crown as Head of the Commonwealth has brought India, we find ourselves baulked. It was intended that this relationship should, in fact, be uninterpretable. It is, therefore, necessary to inquire what is the minimum content which entitles us to recognise unity at all, and then to ask whether that necessary minimum content is applicable in the case of India.

I assert that the essence of unity, whether it be in a close-knit country or in a loosely-knit federation, is that all the parts recognise that in certain circumstances they would sacrifice themselves to the interests of the whole. It is this instinctive recognition of being parts of a whole, which means that in certain circumstances individual, local, partial interests would be sacrificed to the general interest, that constitutes unity. Unless there is some such instinctive, deliberate determination, there is no unity. There may be alliance, indeed. We may have alliance between two sovereign Powers for the pursuit of common interest for a particular or for an undefined period, but that is not unity. That is not the maintenance or the creation of any such entity as we refer to by the name 'Empire' or 'Commonwealth'.

I deny that there is that element, that minimum basic element, of unity binding India to Her Majesty's dominions. I deny that there is present, in that former part of Her Majesty's dominions which has deliberately cast off allegiance to her, that minimum, basic, instinctive recognition of belonging to a greater whole which involves the ultimate consequence in certain circumstances of self-sacrifice in the interests of the whole.

I therefore say that this formula 'Head of the Common-wealth' and the declaration in which it is inscribed, are essentially a sham. They are essentially something which we have invented to blind ourselves to the reality of the position. Although the changes which will be made in the Royal titles as the result of the Bill are greatly repugnant to me, if they were changes which were demanded by those who in many wars had fought with this country, by nations who maintained an allegiance to the Crown, and who signified a desire to be in the future as we were in the past; if it were our friends who had come to us and said: 'We want this,' I would say: 'Let it go. Let us admit the divisibility of the Crown. Let us sink into anonymity and cancel the word "British" from our titles. If they like the conundrum "Head of the Commonwealth" in the Royal style, let it be there.'

However, the underlying evil of this is that we are doing it for the sake not of our friends but of those who are not our friends. We are doing this for the sake of those to whom the very names 'Britain' and 'British' are repugnant –

Mr Gordon Walker: Would the hon. Gentleman –

Mr Powell: We are doing this for the sake of those who have deliberately cast off their allegiance to our common Monarchy.

Hon Members: Who are they?

Mr Nicholson: They died in thousands during the war.

Mr Hector Hughes (Aberdeen, North) *rose* –

Mr Nicholson: I appreciate my hon. Friend's giving way, and I thank him. I beg him to measure his words and to remember the vast sacrifices and the oceans of blood that India has poured out in the past, and to recognise the deep affection and feeling that exist throughout India towards this country.

Mr Powell: I am obliged to my hon. Friend. I, who have had the advantage and privilege of serving with the Indian Army in the war, am not likely to be unmindful of it; but it was an army which owed allegiance, an enthusiastic allegiance, which was its very principle of existence and its binding force, to the Crown. That allegiance, for good or for evil, has been cast off, with all that follows.

Now, I am not under any delusion that my words on this occasion can have any practical effect, but, none the less, they are not, perhaps, necessarily in vain. We in this House, whether we are the humblest of the back benchers or my right hon. Friend the First Lord of the Treasury himself, are in ourselves, in our individual capacities, quite unimportant. We have a meaning in this place only in so far as in our time and generation we represent great principles, great elements in the national life, great strands in our society and national being.

Sometimes, elements which are essential to the life, growth and existence of Britain seem for a time to be cast into shadow, obscured, and even destroyed. Yet in the past they have remained alive; they have survived; they have come to the surface again, and they have been the means of a new flowering, which no one had suspected. It is because I believe that, in a sense, for a brief moment, I represent and speak for an indispensable element in the British Constitution and in British life that I have spoken. And, I pray, not entirely in vain.

HOLA CAMP

27 July 1959

Mr J. Enoch Powell (Wolverhampton, South-West): Many aspersions have been cast and many imputations made by hon. Members opposite in the course of this debate with which I could not for an instant associate myself. And yet I cannot regret that even at this hour the House is once again considering the affair of Hola Camp. For the further documents relating to the deaths which were issued as a White Paper last week confirm what was already pretty clear from the earlier evidence, that it could be to the credit neither of this House nor of this country that the matter should rest where it now stands.

The affair of Hola Camp was a great administrative disaster, and to that administrative disaster there were three aspects. There was the authorisation of an operation which in its nature was likely to have fatal results; there was the failure to see that that operation, such as it was, was at least carried out with the minimum of risk; and, finally, there was the incident, which it is difficult to find a word to describe, of the water-cart communiqué. The new documents show that the responsibility for all three aspects of this administrative disaster goes higher than can be discharged by the premature retirement of the officer in charge of the camp or by the retirement, accelerated by a few weeks, of the Commissioner of Prisons.

The central document in the White Paper of last week, and it has often been referred to in this debate, is the minute of 17 February addressed by the Commissioner of Prisons to the Minister of Defence. That Minute enclosed two other documents. Folios 9 and 10 on the file. Folio 9 was the Cowan Plan as drafted and intended by Cowan and put up by him as a proposal to his senior officers. Folio 10 was the extraordinary message which Sullivan had sent to Cowan on the 14th which can hardly be described otherwise than as a *cri de coeur*. It is impossible to read that document without sensing through it the state of mind of the man who wrote it or being aware of the risks which were attendant upon the situation which it reveals.

I will only remind the House of the ominous facts which it disclosed, that the Ministry of Works on the site had asked to be 'disassociated entirely from any such operation' and the request for a senior superintendent, 'with appropriate powers of summary punishment', to 'be present when the policy outlined is implemented'. It was clear evidence, among other things, that the Cowan Plan, Folio 9, was not what Sullivan, *vide* Folio 10, thought he was expected to implement. Incidentally, therefore, if there is blame for the failure to implement the Cowan Plan accurately, that responsibility must rest on all those who should have became aware, through seeing Folio 10, that Sullivan had misunderstood the Cowan Plan. With these two documents underneath, went this Minute, Folio 11, from the Commissioner of Prisons to the Minister of Defence. The Commissioner of Prisons had not yet taken a decision on the Cowan Plan. Indeed, when he saw it he gave instructions that 'no action should be taken until authority was given' by his office. When he looked at 9 and 10 together, he decided that he, on his responsibility, could not authorise any action to be taken, and submitted it to his Minister, saying – and I am sorry to quote these words again, but they are essential –

> The plans Mr Cowan worked out at (9) could be undertaken by us, but it would mean the use of a certain degree of force, in which operation someone might get hurt or even killed. I think this situation should be brought to the notice of the Security Council and

a direction given on what policy should be adopted.

He then again referred to the 'action as planned at (9) with the risk of someone getting hurt or killed'.

Those were not idle words, the reference to someone getting hurt or killed. He said in evidence to the Committee of three that the risk he had in mind that someone might get killed or hurt included 'warder staff as well as detainees'. Since the Commissioner of Prisons knew that in the Cowan Plan the numerical superiority of the warders to the detainees was to be overwhelming, the fact that he regarded the likelihood of being killed as applying to warders as well as to detainees is evidence of the degree of risk and danger which he associated in his mind with the Cowan Plan – the original, correct Cowan Plan, Folio 9. This was apart from the evidence in Folio 10 that things were going wrong, that it would not be that plan which would be put into effect, and that Sullivan had misunderstood.

He considered the responsibility for putting this into effect was not only one that he could not take, but it was one he could not advise his Minister to take alone, without reference to the Security Council.

Incidentally, the action of the Commissioner of Prisons disposes of the notion that the Cowan Plan for Hola was, as has often been said – and I quote the expression in the leading article in the *Daily Telegraph* yesterday – 'the application of a long-standing and highly successful technique of rehabilitation'. The truth is that it was the application of a modification, and a very important modification, of the technique which had elsewhere yielded good results.

When my right hon. Friend spoke in the debate on 16 June last, he was careful to put that correctly. He said: 'The proposals were the adaptation of a proved and successful technique to the circumstances of Hola' (*Official Report*, 16 June 1959; Vol. 460. *c*. 280).

They were, in fact, as proposed now in the Cowan Plan, something which represented such a serious departure from anything attempted before, something so dangerous in themselves, that he could not envisage the responsibility to carry them out being taken otherwise than by the Security Council itself.

The Minister of Defence decided that it was not necessary, and the Minister of Defence and the Minister of African Affairs took upon themselves the responsibility for authorising an operation which they had been warned involved the risk of death, in a minute accompanied by a paper which showed to anyone who cared to read it that not even that operation, dangerous as it was, was the one which Sullivan contemplated carrying out.

The hon. Lady the Member for Blackburn (Mrs Castle) was a little too kind to the Minister for African Affairs. She overlooked the fact that he as well as the Minister of Defence had all the relevant papers in front of him. Those two men took upon themselves, with their eyes open and with full knowledge, not only the responsibility for the Cowan Plan but the responsibility for allowing the deformed version of it to go forward. It was authorised – now we come to the second phase, the execution – with the indication that it should go forward 'subject to the proviso that' the Commissioner 'should first ensure that he has a sufficient number of warders at Hola to cope with possible eventualities'. So, warned of the danger implicit, aware from the SOS that all was not well, the Ministers responsible, the Ministers who had given the decision, left the matter there and just sent it down the line.

Those two men, who knew that they had authorised – without reference, as advised by the Commissioner of Prisons, to the Security Council – an operation involving the risk of death, learnt on the afternoon of 3 March that on the day on which that operation was carried out ten men had died at Hola Camp; and on 4 March, after – and these are the words of the publicity officer: 'a good deal of discussion as to whether violence was the cause of the deaths of these men' in a meeting presided over by His Excellency the Governor, they were parties to the issue of the water-cart communiqué.

Those documents, that evidence, prove to me conclusively that the responsiblity here lies not only with Sullivan and Lewis, but at a level above them. It lies with those to whom they actually appealed for help, whom they warned of the danger, from whom they received indeed a decision which transferred responsibility upwards, but no other help or guidance. That responsibility, transcending Sullivan and Lewis, has not been recognised; but it cannot be ignored, it cannot be burked, it will not just evaporate into thin air if we do nothing about it.

I am as certain of this as I am of anything, that my right hon. Friend the Secretary of State from the beginning to the end of this affair is without any jot or title of blame for what happened in Kenya, that he could not be expected to know, that it could not be within the administrative conventions that these matters should be brought to his attention before or during the execution. When I say my right hon. Friend was in this matter utterly and completely blameless, that is of a piece with his administration of his high office generally, which has been the greatest exercise of the office of Colonial Secretary in modern times. It is in the name of that record, it is in the name of

his personal blamelessness, that I beg of him to ensure that the responsibility is recognised and carried where it properly belongs, and is seen to belong.

I have heard it suggested that there were circumstances surrounding this affair at Hola Camp which, it is argued, might justify the passing over of this responsibility – which might justify one in saying, 'Well, of course, strictly speaking, that is quite correct; but then here there were special circumstances.'

It has been said – and it is a fact – that these eleven men were the lowest of the low; sub-human was the word which one of my hon. Friends used. So be it. But that cannot be relevant to the acceptance of responsibility for their deaths. I know that it does not enter into my right hon. Friend's mind that it could be relevant, because it would be completely inconsistent with his whole policy of rehabilitation, which is based upon the assumption that whatever the present state of these men, they can be reclaimed. No one who supports the policy of rehabilitation can argue from the character and condition of these men that responsibility for their deaths should be different from the responsibility for anyone else's death. In general, I would say that it is a fearful doctrine, which must recoil upon the heads of those who pronounce it, to stand in judgment on a fellow human being and to say, 'Because he was such-and-such, therefore the consequences which would otherwise flow from his death shall not flow.'

It is then said that the morale of the Prison Service, the morale of the whole Colonial Service, is above all important and that whatever we do, whatever we urge, whatever we say, should have regard to that morale. 'Amen,' say I. But is it for the morale of the Prison Service that those who executed a policy should suffer – whether inadequately or not is another question – and those who authorised it, those to whom they appealed, should be passed over? I cannot believe that that supports the morale of a service.

Going on beyond that, my hon. Friend the Member for Leicester, South-East (Mr Peel) reminded the House how proud the Colonial Service is of the integrity of its administration and its record. Nothing could be more damaging to the morale of such a service than that there should be a breath or a blemish left upon it. No, Sir; that argument from the morale of the Prison Service and the Colonial Service stands on its head if what we mean is that therefore the consequences of responsibility should not follow in this case as they would in any other similar case.

Finally it is argued that this is Africa, that things are different there. Of course they are. The question is whether the difference between things there and here is such that the taking of responsibility there and here should be upon different principles. We claim that it is our object – and this is something which unites both sides of the House – to leave representative institutions behind us wherever we give up our rule. I cannot imagine that it is a way to plant representative institutions to be seen to shirk the acceptance and the assignment of responsibility, which is the very essence of responsible Government.

Nor can we ourselves pick and choose where and in what parts of the world we shall use this or that kind of standard. We cannot say, 'We will have African standards in Africa, Asian standards in Asia and perhaps British standards here at home.' We have not that choice to make. We must be consistent with ourselves everywhere. All Government, all influence of man upon man, rests upon opinion. What we can do in Africa, where we still govern and where we no longer govern, depends upon the opinion which is entertained of the way in which this country acts and the way in which Englishmen act. We cannot, we dare not, in Africa of all places, fall below our own highest standards in the acceptance of responsibility.

SUPPLY DEFENCE

6 March 1967

Mr J. Enoch Powell (Wolverhampton, South-West): I am very grateful to the hon. Member for West Stirlingshire (Mr W. Baxter) for piping me in so briefly and so cheerfully.

This at times has seemed to be a rather Parkinsonian debate in that it might have been designed to illustrate Parkinson's Law that the number of speakers expands to fill the time available. It was opened by the Under-Secretary in an often interesting and informative speech which has been referred to as of being of a nuts-and-bolts character, though it was disappointing that he did not seem to be informed on one or two questions, not very recondite, which were put to him. But it was my hon. Friend the Member for Stroud (Mr Kershaw) who, in a most valuable speech, carried the debate to a much higher level and who set its tone.

Mr Archie Manuel (Central Ayrshire): Unusual for him.

Mr Powell: I was about to say that I was rather shocked by the levity with which it was greeted by the Secretary of State when my hon. Friend trenched upon some of the deepest questions which have to be decided in this country's defence policy. It was a levity which ill-matched the responsibility which the right hon. Gentleman bears.

Mr hon. Friend sounded the note, which has been frequently repeated throughout the debate, of anxiety and uncertainty as to the whole role and future of the British Army. It is not surprising that there should be that anxiety and uncertainty, because we have had a White Paper which has simply told us that we must now await the outcome of various discussions before knowing 'the shape and size of our defence forces in the 1970s' and referring to the intention to 'cut supporting services . . . as reductions are made in the combat forces'.

The evident embarrassment and insincerity of the Government on a number of matters relating to the future size of the Army were bound to intensify this anxiety and suspicion. For example, there is the question of the accommodation of troops returning to this country. In that period of fret and bluster last July, when we were to bring back the troops from the Continent in a matter of weeks if not days, the public was told by the Ministry of Defence that there were fourteen camps on a care and maintenance basis, earmarked – that was the word – for an eventuality such as this.

That was last July, but when last week I asked the Minister of Defence (Administration) about those fourteen camps, he told me that they had 'now been included in a larger list of camps to meet planned withdrawals as a result of the Defence Review as well as possible withdrawals from BAOR' (*Official Report*, 2 March 1967; Vol. 742, c. 154). It is perfectly obvious that most of this accommodation is being used, and will be required, for the Defence Review withdrawals, as they are called, alone. It was a piece of bluff last July.

It is a vast operation on which the Government are engaged, to accommodating the 30,000 troops which they expect to bring back from outside Europe. It is an operation for which we have not had the slightest suspicion of a costing. We have been told that it is the equivalent of producing a whole new town, but the question which my right hon. Friend the Member for Barnet (Mr Maudling) put, as to what was to be the cost of this new town has so far not been answered. Yet this concerns only the Defence Review withdrawals.

It must raise a question in one's mind and is bound to excite suspicion when it is realised that, in addition to all this, would come at least an equal operation, if not a greater one, if substantial withdrawals were to be made from BAOR, and if those troops were retained in the Services and not disbanded.

Then there was the matter of training ground. In March 1965, the Minister of Defence (Administration) said: 'We are desperately short of land where tracked vehicles can manœuvre' (*Official Report*, 8 March 1965; Vol. 708, c. 195). This was a very forthright statement, and after a time we started to inquire what had been done to meet this desperate shortage of land where tracked vehicles could manœuvre. In the debate last week the hon. Member attempted to say that everything was all right for the time being because of a reduction in the size of the Territorial Army.

When I challenged him and asked, did he really mean that the reduction in the size of the Territorial Army had met the deficiency of land for training with tracked vehicles, he said, quite candidly: 'To a slight extent that has happened . . .' (*Official Report*, 27 February 1967; Vol. 742, c. 216). To a slight extent. Of course, this is an enormous problem, a problem to which the Government have not yet seriously addressed themselves, how training land, particularly for tracked vehicles, could be found if substantial forces were to be brought back to this country from the Continent and retained with the Colours. They would need training land on which not only units, but whole formations can manoeuvre, formations including armour as well as infantry.

It was in this connection, the question of availability of training land, that the hon. Gentleman twice used his significant 'if'.

'If,' he said, 'it is necessary . . . to bring troops back from Germany, and if' – a further condition – 'such troops remain assigned to NATO . . . then there will have to be training land for them, including the armoured formations.'

And again: 'We would probably require additional land for tracked vehicle training if these troops come back from Germany and remain assigned to NATO . . .' (*Official Report*, 27 February 1967; Vol. 742, c. 216).

It is impossible to listen to that repeated hypothesis on the part of the Government without realising that this great threatened operation has barely been considered by the Government in its practical bearings – unless, of course, it is to be coupled, and there are all these indications that it is, with a reduction in the size of the British Army as a whole.

The right hon. Gentleman the Secretary of State asked in an intervention this afternoon where, in the matter of bringing forces from the Continent to this country, did this party stand? The answer has been given repeatedly, and I will give it again. In

the first place, we are resolutely opposed to any unilateral decision by this country to withdraw troops from the Continent. In the second place, we do not believe that the strength of British forces on the Continent ought to be determined by short-term foreign exchange considerations, especially when we are entering upon a year in which – the Chancellor of the Exchequer told us, a day or two ago – we shall have a surplus on our balance of payments sufficient to make massive repayments of debt. Finally, we believe that this is a matter which must be decided with our allies, upon a long and profound view, both of the military and political implications.

This brings me to the great central question which seems to dwarf all others in the field of defence. I raise it particularly within the framework of the Army Estimates and the manpower Vote, for though the answer which is given to this question must affect profoundly the future of all three Services, its effect upon the future of the British Army is beyond all comparison far reaching.

Mr Denis Healey: With respect, the question I put to his hon. Friend referred not to possible withdrawals from Germany, but to the withdrawals already planned from outside Europe. [Hon. Members: 'No.'] Oh, yes. His hon. Friend was arguing that the cost of accommodating those people would offset the savings. The question I asked him was, was he in favour of moving those people outside Europe back to the United Kingdom or not? We have not had an answer to that question yet.

Mr Powell: It appears from the sounds from behind me and elsewhere that my recollection is not the only one that it was the issue of the size of BAOR on which that question was put. However, this can be settled when we look up the record.

I am referring to what I may perhaps for convenience call 'the nuclear assumption'. Stated in bald terms, this assumption is that there can never again be a war which threatens the safety of this nation, because if such a war were ever to commence it must speedily be terminated by the inconceivable catastrophe of the nuclear exchange. To accept this assumption is to take a decision of the utmost gravity for the future of our country. For if our military preparations were based on it – and logically they must be, if it is accepted – then, in the event of its proving to be wrong, we should have thrown away the means of rational self-defence and stand, like Wolsey, 'naked to our enemies'.

It would be the ultimate, unforgivable miscalculation, and an awe-inspiring responsibility is entailed upon those who accept this assumption. Clearly, it is the duty of us all not only anxiously

to examine and re-examine it, but to give the benefit of any doubt rather against than for it. It is in this spirit and with that sense of responsibility that I want to challenge the sway of the nuclear assumption tonight.

The assumption is accepted by the Government: 'It is difficult to believe' – they say in the White Paper – 'that any rational government . . . would reckon to achieve by the use of force against Western Europe any political objective whose value would be remotely commensurate with the appalling risks.' That is, the risks of going nuclear. In the Minister's words, '. . . a Western nuclear response to deliberate aggression in Europe is inevitable . . .' (*Official Report*, 27 February 1967, Vol. 742. *c.* 113).

Inevitable – that is his word. Hence the only war, in the ordinary sense of the word 'war', for which we have ever to be prepared is the brief pre-nuclear phase of a few days or even a few hours. That is why, for instance, the White Paper says that 'it is no longer realistic . . . to attempt to provide maritime forces for conducting a prolonged war at sea after a nuclear exchange', dismissing as non-existent the possibility of a prolonged war at sea without a nuclear exchange or before a nuclear exchange.

Mr Emrys Hughes: Before the right hon. Gentleman leaves the nuclear assumption –

Mr Powell: I think that I am going to take most of the questions which the hon. Gentleman would think of putting to me. I shall be on the nuclear assumption for the next twenty minutes, so perhaps the hon. Gentleman will be a little patient.

No wonder that the right hon. Gentleman the Member for Easington (Mr Shinwell), with his octogenarian common sense, pointed out last Monday that in this case one needed very few forces at all.

In my submission, this assumption is untenable, and is only, in modern dress, our old friend, the hoary, perilous delusion that 'There will never be another war', which those of my generation remember having heard before, just as we remember two wars that were going to be 'over by Christmas' because a long war was supposed to be no longer possible. The first one lasted four and a quarter years, and the second lasted six years.

But let me, at the outset, identify if I can as many areas of agreement as possible before I come to the difference. First, I accept that as long as nuclear weapons exist, there is always a possibility that they will be used at some stage in a conflict. I do not see how this can be denied. If the nuclear assumption asserted no more than that – that is, that the possibility of the nuclear exchange cannot be excluded – I would have no quarrel with it. Secondly, I accept as self-evident that the existence of nuclear weapons other than one's own is a deterrent to using them. In the words of Part II of last year's Defence White Paper,

> . . . the nuclear strategic forces exist to deter any nation from mounting a nuclear attack against ourselves or our allies. To achieve this, the nuclear forces must be seen to be able to inflict an unacceptable degree of damage on any nation contemplating a nuclear attack.

Notice the careful, and in my view logically correct, insertion each time of the word 'nuclear'. Whoever drafted those sentences might well have had in mind Sir Basil Liddell Hart's dictum that the nuclear weapon is a deterrent to nuclear war but not to war.

Here I part company with the hon. and learned Member for Northampton (Mr Paget) at that point of his important argument on the Navy Estimates last Wednesday when he dismissed the British Polaris fleet as void of effect because of its relatively small scale. Certainly no deterrent is absolute; but I suggest that if in August 1945 Japan had been known or even suspected to possess and to be able to deliver a fraction of the atomic power of the allies, the horrors of Hiroshima and Nagasaki would very likely never have happened. However the efficacy of nuclear weapons to deter nuclear war and the worth-whileness of Britain's nuclear weapons for this purpose is common ground with the Government, if not with their so-called supporters.

Mr Mayhew: The right hon. Gentleman said that nuclear weapons never deter conventional war. Does he suggest that if Nasser had had nuclear weapons, Suez would have taken place?

Mr Powell: I am about to deal with the question whether nuclear weapons deter non-nuclear war. I have admitted so far, and I accept, that they are a probable and valid deterrent to nuclear war.

Finally, before I come to the point to which the hon. Member sought to bring me, I go further, and I agree with the right hon. Gentleman that there is no significant hurdle between tactical and strategic nuclear weapons, to use those horribly inappropriate adjectives. As he said last week: 'within days of starting to use nuclear weapons, organised warfare would become impossible' (*Official Report*, 27 February 1967; Vol. 742, *c*. 111). In other words, I accept, as he does, if not the inevitability, the high probability of nuclear escalation. Once you go nuclear at all, you go nuclear for good; and you know it.

Here is the parting of the ways, for from this point two opposite conclusions can be drawn. One is that therefore there can never again be serious war of any dur-

ation between Western nations, including Russia – in particular, that there can never again be serious war on the Continent of Europe or the waters around it, which an enemy must master in order to threaten Britain. That is the Government's position.

The other conclusion, therefore, is that resort is most unlikely to be had to nuclear weapons at all, but that war could nevertheless develop as if they did not exist, except of course that it would be so conducted as to minimise any possibility of misapprehension that the use of nuclear weapons was imminent or had begun.

The crucial question is whether there is any stage of a European war at which any nation would choose self-annihilation in preference to prolonging the struggle. The Secretary of State says, 'Yes, the loser or likely loser would almost instantly choose self-annihilation.' I say, 'No. The probability, though not the certainty, but surely at least the possibility, is that no such point would come, whatever the course of the conflict.'

The right hon. Gentleman has expressed the core of his argument in those two terrifying sentences to which my right hon. Friend the Member for Flint, West (Mr Birch) devoted a brief but trenchant analysis last week. I must read them again: '. . . there is no country on the Continent,' said the right hon. Gentleman, which does not believe that a prolonged conventional war would inflict damage on it quite as difficult to bear as the damage resulting from a strategic nuclear exchange. This is not an option which any of our European allies has the slightest intention of accepting (*Official Report*, 27 February 1967; Vol. 742, *c*. 112).

Those are the right hon. Gentleman's words. In other words, every European nation has resolved to choose nuclear annihilation rather than fight to win or lose.

Mr Healey: No.

Mr Powell: Let me translate that into terms of a real situation which we all remember. Suppose that in September, 1939, all parties had possessed whatever nuclear capability one chooses but that otherwise everything was as it was in reality. I ask, would Reynaud, in June 1940, have destroyed his country? Would Churchill have destroyed ours in September 1940, if the Battle of Britain had failed to deny the Channel to the invasion barges?

If that seems to be making it too easy, take Poland in 1939. Would the Poles, even if they had foreseen the years of crucifixion which lay before them, have chosen rather not to exist? In all these cases the answer, I believe, is 'No, in all human probability not.' If so, it follows that as reasonable beings we have to be prepared to fight for our country,

not despair of it and make ready to destroy it. In making and being seen to make preparations to fight with reasonable prospect of survival and victory lies the longest hope of peace.

To those who argue as I have just done, two great objections are always made. One is that no such European war is in prospect; that in the words of the White Paper, 'Though it is not, perhaps, inconceivable that because of some fundamental change in the world situation the threat to Western Europe might revive, such a change is most unlikely to develop overnight.'

Very likely. We are not today, to use analogy, at 1935, let alone 1937 or 1939. But there is a relativity which is vital to all thinking about defence. It is that political circumstances can change, and the assumptions of foreign policy can be stood on their heads, in a much shorter time than is required to gain a new military capability or to regain an existing one which has been lost. If we were to dispossess ourselves of the capability of fighting a conventional war for the safety of these islands and Western Europe, we might not be in a position to acquire it again once a specific threat became unmistakable.

Mr Healey: I should like the right hon. Gentleman to make clear to the House and the country whether he believes, therefore, that the British Government should prepare itself to fight and win a purely conventional war in Europe.

Mr Powell: I will not leave that point undealt with.

Mr Healey: Answer my question, 'yes' or 'no', now.

Mr Powell: This is my speech. I will make it in my own time and in my own order.

As I was saying, this is the reason why those hon. Gentlemen opposite are so mistaken and so dangerous who demand imperiously to be told who is the enemy before they will consent to a defensive capability being required or maintained.

There is, moreover, a certain relationship of cause and effect. The declaration, as a matter of settled policy, that a nation does not contemplate defending itself otherwise than in the sense of committing suicide is bound to affect the balance of power of which that nation is a part. I adopt some wise words spoken last week by the Foreign Secretary, they contain a sentiment expressed by a number of my hon. Friends, and I commend to the House the whole passage in which they appear. He said:

We cannot leave Central European countries to face by themselves the problems they have had to face before. So long as we and the United States are there in sufficient strength, some of the things which we all of us think dangerous – even disastrous – will not happen. (*Offical Report*, 28 February 1967; Vol. 742, *c*. 288).

As we learnt between 1918 and 1939, mortal danger to a nation does not arise suddenly like a summer thunderstorm. It creeps upon it, stealthily, by gradual stages, at none of which extreme measures appear either necessary or justified – until, at last, simply because we had rested our safety upon the theoretical alternative of no war or the nuclear exchange, we might find ourselves one day faced with that very alternative in practice; and be forced to resolve it by choosing surrender.

I come to the other objection, in which the right hon. Gentleman sought to anticipate me. It is alleged that to provide the reasonable means to defend ourselves and Western Europe, along with our allies, in a perhaps prolonged conventional war would be altogether beyond our capability or, at least, beyond our will. There are several fallacies in this argument, all rolled up together.

It is true that the nuclear assumption is the cheapest form of defence ever thought of. Taken literally, it makes it possible to dispense with the great bulk of all military forces and preparations other than nuclear. It is, of course, cheaper still if, like some hon. Gentlemen opposite, one is prepared to leave even that to somebody else. But whereas between two courses of action within our own control we are entitled, if we wish, to choose the cheaper, we are not entitled to choose the cheaper of two assumptions about the future course of events and the behaviour of others. There we dare take only reason and probability for our guide, for there is no ground for supposing that what is cheap and convenient for us is therefore probable.

Of course, if it were true that it would be quite beyond our capability to fight a European war with any rational chance of victory, then that might have to be accepted. But what reason is there for supposing that to be true? There is no such inferiority either of industrial capacity or of manpower on the part of Britain and any likely combination of allies, compared with any likely combination of enemies, as to make the contest a priori unsustainable, expecially if we take into account the degree of superiority which it is generally considered necessary for a successful aggressor to possess.

It may indeed be that the present conventional forces in Europe, of the present North Atlantic Alliance, are not capable of defeating an aggression by the Warsaw Pact Powers, though even this is by no means as self-evident nor so firmly held by professional opinion as is commonly supposed; but that is not what the argument requires. The Government themselves regard such an aggression as far from imminent. As the right hon. Gentleman said, if Soviet policy '. . . were to change, all sorts of political indications that a change was under way would reach the West long before military intelligence was received on the physical movements of forces which must precede aggression' (*Official Report*, 27 February 1967; Vol. 742, *c.* 111).

What the argument does require is that we should have the ability, by the time such aggression was mounted, to oppose to it, with our allies, such forces as might have a rational prospect of eventual victory.

For the Service whose Estimates are before the House that means, to adopt a famous phrase from naval theory, that Britain must have 'an army in being', an army equal in armament, training and philosophy to any other in Europe, and of such dimensions and structure, and supported by such reserves, as to be able, and to be seen to be able, to play an important and continuing part in Continental warfare; a part which would make it the cement and fulcrum of the indispensable alliance.

If there is to be a British Army in the years to come – and I confess I cannot conceive that a nation such as ours in size, position and potential could be without a substantial military capability on land – then to be such 'an army in being' must be its *raison d'être* and its principal purpose.

I sometimes think that the magnitude of the reorientation which lies before the British Army, far beyond what is imposed on either of the other Services, is rarely grasped. It has been concealed from us in the last twenty years by the very existence of BAOR and NATO as they emerged, without a decisive break, from the circumstances in which the last war terminated. This has enabled us to forget that in 1939 there were 46,000 British soldiers in India, large numbers in Egypt and the Far East, as well as in garrisons east and west right round the world. The British Army was then, as it had been for the greater part of two centuries – except when we were fighting for our lives – a colonial or imperial army, with the establishments in Europe serving to recruit, train, reinforce and relieve it.

That Army has gone for ever. On any possible view, the proportion of British troops outside Europe in a few years' time will be only a minority. There has to be a new basis, a new concept of what the Army is about, a new main purpose. This main purpose can only be to provide such 'an army in being', as I have defined, for the defence of Britain in Western Europe. From that main purpose all else – organisation, training, location, reserves – will fall logically to be derived.

But there is an underlying prior decision which has to be taken first. It is a question which the hon. Member and I resolve in an opposite sense – whether we intend to be able to defend ourselves at all, in the rational, human sense of that term. That is why it is vital that the issue of nuclear assumption, which denies alike the possibility, the desirability and the necessity of rational defence, should be fought through to a finish. On the rightness of our answer may hang not only the future of the British Army, but the existence of the nation.

EUROPEAN COMMUNITIES BILL

17 February 1972

Mr J. Enoch Powell (Wolverhampton, South-West): This Second Reading debate is the first occasion upon which the House of Commons has ever had before it as a specific proposal the proposition of British membership of the European Economic Community. It is the first time that we have ever debated this matter in the form and in the way in which this House historically takes its decisions; for it is part of its habit and its shrewd wisdom that it does not take its decisions on matters of theory, on hypothetical possibilities, upon approving or disapproving White Papers. It takes its real decisions – and examination of its history at the moments when it has asserted its power and vindicated the liberties of the people will prove this – on the occasions when specific legislative propositions are put before it. Now is the first time that we are asked in that form to consider British membership of the Community and its consequences.

This is why it has been – worse than a waste of time – a vanity and vexation of spirit, to listen to the cross-fire of quotation and counter-quotation. It does not help us or rescue us from the necessity of taking our decision now, and perhaps in the days to come, to refer to a White Paper of last year, or three years ago or ten years ago, or to what some other right hon. Gentleman said several years before. We are approaching this question for the first time as a practical one. Never till now has the House of Commons had placed before it proposed legislation on which it must take a definitive view and on which it must envisage as a pratical issue what it will mean for this country if we accede to the Community.

The Bill, whatever its defects, does manifest some of the major consequences. It shows first that it is an inherent consequence of accession to the Treaty of Rome that this House and Parliament will lose their legislative supremacy. It will no longer be true that law in this country is made only by or with the authority of Parliament – which in practice means the authority of this House. The legislative omnicompetence of this House, its legislative sovereignty, has to be given up.

The second consequence, which is equally manifest upon the face of the Bill, is that this House loses its exclusive control – upon which its power and authority has been built over the centuries – over taxation and expenditure. In future, if we become part of the Community, moneys received in taxation from the citizens of this country will be spent otherwise than upon a vote of this House and without the opportunity, necessarily preceding such a vote, to debate grievance and to call for an account of the way in which those moneys are to be spent. For the first time for centuries it will be true to say that the people of this country are not taxed only upon the authority of the House of Commons.

The third consequence which is manifest on the face of the Bill, in Clause 3 among other places, is that the judicial independence of this country has to be given up. In future, if we join the Community, the citizens of this country will not only be subject to laws made elsewhere but the applicability of those laws to them will be adjudicated upon elsewhere; and the law made elsewhere and the adjudication elsewhere will override the law which is made here and the decisions of the courts of this realm.

Those three facts, those essential sacrifices of sovereignty, are evident upon the face of the Bill;

and they are not disputed, although they are sought to be qualified, and I will come presently to the qualifications. There is, however, a fourth consequence which, though not manifest, is inherent and implicit. That is the progressive strengthening of the Executive as compared with this House, or, to put it the other way, the continuing diminution of the power of this House to influence and control the Executive, as I will presently prove.

Let me come first to the two grounds on which the propositions I have stated are – not disputed; they cannot be, they are in the Bill – but upon which it is sought to palliate them and render them palatable. The first is the *de minimis* argument – 'Don't worry; it's not very important, because it will not refer to many subjects or very important matters.' The second is the remonstrance: 'Don't worry, because, at any rate in future, we' – whoever 'we' is – 'will be participating in whatever decisions result in the overriding authority of the Community being exercised in this country.'

I will take those two arguments in order. First, the *de minimis* argument. Of course, it is true that at present the great majority of Community law which will become part of our law, either directly and automatically under Clause 2 (1) or by directive through legislation or the regulation-making process, refers to two subjects. It refers to the common tariff and what is implicit in that; and it refers to the common agricultural policy, in the broadest sense of the term. Although these are important matters – many of us would consider that they are far-reaching in their consequences – they are still relatively narrow compared with the whole sweep of administration and legislation.

But this is intended to be only a start. Of course, the receptacle which is formed by Clause 2 will not initially have much put inside it. It starts life by no means full; but it is a receptacle which is intended progressively to contain more and more external powers, legislation and decisions. It is a receptacle created to be progressively filled.

Let me put it in practical terms to my right hon. and learned Friend. Imagine it was proposed to him during subsequent stages of the Bill: 'Very well; we take you at your word, that it is only on these two subjects, broadly speaking, that these cessions of sovereignty are to occur. Let us then have an amendment; let us write in words which will limit the applicability of Clause 2 to those two subjects.' My right hon. and learned Friend would instantly repudiate any such proposition. He would have to, because the argument, the ground, on which British membership of the Community has been eloquently argued by himself, the Prime Minister and all its greatest advo-

cates is not that the effect will be minimal but that this is intended to lead progressively to the political unification of this country with the countries of Western Europe. That has been said candidly, frankly, over and over again. So, although this surrender begins as minimal, it is intended to become maximal: and that intention is implicit in the policy and declarations of the Government.

Then they say, passing to the other defence, 'Ah, yes: but then, as this develops, as we go from the minimal to the maximal, at each stage – in the making of each new regulation, in the entry of the Community into each new area – we, the United Kingdom, will be a party to the decision; and since the Government are sitting in this House, since the Government will still be responsible to this House, it will be this House which will, in effect, still control the elaboration of Community law and Community powers and the progress of political unification at each stage.'

This is the argument – that we in this House will still be in charge. Let us examine this process stage by stage. Let us take it for convenience in the case of a regulation – not one of those regulations which, as the right hon. Member for Battersea, North (Mr Jay) pointed out, can be made by the Commission by itself, but one of those more substantial regulations which are made by the Council of Ministers. My right hon. and learned Friend announced that it was intended to consider ways in which this House could be 'apprised' of proposed regulations. This is generous, that we should at least have the opportunity of knowing what is going on. But it is not by being 'apprised' of what is proposed that this House exerts its control or ever has done. It has been done by the power to vote upon it and, potentially, to throw it out. However, at that stage, it would be only a draft: there would be no point, when we were 'apprised' of the proposed regulation, for example, or of the proposed development of the Community, in throwing it out. We should be invited to take note of it. The views expressed on both sides of the House would be taken into account, 'with great interest'. One can almost rehearse the wind-up speech which would be heard from the Government Bench.

Then the Minister goes to the Council of Ministers and eventually, sooner or later, he comes back with the decision, the common decision. If it is in the form of a regulation or if it involves legislation or if it is merely an act which can be implemented by the Executive, this House once again can address itself to it. We can address ourselves to it, but can we deal with it as we now deal with every proposition which comes from the Executive? There

was an interesting exchange on Tuesday between the hon. Member for West Stirlingshire (Mr W. Baxter) and my right hon. and learned Friend. The hon. Member for West Stirlingshire asked: '. . . if when the Minister reports back and a debate takes place . . .' – that is the stage we have reached in our imaginary journey – '. . . the decision of Parliament is against the decision of the Common Market Communities, how would we resolve that situation?' My right hon. and learned Friend correctly replied: 'That would be in breach of the treaty' (*Official Report*, 15 February 1972; Vol. 831, *c.* 275). A fine basis for asserting the continued control of this House over the Executive, to be able to say, 'But we can break the treaty'! Of course all treaties can be broken. In that sense no parliament can bind its successors. All agreements can be scrapped, all engagements can be reneged upon. Is that the dishonour that this House intends – to enter into this with the *arrière pensée* that if we do not like anything that comes out of it we can always break the treaty?

No, the clear fact is that at no stage will the House of Commons be able to take a decision with binding effect, neither before consideration in the Council of Ministers nor after a Community decision. Not only can this House in those circumstances take no binding decision, but neither it nor any future House can revere that decision. And here we come to one of the most fundamental truths of this whole debate, that the power of this House depends, in the last resort, upon its power, humanly speaking, to reverse previous decisions; and not only the power of this House, but the power of those whose servants we are – the electorate. What meaning has the right of the electorate to send hon. Members here unless, so far as legislation and administration can bring it about, what has been done in the past can, if the electors desire it, be reversed?

So it is implicit and inherent in the nature of the Community that the control of this House over the Executive is progressively diminished, and consequently that the self-government of the electorate is diminished.

Let no one say that it is rare for something proposed by the Government to be thrown out. This would be a very simplisitic objection. How often does it happen in a game of chess that the king is actually taken off the chess board? Yet one could not play a game of chess if it were not possible to take the king. It is the knowledge that this House can defeat the proposals of the Executive – and if not this House, then a future House of Commons – upon which the power and authority of this House depend, and upon which depends the thing that we in this country call democracy.

There is something else. Criti-cism of the Executive is not always, perhaps not mostly, negative. We do not only come to the House and say to the Executive, 'Why have you done this, or why are you proposing to do this? We do not like it.' We also say often enough – it is the stuff and matter of Supply debates – 'Why don't you do what you are not doing or are failing to do?'

In the Community, however, the Executive has no initiative. The initiative lies, by the consti-tution of the Community, with the Commission. We cannot say to the Government, 'Why do you not do this?', just as, when some-thing is done by the Council of Ministers and by the Community, we cannot effectively call them to account for what they have done. So it remains a fact that, as the Community develops with this country as a member of it, so the control of this House and of the people of this country will dimin-ish and shrivel.

Now, I am very far from saying that there are no circumstances in which it would be right, wise, beneficial, for a country with its eyes open to surrender its sover-eignty; that even for Britain – the extreme example perhaps – there are no circumstances in which it would be right, necessary per-haps, to say that we would give up all we have historically clung to, the sovereignty of this House, or judicial independence, the control of the House of Com-mons over taxation and expenditure, in return for something which we hope to gain thereby. There is nothing inherently impossible in such a proposition. But there is a condition attached to such a course being embraced. What is given up, what is paid, is not the personal property of hon. Members of this House or of any one Parliament, but comes from and is held as a trust for the entire people of this country.

It follows that for such a course to be taken it is indispensably necessary that it should be seen to be willed, and heartily willed, by the overwhelming majority of the people.

Mr Wilkinson: Will my right hon. Friend give way?

Mr Powell: We are all in this debate speaking under great constraint of time, and I hope that on this occasion my hon. Friend will excuse me.

Such is the nature of this decision, that that condition necessarily attaches to it. That, of course, is the significance of the famous words of my right hon. Friend the Prime Minister about the full-hearted consent of Parliament and people. Those words were not plucked up as a verbal infelicity for which he was to be held to account. They have become so famous because they enshrine a manifest and necessary truth.

That condition does not exist. I will take it in its two parts – the people first. I do not think that any hon. Member would be bold enough to say that he believed he could claim the full-hearted consent, the strong positive will, of the people of this country to give up all the things we know we have to give up in order to join the European Community. Let me put it more personally to my hon. and right hon. Friends here. Most of us in this Chamber, not myself, did not happen to mention the European Community in their election addresses –

Sir G. Nabarro (Worcestershire, South): I did.

Mr Powell: Some did, but most did not. I ask hon. and right hon. Members to address to themselves this question: 'Did I tell the electorate in June 1970, whether or not I was in favour of entry?' – [Hon. Members: 'Yes.'] I will complete the sentence. 'Did hon. Members tell their electorate, whether or not they were in favour' – [Hon. Members: 'Yes.'] I will start again; the syntactical construction was apparently a little too difficult. 'Whether or not hon. Members were, or expressed themselves, in favour of joining the Community, did they say to their electors plainly that they were in favour of this House giving up its legislative supremacy and surrendering its control over taxation and expenditure and of an overriding superimposition of courts and laws over the courts and laws of this country?' If they said that – and only if they said that – and if, moreover, they said that this would be done without further reference to the electorate, then they had some excuse at any rate for neglecting the evidence, which I do not believe anyone can seriously neglect, that the people of this country have not given their full-hearted consent to any such thing.

Mr Rippon: But surely my right hon. Friend must understand that we all made our position perfectly clear about parliamentary power and sovereignty when we, like my right hon. Friend, supported the original application to join?

Sir T. Beamish: And in 1967, too.

Mr Powell: If my right hon. and learned Friend believes that it was made clear to the electors at the last election that this was to be the price of British membership of the Community – a membership which was proposed to them not, as it is now for the first time being proposed to this House, as a practical proposition, but only as something which would be negotiated – then indeed he belongs to a very small number of exceptions.

However, it is said, 'Let it be Parliament that decides. Let us wrap it up, so that what we are talking about is the full-hearted consent of the House of Commons.' There was a debate in October – a debate which did not

deal with a precise proposition such as this – when the House decided affirmatively by a vote of seven-twelfths in favour. In no country with a written constitution, in none of the other countries which are participating in this operation with the United Kingdom, would such a proportion justify the major step which is involved in joining the Community. All of them have safeguards which require a much more generous margin even than that on which the House voted on 28 October.

Sir T. Beamish: May I ask my right hon. Friend why he voted for the principle of entry in 1967 when there was a majority of more than 400 in this House? He has not answered that question.

Mr Powell: That vote was in favour of negotiation – [An Hon. Member: 'Genuine negotiation.'] – In favour of genuine negotiation but, as I said earlier – and I do not know whether my hon. and gallant Friend the Member for Lewes (Sir T. Beamish) was here – we none of us have the right, faced with this Bill, to go back to White Papers and declarations in previous years. [Hon. Members: 'Oh!'] None of us can shelter behind the past. We each have to take our decision in the open upon the proposition which is now before the House.

Before I conclude, I want to glance at the state of full-hearted consent in this House now. Is it a full-hearted consent which is anticipated from this House as the necessary legislative condition of British membership of the Community? My right hon. Friends on the Front Bench do not think so. My right hon. Friend the Prime Minister does not think so. In order to secure a narrow majority in the Division tonight, they have brought to bear upon hon. Members of different views, despite my right hon. Friend's assurance that they would have an absolute right to vote as they so decided on this question, every available form of pressure. Is that a sign of belief? [*Interruption.*] One hon. Friend behind me says that we are not voting on the Common Market.

Indeed we are, and it is on the Common Market that it will be shown tonight that there is not full-hearted consent in this House.

For this House, lacking the necessary authority either out-of-doors or indoors, legislatively to give away the independence and sovereignty of this House now and for the future is an unthinkable act. Even if there were not those outside to whom we have to render account, the very stones of this place would cry out against us if we dared such a thing. We are here acting not only collectively but as individuals; and each hon. Member takes his own responsibility upon himself – as I do, when I say for myself, 'It shall not pass.'

FALKLAND ISLANDS

29 April 1982

Mr J. Enoch Powell (Down, South): Earlier this week the right hon. Gentleman the Leader of the Opposition said: 'We are supposed to act under the authority of the United Nations. Indeed, it is the only authority under which we are supposed to act.' And again, that 'we act in this matter only under the United Nations charter' (*Official Report*, 27 April 1982: Vol. 22, *c.* 720–23). In fact, that was also the purport of much of his speech this afternoon.

With the greatest possible respect, I doubt whether that definition by the right hon. Gentleman is correct. The right of self-defence – to repel aggression and to expel an invader from one's territory and one's people whom he has occupied and taken captive – is, as the Government have said, an inherent right. It is one which existed before the United Nations was dreamt of. True, it has been accommodated and given a definition in the United Nations charter. However, it is not under that authority that we exercise it: we exercise it as a right which is inherent in us. It is as such that both the British Government and, in large measure, the British people have resolved that we ought to place ourselves in a position to exercise that right, namely, by force, if necessary, to repel the aggression and to repossess our territory.

That resolve, which I believe is widespread not only in the House but outside it, carries with it some important implications. One is that having willed and approved that action we must, as a nation, be prepared to take the consequences. It is much easier to overestimate the ease than to overestimate the difficulty of any military operation. No course of armed action, however justly embarked upon, however necessarily embarked upon, can be foreseen in all its consequences and repercussions. When we took the decision which we did two or three weeks ago, and which we are following through now, it ought to be understood that we were accepting and expressing the will, if necessary, to maintain a long and difficult course of action in which there may be reverses and severe losses. We must not allow that to be misunderstood or played down outside the House.

There are two other grave implications of our having taken

this action, of our having resolved that, if necessary, we will place the lives of our forces, as well as of other human beings, at risk. It has often been said in the last few weeks that, even if we repossess the Falkland Islands, that outcome is unstable because we cannot stay there, cannot maintain possession. If that were true, it would be highly irresponsible, if not absurd, for us to say that we are ready to face what we have willed and decided, with all its implications, in order to make good a right which we cannot thereafter maintain.

However, the proposition is unsound. The notion that if, by whatever means, we regain the administration of the Falkland Islands and reassert our sovereignty in practical terms it will be a mere passing phase is demonstrably false; it is false because if this Argentine adventure ends sooner or later in the fiasco that it deserves, it will be a long time before anyone will think of repeating it. It is wrong also because if we, the third naval power in the world, a country in the North Atlantic uniquely dependent for its existence upon the ability to command the seas and the air which are relevant to its defence, are unable, in defence of a island group hundreds of miles from the nearest continent, to maintain the necessary availability of strength, and the necessary command of the sea, so that our possession of the Falkland Islands is of a precari-

ous character, we had better resign any notion that we might have had of being able to defend ourselves in our island home in the North Atlantic. The ocean is one, and the ability to command the ocean is one. The interests and the power of a maritime nation are wherever the sea is. Therefore, when we repossess the Falkland Islands –

Mr Andrew Faulds (Warley, East): Hong Kong, Gibraltar.

Mr Powell: The words 'Hong Kong, Gibraltar' are being voiced by somebody who evidently does not use an atlas. Hong Kong is under the lee of a continent.

Mr Faulds: No ocean around it?

Mr Powell: It is commanded by a continent. Gibraltar –

Mr Faulds: No ocean?

Mr Powell: Gibraltar is also under the lee of a continental land mass and effectively commanded by it. There is no serious comparison – perhaps I might stress the word 'serious' – between the situation of a group of islands hundreds of miles from the nearest continent and those two other positions, which it is doubtful whether, if a major enemy seriously threatened them, we would be able physically in the last resort to defend.

We owe it to those whom we have involved by our decision –

our governmental decision, our parliamentary decision, our national decision – to be clear with ourselves that the possession of the Falkland Islands is integral to our national defence and interests and that it is, if necessary, indefinitely sustainable.

The second implication concerns what follows after repossession. The expressions 'diplomatic solution', 'solution of the problem', 'solution by negotiation' have frequently been used in these last few weeks. If those phrases mean that preferably diplomatic and other pressures should induce the aggressor to reverse his act, there would be no problem whatever raised by their use. However, that is not all there is to it. The House has become aware, perhaps belatedly, of the extent to which, in the months and years previous to the aggression at the beginning of April, negotiations had been engaged in on behalf of Britain in which the possibility was envisaged that our sovereignty and possession of the Falkland Islands might be compromised or even surrendered.

However, the House has at no time authorised, or been given the opportunity to authorise, any decision to compromise or part with our sovereignty of the Falkland Islands. It is true that from time to time the injudicious expressions of a junior Minister have allowed us to suspect what might perhaps be being carried on in our name; but there can be no dispute that the House has not authorised anyone, any Government or Minister, to engage in any way in compromising or in trading away our right to the possession of the Falkland Islands.

Mr Frank Allaun (Salford, East): Did not Lord Carrington report that cordial negotiations were taking place with the Argentine?

Mr Powell: I repeat – and it is consistent with the hon. Gentleman's correct observation – that the House has never been invited to authorise, and has never authorised, any negotiating away or compromising of the present status of the Falkland Islands.

If the consequence of exerting our right – in the way in which we are prepared to exert it if necessary – is that the rightful repossession of the Falkland Islands is only a prelude to a course of action that in due course will place the aggressor in more or less the position that he wished to attain by means of his aggression – if we are exercising our inherent right to recover our own, only in order, thereafter, to trade our own away – how can we face the men whom we are asking to take part in that operation? If we support that operation, we owe it to them, as well as to ourselves, to make it clear that that which we regain if necessary by force – although we hope to regain it without force – will not be cast away, negotiated away or given away by this country.

The fact that we are resolved on exercising that ultimate, inherent right of ours implies that we cannot allow the power to exercise it to be whittled away by the passage of time; for if we allow it to be whittled away, that will be tantamount to renouncing the very exercise of the right upon which we are resolved. No hon. Member – except perhaps one or two right hon. Members on the Front Bench – has much notion of what is the true time factor in this critical process of whittling away of the power to exercise our right. However, somewhere – be it near or far – there is such a point at which our power to exercise that right begins to diminish and to be sacrificed. The Government, who have, on the whole, been supported by the House and the country thus far, have the right also to expect that they will be supported when they refuse to allow our ability to exert our right to be taken away from us by stealth and by the passage of time.

The right hon. Member for Cardiff, South East (Mr Callaghan), to whose authority – he being Royal Navy and I a mere 'brown job' – I gladly defer, has marked out rightly for the House the different gradations of pressure and force that can be brought to bear in this situation. But over and above those gradations and the manner in which, subject to the support of the House, they might be used by the Government there lies the overriding duty on the Government not to allow the power that we have to enforce our right to be taken away from us.

I hope that the Government will make it clear that they remain resolved to retain the power to exercise that right. If they make that clear, I believe that the nation will support them.

'FROST ON FRIDAY'

London Weekend TV, 3 January 1969

DAVID FROST: If you had to pick an achievement thus far, that you picked out as your greatest achievement in politics thus far, what would that be?

ENOCH POWELL: I think of – can I have two goes at this?

FROST: Yes.

POWELL: One parliamentary, and the other non-parliamentary. The thing that I'm most glad I was in Parliament to do was to make the speech against the Queen's Titles in 1953, when I argued that the pretence of headship of a Commonwealth was part of a humbug for which we should, in the long run, be punished. Though, I must admit that a close runner-up was the speech I made on Hola Camp. So I put those two on the parliamentary side. On the political side, I think I have severely damaged the prices and incomes policy, and I think I have given a good shake to the complacency with which people were assuming that a planned economy and a largely and increasingly nationalised structure of industry had come to stay and were inevitable. Let me put it this way: I think I've shaken some inevitabilities. I hate inevitabilities.

FROST: Is there anything you regret in politics having done?

POWELL: Yes. I regret a speech that I didn't make. It was in 1953, at the time when the Federation of Rhodesia and Nyasaland was being created, and I was – I had a speech prepared to make against it, and in the end I said to myself, 'Well, look, I've got four rebellions on hand at the moment. Really, I can't go out on a limb on this as well,' and I didn't make it, and I've regretted it ever since.

FROST: That's things that we ought to have done that we have not done; what about things that –

POWELL: Yes, things that we've left to be done.

FROST: – we've done, things that we have done that we ought not to have done?

POWELL: You know, I do think it's part of my answer, that my answer was a thing left undone, but –

FROST: Yes. What about something that was a positive mistake? Anything you'd like to – an episode you'd like to rewrite? A phrase you'd like to retract?

POWELL: Of course, every man would like to polish up his speeches, if he got the chance. But I come back to saying that – and I'm sure this is – has got a proof – not just about me perhaps but about politics as well – in it. I'm sure that you really go wrong in politics, you're really untrue to what you're there for when you say what comes to you to say at that time. And it's terribly hard to go back and say, 'Well I could have said that better, I could have left that out' and I don't –

FROST: You're almost saying you don't really think you've made a real mistake, really done anything wrong.

POWELL: Ah, now you've pushed me in a corner. That sounds too self-satisfied, doesn't it. All right, well, I'll have to be self-satisfied. (*laughter, applause*) The –

FROST: Everybody said you wouldn't find a mistake, actually. People predicted that of you.

POWELL: Ah. They knew me too well.

FROST: Yes, 'fraid so. (*laughter*) What about the two inevitably – in my mind – would come to – some of the phrases you used in the two speeches on immigration; is there anything in either of those that you'd like to rephrase or withdraw?

POWELL: Well, let me take the Birmingham speech, because – and this illustrates how very slight indeed are the retouchings that one might like to go back over – there are in that speech only two things which, in the issued script, I would alter. The first is that in the letter which I quoted, I would put inverted commas in front of every paragraph, instead of just at the beginning and the end, so that it would have been clear – and I'm sure this was misunderstood by a vast majority of reporters and readers – that it was quotation throughout and that none of the words were mine. And the second –

FROST: Just carry on with that, yes.

POWELL: And the second, equally minor, thing, is that I would have put the quotation about the Tiber into Latin in the hand-out, as I spoke it. And those two points, tiny, but they have caused considerable, unnecessary misunderstanding, and if I had my time again, I'd certainly make those typographical changes.

'WHITEHALL AND BEYOND'

BBC TV, 1964

NORMAN HUNT: Mr Powell, as a former Minister of Health what area of manoeuvre did you have in making policy decisions in your department?

ENOCH POWELL: There is a good deal of popular misconception, you know, about ministers and policy decisions. I think a large section of the public imagines the competent minister bustling into his office on a Monday morning with a neatly written list of the new policies which he is going to put into force. In real life nearly all policy decisions emerge out of an existing situation. I don't say that the answer is thrust upon you, but the problem and the necessity of taking the decision emerges from life itself, and I would say that this is even true in the extreme instance of a new government moving in after a decisive General Election in which they've defeated their opponents. They would still find most of the decisions they were taking had arisen out of a pre-existing situation.

HUNT: How far, in the light of the facts which the civil servants have presented you with, can you go outside that range of advice in making your final decision?

POWELL: As far as the facts of life permit. You may, for example, come to the conclusion that you haven't got enough information or that the information, unintentionally no doubt, is slanted one way. In that case you will seek other information. You may feel that although the information is complete, the deduction which you intend to draw from it, either for reasons of political ideology, personal idiosyncrasy or just because you come to a different view, will not be that of your department. But any wise minister, any competent minister, will not just disagree with his department by crossing out 'yes' and writing 'no' on the papers. If he finds himself in disagreement with the advice which is tendered to him, he will seek to probe the reasons, both in his own mind and in the departmental mind, by a process of discussion. It would be a very foolish minister who just overset the advice that he was tendered without having worked back to the constituents of that advice, and having decided that the alternative which he wanted to adopt was soundly based and rationally defensible.

HUNT: How far – if you're countering the advice that your civil servants are giving you – is it useful to you to draw on the assistance of the other political members of the department?

POWELL: Certainly the junior minister – or ministers, as the case may be – can be very important in this, and again it would be an unusually abrupt minister who came to major decisions in his department, especially if he was taking a line other than the traditional line or the departmental line, without putting all the problems through another political mind as well as his own, namely that of his junior minister. It's a tremendous asset to have another politician or two as a longstop in the department.

HUNT: Would it be an even bigger asset if there were rather more politicians, more junior ministers, in a department to help the minister? Would this enable the minister perhaps more regularly to go against the advice of his top civil servants or more effectively to evaluate that advice?

POWELL: Well, there's no virtue in going regularly against the advice of one's civil servants. But I think it's a mistake to assume that just because it is essential to have at least one other political mind applying itself to the policy problems, one would be helped by multiplying the political mind. After all, if your parliamentary secretary is going to help you in this, he must be very closely in touch with all that you are doing and thinking. It very soon becomes difficult to do this if the number increases. I personally would sooner operate in a department with one junior minister than with more than one. It's astonishing how much more difficult it is to keep even two people in touch with what you're doing and thinking than one.

HUNT: So you're very much opposed then to the idea that some people have been suggesting that ministers should have a little private *Cabinet* of ministerial colleagues within a department to help them in getting material through the department?

POWELL: Yes, I'm very much opposed to this, because I think it would result in the junior ministers ceasing to be political longstops or political understudies of the minister, which I believe is their true function in the machine. They would start to become departmental sub-heads divorced from the minister. What I'm emphasising is that in helping the person who is the minister, you want a political mind that is as near as may be his double, so that he doesn't bear the burden unshared – so that the slips are picked up, if you like, by the longstop.

HUNT: So that if the area of activity of a department becomes too big for one minister to control, assisted by perhaps one or two junior ministerial colleagues, you would be in favour of splitting the department rather than introducing more junior colleagues to help you?

POWELL: I would rather do that in principle, though one has got to look, in order to answer that completely, at the resultant size of the Cabinet; but that's a different question.

HUNT: You said that even a minister taking over a department after an election, coming into the department new, even that man can't do just what he wants within a department – but isn't he in a stronger position if he's got a distinct party line behind him than when there isn't a strong party line on the question?

POWELL: Certainly there is a great advantage in being new to a department, and this is why it is important that ministers should not stay too long in departments. The impact of a minister is always greatest (and his value I believe is always greatest) when he comes fresh from outside and can say: 'Good Lord, is that what you've been doing? Well, I'm afraid you won't go on doing that under me.'

HUNT: When he comes fresh from outside like that, does he really know enough about what's happening in the department to be able to be a new broom in that sense against all the very able civil servants who really do know what's best for the department?

POWELL: Well, naturally, you can't make such a remark as that which I have just imagined unless you are going to go on from that to discover the facts. And you will expect the department to explain to you why it is that this is happening and what all the attendant facts are. But any minister should be coloured in his approach to decisions which have any political flavour or overtones by the general policy of his government and his party. I don't think there's any difference in that respect between a new government and an old government.

HUNT: How important are advisory committees in the shaping of a department's policy and in the assistance they give to a minister?

POWELL: There are a lot of different kinds of committee, you know. Take for instance the ad hoc committee, as it's rather horribly called. The minister may genuinely feel that the department with its own resources isn't sufficient, that he really needs a wider spread of experience and of viewpoint to put before him the material for a policy decision by himself or by the Government as a whole. Conversely he may feel: 'There is a big change to be made here, quite clearly, or a big advance. It will be much easier to commend it to Parliament and the country if I have set up a group of reasonable beings well experienced and so on, and they have come to that conclusion.' I'm sure in many cases a policy which was broadly inevitable has been greatly assisted by an independent committee coming to the conclusion that it *was* broadly inevitable.

HUNT: And the independent committee there helps you not only with Parliament and with your colleagues in the Cabinet, but with the department civil servants as well?

POWELL: Yes, though I wouldn't say that one was thinking of it primarily as inward-looking. I think of it mainly as an outward-looking instrument.

HUNT: How much notice does a minister take of the views of his own colleagues in Parliament who are perhaps on the specialist party committee concerned with that minister's activites?

POWELL: Well, he ought to be in constant touch with them and there ought to be mutual confidence between them. He is failing if either their opinions are getting out of line with his without his knowing it, or if the growth of this thoughts isn't being shared, as far as it properly may be, with them. I think this is a matter of the very greatest importance and here the parliamentary private secretary is very important, because, even more than the parliamentary secretary, the PPS is himself a back-bencher, and so he does a great deal in keeping the harmony of understanding that there should be between minister and party on the benches.

HUNT: Did you as Minister of Health, Mr Powell, have regular meetings with the Conservative Health Committee?

POWELL: Oh yes, and indeed this is the normal practice. The minister will usually welcome the chance to meet the committee several times in a year and he will always be talking with its officers and with prominent members of it.

HUNT: Did you put before them your ideas about future policy?

POWELL: Yes. I don't want to be misunderstood here. Clearly a minister mustn't treat them as a Cabinet – the Cabinet has its responsibilities quite distinct from those of the party on the back benches – but he must be sure that he is aware of their point of view and their pressures and their reflection of feeling in the party and in the country, and he must also be sure that his policies are seen as growing out of their views and the situation as they understand it.

HUNT: What use did you as a minister, Mr Powell, make of the press as a means of (perhaps), getting your policies through a department?

POWELL: Oh, through a department? I'm not sure that I like this expression that you use of 'getting one's policy through a department' as though it were a kind of resistant material. It isn't a resistant material, it's an indispensable instrument for the preparation of decision and of course it's an indispensable instrument for the execution of decision. It's quite a misconception to treat it as a kind of almost impermeable substance that you have to punch away at, and I think it would be a very strange situation in which the minister was using the press – an outside body – to work upon his own advisers.

HUNT: But did you ever do any kite-flying in the press with a view to establishing favourable publicity for an idea which you very much wanted to follow up?

POWELL: Ah, that's quite different. This is an outward-looking use of press publicity. Well, just as a minister will want the party in the House not to be taken by surprise by something, so he would wish the public not to be taken by surprise by a policy decision.

HUNT: When you receive advice from within your departmental machine how can you be sure that way down in the department there isn't a conficting view which you as minister have not been made aware of?

POWELL: This is one of the tests, I think, of ministerial competence – to be able to detect, when a problem comes forward, whether hidden in it somewhere there is a contradiction, an unresolved discord. And certainly, as there are two or more sides to almost any question, it is often helpful, when a policy decision has to be arrived at, to get the process of dialectic going again inside the department. The advice tendered to the minister is, of course, unitary. You can't give a man two opposite pieces of advice at the same time, and therefore it is the function of the department, when the advice comes to the minister, to come down on one side or the other or to commend one course of action. But it may well be that the minister will wish himself to unravel again the 'yeas' and the 'nays' which have been resolved in arriving at that unitary advice. This process of discussion round a table in the minister's room, where even relatively junior officials can have their say, is tremendously important in the logical process of making sure that all the facts are deployed, and that the course of action on which one is going to embark is defensible and practical and one which can be commended to the country.

HUNT: But you, as a minister, would have time to do this only on a relatively small number of issues, wouldn't you, to have the 'yeas' and 'nays' confronting you with their conflicting advice so that you can unravel it and get to the heart of the problem?

POWELL: Part of the art of being a good or successful minister is to know what the subjects are that require one's personal attention.

HUNT: Looking back on your time as Minister of Health, Mr Powell, was there anything that you wanted to do which you believed right, but were overborne in the end, perhaps by the weight of advice against it – as Winston Churchill was sometimes during the war?

POWELL: If by being overborne you mean that an intention which I still held was frustrated by those advising me, the answer is 'No'.

There might have been instances – I don't at the moment recollect any of importance – where one started with a gleam in one's eye and then discovered that the facts were very different from what one had supposed. But then of course that is not being frustrated by a department. The department is there performing part of its essential function in confronting the minister with the facts on which he has to work.

HUNT: The Civil Service has often been criticised, Mr Powell, for the shortage of scientists. Now to what extent was it a disadvantage in the Ministry of Health that presumably so few of your top administrative class officials were scientifically or medically trained? Particularly when you yourself, your previous training was as a professor of Greek.

POWELL: Well, there would be no advantage in the administrators having medical training. Indeed that would be a positive disadvantage. That would be the little learning which is a dangerous thing. And certainly it's important in my view that the minister should be strictly a layman. Because in the last resort government decision is lay decision. Now, if that is so at ministerial level, there must be something which corresponds to it in the structure of a department. The minister who has got to take the ultimate layman's decision requires the administrative lay mind applied to his problems – even though the content of the problems may be technical and professional. The professional advice should be in a sense subordinate to the administrative advice.

HUNT: But can these administrative lay minds at the top of the department really understand properly the scientific problems which they are supposed to be solving?

POWELL: If they can't, neither can the minister. If it's going to be – I repeat my expression – a lay decision, then the problem has got to be reduced to terms in which the layman can exercise his judgement upon it.

HUNT: But why aren't scientists the well-equipped people to reduce a problem to lay terms?

POWELL: Because that's not their business.

HUNT: But why?

POWELL: Their business is to deal with the content of their subject – whether it be medical or scientific or architectural or engineering or military. I'm thinking of various departments of government. But it is a different activity of the mind to say: 'Now, given that these are the scientific data, what are the implications of these data for the management of men?' That is the function of government.

HUNT: But are you saying that a man trained in science can never become a manager of men?

POWELL: No, but he then ceases to be specifically a scientist and becomes an administrator or a politician. I'm not saying that a man can't be both, though in a department it is useful that the two should be kept apart. There's something else here. Suppose you've got a minister who is an expert. We say: 'We'll make so-and-so Minister of Health, he was a doctor, he knows all about hospitals.' Well, you make him Minister of Health and what do you do with him after that? You can't take him to the Foreign Office or the Treasury or anywhere else. Where do you find your team of ministers if they all start by being appointed because they are experts? And the same applies to the administrator. Your argument would lead to departments which were water-tight, where a man stayed in one department from entry to the end of his career. Now I think it's one of the advantages of our system that your administrative civil servant moves around from one department to another and sees the problems of administration and government from many angles in the course of his administrative career.

HUNT: No, I'm really suggesting that a man with a general scientific training would be able to make men-management type of decisions in a number of departments at least as well as a man who has been trained in Latin and Greek.

POWELL: This is the proposition that man-management derives from scientific rather than from humanistic considerations. I don't agree.

HUNT: But you're regarding scientific qualifications as a bar to man-management?

POWELL: No, I didn't say that. It might well happen that a man with scientific training also had a broad administrative outlook. But I am maintaining that it's difficult to combine in one person the function of giving professional advice and the function of giving administrative advice, and that you would lose by attempting to do it.

HUNT: If one looks at the content of the Civil Service from another angle, it's often criticised because it contains virtually no men with practical experience in business. Now, would the Ministry of Health have benefited from bringing in businessmen as top civil servants?

POWELL: Businessmen, I suppose, are men whose training is related to the making of a profit.

HUNT: Yes.

POWELL: I can't see that that has a very close relationship with the functions of a department which is not orientated in that way. I think there's a lot of misunderstanding about this. Business administration is administration of a particular kind, dealing with a particular material – profit and loss, supply and demand, and so on – and this is a specialised administrative training. I would rather see the civil servant trained by applying his mind to the problems of government which are those on which he has to advise.

HUNT: But isn't one of the problems of the Ministry of Health controlling the drug industry? And wouldn't it have helped rather more if you'd had more businessmen and more scientists to help you in that?

POWELL: No, it wasn't the lack of either business knowledge or scientific knowledge which was the problem. It was an administrative problem arising out of the organisation of the Health Service.

HUNT: But your problem was to buy drugs for the National Health Service at rather lower prices than the drug companies were wanting to charge you. And wouldn't it have helped in your negotiation with the drug companies if you'd really had men of business experience conducting these negotiations?

POWELL: I wouldn't have thought that in maintaining the delicate balance which had to be maintained in procuring supplies of drugs for a service responsible to Parliament, one needed the point of view of a businessman, unused to operating in a sphere where public responsibility and accountability are decisive factors. I would have thought that he would have been a fish out of water.

HUNT: You don't think he'd have been able to help you drive a harder bargain?

POWELL: I don't think so.

HUNT: A minister, besides having to run his department, has to deal with the Cabinet too. How do you decide what to bring before the Cabinet for approval before you can go ahead with it in your department?

POWELL: There may be several grounds on which a minister ought to share a decision with his colleagues. For instance, he may be in disagreement with one of his colleagues on a matter which is common to both their departments. Now normally they should be able to resolve that disagreement. But clearly, if they cannot resolve it between them, then they must ask their colleagues to decide which of the two those colleagues are prepared to support. Then there are the decisions which are important in themselves. I would naturally wish to say to my colleagues: 'Look, there's something very important going on here. It's bound to bulk large in the public eye and I would like you to know broadly what is happening, why it's happening, when it's going to happen, and so on.' And then thirdly, there are the insoluble problems – and most of the Cabinet's time is spent in dealing with matters which are insoluble, in the sense that there are serious disadvantages attaching to any possible course of action. And there, politically charged as these issues are, so that the result will have to be defended, perhaps fought through, in the House and the country, clearly colleagues have got to be agreed first before they go forward.

HUNT: But how far is the Cabinet really a centre of decision on these matters? Or is it just a question of chewing them over, and eventually accepting the minister's advice from the department concerned? If there's, say, a Health Service matter up for discussion before the Cabinet, can the Foreign Secretary, for example, really know enough about it to perhaps argue against the advice which you as Minister of Health are tendering to the Cabinet?

POWELL: Oh, if *he* doesn't know enough about it, then certainly the back-benchers won't know enough about it and certainly the country won't know enough about it. And he is likely to be expressing a point of view which I, as Minister of Health, shall need to have a good answer for. If I haven't got a good answer, then it's not a good policy.

HUNT: But who will have briefed the Foreign Secretary on the health problems which he'll be expressing views on in the Cabinet?

POWELL: He – this is an imagined instance, of course – like any other member of Parliament, or member of the public, is looking at these things from the outside. He's saying, 'What impact will this have on me, on the country? What will the consequences be for the people who need treatment, and so on? If such and such a question is raised by my constituents, or is raised in the House, or is raised in the press, what is your answer going to be?' Of course, where there is a difference of opinion between two ministers, then they naturally will present to their colleagues the full range of the basic facts. On these they should be agreed. In any confrontation of ministers you've got to start with the agreed facts. You often have instances where two ministers have met to discuss a problem but find that their facts don't agree. Then they won't go on and argue. They'll say: 'Well, we've got to get our departments to sort the facts out, and I'll see you next Thursday, old boy.' So agreed facts have always got to be presented as the basis for the decision.

HUNT: Yes. I can see the Cabinet acting as an adjudicating body when there's a conflict between a couple of ministers, and sorting that one out. What I find a bit difficult to understand is how the Cabinet, faced with an intractable problem which a minister in a particular department puts up, unbriefed on that problem except as far as the minister himself is concerned, and nevertheless advised by that minister to follow a certain course of action, can really go against the minister's advice?

POWELL: If it is a purely departmental question, then indeed the data will come from that minister and that department. But reasonable men can arrive at different views on the same data; they can take a different view of the balance of public advantage, and of the relation of the decision in this particular department to the policies of the Government as a whole. They might, for example, say, 'Well, this is a perfectly possible line for you in the Ministry of Health, but you can't be doing that in the Ministry of Health while we are doing X, Y and Z in the ministries of – what shall I say? – Transport, Foreign Affairs, and so on.' One rarely loses – this is something that is borne in on a man the more he lives in politics and in government – one rarely loses by consultation. One human mind is rarely capable of surveying all the aspects of a subject, and although it's often irritating to have to go through committees and discuss with colleagues, in the end if you're candid with yourself you will admit that you've seen and understood things – not expert things – which otherwise your mind would have remained closed to.

HUNT: How far did you feel that you'd got time to, say, master broad economic problems or broad foreign affairs problems which your other colleagues were presenting to the Cabinet, when you were so inevitably immersed in your own department?

POWELL: I don't like that word 'immersed'. A minister has no business to be immersed. Of course there are periods of very high pressure, but it's his duty not to be immersed. It's part of his job to select those aspects of the work of his department which require his attention, to know which they are, to sense which they are, and to focus on those and to do so in a way which leaves him time and freedom of mind to be what he also is, a member of Parliament – don't forget that: a member of Parliament with responsibilities to his constituents and so on – and also a member of the team which is governing the country.

HUNT: Well how, as Minister of Health, how did you set about briefing yourself on foreign policy matters and, say, general economic matters outside your department?

POWELL: Well, we've really answered this, haven't we, in investigating what it is that a departmental minister's colleagues bring to bear in Cabinet upon his problems. They are not bringing to bear the results of separate briefing. They are bringing to bear, if you like, a fresh mind, a political mind, a mind conditioned perhaps by the outlook of an entirely different department, upon the material which he presents to them candidly and as fully as he can.

HUNT: If you yourself had a tricky matter that you wanted to bring to the Cabinet, to what extent would you discuss your proposed line with the Prime Minister first?

POWELL: I don't think there's any rule you can lay down in this. Personalities vary – personalities of a Prime Minister, personalities of individual ministers. I must also point out that I've only sat in Cabinet under one Prime Minister, and I would imagine there are very big differences in the texture of Cabinet Government according to the personalities involved.

HUNT: But also would there be discussion between a minister and the Prime Minister on a personal basis before matters come to Cabinet?

POWELL: I don't think you can make any rule, even after taking account of the qualification about personalities. This will depend on such things as the hotness of the topic, which may not be related to its importance. I am sure there's no rule here, and it would be misleading to attempt a summary.

HUNT: To what extent, though, does the Prime Minister control the agenda of the Cabinet? And don't things have to be discussed with him first before they can actually get on to the agenda?

POWELL: Oh no, no. A minister clearly has a right to bring a matter to his colleagues if he wants to. The very nature of collective responsibility implies that if a man wants his colleagues' assent or advice he can have it.

HUNT: To what extent is a minister really conscious of the fact that the Prime Minister in a very real sense, perhaps, is the real boss of the Cabinet?

POWELL: A minister ought to be all the time conscious of his colleagues. Now, in so far as the Cabinet is the creature, in a sense, of the Prime Minister – in that it stands and falls with him – then you might say that a minister is all the time conscious of the Prime Minister. But this is derivative from a minister's consciousness of his colleagues. I would put it that way round.

HUNT: But the Prime Minister's ability to hire and fire or promote really does give him enormous power over his colleagues, doesn't it?

POWELL: Yes, that's the implication of this form of collective responsibility whereby the Government stand or fall together, and stand or fall with the Prime Minister.

HUNT: But they don't necessarily stand or fall together, because he can sack half of them without the rest falling, can't he?

POWELL: Yes. But it's really grotesque to think of him as therefore wielding a lever to manipulate the decisions and behaviour of individual ministers, so that they would have recourse to him as a departmental head might to a managing director in a firm.

HUNT: But –

POWELL: I bring you back again, if you want to have a real picture of it, to the collective nature of this group of men. They may indeed be dominated, in the perfectly correct constitutional sense that you have explained, by the Prime Minister; but it is the collective view which is at the back of the mind of the individual minister all the time.

HUNT: Looking back, Mr Powell, at the government machine, is it really capable of doing the job nowadays, or would you like to see changes in this?

POWELL: I believe we have to be very careful to limit the increase of ministers in individual departments. I'm also sure that you can't see an indefinite extension of the size of the Cabinet without losing its truly collective nature that I've emphasised all the time. Indeed, there's one reform I'd like to see, though I doubt if it's a practicable one in modern times – I should like to see the Cabinet dine together regularly. After all, the Cabinet started as a kind of dining club, didn't it? I think that that kind of interchange of opinion and sentiment is essential to the success of government. Anything which installs ministers as separate powers in remote departments and brings them together only in an official atmosphere is very dangerous. So I want to see it not merely remain matey. I would like it to become matier still, or to become matey again.

HUNT: So you'd like to see, in fact, the size of the Cabinet reduced rather?

POWELL: I think it's on the high side at the moment. Somewhere between fifteen and twenty I would guess is the size where this atmosphere flourishes best, given that there are a considerable number of departmental viewpoints which have to be reconciled.

HUNT: But if you're keeping the size of the Cabinet down and government business is proliferating, isn't this going to mean that you have more ministers outside the Cabinet?

POWELL: Only if the proliferation of government business means the proliferation of political heads. I doubt this, and I think it is often too readily assumed that because there is a new subject, a new development, therefore we must have a new minister for it. I would question this.

HUNT: Do you think that the tendency in the twentieth century really is going to continue to be for the power of the Prime Minister to continue to increase?

POWELL: I'm not sure that it has been increasing, you know. I regard this notion of the Prime Minister's power or potential power increasing as a myth. As long as it has lain in the hands, as you said, of the Prime Minister to decide the political life or death of a colleague, or indeed of a Cabinet, I would have thought that the power of the Prime Minister has been constant – if he liked to exercise it. No doubt different personalities exercise it to a different extent and in different ways; but that's another question.

'THE ENEMY WITHIN'

Birmingham, 13 June 1970

Britain at this moment is under attack. It is not surprising if many people still find that difficult to realise. A nation like our own, which has twice in this century had to defend itself by desperate sacrifice against an external enemy, instinctively continues to expect that danger will take the same form in the future. When we think of an enemy, we still visualise him in the shape of armoured divisions, or squadrons of aircraft, or packs of submarines. But a nation's existence is not always threatened in the same way. The future of Britain is as much at risk now as in the years when Imperial Germany was building dreadnoughts, or Nazism rearming. Indeed the danger is greater today, just because the enemy is invisible or disguised, so that his preparations and advances go on hardly observed. When Czechoslovakia was dismembered or Austria annexed or Poland invaded, as least one could see that a shift of power had taken place; but in the last three years events every whit as pregnant with peril have given no such physical signal.

As we prepare to elect a new Parliament, the menace is growing, as such dangers do, at an accelerating pace. Other nations before now have remained blind and supine before a rising danger from within until it was too late for them to save themselves. If we are to escape the same fate, it is high time we opened our eyes; for the first condition of self-defence is to see what it is we have to fear.

I assert, then, that this country is today under attack by forces which aim at the actual destruction of our nation and society as we know or can imagine them. The same forces are at work in other Western countries too. Indeed, in some other countries they are more advanced than in this country. However, just as it is no consolation to be told by the Prime Minister that other nations have inflation too, so here there is no salvation in common peril. A plague is not less deadly because it is not confined to a single country. Nevertheless, it is useful to be able to register in terms of other countries as well as our own the advances which the enemy has made in the last three, or at most four, years. Let me remind you of them.

In those three or four years we have seen the universities of America being destroyed. Those institutions are now not merely the permanent scene of violence and disorder, but they only exist and are administered upon terms dictated by the enemy; they have passed out of the control of authority. In the same period we have seen the same enemy in his student manifestation not only terrorise one European city after another, but bring down one of the strongest European governments. In this country we have seen the institutions of learning systematically threatened, browbeaten and held up to ridicule by the organisers of disorder.

So much for the universities; but civil government itself has been made to tremble by the mob – in its modern form, the demonstration. The actual policy and administration of the United States has been altered, and altered again, not by the votes of the electors or the decisions of Congress, but by the fact or the fear of crowd behaviour. Nor need we go abroad for our examples. We have seen in this country in the last few weeks how the menace of organised disorder could threaten the morale of the police and wield the authority of the state itself not in favour of the peaceable citizen but against him. When the *Prince of Wales* and the *Repulse* disappeared beneath the waters of the Gulf of Siam, at least we knew that Britain had suffered a defeat. We suffered no less decisive a defeat when Britain's Home Secretary surrendered the rule of law in order to buy off demonstrations; but do we know that it was a defeat, or are people so foolish as to suppose that such an event is the end of a humiliating story, and not rather the beginning?

A considerable portion of the British Army is at this moment on active service in a province of the United Kingdom. But it is not in Northern Ireland to put down rebellion, nor is it there to repel invasion, though both those things may be woven into the future pattern of events. It is there because disorder, deliberately fomented for its own sake as an instrument of power, had come within an ace of destroying the authority of the civil government, and because the prospect of that authority being easily recovered is not foreseen. That the enemy has utilised the materials of religious division is almost as fortuitous as that a mob should use missiles from a nearby building site.

Nor is religious difference the only material that can be made to serve this purpose. On this side of St George's Channel combustible material of another kind has been accumulated for years, and not without deliberate intention in some quarters. The exploitation of what is called 'race' is a common factor which links the operations of the enemy on several different fronts. In the last three or four years we have seen one city after another in the United States engulfed in fire and fighting, as the material for strife provided by the influx of Negroes into the Northern States, and their increase there, was flung into the furnace of anarchy. 'Race' is billed to play a major, perhaps a decisive, part in the battle of Britain, whose enemies must have been unable to believe their good fortune as they watched the numbers of West Indians, Africans, and Asians concentrated in her major cities mount towards the two million mark, and no diminution of the increase yet in sight.

One of the most dangerous characteristics of any aggressor is the ability to make his intended victim underestimate his power. This characteristic the present enemy possesses to a high degree. 'Fortunately,' people are heard saying, 'it is only a small minority which is involved.' There could be no greater ineptitude. In any event, all revolutions are made by minorities, and usually by small minorities. But those who talk in this way have not grasped the force and novelty of the new psychological weaponry with which they are being attacked. It is as if someone were to dismiss the discovery of the nuclear weapon with the offhand observation that 'the bomb is only a very small one'. It is small, yes, but it is nuclear.

The power of the minority, which, though still only in its infancy, we have watched being exerted here and elsewhere during the last few years, derives from its hold over men's minds. The majority are rendered passive and helpless by a devilishly simple, yet devilishly subtle, technique. This is to assert manifest absurdities as if they were self-evident truths. By dint of repetition of the absurdities, echoed, re-echoed and amplified by all the organs of communication, the majority are reduced to a condition in which they finally mistrust their own senses and their own reason, and surrender their will to the manipulator. In all war the objective is to break the opponent's will. Our danger is that the enemy has mastered the art of establishing a moral ascendancy over his victims and destroying their good conscience.

People observing the advance of anarchy call for more police, more punishment, more force. These may indeed be necessary; but in themselves they are impotent – in fact, they can become additional weapons in the enemy's armoury – unless the battle is simultaneously fought and won in the moral sphere. The decisive act is to put sense and nonsense, truth and absurdity, back into their right places; and that act is already so difficult that conventional wisdom and polite society have come to regard it as impossible. Have you ever wondered, perhaps, why opinions which the majority of people quite naturally hold are, if anyone dares express them publicly, denounced as 'controversial', 'extremist', 'explosive', 'disgraceful', and overwhelmed with a violence and venom quite unknown to debate on mere political issues? It is because the whole power of the aggressor depends upon preventing people from seeing what is happening and from saying what they see.

The most perfect, and the most dangerous, example of this process is the subject miscalled, and deliberately miscalled 'race'. The people of this country are told that they must feel neither alarm nor objection to a West Indian, African and Asian population which will rise to several millions being introduced into this country. If they do, they are 'prejudiced', 'racialist', 'unchristian' and 'failing to show an example to the rest of the world'. A current situation, and a future prospect, which only a few years ago would have appeared to everyone not merely intolerable but frankly incredible, has to be represented as if welcomed by all rational and right-thinking people. The public are literally made to say that black is white. Newspapers like *The Sunday Times* denounce it as 'spouting the fantasies of racial purity' to say that a child born of English parents in Peking is not Chinese but English, or that a child born of Indian parents in Birmingham is not English but Indian. It is even heresy to assert the plain fact that the English are a white nation. Whether those who take part know it or not, this process of brainwashing by repetition of manifest absurdities is a sinister and deadly weapon. In the end, it renders the majority, who are marked down to be the victims of violence, or revolution, or tyranny, incapable of self-defence by depriving them of their wits and convincing them that what they thought was right is wrong. The process has already gone perilously far, when political parties at a general election dare not discuss a subject which results from and depends on political action and which for millions of electors transcends all others in importance; or when party leaders can be mesmerised into accepting from the enemy the slogans of 'racialist' and 'unchristian' and applying them to lifelong political colleagues.

But this is only one, if the most glaring, example; for there is no end to the use of absurdity, like obscenity, as a weapon for brain-smashing.

In the universities, we are told that the education and the discipline ought to be determined by the students, and that the representatives of the students ought effectively to manage the institutions. This is nonsense – manifest, arrant nonsense; but it is nonsense which it is already obligatory for academics and journalists, politicians and parties, to accept and mouth, upon pain of verbal denunciation and physical duress.

We are told that the economic achievement of the Western countries has been at the expense of the rest of the world and has impoverished them, so that what are called the 'developed' countries owe a duty to hand over tax-produced 'aid' to the governments of the underdeveloped countries. It is nonsense – manifest, arrant nonsense, but it is nonsense with which the people of the Western countries, clergy and laity – but clergy especially – have been so deluged and saturated that in the end they feel ashamed of what the brains and energy of Western mankind have done, and sink on their knees to apologise for being civilised and ask to be insulted and humiliated.

Then there is the 'civil rights' nonsense. In Ulster we are told that the deliberate destruction by fire and riot of areas of ordinary property is due to dissatisfaction over allocation of council houses and opportunities for employment. It is nonsense – manifest, arrant nonsense; but that has not prevented the Parliament and government of the United Kingdom from undermining the morale of civil government in Northern Ireland by imputing to it the blame for anarchy and violence.

Most cynically of all, we are told, and told by bishops forsooth, that communist countries are the upholders of human rights and guardians of individual liberty, but that large numbers of people in this country would be outraged by the spectacle of cricket matches being played here against South Africans. It is nonsense – manifest, arrant nonsense; but that did not prevent a British Prime Minister and a British Home Secretary from adopting it as acknowledged fact.

It may have been a happy chance that this particular triumph of organised disorder and anarchist brainwashing coincided with the commencement of this general election campaign. For many people it lifted a corner of the veil; for the first time, they caught a glimpse of the enemy and his power. If so, it was timely. That power lies in what we are made to say (or not say), and thus ultimately made to think (or not think). That power can only be broken by plain truth and common sense, and the will to assert it loud and clear, whoever denies, whoever jeers, whoever demonstrates. Without that, there is no escape from the closing trap; no victory over those who hate Britain and wish to destroy it. Next week the people have it in their hands, perhaps for the last time, to elect men who will dare to speak what they themselves know to be the truth.

'THE STATE OF THE NATION'

Granada TV, 1973

JOHN JENNINGS: The question is '*That Members of Parliament are too ignorant to do their job properly*'. I call the Rt Hon. Enoch Powell.

THE RT HON. ENOCH POWELL: Mr Jennings, if I were a Prime Minister whose object was to turn himself into a dictator, if I hated the House of Commons as much as I love it, and if I wanted to deprive it of all real political effectiveness, then I would seize with both hands and with gratitude the arguments, the line of thought, and the developments foreshadowed by the hon. Member opposite. I should encourage the House of Commons to set up as many committees as possible. My object would be, especially in the afternoons and evenings, to have hon. Members busily and I am sure happily employed upstairs. As long as they didn't come into the Chamber I wouldn't mind what they were doing upstairs in the committee rooms. Of course I would bring them into consultation on all the legislation beforehand, naturally in the form of a Select Committee: balanced, of course, in party terms, but hand-picked by the Whips. And therefore by the time my legislation came before, as a perfunctory last stage, the House of Commons itself, I would not only have allies on both sides of the House, who had been through it all, who were committed to it, but my Ministers would be able to confront the House with the undeniable fact that really all the work had been done. There's no point in the ignoramuses on the floor of the Chamber – of course they might be allowed to ask a question occasionally, satisfy a little ignorant curiosity. But the main work of course had, as would be quite logical, been fed into the preparation of the legislation itself. And as for information, of course I wouldn't be satisfied with the present excessive services provided by the House of Commons library. I would take hon. Members and I would stuff them with information as one stuffs a goose to produce *pâté de fois gras*. They should have information until it was coming out of their ears. Because they would be quite unable, with absorbing the information and working the computers and keeping their staff of researchers and secretaries well occupied, they would be quite unable to get together in the lobbies, to meet, to talk to one another. And above all, they wouldn't come into the Chamber very often. (*Interruption:*

JOHN MACKINTOSH: They don't anyway!) Aha! But it's the people that do come into the Chamber – and the occasions when what's happening in the Chamber draws hundreds of other Members there – that I should be really afraid of. I say, Mr Jennings, above all they wouldn't come into the Chamber.

Now I went along partly with the analysis of the hon. Member, of the function of Parliament, of the House of Commons. That it is a political forum which protracts the essential debate in the electorate, that it is a representation of the people which is constantly watching Government, constantly asking it questions, striking the finger upon the weak places. But it does this in a particular way. It is the power to force a Minister in the Chamber to make a case and to sustain that case, whether he is arguing the question that Clause 33 of a Bill Stand Part or whether he is arguing a major matter of Government policy.

Now I would like to take very briefly some of the cases, because they are very instructive, which the hon. Member raised. He mentioned Concorde. I'd like to throw in another couple for good measure. He mentioned the ignorant approach of Michael Foot in a defence debate. Well I was for a period spokesman for the Opposition on Defence, and two of the proposals of the then Government were in the range of advanced weapons, the purchase of an American aircraft called the F–111, and the construction of an Anglo-French variable geometry aircraft. And I said they were nonsense. I said they wouldn't happen, and I said that the policy based upon them would collapse in ruins. Not only did I not need the advice of Air Vice-Marshals, Air Marshals, or experts from the aviation industry in order to do this; they would have been a positive nuisance. Indeed I had to restrain my colleagues from going and getting that sort of misleading advice. I said, 'No, just read the White Paper. And you will see that when a politician, when a government has to write paragraphs like that, then there is nothing behind it and they know there is nothing behind it.' And sure enough, there was nothing behind it, because the simple questions, the simple questions which any intelligent member of the public could have asked, but wasn't in the House of Commons to ask, could not be answered. What the devil are you going to do with fifty of those aircraft? Whatever they were like, however good they were. The Government could never answer that question, and in due course, in incredible humiliation, the policy collapsed.

Now debate. I come back to this central point. Mr Jennings, everything which diminishes true debate on the Floor of the House of Commons strengthens the Executive and weakens Parliament. We must in order to do our business, be uninvolved. We are not participating in government, we are not experts, we are even less the puppets of the experts. We have our own expertise, and our expertise is as politicians and would-be Ministers facing other politicians and actual Ministers, to strike our finger upon the places where it hurts, or upon the places where the great clash of politics is going to take place, and fight it out. We can only do that through debate, we can only do that on the Floor of the Chamber. And those who wish Parliament and the House of Commons ill, will support this motion. (*Hear, hear*) [. . .]

Mr Jennings, I cannot help being struck by what wonderful friends hon. Members opposite are to the Executive. (*Hear, hear*) As, if I were a governmentalist, of course I'd be on that side every time. And I noted during Mr Crosland's speech at least three major benefits which an extension of the Select Committee and the expert committee procedure on legislation would confer upon an Executive. He complains about repetition. Repetition is what governments fear most. When they're on a weak point they'd be only too glad for it to be disposed of at Second Reading. And for the Chairman to say, 'Now now now now, we're only here to consider detail in Committee.' It is the fact that in Committee on Clause 1, Clause 2, oh the same point comes up and up again and again until eventually the Government gets rattled on it and the weakness of their case begins to appear. I happen to be sitting at the moment on a Select Committee on a Bill where the Government was defeated yesterday.

ANGUS MAUDE (*Interruption*): Standing Committee.

POWELL: On a Standing Committee on the Bill. Now that wasn't the first time that point had been raised. It had been raised, I imagine just on the edge of order, about half a dozen times before during the proceedings. And by the time the Government got to the particular amendment, they knew they were beaten. I very much doubt if they would have been beaten on it if there hadn't been that constant rattling process of repetition. Repetition, whether we like it or not, boring or not, is part of the parliamentary process and it's very effective.

Then there was his second point, that Ministers are often incompetent to explain their Bills. Quite true. And what's his solution? Why the poor dears, they oughtn't to be expected to. (*Laughter*) They ought to be able to bring their officials. But one of the effects of the parliamentary process is to show up the incompetence of Ministers. (*Hear, hear*) A Minister has no right to come before the House of Commons with a Bill if he can't explain the provisions of it. And he has no right to be allowed to say – 'Oh this is very complicated, this is a matter for experts.' After all he's making law

by which people are to be bound; at least it's a minimum requirement that he should u erstand it himself. (*Hear, hear*) And in
the Committee we have the opportunity to show him up. And we
have all of us seen Ministers whose career was ended by being
pulverised because it was realised that they couldn't explain their
own Bills. I want to keep them there, and there's no place for it
like a Standing Committee, which is the microcosm of the House,
and the House of Commons itself. (*Interruption*)

ANTHONY CROSLAND: Perhaps I could point out to Mr Powell that
the Minister whose incompetence on the Housing Finance Bill
prevented any proper explanation of the Bill at all, has subsequently been promoted.

POWELL: Well there are ways (*Laughter*) – there are ways and ways
of dealing with – well – I don't want to use the word 'incompetence'
in a personal context. (*Hear, hear*) But I think the Rt Hon. Gentleman has helped me to make my point. (*Laughter*)

And finally his notion was astonishing that you can separate the
political part of a Bill from the non-political part. Surely all of us
know by experience that quite suddenly in examining an apparently
innocuous clause, first of all Members discover that it means something different from what they've imagined and is more important,
and secondly they realise there is a political intention behind it.
That lurking beneath the apparent technicalities there was a political will. No, we're here to do a political job. We cannot shift that
political job over (and it is one hundred per cent political) either
to the interrogation of experts, nor can we delegate it to a committee of ourselves, whose business is not to be political but to be
expert. And once again I say, this would be the dream of all
governments, to have an extension of this development. That is
why we shall oppose it. (*Interruption*)

RICHARD CROSSMAN: Could we have one question?

JENNINGS: One question, Mr Crossman.

CROSSMAN: I was just listening very carefully to the point about how
you can't separate off what's called the political from the non-
political. Now I am surprised at the gentleman saying this, because
I had thought that the compromise we reached on the Finance Bill
Committee Stage was broadly acceptable to people on the other
side here, where we have in fact kept the controversial on the
Floor of the House and put the less controversial into Committee
upstairs. Is he saying we have done a bad reform there, because I
think it would be highly relevant to have that made clear?

JENNINGS: Mr Powell.

POWELL: In my opinion no single change has been more disastrous to
the House of Commons than the splitting of the consideration of

the Finance Bill into four or five purely formal general debates – that is what they are – and an examination of what is called the 'detail', in Committee. And this is wholly on the Government's side, which is why one Government after another proposes and continues it. It prevents whatever time may be necessary being taken by ordinary Members of the House of Commons to discuss which clauses and which aspects they want to discuss. The all-night sittings, the series of all-night sittings on the Finance Bill, the fact that the Government couldn't guillotine the Finance Bill on the Floor of the House has been the strength of the individual Member and has been the strength of the tiny minority perhaps of members of the public who were affected by Clause 123. Because, sure enough, at three o'clock in the morning, when we were all groaning, nevertheless their case was going to get put. That case has no assurance, indeed somebody opposite said that, of being put under this system. (*Hear, hear*) [. . .]

I only want to make one point briefly, Mr Jennings, but it is I think the crucial one and is the test question. I just put this question. And I put it with confidence to honourable Members on both sides who have been in office themselves. Of what is it that a Minister and the Cabinet are most afraid? What test is it that they have in their minds, other than that of the next election, when they elaborate policy and legislation? Do they say, what if a Select Committee were to get at this? Do they say, what would (*Interruption*) . . . yes, but what are they afraid of?

CROSSMAN: Being found out.

POWELL: Being found out – and where are they afraid of being found out and exposed?

CROSSMAN: In the Select Committees.

POWELL: No, the right honourable gentleman cannot say that. That is the test about which – (*John Selwyn Gummer rose*) – the honourable Member needn't intervene. He hasn't got this experience. I am putting this to those who have experienced it. Of what is it that Governments are most afraid? I say they are most afraid of the House of Commons and it is only the House of Commons that ever destroys a Minister or – outside an election – an administration.

TO SOUTH KENSINGTON
YOUNG CONSERVATIVES
Kensington, 30 September 1976

'I never understood, Mr Powell, why you gave up your seat at Wolver-hampton.' 'I never heard the reason, Mr Powell, why you advised the electors to vote Labour in 1974.' It would be natural, but it would be foolish, for a politican who found these sentences constantly recurring in a far from negligible proportion of the abundant mail which he received from the general public to be assailed by feelings of surprise or even exasperation. Just because politicians are absorbed in political events and vicissitudes, there is, mercifully, no reason why their fellow mortals should share the same taste or suffer from the same depraved inclination: other people's lives are filled with their own business, and they attend only fitfully and superficially to what fills the columns of Hansard and provides the political journalists and commentators with a livelihood. Nor, just because events by which one's personal life has been turned inside out remain indelibly fixed, with all the relevant dates and details, in one's memory, is there the slightest reason why those events should keep a foothold, even if they ever had it, in the recollection of the rest of the world.

It is therefore with uncomplaining humility that I propose this evening to answer – or rather, to answer yet once more – these two questions, which evidently puzzle and dismay considerable numbers of people who, after all, do me the honour of attaching some interest and concern to my words and actions. Nevertheless, I would not have been tempted into doing this simply by the fact that your invitation, as Young Conservatives, to me, a non-Conservative, affords an appropriate and indeed rather piquant opportunity for public expla-nation. If the matter were one of purely personal and biographical interest, I would have been quite content to leave it to the biogra-phers, the historians and the writers of dissertations in university departments of political science to get the answers right or wrong – or more likely, as is the case in human affairs, part right and part wrong. I claim your attention to these questions and to my answers not on any personal grounds but because issues profoundly important to the health and perhaps survival of parliamentary democracy are involved. It is rather like those leading cases in the law books which are important because of the principles they enshrine and not because of the criminals or litigants by whose names they happen to be known.

All my political life I have commended to those from whom I sought election what I believe to be the essential function of party in parliamentary democracy. A party, namely, is not a faction or club of individuals who associate for mutual assistance in acquiring and retaining office. It is a body of persons who hold, advocate and desire to bring into effect certain political principles and policies. The Romans, no more than the Greeks, had a word for party in that sense; but in the days of the republic they understood the thing very well, and Cicero used to express it accurately if somewhat clumsily by his recurring phrase *idem sentientes de re publica*, 'those of like opinions about the public interest'. It is because of party in this sense that the electorate at a general election is, or ought to be, able to choose, by a majority, not only its government but the purposes of its government. They vote thereby not for persons but for policies.

There can be no body of men, especially of the number and diversity comprised in a parliamentary party, who, despite their general affinity and agreement, can be at one on all subjects. The individuals will not merely give different emphases to different parts of their party's policy, but there will be elements from which they actually dissent. Unless and until they become members of an administration and thus accept collective responsibility for all the administration's acts, a candidate or member can – and normally should – indicate his points of disagreement without impairing thereby the effectiveness of the electoral process. While he retains his Burkeian independence and judgement, the electors retain their equally Burkeian privilege of choosing policy. Whatever the personal reservations of Candidate A or Candidate B, the electorate know for what sort of government they are opting when they vote for him as party candidate. The only qualification is, of course, that a candidate's dissent must relate to particular subjects, however important, and cannot amount to dissent from the general principles and programme on which his party aspires to govern.

Most general elections do represent the offer of a choice between such broad principles and programmes. From time to time, however, an election is called specifically to test the country's acceptance or rejection of an individual policy, even though nothing can prevent other issues being raised and though most electors may still make their decision on the basis of their general view of the respective party images. The general election of February 1974 was a classic case in point. It was expressly called with the object of seeking support and authority for the Heath Government's prices and incomes policy. That being so, no Conservative Party candidate could declare himself opposed to that policy without rendering the electoral process meaningless. On many other matters – from aid to developing countries to tactical nuclear weapons – he was free to state a personal and, if necessary, a dissenting view: on the Government's prices and incomes policy, by the nature of the case, he was committed.

Now I had not only, along with all other Conservative candidates, fought the 1970 election on a party manifesto which 'utterly rejected the philosophy of compulsory wage control'. I had been for many years previously one of the most vocal public critics of the very principle of prices and incomes policy. What mattered was that from the moment in September 1972 when the Conservative Government embraced such a policy, I had attacked, denounced and ridiculed it, I had predicted its failure, and I had voted against it in the lobbies. How, short of humiliating and insincere recantation or open defiance of the very meaning of party and parliamentary democracy, could such a person stand as a Conservative candidate at any election fought primarily and explicitly on that very issue?

What I have said already makes it unnecessary to waste many words on the fatuous suggestion that such a person might stand as an Independent Conservative or an Independent. 'Independent Conservative' would be disreputable use of a designation in order to secure party votes while opposing party policy. As for 'Independent', the basic mechanism of party as the lynchpin of parliamentary democracy makes the independent candidate an irrelevant absurdity. A single imaginary question settles the point. 'Mr Candidate, if you find you have the deciding vote in an evenly balanced new House of Commons, will you use it to turn the Government out or to keep them in?' The candidate cannot refuse to answer; when he does so, he ceases to be an independent candidate.

I have, then, answered the first of my two questions – why I did not stand in February 1974 and thereby of necessity ceased to be a Conservative; for one cannot belong to a party whose cause one cannot advocate. But before I turn to the second question, there are some reflections which obtrude themselves. I was not the only Conservative Member of the 1970 Parliament who was opposed to prices and incomes policy and shocked by the Conservative Government's adoption of it. If the logic of parliamentary democracy was irrefutable and inescapable in my case – as it was – what of them? 'Where,' as someone might have remarked, 'are the nine?' All human institutions have their dark side; and the question I have just posed turns up the rough and seamy reverse side of the garment of parliamentary democracy. Of course, it is true that no one had been quite so explicit, notorious and unqualified as I had in condemning and opposing the Government's prices and incomes policy; but there was no material doubt that a number of men stood and were elected as Conservative candidates, in February 1974, who were opposed to the very policy for which, by the fact of being Conservative candidates, they were asking the support and approval of the electorate. They did so because the only alternative to the self-contradiction which they accepted, and of which the more sensitive will carry the scars as long as they live, was the end of their political life and career – something which can be contemplated with more equanimity at sixty-one than at fifty-one or forty-one or thirty-one. For that reason among many others, I point no finger and imply no judgement; but the fact remains that we are face to face with the price that must be paid – I said 'must' because the article cannot be had at any lower price – for parliamentary democracy. The more crucial an issue is to the life not just of a government but of the nation itself, the more cruelly and ruthlessly is the possibility of public dissent from those inside a political party eliminated.

It is only by an exception which proves the rule that I am alive to tell the tale – and that brings me to the second question I must answer.

I preface it by a confession. Until a few years ago I had always taken it for granted that for any Conservative of any description, let alone for any Tory, the political independence of the United Kingdom was an unconditional presupposition in peace, as well as in war, and that its preservation was a cause which justified and indeed demanded any sacrifice, individual or collective, including the sacrifice of life and limb. I accepted that Conservatives and especially Tories might question the extension of that ultimate and instinctive loyalty to what the nineteenth century knew as Greater Britain and the twentieth century has known successively as the Empire and as the Commonwealth. But I confess that as to the essential nation itself, this realm, it had never occurred to me to doubt the Conservative Party's total commitment.

I was wrong; evidently I was wrong. With incredulity and then with angry astonishment I saw the Conservative Party not merely agree to cede, in the most complete and formal manner, that sovereign omnicompetence of Parliament which for Britain is the essence of political independence, in order to become a member of the European Economic Community, but proclaim that to amalgamate the United Kingdom into a new West European state was the very object and justification of this act. Through the mouth of its leader in the highest office under the Crown the Conservative Party declared that the nation state as exemplified by an independent and self-governing United Kingdom was obsolete. Thereby for me the Conservative Party ceased to be the Conservative Party which I thought I knew and to whose causes my political life had been devoted. It became an incomprehensible stranger to me, though apparently the incomprehension was mutual, because despite all that I said and did the Party seemed unaware that anything had happened. I remember that in June 1973, in a radio programme widely reported and commented on, I declared that I would sooner live my life out, if I must, in a Socialist Britain if that was the price of Britain not losing its political independence. I remember that in the same month of June 1973 I explicitly identified membership of the Community as one of those supreme questions over which, like Joseph Chamberlain over Home Rule, politicians not merely quit but destroy the parties they were reared in. The speech was carried in blaring headlines in the entire national press; but it later became apparent that, if many had heard, few had been listening.

No man can decide what others are to regard as the supreme objects – in life or in politics. Indeed we do not decide for ourselves. The decisions are taken for us already by our make-up, which is why nations are born and not made – and perhaps why they die and are not destroyed. For me, however, there could be no hesitation: no means of preserving or recovering the independence which Britain had lost and was losing in the Common Market must be neglected – any more than means of survival in war could be neglected. The Labour Party in Parliament with negligible abstentions opposed the European Communities Bill tooth and nail in the session of 1972, and I went through the lobbies with them 104 times, in every division that was called. By 1983, the Labour Party, which in the country was strongly opposed to British membership, had adopted as its official policy a renegotiation of the Treaty of Brussels which, in the terms proposed, would be tantamount to withdrawal and it offered to comply with the decision of a national referendum if that were adverse to membership. It was clear to me that at a General Election I could not stand against a Party putting forward these proposals in favour of a Party whose continuance in office would make Britain's membership as far as humanly possible an irreversible fact.

I knew therefore by the end of 1973 that unless some incalculable change came over the Conservative Party I must give my supporters timely warning that I should not be defending my seat; and I had fixed upon May of 1974 as the latest date by which in all reason and fairness I must do so. In the event the matter was struck out of my hand by the unforeseen event of the Prime Minister suddenly dissolving Parliament upon an issue which as I have explained, made it in any case impossible for me to defend my seat as a Conservative candidate. This left me with only one question to answer, and that not a difficult one, namely, whether to keep silence as I stepped out of public life or whether, at this supposedly last moment of it, to exert what authority and influence I still possessed in the cause, which to me was supreme and all-embracing, of national independence. I chose the latter, not imagining that an unforeseeable and improbable outcome would shortly afterwards bring me back to Parliament as a Member of a small independent party committed to opposition to Britain's loss of independence by membership of the European Community.

Unlike the issue on which the then Prime Minister fought the February 1974 election, the issue on which I sought, and perhaps secured, his defeat in it has not become obsolete or been carried away down the stream of events. It remains, despite the sham renegotiation of 1974–75 and the 2 to 1 outcome of the 1975 referendum, at the centre of British politics, inasmuch as the existence of the state itself is the major premiss which subtends all lesser questions. It has not lain down; it will not lie down; and it will subject the political parties and thereby parliamentary democracy itself to a gruelling and, in recent history, unprecedented test.

At the time of the referendum more than half the Parliamentary Labour Party, including more than half the members of it who held office, were opposed to British membership. Debate after debate has shown that the grounds of that opposition were overwhelmingly the determination not to allow political decision in Britain to be transferred away from the British electorate. In short they are the reasons which I and no doubt others had supposed to be inalienable – though not of course exclusive – to the Conservative Party. In the last year there is not the slightest doubt that the majority of which I speak in the Labour Party has increased, not diminished. Meanwhile opposite there sits a Conservative Party in which the spokesmen of parliamentary self-government and national independence have dwindled to a little group contemptuously tolerated by their colleagues and numbering, when mustered, barely a dozen. Whatever doubts or traumas are nursed by the remainder, they are estopped not so much by their votes in a former Parliament as by the very fact that they twice offered themselves as Conservative candidates in 1974 from resisting the institution of direct elections to a European Parliament which will seal the acceptance of Britain's relegation to provincial status in a European federal state.

No doubt in this proportion the Conservative Party in Parliament does not correctly represent the rank and file of its voters, though alas, it is evident that it all too well represents financial and commercial interests and some of the social classes who are associated with it. On the other hand, the majority of the Labour Party in Parliament is in this supreme matter backed by a probably larger majority still of those in the country whom it represents and who furnish its electoral base. By an incredible and for many a heart-rendering reversal of roles it is the Labour Party which is now the patriotic party. In 1940 the voice which cried 'Speak for England' came from a Tory bench. It comes from there no longer. I do not presume to forecast what is portended by this crucial inversion of the functions of the political parties. I only say that they misjudge the significance of party in our parliamentary democracy who imagine that the consequences of that inversion will be easily undone.

'THE PARLIAMENTARIANS'

BBC TV, 4 February 1979

ROBIN DAY: From the volumes of his much-quoted oratory I have chosen this as an opening to our conversation: 'Take Parliament out of the history of England and that history itself becomes meaningless. The British nation could not imagine itself except with and through its Parliament.'

Consequently Mr Powell argues that the sovereignty of our Parliament is something other for us than the assemblies of other nations are for them. Mr Powell, would it be right, broadly speaking, to say that you're less interested in the reform of the way Parliament works than in the need to uphold the sovereignty of Parliament and to protect it against erosion and surrender?

ENOCH POWELL: You don't have to worry about the reform of Parliament because Parliament or the House of Commons keeps on reforming – it would only be a slight exaggeration to say that almost every day it reforms itself. Its procedure, its conventions and so on are a living, changing body from generation to generation. So reform is – the use of the term 'reform' in the sense of organic change or deliberate change is a misconception of the creature with which we are dealing. But power, sovereignty, the fact that the ultimate power is there in that Chamber, that's of the essence. Everything else – the institution, the rules, the customs, the unique combination of intimacy and solemnity which is the House of Commons, that would be worth nothing if power did not ultimately reside there. It's about the exercise of power, it's the unique form of the exercise of power, the self-conscious exercise of power by a nation. [. . .] The House of Commons is not a photograph of public opinion at a moment of time – a picture we know very well from the opinion polls to be as shifting as the shifting sands. It is a delegation from the nation, place by place, of authority to assent or to withhold assent to the proposals and the acts of government. It is a representation in local terms, place by place of the nation, but it is a representation for the purpose of saying yea or nay. It is not an attempt to find out the exact shadings of opinion across the whole spectrum. It is a means of arriving at valid, sustainable, decisions. And it does so by a method which indeed is rough and ready, which one might say is harsh and peremptory, but which, for its validity, rests upon its acceptance. But despite all these apparent arithmetical contradictions and imperfections people accept what the House of Commons votes until they secure a change in what the House of Commons has voted.

DAY: Well, there are various – we have seen increasing signs of a number of people not accepting what the House of Commons votes –

POWELL: Well, not on that ground.

DAY: Well, one of the arguments, of course, for proportional representation is that this would give Parliament greater moral authority.

POWELL: Well, I must say that you need to be pretty credulous to suppose that if this present House of Commons – if this Parliament had been elected on some form of proportional representation what's going on at the moment would not be going on in similar terms. The difference would be that lacking though the majority may be in accepted authority, the Government would then lack all credibility, since it would be a Government which existed by the tolerance of those elected to represent opposite or different points of view.

DAY: But of course those who advocate electoral reform, as it is called, do so on the grounds that they say this would be just another stage in the continuing development of the electoral system that we've seen over the last hundred and fifty years, for instance – the Reform Bill, universal suffrage, votes for women at thirty, then votes for women at twenty-one, then votes for people at eighteen. Next they say we've got to make it an even fairer system.

POWELL: To change the franchise has nothing to do with changing the electoral system. The implications of the single representative of a single constituency entitled on behalf of that constituency as a whole to say yea or nay are just the same whether it is a restricted franchise, a potwalloper franchise of the early nineteenth century in some places, or whether it is the universal franchise of today. But you alter something radical when you say that the House of Commons is intended to be a mathematical representation of the spectrum of opinion, and we will only have a Government which can obtain a majority, draw a majority from that represented spectrum. That would be a different constitution altogether.

DAY: What do you say to the view which is quite commonly held nowadays that the parliamentary system that we have at the moment is to blame to a very great degree for our economic and industrial problems and the decline of our nation in some ways, particularly because, it is said, of the adversary system which dominates our present parliamentary atmosphere. Indeed it is supported by the very physical layout of the Chamber.

POWELL: Well, if I had to attribute blame for the mess we are in, it would be to a lack of the use of the adversary system. It is that both sides of the House over so many years have connived in fictions which, as politicians, workers in the same trade, they found convenient, but which increasingly they knew to be false and yet the falsity of which they have not been able to renounce. But then in the last resort that is a reflection – I fear a rather truthful reflection – of the makers of Parliament out of doors. They wanted to be deceived. They wanted to be told that you can have public expenditure and not finance it by taxation. They wanted all these tales to be told to them and so the House of Commons, which is their creature and their reflection, told them the tales they wanted. And only when the people say, 'We're sick of that tale', only when the people turn on those who told them the tales as they sometimes unfairly do, will we be freed to face our difficulties and to deal with them.

DAY: So it is not the parliamentary system which has failed the nation, but it is the nation and the people it elects who have failed the parliamentary system.

POWELL: No, but I never claimed more for the House of Commons than that it was the most authentic expression of the British people.

DAY: How important in the scale of issues confronting the British people at the coming general election do you place the dangers to the sovereignty of Parliament and our system of government?

POWELL: I will place them as high as I possible can, since however long a time one may have still realistically can change, can repeal, can amend, the '72 Act.

DAY: The European Communities Act?

POWELL: The European Communities Act. However long or short a time we may have, that must be the question which subtends all others. What Parliament can do must be more important than the particular way in which, Parliament by Parliament, Parliament exercises its powers.

DAY: So you would say, would you – I hope I am not misrepresenting you – that the question of parliamentary sovereignty and national sovereignty as affected by our membership of the EEC, is the issue on which you would like to see most people have as their reason for voting one way or the other?

POWELL: Yes, for – in peace as in war, it is the great, the ultimate, question for any nation. If we still are a nation. So really I am inviting the British people and have been these many years, to say whether they intend still to be a nation.

'JEWEL IN THE CONSTITUTION?'

BBC Radio, 6 April 1989

ENOCH POWELL: I must say I'm really quite shocked at the idea of Tony Benn approving of an unamendable motion before the House of Commons. Surely the essence of debate in the House of Commons is that you debate amendable motions. You debate motions to which you can propose amendments. If the House of Commons is really going to control honours, then it has to have the right to pick and choose on a list which is submitted to it and say, 'We're not going to have so and so, we're going to have somebody else instead' and you must be in the position if the thing is genuine at all, to debate that. I think this is the underlying practical difficulty of the objective which I think we achieve as far as it's practicable to achieve it by the principle of confidence and that's what worries me about Tony's approach.

TONY BENN: Well, Cromwell had a parliamentary medal and I think we don't agree really historically as much as you made out at the beginning, because for me it's the sovereignty of the people, for you, the sovereignty of the House of Commons. I'm really a Cromwellian, you're a 1688 man. But that isn't to say that we don't come together on the tyranny of Brussels, where we're governed by a re-creation of the Holy Roman Empire over which we had no real say.

PETER HENNESSY: Can I bring it back from the Holy Roman Empire to our own former empire and King, but now the Queen. Do you think, Mr Powell, that Tony's suggestions would jeopardise the utility and, therefore, the survivability of the British monarchy if there was this fundamental change in the ground rules which he's proposing?

POWELL: The utility of the monarchy and its necessity in a sense to our parliamentary institution is that it is the unlimited, because unwritten powers of the monarchy which are, as it were, in commission with Parliament. If the monarchy was a creature as monarchies in most other countries are, of a written constitution, then those powers and therefore the powers of Parliament controlling the monarchy would be circumscribed and what they were would have to be decided by a court sitting in judgement upon the constitutional foundation.

HENNESSY: Do you accept that, Tony Benn?

BENN: No. [. . .]

POWELL: I hardly feel that the present administration is operating in secret. And of course, he's now raised the other act of genius of a British people in the development of a feudal constitution which inherently – and he's quite right, it is – into the modern British democracy, namely representation. The nature of representation. The underlying sense of a British people, as to what they're prepared to put up with and what they're not prepared to put up with, which they have this curious habit of conveying through the ballot box and through the elective process in the House of Commons. I think our security lies upon this combination of representation and Tony really isn't fair to me over my attitude about the electorate. In the end, as I've always said . . .

BENN: I know.

POWELL: . . . it is about the electorate, it's about the people out of doors. Those are the people ultimately who are our masters. Those are the people ultimately to whom we report and refer. Representation *and* the confidence of the House. These are the two pillars on which – and I'm prepared to call it democracy just to keep in with the Americans – our system rests.

HENNESSY: The common people have had more than a walk-on part in our discussion this afternoon. But Mr Powell you once said 'the common precious and hereditary jewel of every British subject' was the Crown, the hereditary monarchy. You put it as one of the great glories of the common people.

POWELL: Until 1972 I thought we had inherited, all of us, the poorest of us, the right to be governed only by laws and to pay only those taxes which were voted in the House of Commons. That has been taken away from us by treaty, yes by treaty, but by a treaty which could not have been made unless a craven House of Commons had voted for it. And on to this craven House of Commons, he wants to heap more functions, more duties, more individual decisions, more invigilation. I don't think it's practicable, I think it would just pull down the House of Commons as well.

'DIMINISHED RESPONSIBILITY?'

from *Strathclyde Papers on Government and Politics*, 1991

It is a matter of legitimate political concern that she is concentrating power in No. 10 Downing Street and in a most dictatorial way.

Denis Healey, 1987

Why has Mrs Thatcher had this impact? I think it is force of will combined with intolerance; and combined with this ability to see a number of limited things, like Neville Chamberlain, to see them very clearly but not to be assailed by doubt or excessive respect for views one does not agree with.

Roy Jenkins, 1988

My self-imposed business in my political life has been telling the English about themselves – who they are and what they are, how they govern themselves, why they govern themselves in that way, and why they do it.

Enoch Powell, 1987

PETER HENNESSY: Mr Powell, what's Cabinet government for?

ENOCH POWELL: It's for the tendering of advice to the Sovereign which has to be unitary advice because otherwise the Crown would be making itself a decision between alternatives. That advice has to be single advice if we are to maintain the principle of government on advice and this is underpinned by the principle of collective responsibility. The Cabinet is the means of tendering collective advice to the Crown. [. . .]

HENNESSY: Enoch Powell, looking back, do you think collective responsibility was easier when ministers in, say, the early part of this century came from roughly the same social background and they all had similar backgrounds and interests and it could be a kind of club at the summit of public and political life? And, if you think that is so, do you think it has diminished because of wider social and political factors as the century has progressed?

POWELL: I think what we're dancing around is the phenomenon of debate and what one particular sort of debate does. Of course 'debate' means something different according to the context. Debate in the House of Commons is different from debate in a university union, and debate undoubtedly takes place in Cabinet; but it doesn't take place in order to resolve differences.

HENNESSY: Can you explain?

POWELL: It sets people to talk under the ever-present necessity of arriving at a conclusion, and secures by some kind of mutual pressure and internal mechanics, an upshot. After all, debate in the House of Commons is conditioned by the fact that everybody knows – unless the Government is falling – what the outcome of the division is going to be. You debate under the shadow of knowing what the outcome has to be. So debate is a conversation influenced by that knowledge. Likewise I think conversation in the Cabinet is a conversation influenced by the knowledge that we have to all hang together.

HENNESSY: Though government by conversation, surely, can be diminished in the knowledge that every Cabinet Minister who has that patronage is in the hands, in the end, of one person, the Prime Minister – that that is the ultimate weapon of hire and fire. Doesn't that diminish it?

POWELL: Oh yes, it's like having a debate with Henry VIII in the chair. I always used, in Macmillan's Cabinet, to imagine I was sitting in Henry VIII's Council. I was conscious that he had the axe down by his chair. Undoubtedly the necessity of unitary advice to the Crown is the ultimate, logical source of the power of the Prime Minister to hire and fire.

HENNESSY: Denis Healey.

DENIS HEALEY: I don't entirely agree with that. I think, first of all, people being at the same school is not very relevant. The disagreements between people who'd been at public schools in the nineteenth century and people who are from a mix of schools in the twentieth century, are not notably fewer. What I think is important about patronage is that in a democratic system, the real power of the Prime Minister to fire depends on the political constituency or weight of the minister concerned. I think Wilson was very tempted to fire Callaghan on many occasions but came to the conclusion that he'd be more dangerous outside the Cabinet than in. Callaghan, himself, was tempted to fire Tony Benn but decided not to for the same reason. And in the United States, President Johnson, whose power was *much* greater to hire and fire than that of any British Prime Minister because his ministers, as a rule, have no constituency, always used to say: 'I'd rather have a fella inside the tent pissing out than outside the tent pissing in', and this is a very important consideration.

POWELL: . . . so what is in form debate is in fact a sort of power struggle.

HENNESSY: How do you see it Roy Jenkins?

ROY JENKINS: I think there are two major fallacies floating around in this discussion. The one is the view that the great rows have been Labour Party rows and the Tory Party's secret weapon is loyalty which is the cliché in which it's often expressed.

POWELL: Who said that?

HENNESSY: Lord Kilmuir.

JENKINS: Lord Kilmuir. In fact, in fact all the great, the really great leadership rows of this century have been Tory rows compared with which the Bevan/Gaitskell row, and all the various other disputes, fade into relative insignificance. The great rows have been the 'Balfour must go' movement in which Balfour eventually flounced out. Then the bringing about the downfall of the Lloyd George Coalition – who admittedly was not a Tory but was presiding over a largely Tory Government – by the revolt of Baldwin and Bonar Law in 1922. Then a *major* revolt against Baldwin in opposition, not in government, in 1930 which meant he was absolutely on the verge of resignation when suddenly he decided to fight back and now this row, this *major* row which perhaps transcends them all and takes one's memories back to Peel in 1846, at the present time. And the four great leadership rows of this century have been Tory rows and not Labour rows.

HENNESSY: The other fallacy, Roy Jenkins? You said there was another one that we were succumbing to.

JENKINS: Well, the other fallacy I think that we were confusing in our discussion of Cabinet government, the need to get a collective voice, as Enoch Powell would put it, to advise the Sovereign, or as Denis Healey put it, more to give a coherent view to the public, with the other function of Cabinet government which is to deal with the fact that all party government is in fact, to a greater or lesser extent, coalition government. In other words parties do not, certainly if they're going to be governing, successful governing parties, they don't just represent a very narrow segment of opinion which is totally united. All governments, certainly all the best governments, have quite a wide spread of opinion within them. In my view all the best governments are governments in which it leads on to the question we've just been discussing, in which you have two or three or four people who have an independent constituency of their own whom the Prime Minister needs as much, or maybe more sometimes, than they need the Prime Minister and who are, effectively, unsackable. And, therefore, their advice can be given, not as middle-grade executives in a business concern, but as people with an independent political position as a whole. In my view one of the great things which has been wrong with this Government is that you have not had people in that position until very recently. And the main reason that you've had the crisis that you have now is by the Prime Minister by trying to prevent that happening has built up a dam of resentment and when resentment bursts then the inundation is greater than if you haven't built up the dam.

HENNESSY: Denis Healey.

HEALEY: I think there are two key elements which we've slightly neglected so far. The first is that every government wants to win the following election as well as carry out whatever policies it won the previous election on, and the means they've got to be very attentive to movements of public opinion. I'm not sure the Labour Party's all that different. We've been in office, let's face it, very much less often this century than the Conservatives and I think when we've been in office, and even more in opposition. After all, we've wasted twenty years of the fifty years since the war, fighting one another rather than the Tories, but in both cases in opposition we stayed in opposition because we fought one another. But the other factor which has been ignored is that there's a very powerful factor making for coherence in Britain and that is the power of the civil servants who advise ministers who tend to have a built-in coherence, partly because of the influence of the Treasury which tends to put its agents into other departments and the private secretaries' mafia who exchange information with one another so that ministers can be warned where problems are going to arrive. And that's why I think, on the whole, our system of Cabinet government normally has worked quite well. It has very, very obvious defects which probably are not a subject for this programme. But on the whole it works well, providing people keep their eye on the constituency outside Parliament and that applies above all to the Prime Minister. If she loses touch with the outside world or insulates herself or himself from the outside world with a little clique of appointed officials, then there's trouble.

HENNESSY: Enoch Powell, I think that perhaps the only really nice thing you've ever said about Harold Macmillan, your Prime Minister, is that he believed in having his enemies in the Cabinet Room with him, in other words; yourself, although he did move you 'cos he couldn't stand your eyes staring at him.

POWELL: 'Good jockeys ride difficult horses,' as Julian Amery once put it to me. But I can verify what Denis said about the importance of Civil Service briefing from the event of the Thorneycroft resignation in 1958. Watching that from the outside, it was quite clear that the breakdown in Cabinet occurred because the old-boy net between the civil servants simply was not working. Those who sat round that Cabinet table were not briefed on the basic assumptions which the Chancellor of the Exchequer, and to a certain extent, the Prime Minister were making in conducting the discussion.

There was breakdown at several levels, but one of the levels at which there was the breakdown which frustrated the achievement of Cabinet solidarity was the breakdown of the old-boy net, the behind-the-scenes Civil Service briefing.

HENNESSY: Isn't there another problem, though, in the sense that, under our system, the statutes vest powers in individual Secretaries of State. There's only two laws that mention the Prime Minister. I think one is to do with Chequers and the other is the Ministers of the Crown Salaries Act. So, in a sense that, one way of looking at Cabinet government is that all the statutory power, with the departmental back-up that you've been describing as so important, shoves power to the periphery. It's the antidote to an over-mighty premiership that's built into the system.

POWELL: I don't think this is realistic. I don't think that those people sitting around the Cabinet table are saying, 'I'm Minister of Health; sucks to you, how dare you interfere in my department? I'm going to take the decisions in my own department.' In fact, rather the contrary. My experience as a departmental minister in the Cabinet was that, occasionally, I had to take something to my colleagues in Cabinet, and before I took it to them I used always to feel this is a waste of time, why on earth should I have to bother with putting this to these people? After all, I've been through all this, I've worked through every aspect of it. I really understand the ins and the outs of the subject. Why should I talk about it to twenty people, who really couldn't care and don't know about it? Yet there was never a case when I'd taken anything to Cabinet that I wasn't grateful afterwards that I'd had to do so because they'd asked me questions which I hadn't asked myself. They'd asked the questions which are asked by people who aren't departmentally responsible. They asked: 'When we have to meet these questions from the public, what do we say?'

HEALEY: I agree very much with that.

HENNESSY: Roy Jenkins.

JENKINS: Whatever the formal position, I don't think a Secretary of State or any other minister can, for the most part, do much without carrying the Cabinet with him on points. He can't legislate without getting approval within a Cabinet committee or the Cabinet itself and he can't spend money without getting the money from the Treasury and he then . . .

POWELL: And he's got to have a majority.

JENKINS: . . . and his only appeal against the Treasury is to the Cabinet as a whole . . .

HENNESSY: But isn't the Treasury the department that breaks the rules in the sense, you as a Chancellor and Denis the same, could by and large get away with a great deal because you had the money sanction . . .

HEALEY: No.

HENNESSY: . . . and a great deal of that didn't reach Cabinet level.

HEALEY: No.

JENKINS: Well, yes, there is something in that. The other department over which I've twice presided which is probably the most detached from the Cabinet is the Home Office which is probably the best department in which to pursue a semi-detached position and I, indeed, the second time I was Home Secretary was, pretty semi-detached from the Government of which I was then a member. And it's a good department from that point of view because you don't spend a vast amount of money except on the police, and people are slightly frightened about cutting down money on the police, and you can do things on your own there. There are a lot of prerogatives which you can exert. But even *there*, if you get on really bad terms with your colleagues, there's a great limit to what you can do. But I must say, although in theory, you may say the Treasury can do a great deal and, of course, the Treasury does have a powerful machine as Denis says, powerful machine within the Treasury and also with its former members who are outside strategically placed in Government departments . . .

HEALEY: Double agents.

JENKINS: None the less my total conviction is that in the Treasury, as compared with the Home Office, a Chancellor is an absolutely busted flush unless he can maintain his authority over his colleagues in Cabinet and a Chancellor who has lost that, if in the first place he comes into a position in which he can only hope to maintain it with the support of the Prime Minister, then he's in hock to the Prime Minister a little too much (though he does need the support of the Prime Minister). But if he can't do it in general, then there is no position in which it is less desirable to be in government than a Chancellor without authority.

HENNESSY: But Denis Healey, compare the time when you were Defence Secretary with when you were the biggest baron in the street at the Treasury. There really is no comparison is there because you just talked about what you called your 'double agents' under your breath – the Treasury's men in other departments and so on?

HEALEY: Well, I had some in mine, of course, when I was Defence Secretary. No, I think everything depends on the situation and the political temperature, as it were, of the issues with which a minister's dealing. I was very lucky when I was at Defence because Wilson left me much more to take my own decisions than the others and things became major issues in the Cabinet when, for example, I used to have terrible rows with Roy about the future of the aircraft industry when he was Minister of Aviation and those had to go to Cabinet. But the real thing is that the process of argument is a geniune one in Cabinet. Ministers do tend to get ministry-bound very often, especially if it's a very time-absorbing department. And to be compelled to argue your case in front of colleagues who are equally able to have often greater political common sense and see their thing is a very important contribution too.

POWELL: And to argue it with laymen.

HEALEY: . . . absolutely. Because in a way, Cabinet ministers represent the public better than you do . . .

POWELL: That's right.

HEALEY: . . . because they are lay.

HENNESSY: Can you explain that, Denis Healey, because some people might think that was proof positive of a British devotion to the amateur? That if you go native on a subject you go native because you know something about it and this needs watching.

HEALEY: Yes, I think so because the job of government is to run the country well so that, you know, we keep out of war and we enjoy prosperity while maintaining the support of the public as a whole. If you don't do that you're thrown out. Now, in a sense, departmental ministers rightly get very absorbed with the extremely difficult and time-consuming problems in their own department, and, therefore, they tend often to lose touch. And I think in our country that is less dangerous than some countries where a minister has to abandon his constituency to become a minister. I used to find my monthly visits to my constituency, especially when I was Chancellor, were *absolutely* invaluable, keeping my feet on the ground. But you keep your feet on the ground also by having to argue your problems through with people who are not overladen with this tremendous burden of departmental responsibility and administration and, from that point of view, take a view very much more like the public, and that is really what democracy is about.

JENKINS: I'll tell you another thing, if I may, which is that, in my view, Cabinet government, the fact that you have to go to the Cabinet and get Cabinet approval for issues, and to some extent parliamentary government, though one can exaggerate the power of Parliament, in my view, but the fact that a minister has to go to the Cabinet and has to defend things in Parliament is, in fact, a great maintainer of ministerial authority within the department. If the Cabinet and Parliament didn't exist, then a minister would find it very difficult to maintain his authority *vis à vis* civil servants who were much more expert than he was. The value of a minister to the officials in his department is that he can get his way in the Cabinet, and that he can defend the department and make the department look respectable before the House of Commons too.

HENNESSY: Mr Powell, do you not think this sounds like vested interest and logrolling in the sense that the description Roy Jenkins has just given of the department wanting the minister to win and so on, is like a constellation of organised pressure groups? In other words, government departments all trying to put their hands in the public purse and win. . . .

POWELL: If it's the expression of a vested interest it's an expression of a vested interest in parliamentary government. After all, democratic government is lay government – government which makes sense to the laity, which makes sense to the governed. . .

HEALEY: Government by amateurs.

POWELL: The application of lay judgement by the House of Commons to the minister at the box and, by the Cabinet to the minister with the proposal, is a safeguard for the subject.

HEALEY: In my experience, civil servants like a strong minister even if the minister rejects their advice, providing he can carry his views through the Cabinet and through Parliament. When things go very badly wrong, and I think that's happened in Britain in the last few years, is when the department itself is giving very bad advice to the minister. I do not know, precisely, how Lawson went so *terribly* wrong after 1987, but I could see as an outsider talking to people over the world, that the deregulation of the financial institutions was going to lead to an explosion of unwise lending and unwise borrowing. And the thing which has sent our economy spinning in the last few years has been this colossal increase in private borrowing, both by individuals and by business, and it appears to me from what Lawson has said that he was not told by the Treasury that this was happening and yet every outsider who was watching the scene saw it happening and was deeply worried about it.

HENNESSY: Mr Powell, Roy Jenkins and Denis Healey, in different ways, have been critical of the last ten years of Cabinet government as it's been practised and the way Whitehall has worked and so on, and Lord Jenkins, in particular, was describing the damage that can be done if you don't have strong independent figures in the Cabinet – figures in their own right, semi-independent of Prime Ministerial patronage. Do you not think though, to be fair to Mrs Thatcher, that modern tendencies, whichever party has formed a Cabinet, have been pushing us in the direction of Prime Ministerial government? I mean I think it's for the last thirty years only we've had regular Prime Minister's Questions twice a week. The elections have become ever more presidential in style and the media has focused more and more on interpreting events through one pair of eyes, the Prime Minister's. So do you think, to be fair to Mrs Thatcher who's come in for a degree of stick in terms of classical Cabinet government in this discussion, that it's not just a strong character in the Prime Minister's chair, it's external events as well?

POWELL: I'm suspicious of detecting trends in periods as short as ten or even fifteen years. I think we can easily deceive ourselves. After all, there isn't a trend between one personality and a different personality who accidentally succeeds. So I don't really accept your notion of a trend, though I do think you have a valid point when you say that the institutionalisation of Question Time has placed an unhealthy spotlight upon the Chairman of the Cabinet.

HENNESSY: Do you think we have seen though, Mr Powell, an accretion of Prime Ministerial power in the last ten years?

POWELL: I doubt it. I doubt whether, in practice, the Prime Minister has got away with a personal view or policy or intention more than would have happened if the Prime Minister were Harold Macmillan or if the Prime Minister were Attlee. I very much doubt that.

HEALEY: If you go back to the nineteenth and even more the eighteenth centuries, the really striking thing was that about the only minister advising the Sovereign and of course that function of advising the Sovereign was more important in the eighteenth century . . .

POWELL: He was 'The Minister', which is what they called him.

HEALEY: . . . yes, 'The Minister', and a lot of the departmental ministers were lazy clots, they knew nothing about what they were doing . . . didn't work at it at all and the real power . . .

HENNESSY: Good amateurs, Denis?

HEALEY: . . . no, bad amateurs. There's a distinction which is quite important as you may have discovered if you ever follow some of the games which are performed by amateurs. Good and bad. No, I think the really striking thing is that the quality of people who reach the top in politics and become ministers is probably a good deal higher than it was, certainly, in the thirties or twenties of this century, certainly most of the nineteenth century if you read the memoirs of the time. And I think its perfectly true that the television, by focusing on the personality of the Prime Minister, has tempted the Prime Minister to assume excessive powers. But whether the Prime Minister can get away with the powers he or she assumes is another question. The really striking thing in the United States, where the President, in theory, has all the power, is that, in practice, he has almost none. Bush's failure to get Congress to agree either his domestic policy, the budget or even his policy in the Gulf now. And Mrs Thatcher's attempt to impose her personal prejudices on her Government has proved to be a disastrous failure.

HENNESSY: Roy Jenkins.

JENKINS: I'm afraid I think Denis's view that the quality of governments has got strikingly better is the reverse of the truth. It's nonsense if you like to put it bluntly. I mean I don't think you've seen a government of anything like the quality of the Asquith Government in the modern period – a Government which contained Churchill, which contained Lloyd George, apart from Asquith himself, which contained Haldane, which contained Bryce, if you're looking at outside the intellectual figures, which contained a whole range of other people and I think . . . that . . .

HEALEY: But, with respect, that is the only government you can point to of which this is true.

JENKINS: No.

HEALEY: It wasn't true of the Disraeli Governments or the Gladstone Governments.

JENKINS: Oh, I think there were quite considerable figures in both those governments. I mean which government would you like to take and I'll give you the example of the people I think are a *great* deal more considerable than Mr Parkinson or . . .

HEALEY: No.

HENNESSY: The Attlee Government?

JENKINS: The Attlee Government was a very powerful government. The government of Bevin, Morrison . . .

HEALEY: Cripps.

JENKINS: . . . and Dalton, Cripps, Gaitskill and Aneurin Bevan, too, was a government of exceptionally strong political personalities and I think it was more or less equal in that respect to the Asquith Government pre–1914. But the Asquith Government had these two incredible stars in the shape of Lloyd George and Churchill in it which puts it ahead, and it also had two or three people of greater outside distinction, greater non-political distinction.

HEALEY: Churchill was only a star in that government in retrospect. I mean he didn't appear to be a star at the time.

HENNESSY: Mr Powell, do you accept there has been a decline in the quality of the political class as Roy Jenkins implies?

POWELL: There's been a change in quality, in that the notion of a career structure is more important and more effective than it certainly was in the last century. I don't think that the members of Gladstone's Cabinet in 1880 regarded themselves as being on the rungs of a ladder. I think they regarded themselves as there in their own right, their own personality, their own background, their own representation. This may be where a change has taken place and it's a change which has affected the House of Commons too. [. . .]

HENNESSY: Enoch Powell, though, even if considerable figures are produced by the party system, a Prime Minister doesn't necessarily have to pick the brightest and the best and the most capable. In fact, it's in a Prime Minister's intersts, is it not, to surround himself or herself by the people who perhaps aren't going to be a personal threat to them?

POWELL: You want good politicians and you want to be lucky. It's like any other branch of human life, you need to be good and you need to be lucky. There's no machinery which will guarantee that you achieve that result.

HENNESSY: Roy Jenkins.

JENKINS: You implied that a Prime Minister is tempted, maybe a Prime Minister sometimes is tempted, to be surrounded by weak sycophants to provide him or her with an automatic majority in the Cabinet. But that is, in fact, a heavy criticism of a Prime Minister. The better a Prime Minister is, the better the ministers with whom they will want to be surrounded.

HENNESSY: I feel I have on my hands three total romantics about the system. You see a danger of succumbing to expertise, a danger of succumbing to arid machinery of government questions. It strikes me that, in essence, what you're saying is a sort of classical nine-teenth-century conception – get the good and the big people and the independent-minded people in the Cabinet and the system runs fine. The rest are peripherals.

POWELL: Maybe this is because we enjoyed it. Enjoyed it so much that we miss being parted from it.

JENKINS: I think you're very polite in saying we're three romantics. What you really mean is we're all three extremely complacent about the system.

HEALEY: No, what you really mean is we're all pragmatic because we have experience.

JENKINS: No, what I do not believe is that you will improve British government by changing the system of administration in the struc-ture of a Cabinet. I think, myself, that the party system, the party system as it has operated recently, has done a great deal of harm to British government on the whole. The rigidity of the two-party system in which people are forced to *pretending* they agree with people in which you produce Cabinets of incompatibles, and, I think, that has done a good deal of harm. But it is that, rather than the structure of government or whether you have a few busi-nessmen from outside or whether you have *Cabinets*, that is the fault and that's a wider fault, too. But I think, as I say, you were polite in what you said. But, although I may be, as you see it, complacent on some of the detailed points, I'm not on the whole complacent about how British government has operated which I think is fairly badly.

HEALEY: We've been complacent about your suggestions because we're pragmatists and we have experience which you don't have. But I don't think the situation's perfect. I think it's far from perfect. But I think the weaknesses of the system are not weaknesses of Cabinet government or of the constitutional arrangements under which we operate. The weaknesses are due to much more deeply rooted things, the strength of the class structure in our culture. All sorts of issues we haven't time to discuss.

POWELL: Don't blame the system if you don't like the results.

HENNESSY: One of the implications then, Denis Healey, of what you're saying is that, if only the Secretaries of State in the 1980s had stood up to the strong Prime Minister, there simply would not have been a problem. That you're saying it's an individual problem and it's all very well for them to come out like veterans of the Somme and tell us, once they've resigned or been sacked, just how frightful it was serving in Mrs Thatcher's trenches and they all continually put collective responsibility in their resignation letters. Do you think it's largely been a failure of individual temperament and strength?

HEALEY: Well, I don't want to talk too much about failures. As I say, it's a very complex matter but I think if you look at the history of *this* Government, there was first of all the determination of the Prime Minister to be surrounded by people she could describe as 'one of us', and then the inability of people who disagreed with the way she was running the Government to work together to stop it – the fact that, for example, Howe and Lawson didn't work together five years ago, rightly or wrongly, on the issue . . .

POWELL: I think Denis is in danger of falling into the error into which, with respect, you fell, of trying to generalise from specific instances.

HENNESSY: Mr Powell, Cabinet government alive and well, solely dependent on the personalities around the table, restorable at the kissing of hands of a new Prime Minister?

POWELL: Yes.

HENNESSY: Roy Jenkins. Cabinet government?

JENKINS: Maybe. Maybe you'll have a different style of Cabinet government, a reversion of an old, rather calmer, more collective style. I mean, I think the lesson of the last few years can be put quite bluntly that, at the end of the day, everybody finds her impossible to work with for long.

HENNESSY: Lord Jenkins, Denis Healey, Enoch Powell, thank you very much.

PREDECESSORS AND CONTEMPORARIES

It is doubtful whether there are such things as friends in politics in the same sense as friends outside . . . As for enemies – enemies in the sense of hating a person, not being able to bear the sight of him, that's very rare indeed.

'A Life in the Day of Enoch Powell'
Sunday Times Magazine, 11 May 1986

'IMPROBABLE PITT'

Books and Bookmen, August 1979

The younger Pitt is so large a figure in British history that we need to make a special effort to understand how breathtakingly improbable his whole career was. Alexander conquering the Eastern world and dying at thirty-three is really easier to come to terms with than Pitt becoming Chancellor of the Exchequer at twenty-three and Prime Minister at twenty-four, less than three years after he entered the House of Commons, and remaining Prime Minister through peace and war until he died aged forty-six in 1806, with an intermission of no more than two and a quarter years out of office between 1801 and 1803.

It is a common characteristic of British Prime Ministers, with few and markedly inglorious exceptions, that nobody can 'see them coming' for very long beforehand. How randomly the lottery wheel of accident chooses, would be better seen if *fait accompli* was not invested with inevitability by the falsifying spectacles of history, as well as by the vested interest of nearly all those concerned in the transactions. But the phenomenon of Pitt the Younger simply cannot be passed off as the usual 'luck of the draw' which happened to work out brilliantly. An attempt at least has to be made at understanding.

The materials for the attempt are sufficiently assembled in Reilly's admirable biography,* plain, thorough and well written, which treats with evenly distributed emphasis all the phases of Pitt's career and all the aspects of his character. He presents us at the outset with what is surely a major ingredient of the explanation – the magic of the name of Pitt and the halo of national sentiment and patriotic ardour which surrounded the head of the future Prime Minister's father both before and after his death in 1778 less than three years before the son entered the House of Commons. The Elder Pitt's catastrophic error in becoming a peer and his temperamental and physical inadequacies in the mid-1760s never dethroned him from his seat in the nation's heart.

The national glory of the Seven Years' War had been followed by the national humiliation of the American War. As it drew to its close, figures like Fox, North and Shelburne were thrown into grotesque

---

* *Pitt the Younger*, by Robin Reilly, Cassell

silhouette, like witches around a cauldron, against the ruin and disgrace into which Britain was subsiding. In 1783 it was almost as if our victory in the Second World War had been followed in the 1950s by another war, as exacting as the former but ending in calamitous defeat, and as if then in the early 1960s there had appeared in Parliament a young Churchill, endowed with all and more than his father's eloquence and stainless integrity. In such circumstances, even under the infinitely different system of party government and universal franchise today, the name of Churchill might have had the power to break down barriers and shatter precedents. In 1783 that system hardly yet existed in outline: the nomination of the Crown could, in that transitional phase between Hanoverian and Victorian times, secure for its choice at least the chance to succeed or fail with a House of Commons and an electorate where patronage and individual judgement were not yet mutually destructive forces. George III had had no love for the Earl of Chatham – the King had been ostentatiously unrepresented at his funeral – but amidst his preoccupations with securing a ministry less odious to him than Fox, North or Shelburne could offer, he was not untouched by the national sentiment and instinct. George III could, and he did, invoke the name of Pitt in the person of Chatham's son. The King and the ghost of Chatham had made the first step possible.

Once he was in the saddle, the hour was peculiarly propitious for the talents and character of the Younger Pitt. I find it impossible to study the triumphant years of the Elder Pitt or the earlier part of the Younger Pitt's career without feeling that in the second half of the eighteenth century Britain may well have been as near to revolution as France. Corruption and incompetence, cumulated by disaster, tested almost to destruction the natural and native bonds between government and people and between the respective elements of the national society. The Elder Pitt restored to the nation its tone and coherence by his manifest patriotic aloofness from the pygmy politicians who surrounded him: the Englishman had in Pitt someone in whom he could feel himself personified.

In 1783 ruin financial as well as ruin military stared Britain in the face: she was impoverished, isolated and – except at sea – ignominiously helpless. The nation wanted financial and personal integrity in government, a break with the politics and the politicians that had betrayed it, and a lengthy period of uninterrupted convalescence. The bleak independence of the Younger Pitt, his superb parliamentary and economic talents, and the aura of authority which he diffused gave Britain what she needed, and knew that she needed, in the years between peace in 1783 and war in 1797. The man fitted the moment. If there had been no Pitt, Britain could well have been the image, instead of the antithesis, of contemporary France. The essence of what Pitt did for Britain lies in the Chapter 'Retrenchment and Revival 1784–92'; in order to understand the influence which Pitt continued to influence from beyond the grave over Peel, over Gladstone, over Britain of the high nineteenth century, one needs to study and study again the budgetary and fiscal measures of those eight years.

It is the characteristic, and part of the fascination, of all great political careers, that lines which stretch far beyond them into the future enter visibly into their texture. In Pitt's career such strands were Ireland, slavery, parliamentary reform. Ireland, indeed, was for Pitt, as it was to be for others, the cause of his biggest mortification and defeat. The impractability of the legislative devolution (as we might inaccurately call it today, for in reality it was legislative independence) conferred in 1782 upon the Irish Parliament was immediately understood and the only logical and workable constitutional arrangement discerned: Pitt's Viceroy, the Duke of Rutland, was reporting in 1784 that 'without a *union* Ireland will not be connected with Great Britain in twenty years longer'. Before it came in practice, it was necessary to work through the perennial delusion that 'the internal poverty and distress of the country is the radical cause of all the discontent that prevails' (Pitt's own words), and to face and quell a rebellion abetted and supported by an external enemy. The logic of *union*, however, implied equality of citizenship and this in turn effectively presupposed emancipation. In the event the Union came into existence without those logical conditions being fulfilled: Pitt's sovereign, and in consequence Pitt's Cabinet, had refused them to him, and he had resigned (February 1801). How different the history of these islands would have been if the logical implication had been accepted, no man can judge; but the calamity was in itself stupendous.

Pitt's Irish policies – both the economic proposals of 1784 and the union of 1800 – illustrate a facet of his character to which the biographer constantly refers: an optimism which frequently bordered on the irrational, and which over and over led him into advanced positions – on slavery and reform no less than on Ireland – in which defeat and withdrawal were inevitable. It comes as something of a shock, used as one is to the legend of 'The Pilot Who Weathered the Storm', to discover how dangerous in war was this quality of Pitt's, especially when joined with a naïveté in things military so opposite to his subtle instinct in things political. Pitt was no war Prime Minister of the stamp of Lloyd George or still less Churchill: his contribution to the achievements of Nelson and Wellington had been made, in economic terms, before Britain went to war with France, though in the wake of Trafalgar the City toasted him as 'the Saviour of Europe'. The judgement of the author is well-founded that 'as a war minister Pitt displayed none of the vigour and understanding of priorities that had distinguished his father's policies'.

As Reilly's biography, by its balance of chronology and emphasis, restores the correct proportion to a career too often viewed from 1806 backwards, so his severe and seaching analysis of Pitt's personal characteristics and habits produces a portrait which is fair and convincing but, just for that reason, heightens to the limit of credibility the improbable quality of Pitt's life, in which the burdens and tensions of supreme office during twenty years were borne under the handicaps of alcoholism, homosexual inclinations (if not more), persistent and disabling ill-health, and an incompetence and carelessness in the management of his private affairs almost unbelievable in the restorer of Britain's credit.

'DISRAELI'

Objective, January 1954

Of all our Prime Ministers, Disraeli is unique in having founded a political faith. For a time after the death of the younger Pitt, adherence to 'Mr Pitt's principles' was a party test: but that time was at an end within a decade of his death. Disraeli's rival, Gladstone, made as great an impression or greater in his lifetime; but it would have occurred to no one in 1900, let alone in 1950, to define Liberalism by reference to Gladstone. Disraeli, dead now seventy-two years, still gives inspiration to a great political movement, and evokes an affectionate veneration which grows rather than diminishes with the lapse of time. His sole possible competitor, Bolingbroke, is an exception which doubly proves the rule: for it was Disraeli himself who did most to stamp Bolingbroke's work as a gospel of Toryism, and it was as an exile and a failure, not as a present or future Prime Minister, that Bolingbroke did his thinking and writing.

In fact, it is to the men of thought, not of action, that we must go to find Disraeli's equals in lasting influence: to Burke, the unsuccessful politician; to Locke, the secretary and scholar; to Marx, the year-long denizen of the British Museum.

His contemporaries could not see Disraeli as posterity can. The passions aroused by the great party split over Repeal, or by the *volte face* of the Second Reform Bill, never quite subsided while he lived. His exotic aspects, both those which were real and those which were assumed, distracted or irritated the observer. His final term of office opening triumphantly ended for his party in reverse, and office enforced even upon him, as it does upon all, certain standards of platitude and convention.

But afterwards those who had scarcely known him, or to whom he was solely a character of history, found in his writings – the novels, the speeches, the essays, especially those of his earlier and middle years – a deposit of pure instruction and delight; and a hitherto hidden consistency and connection of principles and practice, reflection and act, came to light. Like Joshua, he appeared as both prophet and captain.

Disraeli is unique among our Prime Ministers in other respects – that of being a Jew; and it is a temptation to make the one peculiarity account for the other. That, of course, would be ludicrously over-simple. But two characteristics of Disraeli which are specifically Jewish do help to account for the lasting importance of his thought. They are characteristics exemplified in Sidonia, the nearest approach to self-portraiture in Disraeli's novels. They are intellectual aloofness, and a belief in the significance of race.

Passionately though Disraeli played the game of politics and cared for its glittering prizes – there is no politician who does not – he could yet survey the scene with an extraordinary detachment, like that of a historian fitting a past epoch into the causation of what preceded and followed it. Unassimilable himself and aloof from the Gentile nobility and squirearchy among whom he sat on the Commons benches, he looked back over millennia of the history of his own race, and from that standpoint saw the politics of his day in a dry, cold light. 'A thousand ages in thy sight . . .'

His own race; and what of theirs? 'Race,' says Sidonia to Coningsby, the idealised young Englishman, 'is everything,' and he proceeds to dilate upon the parallel between the Jewish and English 'races', guided along the path of their respective destinies by instinct. Thirty years later, a *Punch* cartoon was to show the Duke of Abercorn asking Disraeli, 'What shall I tell them is our policy?' and Disraeli replying, 'Say – er – that we will rely upon the sublime instincts of an ancient people.'

It all sounds to us fanciful and rather Hitlerian, but only if we fail to see that the desire to produce a parallel between Britain and Judah had led Disraeli to say 'race' where we should say 'nation', and, incidentally, that 'race' has overtones for us which it had not for our grandfathers. 'Instinct', too, is the word we should use; for biology and anthropology have given us new categories of thought and language. Disraeli claimed to be 'on the side of the angels'; but when he talked about 'relying on the instincts of the race', he was actually dealing in the ideas of evolution.

Disraeli by observation of the present and study of the past had grasped the underlying nature of the British nation. He knew its lineaments which, like those of a human face, remain recognisable despite the vicissitudes of time and events. His own political acts were guided by faith that he perceived aright the laws of the nation's being; and so deep and sure was his perception that when we turn to his words in the perplexities of our present generation, we start as though a live voice sounded at our elbow.

'DISRAELI'S ONE NATION'

BBC Radio, 19 April 1981

Despite the strong, competent and confident adminstration of Sir Robert Peel, the early 1840s were uneasy years of turbulent change and revolutionary anxiety. The first half-century of intense industrialisation had wrought its social havoc; there was both agrarian and urban unrest and distress. The railway mania was just commencing. And the agitation which had declined after the First Reform Act of 1832 was rising again under a House of Commons in which the middle classes were beginning to preponderate and in which the 'Conservative' majority – the word was barely ten years old – uneasily straddled the older and the newer governing classes.

There were many in the 1841 Conservative intake to Parliament who found themselves wondering, vaguely, what it was that they distinctively stood for. Sitting among them on the back benches behind Sir Robert Peel was a man who undertood to give them an answer. It was Benjamin Disraeli, to whom Peel had refused the government office which he – and his wife – had humiliatingly solicited. A few years earlier, Gladstone had been sure that he knew the answer to a similar question, and he had laid it on the line in his now unread book *Church and State*. Disraeli's mind was differently attuned. Fascinated from boyhood with aspirations to novelistic authorship, he cast what he had to suggest into romantic shape. Two love stories, lavishly adorned with scenes from high society but interspersed with didactic passages by way of political commentary, followed one another in 1844 and 1845: *Coningsby* and *Sybil*.

It is always useful in dealing with a Disraeli novel to turn straight to the end, to find out who is going to finish up by marrying whom. *Coningsby* concludes with a marriage of the eponymous hero, a scion of the aristocracy, to Edith Millbank, daughter of an enlightened mill owner and sister of his best friend at public school. *Sybil* ends with a more melodramatic marriage between Egremont, Earl of Marney, and Sybil Gerard, daughter of a Chartist leader and a dispossessed Roman Catholic. In allegoric form, the two plots expressed Disraeli's answer to the question: What is the Conservative Party for? Through a reinterpreted Conservatism, the hereditary or prescriptive element in the constitution was to temper the brashness of the new industrial classes and was to ally itself with the aspirations of the organised workers. The Conservative Party, as Disraeli was to declare more pompously thirty years later, 'was a national party or it was nothing'; and in the romances was signified the reunification of the nation around its historic institutions – the reunion of those 'Two Nations' from the famous passage in *Sybil*, which has passed into the common repertoire of politics.

> 'Well, society may be in its infancy,' said Egremont, slightly smiling, 'but say what you like, our Queen reigns over the greatest nation that ever existed.'
>
> 'Which nation?' asked the younger stranger, 'for she reigns over two.'
>
> The stranger paused; Egremont was silent, but looked enquiringly.
>
> 'Yes,' resumed the younger stranger after a moment's interval. 'Two nations, between whom there is no intercourse and no sympathy, who are as ignorant of each other's habits, thoughts and feelings as if they were dwellers in different zones or inhabitants of different planets, who are formed by a different breeding, are fed by a different food, are ordered by different manners and are not governed by the same laws.'
>
> 'You speak of – ' said Egremont, hesitatingly.
>
> 'THE RICH AND THE POOR.'

There is a less-quoted companion dialogue, also in *Sybil*, which points to that element in Disraeli's prescription for the Conservative Party which a more recent political vocabulary would call populist.

> 'And yet,' said Egremont, 'a great family, rooted in the land, has been deemed to be an element of political strength.'
>
> 'I'll tell you what,' said Gerard, 'there is a great family in this county and rooted in it, of which we have heard much less than they deserved, but of which I suspect we shall very soon hear enough to make us think a bit.'
>
> 'In this county?'
>
> 'Ay, in this county and every other one: I mean the PEOPLE.'

In each of the two novels, *Coningsby* and *Sybil*, two other themes are interwoven with the main allegory of a nation reunited and a working class elevated. They are themes that were never far away from Disraeli's political thinking; and in later novels, as we shall see, they were to form the main themes. They are race and the Church.

Near the beginning of *Sybil* one whole chapter is devoted to a highly idosyncratic presentation of English history from the time of Henry VIII. As history-writing it is preposterous; but recognisable among all the extravagances are the essential elements of historic English Toryism, on which the novels are a rhapsody and which Disraeli intended to hold up to his Party. This is how the passage goes:

> If James II had really attempted to re-establish Popery in this country,

the English people, who had no hand in his overthrow, would doubtless soon have stirred and secured their 'Catholic and Apostolic Church', independent of any foreign dictation, the Church to which they still regularly profess their adherence; and, being a practical people, it is possible that they might have achieved their object and yet retained their native princes; under which circumstances we might have been saved from the triple blessings of Venetian politics, Dutch finance and French wars, against which, in their happiest days and with their happiest powers, struggled the three greatest of English statesmen, Bolingbroke, Shelburne and, lastly, the son of Chatham.

The people, you see, could have been relied upon to secure their independent national church, and it was unnecessary, by invoking a Protestant Hanoverian dynasty, to involve England in the triple evils of a closed Whig oligarchy (Disraeli calls it 'Venetian politics'), the money power of the City (he calls it 'Dutch finance') and continental alliances (called 'French wars'). The mere fact that Bolingbroke and Shelburne and not the Younger Pitt either would not have had a notion what Disraeli was talking about does not matter.

'The English people', 'their native princes': it is the determinism of race. Into *Coningsby* is introduced, as the exponent of race, the figure of Sidonia, half Rothschild, half Wandering Jew, who undertakes to enlighten the young nobleman on a factor to which his education had omitted to point him. 'Where, then,' asks Coningsby, 'would you look for hope?' 'In what is more powerful than laws and institutions,' replies the Jew, 'and without which the best laws and the most skilful institutions may be a dead letter or the very means of tyranny. In the *national character*. It is not in the increased feebleness of its institutions that I see the peril of England: it is in the decline of its character as a community . . . A political institution is a machine; the motive power is the national character. With that it rests whether the machine will benefit society or destroy it.'

In words such as those lies perhaps the one political mission to which that kaleidoscopic and enigmatical character Benjamin Disraeli genuinely felt himself called: to teach the English their nationhood. It was as a Jew that the mission had been assigned to him. 'Sidonia and his brethren,' he observed, 'could claim a distinction which the Saxon and the Greek and the rest of the Caucasian nations have forfeited. The Hebrew is an unmixed race, and an unmixed race of a first-rate organisation are the aristocracy of nature.' Of course, like the business about 'the three greatest English statesmen', it is a flight of fantasy; but Disraeli would not take that for refutation. 'How limited is human reason,' says Sidonia to Coningsby, 'the profoundest enquirers are most conscious. Man is only truly great when he acts from the passions, never irresistible but when he appeals to the imagination.'

In that sentence Disraeli sounds the authentic Tory note of faith in instinct – not instinct disembodied and abstract but the national instinct of a homogeneous people. 'Tell them,' says Disraeli as Prime Minister in a *Punch* cartoon when asked what answer to give to enquirers who want to know Conservative policy, 'tell them that we shall rely upon the sublime instincts of an ancient people.'

Notwithstanding Disraeli's advancement into the front rank of the Conservative Party after the fall of Peel, he went on writing novels; and his next two novels, *Tancred* and *Lothair*, were dedicated to examining in romantic guise the two principles of the Church and race.

Tancred was published in 1847; *Lothair*, not announced for publication until 1870, is located amid the events of the years immediately before that, and yet in 1870 its theme already lay twenty years back: it belonged to the so-called 'papal aggression' of 1850. It is worth making the effort to penetrate the more difficult allegory of these two novels.

As always, we get our bearings by observing who marries whom. In *Lothair* the hero (need one say?) is the orphaned heir to a great dukedom. The girl who eventually gets him turns out not to be Miss Arundel ('whatever you think', said Miss Arundel, 'you will go to Rome, mark my words; I summon you to meet me at Rome'). It is the equally aristocratic but impeccably Anglican Lady Corisande, the one-time object of his adolescent admiration. His two guardians were a Scottish protestant lord and a clergyman who has gone over to Rome and become a cardinal. Lothair, of a naturally religious temperament, falls, first in England and then in Rome, into a trap designed to secure his submission to Rome and to make him champion of the reconversion of England. Horrified on discovering the trickery, he draws back at the last moment, takes flight on a Mediterranean journey, and regains his balance in the Holy Land itself, while his lawyer, on his instruction, 'commences building two new churches on his estate, subscribes in his name to all the diocesan societies, and accepts for him the office of steward for this year of the Sons of the Clergy'.

Disraeli, according to his habit, has escaped from our and his contemporaries' questioning behind a smokescreen of badinage; but the pattern is recognisable through it. The generous enthusiasm of the rising political generation has to be tempered by insight into nationhood. Where better to be learnt than from the greatest exponents of the principle of race and religion?

And so we turn to *Tancred*, which also has its denouement in the

Levant. Its last sentences have become deservedly immortal: ' "I am here," said Tancred, pale and agitated. "Why am I wanted?" Colonel Brace began to explain, but all seemed to speak at the same time. The Duke and Duchess of Bellamont had arrived at Jerusalem.' Tancred – needless to say, the only child and heir of an immensely rich duke of recent ennoblement – has won for bride a Levantine Jewess, at the end of a course of education which parallels that of Coningsby in the industrial revolution and of Egremont in Chartism, not to mention that of Lothair in Anglicanism.

As the novel opens, Tancred – Lord Mantacute by courtesy title – astonishes his father by declining the intimation that it is time for him, being now twenty-one, to assume his rightful seat in the House of Commons. The dialogue which follows between them is, taken as a whole, the most sustained political critique in all the novels. It might serve as a kind of catechism which summarises the very question Disraeli heard his contemporaries asking in the 1840s, to which he offered them his answers in his own peculiar form.

'I cannot find,' Tancred tells his father, 'that it is part of my duty to maintain the order of things which at present prevails in our country. It seems to me that it cannot endure, as nothing can endure that is not founded upon principle; and its principle I have not discovered. Is there such a thing as religious truth? Is there such a thing as political right? Is there such a thing as social propriety? If they are facts, where are they likely to be found in England? Is there truth in our Church? Why, then, do you support dissent? Who has the right to govern? The monarch? You have robbed him of his prerogative. The aristocracy? You confess to me that we exist by sufferance. The people? They themselves tell you that they are nullities.'

After some more of this, the duke protests, 'You are going into first principles.' 'Give me then second principles,' replies his son; 'give me any.' So the duke draws attention to the beneficial effect upon the condition of the people of the expansion of the railways, only to be told: 'You have announced to the millions that their welfare is to be tested by the amount of their wages. You propose for their conduct the least ennobling of all impulses. If you have seen an aristocracy invariably become degraded under such influences; if all the vices of a middle class may be traced to such an absorbing motive; why are we to believe that the people should be more pure or that they should escape the catastrophe that confounds the happiness with the wealth of nations?'

Instead of going into the House of Commons Tancred's decision is to go to Jerusalem. He seeks out (whom else?) Sidonia-Rothschild.

'I am born in an age and in a country,' he complains to him, 'divided between infidelity on one side and an anarchy of creeds on the other: I would appeal to that comforter promised to man on the sacred spot on which the assurance of solace was made.' 'It appears to me, Lord Montacute,' observes Sidonia, 'that what you want is to penetrate the great Asian mystery.'

And did he? The reader would be hard put to it, if so, to formulate the result. The first encounter at Bethany with the eventual heroine ends in the air: ' "We have some conclusions in common. We agree that half Christendom worships a Jewess and the other half a Jew. Now let me ask you one more question. Which do you think should be the superior race, the worshipped or the worshippers?" Tancred looked up to reply, but the lady had disappeard.' By the end of a tangled tale, Tancred is as disillusioned with the Levant (called 'Arabia') as Lothair was with Rome. Just before his father and mother the duke and duchess make their triumphant entry, a last passionate declaration has occurred. 'Fly from me,' says Eva, 'son of Europe and of Christ.' ' "I am a Christian in the land of Christ," said Tancred, "and I kneel to a daughter of my Redeemer's race. Why should I fly?" ' He doesn't; he's going to take her home to England with him to yet another one of those Disraelian marriages which stand in the place where we might have expected a solution.

Few political treatises, even in romantic form, could conclude so unsatisfactorily. The reader, entertained by the ebullient, ironical humour and the scenes of government, Parliament and of high society mischievously but accurately delineated, not to mention the far-fetched escapades and adventures, could be forgiven for wondering if this and the other novels are really political at all, or just a mockery by the arch-mocker and a piece of illusionism by the old magician. Looking back, however, it is the questions that Disraeli put into the persons of Coningsby, Egremont, Tancred and Lothair which mattered, and still matter, more than the fanciful, evasive and roman-tic answers which he gave to them. There are many generations of younger politicians yet to come who will recognise in the novels of Benjamin Disraeli MP their own bewilderment at the gap between the practice of politics and those aspirations and imaginings without which politics itself is a sordid occupation. Like his hero, they will say, 'Then give me second principles, give me any principles.' They will ask how authority can inhere in institutions which continually change and are called in question. They will recognise the nation as the be-all and end-all of politics, and yet seek in vain for a tenable definition of it.

Perhaps the secret of the strange vitality of Disraeli's memory, of why he remains a living political presence when his contemporaries, even the greatest of them, are mummified in history, is that, like life itself, he gave no answers or, if he gave them, gave them only in enigma.

'ENOCH POWELL TALKS TO DISRAELI'

'Weekly Review', *The Sunday Times*, 22 December 1963

Three steel engravings hang on the wall a foot or two in front of my writing desk. I hesitated which of them I should summon to life. Richard Porson, the ornament of every Porson prizeman's study? No: Greek iambics are far away now, and anyhow he would most likely be too drunk for conversation. The Right Honourable William Pitt in 1804? No again: our worlds are too strange; we would pass the brief allotted time in preliminary explanation.

So, then, the third: Benjamin Disraeli, Earl of Beaconsfield, KG in the year 1878.

Myself: Dizzy – please forgive the affectionate familiarity; it is hard for me to call you anything else. You see, the Young England of my own day – One Nation we called it, thinking of *Sybil* – found in you its prophet and its friend, like that earlier Young England of yours a century before. Besides (though we won't go into the details now), there has been a little local difficulty here about earls and prime ministers – Dizzy, tell me: how much was truth, how much was humbug? All that imperialism, the 'empire of England' at the Crystal Palace, and Victoria Empress of India. A quarter of a century earlier you had been talking about 'these wretched colonies, a millstone round our necks' which 'will all be independent in a few years'.

Dizzy: Well, and aren't they? No, I never forgot that our possessions overseas were transitory. I knew it of Canada no less than Durham did; I knew it of India no less than Metcalfe and Elphinstone. But when, beyond all expecation, our power grew instead of waning, and England, not for the first time, confronted Europe as an *alter imperium*, their military autocracies outmatched by Asia and Africa opening to our fleets and our administrators, then I gave this miracle its name and its voice – not, I think, ignobly. A statesman speaks for his day, not for eternity.

Myself: No doubt: yet – without impertinence – some politicians' words last, others' die as they speak them. Yourself and Gladstone, for instance. Goodness knows, back Hansards are dreary stuff at the best of times; but Gladstone has left nothing that lives, while some of your speeches and some of your books are read, quoted, reprinted still. What is the vital secret?

Dizzy: Ah, poor Gladstone! A wonderful career, far more wonderful and romantic than mine, with many more unexpected turns; yet no one thought so, because somehow he dried every drop of romance out of it. I made mine into a romance, conciously, deliberately, artistically; and not only my own career, but everything that came its way: English political history in the previous sixty years – you remember all that about the 'Venetian oligarchy'? Peel and Lord George Bentinck – no romance in *him*, but I turned him into the hero of my finest novel. (You have read my *Life of Lord George Bentinck*, I hope? *I inclined my head.*) Queen Victoria herself – you remember that business about 'the Fairy', though unintentionally she paid it back with 'his favourite flower' (I loathe primroses). Above all I made a romance of the nation itself. That was what it wanted. That is what a nation does want from its politicians, who after all are its priests, its hierophants, its witch-doctors. I gave it them; and they have rewarded me by remembering me.

Myself: 'The throne, the altar and the cottage'?

Dizzy: Precisely, 'the throne, the altar and the cottage': the simple essentials of every national existence – loyalty to its institutions, faith in its God, love of its homes. I only gave these things a concrete, a visible, above all a romantic expression.

Myself: Only?

Dizzy: You mean, did I not by policy and administration bring about all the amelioration that the characters in *Coningsby* and *Sybil* looked forward to, the 'improvement of the condition of the people', as I called it in my Crystal Palace speech? No. I discerned dimly what was coming to pass under the impulse of innumerable, complex, yet often mechanical causes – have you ever reflected how little 'improvement of the condition of the people' would have been possible without iron pipes? – and I gave it a name, I gave it a welcome and a good conscience, I gave it romance. There was my work. The statesman or, to call him by the more honourable name, the politician, is not like the engineer or the architect or the sculptor. He is more like the master of a sailing barque on the ocean. The winds, the currents, the storms of events are not his to govern or decide or even, except at short range by good luck or practised judgement, to foresee. He pits his puny strength against these huge blind forces to keep the ship of opinion afloat and unharmed and to steer it no man knows whither! The helm is men's imagination.

Myself: But you, of all people, cannot mean that a man sets out in politics, or lives a life in politics, without principles, objects or even ambitions – ambitions, that is to say, for his country, not for himself? ' "These are first principles you are asking for," said the Duke. "Then give me second principles, or any principles," replied Lothair.' I quote from memory.

Dizzy: And your quotation is nearly accurate. No, I do not mean that. It is a politician's principles, or objects, or ambitions which his imagination ought to play upon and endow with the indispensable romance. Without them imagination would work in the void. What I do mean is that at the end of a lifetime in politics – you, too, will find this one day – when a man looks back, he discovers that the things he has most opposed have come to pass and that nearly all the objects he set out with are not merely not accomplished, but seem to belong to a different world from the one he lives in. Yet he need not think this a refutation or a mark of failure. However much his objects were deflected or defeated by events or the facts of the world, he may still feel that his pursuit of them was the important thing about him. The aspirations of *Coningsby* and *Sybil* belonged to a world which, if I could but have perceived the fact, scarcely existed when I wrote; a generation later the last landmarks had disappeared. But it would not have been worth a lifetime's struggles and disappointments to be Prime Minister in 1874 if I had not dreamt those dreams thirty years earler.

Myself: Yet when one lives in politics, so much – as you well know – is seen to be the outcome of utter chance: the unexpected that always happens was one of your own themes.

Dizzy: There is no inconsistency. No one was to know that England would want a novel-writing Jewish romantic to be its Prime Minister. A vast series of accidents, which only the historians will mistake for inevitabilities, was needed to make him so. I sat at the gaming-table with scores of others; I learnt the rules – and tricks – of the game, and played it with a delight that I need not describe to you; for its fascination is the same in every age and generation. (I assume, with some confidence, that 'dishing the Whigs' is not yet out of fashion?) But to the hazards of the game I brought an inner continuity and certainty, deeper even than the principles – or the romances – in which it sought expression.

Myself: A certainty – of what? It was too late. The eyes, that had seemed to move and twinkle in harmony with the puckish lips, had resumed the distant, fixed, inscrutable gaze of the steel engraving.

'CHURCHILL AND WAR'

BBC Radio, 29 July 1983

With its fifth volume of over 1,300 pages, the *Life of Winston Church-ill*, started by his deceased son Randolph and now carried on by Martin Gilbert, has reached its climax in *The Finest Hour 1939–41*. The volume takes its name from a phrase in a Churchill speech of the time, which, like so many others, passed into the mouth of the English people. But for the events of 1939–41, there would have been no such majestic biographical monument, and no such voluminous archive as the parallel-running *Companion Volumes* of source material. The *Companion Volumes* aim at being a comprehensive collection of the evidence on which the *Life* is based. Unfortunately, they have fallen out of phase with the actual biography, and the last volume of them just published – No. V.3, of nearly 1,700 pages – just comes up to the first day or two of September 1939, where *The Finest Hour* commences.

The *Life* itself is a hybrid. It is less than a biography, because the author has not given to the material a shape or form beyond those which simple chronology and the succession of the events impose. On the other hand, it is more than a chronicle, because the author has not refrained from allowing his own opinion and judgement occasionally to appear, although he mainly uses quotations from the diaries, memoirs and letters of his eye-witnesses to do the taking for him. Illustrations of this are to be found everywhere in the book. I will take just one.

Churchill was often accused of insisting upon interfering too much in minute details. Gilbert takes this charge seriously, and points out that before 1939, when Churchill was politically isolated, he had to accumulate for himself much of the detail necessary to buttress his arguments. The same habit, however, became a source of strength to him as a wartime Minister and Prime Minister, because it equipped him to probe and to prod. At this point the biographer hands over to one of his sources, and quotes directly from Colonel, later General, Jacobs, who was Churchill's staff officer at the Defence Ministry. 'As Jacobs later recalled', writes Gilbert, ' "Churchill pushed and pushed and pushed, which was all to the good – the admirable wish for the offensive – provided he had people to keep him on the rails".' As Prime Minister the restraints were there: ' "That," Jacobs reflected, "is one of the reasons why we won the war." ' So there is a judgement, and quite a striking one, which the biographer has pronounced, but not in his own person.

By such presentational methods the *Life* creates a powerful cumulative impression of the day-to-day operations of the man upon whose shoulders the British war effort uniquely rested. For those of us who, like myself, were on the periphery of that effort but can match date for date in our lives, such a narrative has an irresistible fascination. No doubt on subsequent readings different conclusions, even for us, would predominate; but at first encounter I found two conclusions overwhelming.

It was not only Neville Chamberlain but the Conservative 'establishment' in Parliament and in government who, for two pins, would have made peace with Germany after the fall of France. In fact, the record shows that the 'appeaser', Neville Chamberlain, when serving in Churchill's Cabinet after Churchill superseded him as Prime Minister in 1940, became surprisingly tough and bellicose. On the other hand, Lord Halifax (the Foreign Secretary) and his junior in the Commons, 'Rab' Butler, were far from being 'above suspicion', though both were perceptive enough to keep on the right side once they realised – to borrow a phrase from Chamberlain's young aide at the time, Alec Home – 'the way the wind blew'. One of the reasons for the immense popularity of Churchill in 1940 was the not unfounded instinct of the common people that, but for him, their rulers would have betrayed them. There is a certain fallacy in attempting to decide what was Churchill's one crucial contribution to the survival of Britain. Great historical events are determined by a whole array of causes, each of which would be entitled in isolation to be regarded as crucial. But I feel sure that many people besides myself believe it was by being an immovable obstacle to compromise or surrender in 1940 that Churchill saved his country.

The other overwhelming conclusion I draw from this volume may seem a paradox alongside the first. It is that the conquest of the British Isles was inherently impracticable for Germany even at the height of her domination of Western Europe. Once the flow of British aircraft production reached wartime levels, the Luftwaffe was not going to get air superiority over southern England; and even if it had done so momentarily, the Royal Navy, at however great sacrifice, would probably still have reduced invading forces to a condition in which they would not have been able to make good a bridgehead on the island. Discount such windfalls as the breaking of the ULTRA code and the (fairly tardy) American provision of arms and ammunition, and still the equation between Churchill and Hitler would have stood in 1940 as it stood between Pitt and Napoleon in 1805:

the Grand Army across the Channel must perforce wheel eastwards, to initial triumph and eventual destruction in Russia. If Germany ever had a chance of conquering Britain it would have been by repeating and surpassing her submarine achievements of 1917 and seizing command of the Atlantic, which no continental enemy of Britain ever achieved.

These things are not lost upon the elderly gentlemen who inhabit the Kremlin and who, or whose advisers, are dedicated students of World War II. Supposing – what I confess is beyond my own capability to imagine – that the Russian rulers include among their purposes the conquest and subjugation of the United Kingdom, their studies must surely have led them to the conclusion that, if Germany, after conquering Western Europe and with Eastern Europe still neutral, could not invade and occupy the British Isles, then neither would Russia be able to do so after conquering continental Europe but with a hostile China on her eastern border. The Russians would moreover have learnt that, if they intend to create even the appearance of such a possibility, they must be able to dispute the command of the eastern Atlantic with the Royal Navy. In short, don't try to frighten me with Soviet tanks; frighten me, if you must, with Soviet submarines.

Just now, I substituted 'British Isles' for 'Britain'. To an observer of Britain's proceedings in Northern Ireland at the present time, it is enormously instructive to be reminded of the preoccupation amounting almost to an obsession, of the British Government in 1939 and 1940 with the Irish Free State. Because the Irish Free State never actually was drawn into World War II, it is perilously easy to overlook the glaring menace which its existence presented on the map to the eyes and thoughts of a British High Command confronting a hostile Continent. Hence the axiom of British statecraft before and since World War II that, if a price exists at which the strategic co-operation of the Irish Republic can be purchased, that price ought to be paid, by finding means to transfer Ulster to an all-Ireland state.

This is how the lines of history run out of the past into the future. When Mrs Thatcher was asked during the recent general election if she would resume her bilateral talks with the Irish premier, she replied: 'It is obviously better for all of us that we enjoy friendly relations between the UK and the Republic of Ireland.' In saying that – whether she knew it or not – she was repeating a refrain which had many years of history behind it. We can read at large in Gilbert's biography how Churchill at the time of our 'finest hour' cast about for means to pay the price of Irish neutrality. Yet in the end he knew the score: 'All this talk,' he minuted in September 1939, 'about partition and the bitterness that would be healed by a union of Northern and Southern Ireland would amount to nothing. They will not unite at the present time, and we cannot in any circumstances sell the Loyalists of Northern Ireland.'

As a politician, I am constantly and embarrassingly reminded that one can never have read enough. What nourishes the working politician best is the raw material of biography such as Gilbert provides much more than the polished and pre-digested pages of period history.

'LOSING THE PEACE'

The Sunday Times, 1983

In 1983 the record of Ernest Bevin as Foreign Secretary between 1945 and 1951 in Attlee's Labour Government is of burning contemporary interest. These were the years in which Britain became committed to that axiomatic identification with the philosophy and strategy of the United States which a whole series of current events – Grenada, Beirut, cruise missiles, a South Korean airliner – are conspiring to undermine and discredit.

How did the sceptical and pragmatic British, with interests traditionally and inherently hard to reconcile with those of the United States, come to be entangled in an American world-view, and American hegemony and an American nuclear embrace? As one reads the story of a robust trade union leader, shrewd and bluff, patriotic and intelligent, presiding over the foreign relations of the United Kingdom in the immediate aftermath of the Second World War, the question begins to get itself answered. Hindsight detects in embryo the assumptions and the attitudes that developed into the dominant orthodoxy which was to determine in the subsequent thirty years almost every phase of Britain's policy.

On the morrow of victory Britain grossly overestimated what its power and potentialities would be around the world in the coming years. It also grossly underestimated the speed and irresistibility with which former colonial territories down to the smallest specks on the map would become finally and formally independent. These were natural errors. It would have been superhuman if the British had avoided them. Yet, right from the ending of hostilities Britain was left under no possible misapprehension as to its financial and economic debility: we could not afford, we realised at once, the cost of what still seemed our manifest destiny in the Mediterranean, in the Middle East, in the Far East, in Africa.

The conclusion drawn was that we had to get the Americans committed at our side. From an early turning-point in 1946 the Americans were nothing loath; but with their seemingly unlimited economic power and their naïve self-confidence, it was inevitable that they would be the predominant partner. It was they and not the British who would call the shots – in Palestine, in Iran and the Arab countries, in the Indian Ocean and (disastrously) in South East Asia. They would do so, moreover, within the framework of a vision of the world which Britain did not naturally share, but in which it felt itself obliged to concur. This was a result of what had happened in Europe in 1945.

The German invasion of Russia had stimulated the transforming of Soviet Russia into a formidable military power, and the Russian counter-invasion left that power in physical control of Eastern Europe. The combined effect of the German victories in 1940–2 and the Russian victories in 1943–5 destroyed the materials for reconstructing that European balance of power and 'concert of Europe' which had been Britain's historic mainstay. It seemed to Britain that the balance had to be restored from outside Europe; and that, again, meant 'getting the Americans committed'.

Unlike Germany, however, Russia represented an exportable philosophy and, as Bevin put it to the House of Commons in June 1946, 'the idea that the security of Russia can only be maintained when every country in the world has adopted their Soviet system'. Thus did the balance of European power become transformed into a worldwide American *cordon sanitaire* and America into the St George of democracy and what is called 'freedom'. Bevin's successor, Eden, was even more sceptical and agnostic than he; but the Suez adventure marked the completion of Britain's absorption into the American hegemony and its accompanying *Weltanschauung*. Only after the passage of a generation is Britain beginning to experience a growing alienation from both and the close of the era over whose inception the Labour Government of Attlee and the Foreign Secretaryship of Ernest Bevin presided.

There is no substitute for details; it is details not generalities which demonstrate and illuminate currents in history. There is an immensity of detail in the 857 pages of the third and last volume of Alan Bullock's biography of Bevin,* which cover the first six years of the peace and the last six of Bevin's life. But Lord Bullock has digested and mastered it totally, so that the book reads like a running narrative and stands up, solid as its subject, like a piece of sculpture. For members of the present-day Labour Party it will be haunting reading, for it is also the story of a romance out of their past which can never be repeated, the tale of how Labour's leaders helped to fight the greatest war in Britain's history and then were called to govern, firmly but peaceably, a Britain in unparalleled transition, the tale of how an old-fashioned Labour dream came true and a destitute Bristol lad

Ernest Bevin: Foreign Secretary 1945–51 by Alan Bullock, Heinemann

born out of wedlock dealt on more than equal terms with monarchs, ambassadors and plenipotentiaries.

If the seeds of our present discontents were sown in the errors and illusions of that time, the fault was not his; but the instruction can still be ours.

'CURIOUS CHANCES IN POLITICS'

Books and Bookmen, August 1976

Anthony Eden would not have expected when he left office in January 1957 to be still writing books of reminiscences twenty years later – which is why he made haste and published the conclusion (*Full Circle*, 1951–7) first, in 1960. Here at last is the slim initial volume,* the first twenty years of his life. The pre-war chapters, boyhood as a younger son in the Eden family home at Windlestone in Co. Durham, are pleasant enough but unremarkable: descriptions of well-to-do Edwardian youth have often been done, and done better, though one can never look at too many of those old photographs.

When it comes to the war, with Captain Eden adjutant of his battalion in the Battle of the Somme at age nineteen, it is the real thing, and the more so for the artless directness of the recollections. There are plenty of narratives, especially in the spate of war books in the late twenties and early thirties, of trench warfare in the First World War; but this is as good as any but the classics like Sassoon, or Remarque, or Lyttelton.

Much more than when reading those books at the time, one is now struck – overwhelmed – with astonishment at the mere boys who overnight in their hundreds of thousands, as it were effortlessly, turned into soldiers, officers and heroes. It must have had far more than the merely superficial consequences for that generation, and perhaps for the next, which are part of the conventional wisdom. 'I had entered the holocaust,' Eden concludes, 'still childish, and I emerged tempered by my experience but with my illusions intact, neither shattered nor cynical, to face a changed world.'

There is something deeply revealing of Eden in that inadequate, near platitudinous reflection. Quite probably, like most things which people tell you about themselves, it is accurate. 'With my illusions intact'! Eden's illusions were always intact. That the lessons of experience and the rules of the game were not perhaps applicable, perhaps not even ascertainable, did not occur to him: and this, intellectually speaking, was his undoing in 1956. All the same, the impression of

*Another World, 1897–1917 Anthony Eden, Allen Lane

judgement in middle-life being simplistically perverted for the 1914–18 generation by the recollection of the trenches is shared with Eden by – of all people – that very different character, his supplanter, Harold Macmillan.

The tragedy of Eden – and he is in the Greek tragic mould – is that the gods gave him charm and bravery and intelligence, and oh! what a hold over the House of Commons; but they did not give him the cynicism nor the strength and ruthlessness nor the self-reliant insight that should have gone with the other qualities. One is never fair to one's leaders till they have fallen: and in my young, irreverent early years in Parliament I was wont to describe Eden as not a person but 'an arrangement of coloured lights'. I was wrong, of course, cruelly and atrociously wrong: but alas for 'the worm that never dies', the residual element of truth.

It is strange – or should it be? – of how many Prime Ministers one ends by wondering how they got to be Prime Minister at all. Most were made so by an unlikely chance, or string of chances, a lucky moment at which their number was opposite to the red. Eden was the exception. Of all Prime Ministers since Balfour and even since Gladstone, he was the one who was seen coming the farthest off; and the accident of ill-health, which might have transferred the crown to 'Rab' Butler at that fantastic juncture in 1953 when Churchill, Eden and Macmillan were all ill at the same time, just managed not to produce the expectedly unexpected outcome.

Surveying Eden's career once more, in the not very satisfactory medium of Weidenfeld's *Prime Ministers*† series – unsatisfactory because they are too long to be biographical essays but too short to have the revelatory quality of new biographical detail – one is still unable to escape the contrast between Prince Charming, the heir apparent of a decade or more, and the Winter King of 1955–6 into whom the alchemy of the supreme office seemed to transform him, a contrast too brusquely sketched in A. J. P. Taylor's introduction. External circumstances and the chance pattern of events will not explain it, because nothing in the Suez crisis precipitated by Nasser in 1956 was out of scale with the kind of events with which Eden had been almost professionally coping during his long apprenticeship and masterhood as Foreign Secretary.

I used, as one of the 'Suez rebels' of 1954 (rebels, that is, against the Treaty of evacuation), to believe that Eden's personal identification with the Treaty, and the commitment to it of his personal credit against the doubts of his own party and of Winston Churchill himself, produced the uncharacteristically rash reaction when events

†*Anthony Eden* by Sidney Aster, Weidenfeld & Nicolson

so promptly invalidated his judgement. In longer retrospect I am inclined to place much less weight upon that humiliation, and instead to seek partial explanation in the concurrence of a recent physical cause with a permanent temperamental one.

From 1952 onwards, and especially after his operation in April 1953, Eden was never again in reliable good health, but exposed, through the permanent impairment of his biliary system, to sudden and severely disturbing fluctuations of physical condition. This interacted with a temperamental defect which only actual occupation of the highest office could fully disclose. This was an unsureness which enabled its possessor to function successfully only when ultimate responsibility was being taken by someone else. It was a curious blend of hesitation and gallantry that depended upon being anchored, or 'earthed', and which therefore left him in the lurch once he gained the summit. Perhaps, all of us end as we began, and the story of the precocious boy-adjutant in the trenches of the Somme is the frontispiece to the whole history.

Baldwin comes aptly in the same series* as a study in contrast, an extreme instance of the opposite, but much more common, enigma of the man who nobody suspected would or could become Prime Minister till a month or two before it happened. Curzon was justified in describing him as 'a person of the utmost insignificance', and he himself attributed to 'a succession of curious chances' his accession to an office which he 'never sought or planned or schemed for in his life'.

After eight undistinguished years as a back-bencher he became PPS to Bonar Law (1916); then, almost by accident, Financial Secretary to the Treasury (1917); then, when Law left Lloyd George's Coalition Government on health grounds, he was made President of the Board of Trade (1921). When the Coalition broke up (through no doing of Baldwin's), be came Bonar Law's Chancellor of the Exchequer (1922), and when Bonar Law died six months later, he succeeded him. Once at the head of the Conservative Party, Baldwin stayed there like a limpet on the point of a rock: he made a hash of his first general election (1923), won the next (1924), lost the next (1929), lived out the years of opposition (1929–31) and of National Government under Ramsay MacDonald (1931–5), and was then Prime Minister again during the two years, 1935–7, which made the Second World War inevitable and the defeat of the British Empire all but inevitable. Whereupon he disappeared into silent retreat, whither presently he was pursued by disproportionate execration.

No doubt there was a man there – sentence after sentence in his

Stanley Baldwin by Kenneth Young, Weidenfeld & Nicolson

speeches betokens a more than ordinary emotion and perception – and no doubt the relationship he made with the nascent Labour Party, foreseeing and desiring for it a great place in Parliament, was a political work in the great tradition. No doubt, too, there was a shrewd and tough political operator, and alert to boot, inside the carefully cultivated persona of the plain Worcestershire Englishman. But – why should *he*, and not some other out of twenty or thirty at the least, have led the Tory Party for fourteen years and been three times Prime Minister? Hindsight, which usually has a deceptively rational answer to such questions, had in his case already withdrawn its sanction long before his death, and retrospection has not seriously offered to renew it since. The true answer is the irrational one that Baldwin himself gave: 'a succession of curious chances'.

Sir Dingle Foot, one of Harold Wilson's Solicitors-General (1964–7), has set out† to examine in some depth five of these 'curious chances', crises after which, using *crisis* exceptionally in its correct sense, everything was visibly different for ever. This is a much more fearsome and demanding operation than in biography to point out the simple succession of unpredictable causes and effects. e.g. that 'A was standing on one side of the road instead of the other, and was therefore knocked down and killed by a runaway horse, with the consequence that B, who happened to be at home when C could not be found, was appointed to the post for which A had seemed predestined.' In order to define political causation at all rigorously, one must, for one thing, be able to detect and isolate the great trends and laws which operate irresistibly and are only diverted slightly or briefly by personalities and chances, as a river is diverted by a rock or fallen tree.

Let me illustrate from Sir Dingle's first crisis, the Liberal Unionist defection led by Chamberlain, which defeated Gladstone's first Home Rule Bill in June 1886. 'In retrospect', he says, 'it can hardly be disputed that this was the most disastrous vote in British parliamentary history,' because, if the Bill had passed, 'it would have averted ninety years of continuing bitterness and bloodshed'. Leaving aside the question whether the Bill could have been got through Parliament and put into force at all, 'it can hardly be disputed' that the refusal of Ulster to participate and the consequent civil war in Ireland would merely have been brought forward from 1912–22 to an earlier period. The great factors – the nationalism of the majority in the island, the unionism of the minority, the absence of any logical or durable middle position between union and independence – existed independently of the protagonists, Gladstone and Chamberlain, who were like actors

†*British Political Crises* by Dingle Foot, William Kimber

playing out one version among many possible versions of a predetermined stark and tragic plot.

How little Sir Dingle comprehends the simple but inexorable mechanics, the following comment of his shows:

> The most extraordinary contribution [to the Home Rule debate of 1886]
> came from Chamberlain himself. To the universal amazement he advo-
> cated a Federation on the Canadian model. Britain was to become a
> Federal State. Since this would have involved the creation of a subordinate
> Parliament in Dublin, it was difficult to see where the fundamental differ-
> ence lay.

Leaving aside the fact that the federal option had been widely can-
vassed previously, by the Home Rulers (Isaac Butt etc.) and others,
the 'fundamental difference' is plain enough. In fact, it will dominate
the forthcoming debates on the same constitutional issue (though we
call it 'devolution') in 1976–7. A federation preserves the unity of the
state by dividing the functions of government into an upper and a
lower tier, and thereby enables all parts to be equally represented
in the union assembly, while separately represented in their local
assemblies. The weakness of the proposition was not in its logic,
which was impeccable: it lay, even if Great Britain would emotionally
have accepted federation, in the fact that the Irish majority rejected
the union as such. Chamberlain was right:

> Once granted that Ireland is entitled to be considered as a nation and not
> as a member of a nation or a State within a nation, then you must follow
> this to its logical conclusion and give them the rights of a nation, including
> separate taxation, foreign relations and military forces.

Without a firm historical grasp of fundamentals, the attempt to identify and analyse political crises, formidable enough anyhow, degener-
ates into mere anecdotal description; and that is the nature of Sir
Dingle's treatment of all his other crises too. December 1916, which
made Lloyd George Prime Minister, destroyed the Liberal Party –
'the principal tragedy of British politics in modern times'. The description is a matter of political taste: but what 'can hardly be disputed'
is that, even if Lloyd George had never lived, the Liberal Party was
destined to be ground in the twentieth century between the upper
and nether millstone of capitalism and socialism – a truth proved
again and again by the manner in which successive attempts to revive
it have failed.

So it is with the rest of the crises – the Carlton Club meeting in 1922,
which 'completely changed the style of government' and ushered in
'the reign of mediocrity'; the financial crisis of July 1931, which laid
the foundation for 'acceptance of Treasury orthodoxy, appeasement,
and the domination of the party whips'; the vote of May 1940, which

made Winston Churchill Prime Minister, 'incomparably the most important decision in 700 years of parliamentary history' because it made 'complete victory' possible in World War II. Every one of these presumptions, on which Sir Dingle builds his crisis theory, is unexamined and in the larger perspective unsustainable.

Paradoxically, in the case of individuals, the author seems to have an almost Calvinistic conviction of predestination. Asquith at Oxford 'was about to become a Member of Parliament. Who could have doubted that here was a future Prime Minister?' And sure enough, 'when Campbell Bannerman died in 1908, Asquith inevitably became Prime Minister'. Strange notions indeed in someone who believes that a single committee meeting creates ninety years of bloodshed, and a misunderstanding between two Cabinet colleagues destroys an historic party!

The book is atrociously proof-read. I mention this only because of a curiosity that I have been unable quite satisfactorily to explain. The text swarms with errors which are not misprints, but either misreadings or mishearings, e.g. 'expand' for 'extend' (page 29) 'position' for 'possession' (page 30), 'steeples' for 'steppes' (page 50), 'projector' for 'projectile' (page 54), 'sanatorium' for 'sanctum' (page 69). Perhaps the most curious of all is 'bolting' for 'coalition' (page 103). The real puzzle, however, is that these and deeper corruptions occur predominantly, though not exclusively, not in the main text but in the quotations, some of which are unintelligible without intensive emendation. I am inclined to think that the text must have been typed or set up from the author's handwriting and never corrected by him – or indeed by anyone who was awake at the time. Perhaps, however, it was dictated over the telephone as well.

'BEVAN AGONISTES'

Listener, 11 October 1973

Michael Foot is a master of English. Both in parliamentary debate and in the written word his diction has the qualities of purity and terseness which the Augustans admired and sought. Indeed, it is of the age of Dryden and Pope, Addison and Swift, where he personally feels most at home, that he is the foremost modern heir and representative. His writing, like his speaking, is almost invariably perspicuous and graceful, offering no avoidable impediment to the reader, and concealing its imaginative quality with the artist's art. Only occasionally, in the House of Commons as on the page, does over-excitement get the better of him and betray him into an exaggerated expression or a faulty metaphor.

These characteristics of the biographer's style throw into relief the very different eloquence and linguistic power of his subject. Those who heard Aneurin Bevan command the House of Commons, in his great days, with an eloquence surpassed, if at all, only by Churchill, are reminded by the biographer's quotations how strangely similar those two antagonistic orators were. Their marvellous and often unexpected vocabulary was that of the self-educated; their oratory often approached, and sometimes crossed, the bounds of intemperance; and they were capable of descent from flights of true imagination to depths of bathos. Bevan's style belonged, like Churchill's, to a more spacious parliamentary and political era, already past before he died. It is in that literal sense that we shall not listen to their like again.

Foot's *Bevan** will be among the outstanding biographies of the twentieth century, even for readers whose interest is neither historical nor political. The proportions and balance, as well as the style, ensure it a place in literature in its own right. Perhaps, as so often, the inherent difficulties of the task promoted the achievement. One of these difficulties was the nature of the material, consisting, on the one hand, of speeches recorded in Hansard or newspapers, and, on the other hand, of anecdote and recollection with only the most meagre survival of documents. Another difficulty was presented by the man's career itself: six years' coruscation in Cabinet office, islanded in a lifetime of opposition before and after. This would be

*Aneurin Bevan, 1945–60 by Michael Foot, Davis-Poynter

no memoir of a successful statesman, tracing his orderly progression from one achievement to the next. At the same time, for Aneurin Bevan's role as a thinker and inspirer the written materials were slight – little beyond the speeches and the single essay, *In Place of Fear*, published in 1952 but largely drafted in 1944 and 1945.

Michael Foot's solution was to write the drama of Bevan Agonistes, the tragedy of the political prophet, cheated by the pattern of events of his practical fulfilment. He is not, therefore, writing a history of the politics of 1945 to 1960, though the book opens one window on to it after another. He is not 'fair' to the other actors on the stage, but brings them on as Agonistes himself imagined them and strove with them. Attlee, Morrison, Cripps, Churchill – these and the lesser figures are presented as they peopled the world of Bevan's mind: for it is the story of that mind that the biographer is attempting.

For this purpose, the biographer had to cross the perilous divide between the two sections of Aneurin Bevan's post-war life, which is also the divide between two types of source-material, the official and the personal. It is part of the success of the book that Michael Foot does not shrink from including a proportionately full description of the housing programme of the later forties and of the creation of the National Health Service, and manages to do so without perceptible change of gear or alteration of style. The reason why he has succeeded lies not only in his literary craftsmanship: that in itself would not have carried him through. It lies also in his partisanship.

It is not as a historian or professional biographer, nor even as Chorus of a drama which he himself observed throughout the years of this second volume, that Foot writes Bevan's life. He writes as a disciple, as a devotee, as a polemicist. This enables him to infuse the narrative of Bevan's ministerial life with the passion of personal conviction. The debates of the later forties are fought over again, as they might have been fought by Michael Foot speaking from his old seat below the gangway in the Commons. What is more, the evident affection between the older and the younger man sheds over the candid partisanship a humanity which forestalls the protest of those who do not share the philosophy. Less remarkable men than Aneurin Bevan have been good company in a punt at Stratford-on-Avon, or escaped from politics into enthusiasms with which the world would not have credited them: but the reader would not have wished to miss these recollections, only because they are less significant than the admirer seems to think.

In the end, what are we to think that Aneurin Bevan was? As one with a low power of visual memory, and therefore obliged to store abstractions rather than images, I found that the photographs in the book helped remarkably to recall judgements made fifteen, twenty and twenty-five years ago and laid aside in the interval. I was struck again with an old impression: that of the conflict between the disorderliness of Bevan's mind and character and his yearning to formulate truths and principles in a manner at once satisfying to himself and convincing to others. One was not mistaken: the face is that of an impulsive man. Yet that is not the main thing. It is the face of a man emotional, clever, affectionate, humorous – all these, yes, but, above all, of a man with a mind and character undisciplined.

In essential tragedy, the hero's catastrophe is the intersection of circumstance with the strengths and weakness of his own character. In Nye Bevan it was the inner indiscipline which denied to his other qualities – his eloquence, his courage, his idealism – the effect they might have left behind them. This inner indiscipline has nothing to do with common-or-garden rebelliousness. Maybe Bevan had the temperament of a born or natural rebel: but that is something different altogether and can co-exist with the strictest self-discipline.

It was this failing which made the book *In Place of Fear* a disappointment to so many eager readers. The book displayed a mind which, for all its insights and fervour, was not disciplined to organise and enforce a continuing and consistent argument and theme. There was a sense in which Bevan's oratorical gifts pandered to this central weakness and enhanced it. Not that his oratory came easily: only the ignorant imagine that such virtuosity is easily acquired and perfected. Nor that his speeches were superficial: on the contrary, his best thoughts and deepest conclusions were stored up in them. The trouble is that a speech – above all, a parliamentary speech – comes to seem like an achievement in itself: not only has the opponent been dialectically routed but the argument has been stated, the truth has been asserted. What more is necessary? Yet in reality the hard thinking and the difficult doing still lie in the future.

The weakness appeared to grow upon Bevan, as such weaknesses do with years and disappointment, during the long and dreary fifties. Nothing seemed to be followed up or followed through. The smoking-room grew more comfortable, the hard slog on the benches less and less attractive. The captain of the small band, the leader of the forlorn hope, the lonely pathfinder, must be found at their unrewarding post through the watches of the night. The heavier the odds, the more patient and persistent must be the politician who intends to make his own ideas the ideas of his party. Nye was not like this. His mind and his character were alike attuned to brilliant forays inside or outside the Labour Party and the House of Commons: but, in the intervals between, he seemed not to be there. Yet in the end he has been fortunate, and what he cast on the waters has been returned to his memory with interest. It is the fate of many who loom large in the eyes and ears of Parliament during their lifetime to become, first, a legend; and then, as those who knew them depart, a name; and finally to become non-persons in the records of the time. This will never happen now to Aneurin Bevan. He owes that to Michael Foot.

'HOW MACMILLAN DECEIVED THE QUEEN'

The Spectator, 13 October 1973

'I was sad that Macleod, for whom I had the highest regard, did not feel able to join' – so said Macmillan, on the formation of Alec Home's Government in October 1963. There was another member of Harold Macmillan's Cabinet who, though not mentioned in the ex-Prime Minister's narrative* of those events, also 'did not feel able to join'. Evidently Macmillan was not 'sad about' him; but there is just this difference – that he is alive to put the record straight.

I agree with Humphrey Berkeley (*The Times*, 29 September 1973) as to the gross impropriety of the communications between Mr Macmillan and the Sovereign being disclosed in his memoirs and the unwisdom of those on whose advice she consented to it. But at least the documents confirm that in the unconstitutional proceedings whereby Harold Macmillan effectively designated his successor while still in office and thus deprived the Queen of the exercise of her principal prerogative, the crucial information which he tendered to her was gravely at variance with the facts of the situation.

On the evening of Thursday 17 October, the Prime Minister in hospital drew up a memorandum for the Queen on the result of his consultations, of which he had formally notified her two days earlier. ('Your Majesty need not be troubled by the matter until these processes have been completed.') In that memorandum, he states, he informed her that there were 'in Cabinet ten for Home; three for Butler; four for Maudling; and two for Hailsham'.

As Macleod set out in a narrative published in *The Spectator* of 17 January 1964, that could at no time have correctly represented the facts, and it had been disproved by events before the memorandum reached Her Majesty's hands on the morning of Friday 18 October.

When Macleod's narrative was published, I publicly confirmed that it was to my knowledge accurate; and I have been able, since reading Macmillan's book, to refresh my memory from my own detailed record of the events of which I was personally witness at that time. The record was dictated immediately after 18 October 1963, and has

At the End of the Day by Harold Macmillan, Macmillan

since been kept at my bank, for publication when the time comes which I or my executors consider appropriate.

On Friday morning, 18 October 1963, the following declared, to Mr Butler and to one another, that they did not consider Lord Home should be Prime Minister, that they would serve under Mr Butler, and that they would not serve under Lord Home unless Mr Butler had previously agreed to do so: Iain Macleod, Reginald Maudling, Quintin Hailsham, John Boyd-Carpenter, Frederick Errol, Edward Boyle, Enoch Powell.

With Mr Butler himself, this makes straight away eight Cabinet ministers opposed to Home and agreed on Butler; but that takes no account of other Cabinet ministers who, while not prepared to take the same personal stand as those seven, had nevertheless advised against Home and expressed Butler as their preference.

In effect, with all the contenders agreed – and Macmillan himself admits that on receiving the information Lord Home 'felt like withdrawing' and had to be 'urged not to do so' – a Butler Government enjoying general acceptance was available by the time Macmillan's resignation reached the Queen; and it is pertinent to recall that at the time Macleod was joint chairman of the Conservative Party and Leader of the House of Commons.

So much for Macmillan's alleged 'general impression' from the selection of Cabinet ministers (including Macleod, Maudling and Hailsham themselves!) whom he had summoned to the hospital on 15 and 16 October, that 'if Lord Home would undertake the task of PM the whole Cabinet would cheerfully unite under him'.

The head and front of Macmillan's offending on the plane of constitutional history is not that this personal preference fell on one potential successor rather than another, nor that he held himself in readiness to give advice, if the Queen should seek it (which she did not constitutionally need to do) *after the premiership had become vacant*, but that he publicly, with the authority of the Prime Minister in office, carried out a process designed to produce the answer, so that the Queen then would be obliged both to ask his advice and to take or seek no other. It is an uncomprehending quibble to say that Macmillan resigned at 9.30 a.m. on Friday, 18 October and the Queen asked his advice at 11 a.m. Weeks before, when he broached resignation to the Queen, Macmillan had noted in his diary: 'She feels the great importance of maintaining the prerogative intact. After all, if she asked someone to form a government and he failed, what harm was done?' Just so. What Macmillan did was deliberately (and, in retrospect, conclusively) to destroy the very prerogative which his Sovereign had thought of great importance to maintain.

In order to put these facts on record, I have used up nearly all my allotted space on the last episode in this concluding volume of the six.

The later volumes, at least, are books which no one will ever read for pleasure. As the autobiographer has drawn on through the years, the style has become more wooden, cliché-ridden and pedestrian than ever, until in this last volume the reader has a recurrent sensation akin to that of chewing cardboard. Confronted with the virtuosity of the man himself in person and on television, this drives one back upon the old riddle: is it all an elaborate pose? is he laughing up his sleeve at us? can he really think and feel as he writes?

I confess I still wobble; but in the end, accepting that all personalities are complex and consequently admit self-contradictions, I come down against the pose theory. For all his finesse and subtlety as a political operator, and his acutely observed experience, I conclude that Macmillan did really visualise politics and the world much as he describes them, in a series of clichés. The convincing evidence is that the extracts from his diaries are of exactly the same texture as the surrounding narrative; and when you find that someone, in the privacy of his diary and the midst of events, talks to himself in the same platitudes and phrases as he uses in a party speech or a press communiqué, you have to believe it is the genuine article.

Men in politics and government – for all I know, in other walks of life too – work on the rule-of-thumb assumption that the other fellow is basically like oneself. The opposite assumption would be nearer the truth. Once get beyond the fundamentals of human nature, and the endlessly astonishing pattern of affairs is woven by men who are more unlike one another than they ever realise at the time. How much bitterness, resentment and misunderstanding comes from underestimating that unlikeness. Only afterwards, when all is done, do we begin to suspect how great it was, and so to understand.

There is another reflection which the reading of this last volume enforces – the more so because it comes nearest in date. This is how fast the relative importance of issues and events can alter. We fail to observe this because we ourselves are moving with the stream. Today, after only ten years, it is impossible even to imagine, let alone to regain, the atmosphere in which the Test Ban Treaty with Russia could appear to be the 'fair flower safety', plucked by statesmen out of imminent international catastrophe. Evidently it dominated Macmillan's mind from first to last in 1961–3, and was the political thought most often present with him as his premiership ended.

Though 'wind of change' is irretrievably embedded in the journalistic vocabulary which serves as a sort of popular potted history, it is equally impossible to retrieve the heart-searching over the demise of the ill-fated Central African Federation or to understand how it could have devoured so great a slice of the time and energy of government. Yet at the time it seemed, as I can well recall, a tightrope with disaster on either side, along which we were painfully edging our way.

Russia and Africa – these occupy a good half of the text, and South East Asia makes it up to two-thirds, reminding us as fact, though it seems no longer credible, that much less than ten years ago the fortunes of Malaysia and Borneo seemed scarcely less the direct concern of these islands they they had been in 1941–2. The echoes continued in the weird 'East of Suez debate' which still made so much noise in the later 1960s, only to vanish almost overnight from British politics. Of all the subjects which bulked largest at the time, and on paper in Volume Six, two only survive after a decade. One is the first abortive Common Market negotiation of 1961–2, as the foil and counterpoint to the different outcome of 1971–2. The second, sad to relate, is inflation and the squirrel's cage of 'prices and incomes policy', complete with every turn and twist so often explored in after years. Who knows, however, but that when Heath's memoirs are written and read, this too will not have found its place in history's limbo? 'There's comfort yet.'

'SUPERWHIG?'

The Spectator, 1 March 1980

'Edwardian'* is too insubstantial a concept for purposes of political classification. It may do for clothes; it will not do for ideas. The question is not: was Mr Macmillan an Edwardian? The question is: was he a Whig? And the answer to that is, Yes. If, as is reputed, the reviewer and Harold Macmillan did not 'hit it off', that would be only to be expected. Of all political categories the Grand Whig and the High Tory are the least compatible.

I would have said that, apart from being married, not born, into aristocracy, Macmillan possessed all the classic notes of the Grand Whig; but before putting that proposition to the test, I must enter a caveat which grows on one as time passes. I suspect that Macmillan was neither so posed nor so tricky as many assumed. We used to think to ourselves: 'He can't possibly *really* believe *that*.' I'm inclined now to think he often did. The suspicion is strengthened by textual study of his utterances, such as his broadcast on becoming Prime Minister, which George Hutchinson quotes *in toto*. (The book consists, in unusually high proportion, of quotations, such as the verbatim reprint of Macleod's famous *Spectator* article on the Home succession, which alone forms no less than one-eighth of the entire text of the book.)

The banality is staggering, and all the more impressive in someone who is undoubtedly a man of taste, perception and education. Consider only two specimens: 'The country that produced men such as James Watt and his steam engine . . . has no reason to quaver before temporary difficulties. After all, this year that has just passed, we have had an all-time record for exports and the best savings for years', or the conclusion: 'Britain has been great, is great and will stay great, provided we close our ranks and get on with the job.'

It would be a mistake to take too seriously or to judge too subtly a politician who habitually addressed his fellow countrymen in such vein.

But to the Whiggism. Like the elephant, it is more easily recognised than described; but among its essentials are cynicism, agnosticism,

The Last Edwardian at Number 10: An Impression of Harold Macmillan by George Hutchinson, Quartet

bread and circuses (provided they are held at a decent distance from the ducal estate), European combinations, a readiness to try any wheeze (provided it helps to keep in power), and a contempt for principle in politics (though some of Mr Locke's ideas may come in handy).

The Suez story was not creditable to Harold Macmillan, though his tracks, so far as he left tracks, have not yet been satisfactorily uncovered. If, as he says, he as Chancellor of the Exchequer 'shared to the fullest extent responsibility for all the decisions because I was one of the circle of colleagues whom the Prime Minister particularly consulted', he was wrong both coming and going: wrong in failing to correct misapprehensions about the importance of the Suez Canal and the practicability of lastingly repossessing it; and wrong in participating in the abandonment of the operation through misjudgement of both the military and the financial position. Still, it worked: and Butler was left at the post.

According to Hutchinson the famous phrase, 'most of our people have never had it so good', used at Bradford in 1957, was appropriated from Lord Robens. Like many such phrases taken unfairly out of context, it nevertheless tells a larger truth. The conflict which six months later resulted in the unparalleled resignation of all Treasury ministers had much to do with that truth. Whether or not he really thought that Stockton in the thirties was lurking round the corner, Macmillan already aimed at winning in 1959 on public expenditure; and when in 1962 he found himself caught in the trap of 'prices and incomes' policy, he planned to repeat the same act in 1963 or 1964, and replaced Selwyn Lloyd by Maudling to do the job, as he had formerly replaced Thorneycroft by Amory. Shortly before the July 1962 'night of the long knives' Macmillan entertained his Cabinet, instead of going through the agenda, with the reading of an essay he claimed to have composed over the weekend. From that paper derived a series of socialist measures, such as 'contracts of employment' and 'redundancy payments', which were seen by him, entirely in the spirit of the Middle Way, as the *quid pro quo* to the workers for co-operation in an inflation-free planned economy. I still relish recalling how the heads which were to roll not long after nodded like cuckoo-clocks in sycophantic approval.

The supreme cynicism was the manoeuvring of Butler out of the leadership succession in 1963. Macmillan's Whig models of 1714 would have admired his deft destruction of one of the last remaining royal prerogatives by the theatrical coup of sending for his Sovereign and tendering advice to her on the succession before resigning instead of waiting to be asked, if at all, afterwards. It was a feat, however, which permanently altered and debased the nature of Conservative leadership and the distinctive internal structure of the party.

'These are high stakes – as high as any that Britain ever contemplated.' The sentence occurs in a passage which Hutchinson claims to have himself had inserted in a speech at Stockton about entry to the EEC. Macmillan, as a true Whig, had always been a 'European'. 'As Prime Minister,' Hutchinson writes, 'he was prepared to surrender a number of United Kingdom and Commonwealth interests for the sake of securing admission to the Community.' The reason why 'in the result it has proved a disappointment – or worse – to many of the original advocates, including Macmillan himself', is that it involved a larger surrender still: the Whiggish surrender of Great Britain's insular sovereignty to a continental alignment, political and ultimately military, towards which the Tory instinct at the end of the twentieth century remains as adverse as it was at the beginning of the eighteenth.

'WINDS OF CHANGE'

Glasgow Herald, 1963

Harold Macmillan warns the reader that his *Winds of Change, 1914–1939** 'is not an apologia'. Certainly anyone who takes it up expecting an intimate autobiography, laying personal motives bare and publishing letters and memoranda that cast a new light upon events, will be disappointed.

Apart from a prologue which surveys the whole period to 1963 – without which it would have been hard to find anything suitable for advance extract in the Sunday press – the volume ends before Macmillan entered a Government. But even from the back-bench politics of the fifteen pre-war years hardly anything is recorded which was not already available in Hansard and a few standard histories and well-known biographies.

The book is, in fact, less an autobiography than a popular account, with autobiographical framework and some reminiscences, of the political history of the quarter-century preceding the Second World War.

No one who knew Macmillan even distantly would anyhow have expected an apologia. More supremely than any other political figure of our time he possessed the quality which Roman historians called 'dissimulation', the art of concealing his real intentions by suggesting others.

It is an art which in some measure is probably indispensable at the summit of affairs. But its great exponent was unlikely to turn Cardinal Newman or J.-J. Rousseau in his old age.

Nevertheless, infinite instruction and enlightenment are to be drawn by the student of the history of British policy in the past fifteen years from just these pages, because they are a reminder, the more striking for being so matter-of-fact, of how early formed, how consistently maintained, and how unchanging were the political ideas which Macmillan held in the 1920s and 1930s and by which he was actuated in the 1950s and 1960s.

From 1958 to 1963 one man placed upon the Conservative Party and Government, and thus upon the political history of our time, his own stamp and express image, which will not for long be obliterated.

**Winds of Change, 1914–1939*, by Harold Macmillan, Macmillan

Not merely the outlines but some of the smallest details of that impress are here in this book, with almost uncanny anticipation.

The year 1958 was even statistically a turning-point in so many trends in the course of events of the last fifteen years. At that point the state's share in the national income, which had been declining since 1951, began to rise again and has been rising ever since.

Up to that point the Government's credit, based on expectation of the future value of money, enabled them to borrow on a massive scale. Since then, their credit has disappeared and their borrowing has turned negative. It is not coincidence that it was just in the first days of 1958 that Harold Macmillan, who had then been Prime Minister for a little under a year, defeated his Chancellor of the Exchequer, Peter Thorneycroft, and settled for inflation.

It was a decision already dictated by Macmillan's basic political past: his old constituency of Stockton-on-Tees and its unemployed, his campaign against deflation and the orthodox budgeting of a quarter of a century earlier, his Middle Way, with its advocacy of state expenditure and state intervention.

'I look back with gratitude to the twenty-odd years of my association with Stockton and the North-East coast. I learned there lessons which I have never forgotten. If, in some respects, they may have left too deep an impression on my mind, the gain was greater than the loss.'

Did he suspect, then? To an observer, like myself, the gulf between a vanished past and the real present seemed to be reproduced in the Cabinet Room. It was a gulf which Macmillan almost studiously emphasised and sharpened, as he does in this book. Reading it, I found constant difficulty in remembering that the writer was a man only half a generation older than myself.

In the great decision Macmillan took with him his Government, his party and the country. From that moment onwards the whole range of policies which he had espoused twenty years before was adopted by the Conservative Party.

Conservatives in 1955 would have been more incredulous than indignant had anyone told them that in seven years' time their political platform would consist of national economic planning, regional economic planning, planning of incomes ('incomes policy'), rationalisation of industries by state intervention, more subsidised housing, and higher public expenditure generally.

Those whom these policies shocked could be heard to say that Harold Macmillan had 'debauched the Tory Party'. Debauch or no, he certainly performed one of the largest mass baptisms in history.

Goethe once quoted a German proverb to the effect that 'what a man sets his heart on in youth he shall have a-plenty in age'. It was abundantly fulfilled in Macmillan's case. Listen to this from 1927:

'An industrial structure with the broad strategic control in the hands of the state and the tactical operation in the hands of private management, with public and private ownership operating side by side. We pleaded for some form of collective bargaining to be given, at any rate in certain industries, statutory authority. We advocated an extension of joint industrial councils with increased powers and, where suitable, of trade boards.'

Or this from 1932:

'I urged that a tariff commission should be something more than a mere judicial body. It should be on the lines of a development or industrial commission, planning the growth of the nation's economic life and helping industries to reorganise themselves in the changed conditions.

'This might involve interference by the state with private interests. But protectionists could not attack it on that score, for the abandonment of free trade surely meant the end of *laissez-faire*. . . . There was need for a central organisation, directing economic effort and the flow of investment.'

The year 1958 was, as I have said, the great turning-point which marked the beginning of the true Macmillan era. The finger of providence might appear to have blessed its inauguration, and the Conservative Party was certainly assisted in swallowing whatever scruples afflicted it by the general election of October 1959, when the party – in words which Macmillan did not use on that occasion – 'never had it so good'.

But there was a later critical point, after which the trends of previous years were intensified. This came in the spring of 1962, when the morale, the by-election results, and the opinion-poll rating of the Conservative Party had plunged to abysmal depths. The pay pause and the 'incomes policy', to which everyone was committed but which nobody could discover, was leading the Government up a cul-de-sac, terminating in the black wall of self-contradiction. Something had to be done, and done quickly, if they were to extricate themselves.

Macmillan did two things. One was the obvious, a drastic reformation of his Government (the so-called 'night of the long knives') in July 1962. The other had already taken place, and was much more significant.

A few weeks earlier Macmillan had promulgated to his colleagues a new programme, which he claimed was 'designed to render counter-inflationary policies acceptable to the general public'. When an otter is hard pressed by hounds it commonly breaks out on to land, though that is actually the one thing bound to result in its death. The reason is that, being originally a land animal, it reverts in extremity to its natural habitat. I often thought of the otter in those weeks.

The new programme, which was hurried into execution, so far from having anything to do with counter-inflation, dotted the i's and crossed the t's and supplied the omissions still outstanding in the Macmillan policy of the 1930s. There were redundancy payments, contracts of service, training schemes, and training boards, above all there was the North-East, with differential tax benefits and all the rest, and its own cloth-cap Cabinet Minister.

In political emergency the Prime Minister had reverted, by a kind of instinct or reflex, to the atmosphere and the ideas of a generation earlier. So it came about that the last eighteen months of the Macmillan era witnessed an almost feverish intensification of what had gone before in the previous four or five years, as if the builder was hastening to put on the mansard roof, from a premonition that time was short.

'I will confess that I was always troubled by the re-emergence, even in a modified form, of this old problem (unemployment) with all its bitter recollections. . . The old memories and fears were not yet altogether dispelled. The underlying anxieties, in these parts of the country, persisted. It was for this reason that, when power came to me I gave what seemed to many, even of my colleagues, undue attention to these problems. I was determined, even in the fifties and sixties, not to forget the lessons of the twenties and thirties.'

Alas, if only we knew what the lessons of our earlier years really were – and if only those lessons, supposing we could know them, were still valid in the world of our later years! But it is rarely so.

'RAB BUTLER: THE MAN WHO SAW HIS PRIZE SNATCHED AWAY'

The Times, 10 March 1982

Rab Butler was a large man. He was large in frame: those who knew him only from photographs or television were surprised, on meeting him, to encounter so lofty a figure. He was large in achievement: for years he moved from one commanding position to another in British government. He was large in mind and spirit, contemplating men and politics with a broad and comprehensive outlook.

Among the swarm of those who, in their own or others' estimation, might or should have been prime ministers, he was the genuine article. The key to his public character is to be found in the dignity and self-control with which he thrice saw the prize snatched away.

I have a right to say so; for I was one of two men who, regardless of consequences, would not submit to serve in a Government which we were convinced personal and public destiny had marked out R. A. Butler to lead.

Born in 1902 and saddled from boyhood with the disabling results of an injury, he missed – and I believe he was always conscious of having missed – the privilege of wearing uniform in either war. That was mere chance; but to some of us it was a chance that seemed to match an aspect of his character. He was not the kind of man for whom any cause – not even his own – was worth fighting to the death, worth risking everything.

When in 1963 a different man would have fought, and won, Rab chose not to. But the premiership, unlike the priesthood of the grove at Nemi, is not the preserve of those who have slain their predecessor or their rivals. Nobody who observed Rab Butler in administration or in the Cabinet could doubt his capacity for government. Nobody who heard Rab Butler interpret the Conservative Party to itself and to the country could doubt that he understood and represented the meaning and purpose of Conservatism in a way that none of his contemporaries did. To call him a 'great public servant' is not cliché: it is an accurate identification of his attitude of mind and of the stronger and of the weaker sides of his personality.

When I look for other examples of the category 'great public servant' to which Rab belonged, I do not find them extant. Ambition and pride are universal human qualities, and Rab possessed them too; but his tenure of nearly all the major offices of state put him in the rank not of the successful political careerists but of those figures, commoner in the eighteenth than in the nineteenth century, who found work to do all their lives in seeing that 'the King's government was carried on'.

Every office and every phase of politics was a challenge to qualities of mind and temper as well as a demand upon industry and endurance. Rab was telling us this about himself when he chose to entitle his autobiography *The Art of the Possible*. In every exigency of government there lies hidden 'the possible', the analysis and the plan of action which will enable society and the nation to cope not unsuccessfully with each succeeding predicament.

It is a business of intellect as well of instinct; and in the sense that he revelled in applying to affairs of state his exceptional powers of mind, R. A. Butler was rightly classed as an intellectual. But his intellect was essentially practical in its bent: his was not a speculative mind, like Salisbury's or even Gladstone's. This is why I think his later years as Master of Trinity were not his happiest. Characteristically, and herein too a 'public servant', he had decided to 'call it a day' when after 1964 long years in opposition loomed ahead. He would take his congé and not stay around to fight on against years and rising odds. I remember, as the only non-member of his family privileged to be with him in the Lodge on the day of his installation at Trinity, being struck by the impression of loneliness and unease: the academic world too was a world of the intellect, but it was not the world of *his* intellect of 'the possible'.

Rab's departure from politics seventeen years ago left a void that has not been filled. He was only sixty-two. What a different and a better House of Commons, what a different Conservative Party, it would have been, if his intellect, his Toryism and his knowledge of 'the possible' had been available longer in that place, and if a whole parliamentary generation – parliamentary generations are natural generations – had not been deprived of his influence, and deprived what is more, of his wit.

I left the mention of his wit till last; but all who were devoted to Rab were affectionate admirers of his 'Rabbisms', remarks apparently innocuous or laudatory, which yet contained some adventitious phrase or adjective that set one wondering 'Did he really mean that?' Of course he did. The 'Rabbism' was the ironical signature tune of a memorable man, powerful in mind, shrewd in insight, faithful in service. His place in our history will not diminish as the years go by.

ON UNVEILING THE BUST OF THE RT HON. R. A. BUTLER IN THE STATE APARTMENTS OF THE SPEAKER OF THE HOUSE OF COMMONS

23 April 1991

The life of a nation, like the life of Parliament itself, is a continual changing of the guard, as one generation steps into the shoes of those that went before it.

A new generation emerged long years ago from seven years of war to take its place in the political life of their country. They had little adult recollection – and that a recollection none too favourable – of the pre-war scene. Some of that generation, as they looked about them and looked inside their own hearts, began to perceive that they were the inheritors of one of the great lines of descent in British politics, the Tory tradition.

One leading figure, at that time and for long afterwards, seemed to them best to personify, and most truthfully to express, their cast of mind. They were grateful to him, and as long as they survive, they will repay him with the tribute of their affection. They are proud and they rejoice today that his likeness will have a permanent place in the halls where Parliament's makers and upholders seem all but physically present.

Toryism is about institutions, and about the authority immanent in them, which makes the unruly spirits of men to be 'godly and quietly governed'. To our central institution, that of Parliament, to using it, honouring it, enhancing it, the service of Rab's life was instinctively given. His towering qualities of intellect were consciously and continuously dedicated to expound and uphold the place of tradition and of historic institutions in the preservation of a people. Those of us who shared that same instinct knew that we would always hear the clear echo of it in his calm, temperate discourse.

Individuals who have been most in tune with the spirit of the nation they served have not always stood on the topmost rung of power and position. Rab stood high enough for long enough to be seen, heard and remembered; and his wisdom was broad enough to encompass and accept the changes and chances of political life to which he, like all beside, was subject.

His eyes will now continue to survey those movements with interest, with benevolence and with that old familiar touch of irony from the place within this building where his own achievements and the esteem of his contemporaries have installed him.

'THE MAUDLING I KNEW'

Sunday Telegraph, 18 February 1979

In those early days of 1946 there were the three of us in the big first-floor room at 24 Wilton Street, the Conservative Parliamentary Secretariat. One is left. First Iain Macleod departed; and now Reggie Maudling is gone.

He was there before the rest of us. His war had been in the Air Ministry; and he moved over not long after peace to start, almost single-handed, the Parliamentary Secretariat, which later merged into the better known Research Department. He was also the first of us to become a parliamentary candidate himself – for the conveniently accessible Barnet, which through various mutations remained his secure base until the end.

Not even Macleod found his way so soon into the confidence and inner circle of the leading men of the party: Rab Butler, of course, but Oliver Lyttelton, Oliver Stanley, Winston himself, and above all Anthony Eden, whom he faithfully advised, guided and ghosted through the difficult years in defeat and opposition. The popular quip 'Eden and Maudling' for 'Eton and Magdalen' – he was a Merton man actually – was near enough to the mark.

He was an admirable colleague at work: easy-going outwardly and unruffled, always with time to listen to other people's problems, and genuinely kind in matters personal. His large, relaxed physique did not belie him; his enjoyments were peaceable, if not passive, and he loathed all things violent, whether physical or mental. I recall once describing to him how the pleasure of a fox-hunt was heightened by the sense of physical risk: 'that,' he observed, 'would kill it stone dead for me'. From the first to the last his family – parents, wife and children – were what touched him nearest, and his sympathy for a friend in domestic trouble, small or grave, was instant and unforgettable.

The trio entered Parliament together in 1950; and when the party gained power at the end of 1951, Maudling was the first of us to be given office. His career thereafter was an uninterrupted progress, rung by rung, to its culmination at the Exchequer in 1962–4. When the thirteen years of Conservative government ended in 1964, Maudling had been in office for twelve of them. In competence, and much more than competence, he was equal to each stride upwards as it came. In Parliament he made no enemies: as a speaker he was persuasive, attempting no more than to confute and convince as economically as possible. He had a good debating technique, exposing the essential weakness of his opponents' case to quiet but withering humour, calculated to make any reasonable person feel half-ashamed not to agree.

He failed only on occasions to which it was necessary to rise; for something in his make-up denied him the ability to stir emotion. The gifts Macleod had were not his – and he knew it. I remember his utter misery at the Blackpool Conference of 1963 – the Conservative Party's first and last 'primary' – when he had a major speech to make and knew that he was going to flop, which he duly did. Danger, challenge and mortal combat, which lift some men above themselves, were not Reggie Maudling's natural environment.

That was the turning-point in his life; success thereafter was to be scanty, and laced with bitterness. The picture in my mind is of July, 1965, when Heath beat him in the first ballot for the leadership and I came to agree with him that we should both withdraw. 'What went wrong?' he kept asking. 'Why did I lose?' I told him; perhaps I shouldn't have done. When the party went into opposition he had taken three major directorships (including one full-time) instead of living in the House and on the front bench. 'People concluded,' I said, 'that you weren't really interested any longer.'

In the next five years of opposition Maudling pulled his weight under the leadership of a man he 'really didn't like'. His debating talent and economic quick-footedness were indispensable to the party; but some of us were surprised how much of his attention seemed to be devoted to the Mediterranean and the Middle East. They were, I believe, not happy years; for Reggie liked office, he liked comfort, he liked the good things of life – and time was going by. They were the years in which uncharacteristic failures of judgement sowed the seeds of the whirlwind.

In 1970 he returned with the party to the top rank of Government as Home Secretary, which his humane and sceptical temperament well fitted him to be. With Macleod early departed, Thorneycroft in the Lords, and no one else of comparable stature around Heath, Maudling might have long been a power in the land and (who knows?), perhaps more. But the shadow of Poulson had already fallen across his path. It constrained him to leave the Home Office and the Cabinet in 1972; and though it did not prevent him from joining Margaret Thatcher's team as Shadow Foreign Secretary in her first year or two as leader, people doubted whether he would occupy high office again, at any rate in the Commons.

Something else too seemed to happen in the years after 1972.

Though he intervened in major debates not less often than a senior member of his experience might have been expected to do, a certain rigidity appeared to enter into his thinking: economic positions of earlier years were no longer examined with his old brilliance and agility, but expounded and defended almost as canons of morality. It sometimes seemed as if the effort of keeping his courage and serenity under crueller disappointment and calumny than most men have to suffer had left him little energy to spare.

The last glimpse I caught of him is the one I shall remember: the unmistakable silhouette, broad and erect, walking slowly away from me down the corridor which leads from the Chamber to the Members' Smoking Room. Now the division bells may ring, but he will not hear.

'HAROLD WILSON: A VERY SPECIAL KIND OF POLITICIAN'

The Director, September 1975

How much easier it is for the working politician to write an obituary of a political colleague than an appreciation – or even a depreciation. True, there is the business over the rule of *nil nisi bonum*. On the other hand, one is secure against having one's subject sitting there afterwards staring one in the face week after week and year after year, and, what is worse, disproving by his subsequent behaviour one's most confident psychological perceptions.

Certainly, anybody who had written this sort of essay about Harold Wilson ten years ago, in the early stages of his first premiership, would now, in the early stages of his second, have wanted to alter some of the most salient features. There he was, ten years ago, bustling here and bustling there, with a self-publicising gimmick ready for every emergency and the cartoonists drawing him as their music-hall one-man band, while his Cabinet ministers found themselves relegated to the position of guests or butlers at a series of No. 10 tea-parties. Where is that Harold Wilson now? The complaint now – much less justified, I think – is that one Cabinet colleague after another is cast by a self-effacing chief in the uncomfortable role of Uriah the Hittite and left to make shift as best they can 'in the forefront of the hottest battle'.

We have thus come straight away upon one of the most remarkable qualities of the Prime Minister – his extraordinary capacity for learning from experience and not merely modifying his methods, but replacing one set of characteristics by their opposites. Nearly all the rest of us in politics remain distressingly like ourselves from one decade to another: when we spring surprises, it is not because we have altered, but because altered circumstances have refracted the light in which our constant qualities are placed. One would need to look a long way to find a parallel to Wilson's radical change of style in the office of premier between 1964 to 1970 and 1974 to whenever it may be. The more one reflects on this characteristic, the more it begins to dovetail, as it ought, into other salient qualities.

Clearly, it is related to Harold Wilson's remarkable quickness of perception. He is not a person to whom you have to explain things twice over. On the contrary, before you are halfway through the exposition of a train of thought not necessarily either familiar or congenial to him, he interrupts to finish it off for you and for good measure to suggest off-the-cuff, as if involuntarily, the political slogan to match it. Whatever mistakes Harold Wilson makes, he does not make through slowness or incomprehension, though he will be quick as lightning to feign incomprehension where he judges that to be the appropriate reaction. Let nobody imagine that in dealing with the Prime Minister he is dealing with someone who perhaps has not quite understood: the likelihood is that he has understood all too well.

This quickness and mobility of comprehension would not by itself account for Harold Wilson's power, Alberich-like, to change himself, if it were not for the concurrence of other characteristics, equally marked.

Harold Wilson is a deeply sensitive man, but at the same time a man without pride. We all in politics are much less pachydermatous than we appear; but some are protected against the slings and arrows of the outside world by a good thick carapace of the mortal sin of pride, not to call it arrogance. The Prime Minister has never had this sort of protection, and I believe he feels insult and hostility more than most. The converse of this sensitivity to his own hurt is a real sympathy for the hurt of others. This is, at heart, a kind and kindly man, and there are many who could record, as I can, spontaneous evidences of it. The fact that he could nevertheless survive, beyond all expectation, the humiliations that were heaped upon him between 1970 and 1974, to emerge once more as Prime Minister, was due to something more than simply persistence and staying-power, not to mention the natural propensity of the man at the top in politics to cling limpetlike to his piece of rock. A proud man could never have lived through those years. Only the total absence of pride could enable any human being to survive that terrible rain of insult – absence of pride, allied to an infinite suppleness and resource.

The absence of pride on his own behalf has its counterpart in a certain lack of scruple in the choice of weapons against others and a preference for striking the lower notes of the political scale rather than the higher ones. He is always in more danger of falling into vulgarity than pathos. As a parliamentary performer he is redoubtable for the sureness of his instinct for the behaviour of the House of Commons; but he puts that instinct to a use from which those prouder or more fastidious would shrink. Time and again Harold Wilson deliberately sets out to bore the House by reading long, White Paper-like speeches of unrelieved monotony; but his disposition to do so springs not from incompetence, but from a judgement – usually a right one – of where tactical advantage lies. Even as they ache with *ennui*, the more knowing Members can be heard saying to one another: 'Isn't Harold a marvel? He's on the top of his form today!'

The resourcefulness and suppleness are in turn the counterpart of a complete lack, so far as the outside observer can judge, of long-term objectives or political convictions. This observation is intended to carry no tone of moral condemnation. Nobody in politics – any more than anywhere else – is under a legal or moral obligation to entertain distant aims or a profound political faith. Some do, some don't; Harold Wilson belongs to the ranks of those who don't, and he practises his trade and exerts his energies and abilities accordingly in that station to which it has pleased God to call him.

Some years ago, Paul Foot wrote a brilliant (I thought) biography of Harold Wilson (published in 1968 as a Penguin Special), which was obviously intended as a hatchet job. The effect was the reverse. One closed the book with a sweeter tolerance towards the subject, because it had proved so conclusively that he was totally lacking in deep convictions. It followed that he did not (as one had uncharitably or ignorantly assumed) betray his principles or abandon his beliefs under pressure or from self-interest: he just had no principles or beliefs to abandon or betray. The U-turn is Harold's normal mode of progression: it is as natural to him as it is to a crab to walk sideways. It is no truer to level the charge of faithlessness for saying one thing and doing the opposite against Harold Wilson than against a civil servant.

In fact, the Prime Minister would have made a wonderful bureaucrat, but that the talents of political management, with which nature has so lavishly endowed him, would have been criminally wasted in the Civil Service.

In watching the Prime Minister one must shorten one's perspective abnormally if one is not to misunderstand or misjudge him. I illustrate by two recent major political issues: inflation and the EEC.

Twice over now, Harold Wilson has forsworn compulsory control of incomes and then, within six months, persuaded his Cabinet to enact it. This is a phenomenon totally different from the superficially similar case of Edward Heath, whose behaviour was the reaction of a proud and stubborn man to the insolent refusal of men and things to behave as he 'absolutely clearly' ordered them to behave.

But Wilson has less in common with Heath than a whale with an elephant. There is nothing I can teach Harold Wilson about the fallacy and impracticability of prices and incomes policies, voluntary or compulsory – he knows it all as well as I do, if not better. Only he cannot see that that is any reason against adopting them, in any of their Protean forms, if one can thereby talk oneself round the next corner. What more evident than that our business is to get round one corner, and then the next, and then the next? Like all people who do something really well, Wilson enjoys getting round corners. He has the joyousness of the virtuoso, which can almost infect with its gaiety those grim people who believe in political aims and principles.

Nothing is farther from the Prime Minister's intention, here and now in the early autumn, than to bother his head about the subsequent phases of his voluntary/compulsory incomes policy or about the when and how of 're-entry'. Like the apostles, he has a sublime confidence that 'it shall be given you in that hour what ye shall say' – and being a true politician he knows that saying is to doing as three is to one.

For Harold Wilson 'keeping all options open' is not so much a cliché, more a way of life. He was grievously misunderstood over the Common Market. Those who argued over whether the Prime Minister was a pro-European or an anti-European were both wide of the mark. He was – and is – neither. This was a dangerous subject, and one, therefore, to be played most carefully by ear, not to attain a predetermined result but, like the French Abbé, 'to survive' – and preferably to survive as Prime Minister.

Having heard and watched every syllable and gesture from the beginning of this Parliament until the declaration of the Cabinet's majority decision, I am convinced that at least as late as the end of 1974 he was 'keeping his options open', and that some of his Ministers believed he was doing so later still. It is a very special kind of politician – and personality – for whom the choice between Britain belonging or not belonging to the EEC can be handled in this way – by the toss of a coin, as it were.

He is now repeating the same process in relation to economic and monetary union and in particular to the frowning obstacle of 'direct elections to the European Parliament'. Once again let no one ask 'Is Harold Wilson a federalist or an anti-federalist?' He is neither. Harold Wilson is not that sort of politician.

The sketch which I have drawn of Harold Wilson will give most readers the impression of being more unsympathetic than it either is or is intended to be. This is because we are so saturated with the over-dramatised presentation of politics by the media, whereby nothing happens whithout being deliberately willed, for preference by the Prime Minister, who is visualised as sitting with crown and sceptre on the apex of a pyramid of power. The reality is very different and always has been. While the great historical forces, which we can neither foresee nor more than dimly assess, continually and sometimes violently alter the political and human landscape, a process of rationalisation – of talking it along – keeps up a sort of accompaniment. 'The Queen's government,' they say, 'must be carried on.'

Through fifteen years as tumultuous as any this generation has known, a succession of Cabinets was headed by someone called the 'Arch-Mediocrity' – Jenkinson, the Earl of Liverpool. I would not call Harold Wilson an arch-mediocrity, nor even a mediocrity – not at all. But he stands in a long tradition.

'HAROLD WILSON'

The Spectator, 31 July 1971

It is an astonishing monument, of its kind, and surely unique in its kind. A Prime Minister, a year after losing office, has published in eight hundred pages, at over five hundred words to the page, an account of his six years' premiership. As one handles the massive book* the questions 'Why on earth did he do it?' and 'How on earth did he do it?' contend for pride of place, followed shortly after by the third question. 'What on earth *is* it, now that he has done it?' Perhaps the last is the easiet to start on.

It is basically autobiography, since the thread which runs through it is the first person. Because the first person is that of the Prime Minister, the story of six years which is strung upon that thread amounts almost to chronicle history of events parliamentary, British and foreign. On the other hand, the self-revelation of the first person is intended to be strictly political, and even within that intention strictly limited. The intimacy is deliberately skin-deep: these are neither reflections nor confessions. The impression of chronicle-autobiography is strengthened by the almost unbroken rigour of the chronological sequence: the framework is that of a diary, and connected events are rarely allowed to overlap even a few days in the order of the narrative. In practice surprisingly, this strict chronology gives to the book the form and continuity which it undeniably possesses: the reader does not often have the sense of being jerked from one subject to another – or no more than reflects the Poo-Bah nature of a Prime Minister's office.

Quotation is lavish. Speeches and statements in the House of Commons: political speeches in the country; prime ministerial speeches at home and abroad; occasionally, speeches by others; rarely, letters and other documents – there are not many pages of the book on which one or more of these do not feature.

> The following Sunday 22nd January [1967], we left for Strasbourg, where I addressed the Assembly of the Council of Europe. I had dictated the speech at Chequers before our visit to Rome, and it was intended as a

---

The Labour Government 1964–1970: A Personal Record by Harold Wilson, Weidenfeld and Michael Joseph

major declaration. Certainly it was so regarded in Strasbourg. I began
with an excursion into history . . .

Or again:

> I decided at once that I must reply to Mr Powell in a major speech. My
> only engagement in the following week-end was a non-party civic dinner
> in my constituency. It would have been wrong to use such a platform, as
> my reply would have to be strongly political. I therefore gave notice that
> I would be saying the following week-end what needed to be said. Taking
> as my May Day theme the brotherhood of man, I decided to challenge
> racialism directly . . .

This is stirring stuff, and the immediacy of these slabs of the spoken
word, embedded in place, time and date in the gargantuan narrative,
gives them a strange life and interest for which neither originality of
content nor distinction of diction account and which they possibly did
not possess when originally pronounced.

The narrative, however, is a genuine narrative, and not a concat-
enation of pre-existing texts, and from time to time there are episodes
where the author seems to drop his self-consciousness and becomes
an interested, and interesting, relator. Good examples are the two
visits to President de Gaulle, in January 1967, before the commencement of the European negotiation, and in June 1967, after it had
begun. They are of special contemporary relevance, and betray an
unexpected sympathy and admiration for the General on the part of
the Prime Minister:

> I then asked if it was agreeable to him that we should discusss the next
> ten years. I asked him how he would forecast a France without de Gaulle.
> Almost repeating the words he had used to Mr Macmillan, who had
> recently told me of it, his forecast was again '*Les délices de l'anarchie*' . . .
> Did he not fear that post-de Gaulle France would be relegated to a second-
> class status against the power of a strong Germany? He warmed to his
> theme. '*Les Allemands,*' he said, '*seront toujours les Allemands.*' He had
> no doubt what would happen – but he would not be there to prevent
> it . . .

But the whole of these passages is prescribed reading (which might
with advantage include the entire narrative of the Wilson-Brown
Odyssey), during the forthcoming holidays.

The size and detail of the narrative throw of their own accord
certain features of the six years into relief without this being deliberately contrived. Even a reader who had not, like the reviewer, been
a 'floating pounder' since before 1964 would be struck by the recur-
rence of the theme of the sterling parity and by the way in which
almost every phase of the Labour Government's existence was saturated and dominated by the pound sterling. It is like one of those

dramas in which an action in the first moments of the first scene pursues the central characters till the final curtain: the decision not to devalue in October 1964, a decision to which the Labour Party came intellectually and philosophically unprepared, contained within itself almost all that was to follow. There is a sense in which the Labour Party lost control over events on the morrow of victory and never regained it. From that moment, Harold Wilson was an Orestes hunted by the Furies. Sometimes he gained a little breathing space, but they soon caught up; and it was only too late to escape defeat that he outdistanced them in 1970.

That the narrative is, upon the whole justificatory, goes without saying. Anything else was, personality apart, inconceivable in an instant autobiography; but the diligent searcher will find, among the normal and natural reflections upon foe and friend, gobbets of retraction or explanation worth the seeking. I offer two as specimens, one at the author's own expense, one at others':

> When I was asked about mistakes I had made in office, I instanced my clinging to our east of Suez role when facts were dictating a recession. I was, I said, one of the last to be converted, and it needed a lot of hard facts to convert me. Others of my colleagues, left-wing and pro-European alike, were wiser in their perceptions.

> On 6 September [1965] fighting began across the Indian border with West Pakistan. CRO officials briefed me on the situation, and inveigled me into issuing a statement – justified, as they said, by cast-iron evidence – condemning India for an act of aggression. I was wrong in this . . . I had been taken for a ride by a pro-Pakistani faction in the CRO: it did not remain there for long.

The nature of the work renders all the more problematic the question: 'Why did he write it?' In scale, in pages per year, it greatly exceeds Harold Macmillan's autobiography, which now awaits the concluding volume. While Macmillan has been able to be free in the use of official material, the total impression is that Wilson's book much surpasses Macmillan's in candour and informativeness. The statesman in definitive retirement, has been less copious than the party leader with time for more than one premiership still before him. The paradox enhances the puzzle.

Personality accounts for something, no doubt: Harold Wilson is by inclination given to diffuseness and documentation; he is not the man to use fewer words where more will do, nor instinctively to prefer silence to speech. Something more must be attributed to the different nature of those two animals, the Tory Party and the Labour Party. The public ventilation of facts, allegations, disagreements, personalities, which would appal the Conservative Party is perfectly normal and socially acceptable in the Labour Party – a difference which at times (such as the present) can mislead the commentators and the Labour Party's opponents. What, in short, would be indecent exposure in a Tory ex-premier may be no worse than informative candour in his opposite number.

Still, when these allowances have been made in full, it remains remarkable that even a Labour ex-premier, and even this one, takes up his pen to such effect on the morning after. Perhaps, however we have not read the sub-title of the book: 'The Labour Government 1964–1970.' I think we should. It may be that the more we reflect on the book in terms of that sub-title the more we shall be inclined to see it not at all as the lucrative valediction of a man who knows he is finished but rather as the first act of regaining power for himself and his party – a kind of historical preface to the manifesto for the next general election. Here again, a Conservative can easily go wrong in understanding Labour. The Conservative regards it as natural anyway that there should be a Conservative government: what's one more or fewer? A Labour government is still an event which makes history, a fact which moulds and transforms and energises the Labour Party itself. A peer of the first or second generation may hasten to adorn his new mansion with an escutcheon of a size and splendour which the ancient aristocrat would think superfluous, if not vulgar.

Finally, how did he do it? I cannot imagine. For many temperaments it would be psychologically impossible to spend the early months of defeat and dejection in the detailed reconstruction of the hours of activity, of excitement, of success and of power. Even to a personality impervious or resistant to dejection and chagrin, the mental as well as the physical effort must have been crushing. No wonder, in those months, encountering Harold Wilson on occasion in the corridor behind the Speaker's chair, one felt that one had met a ghost. Well, it is over now. In one year flat the ex-Prime Minister has exorcised the immediate past by externalising it. Sinbad has got the Old Man of the Sea down from his shoulders. But what will Sinbad do now? Who knows?

'NO ANSWERS BLOWING IN THE WIND'

The Spectator, 9 October 1976

The publishers, with a candour exceptional in a blurb, describe Lord Home's autobiography* as 'utterly unpretentious'. Even so, they have not hit upon quite the right adjective. The right adjective is 'naïve'; but one is 'utterly' at a loss to find an adverb adequate to qualify it. When a politician who throughout his life has gone 'the way the wind blows' actually chooses that phrase as the title for his autobiography, it is difficult to know whether one is in the presence of fantastic candour or fantastic innocence.

My first inclination after getting through the first two chapters was to wonder if this was not an exercise in sustained autobiographical parody which had not quite 'come off' – a sort of *Don Quixote* or *Orlando* manqué. There are whole pages of pure old-boy visiting speaker at Speech Day, which approach perfection in their genre:

> What did Oxford do for me? It provided understanding of life and more independence of judgment. It was impossible . . . to dine in Hall in the company of portraits of great men without realising that it matters what people do. Impossible too to rub shoulders with brain and brawn, artists, scientists, classical scholars, historians, mathematicians and churchmen without broadening one's mind. An honorary fellowship at Christ Church and an honorary degree at the University later set the seal on a most rewarding part of life.

Or this:

> My father's butler, Collingwood, who was faithfully produced in my brother's play *The Chiltern Hundreds*, was a splendid character and what we should have done without him I do not know.

Gems of this order are offset by recitals of the autobiographer's cricket scores at school and varsity, and even of game bags:

> One day I recall with particular pleasure was with Henry, David Bowes-Lyon and Cosmo Crawley (the Harrow cricketer). The game-book entry ran: 20 grouse, 5 black game, 1 partridge, 1 woodcock, 15 snipe, 5 mallard,

*The Way the Wind Blows by Sir Alec Douglas-Home, Collins

5 teal, 2 gadwall, 4 golden plover, 5 pigeon, 18 hares and 26 rabbits. Such sport was undiluted fun.

Alas, as the narrative progressed from early manhood, it became painfully clear that the whole thing was meant seriously and that this was, and is, the man himself and not intentional satire.

We have a chapter (Chapter Five) on religion ('There comes a moment when one has to confess one's faith, *for testing trials were ahead*'†), which contains whole slabs from the author's contribution to a 1946 seminar on 'Why I believe in God'. 'I was and am,' he says in this chapter, 'impatient of the muddle and confusion and division which the churches have made of the simple message of Christ,' of which 'men have made unbelievably heavy weather'. It is an almost terrifying piece of self-revelation. Here is this nice, honest, honourable schoolboy who never grew up finding nothing but what was plain and simple in the gospel and marvelling at those who made 'heavy weather'. I wonder what he thought when he came to the words 'Take, eat, this is my body'? – just read on, I suppose, seeing nothing out of the ordinary:

At any rate I have in my profession and in my work and play found myself happier and more relaxed and more confident by reason of faith in God, and *a set of positive values is certainly useful*‡ when trying to decide – in terms of my father's exhortation – what effect my action would have on the other fellow.

When one encounters a man who has lived through forty years of public life and risen to the highest offices of state without having apparently perceived anything not reducible to the ethics of the public school, the temptation is almost irresistible to assume that the whole thing has been a consummate exercise in dissimulation, and that behind the mask is concealed a calculating and ruthless intellect. That is what the knowing ones whisper to one another in the Smoking Room with a chuckle. That is what contemporaries have every motive of *amour propre* to believe. But, historians, beware! Men high and low are nearly always more or less what they seem to be; and if the former Foreign Secretary and Prime Minister, as revealed in these pages even more clearly than in personal intercourse, is a paradox, we ought not to pretend the paradox away, but learn from it anew the old, old lesson that any sort of person can be found in any sort of position and that it is the holder who makes the office, and not the office the holder.

This is not to say it makes no difference what manner of person

†Reviewer's italics. I apologise; I couldn't resist it.
‡Reviewer's italics again.

occupies a position. In 1961 Lord Home wrote: 'I have no doubt what would be best for Nyasaland and Northern Rhodesia; they should be in a tight economic and a loose political federation' [viz with Southern Rhodesia]. In 1968 he reported that Scottish aspirations should be met by a directly elected assembly which would take Scottish Bills through some of their legislative stages and 'decide priorities in expenditure', whereby 'Scotsmen would feel that their influence over their own affairs had substance and was real'. This degree of incapacity to perceive contradiction and to analyse problems is not rendered harmless because it is the innocent projection of a mind which cannot understand how others make 'heavy weather' of what it finds plain and simple. In real life such a personality is peculiarly disaster-prone.

It is not likely that *The Way the Wind Blows* will be a serious historical source. The chapter on 'The Diplomacy of Suez' – another unintentional irony – is exactly four pages long, totally uninformative and ends with the opaque conclusion that 'whatever the final verdict of historians on the British occupation of the Canal Zone, they will be bound to record that, had it not been for a sad lapse on the part of American diplomacy, peaceful persuasion had a good chance of gaining the day'. However, I believe that where a reviewer has been an eye-witness, he should add his mite of correction to the record.

My own appearance is limited to the succession to Macmillan in October 1963, where the narrative is remarkable for the size and number of the vital gaps. It is doubtful, however, how much Lord Home understood the inwardness of what was happening. 'With kindness,' he says, 'and loyalty and sacrifice they [Butler, Hailsham and Maudling] gave me their support, as did all but two of my colleagues in Mr Macmillan's cabinet. They were Mr Iain Macleod and Mr Enoch Powell, who were not natural bedfellows but who for the moment had got into a huddle.' Anybody who was unaware of the long and exceptionally intimate association and collaboration between the late Iain Macleod and myself, or of our close sympathy and indentity of political views until a period later than 1963, could not have known much about what had been happening in the Conservative Party since 1945. Little wonder that Lord Home did not understand the reason why both of us said we would not join the new Government unless it was Butler's.

Another error which is also the fruit of incomprehension ought to be corrected. 'In Cabinet [8 October 1963] in the Prime Minister's absence we had a short discussion. The Lord Chancellor said that he was not a candidate for the leadership . . . I said that the same applied to me. Enoch Powell later cited this indication of my position as a kind of pledge from which, when events turned out as they did,

I should have had the whole Cabinet's leave formally to withdraw.' When I read this passage I wrote to Lord Home as follows:

House of Commons
16 August 1976

Dear Alec,

I am reviewing *The Way the Wind Blows* and think that one should use such reviews at least in part for the benefit of future historians. That is why I hope you can let me have a reply to the following query.

On page 181 you say that I 'later cited' the indication of your position which you gave to Cabinet on 8th October 'as a kind of pledge, etc'. I have no recollection of entertaining such an opinion as you attribute to me, nor do I see how such an opinion could reasonably be held. However, I know from experience how fickle one's memory can be and I would therefore be grateful if you could tell me what is the nature of the 'citation' to which you refer since the language appears to indicate much more than recollection of a verbal or second-hand communication, but rather written or spoken words which are somewhere on the record.

Yours ever,
Enoch.

I received the following reply.

Castlemains,
Douglas,
Lanarkshire
21 August 1976

My dear Enoch,

Thank you for your letter.

I used the word 'cited' in the sense of 'quoted' which I think is accurate. The position is this. It was reported to me from one of the meetings which you and some colleagues had that you had said that I ought to have brought the Cabinet together so that I could withdraw the statement which I had earlier made that I was not in the contest for the leadership. I recall it vividly because I was genuinely worried that I might have done something reprehensible. I soon decided, however, that as I had seen every member of the Cabinet separately and you and Iain together* that I should leave the matter alone.

You must, of course, feel absolutely free to say that this is not your recollection of the matter, unless, of course, what I have written now has touched a chord in your memory.

It was nice of you to write.

Yours ever,
Alec.

The interest of this exchange lies not so much in that it disposes of a second- or third-hand rumour, which as reported might have been

---

*In fact, Lord Home saw us separately – as indeed was proper.

taken by readers for factual, but in the incomprehension of the constitutional position, not only on my view but on almost any view which
it reveals. In the first place, a Cabinet cannot as such be concerned
with the behaviour of its former members after it has been dissolved;
and secondly, once Macmillan's resignation was accepted by the
Queen, neither Lord Home (either before or after receiving her
commission) nor anyone else could bring it together again for any
purpose. The view mistakenly attributed to me is therefore one which
neither I nor anyone constitutionally literate could hold or argue.

Lord Home clearly never understood the historical significance of
the events of October 1963, which was that Macmillan, by publicly
carrying out while still in office a process purporting to indicate who
should succeed him and by communicating the result to the sovereign
when relinquishing his office, effectively destroyed the royal prerogative of selecting a Prime Minister which until that time still existed
except when the Labour Party was in a majority.

Having referred to two points at which I do feature in Lord Home's
narrative, perhaps I may mention two incidents involving us both,
which he does not happen to record. One is the occasion in July 1965
when he informed me, as he was informing the other members of his
shadow cabinet, that he was about to resign the leadership of the
Opposition. I remember saying to him, and perhaps he recalls it too,
that, whatever had happened in 1963, having joined his shadow team
in 1964, I would the 'the last man to leave the ship' if he decided, as
I hoped he would, to remain in command.

The second occasion dates from early 1971, when I was embarking
on a campaign of speeches against the proposition that Britain should
join the EEC. Since he was Foreign Secretary I gave him due and
friendly notice of my intention. His reply was this: 'I do wish that
instead you would concentrate on making speeches on immigration,
because that is so vitally important and you are so right about it.'
The friendly candour was characteristic of the man. But so also was
the fact that no hint ever reached the public that that was what the
Foreign Secretary thought. After all, it was not the way the wind was
blowing.

'ON BEING A MINISTER'

Books and Bookmen, April 1976

The public has a quite mistaken idea about the friendships between politicians of opposing political parties. It thinks of them slapping one another's backs and going off arm-in-arm on common pursuits out of working hours. The reality is quite different. What usually happens is that a liking – rarely unaccompanied by some degree of admiration – is conceived, often across the Chamber or in a debating forum, and thereafter maintained and increased over the years and mostly by mutual observation at a distance. It is largely independent of personal association in private life, which is the rare exception; and yet so searching is the exposure of character in politics, each actually does know the other, much as friends in ordinary life know one another.

Richard Crossman was a person, one of no more than three or four, with whom I had this sort of friendship for a quarter of a century. We met first, characteristically enough, doing a panel discussion on House of Commons procedure in 1950. I remember our last meeting too. He came as a dying man to report for the BBC the rally held in Birmingham during the February general election of 1974, at whch I denounced the EEC and the Conservative Party for supporting it. As we went our several ways at the finish, he called out to me a few last friendly words.

All his life Richard Crossman was the academic and the intellectual in the best meaning of those words. Curiosity to understand the behaviour of men in their political aspect was with him a passion which overpowered the common political passions of ambition, envy, emulation, pugnacity. He was an unrivalled observer and critic of political situations, because observing was his supreme intellectual enjoyment; and he brought the same dispassionate and searching scrutiny to bear upon himself as upon others. His insight was none the less fallible for being that of a man fundamentally charitable and kindly disposed towards his fellow human beings. To some of different natures it seemed that in his enthusiasm and also in his good-heartedness he remained a boy to the day he died.

He has built himself a monument; for the book he left* will be no

*The Diary of a Cabinet Minister. Vol. 1, by Richard Crossman, Hamish Hamilton/Jonathan Cape

less memorable as a self-portrait of the author than as a record of six years in British politics seen from the inside of a Cabinet minister's mind. There has never been anything like it. Political diaries are not the same thing at all, let alone memoirs, biographies, autobiographies and the rest. There is something Proustian, not indeed about the language of the work, but about its meticulous self-observation and deliberate embalming of the momentary impression, judgement or expectation. It is Proustian, too, in that kind of authenticity which only sheer volume – life-size volumes – can convey.

It is a great shame that it was serialised before publication and that many will consequently have formed their first and their only impression of the book from those extracts. I am glad that, knowing I would have the volumes to review, I was careful to refrain from reading a sentence of the extracts. The essence of this work is destroyed by extracting: for the essence is that it is six years of a lifetime uncompressed. Nowhere else can be read – illuminated by trained and unsparing observation, but uncontaminated by hindsight or by the mythologising which sets in almost immediately after experience as the wake follows foaming behind a steamer, what it is actually like to be a member of a British Cabinet. No one else that I know could have achieved that result, and by no other method.

It was characteristic of Crossman that when, after twenty years on the back benches or in opposition, he found himself all at once a Cabinet minister in 1964, his dominant idea was to keep a continuous contemporary record of what happened to him, in private life and in political life, so that he could test his theories against the reality but also, still more, so that here should be a great chunk of reality against which any theory could be tested. He set about it, knowing what he was doing and determined to let nothing interfere with the purpose or frustrate its outcome, rather like Richard Wagner setting out to create and stage *The Ring*. When 'sent for' by Harold Wilson, he had already made the 'preparations which concerned my diary. Jennie Hall, my secretary, agreed to become my archivist and to look after the tapes on which the diary would be dictated each weekend in my home in North Oxfordshire, a 'task to which I devoted most of Saturday evening and Sunday morning each week', with 'a careful selection of all the relevant Cabinet and departmental papers – a task to which one member of my Private Office was always assigned' (pages 12–13). By 22 June 1966, he could note that 'the arrangements with the publishers are nearly completed' for a book which was then already envisaged not as a work based upon the raw material of the diary but as the diary itself. It was this diary which replaced, or rather accomplished, Crossman's 'ambition to write a book which fulfilled for our generation the function of Bagehot's *English Constitution* a hundred years ago'.

As a friend of Crossman (in the sense before defined) I was shocked to learn last year that the diaries were to be published so soon after the events: for I believe, contrary to currently popular notions about 'open government', that secrecy – that is, secrecy of deliberations – is essential to all government, so much so that as soon as a zone of deliberation is invaded government must and does retreat behind more interior fortifications. It was for that reason that I (vainly) argued against the Conservative opposition consenting in the 1960s to the replacement of the 'fifty-year rule' by the 'thirty-year rule'. I was therefore instinctively on the side of the establishment and the Attorney-General in their unsuccessful endeavours to prevent publication, and was saddened that Michael Foot, a Cabinet minister himself, could, as a trustee of the *Diaries*, not be sensitive to the mischief of so early publication of what the lapse of time would not render less valuable.

When I read the book, I realised I was wrong. Not only is it inconceivable that damage to the interests of the state could flow from the Crossman *Diaries*, but I find it difficult to imagine how the deliberations of the existing Cabinet – let alone a Cabinet formed by another party – could be inhibited by the fact that these *Diaries* are in print and on sale. The participants in Cabinet discussion know that they are more at risk from a deliberate leak to the press by one of their number than from consultation of the Index to Crossman, and they at least do not need his characterisations to open their eyes to the moral and intellectual qualities of their colleagues. No doubt some of the named civil servants who play their part in these pages would prefer to be anonymous or absent; but the disclosure or allegation of their modes of proceeding is not likely to injure them in their career and is easier to argue against on grounds of convention than of the public interest.

True, it is all made easier by the author's death – that, and a Crossman characteristic which comes through constantly and endearingly, namely, that his severest and unfairest criticism is levelled at himself. In short, I cannot but rejoice that these three volumes have begun their long career in 1975 and have not had to wait till 1985 or after, though they will be no less compelling to later readers than they are now.

The editing consisted in redictation by Crossman of the text as transcribed from the tapes, to omit repetition and circumlocution, but nothing else. This was guaranteed by a comparison of the second script with the first by the editor, Dr Janet Morgan. There are astonishingly few errors in the text. One or two of fact: the Registrar-

General's Department was not, as Crossman thought (page 31), under him but under the Minister of Health; Wolverhampton was not won (by Labour) after Patricia Llewelyn-Davies left it in 1951 (page 496) but continued to be held by large majorities by the present reviewer until he relinquished it in 1974: an address to the Town Planning Institute in April 1965 (pages 192, 194) comes twice over in successive weeks. One or two errors perhaps of hearing: 'deflation' twice for 'devaluation' (page 318); 'the thousand' for 'ten thousand' (page 332); 'three weeks' for 'three months' (page 515). And practically no misprinting.

The same cannot be said of the historical link passages – were they really necessary at all? – and the brief footnotes added by the editor, which swarm with unnecessary errors. The Commonwealth Immigrants Act was 1962, not 1961 (pages 60, 173); orders do not 'give authority to legislation delegated to Ministers' (page 72): it was Michael Hamilton, not 'Heseltine', who held Salisbury in 1965 (page 151); Ramsay MacDonald did not 'resign' in 1931 (page 161); the Hartley decision in 1969 was a planning not a boundary decision (page 163); Aidan Crawley has not been an MP for West Derbyshire 'since 1962' (page 405), and if his seat was to be mentioned at all, his Labour membership for Buckingham 1945–51 should have been recorded also; a majority of 'only' 8,300 for Newport, Mon. (page 411) is absurd; it is not 'the commanding heights of the economy' of which Labour's Clause 4 'pledges' nationalisation (page 445); Christopher Soames was not 'appointed an EEC Commissioner in 1970' (page 487); Mackintosh's *British Cabinet* was published in 1962, not '1968' (page 561); there is no such thing as 'a Standing Committee of the Whole House' (page 602).

It is to be hoped that the editing of the remaining two volumes will be more carefully checked. The indexing, by contrast, is first-rate.

Any politician who has served in a ministry or sat in Cabinet will testify to the vivid authenticity of the *Diaries*. As page succeeds page, one recalls: 'this is exactly how it was'. Having as it happens served at the Ministry of Housing and Local Government with Duncan Sandys and with (or should it be 'under'?) Dame Evelyn (now Baroness) Sharpe, eight years before Crossman, I can depose that it was all just the same then. But indeed, apart from minor variations of personality, Crossman's picture – or camera-reel – of ministerial life in a department is valid horizontally across the ministries as well as vertically down the years. So is the psychology – the gradually alternating perceptions of oneself, of one's family, of the House of Commons, of government, of the public. It happens more or less the same way to everybody. Only, until now, there was no record or description in any comparable mode with this.

Even at the supreme level of the inner few in Cabinet, in the parallelograms of forces set up within that body, I wonder if there is as much variation as we all – including Crossman himself – are tempted to assume between human nature under a Winston Churchill and a Harold Wilson, a Clement Attlee or a Harold Macmillan. The institution, and the constitutional setting in which it is placed, do wondrously sort and classify all human types into the few standard roles which they are to play out in Cabinet, much as the infinite variety of possible games of chess is all achieved by the movement of no more than six kinds of pieces. In any Cabinet the rooks, the knights and the bishops soon identify themselves: and so do the pawns, who, as always, are in the majority. I remember agreeing with Iain Macleod (he was a 'king's black knight') how much we both enjoyed Cabinet and looked forward to Tuesdays and Thursdays as the best days in the week; but not all, nor most, Cabinet ministers are made that way.

Crossman often records as special what is in fact general, and as peculiar to the Labour Party and a Labour government what is in fact the norm. He even has his little daydreams in which he imagines how different other governments would be. 'How much we in the Labour Party miss the country houses which we don't have! How much Harold's personality accentuates the fragmentation to which we've been submitted' (page 98). He indulges the never-never notion of a Cabinet which really gets down to some strategic thinking and planning for the future. Maybe there have occasionally been such Prime Ministers, but I would take leave to doubt if there have ever been such Cabinets. However, these fond illusions in no way detract from the documentary veracity of the record; in fact, they are a part of it.

The *Diaries* will not in themselves be an important source for political history: they are not that kind of book. That indeed is why one realises that they give away no historical secrets, while they expose so many psychological ones. What is nevertheless of historical value – though I emphasise that this is not the central merit of the book – is to be able to observe chronologically when and in what forms themes which afterwards assumed major, not to say dominant, importance first impinged on the consciousness of at least one Cabinet minister, and that a highly sensitive and introspective one. I choose two themes to illustrate this effect: New Commonwealth immigration and EEC membership.

In examining the first of these two themes one must remember that Crossman's Coventry constituency, though negligibly affected compared with Birmingham or Wolverhampton, was no stranger to the phenomenon, either by proximity or direct experience. This only makes more striking the total disappearance of the subject after the election of March 1966, at which Crossman believed (page 475) that 'if the Conservatives were to launch a strong anti-coloured-immigration line, they might really start winning votes', but discovered in West Bromwich, 'a Black Country town where immigration is the strongest issue' that, whereas, 'in 1964 the pro-Tory undertow against Labour on the ground that we were soft on immigration was what prevented us achieving any swing in the West Midlands, there was a chance of getting a swing this time' (page 477). That is the last mention of the subject.

No doubt in 1964, with the trauma of Gordon Walker's ejection from Smethwick and rejection at Leyton, the Labour Government were highly conscious of immigration. They ditched their pledge to repeal the Commonwealth Immigrants Act 1962, which Gaitskell had fought line by line, and they greatly tightened its administration. What is less known, if at all, is that the 1964–6 government was preparing further anti-immigration legislation of its own. By February 1965 the Home Secretary Soskice

> has been gradually dragged [by the Cabinet Committee on Immigration] out of his purely liberalistic attitude and [taught] that we have to combine tight immigration controls, *even if it means changing the law* [my italics], with a constructive policy for integrating into the community the immigrants who are here already,

and 'George Wigg ran up asking urgently that when I went to Stoke at the weekend I should do a hand-out on immigration', because 'it has been quite clear that immigration can be the greatest potential vote-loser for the Labour Party. If we are seen to be permitting a flood of immigrants to come in and blight the central areas in all our cities' (pages 149–50).

In June 1965 Maurice Foley, the Minister with special responsibility, proposed 'a twelve-month moratorium on all entries, including wives, children and dependants' (page 258), and in July the Cabinet decided with only three dissentients 'to cut down vouchers and stiffen up control of dependants'. The Prime Minister suggested excluding dependants in future, failing evidence of suitable housing (pages 271, 272).

> Like Bert [Bowden, a Leicester MP], George Wigg and I are Midlands MPs and because we see the effect in our constituencies* we all realise that we have got to control the rate of immigration into this country – we can't digest the number who are now arriving in the West Midlands.†

After the administrative measures were announced on 2 August 1965, Crossman reflected:

*Immigration, as it happens, was lower in Dudley, George Wigg's constituency, than in any other part of the Black Country or in Birmingham [Reviewer's note].
†New Commonwealth immigration in 1965 was 51,000 [reviewer's note].

Politically, fear of immigration is the most powerful undertow today. Any attempt now to resist demands for reduced quotas would have been fatal. We felt we had to out-trump the Tories by doing what they would have done and transforming their policy into a bi-partisan policy. I fear we were right; and partly I think so because I believe that anti-Semitism and racialism are endemic, and that one has to deal with them by controlling immigration when it gets beyond a certain level [page 299].

In October 1965 (page 366) a Home Office proposal for a Royal Commission on immigration was shot down because it would 'announce our determination to postpone any action at all for years'; and there was an Immigration Bill, of which it would be fascinating to know the contents, dropped at the last moment out of the programme for the 1965–6 session (page 365). Once the 1966 election was over, however, action was not to come till 1968 and was then to take a very different form.

The theme of the EEC describes an opposite curve in the *Diaries*. In February 1965, discussing Harold Wilson's tolerance of a pro-American line over Vietnam, 'he just saw that one must either go into Europe or become a subsidiary of the Americans, and he chose the latter' (page 156). Then in the draft Queen's speech in October 1965, 'I spotted a very sinister phrase about entry into the EEC and said it had to go. It did' (page 365). By 31 January 1966 the alarm bells were sounding furiously:

I was aware that if I forced a straight vote on whether we should apply for entry to the Common Market or not, the pro-Marketeers would win. They have been pretty busy during the last weeks. I learnt from Tommy [Balogh] that at the beginning of December Michael Stewart had approached the PM urging that we should make an immediate application to enter the EEC and this had only been frustrated when the PM point-blank refused to permit the paper to be circulated. This had already aroused the wrath of Douglas Jay and Fred Peart who approached me over Christmas [page 443].

Three weeks later, when the election is plainly imminent, the PM appears in a different light (page 461):

Harold expects to bring something back from Russia with him and he may be able to link with this a Common Market initiative. He has been under tremendous pressure over the EEC from Stewart and George Brown ever since last December. He has been trying to get them out of their purely anti-French position: and it looks to me as though he is right in thinking that there are reasonable chances of a new approach to Europe. As he sees it, the difficulties of staying outside Europe and surviving as an independent power are very great compared with entering on the right conditions.

The March 1966 election and the post-election reshuffle over, 'I feel there will be much less difference in Cabinet about an approach to the Common Market; and he [the PM] knows that on this issue he has in me a person who takes exactly the same line as himself. Yes to entry, but only on the right terms' (page 492). And so there it was, in the Queen's speech on 18 April 1966: 'My Ministers would be ready to enter the EEC provided essential British and Commonwealth interests were safeguarded.'

This is how, in real life, a non-fact becomes a fact almost overnight and an impracticability has turned, when we next look, into a commitment. But I must not go on quoting, even to follow the EEC through its exciting and ever more frequent appearances, playing hide-and-seek with George Brown. I will finish instead with a beautifully characteristic piece on being a Minister, written only two months after Crossman set out upon the period of office which his *Diaries* will render memorable when most of the public events of that period are out of mind:

> When I went to lunch last week I was asked what it felt like to be a Minister and I replied I hadn't realised how frustrated I was before I got office. I feel better, physically healthier, far less tired, on top of my form by day, even though I have very long days – I may sit in conference almost without a break from nine in the morning until six in the evening. But this doesn't tire me. It exhilarates me and I feel the better for it, whereas a morning at one's desk writing an article is nearly always exasperating and frustrating because one is always striving to improve it and one always knows it could be better than it is when one's finished it. In my life as a journalist I used to wake up after a night's sleep to find I had been pounding away at an article all night, writing, rewriting paragraphs in my sleep. I haven't so far found myself taking planning decisions in my sleep. Indeed I sleep all the more soundly for having had those decisions to take during the day, for having written 'OK' on that policy document, for having been a man of action in that sense of the word.

'THE SHALLOW DIARY OF A CABINET LADY'

Now!, 26 September 1980

Times are changing for historians – for future historians of our present age, that is to say.

Hitherto the historians of political events, besides having recourse to the official records (which included, in this century, the belatedly released records of the Cabinet), were obliged to quarry memoirs and biographies written years after the events by the participants or others.

Even the letters and other contemporary material which such books contain were suspect for omission and manipulation. As for the facts, as alleged or recollected, memory had ample time to play its tricks, innocent or less innocent. Two things have changed. Cabinets nowadays, at any rate Labour Cabinets, are largely composed of diarists; and by that I do not mean people who keep jottings and daily records like those, for instance, of Gladstone, which have recently been voluminously published. I mean professional diarists, people who write diaries as a main ingredient of their daily work just as novelists write novels or journalists write columns.

The second change is that these diaries are no longer consigned to lengthy and profound confidentiality. They are written, quite deliberately, for publication – and preferably lucrative publication – at the earliest possible moment.

We have as yet no evidence of the diarism under Heath or Thatcher to compare with that under Wilson and Callaghan; but even if the disease has made fewer inroads into Conservative government, it already represents a far from negligible alteration in Cabinet morality. The mere diversion of effort and attention from the diarist's duties in his capacity as Minister and member of the Cabinet must be serious.

Mrs Castle's diaries,* which cover her period in office from 3 March 1974 to 13 April 1976, little more than two years, occupy more than 700 pages of this book and well over half a million words. The sheer

*The Castle Diaries 1974–76 by Barbara Castle, Weidenfeld

nervous and physical energy expended in maintaining that output must be considerable.

More serious is the altered attitude of mind. The diarist lives his or her life, in Ministry, in Cabinet, and in the more private political relationships, thinking all the time, first and foremost: 'That must go into my diary; that is a phrase I must remember, a revelation I must record.'

Not only will this colour his own behaviour; it is bound to colour that of his colleagues as well. Henceforward colleagues have to assume that what they say in their most disarmed moments will be public property before a few years are out. Even one such diarist in a Cabinet would be enough to change its nature. But six or seven!

Diarism, in the sense in which I have defined it, is no less than a deliberate subversion of the personal and constitutional duty of a Cabinet. It is a breach of the Privy Councillor's oath or (if that expression be found too romantic) it is a denial to the Sovereign and to the nation of that confidentiality and collective responsibility of the Cabinet which is basic to modern British parliamentary democracy.

Even if Mrs Castle, as one would hope, had accepted no money for systematically betraying the confidence of her colleagues and the secretary of the Cabinet, the publication of her diary is still a totally inadmissable action.

The classic case in this area is Richard Crossman, who deliberately, and with the knowledge of the Prime Minister, recorded weekly what had passed in Cabinet and among colleagues. At first his idea had been that it would form the raw material for an academic study of government. But presently, under the shadow of death, he resolved on direct publication.

It was that publication which tore a hole in a wall of the constitution. The question is whether the precedent can allow repetition, and in particular this repetition. I say not.

Crossman's diarism was not diarism for its own sake. It arose from a conviction, justified or not, that the working of British government can only be rigorously understood, 'if one rose from the dead' – in other words, if one day somebody from within would part the curtains and 'tell it how it was'.

Given that conviction, Crossman, with all his faults, brought to its implementation a sincere desire to advance knowledge and a high intellectual capacity. That cloak will not cover Barbara Castle.

The overpowering impression left on the reader's mind by her diary is that of triviality: the largest decisions and the profoundest issues are effortlessly trivialised.

As a strong and doubtless sincere opponent of Britain's membership of the EEC, Mrs Castle lived through Harold Wilson's reduction

of Labour's promised 'renegotiation' to a charade, through the unprecedented Cabinet 'agreement to differ', and through the capitulation
of a reluctant Cabinet to the Foreign Secretary and the Prime
Minister.

'As someone said afterwards, a historic Cabinet!' – that was 21
January 1975, when the 'agreement to differ' was proposed and
accepted. Mrs Castle's contribution was that she 'certainly wasn't
going to let such an important thing as the Common Market wreck
her political work or her party's socialist unity', and her 'morning
was made by a friendly note John Silkin tossed' to her at the end,
consisting of doggerel in praise of her 'commonsense'.

Her general conclusion was that 'it really does look as though
Harold's long period of humiliation has not been in vain and that the
party's unity is emerging as an exercise in genuine party democracy'.

Could it be that Mrs Castle failed to comprehend that it was the
'agreement to differ' reached in January which reduced the substan-
tive decision of the Cabinet in March 1975 to a foregone conclusion?
'We all knew that everybody had made up their minds and that
nothing anyone said would change anything.'

Though intended as ironical, there is a damning appropriateness
about Mrs Castle's epitaph on the Cabinet decision: 'Anyway, history
has been made this morning. We actually had a break at 11 a.m. for
coffee to be served!'

The Prime Minister himself, who contrived the typical device of
the 'agreement to differ', was startled, or pretended to be so, by the
vigour with which Mrs Castle and others availed themselves of it.
After summoning her rudely late in the evening, he apologised in
the presence of Callaghan and Foot. 'I went over and kissed him
affectionately on the forehead. "And I'm sorry if I have upset you,
but I'm afraid I can't withdraw." I replied. "Don't I get a kiss?" said
Jim Callaghan gloomily. "God knows I need it." So I kissed him too
and sat down next to him. "I can't understand why Barbara is so
chirpy," he almost groaned. "Because I don't think the situation is
tragic," I replied.'

Tired as Mrs Castle must have been when she got home after all
that in the early hours, between long sittings of the House and the
piloting of a Bill of her own, this was the sort of stuff that she
recorded verbatim forthwith. It is hard to know whether to marvel
more at her industry or her shallowness.

She records having told Harold Wilson: 'I'm the best Minister
you've got.' Perhaps the best commentary is that of Edward Short
(Lord Glenamara) when Callaghan had dropped them both on
coming into office: 'I feel at the top of my powers. I expect you are

the same. You ought to have been allowed to finish your pay beds legislation. I would have liked to finish my work on devolution. I have spent months on it.'

That is just about the level.

'THE ARCHETYPAL DEMAGOGUE'

The Spectator, 22 November 1986

A detailed biography* of Paisley is well worth reading for anybody who became a spectator of the Northern Ireland scene or a participant in it after the story was already well in progress. The plot of the story is so repetitive, and the Paisley act is so repetitive, that one stands amazed to find how far back the same pattern can be recognised running along the carpet. Biographers Ed Moloney and Andy Pollak have been industrious in interviewing witnesses and working the seams of the *Irish Times* and the *Belfast Telegraph*. They are not pro-Paisley – a biographer is bound to be either pro or anti – and Paisley receives anything but sympathetic handling from authors whose view of events is limited by a conventional Irish nationalism which still believes that King James I sent 200,000 people to settle Ulster or can write of Paisley's Free Presbyterian Church that 'like some poisonous growth on a sickly plant, their bright new temples to separatism and sectarianism were among the very few beneficiaries of the collapse of Terence O'Neill's timid attempt at reform'.

In retrospect 'Terence O'Neill's timid attempt at reform' which launched Paisley as a political party leader doubling with the role of perpetual moderator of the church that he founded, is recognisable as the first in the series of initiatives since then which have now culminated in the Anglo-Irish Agreement. The underlying proposition, posed to one Ulster politician after another, has been constant: 'The UK,' it runs, 'is determined to transfer Ulster into an all-Ireland, probably confederal, state. You cannot prevent this, but you can co-operate to ensure that it takes place in easy stages and produces the most favourable terms possible for your people.' The tactics are as unvarying as the objective. They consist of a one-off Ulster assembly on a power-sharing basis, plus an umbrella contraption by way of a Council of Ireland, Anglo-Irish Council, etc., etc., under which the seed of confederation can be sown and cultivated.

After O'Neill choked to death trying to oblige, the same chalice was handed to Brian Faulkner, notably at the Chequers summit with Heath and Lynch in September 1971. When that attempt foundered

---

* *Paisley* by Ed Moloney and Andy Pollack, Poolbeg Press

in 1974 on overhaste and on Protestant worker resistance, not to mention the Westminster election débâcle, Faulkner too was bust. Thereafter the Foreign Office – sorry, the Northern Ireland Office! – went on hawking the cup around to one blue-eyed candidate after another. William Craig was given a gulp of it. After it poisoned him in 1975 the cupbearers tried a whole procession of others down to the present day, whose names for reasons of decency I do not here propose to supply.

It is a process which has to be kept constantly in mind by those who wish to study and understand Paisley's political role from the mid–1960s onwards. At each stage he was in the right place at the right time, to articulate the well-founded instinctive suspicion of Ulster Unionists that they were being sold down the river, and to stand forth as the 'seagreen incorruptible' who mobilised Protestant resistance in the nick of time – under a bewildering array of ever new titles.

It may be said of Paisley, as someone – was it Voltaire? – said of God, that if he had not existed it would have been necessary to invent him. He incarnates and he appeals to certain characteristics typical of Ulstermen and dangerously unshared by their English fellow countrymen, which have rendered them vulnerable, despite all their courage and steadfastness, to the wiles and cynicism of their enemies. One such characteristic is a propensity to mistake words for deeds and to be more impressed by words when they are shouted than when they are spoken softly. In a commonplace Ulster phrase, Paisley has been the 'mon who speaks out', and his audiences love it to the point of not observing what, if anything, happens afterwards. Another of those characteristics is the habit of dealing in threats and the preference for a deliberately rough approach, which belies an underlying reasonableness and even kindliness. Threatening and derogatory language does not lose Brownie points but actually adds to credibility; and that links up with yet another characteristic – a tendency to take appearances on trust and an unwillingness to assume that externals probably conceal a very different inner reality.

All these qualities are abundantly documented in the biography of the most outstanding, archetypal and talented exponent, in Ulster terms, of the art of demagogy. It is a career that would be unthinkable in any English context. Indeed, it is for that reason uncomprehended and persistently misinterpreted on the British mainland. Nevertheless it repays a study which, after due allowance for easily discountable bias, this new biography makes possible.

A Shankill businessman and supporter of Paisley's Democratic Unionist Party is quoted saying of him: 'He has never led the people into a blind alley yet.' That may seem a remarkable statement, not least in the light of the abortive strike into which Paisley plunged the province in 1977, declaring as he did so that, should it fail – which it did – he would quit public life for ever. It seemed at the time an inexplicable and foredoomed miscalculation. Yet random misjudgement is not a characteristic of Paisley: shrewd foresight and cautious calculation would be nearer the mark. If it were that he stands in the line of those who have been vouchsafed an insight into the purposes and the determination of the British state, the 1977 strike (to which the biography devotes inadequate attention) and much else that otherwise appears contradictory about Paisley would cease to be so: his abandonment of the integrationist policy which he espoused in the 1970–4 Parliament; his offer in 1981 to accept the verdict of a referendum in Great Britain upon the union with Northern Ireland; his valediction to Jim Prior in 1984 as having 'done a good job' as Secretary of State; his current hankering after round-table talks between all the political parties in the province.

Of course, the play is not over yet, though rumours that Paisley is immortal are probably exaggerated. One's mouth waters at the thought of what future biographers and historians will be able to make out of these troubled decades in Ulster's history with the benefit of hindsight when the seals are opened.

'A STRANGE CHOICE OF HERO'

Independent, 27 March 1991

'Since Mrs Thatcher's fall,' declared a political correspondent recently, reporting an interview with Norman Lamont, 'it has become fashionable for ministers to cite Iain Macleod as a political idol.'

This is a strangely paradoxical happening, especially viewed in the aftermath of a Budget which reverted to the socialist hosepipe method for allocating welfare payments (child benefit) in preference to any attempt to target the recipients selectively and eliminate flat-rate largesse.

I remember Iain Macleod telling me with a chuckle when he was catapulted in 1952 into the office of Minister of Health, how he sat down at the desk of his predecessor Captain A. Crookshank, pulled open a drawer and found there a well-used copy of *Needs and Means*, a pamphlet, written in 1951 by Iain Macleod and myself, that addressed itself to the method of providing 'means' on the basis of 'needs'. It was indeed upon exposing the Labour Party's lack of a consistent philosophy of needs and means that Iain based the famous philippic against Aneurin Bevan in the House of Commons, which set him off on a meteoric ministerial career little more than two years after he first got into Parliament.

I suspect that the unhistorical invocation of Iain Macleod's name by those in retreat from the Thatcher years, to cast a mistily romantic 'wet' vapour around the Conservative Party, may have something to do with the much-bandied expression 'One Nation'. Its history is worth recalling.

In the years after the Conservative defeat of 1945, the memory of Benjamin Disraeli, primroses and all, enjoyed a springtime among young aspirants in the Tory ranks. Here was the man whose novels had supplemented the more august writings of Edmund Burke, giving flesh and blood to the Tory tradition in Britain and British politics. The pushful adventurer who had written novels revealing sympathy and understanding of the Chartists and their riots more than for the 'great nonentities' of the Conservative establishment, had indited a celebrated passage in his novel *Sybil*, where the Tory hero is confronted with the existence of 'two nations' and informed that they are 'the rich and the poor'.

What comfortable words for struggling youth in a Conservative

Party reeling under the combined impact of electoral defeat and the popularity of the welfare state – universal health service, universal pensions, universal education and what else! Here was the evidence that the heirs of Toryism, with their rooted belief in the nation as a homogeneous, organic phenomenon of nature, could recognise concern for all its members as an essential mark of society – and Tory society, mark you, not socialist society. So what to say amid the ravaging storm which beat about their heads as Churchill, Macmillan and Butler were cautiously erecting a lightning conductor called the *Industrial Charter*? What to say about all that on the forthcoming hustings? What, more urgently still, to say in the unavoidable debates in the House of Commons?

Slinking out of the chamber disconsolately after yet another failed frontal attack upon the Labour Party's welfare state, Iain Macleod and Angus (now Lord) Maude put their heads together and said 'Let's write a book about One Nation.' 'As one,' like St Paul, 'born out of time', I was the last to be recruited to the noble nine who toiled week by week in a committee room and produced the Conservative Party's bestseller of that autumn of 1950, during which Attlee's government lay a-dying at last and none too peacefully. We have been a longevous lot; for seven of us still survive to verify the tale, in or out of the House of Lords. The subtitle to *One Nation* was 'A Tory approach to social problems'; Rab Butler (who else?) wrote the foreword.

What were we trying to do? A cynical commentator once précised the contents as 'higher rents and more Morris dancing'. It was anything but a wets' charter; but he had a point. Need, suffering, poverty, deprivation – how does a Tory confront them without throwing a welfare state at them and baptising them with an undiscriminating financial hosepipe? As I piece the answer back together, I am astonished to realise how deep and how long was the germination in the Conservative Party of the policies and attitudes which are now irretrievably going to be labelled 'Thatcherite'. The 'dry' years 1979–90 did not come from nowhere.

Well, first one must look to see if some dislocation, some damage being inflicted on the functioning of society itself, was to blame for the perceived evils. This was the 'higher rents' end. *One Nation* rediscovered the market and the evil consequences of destroying it. That, indeed, was the subject of the group's next book. *The Change is Our Ally* (1954). Misery and deprivation might actually be inflicted or prolonged by refusal to let society's mechanism operate. Then there was the problem of identifying and locating those ills which no market system can alleviate. There was no pussy-footing over discretionary state help, with the emphasis on discretionary; nor was there over the voluntary sector. My eye falls on the sentence in *One Nation:* 'Voluntary effort must provide much the greatest part of the services needed [for the old].' That perhaps is the 'more Morris dancing' – the conviction that society as a whole with its inherited means confronts the predicament of its parts.

Iain Macleod bequeathed no testament. Like Gladstone, but unlike Disraeli, he left no written political memorials of his own beyond the record of speeches on public platforms and in the Commons. They were acclaimed, for he excelled in that medium; but they do not provide those who seek to reconstruct his political philosophy with adequate material for the task. That perhaps accounts for his name having been so inappropriately inscribed in the banners of a Conservative Party fleeing from beneath the fall-out from the Thatcher detonation. Alas, poor Iain; how surprised he would be to find himself the darling of the refugees from Thatcherism.

'FACE THE PRESS'

Channel 4 TV, 9 October 1983

ANTHONY HOWARD: What general view do you take of the Prime Minister [Mrs Thatcher] in her second term? You've been said to be quite close to her. She regards you, perhaps, as somebody who she listens to, and some people have said that she is simply carrying on Powellism by other means.

ENOCH POWELL: Then I'm not sure that she's ever meant, by Powellism, what I meant, though it was others not I who called it Powellism. I'll tell you what worries me. I would wish that the Prime Minister had been able to digest her victory with more relaxation and greater magnanimity. After all, great affirmation has been conferred upon her. And yet, it seems to be that she's often behaving like someone who still has to fight for it. I don't mean to be self-satisfied, I mean the opposite. That it would be a time where stridency was less necessary or understandable than before. I do find myself anxious at the effect of that success and the manner in which she has coped with it.

FRANK JOHNSON: It's a lack of Christian humility, are you suggesting?

POWELL: Well, what's Christian humility as opposed to humility might take us into a larger debate, but I don't even mean humility. It's, after all, natural that a person whose life has been lived in British politics and who finds something like four more years in the greatest position opening out before her, to view that scene with a benign, relaxed attitude and a sense which is perceptible of magnanimity. I wish that were more so.

PART THREE

POWELL THE POLITICIAN

IMMIGRATION

HUDDLESTON: . . . What I still want to know from you, really, is why the presence of a coloured immigrant group is objectionable when the presence of a non-coloured immigrant is not objectionable.

POWELL: Oh no, oh no! On the contrary I have often said that if we saw the prospect of five million Germans in this country at the end of the century, the risks of disruption and violence would probably be greater, and the antagonism which would be aroused would be more severe.

'The Great Debate', BBC TV, 9 September 1969

'PANORAMA'

BBC TV, 12 February 1968

ROBIN DAY: In the 'Panorama' studio, the Right Honourable Enoch Powell on coloured immigration. Do we need much stiffer controls? And, across the Channel, after de Gaulle's veto, how do the French people see the British?

(music)

DAY: Good evening. First, coloured immigration and the views of Mr Enoch Powell, Conservative Front Bencher and Member of Parliament for Wolverhampton, South-West. Last Friday, Mr Powell denounced Britain's immigration policy as crazy. The nation, he said, was menaced with a racial problem which, at the present rate, would be, by the end of this century, as big as America's is now. And this evening, in Parliament, five Conservative Privy Councillors, including Mr Duncan Sandys, tabled a Commons motion calling for immediate legislation to curtail the influx of immigrants into Britain. Now Mr Powell, may I ask you first of all, what changes would you like to see? Would you in particular want to cut down altogether on the immigrant vouchers we now have and on the dependants who come in as well?

ENOCH POWELL: Well there are three aspects of Conservative policy on this subject which, as it's of particular importance and interest in my own area and to the immigrants themselves who've settled in my own area as well as to the rest of the population, I wanted to emphasise. One is as regards illegal entry, that it seems to be absurd that it should not be a cause for deportation that a person has made good an entry to this country against the law . . .

DAY: Could I come on to that in a moment because I was going to raise that separately?

POWELL: I'm sorry.

DAY: On this point about cutting down: do you want to cut down?

POWELL: The second is that we ought to have power of control over dependants. At the moment, as you know, the number of dependants is unlimited, there is no limit or control over dependants within the definition of the 1962 Act. Now the number of dependants seeking to come in is ultimately dependent . . . ultimately a result of the numbers who are admitted from year to year. And on present rate of inflow, the official estimate is that the numbers of immigrants will have risen to 3½ million by 1985. That's in seventeen years' time, 3½ million, at the present rate of inflow. So, I re-emphasised our policy that the rate of inflow has got to be cut down and that in particular it has to be done by taking power to control the numbers of dependants who are admitted. And, finally, if I could just mention the last point, we have proposed that there should be power, and generous power, to assist voluntary repatriation of those who want to go home, which I mention because of course it is one of the ways in which a divided family can, not necessarily would but can, be reunited and it belongs in this context.

DAY: But I'm still not clear. Do you want to stop all immigration now, because there was one interpretation of your speech which gave that impression?

POWELL: No, what I said was that if the present rate of inflow is excessive and I believe that it is and I believe that those figures show that it is, and we as a party believe that it is, then you can tackle this in two ways or both. You can tackle it by cutting down vouchers or you can tackle it by cutting down the number of dependants admitted when you have the power to control them, or both.

DAY: Well now, knowing the problem as you do from your experience in Government, and as your local experience in your constituency, what action would you take on those alternatives if you were responsible?

POWELL: Well in the first place, we have got to have legal powers to control dependants. That's the first thing and that involves legislation. If you have that power, it means that you can use the rights to admit dependants selectively, you can look at the circumstances and, indeed, you can obtain very much better documentation than at the moment we are able to obtain of the actual or alleged dependants. And then, thirdly, there's no doubt that if eventually one is going to reduce the flow, the number of vouchers must be further restricted. But, of course, to say nil per annum is an absurdity.

DAY: Do you think this goes further than the official Conservative policy?

POWELL: No certainly not, certainly not.

DAY: Mr Heath didn't quite spell it out in the way you have spelled it out though, did he?

POWELL: Oh well, I have refreshed my memory of what he said precisely in a speech in September at Ipswich and I would say that what I have said is entirely within the lines of his speech.

DAY: What about . . . on the question of illegal entry, what do you want to do about that?

POWELL: That it should be an offence which renders a person liable to return to the country from which he came, to have entered this country by false practices or in other ways illegally.

DAY: Do you know why this loophole exists in the law which the Conservative Government, of which you are a member, passed?

POWELL: Oh there were a good many loopholes. I'm afraid that if you have to pass legislation amid the storm of a very largely misguided opposition that there was at the time you are liable to find that you end with some loopholes.

DAY: And, briefly, what about this very important question of the two hundred, or thousand . . . two hundred thousand or so Asians in East and Central Africa who have passport and citizenship status which enables them under present law to come into this country outside the Immigration Control?

POWELL: Yes the position is that as a result of a combination between a provision in the 1962 Commonwealth Immigrants Act and a provision in the relevant Kenya and other legislation, passports issued after independence by the High Commissioner are regarded as United Kingdom passports. Now I think it's impossible to say that this possibility wasn't envisaged at the time when both laws were passed, but what certainly was not anticipated or taken account of was the large and sudden influx which might result from it.

DAY: Do you think this should be restricted?

POWELL: Now what I say is that it is absolutely absurd for the Government, in the face of this, to have remained absolutely inactive. Now in months after months this has been pointed out and the flow has been increasing. Now there are various ways one can approach this, and one perfectly elementary way, which so far as I know there's been no move to take, is that the Government should make some contact with the Government of these countries, first of all to see whether the causes which are leading to this influx into this country can be dealt with in other ways. It's one thing to say the people should be accorded an ultimate right, an ultimate resort . . . it's quite a different thing to remain perfectly passive while an inflow of dimensions which is, I suppose, what two or three times perhaps the rate of Commonwealth immigration continues.

DAY: But are you saying their entry should be restricted?

POWELL: I'm saying that we cannot remain passive when there is a possibility from Kenya of up to some 180,000 people entering this country completely outside the controls. Now the first thing to do is to see whether without direct control or intervention, you can do something about this. I believe in taking fences when one comes to them, but my charge against the Government is that they've done absolutely nothing and haven't shown any realisation that there is a problem here.

TO THE ANNUAL GENERAL MEETING OF THE WEST MIDLANDS AREA CONSERVATIVE POLITICAL CENTRE

Birmingham, 20 April 1968

The supreme function of statesmanship is to provide against preventable evils. In seeking to do so, it encounters obstacles which are deeply rooted in human nature. One is that by the very order of things such evils are not demonstrable until they have occurred: at each stage in their onset there is room for doubt and for dispute whether they be real or imaginary. By the same token, they attract little attention in comparison with current troubles, which are both indisputable and pressing: whence the besetting temptation of all politics to concern itself with the immediate present at the expense of the future. Above all, people are disposed to mistake predicting troubles for causing troubles and even for desiring troubles: 'if only', they love to think, 'if only people wouldn't talk about it, it probably wouldn't happen'. Perhaps this habit goes back to the primitive belief that the word and the thing, the name and the object, are identical. At all events, the discussion of future grave but, with effort now, avoidable evils is the most unpopular and at the same time the most necessary occupation for the politician. Those who knowingly shirk it, deserve, and not infrequently receive, the curses of those who come after.

A week or two ago I fell into conversation with a constituent, a middle-aged, quite ordinary working man employed in one of our nationalised industries. After a sentence or two about the weather, he suddenly said: 'If I had the money to go, I wouldn't stay in this country.' I made some deprecatory reply, to the effect that even this Government wouldn't last for ever; but he took no notice, and continued: 'I have three children, all of them been through grammar school and two of them married now, with family. I shan't be satisfied till I have seen them all settled overseas. In this country in fifteen or twenty years' time the black man will have the whip hand over the white man.'

I can already hear the chorus of execration. How dare I say such a horrible thing? How dare I stir up trouble and inflame feelings by repeating such a conversation? The answer is that I do not have the right not to do so. Here is a decent, ordinary fellow Englishman, who in broad daylight in my own town says to me, his Member of Parliament, that this country will not be worth living in for his children. I simply do not have the right to shrug my shoulders and think about something else. What he is saying, thousands and hundreds of thousands are saying and thinking – not throughout Great Britain, perhaps, but in the areas that are already undergoing the total transformation to which there is no parallel in a thousand years of English history.

In fifteen or twenty years, on present trends, there will be in this country 3½ million Commonwealth immigrants and their descendants. That is not my figure. That is the official figure given to Parliament by the spokesman of the Registrar General's office. There is no comparable official figure for the year 2000, but it must be in the region of 5–7 million, approximately one-tenth of the whole population, and approaching that of Greater London. Of course, it will not be evenly distributed from Margate to Aberystwyth and from Penzance to Aberdeen. Whole areas, towns and parts of towns across England will be occupied by different sections of the immigrant and immigrant-descended population.

As time goes on, the proportion of this total who are immigrant descendants, those born in England, who arrived here by exactly the same route as the rest of us, will rapidly increase. Already by 1985 the native-born would constitute the majority. It is this fact above all which creates the extreme urgency of action now, of just that kind of action which is hardest for politicians to take, action where the difficulties lie in the present but the evils to be prevented or minimised lie several Parliaments ahead.

The natural and rational first question with a nation confronted by such a prospect is to ask: 'How can its dimensions be reduced?' Granted it be not wholly preventable, can it be limited, bearing in mind that numbers are of the essence: the significance and consequences of an alien element introduced into a country or population are profoundly different according to whether that element is 1 per cent or 10 per cent. The answers to the simple and rational question are equally simple and rational: by stopping, or virtually stopping, further inflow, and by promoting the maximum outflow. Both answers are part of the official policy of the Conservative Party.

It almost passes belief that at this moment twenty or thirty additional immigrant children are arriving from overseas in Wolver-hampton alone every week – and that means fifteen or twenty additional families of a decade or two hence. Those whom the gods wish to destroy, they first make mad. We must be mad, literally mad, as a nation to be permitting the annual inflow of some 50,000 dependants, who are for the most part the material of the future growth of the immigrant-descended population. It is like watching a nation busily engaged in heaping up its own funeral pyre. So insane are we that we actually permit unmarried persons to immigrate for the purpose of founding a family with spouses and fiancées whom they have never seen. Let no one suppose that the flow of dependants will automatically tail off. On the contrary, even at the present admission rate of only 5,000 a year by voucher, there is sufficient for a further 25,000 dependants per annum ad infinitum, without taking into account the huge reservoir of existing relations in this country – and I am making no allowance at all for fraudulent entry. In these circumstances nothing will suffice but that the total inflow for settlement should be reduced at once to negligible proportions, and that the necessary legislative and administrative measures be taken without delay. I stress the words 'for settlement'. This has nothing to do with the entry of Commonwealth citizens, any more than of aliens, into this country, for the purposes of study or of improving their qualifications, like (for instance) the Commonwealth doctors who, to the advantage of their own countries, have enabled our hospital service to be expanded faster than would otherwise have been possible. These are not, and never have been, immigrants.

I turn to re-emigration. If all immigration ended tomorrow, the rate of growth of the immigrant and immigrant-descended population would be substantially reduced, but the prospective size of this element in the population would still leave the basic character of the national danger unaffected. This can only be tackled while a considerable proportion of the total still comprises persons who entered this country during the last ten years or so. Hence the urgency of implementing now the second element of the Conservative Party's policy: the encouragement of re-emigration. Nobody can make an estimate of the numbers which, with generous grants and assistance, would choose either to return to their countries of origin or to go to other countries anxious to receive the manpower and the skills they represent. Nobody knows, because no such policy has yet been attempted. I can only say that, even at present, immigrants in my own constituency from time to time come to me, asking if I can find them assistance to return home. If such a policy were adopted and pursued with the determination which the gravity of the alternative justifies, the resultant outflow could appreciably alter the prospects for the future.

It can be no part of any policy that existing families should be kept divided; but there are two directions in which families can be reunited, and if our former and present immigration laws have brought about the division of families, albeit voluntary or semi-voluntarily, we ought to be prepared to arrange for them to be reunited in their countries of origin. In short, suspension of immigration and encouragement of re-emigration hang together, logically and humanly, as two aspects of the same approach.

The third element of the Conservative Party's policy is that all who are in this country as citizens should be equal before the law and that there shall be no discrimination or difference made between them by public authority. As Mr Heath has put it, we will have no 'first-class citizens' and 'second-class citizens'. This does not mean that the immigrant and his descendants should be elevated into a privileged or special class or that the citizen should be denied his right to discriminate in the management of his own affairs between one fellow citizen and another or that he should be subjected to inquisition as to his reasons and motives for behaving in one lawful manner rather than another.

There could be no grosser misconception of the realities than is entertained by those who vociferously demand legislation as they call it 'against discrimination', whether they be leader-writers of the same kidney and sometimes on the same newspapers which year after year in the 1930s tried to blind this country to the rising peril which confronted it, or archbishops who live in palaces, faring delicately with the bedclothes pulled right up over their heads. They have got it exactly and diametrically wrong. The discrimination and the deprivation, the sense of alarm and of resentment, lies not with the immigrant population but with those among whom they have come and are still coming. This is why to enact legislation of the kind before Parliament at this moment is to risk throwing a match on to gunpowder. The kindest thing that can be said about those who propose and support it is that they know not what they do.

Nothing is more misleading than comparison between the Commonwealth immigrant in Britain and the American Negro. The Negro population of the United States, which was already in existence before the United States became a nation, started literally as slaves and were later given the franchise and other rights of citizenship, to the exercise of which they have only gradually and still incompletely come. The Commonwealth immigrant came to Britain as a full citizen, to a country which knows no discrimination between one citizen and another, and he entered instantly into the possession of the rights of every citizen, from the vote to free treatment under the National Health Service. Whatever drawbacks attended the immigrants – and they were drawbacks which did not, and do not, make admission into Britain by hook or by crook appear less than desirable – arose not from the law or from public policy or from administration but from those personal circumstances and accidents which cause, and always will cause, the fortunes and experience of one man to be different from another's.

But while to the immigrant entry to this country was admission to privileges and opportunities eagerly sought, the impact upon the existing population was very different. For reasons which they could not comprehend, and in pursuance of a decision by default, on which they were never consulted, they found themselves made strangers in their own country. They found their wives unable to obtain hospital beds in childbirth, their children unable to obtain school places, their homes and neighbourhoods changed beyond recognition, their plans and prospects for the future defeated; at work they found that employers hesitated to apply to the immigrant worker the standards of discipline and competence required of the native-born worker; they began to hear, as time went by, more and more voices which told them that they were now the unwanted. On top of this, they now learn that a one-way privilege is to be established by Act of Parliament: a law, which cannot, and is not intended, to operate to protect them or redress their grievances, is to be enacted to give the stranger, the disgruntled and the *agent provocateur* the power to pillory them for their private actions.

In the hundreds upon hundreds of letters I received when I last spoke on this subject two or three months ago, there was one striking feature which was largely new and which I find ominous. All Members of Parliament are used to the typical anonymous correspondent; but what surprised and alarmed me was the high proportion of ordinary, decent, sensible people, writing a rational and often well-educated letter, who believed that they had to omit their address because it was dangerous to have committed themselves to paper to a Member of Parliament agreeing with the views I had expressed, and that they would risk either penalties or reprisals if they were known to have done so. The sense of being a persecuted minority which is growing among ordinary English people in the areas of the country which are affected is something that those without direct experience can hardly imagine. I am going to allow just one of those hundreds of people to speak for me. She did give her name and address, which I have detached from the letter which I am about to read. She was writing from Northumberland about something which is happening at this moment in my own constituency:

Eight years ago in a respectable street in Wolverhampton a house was sold to a negro. Now only one white (a woman old-age pensioner) lives there. This is her story. She lost her husband and both her sons in the war. So she turned her seven-roomed house, her only asset, into a boarding house. She worked hard and did well, paid off her mortgage and began to put something by for her old age. Then the immigrants moved in. With growing fear, she saw one house after another taken over. The quiet street became a place of noise and confusion. Regretfully, her white tenants moved out.

The day after the last one left, she was awakened at 7 a.m. by two negroes who wanted to use her phone to contact their employer. When she refused, as she would have refused any stranger at such an hour, she was abused and feared she would have been attacked but for the chain on her door. Immigrant families have tried to rent rooms in her house, but she always refused. Her little store of money went, and after paying her rates, she has less than £2 per week. She went to apply for a rate reduction and was seen by a young girl, who on hearing she had a seven-roomed house, suggested she should let part of it. When she said the only people she could get were negroes, the girl said 'racial prejudice won't get you anywhere in this country'. So she went home.

The telephone is her lifeline. Her family pay the bill, and help her out as best they can. Immigrants have offered to buy her house – at a price which the prospective landlord would be able to recover from his tenants in weeks, or at most a few months. She is becoming afraid to go out. Windows are broken. She finds excreta pushed through her letterbox. When she goes to the shops, she is followed by children, charming, wide-grinning piccaninnies. They cannot speak English, but one word they know. 'Racialist', they chant. When the new Race Relations Bill is passed, this woman is convinced she will go to prison. And is she so wrong? I begin to wonder.

The other dangerous delusion from which those who are wilfully or otherwise blind to realities suffer, is summed up in the word 'integration'. To be integrated into a population means to become for all practical purposes indistinguishable from its other members. Now, at all times, where there are marked physical differences, especially of colour, integration is difficult though, over a period, not impossible. There are among the Commonwealth immigrants who have come to live here in the last fifteen years or so, many thousands whose wish and purpose is to be integrated and whose every thought and endeavour is bent in that direction. But to imagine that such a thing enters the heads of a great and growing majority of immigrants and their descendants is a ludicrous misconception, and a dangerous one to boot.

We are on the verge here of a change. Hitherto it has been force of circumstance and of background which has rendered the very idea of integration inaccessible to the greater part of the immigrant population – that they never conceived or intended such a thing, and that their numbers and physical concentration meant the pressures towards integration which normally bear upon any small minority did not operate. Now we are seeing the growth of positive forces acting against integration, of vested interests in the preservation and sharpening of racial and religious differences, with a view to the exercise of actual domination, first over fellow immigrants and then over the rest of the population. The cloud no bigger than a man's hand, that can so rapidly overcast the sky, has been visible recently in Wolverhampton and has shown signs of spreading quickly. The words I am about to use, verbatim as they appeared in the local press on 17 February, are not mine, but those of a Labour Member of Parliament who is a Minister in the present Government.

> The Sikh communities' campaign to maintain customs inappropriate in Britain is much to be regretted. Working in Britain, particularly in the public services, they should be prepared to accept the terms and conditions of their employment. To claim special communal rights (or should one say rites?) leads to a dangerous fragmentation within society. This communalism is a canker; whether practised by one colour or another it is to be strongly condemned.

All credit to John Stonehouse for having had the insight to perceive that, and the courage to say it.

For these dangerous and divisive elements the legislation proposed in the Race Relations Bill is the very pabulum they need to flourish. Here is the means of showing that the immigrant communities can organise to consolidate their members, to agitate and campaign against their fellow citizens, and to overawe and dominate the rest with the legal weapons which the ignorant and the ill-informed have provided. As I look ahead, I am filled with foreboding. Like the Roman, I seem to see 'the River Tiber foaming with much blood'. That tragic and intractable phenomenon which we watch with horror on the other side of the Atlantic but which there is interwoven with the history and existence of the States itself, is coming upon us here by our own volition and our own neglect. Indeed, it has all but come. In numerical terms, it will be of American proportions long before the end of the century. Only resolute and urgent action will avert it even now. Whether there will be the public will to demand and obtain that action, I do not know. All I know is that to see, and not to speak, would be the great betrayal.

'THIS WEEK: THE WORLD OF ENOCH POWELL'

Rediffusion TV, 4 July 1968

PETER JENKINS: Mr Powell, you're always very precise in your use of words – you were in reply to the opening question of this programme. I wonder if you understand the power of words – when you made that speech did you anticipate that you speaking as a rational, educated man would incite a violent and irrational response in the streets?

ENOCH POWELL: I've no reason to suppose that I did incite a violent and irrational response. If you're referring to the many workers in many parts of the country as well as the dockers and the Smithfield men who demonstrated and came out on strike, well, I met quite a number of them and I can only say that I found no evidence whatsoever in their behaviour and in the way they talked of violence or – I suppose we've got to have the word sooner or later – racialism. And I'm not at all satisfied with the allegations that as a result of anything I said any violent action took place.

JENKINS: Your moral position on this confuses me somewhat because you were justifying yourself a moment ago in terms of representing the wishes and concerns of the people, but on another issue, capital punishment, you were in favour of abolition. Now probably the majority of the people in this country are in favour of capital punishment.

POWELL: No, I wasn't justifying myself on that ground at all. I was asked what I thought had been the effect of my speech and I said it had been that a great volume of opinion had been expressed. I also said that undoubtedly in this matter I am speaking for the immigrants in my constituency as well as for the indigenous inhabitants. I wouldn't seek on that ground to say something I didn't believe, and I agree with you, I am obliged to you for the example, on many cases I have thought it my duty to express views which I knew were not shared by a majority of my constituents. I regard that as my right. But let me put this to you: would it not be a very dangerous position if, there being widespread feeling in the country for the retention of capital punishment, nobody was allowed to argue the case for retention without it being treated as almost an unmentionable, and without his becoming the subject of violent abuse. That surely would be a dangerous situation and in that sense, someone who expresses a widely held view, is performing a function in public debates.

GEORGE FFITCH: Does that depend upon how much he exaggerates the facts, though? I mean let's take the Kenya Asians – you have had dire warnings of this flood of Asians from Kenya that were going to come here and the Government took – was probably panicked by you and Mr Sandys into taking action. Yet since that Immigration Bill, Commonwealth Immigration Bill came into law nobody, almost nobody in Kenya has applied for vouchers to come to this country. And the vouchers are not being taken out to such an extent that they are now going to unwind the appeals machinery they had in Kenya.

POWELL: But you're not seriously saying, are you, that without that legislation there would have been no influx from Kenya –?

FFITCH: I'm only saying as a result of your speeches you panicked these people into coming here in very greater numbers when they might have spread it over a number of years.

POWELL: I don't think there's the slightest ground for believing that, and let me give you a fact, and that is that before I spoke on that subject at Walsall the weekly inflow of children into Wolverhampton from overseas had gone up from twenty to thirty a week to eighty a week, large numbers were already arriving direct in the Midlands, and this was a flow which was being stimulated by the Kenyatta Government. This was being organised. Of course it was being organised.

TO THE ANNUAL CONFERENCE OF THE ROTARY CLUB OF LONDON

Eastbourne, 16 November 1968

Seven months ago I made a speech in Birmingham which attracted some considerable attention. I discussed in it the present and prospective consequences of the immigration of Commonwealth citizens into this country during the last fifteen years which took place because, until 1962, this country, alone of all the nations in the world, had no definition of its own people, so that for all purposes an Englishman born in Birmingham and a tribesman from the North-West Frontier were indistinguishable in the law of the United Kingdom. It was a subject on which I had spoken and written on a number of occasions over the preceding months and years. The immediate occasion was the imminent Second Reading of the Government's Race Relations Bill, which the Conservative Shadow Cabinet, then including myself, had decided, and publicly announced its decision, to oppose, on the ground that the Bill would do more harm than good. My speech was made in support and in defence of that decision from the point of view of a Member representing a constituency in one of the areas most affected; and it was so understood both by those to whom it was delivered and by the party officials who, in the normal course, were aware of its contents in advance.

In the seven months which have elapsed since I spoke I have been the target of endless abuse and vilification. No imputation or innuendo has been too vile or scurrilous for supposedly reputable journals to invent or repeat. On the other hand, I have been borne up by an astonishing manifestation, from among all classes of people and from all areas of the community, expressing relief and gratitude that the speech was made. Through all this I have kept silence. With the exception of a five-minute intervention at the Conservative Party Conference last month, and the unavoidable necessity of answering questions put to me at public meetings, I have not once returned to the subject until now.

Sooner or later, however, I was in duty bound to take up the theme again and since beyond dispute the question – whatever view be taken of it – is of deep national concern and since divisions of opinion upon it do not follow normal party lines, it seemed to me a subject appropriate to the platform of an organisation which is both non-party and devoted to whatever concerns the public interest.

I am concerned with the future. I will waste little time upon the past. Only one domestic thing I ask your indulgence to say briefly in my own defence. It has been freely alleged that I was somehow guilty of a breach of discipline or of disloyalty, either to my colleagues generally or to the party's spokesman on home affairs in particular, in speaking as I did. There is no substance in this charge. No rule or convention forbids front-benchers to advocate or defend, even before parliamentary debate, the line which the leadership of the party has publicly decided to take. There is none which requires them before doing so to consult or even inform their colleagues. Such speeches are continually made and indeed expected. It is, of course, different if they intend to recommend a divergent policy; but this it was not suggested I had done. It was to the 'tone' of my speech that objection was taken, so strongly indeed that I was excluded from the Shadow Cabinet. Now, 'tone' is a matter of personal taste, *de gustibus non est disputandum*, and a leader is entitled to be guided by his own taste in the choice of his colleagues. What is matter of fact and not of opinion, is that neither in making the speech, nor in any of the circumstances attendant upon it, did I neglect or break any of the rules or conventions which govern honourable behaviour between colleagues.

The reaction to that speech revealed a deep and dangerous gulf in the nation, a gulf which is I fear no narrower today than it was then. I do not mean between the indigenous population and the immigrants. On the contrary, over the months and years the pressure upon me to oppose the growth in the number of immigrants has come as much from my immigrant constituents as from the rest, if not more so: in this matter I was convinced of speaking for and in the interest of all my constituents. Nor do I mean the gulf between those who do, and those who do not, know from personal experience the impact and reality of immigration. Knowledge of the facts and concern about them has been spreading rapidly in parts of the kingdom where a Commonwealth immigrant is never seen. I mean the gulf between the overwhelming majority of people throughout the country on the one side, and on the other side a tiny minority, with almost a monopoly hold upon the channels of communication, who seem determined not to know the facts and not to face the realities and who will resort to any device or extremity to blind both themselves and others.

In an earlier speech in February I had mentioned a class in a school in my constituency where there was only one white child. I mentioned it as a fact calculated to bring home to people the size and concentration of the immigrant population. Immediately, I was denounced as lying or retailing hearsay; and though the truth of what I said was confirmed in open council a few days later by the Chairman of the Education Committee, the national press refrained from reporting it and Roy Jenkins, the Chancellor of the Exchequer, in a speech at Swansea three months later, who had only to lift the telephone on his desk to ascertain the truth, preferred to brand me as a liar by stating that no such school had ever been discovered. However, Nemesis had not long to wait; and in September the very newspapers which had attacked me had the ignominy of having to report the existence not only in Wolverhampton but in Birmingham of such classes, as well as the 90 per cent immigrant school in my own constituency. So quickly does the incredible turn into what everybody knew all the time.

In the context of a Bill which the native inhabitants of this country were bound to see as directed against themselves, an important part of my argument at Birmingham was the fact of reverse discrimination – that it is not the true immigrant but the Briton who feels himself the 'toad beneath the harrow' in the areas where the immigrant population is spreading and taking root. This indeed was the background against which the opposition were justifiably claiming that the Race Relations Bill would do more harm than good. To illustrate it I described the typical situation of the last and usually elderly white inhabitants of a street or area otherwise wholly occupied by immigrants, and I did so by citing an individual case from Wolverhampton in a correspondent's own words.

The outcry which followed illuminated like a lightning flash the gulf between those who do not know or want to know and the rest of the nation. Here were circumstances which those who know the facts know are being repeated over and over again, at this very moment, in the towns and the cities affected by immigration – often with aggravations more distressing than in the case I cited. It was ordinary, not extraordinary. Yet all at once the air was filled with denunciation: I was romancing; I had picked up a hoary, unverified legend; I had no evidence; nobody could find the old lady – no more than the class with the one white child! Where do these people live, who imagine that what I related was so remarkable and incredible that they had to conclude it was apocryphal? What do they suppose happens, or has been happening, or will be happening, as the growing immigrant numbers extend their areas of occupation? They must live either a long way off, or they must live with their eyes tight shut.

I will not betray those who write to me in confidence or expose to publicity those who understandably fear it; but as I have been traduced and defamed, I will select one out of the numerous witnesses who wrote and offered me their own evidence for the truth and typicality of what I described. It is, I repeat, not something rare, not something abnormal, but something which is part of the daily life and experience of fellow countrymen of ours who happen to be less fortunately situated than Mr Rees-Mogg or Mr Bernard Levin.

Dr W. E. Bamford on 17 August writes to me from 408, Garratt Lane, SW18. After describing his experiences in attending a patient aged eighty-four on the second floor of a house owned by an immigrant landlord, as a result of which 'the police have since provided me with a police escort each time I visited the patient', he continues:

I saw her with the consultant geriatrician from St Johns Hospital on Tuesday, 13 August. His advice was that it was best to 'cut one's losses' as she would eventually be intimidated out of her home. He arranged to admit her to St Johns with a view to rehabilitation and finding another home for her. It is very tragic that this poor old lady should now have to leave her home and possessions where she has spent most of her life, but there seems no other solution.

I am most reluctant to cause any racial disharmony. I have many coloured patients on my list and I believe my relations with persons of all colours have always been harmonious.

I would like to draw your attention to a few other incidents which involved my patients:
1. An elderly widow of eighty-plus had the house in which she was living bought by a West Indian lady.
   The old lady was intimidated by having:
   (a) Her bell disconnected.
   (b) Her letters not received.
   (c) When she went out, she would come back to find water had been poured on her bed.
   (d) Her possessions were broken.
   (e) In the darkness when going upstairs she would receive a thump on the back.
   (f) She was accused of behaving immorally when she had a young technician in to do repairs to her broken possessions.
In spite of informing the police – she had no witnesses! – and the fact that I informed the MOH Dr Garland and the Health Visitor, she was intimidated out of her home eventually.
2. A widow with two young children was similarly intimidated by the knocking on the wall and the disturbance of her sleeping children at all hours of the night by West Indian neighbours. Actual damage was caused to her ceilings and walls. She had to leave in spite of appeals to the police.
3. A young English couple were intimidated out of their flat by their West

Indian landlord by verbal abuse and filth smeared on and around their toilet.

There is just one witness, just a few examples; but let no one object that they are 'just a few'. Ask those who know and they will tell you whether all that is exceptional.

Let no one object, either, that there are bad British landlords too, that British people bully and maltreat British people, and so on. I know. I have never said or implied that immigrants are more predisposed to vicious or spiteful behaviour than the indigenous population. Though their customs and their social habits and expectations may be widely different, there is no reason to suppose they are more malevolent or more prone to wrongdoing. That is, however, not the point. With the malefactors among our own people we have got to cope; they are our own responsibility and part of our own society. It is something totally different when the same or similar activities are perpetrated by strangers, and above all when they occur in the course of an increase in the numbers of those strangers and an extension of the areas which they occupy – an increase and an extension to which the victims perceive no end in sight. Surely only very clever people could fail to understand so simple a point.

The issue is not, as some people appear to imagine, one of being nice to the immigrants or strangers in our midst, however diverse their race or culture. The issue is an issue of numbers, now and especially in the future. And so I come to the question of numbers, and of the increase in numbers; for it is the very heart of the matter. As Lord Elton once put it: 'If it were known in my home village that the Archbishop of Canterbury were coming to live there, we should undoubtedly ring a peal on the church bells. If it were known that five archbishops were coming, I could still expect to see my neighbours exchanging excited congratulations at the street corners. But if it were known that fifty archbishops were coming, there would be a riot.'

First, let us get our sense of perspective. Let us look at present numbers. There are today in this country about 1¼ million Commonwealth immigrants, though the basis of the statistics is far from perfect and the number is likely to be more rather than less. Suppose that any Government fifteen years ago had declared: it is our intention that by 1968 1¼ million Afro-Asians shall have entered this country and settled in it. People would not have believed their ears. Of course, no government, no party would have dared to put forward such a proposal; if they had, they would have been hissed out of office. Yet the thing is no less absurd or monstrous now that it has become a reality than it would have seemed to everybody beforehand.

It never was proposed or argued on grounds of supplying labour or skill. Indeed, it could not be; for that has nothing to do with immigration. The doctors, aliens as well as Commonwealth citizens, who have made it possible, by getting a few years of post-graduate experience in Britain, to expand the hospital service faster than would otherwise have been possible, have no more to do with immigration than have the *au pair* girls admitted for a year or two to give domestic help or the workers moving temporarily from one Common Market country to another. Those who still talk about needing immigrant doctors, dentists and teachers, are not really talking about immigration at all. As for unskilled labour, the mere attempt to justify mass importation of it would have been exploded by economists and trade unions alike: the remedy for shortage of labour in a developed economy is more capital and better organisation. In short, it is only now that this has happened and the people of Britain are faced with a *fait accompli*, that all sorts of excuses are invented and we are told in terms of arrogant moral superiority that we have got a 'multi-racial society' and had better like it.

Yet if that were all, it could be endured. With their almost incredible tolerance the English – it is virtually only England which is affected – would settle down to live with what they neither asked for nor wanted nor were warned of nor understood. But the present, this 1¼ million reality – however inconceivable it would have been in prospect – this is not all. People look to the future, and, as they do so, they remember that they have been betrayed and misled in the past. It is our duty not to betray or mislead them again.

It is easy to understand how enormously strong is the temptation for all politicians to baulk at this vision of the future, and not least for my own party, the Conservative Party, which formed the Government of the country during the crucial years and would fain close its eyes and ears to the wholly unnecessary and avoidable havoc its own inaction wrought – a tragedy which need never have been enacted. If Britain had provided herself in 1956 instead of 1962 with what every other nation under the sun possesses – a law defining its own people – what a world of anguish past and future would never have been! Even those of us who inveighed against the British Nationality Act 1948 from the outset and who from inside and from outside Government urged legislation over the years, feel an oppressive sense of guilt and humiliation. The temptation to close our eyes to the future is correspondingly strong. But it is a temptation that has to be conquered.

Even more dangerous is the too common taunt: 'You did the wrong; you have no right to talk about it now.' Woe betide the nation that will not let its rulers admit their errors and try to remedy the consequences: there is no surer way to persist on a disastrous course until it is too late than to attach the penalty of mockery to those who say: 'We have done wrong.'

Let us take as our starting-point the calculation of the General Register Office that by 1985 there would be in this country 3½ million coloured immigrants and their offspring – in other words that the present number would have increased between two- and threefold in the next seventeen years – on two assumptions, current rate of intake and current birthrate. I have been endlessly accused of using this figure without regard to those assumptions. I did not. In my previous speech I expressly qualified it as being 'on present trends', and to the consideration of those two assumptions I now address myself.

The first assumption is that the rate of net inflow continues as at present. It has not, indeed, diminished since the estimate was made, but I am willing to suppose that, especially with the substantially greater limitations which a Conservative Government has undertaken to apply, the rate would be markedly reduced during the period in question. For the purposes of argument I will suppose that it falls at a steady rate from 60,000 in 1968 to nil by 1985. In that case the total in the latter year would be reduced by about ½ million, that is to 3 million.

I now turn to the second and more crucial assumption, the birthrate. There are those who argue that the longer the immigrant population is resident in this country, the more closely their birthrate will approximate to that of the indigenous population, and thus, of course, to a rate of increase at which their proportion to the total would remain static. Now, I have no doubt that an immigrant element thoroughly absorbed into a host population does tend to have the same birthrate, and I have no doubt that among our Commonwealth immigrants the small minority to whom that description can be applied, may soon show evidence of this. But to suppose that the habits of the great mass of immigrants, living in their own communities, speaking their own languages and maintaining their native customs, will change appreciably in the next two or three decades is a supposition so grotesque that only those could make it who are determined not to admit what they know to be true or not to see what they fear. On the contrary, there are grounds for arguing that the immigrant birthrate is more likely to rise during the next two or three decades; for instance, the proportion of females must increase as dependants join male workers, so that a given total of immigrant population will yield more family units.

Let me take you and show you the process actually happening. In the county borough of Wolverhampton, as recently enlarged to a total population of 267,000 in 1967, the proportion of immigrants and their offspring was 5.13 per cent on the basis of the 1966 sample census, though of course, as the borough now includes large suburbs which are wholly white, this percentage gives no idea of the proportions or concentration in the inner zones of the borough. Now, that immigrant population, which forms 5.13 per cent of the whole, produces no less than 23 per cent of the births; that is, while one in twenty of the population is an immigrant, one in four of the births is an immigrant birth. I am not referring to births in maternity beds – there, the immigrant is higher still, one in three – but to total births; and before anyone calls me a liar, I might mention that the figures are those of the borough Medical Officer of Health and may be found reprinted, amongst other places, in *The Lancet* for 26 October.

The procession, and the rate at which it gathers numbers year by year, can be traced as it moves upwards through the schools. Here are the percentages of immigrant children in the Wolverhampton schools last April, reading upwards: infant schools 17.1 per cent, junior and infant schools 12.7 per cent, junior schools 10.9 per cent, secondary schools 9.7 per cent. However, even those figures do not fully reflect the rate at which births have been rising hitherto, because they include not only children born to immigrants in this country but children who have immigrated when of, or under, school age – and Asian and West Indian children of school age are still arriving in Wolverhampton at the rate of eight or nine hundred a year. The idea that the size of the immigrant population – even without any net intake at all – is destined from now onwards to increase little more rapidly than that of the indigenous population cannot seriously be sustained in the face of the sort of reality I have described. The only prudent assumption is that the present trend will continue for at least a decade or two. This is the assumption which underlies the Registrar General's projection, and gives the figure of 3 million for 1985, after allowing, as I have done, for reduction of intake. I am reassured that I am not far from the mark when I notice that a year ago the Home Office spokesman, who can hardly be accused of wanting to play the numbers up, arrived at 2½ million in 1985 as the lowest figure he could foresee after making the utmost allowances both on intake and on birthrate.

After 1985, we may perhaps allow ourselves to hope for a decline in the rate of reproduction; but if the following seventeen years, instead of multiplication by the factor of two, as between 1967 and 1985, resulted only in multiplication by a factor of 1½, the total immigrant and immigrant-descended population at the end of the century – to be precise, in 2002 – would be 4½ million, or three and a half times the present number; and that is assuming no further net immigration at all after 1985. Bearing in mind that the assumptions which produce this figure are deliberately pitched low, it will be seen that my reference at Birmingham to something 'in the region of 5–7 million' for the year 2000 'on present trends' was neither random nor ill-considered.

Now, if that minimum figure of 4½ million is expressed as a percentage of the projected population of the United Kingdom for the year 2000, it works out at a little over 6 per cent. But of course it is monstrously fallacious thus to divide the immigrant population into that of the UK as a whole. I do not know what would be the aspect of a United Kingdom where uniformly one in eighteen of the population – in Easington and Exeter, and in Aberystwyth and Aberdeen, in Antrim and Eastbourne – was an Afro-Asian. But that is not how it would be. The very growth in numbers would increase the already striking fact of dense geographical concentration, so that the urban part of whole towns and cities in Yorkshire, the Midlands and the Home Counties would be preponderantly or exclusively Afro-Asian in population. There would be several Washingtons in England. From these whole areas the indigenous population, the people of England, who fondly imagine that this is their country and these are their home-towns, would have been dislodged – I have deliberately chosen the most neutral word I could find. And here for the first time this morning I offer a subjective judgement, because in the nature of the case there can be no other and because on such a matter it is the duty of a politician to make and to declare his judgement. I do so, I hope, not unduly moved – though why should I not be moved? – by the hundreds – no, thousands – of my countrymen who speak to me or write to me of their fear and foreboding: the old who rejoice that they will not live to see what is to come; the young who are determined that their children shall not grow up under the shadow of it. My judgement then is this: the people of England will not endure it. If so, it is idle to argue whether they ought to or ought not to. I do not believe it is in human nature that a country, and a country such as ours, should passively watch the transformation of whole areas which lie at the heart of it into alien territory.

On these two grounds then – the prospective growth of numbers with its physical consequences, and the unacceptability of those consequences – rests the urgency of action. We can perhaps not reduce the eventual total of the immigrant and immigrant-descended population much, if at all, below its present size: with that, and with all that implies, we and our children and our children's children will have to cope until the slow mercy of the years absorbs even that unparalleled invasion of our body politic. What I believe we can do, and therefore must do, is to avert the impending disaster of its increase.

There are two, and, so far as I can see, only two measures available to this end. Both are obvious; one is far more important, and far more difficult, than the other. If further net immigration were virtually to cease at once, that would reduce the prospective total for 1985 by a further half million, and would have a somewhat more than proportionate effect on whatever is to be the rate of increase after 1985; for, as I have pointed out, the inflow, consisting as it does mostly of dependants, forms the basis for new family units in the future. I say 'virtually cease', because of course no one would wish an absolute veto on the settlement of individual Afro-Asians in this country in future, any more than of other aliens. But let there be no prevarication about what is meant. What is meant is that we would cease to admit not only new settlers and their dependants, but the dependants or remaining dependants of immigrants already here. The first half of this presents no human difficulty: if we admit no new settlers, there is no problem about their dependants. The problem attaches to the reservoir of dependants who have not yet joined immigrants already here. In this case we have to decide between two evils, the denial of entry to an immigrant's dependants and the consequences of the prospective growth in numbers. But here the minor issue merges into the major one, that of repatriation.

I have argued that on any prudent view, quite apart from any subsequent immigration, the future prospect is unacceptable. Hence the key significance of repatriation or at any rate re-emigration. A policy of assisting repatriation by payment of fares and grants is part of the official policy of the Conservative Party. It is a just, rational and humane policy; it accepts that a wrong has unintentionally been done to the immigrant by placing him in a position where the future is as pregnant with trouble for him as for the rest of the population, and it accepts the duty of reinstating him as far as possible. As my colleague, Mr Boyd-Carpenter pointed out in a speech at Blackpool recently which has received too little attention, it would provide the fair answer for the immigrant here whose dependants were not permitted to join him. The question is what would be the practical scope and application of such a policy.

I believe that ignorance of the realities of Commonwealth immigration leads people seriously to underestimate the scope of the policy and thus to neglect and despise the chief key to the situation. Perhaps it is the historical associations of the word 'immigrant' which create in those remote from the facts the picture of individuals who have left their homes behind for ever to seek a new future in a far-off land, rather in the mood of those Victorian pictures of the immigrants' farewell.

Of course, there are many cases where individuals have uprooted themselves to come here; but in the mass it is much nearer the truth to think in terms of detachments from communities in the West Indies or India or Pakistan encamped in certain areas of England. They are still to a large extent a part, economically and socially, of the communities from which they have been detached and to which they regard themselves as belonging. As a recently published study of one of the West Indian islands put it thus:

> Migrant communities in Britain are linked to their home societies by an intricate network of ties and obligations. There are strong social pressures for members of a community to send back money to their families in the island, where most of them expect to return eventually . . . the ideology of migration and the social networks formed around it are so closely connected that it is rare for migrants to abandon one without leaving the other. Thus migrants who decide to stay permanently in Britain often cut themselves off from the others.

This description could apply, even more strongly, to the communities from India and Pakistan, whose total numbers now exceed the West Indian, and whose links with their homes are kept in being by a constant flow not only of remittances, amounting to many millions of pounds a year, but of personal visits and exchanges, the scale of which would astonish anyone not closely acquainted with the actual phenomenon of Commonwealth immigration in this country. The annual holiday 'back home' in the West Indies or in India or Pakistan is no rare feature of life in the immigrant communities.

Against this background a programme of large-scale voluntary but organised, financed and subsidised repatriation and re-emigration becomes indeed an administrative and political task of great magnitude, but something neither absurdly impracticable nor, still less, inhuman, but on the contrary as profoundly humane as it is far-sighted. Under a agreement between Ceylon and India for the repatriation of more than half a million Indians over fifteen years, 35,000 return to India each year with their assets. The Government of Guyana is anxious to promote the re-emigration to that country of West Indians and others who can help to build up its economy and develop its resources. A cursory survey carried out by a national newspaper six months ago indicated that over 20 per cent of immigrants interviewed would contemplate availing themselves of an opportunity to go home. It need not even follow that the income from work done here in Britain would be suddenly lost to the home communities if permanent settlement of population were replaced by what many countries in Europe and elsewhere are familiar with – the temporary, albeit often long-term, intake of labour.

The resettlement of a substantial proportion of the Commonwealth immigrants in Britain is not beyond the resources and abilities of this country, if it is undertaken as a national duty, in the successful discharge of which the interests both of the immigrants themselves and of the countries from which they came are engaged. It ought to be, and it could be, organised now on the scale which the urgency of the situation demands, preferably under a special Ministry of Repatriation or other authority charged with concentrating on this task.

At present large numbers of the offspring of immigrants, even those born here in Britain, remain integrated in the immigrant community which links them with their homeland overseas. With every passing year this will diminish. Sometimes people point to the increasing proportion of immigrant offspring born in this country as if the fact contained within itself the ultimate solution. The truth is the opposite. The West Indian or Asian does not, by being born in England, become an Englishman. In law he becomes a United Kingdom citizen by birth; in fact he is a West Indian or an Asian still. Unless he be one of a small minority – for number, I repeat again and again, is of the essence – he will by the very nature of things have lost one country without gaining another, lost one nationality without acquiring a new one. Time is running against us and them. With the lapse of a generation or so we shall at last have succeeded – to the benefit of nobody – in reproducing 'in England's green and pleasant land' the haunting tragedy of the United States.

The English as a nation have their own peculiar faults. One of them is that strange passivity in the face of danger or absurdity or provocation, which has more than once in our history lured observers into false conclusions – conclusions sometimes fatal to the observers themselves – about the underlying intentions and the true determination of our people. What so far no one could accuse us of is a propensity to abandon hope in the face of severe and even seemingly insurmountable obstacles. Dejection is not one of our national traits; but we must be told the truth and shown the danger, if we are to meet it. Rightly or wrongly, I for my part believe that the time for that has come.

'ANY QUESTIONS?'

BBC Radio, 29 November 1968

ELIZABETH ECCLESHERE: Elizabeth Eccleshere. Does the team think that immigrants damage our national and traditional way of life?

DAVID JACOBS: Elizabeth Eccleshere wants to know whether we think, or the team thinks, that immigrants damage our traditional way of life. Lord Wigg.

LORD WIGG: No, I don't. (*applause*)

JACOBS: Auberon Waugh?

AUBERON WAUGH: I think it's certainly bringing about a certain amount of change in our traditional way of life. I wouldn't have said necessarily this was for the worse. I think that the presence of a large immigrant population will help eventually to create a more diverse, less egalitarian society, and that is one which I personally will welcome. There may be tensions inside that society; I personally won't even mind them much. But then, I am not a democratic politician, and I don't have to survive on the approval of the populace. I am a middle-class person, living delicately by myself, and I don't suppose that there's an immigrant living within ten miles of me. The ones I see I quite like, and I welcome their presence.

JACOBS: Enoch Powell. (*applause*)

ENOCH POWELL: Surely, it must depend how many. Clearly, if the number is relatively small – especially if they are relatively dispersed – then they can probably contribute a new benefit to the community. If their numbers are large, and particularly if they are concentrated, then they may place strains upon the community and may alter its character, in a way which the community itself feels – whether it ought to or not – is intolerable. So I say this is a question of numbers. (*applause*)

JACOBS: Marghanita Laski.

MARGHANITA LASKI: I hope this extraordinarily useful and well-phrased question is going to give us a chance to discuss what we consider to be our traditional way of life. This, it seems to me, is something that's been very much left out of discussion so far. Mr Powell has often spoken about 'culture'–

POWELL: Have I?

LASKI: Yes, you have, Mr Powell.

POWELL: Have I ever used the word 'culture' in this context?

LASKI: I believe you have used the word 'culture' in this context. I hope –

POWELL: I think not. Well, you hope I have?

LASKI: No –

POWELL: Well, I will oblige you by agreeing that I have, even if I haven't.

LASKI: All right. If you'll accept the word. I hope, Mr Chairman, we'll discuss that.

JACOBS: Then you begin the discussion, Marghanita.

LASKI: Right. May I?

WIGG: Just a moment – one second. We mustn't let Mr Powell get away with this. You see, he said – 'Immigrants: it all depends upon numbers.' But it also depends on what kind of immigrants. You see, I have a suspicion about Mr Powell, which may be elaborated as we go along. But, you see, I don't think he would have said anything about immigrants if they had come from the white Commonwealth, or if they'd been Irish. He's only raised the question because he has discovered that talking about immigrants in relation to colour is a popular thing to do, from a political point of view. (*applause*)

JACOBS: Now, Mr Powell didn't actually raise this question. Lord Wigg, Mr Powell didn't in fact raise this particular question – it was raised by Elizabeth Eccleshere. But perhaps Enoch Powell would like to carry on what Lord Wigg has said.

POWELL: Oh, yes, because if – it depends indeed on whether the immigrants are different, and different in important respects from the existing population. Clearly, if they are identical, then no change for the good or the bad can be brought about by the immigration. But if they are different, and to the extent that they are different, then numbers clearly are of the essence and this is not wholly – or mainly, necessarily – a matter of colour. For example, if the immigrants were Germans or Russians, their colour would be approximately the same as ours, but the problems which would be created and the change which could be brought about by a large introduction of a bloc of Germans or Russians into five areas in this country would be as serious – and in some respects more serious – than could follow from an introduction of a similar number of West Indians or Pakistanis. [. . .]

LASKI: Now, it seems to me that people of the working classes of this country, with a long tradition of slums, of under-feeding, of lack of education are in this respect the young, to those of us who are more fortunate, and it is our duty, as the Victorians said, to educate our masters not by making them angry, not by playing on their worst emotions but by – and if this sounds arrogant, I don't mind – by training them in those virtues of liberal tolerance that alone makes a community a decent place to live in. (*applause*)

WAUGH: Yes, that's entirely –

JACOBS: Auberon Waugh, let Enoch Powell –

WAUGH: But that's an entirely different proposition from the original one.

JACOBS: It may be, but let Enoch Powell come in.

POWELL: We've been going round liberal tolerance and tolerant liberalism, and it seems to have centred on that. I'm prepared to say that the tolerance which has been shown by the British people – and, as someone said, it is mainly a working-class people – towards this enormous influx over the last ten years in certain specific areas, has been beyond all praise. The people of those areas have seen the towns which they knew utterly altered, they have seen themselves more or less literally driven from one area after another, and the way in which they have tolerated this thing is incredible and, as I say, it does them immense credit. But this again turns on a matter of numbers. There is always a limit to toleration of any – you used the word 'invasion', Auberon, you used the word 'coloured invasion', and I was reminded of Marghanita Laski's reference in her list to the Danes. Now, we were invaded by the Danes, they did alter the country and we fought them for two hundred years. If that's what is meant – to be allowed to happen?

LASKI: Were we wise to do so? Didn't they add to us in the end? Wasn't there much more suffering and misery because we fought them?

POWELL: Only because we fought them, and eventually subjugated them and Christianised them. (*applause*)

WIGG: . . . not to wander too far from toleration, because of course one of the most tolerant persons in this audience, holding the views he does, is Mr Powell. I sit for a working-class – or, I sat for a working-class constituency. I was in the House of Commons longer than Mr Powell. I well remember his maiden-speech, and you know, in that maiden-speech he pleaded for larger colonial forces, and he used some very striking phrases. I've never forgotten them. He said: 'Let's always remember that the subjects of His Majesty, wherever they happen to be – anywhere in the continent, anywhere in the Commonwealth – owe a duty to their Sovereign, and let us be partners in this question of raising our defences.' And he wanted them irrespective of colour, irrespective of their background. And now, the other extraordinary thing about this is that Mr Powell never talked, as I can discover and well remember, in any disagreeable terms about race until 1964, although a year ago he wrote an article and said this was the most pressing problem in his constituency from 1957 onwards. And he only began to talk about this in the terms which has become a matter of controversy in his Walsall speech.

POWELL: It simply isn't true. I (*talking together*) on the subject – but you can't prove a negative.

WIGG: I don't – oh yes I can. Oh yes I can. (*laughter*) I can prove a negative quite easily because I can look up the press cuttings just as easily as Mr Powell. The only thing, Mr Powell, I get my stories right, but I don't allow second-hand ones when you're proved to be wrong, as you consistently do. But the point is this: Mr Powell in his Walsall speech found he was on a winner. He says – he's told us how many letters he got, 798, the high proportion . . .

POWELL: What do you mean by 798?

WIGG: You said – you are on record, Mr Powell, as saying you had eight hundred letters following your Walsall speech, and only two were in favour, and a high proportion were anonymous. So Mr Powell had his mind made up from him by anonymous letters because . . .

POWELL: What a lot of nonsense you're talking. You talk just as much nonsense now as you used to in the House of Commons. (*laughter, applause*)

WIGG: Mr Powell – Mr Powell, abuse is no use – no substitute for argument. The fact is you were engaged in a competition with Mr Sandys, you found he was winning, and then you brought into your Birmingham speech, the identical speech you made at Walsall, but you introduced a Tiber flowing with blood because you thought you were on a political winner. And the more you talk the better I'm pleased, because you will eventually be exposed, for you are talking nonsense and not me. (*applause*)

LASKI: I came here wanting to ask Mr Powell a question that I gather he's going to answer on Sunday night, so I won't – which is how he can reconcile his Christianity, the Christianity of Paul, presumably, who said there should be neither Greek nor Jew, circumcised nor uncircumcised, barbarian and civilised. But this, I think, he's going to answer on Sunday. So I'd like to ask . . .

POWELL: In that case it's unfair to raise it on an occasion when you know it can't be answered then.

LASKI: Yes, I think it is, I was . . . (*applause*) But I would like to ask you another question, Mr Powell. You've often spoken, I think you'll accept this word, of the danger that this coloured immigration can bring.

POWELL: Yes I have.

LASKI: What specifically is this danger?

POWELL: The danger that if there is a large and increasing concentration of unassimilated immigrants in certain areas in the country, tolerance will break down and there will be violence, that is the danger which I foresee, unless we take steps to ensure that the numbers do not increase, as is foreseeable, and that the concentration does not continue. (*applause*)

LASKI: Would you call Orthodox Jews, who stay in their own communities and practise their own ways of life – unassimilated immigrants?

POWELL: The numbers are relatively small compared with those of the Commonwealth immigrants already – again and again and again I come back to the fact that this is a matter of numbers. Almost any unassimilated element can be tolerated and can live in the community if it is sufficiently small in proportion, either generally – both generally, and in a particular area.

'THE GREAT DEBATE'
BBC TV, 9 September 1969

TREVOR HUDDLESTON: . . . We deliberately recruited West Indies labour, at a time we needed them to do the dirty work.

ENOCH POWELL: Well yes, but, Bishop, who is the 'we'?

HUDDLESTON: The British Government.

POWELL: Oh no! This, as a matter of fact, is not the case.

HUDDLESTON: The Transport Services of this country are nationalised services, and we recruited West Indians to run the Transport Services of this country quite deliberately, and the hospital services.

POWELL: The Government could not have prevented this recruitment, had it so wished, without the fundamental change in our citizenship law first taking place, and it does seem to me very misleading to say that because there is no distinction in the then state of our law between the inhabitants of the four continents which were formerly part of the British Empire and the people who belonged to the United Kingdom, therefore the inevitable recruitment which followed by private and by publicly owned industry was a deliberate act of the state.

HUDDLESTON: Well I would agree that we need a new definition of citizenship but I don't suppose the definition that I want is the same as yours, but I agree with this wholeheartedly, we certainly do, we need a new definition of citizenship in this country badly. But we need a definition of citizenship which carries with it inescapedly the full rights of citizenship, and what I still want to know from you, really, is why the presence of a coloured immigrant group is objectionable, when the presence of a non-coloured immigrant is not objectionable.

POWELL: Oh no, oh no! On the contrary, I have often said that if we saw the prospect of five million Germans in this country at the end of the century, the risks of disruption and violence would probably be greater, and the antagonism which would be aroused would be more severe. The reason why the whole debate in this country on immigration is related to coloured immigration, is because there has been no net immigration of white Commonwealth citizens, and there could be no migration of aliens. This is merely an automatic consequence of the facts of the case; it is not because there is anything different, because there is anything necessarily more dangerous, about the alienness of a community from Asia, than about the alienness of a community from Turkey or from Germany, that we discuss this inevitably in terms of colour. It is because it is that problem.

ELECTION SPEECH

Wolverhampton, 11 June 1970

I have not so far in any speech in this election campaign referred to Commonwealth immigration into the United Kingdom and its consequences, present or prospective. It is in fact a subject on which I speak rarely – three or four times a year at most – and with greater deliberation and care than upon any other. Nevertheless, I have not concealed my belief that this subject exceeds all others in its importance for the future not only of this town and other areas already directly affected, but of the entire nation. I thought it right to say so plainly in my election address, especially as the policies of the opposing parties in regard to it differ sufficiently to offer the electorate a real and substantial choice. It would be absurd therefore if I were to refrain from speaking about this subject here, to my own electorate, before the election comes to an end.

I do not intend tonight to attempt a general survey of the problem. My object is to concentrate upon a few major points which are in danger of being ignored or suppressed.

The first, which cannot be emphasised too often, is that of number. The scale of Commonwealth immigration into this country in the last twenty years – apart altogether from the nature of that immigration – is already in point of numbers out of all comparison greater than anything these islands have ever experienced before in a thousand years of their history. People who talk in this context about the immigration of one or two hundred thousand Jews from Europe before World War I or of the Huguenots from France only reveal that they have no conception of the facts.

What I have said in the last two or three years about the numbers of Commonwealth immigrants and their increase has been treated over and over again with derision and with that abusive obloquy which is intended to obviate the need for rational discussion. But as the facts have at last, grudgingly and partially, been revealed, it has turned out that I was right and my traducers were wrong. Indeed, the figures which have become known in the last year, or year and a half, have in every case proved to be higher than I myself would have guessed. If I have been guilty on this score, it is *under*statement that has been my offence. On this subject, so vital to their future, the people of this country have been misled, cruelly and persistently, till one begins to wonder if the Foreign Office was the only department of state into which enemies of this country were infiltrated.

Earlier this year we learnt that the Government had been grossly underestimating the size of the annual addition to the Commonwealth immigrant population by natural increase. After making all conceivable allowances – some of them quite ludicrous – I showed that the true increase would still be almost 60 per cent greater than the Government had estimated. On the basis of any reasonable assumptions (instead of extravagantly low ones) the true excess is about 100 per cent. This can only mean that the size of the present immigrant population, or its birthrate, or the two combined, are twice what the Government had assured us.

The immigrant population is now certainly nearer 2 million than the 1¼ million which the Government allege. Those who talk about 'only 2 per cent' of the population of England and Wales are misled, however innocently; 4 per cent is already nearer the mark.

Most people have no conception how fast that percentage is growing. Last year there was almost the same increase in the white and in the coloured population of this country. It is not enough to look at the proportion of coloured births to total births. You have also to look at the large net *em*igration of white residents and the large net *imm*igration of coloured residents. When these are taken into account, we find that between 90,000 and 100,000 a year net is being added *on each side*. At that rate the proportion between the two is altering very rapidly.

I know it is dinned into us that net Commonwealth immigration is rapidly falling; but this, like so much else that is fed to the British people by this Government, is misleading. The fact is that net immigration in 1969 was back again to practically the same figure as in 1966, after having been higher – much higher – in the two intervening years, 1967 and 1968. When we are told that the first quarter of 1970 was lower again, that too is misleading. The fall in 1969 only took place in the second half of the year, when the delay took effect which was imposed by the new requirement of entry certificates. In fact, the first quarter of 1969 was actually running above previous levels. No doubt, net Commonwealth immigration will gradually fall. On the other hand, it is not denied that for a time the births will go on rising; and if this Government were to remain in office after the election, I would not care to answer for the effect on the numbers of our own people emigrating.

However, as we in Wolverhampton well know, the total figures, though much larger and growing much faster than people had been led to believe, convey no impression of the reality, when divided into the entire population of England and Wales so as to yield an overall percentage. The reality is what we see emerging before our eyes in the transformation of this and other towns and cities, including the inner part of the Metropolis itself. When I referred, two years and more ago, to 'whole areas, towns and parts of towns across England being occupied by different sections of the immigrant and immigrant-descended population', the prediction was derided and denounced. The facts which have become known since then have proved it true. I have demonstrated that, even after making every concession, however improbable, however unreal, a fifth or a quarter of such towns and cities as Wolverhampton, Birmingham and Inner London will in course of time consist of the Commonwealth immigrants and their descendants. There has been no attempt at refutation. No refutation is possible. Those who mocked two years ago have taken refuge either in silence or in abuse. Once again, I have erred – perhaps all too much – on the side of understatement: the rational probability is much larger. Indeed, what I said is already ceasing to be prediction and becoming current fact. There are at this moment parts of this town which have ceased to be part of England, except in the sense that they are situated within it geographically.

So – number is of the essence, and geographical concentration is of the essence, and each multiplies the effect of the other. Now I turn to the consequences of number and of concentration. These neither I nor anyone else can prove in advance; but if, when the consequences occur, it would be too late to reverse them, it is the politician's duty to form and to declare his judgement of them in time, so that, if possible, they may be averted or modified. I declare, then, that in my judgement, based upon what knowledge I have of human nature and upon what observation I have made of events in the world, the prospective growth in this country of the Commonwealth immigrant and immigrant-descended population will result in civil strife of appalling dimensions, and that institutions and laws, let alone exhortations, will be powerless to prevent it. On the other hand, it is not in my judgement yet too late to prevent or greatly reduce those consequences – namely, by a great reduction of the prospective number.

Like any other man, I can be mistaken; I can be mistaken either about the consequences or, if I am not mistaken about those, then I can be mistaken about the possibility of averting them. What is certain is that whatever the consequences are, my words could not cause them and my silence could not avert them. What is also certain is that anyone bearing the responsibility of a Member of Parliament who judged as I do but held his peace, would be guilty of a crime against his country and his fellow men. There are some so foolish as to imagine, or so malevolent as to pretend, that those who think they foresee danger or disaster, therefore desire it. One might as well accuse a man who warned against a rearming enemy of desiring the war he hoped to avert.

That nation will be ill counselled which allows its statesmen to predict only what it is pleasant to hear.

The reduction of prospective numbers depends upon two courses of action. One is the cessation of further immigration. On this I find nothing to alter in what I said over two years ago: 'We must be mad, literally mad, as a nation to be permitting the annual inflow of some 50,000, who are for the most part the material of the future growth of the immigrant-descended population.' However, I would be deceiving you if I allowed you to suppose that in my opinion the cessation of further immigration would sufficiently reduce prospective numbers to modify at all appreciably the consequences I foresee. I wish I could think so; but I cannot. Therefore it follows that a major re-emigration or repatriation is essential if it is possible. The Conservative Party had adopted the policy of assisting the repatriation and resettlement of all who wish to avail themselves of the offer, without limitation of numbers. My own judgement is that the numbers, if this policy is adopted promptly and wholeheartedly, could be decisive; and I am fortified in this by the fact that my estimate of half was reached by, among others, one of the most brilliant and impartial judicial minds in the country, Lord Radcliffe's. To the doubters I say: since when has it been an argument against adopting measures to combat a danger, to say that they might not, or might not fully, succeed?

The last point that I wish to emphasise is one which certainly does not need emphasising to the people of this town and ought not to need emphasising to any person of intelligence and impartiality. It is that to speak and act as I have done implies no ill will towards Commonwealth immigrants or any section of them, but much the contrary. Like the overwhelming majority of my fellow countrymen, I hold no man inferior because he is of different origin. As the Member during twenty years for a constituency which has had a higher influx of Commonwealth immigrants, and for longer, than almost any other, I have invariably given the same service and shown the same good will to my immigrant constituents as to the rest. They have the same claim upon me, and it has been equally discharged; and many there are who can testify to that. And so it shall always be.

But I owe to them, along with the rest, another and a higher duty. If my judgement of the dangers of the future is right, then the immigrants and their descendants have, if possible, even more to gain than the rest of us from those dangers being averted; for the outcome which I believe is portended would be at least as disastrous for the newcomers as for the indigenous inhabitants. What I have said, I have said in the interest of all.

'RACE AND IMMIGRATION'
BBC TV, 18 February 1973

ROBIN DAY: Good evening. How should we deal with the consequences of Commonwealth immigration? Enoch Powell and Mark Bonham-Carter lead the arguments in this three-part Sunday Debate. The issue is one which raises major questions of national policy and moral principle. The purpose of this debate is not to inflame the strong feelings which this subject can arouse but to examine those feelings and the facts in a way which is both rational and realistic.

The Right Honourable Enoch Powell MP will advocate his proposals for dealing with what he sees as the consequences of Commonwealth immigration. With him, Mr Clifford Thomas, Senior Lecturer in Social Statistics at Southampton University. On the other side are Mr Mark Bonham-Carter, Chairman of the Community Relations Commission and formerly Chairman of the Race Relations Board. With him, Professor Albert Hines, West Indian-born head of the Department of Economics at Birkbeck College, London. They will be questioning Mr Powell and Professor Hines tonight and will put their side of the argument in next Sunday's programme. Our two assessors, in the centre, both live and work in an area of high immigration. Trade-union leader Jack Peel, General Secretary of the Dyers, Bleachers and Textile Workers, whose headquarters are in Bradford. And Patrick Corbett, Professor of Philosophy in the University of Bradford.

I now call on Mr Enoch Powell to open his argument.

ENOCH POWELL: This is a subject that it's no use discussing unless one starts with the magnitude of it. You've got to get the size of it right because everything else follows from the size. Now, in fact, we do know, and I – when I say know, I mean know – that the consequences of Commonwealth immigration will be, unless there are major alterations in policy, that in the foreseeable future, a proportion of the population of major towns, cities and areas in this country, from a fifth to a quarter to a third, will be the descendants of the immigrants from the new Commonwealth. That, to use the word which we shall have to use for convenience, they will be to that extent a quarter or a third coloured.

Now, of course, it isn't a question of fact what the result of that will be. But that's a matter on which, at any rate a politician has a duty to form his judgement. And my judgement is that so profound a change in the population of that sort of area is not likely to take place without the most fearful friction, not to say conflict, and that therefore it is an overriding duty to seek to prevent that situation from arising.

How? Well, quite clearly by two methods. First, and quite obviously, there must be no more, whatever the proportions are, they mustn't be further increased by any addition to that population. But, secondly, as much as possible, that population and the prospective future must be reduced by every form of encouragement and help to those concerned to go home; the first, and their children now, of the second generation. That, in a nutshell, is my submission.

DAY: Would you state your evidence, Mr Powell, for knowing that the consequences will reach the proportions you have mentioned?

POWELL: Yes. This is very simple. There are a good many ways of doing it, and the way that I find easiest is this: let us take a generation. People from age nought to twenty-five or twenty-six. Now that's a generation. Twenty-six being the average age of a mother at the birth of a child. And whatever the population is up to twenty-six will in due course become the pattern of a population as a whole as each generation reproduces itself.

Now in a place like my own town, Wolverhampton, we do know of that generation, the young generation, that it is at least a quarter and more likely a third coloured. We know that that can be proved from evidence that we've got. In Birmingham it is something approaching that, and it is as high as that or higher in certain areas of London and is being approached in parts of Yorkshire and of Lancashire. And so we know that at the very least, that will be the ultimate proportion of the entire population. But I say at the very least, because I have in fact fed in a number of assumptions all of which are unreasonably optimistic. Or at any rate, most are. The first is that you will observe that I have assumed no difference in fertility or birthrate between the new population and the indigenous population. Of course, to the extent to which the birthrate is higher, then the consequences are larger, but I've assumed no difference in that respect. Secondly, I've assumed no further immigration. Thirdly, I've assumed no moving out by the rest of the population from the towns and areas where the coloured population is large and rapidly increasing. Well, both those are unrealistic assumptions.

And, finally, we mustn't forget that from this country as a whole, the white population is emigrating on a substantial scale, it was recently as high as 120,000 a year; it's lower than that now. But of course that also falls into the scale. So we literally do know, as a minimum, what this proportion is going to be, in places like Wolverhampton and Birmingham.

'THE UK AND IMMIGRATION'

Sydney University, September 1988

The story which I have to unfold is unique, and that perhaps is the potential interest of it for nations other than the inhabitants of the United Kingdom, because it exhibits the peculiarity both of British law and of the British character. As such, I offer it here in Australia as a modest contribution to Pommology. The uniqueness of my story is also a caution against the vulgar error of supposing that when we apply the same word (or its relevant equivalent in translation) to the affairs of different countries we are talking about the same thing or even about different things which have any significant commonality.

Every society has a definition to identify those who belong to it – I shall resolutely refuse to define the word 'belong' itself, regarding it as sufficiently understood for my purpose without definition – and to distinguish them from the rest of mankind who do not belong to it. In the case of a club that definition is to be found in the rules. In the case of a state it is to be found in its law of nationality or citizenship. (The two terms, nationality and citizenship, are not exactly interchangeable, but the course of my narrative may cast light upon their difference.)

Until recent times the nationality law of the United Kingdom was essentially feudal. It was based on the conception according to which, between whoever is born in a territory and the lord of that territory, there exists a nexus of reciprocal rights. Those who were born in England were consequently subjects of the Crown, and to be born with that allegiance was to be a British subject. The law of the United Kingdom thus divided mankind into two classes: British subjects, and the rest. (Strictly speaking, there was a third category, namely, 'British protected persons'; but it was of no importance generally and I mention it only to protect myself against anyone complaining that I have overlooked it.)

Of course a person not born within the allegiance could become a British subject by being allowed to undertake that allegiance. This might be a formal legal act of naturalisation, or it might follow as a consequence of some other event. A woman, for example, became a British subject by marrying one, because it was inconceivable in that relationship that she did not share the allegiance which might require him to fight and die for his sovereign.

This law of nationality was a *ius soli*, 'right of the soil', as distinguished from *ius sanguinis*, 'right of blood'. There were, it is true, circumstances in which children born to British subjects but born outside the allegiance were recognised as British subjects; but this anomaly – for such it was – was jealously limited and did not normally extend beyond one such generation. The idea, familiar to the nationality law of other nations, of an inherited status transmissible from generation to generation was, and indeed still is, foreign to the law of the United Kingdom.

To the status of British subject attached the bundle of rights and liberties of the sort which we ordinarily describe by the term citizenship. They included the right to enter or leave the realm at will and to be domiciled in it, as well as such political rights, like holding office or exercising the electoral franchise, as the law attached to the status of British subject, with or without other qualifications.

From the middle of the eighteenth century onwards, notwithstanding the loss of the American Colonies, there occurred a striking expansion outside the United Kingdom of the dominions of the Crown, until those born within a quarter of the land surface of the globe were born within the allegiance and consequently British subjects indistinguishable from one another in the law of the United Kingdom. Britain, be it noted, did not, in that alleged fit of absent-mindedness in which it acquired an Empire, create in its metropolitan law any new status to accommodate the denizens of the Empire. It simply allowed the consequences of the doctrine of allegiance to operate automatically wherever the sovereign of the territory of birth was the sovereign of the United Kingdom. Consequently by the end of the Second World War there were in the world some eight hundred million persons born outside the United Kingdom but endowed in the United Kingdom with all the rights of British subjects.

Every state claims and exercises as a natural aspect of its statehood the right to admit or exclude at discretion those who do not belong to it. In exercising that discretion it may have regard to the present or future interests of its inhabitants or to other considerations, which may include considerations of an altruistic nature. The policy involved in exercising that discretion is commonly and conveniently described as its immigration policy. The United Kingdom had, of course, always exercised this discretion in respect of aliens, as for example when it admitted to the United Kingdom some 200,000 European Jews in the last decade of the nineteenth century and the first decade of this century and a further 50,000 in the 1930s. In respect of British subjects, however – those eight hundred millions to whom I just referred – there neither was nor could be an immigration policy. All possessed under United Kingdom law the same unqualified right of entry and domicile.

This consequence of United Kingdom law applied of course in the United Kingdom only. By a curious irony, entry, including entry by other British subjects, into the territories composing the remainder of the British dominions was controlled by the relevant local government whosever government that was. There was always and everywhere an immigration policy in the rest of the Empire. Acts of discretion underlay Asian immigration into East Africa or, for that matter, into Fiji. Responsibility for immigration policy, as for every other discretion, devolved as part and parcel of self-government.

The populations which eventually amounted to the eight hundred millions I have mentioned made a quantitatively negligible use of their rights of entry and domicile in the United Kingdom until after the Second World War, when economic conditions in Britain, coupled with the enormous capability of air transport for shifting large numbers of persons, opened up the imminent prospect that a movement thitherto negligible would become so massive as to alter substantially the composition of the population of Britain. If this was not to happen, it would be necessary so to alter the law of nationality of the United Kingdom as to detach the right of entry and abode from the status of British subject and attach it to a narrower category, however defined, of those who belonged to the United Kingdom itself.

I have brought my account down to the point where the inevitability of that alteration of British nationality law was fatefully fended off between 1949 and 1961. Before I proceed to describe and explain that drama there is a tale within a tale that must be told first. It is surpassingly bizarre.

When British rule in India came to an end in 1947, it was evident that the principal successor state, the Indian Union, and probably also the other successor state, 'Pakistan', would wish not to recognise the British monarch as their sovereign. In consequence they and their populations would automatically, being outside the allegiance, become foreign states whose citizens were aliens, as had been the case with Burma in 1946. For a Britain which was engaged in telling itself that the Empire was in process of evolving into a worldwide Commonwealth of Nations on which the sun would never set, this was an appalling prospect, and they applied to themselves – nobody else wanted it – a hallucinatory drug. They abolished allegiance as the basis of British nationality. Instead they declared that British subjects would in future be those who were the citizens of a list of self-governing countries which grew longer and longer as colonies became independent. That left the United Kingdom itself and the colonies that were still dependent unaccounted for. To accommodate them the British invented a new category called Citizens of the United Kingdom and Colonies. The whole lot were to be called Commonwealth citizens and equated for the purposes of UK law with British subjects. Thus did the British bravely hold reality at bay, and ensure incidentally that the overhanging entry rights of eight hundred millions would remain intact, however many of their countries became, like India, republics.

This passionate attachment of post-war Britain to the myth of a continuing Commonwealth has to be grasped in all its fullness if the disaster of the 1950s is to be understood. By the time Churchill ceased to be Prime Minister in 1955, a Bill to restrict in the United Kingdom the right of entry and domicile, as every other country on the face of the earth restricts it, to belongers was in draft and awaiting introduction into Parliament. There is no reason for supposing that it would have been particularly controversial there or elsewhere. That the old law was obsolete in modern circumstances was generally recognised at the time. Instead, however, after a year spent searching for alternative wheezes, such as making admission conditional on housing or employment, Macmillan shelved the whole matter for the duration of the 1955 Parliament. Quite suddenly, in the middle and later 1950s, not only did the reform come to be perceived as a threat to the multi-racial Commonwealth, but the idea grew up that there would be actual merit in the presence in Britain of those whom the reform would have excluded if it had been in force already.

It was thus in a different atmosphere and only after the Conservative Government had won a majority of 100 in the general election of 1959, that the original Bill was at last put before Parliament in 1961 and came into force in 1962. That Act created for the first time two classes of British subject – now alias 'Commonwealth citizen' – those who did and those who did not possess in UK law the right of entry and abode. However fate played a malign trick.

There was a flaw in the drafting, which was to have serious and continuing consequences. The category of British subjects who were to retain the right of entry and domicile was basically defined as those 'born in the United Kingdom'; but for convenience and to avoid verification of birth at the point of entry, an alternative definition was provided, namely, those 'who hold a UK passport or a passport issued by the Government of the United Kingdom'. Now, when a Commonwealth country became independent and created its own citizenship, persons belonging to that country who did not obtain that citizenship but remained therefore Citizens of the United Kingdom and Colonies would look to obtain their passports from the local High Commissioner (who else?), who, unlike the former Governor or Governor-General, represented 'the Government of the United Kingdom'. Thus quite unintentionally the right of entry and abode was conferred upon large numbers of persons, notably Asians in East Africa, who did not become citizens of the newly independent states. When substantial numbers availed themselves of this facility it was obvious by 1968 that an amending Act had become unavoidable. By then, however, the whole subject was surrounded by great excitement and the allegation was being widely made, for which no evidence has ever been produced, that the provision was in fact intended in the first place and had even been promised. As a result, the Government were forced to purchase the passage of the amending Bill by promising that, although the right of entry was withdrawn, all such persons would eventually be admitted by discretion.

An important consequence of the absence – indeed, the legal impossibility – of what in other countries would be an immigration policy was the dearth of reliable information as to what had been happening: statistics and a policy of control go hand in hand. Huge numbers of Commonwealth citizens enter and leave the United Kingdom all the time. Theoretically, if you subtract the number who leave from the number who enter, you arrive at the number who stay – whether legally entitled to do so or not. The scope for error, however, when the gross totals were so large, was great and, in the absence of any device for matching individual departures against individual entries, the method was hopelessly inadequate. Moreover after 1972 documentation was to be further impeded when freedom of internal movement within the European Economic Community came into force. In the middle 1960s it would not be unfair to say that no British Government really knew in quantitative terms what had happened.

It was natural, in retrospect, that for a long time attention continued to be concentrated upon the crude numbers of New Commonwealth citizens, who had entered before the Act of 1962 (necessarily an unofficial figure) and of those who were admitted afterwards. Only in the later 1960s did information become available on the proportion of births within the United Kingdom which were attributable to parents who had themselves been born outside it. This information, at first collected locally by the health authorities, was given a statutory basis in 1969, when the place of birth of parents was required to be notified at the registration of all births. The figures thus obtained cast some light upon the prospective future make-up of the population, both locally and for Great Britain as a whole; but these implications were confused by the debate over the likely future pattern of fertility. Moreover, with every year that passed, more and more parents of New Commonwealth origin would themselves have been born in the

United Kingdom, so that births to parents born outside would trend downwards even while New Commonwealth births were increasing.

The focus of interest has shifted in recent years, as the central importance of population profile, or the age structure of the population, has begun to be appreciated. It is the profile of one element in a country's population, compared with that of the rest, which determines future relative magnitudes. This is subject of course to any assumptions that may be made as to differential fertility; but it still holds good and produces a reliable minimal model if that differential is taken at zero. The current official projection of a Great Britain in 2000 A.D. with a minimum 7 per cent ethnic minority population derives from population profiles which have been increasingly based upon direct surveys of the population initially undertaken for other purposes – for employment policy, for example. The existing age profile is, of course, the product of what took place before 1962 combined with the manner in which the policy governing control thereafter was exercised and notably the principle, successively refined but remaining broadly in force, of admitting the children, spouses and dependants of previous arrivals.

These surveys, on which population statistics in Britain are now based, rely upon the visual self-identification of those surveyed in terms essentially of colour. The replacement of more objective classification, such as place of birth, by ethnicity and the supersession of older terminology such as 'New Commonwealth origin' by the now almost standard term 'ethnic minority' are the end product of a process that has extended over thirty years. It was, you will recall, in 1961 by a fundamental change in its law of nationality that the United Kingdom acquired the possibility and therefore the obligation of an immigration policy – something which every other nation, under different systems of law, had possessed. Immigration policies take account *inter alia* of the prospective consequences of a change in the population of the receiving countries and in particular, in the case of long-established and densely populated countries, of acceptability to the existing population and of governability under the existing constitutional modes. When the United Kingdom enabled itself lawfully to control the entry of British subjects not defined as belonging to it, the measure was inherently neutral: the UK differentiated itself thereby for nationality purposes from the whole of the rest of the Commonwealth indiscriminately.

However, the motive which compelled the change was alarm at the consequences anticipated from unlimited entry from the New Commonwealth such as took place between 1948 and 1962 and the implications of further growth of that element in Britain's population. Any attempt therefore to measure and to observe had to be in terms of an element defined not by status but by another criterion. This was an ethnic criterion; and it is significant that in official publications the term 'ethnic minority', which no longer distinguishes at all between those who are Commonwealth citizens and those who are not – it would for example include mainland Chinese and Filippinos – has replaced the older terminologies, 'New Commonwealth', 'New Commonwealth and Pakistan', or even 'New Commonwealth ethnic', which retained a basis in status and embraced, for example, Maltese and Cypriots.

The term 'race' first made its way into the law of the United Kingdom in 1965 in a measure which referred, without further definition, to 'colour, race or ethnic or national origin', and has been pronounced by the courts to differentiate the Scots and the Welsh from the English. Indeed, the introduction of that term borrowed from biology was intended to abort specification of the apprehensions which underlay the decision to legislate in 1962. The 1965 Bill was in fact the earliest essay in the attempt, by the creation of offences and a new distinction at law between one citizen and another, to avert those consequences of which the apprehension had led to the abandonment of the old United Kingdom law of nationality. Thus it came about that the delay between 1954 and 1961 in moving to bring United Kingdom nationality law into consonance with contemporary realities has entailed upon Britain what the modern world understands as the politics of race. A Government decision, albeit a decision by default, in the middle 1950s wears in retrospect all the dignity and significance of tragedy.

AMERICA

ANTHONY HOWARD: Some people say that they detect, in most of the things you say, a vein of anti-Americanism.
POWELL: I don't think that would be entirely unfair.

'Face the Press', Channel 4 TV, 9 October 1983

'DR KISSINGER'S ILLUSIONS'

Sunday Telegraph, 18 November 1979

For eight years from 1969 to 1977 Professor Kissinger of Harvard University was at Richard Nixon's right hand, first as Assistant for National Security Affairs, and then as Secretary of State. He has in less than three years thereafter delivered himself of the first of two volumes in which he bequeaths his memoirs of that period to posterity. If the second volume matches the first,* the whole document will comprise 3,000 pages of text. It is a heavy book physically, as only American books can be, and dense in content, a running account day by day of 'how it happened' to Henry Kissinger from start to finish.

I met Dr Kissinger briefly in London in 1966 after the United States was caught fast in the Vietnam quicksand, and upon his request for my view I replied: 'Go on board ship' to which at the time he replied not at all, but subsequently wrote from America that I was not to assume from his silence that he necessarily disagreed. The following year I addressed his seminar at Harvard, and gained a considerable appreciation of the quickness and sensitivity of his mind.

To an English observer the appropriate title for his memoirs would be 'A Professor at the Court of King Nixon'. But then it is probably beyond the English imagination anyhow to comprehend how university professors – and other sorts of non-politicians, totally unversed and inexperienced in the life and ways of government – can step straight into high office and public responsibility.

It is not so much that our sense for apprenticeship and hierarchy is offended. The trouble is that for Americans the expression 'government of the people by the people', which to us appears a mere catchphrase, is factual description: that anybody can be anything is part of the American idea of democracy, just as it was part of Athenian democracy that Cleon could be a leather-seller one day and a general commanding an expedition the next.

Henry Kissinger is not a Richard Crossman, who, while zestfully and professionally playing a leading role in politics and government, remained throughout essentially the don and philosopher, finding his highest satisfaction in academic contemplation and analysis of the

The White House Years by Henry Kissinger, Weidenfeld and Michael Joseph

scene. When Kissinger entered the White House, he left his Harvard seminar behind him.

His memoir belongs to the style of Caesar's 'Commentaries' rather than that of Marcus Aurelius's 'Reflections'; or, not to pitch the comparison too high, it would bear equation with that of Harold Macmillan and Harold Wilson telling us what happened while they were Prime Ministers and how successful (on the whole) they had been. As a specimen, the conclusion of the passage on Kissinger's visit to Chou in 1971, to prepare the way for Nixon, will do as well as any:

> We had conducted one of the most comprehensive reviews of international relations in my diplomatic experience. In one giant step we had transformed our diplomacy. We had brought new flexibility to our foreign policy. We had captured the initiative and also the imagination of our own people. We had much farther to go, of course; but we had made a new departure and travelled some distance down the road.

Well, well; the transformation of the professor into the politician had certainly gone 'some distance down the road'. As the reader perseveres, he becomes more and more doubtful whether any vestiges of detachment or critical sense survived that transformation. It was Kissinger who negotiated and signed the USA's capitulation which ended the Vietnam War in January 1973 – America's own 'Treaty of Paris', 190 years later, if an Englishman may be permitted that sardonic comparison. Here is his epilogue upon it:

> We [Nixon and I, that is] had no illusions about Hanoi's long-term goals. Nor did we go through the agony of four years of war and scaring negotiations to achieve a 'decent interval' for our withdrawal. We were determined to do our utmost to enable Saigon to grow in security and prosperity so that it could prevail in any political struggle. We sought not an interval before collapse but lasting peace with honour. But for the collapse of executive authority as a result of Watergate, I believe we would have succeeded.

That last sentence crowns the terrifying self-revelation. What? 'No illusions'? Every word is saturated with illusion. Kissinger writes of his quondam patron Nelson Rockefeller, that 'he was quintessentially American in his unquenchable optimism; he could never imagine that wrong could not be righted, or that effort could not conquer obstacles in the way of honourable goals'. Foreign-born though he is, Henry Kissinger is 100 per cent naturalised. And there was Nixon, according to Kissinger, 'envisaging a new international order that would reduce lingering enmities, strengthen friendships and give new hope to emerging nations. It was a worthy goal for America and mankind.'

Heaven save us from such dreamers.

'WHY WASHINGTON HAS ITS OWN PLANS FOR THE FALKLANDS'

The Times, 29 June 1982

There is no aspect of Britain's strategy and defence policy or of Britain's external relations that will remain unaffected by the events of these weeks. Few aspects will be affected more than the future relationship between Britain and the United States.

The action of nations, and the reaction of nations, is often more conditioned than they themselves and others are aware at the time by their self-perception. It can even be unconscious: a picture of themselves which slumbers somewhere in their collective mind.

By the same token, a failure to allow for the self-perception of other nations can be a cause of deep and dangerous misunderstanding. I believe that something of this kind may be at the bottom of the mutual alienation between Britain and the United States which has puzzled both parties since the Falklands affair began. If so, it is worth while attempting a bit of psychoanalysis.

The Falklands have brought to the surface of the British mind our latent perception of ourselves as a sea animal: we floated away from the adjacent mainland and became an Atlantic island, threatened in its very habitat by a sudden and brutal threat to one of our Atlantic 'other islands'; our mental geography altered – sufficiently for *The Times* to title a leader 'We are all Falklanders now'. No assault on a landward possession would have evoked the same automatic defiance, tinged with a touch of that self-sufficiency which belongs to all nations – be it classical Athens or seventeenth-century Holland – who depend for existence on command of the seas around them.

In the Americans the Falklands evoked a very different but just as deep an instinctual reaction. The United States, in this century, has become a naval as well as a continental power. Wide though the oceans may appear to us which separate that democracy from its actual or potential enemies at either end of the Asiatic land mass, the United States has an almost neurotic sense of vulnerability. As a naval power, the United States suffers from a crucial and permanent handicap of a sort unknown to an island power like Britain: its two coastlines, its two theatres, its two navies are separated by the entire length of the New World down to the Horn.

In this respect, as in others, the Americans have something in common with the Russians. The Rozhdestvensky is branded on the Russian consciousness. He was the admiral whose fate it was to circumnavigate half the world in the vain attempt to join what remained of the Far Eastern Fleet and deliver a death blow to the Japanese enemy. Against Russia's three seaboards, America has only two; but she lives with the same nightmare, the nightmare of having one day to fight a decisive sea battle without the benefit of concentration, the perpetual spectre of naval 'war on two fronts'.

Turn the globe so that North and South America face you; and the preoccupation of the United States with the tedious complexities of the Central American isthmus and the larger ambition of the United States to a leadership in the South American continent cease to be occasion for surprise. The Panama Canal from 1914 onwards could never quite exorcise the spectre. In the ultimate worst case, which all contemplation of war must envisage, the Straits of Magellan and Cape Horn lie on the most critical of all routes for American naval strategy. It was the position of the Falkland Islands in relation to that route which gave and gives them their significance – for the United States above all.

The British people have become uneasily aware that their American allies would prefer the Falkland Islands to pass out of Britain's possession into hands which, if not wholly American, might be amenable to American control. In fact, the American struggle to wrest the islands from Britain has only commenced in earnest now that the fighting is over. We should underestimate the seriousness and the motivation of America if we allowed ourselves facile explanations on the lines of old fashioned anti-political prejudice or Monroe Doctrine echoes. The true explanation owes no less to the American people's self-perception than our action in the Falklands did to our own self-perception.

There is another cause conditioning the American state of mind, which is equally inaccessible to us in Britain and of which we therefore need the more forcibly and frequently to remind ourselves.

Historians will one day have the means to show that Britain's fateful failure in the 1950s to change its law of nationality so as to control coloured immigration, owed much to the contemporary inflammation of 'race' in the United States in terms of white versus black. American terminology dominates to this day our debate on the very different circumstances in Britain.

Meanwhile, in the States, that older trauma is being overtaken by another, potentially as large or larger in numerical and political terms:

the Hispanic factor. If we could gather together all the anxieties for the future which in Britain cluster around race relations – from the 'race relations industry' to our relations with the new Commonwealth – and then attribute them, translated into Hispanic terms, to the Americans, we would have begun to comprehend something of the phobias which haunt the United States and addressed itself to the aftermath of the Falklands campaign.

'DANCING TO THE WASHINGTON TUNE'

The Times, 17 September 1983

Nations have an outside as well as an inside, and the behaviour of their outside can at certain periods be more decisive to their well-being than the way they behave on the inside.

I happen to think that we are having an exceptionally bad period in British foreign policy, and a politician who believes that ought not to refrain from saying so.

I don't know if you were as shocked and incredulous as I was when on the second of this month the Foreign Secretary demanded from the Soviet Union an apology, compensation, admission of guilt, and punishment of the guilty. When Lord Palmerston in 1850 issued a similar demand to the Greek Government, there was a widespread sense that he had gone too far. The two cases, however, differ in certain important particulars. Greece in 1850 was much weaker than Britain, which had naval supremacy in the eastern Mediterranean; the sole matter at issue was the treatment of a British citizen; Britain had a gunboat and sent it; Greece gave in.

Sir Geoffrey Howe's situation is unlike Lord Palmerston's. Russia is more powerful than Britain and inaccessible to British forces; the matter at issue concerns Britain only marginally and incidentally; Sir Geoffrey will not send a gunboat; Russia will not give in; and Britain will not do anything about it. How comes it about that Britain's Foreign Secretary in 1983 could court humiliation by issuing a series of demands that might mildly be described as lunatic?

You have read in the newspapers that there is a multinational force in the Lebanon, called a peace-keeping force, which includes a British detachment of nearly 100 men. You have been misinformed. If there is, in the natural sense of the words, a multinational peace-keeping force in the Lebanon, the British troops are not part of it. This is a point on which I have been at pains to establish the facts by a series of Parliamentary Questions.

The British force is stationed in Beirut in pursuance of an exchange of letters last January between Her Majesty's Government and the Lebanese Government. Command authority is exercised over it exclusively by the British Government through – I quote – 'existing

British diplomatic and military channels'. A curious phrase, you might think, to which, as it happens, there is no parallel in the agreement, for instance, under which British forces are in Belize.

More curiously still, it is a condition of the presence of the British troops that the Government of Lebanon and the Lebanese armed forces shall take 'all measures necessary to ensure the protection of the British force's personnel, including securing assurances from all armed elements not now under the authority of the Lebanese Government, that they will refrain from hostilities'.

You may regard that as having been obviously drafted with the object of making the cats laugh; but you will be less amused to learn that the Foreign Office assures me that in their view Lebanon is not in breach of that condition.

As to the purpose of the force, the agreement specifies that 'the British force will not engage in hostilities or other operations of a warlike nature, but may exercise the right of self-defence'. Subject to this, we are told no more than that the force will 'carry out such tasks as may be agreed between the United Kingdom and the Lebanese Government', provided such tasks are 'consistent with' (another peculiar phrase) 'the mandate of the multinational force comprising American, French and Italian troops'.

Enquiring further as to what that mandate is, we learn that the multinational force is 'to provide an interposition force at agreed locations' and by their presence 'facilitate restoration of Lebanese Government sovereignty and authority over the Beirut area'.

When the first British soldier in the force is killed or when the first non-British life is taken by British forces we shall no doubt ask what the blood was shed for. The answer will perforce be: to assist the Lebanese Government to control Beirut. Somebody is then going to have to show what moral or other justification exists for British lives to be lost or for British soldiers to take other lives in that cause, in pursuance with an agreement we have made with the Lebanese Government.

I will not shirk answering that question for myself, and will say that in my opinion there is no justification. It does not matter to the United Kingdom and its people who is in Beirut or who governs Beirut – the matter is one of the utmost indifference for the United Kingdom. Neither is there any general nor specific commitment by which the United Kingdom has bound itself to uphold the sovereignty and authority over Beirut of the Lebanese Government (which, you will observe, means the Lebanese Government of the day, however constituted).

In the absence of any such interest or commitment we have no moral right by even the passive use of military force, let alone by killing and being killed, to attempt to determine the governance of Beirut.

How come we to find ourselves in so absurd and unjustifiable a predicament? The answer is the same as to my earlier question: in order to dance, and be seen to be dancing, to the American tune. In the case of Geoffrey Howe's *demarche* we were so keen that we started to dance before the music began properly to play. In the case of Lebanon we are delivering a token assent on our part to the interventions of the United States in the affairs of Lebanon.

I am reminded of two earlier occasions. One memory is of staying up all night in 1980 to oppose the passing of a palpably futile Act of Parliament imposing sanctions on Iran because the American Embassy in Tehran had been sacked and its inmates confined. The second memory is graver. It is March 1966, when the Conservative Opposition of the day prevented, by exposing just in time, the intention to send a token British contingent to the American forces in Vietnam by way of demonstrating British approval for American policy and actions there.

There is a word 'Finlandisation'. It describes the process to which a state, nominally sovereign and independent, is subjected when it decides that in reality its actions must conform to those demanded or imposed by an irresistibly powerful neighbour.

I make no complaint against whatever courses the Finns may have thought it right to pursue. I do say that successive British governments down the last thirty years have Finlandised the United Kingdom in relation to the US without justification either of national interest or of *force majeure*.

The result has been to associate us with, and subordinate us to, the huge miscalculations and misconceptions which dominate American policy and which have led that country from one failure to another, failures mainly paid for by the inhabitants of those distant territories where the United States mistakenly sought its own interests by the attempt to coerce others into conformity with its invincibly erroneous preconceptions.

There has not even been the compensation, if such it were, of finding ourselves on the winning side. In the last thirty years, whenever we have followed them as in Iran, or been tempted to follow them as in Vietnam, the Americans have been the world's grand losers. We plaster that fact over in vain by telling ourselves that, through it all, the United States has kept the Soviet Union at bay.

Suppose, people say, the United States were to wash its hands of Beirut and the Lebanon, even granted it has no business to be there at all. Would not the Russians walk in next day? The answer to that is No. It is not the Americans that keep the Russians out of Beirut;

common sense would keep them out. The Soviet Union has quite enough joy over one Afghanistan without creating others for itself all round the Middle East.

But surely, it is objected, if we do not do what the Americans tell us, if Britain does not ditto their words and sayings like a court sycophant, surely they will refuse to defend these islands? Rest assured, the reply runs, if the United States believes its own interest calls for the defence of the British Isles, the difficulty will be to keep them out and not to get them in, but if it doesn't, no quantity of sycophancy will make the difference.

It is reason, not pride, that counsels a radical revision of British foreign policy, though self-respect is after all no bad guide to a nation in its dealing with the outside world. The central forum for reasoning about these things is Parliament.

If the opportunities in Parliament are withheld or prove inadequate, then we must seek a forum among the people. The worst fate for a nation's foreign policy is to lie undebated and unexamined in a rut.

'FACE THE PRESS'
Channel 4 TV, 9 October 1983

ANTHONY HOWARD: Would it be fair to say that lately you have emerged as one of the stronger critics of the Government's foreign policy?

ENOCH POWELL: Yes, I think that would be fair. Though, little that I have said in criticising it is novel on my lips. Almost always what I have said is something which I can refer to having said five or ten years earlier. But I have said it perhaps more frequently and perhaps with more emphasis. Why? Because certain aspects of the Government's policy are becoming more visible and more strident, if not more offensive. And also, in so far as they are concerned with defence, there is a definite connection in my mind with the question of Northern Ireland which was the reason why I made two speeches on that subject during my own election campaign in Ulster.

HOWARD: Some people say that they detect, in most of the things you say, a vein of anti-Americanism.

POWELL: I don't think that would be entirely unfair. There are some things which get on one's nerves and some things that don't. And I'm, to use a rather journalistic word, allergic to the things that are typically American. I think that's fairly natural to someone who has just been described as a Tory and is always ready to describe himself as a high Tory.

FRANK JOHNSON: Are you allergic to the things which can be described as typically Russian?

POWELL: I regard them as an outside observer, contemplating something which, from the start, he perceives to be totally strange, interpretable only against a background to which I have had little access. I worked away, in my time, at Russian. In fact, I achieved sufficient facility in reading Russian to be able to translate a Russian handbook on parachute jumping, for the training of our own troops in 1940. But, eh, I haven't the facility to read, readily, Russian literature, and I do see Russia as a different sphere, culturally, intellectually, emotionally.

JOHNSON: But which do you regard as the most maligned force in the world – the Soviet Union or the United States?

POWELL: Maligned to whom?

JOHNSON: To the rest of mankind.

POWELL: I'm not primarily concerned with the rest of mankind. The rest of mankind is a statistical total. It's like –

JOHNSON: To this country.

POWELL: Ah, that's different. Now, that's coming to practicalities.

JOHNSON: To this country and its allies.

POWELL: I do not think that Soviet Russia is dangerous to this country. It can't get at us and, eh, a vast land power like that, which has on, in three periods of our history, by its very existence, arguably been our salvation, is difficult to envisage as presenting a threat to the liberties and the safety and the independence, if we still have it since joining the European Community, of the United Kingdom.

HOWARD: You were very roundly rebuked, was it last week, by *The Times* newspaper, for saying that there wasn't a single Soviet soldier in place who wasn't there in 1948, with the exception of Afghanistan.

POWELL: Ah, yes. There's a lesson here which I suppose the experienced ought not to need. I should have said 'Russian division' and I chose the more plastic word, 'no Russian soldier – the picture of a single Russian soldier'. I shouldn't, of course, but anyone reading what I had to say would understand that I meant Russian forces.

JOHN WHALE: You say that the Russians can't get at us. They surely can with missiles?

POWELL: But what possible point would there be in getting at us with missiles? Because if they were poised actually to conquer the United Kingdom, something which I find an inconceivable objective, then the last thing they would do would be to devastate it with atomic, with nuclear, weapons. If that was not their objective, then they would be concerned with other forces which they had to encounter. And I cannot see that the invasion, if one can imagine it, by the Soviet Union of Western Europe, would be accompanied by a discharge of nuclear missiles. I can make no sense of such a strategy.

WHALE: Would you require no concession from the Soviet Union for a British renunciation of nuclear weapons, of the kind which you seem to have been advocating?

POWELL: And my argument is that I can't see what use they are to us. And it's a little cheap to go and ask somebody to pay for not doing something which is not very sensible, anyhow, to do.

JOHNSON: You said earlier that the Russians were arguably our salvation in the Second World War. Well, couldn't one argue just as plausibly that, with the Nazi–Soviet pact it was arguably our doom? And you say it can't get at us but surely it can get at us via

West Germany, the Low Countries, France and those other powers which are joined with us in the NATO Alliance?

POWELL: Yes. If it becomes the power that dominates Western Europe, then the power which dominates Western Europe is potentially the classic risk to the United Kingdom.

JOHNSON: Now, if you're so critical of the United States, why are you prepared for us to be members of an alliance of which the United States is the head – or, does your celebrated logic suggest that –

POWELL: As a member –

JOHNSON: Yes.

POWELL: I don't know that anyone ever made it the head of the alliance, except the Americans. They tend to assume that they're the head of the alliance but I'm not aware that there's any such official position been organised for them. Eh, they don't necessarily, except in a nuclear context, contribute the lion's share of what there is on the ground in Europe.

TO ROTARY DISTRICT 113

Eastbourne, 18 October 1985

The thesis that I lay before you this morning is one at which I arrived reluctantly and painfully yet with cumulative conviction as I lived, observing and reflecting, through the political vicissitudes of the 1970s and 1980s. I will formulate the thesis at the outset. It runs as follows: 'No Government can hold office in contemporary Britain unless it conforms with the assumptions of United States strategic policy.' Since all necessity resides in the mind, the thesis may be restated slightly differently thus: 'No Government in contemporary Britain *believes* it can hold office unless it conforms with the assumptions of United States strategic policy.'

The thesis holds good irrespective of political party or personalities. It controlled Wilson and Callaghan in government no less than it controls Kinnock and Healey in opposition, and it would operate upon Mrs Thatcher no less if she were as allergic to President Reagan as she is apparently sympathetic to him. It almost attains the dignity of a law of the physical world.

The professional servants of government have no doubt a special role in expounding the thesis to successive masters and enlightening them, as and when necessary, in accordance with it. That however is no more than a mechanical function, part and parcel of the general business of officials to interpret the real world outside to their political superiors. The strength of the thesis and its indefeasibility do not lie in the Civil Service or the Foreign Office or the Ministry of Defence. The thesis derives its force from opinions which are widely shared and deeply rooted in government and governed alike. It is indeed part of the anatomy of Britain itself in the second half of the twentieth century – and not necessarily Britain only, for my thesis knows no parochial bounds.

On 21 September this year the American Government issued a summons to the Finance Ministers of three European nations and Japan to attend at twenty-four hours' notice to receive instructions. Without exception they dropped whatever they were doing wherever they were – the British Chancellor of the Exchequer dashed away from an EEC Financial Conference at Strasbourg – and flew to Washington. There they were told that the exchange rate of the dollar against their respective currencies was too high and that, unless they took immediate steps to reduce it, the United States would retaliate by penalising or excluding their exported goods. Without a murmur they submitted and filed out again. There seem to have been no reports that anybody laughed; but the incident is as instructive as it is ludicrous.

The United States had organised itself into a classic quandary by first of all indulging on a huge scale in deficit financing – duly applauded by the surviving Keynesians here in this country – and then reversing engines with an equally massive bid for loan money. In large measure the loan money was supplied from overseas as the counterpart of America's balance of payments deficit on current account. As for the other countries, short of pushing up their own domestic interest rates, to which they were naturally averse, or selling off what reserves they possessed in the form of dollars, there was nothing whatever they could do about it. So they took refuge in servility and verbiage, hoping the United States would accept the shadow for the substance and let them off with a caution. What nobody had ventured to do was to say to the United States: 'All right, if you want to go protectionist, that's up to you.' So deeply rooted is the conviction of the participants in the overwhelming economic power of the USA.

Both indirectly, through the International Monetary Fund and World Bank, and also directly the United States has lent lavishly to countries in what it calls the Third World, mostly but not exclusively in South and Central America, who have foreseeably turned out to be bad risks. Faced with the consequences of their default, the United States has successfully coerced the other potential lender countries to put up still more loan capital to continue the process and to stave off the default of the debtors. At no point has Britain or any of the rest dared to say to the United States: 'This is a fool's game, and we will play it no longer.' That is a tribute not so much to their conviction of America's economic power as to their subjugation to its grand strategy, of which worldwide development aid forms part.

What the British public, with its relatively relaxed and live-and-let-live attitude to other nations, does not readily understand is the obsessive preoccupation of the United States with its vision of a world in Manichaean conflict between good and evil, free and unfree, West and East. All America's relations with other nations are ultimately determined by the place and role which it assigns to them, or desires for them, in that nightmare drama. They are all in the last analysis pieces on the strategic chessboard, and understood and dealt with as such by the United States according to the rules of its games.

At the beginning of next year Spain and Portugal will become members of the European Economic Community. There is no benefit in this for the existing EEC members. On the contrary, they will in varying degrees be laid under contribution to subsidise the Spanish and Portuguese economies, and the uneasy financial relationships among themselves, which they have just with great difficulty managed to settle, will be thrown into disarray. So why did this unnatural event occur? Spain became a member of the American alliance known as NATO in May 1982 against the strong disinclination of a large part of its people. A referendum next spring could take Spain out of NATO again. At the critical stage of the negotiation with the EEC the Spanish premier deployed the slogan: 'No membership of the EEC, no membership of NATO'. The present premier, Signor Gonzales, whose party campaigned against membership of NATO, was warned of the continuing force of that slogan at the beginning of this month in Bonn when Chancellor Kohl, we are told, 'emphasised the link between EEC membership and NATO'. The link is simple: the benefits extended by the other members are the price to be paid for an Iberian peninsula in the American alliance. And why do the European countries pay up? Because the requirements of America geo-politics are regarded by them as mandatory.

The same theorem explains the story of the EEC and Greece, whose Prime Minister also changed his mind about the Common Market after coming into office. Talking of change of mind makes one feel, all of a sudden, quite at home. It reminds one of three Labour Party leaders in a line, Wilson, Callaghan, Kinnock. In 1974 Wilson and Callaghan moved into No. 10 and the Foreign Office firmly committed against British membership of the Common Market. Within a month they were standing on their heads, a new light had dawned, another imperative had become dominant. The innocent may imagine that they worked out the economic sums again and got a different answer – but Kinnock? What source of economic enlightenment caused him, on becoming Labour's leader after a lost election, to drop overboard as his first act the official, long-standing and detailed Labour Party commitment to quit the Community? He bowed to the same relentless strategic imperative which none before him has been able to resist.

A fascinating glimpse behind the scenes was vouchsafed a year ago by Sir Anthony Parsons, an eminent ex-Foreign Office official and civil servant. In a Sunday newspaper he wrote applauding a colleague's stated opinion that 'a severe strain would be imposed on the code of loyal service to political masters if a future Government were to adopt an extremely radical policy' – what sort of 'radical policy'? – 'such as withdrawal from the European Community or from NATO'. The juxtaposition is significant. In American eyes the European Community, tiresome though some of its economic consequences may be, is the indispensable political counterpart of NATO. Hence the increasing stress beng laid upon the non-economic and external political significance of the Community. Hence the revealing assertion which Sir Anthony Parsons went on to make, that 'if the broad bipartisanship of the past forty years broke down in such a way, many officials in the higher reaches of the Foreign Office would find it impossible conscientiously to implement the new policies and the Government would be obliged to recruit political loyalists in order to carry out its will'.

That is a threat which no British Government so far has been willing to court, a threat more alarming to those holding or coveting office than any risk of alienating electoral support among the public. Its existence is a key which unlocks some of the most puzzling secrets of British politics in these last forty bipartisan years. It contains, for example, the clue to the tangled story of Northern Ireland since 1969 – yes and, I dare say, long before that date.

The island of Ireland is a piece on the strategic board of the importance of which NATO strategists have no doubt: 'a yawning gap in NATO defences' is how the absence of the Irish Republic from NATO (though not from the EEC) has been described and is discerned in the eyes of American Government. The price tag attached to the desired article is the cession of Ulster, under some form or other, to the Irish Republic. To engineer that cession, whatever the cost in human life and political morality, has accordingly been seen by successive British Governments as an inescapable imperative. Twice the main political parties, once Labour and once the Conservatives, have attempted to renege, and twice they have been whipped back into line by intimations, not to be ignored, that they could not be seen failing in loyalty to the strategic requirements of the American alliance. Whatever commitments and policies had been undertaken internally or in opposition were overturned without compunction once that screw was turned. The relationship between London and Dublin has never been bipartite. There has always been a third party, Washington, at least since NATO came into existence.

The philosophy of the alliance necessarily reflects the geo-politics of the United States; but its binding character for Britain and other nations of Western Europe has always depended on the assumed indispensability of that alliance, the starting-point from which all reasoning on British policy in the outside world has proceeded as from an irrebuttable premise. There is no doubt whence that assumed indispensability arises: it derives from the American command of nuclear military power. From that focus has radiated American domination, during forty bipartisan years, over British, and not only

British, policy. The domination has not been economic, it has been military; it has not been military, it has been nuclear.

I see two possible symptoms of that domination being undermined, not perhaps immediately but in the event surely. One is the erosion and threatened collapse of the theory of the nuclear deterrent, of which unquestioned acceptance has been mandatory upon the European members of the alliance. The whole controversy over the Cruise missile, which implies a European instead of global theatre of nuclear exchange and nuclear balance, is not really about the weapon: it is about the credibility of the deterrence theory. The whole excitement about the Strategic Defence Initiative is not about the perfectly logical defensive response which every weapon of attack evokes and always has evoked: it is about the credibility of the deterrence theory. Once that theory is seriously undermined, the whole structure of American political predominance is unbolted and starts to disintegrate.

The other sympton is more recent and less easy to interpret, but it has been sharply brought to people's minds in the recent past. There is an ultimate line of resistance which the assumption of unquestioned power and indispensability inevitably encounters. As long as the direct application of American military strength in support of America's strategic perceptions was relatively remote – enacted, for example, in Central America or South East Asia or the Middle East – uncritical British indifference could be safely assumed. The same will not necessarily hold good nearer home. When the act of blatant aggression committed, unsuccessfully, against Iran by the United States in 1980, was repeated by Israel against Tunisia, its condonation by the United States drew from the United Kingdom a repudiation quite novel in tone. When American military aircraft forced a civilian aeroplane, whose passengers the United States dislikes, to land at an American base in a European country, the event did not pass unnoticed in Britain, where the extraterritoriality of American bases already causes unease. A simple test applied to both occurrences exposes their true character: substitute Russian for American in corresponding circumstances, and then enquire how the actions would have been viewed in the United States and in Britain.

It would be all too easy for the United States to be betrayed by the long unchallenged prevalence of the American factor in British policy into taking British acquiescence for granted and presuming too far upon the logic of an American indispensability which events have begun to call in question.

'A SECOND FIDDLE IN THE AMERICAN ORCHESTRA'

Guardian, 1 December 1986

It is now evident in retrospect that in the later 1950s there took place in Whitehall a radical reassessment of Britain's future place in the world. The Suez fiasco, though not the sole occasion of that reassessment, can conveniently be taken as its starting-point. It has conditioned the major decisions made by British governments during the intervening thirty years and it provides the explanation for much that otherwise would remain unintelligible.

The reassessment was based on two perceptions. First, Britain as such would have no worldwide role: the wind of change would blow away her remaining colonies, dependencies and positions, and she would be effectively reduced to the British Isles. Secondly, Britain would be dependent for her defence upon the shield, including the nuclear shield of the United States. From these two perceptions were drawn certain axioms, the most important of which was that henceforth British policy must be subservient to that of the United States and Britain's remaining power and influence would be whatever impression it could exert upon the United States. Harold Macmillan, the high-priest of the new religion, loved to give a classical garb to this axiom by identifying America with imperial Rome and Britain with the powerless and decadent but still subtle Greeks of the Hellenistic Age.

It was in 1957 that British defence went nuclear. Abolition of conscription and drastic reduction of expenditure on defence were based upon the cornerstone of the American nuclear deterrent, all the more indispensable now that the Russians too had broken into space and into nuclear technology. With acceptance of physical reliance upon America went another surrender. Britain, hitherto supreme in the field of intelligence gathering, threw its resources into the pool of the United States and accepted virtual dependence upon America.

Thus Britain became, conceptually and morally, a satellite of the United States. The first humiliating fruits of that status were reaped in 1962, when two things happened. The cancellation of American Skybolt, as a replacement for British Blue Streak, revealed our dependence and vulnerability in all their nakedness. Almost simultaneously de Gaulle made a monkey of Macmillan by repelling him from the doorstep of the European Community, to which we were asking to be admitted.

The United States has never been satisfied with the untidy independence of its ragbag of military allies in Europe and postulates political unity as the precondition of strategic reliability. Its British satellite had therefore no business to stand aside from absorption into a European political union, to which the twin conceptions of a Britain which had lost an empire and was looking for a role and a Britain dependent henceforth upon American approval would fit snugly. European union and strategic subservience to the United States are the postulates which for the last thirty years Whitehall has imposed with more or less brutality upon successive Governments. From that time to this no Foreign Secretary, no Prime Minister even, has dared to deviate, whatever their private predispositions or their party political commitments. The British score is written out for the second fiddle, and anyone looking over the shoulder of the violinist can observe how obediently the score has been played.

Ireland, for example. From 1919 onwards Whitehall had always been set upon bringing an all-Ireland state into existence; but until the 1950s the motivation was British. Britain after the First World War needed, or thought that she needed, a Commonwealth of nations. Ireland, Britain's oldest dominion, would not be fitted into that structure except upon condition of a state embracing the whole island. Nevertheless, though Churchill would have sold Ulster to de Valera in 1939 for common defence against Germany, the reality of Ulster's separateness was always too plain to be ignored.

With the great reassessment of the late 1950s came a fundamental change. America's purpose was an Ireland in the American alliance: NATO needed Ireland not only to close what strategists called 'the yawning gap' but to afford surveillance and defensive facilities vital to command of the Atlantic. Britain was given its orders: get Ulster out of the UK into an all-Ireland state. Britain believed it had no choice but to comply, and Whitehall set to work to find the line of least resistance by organising a gradual and colourable consensual handover. Brookeborough's successor, Terence O'Neill, received his initiation: 'Look here, this is what the USA and the UK are going to bring about, whether you like it or not. Are you statesman enough to come quietly?' Even so, O'Neill's gambit with Sean Lemass was suspicious enough to cause his downfall. The next intended statesman, Brian Faulkner by name, was more roughly handled – by then HMG had the Army in Ulster – but he proved compliant enough for the patented model to be erected on the cleared site of the old

Stormont Parliament and Government: a manageable assembly, an executive with republican members as of right, and a Council of Ireland ready to embrace its new partner.

That too was seen through. That too collapsed. The operators decided not to push things so fast again the next time round. In the confused politics of the province the search was now on for somebody who could deliver where O'Neill and Faulkner had failed: Puzzle Find the Traitor was the name of the game. The Northern Ireland office has groomed a whole line-up of candidates, none of them any good so far. By 1979, when Britain's pro-American party, the Conservatives, returned to power, the United States was becoming impatient. Mrs Thatcher was tipped the black spot; and a timetabled programme was set up entitled 'A United Ireland in Ten Years'. The year 1982 saw the assembly in place again, and a taker for the bribe to lead Ulster into a confederal Ireland was being desperately but unsuccessfully sought. The bait was tempting but too dangerous as long as the Ulster Unionist leadership kept uncorruptible watch and ward.

The Americans were not amused, especially as the Government of the Irish Republic was threatening to disclose and thus undermine the facilities which NATO intelligence and surveillance enjoys in its territory. Things had to be brought to a head; and brought to a head they were in 1985, with an international agreement by which the UK, acting under American pressure, formally granted the Republic rights within Northern Ireland as an instalment of what one Northern Ireland Office Minister once too candidly described to me as 'the re-unification exercise'.

So far, so good – there was rubbing of hands and shelling out of dollars after Hillsborough – but still not good enough. The contraption of a devolved set-up in Ulster had been built into the Agreement like the second stage of a rocket; and the hunt for the traitor who would undertake to deliver goes feverishly on. The timetable is slipping again. By spring 1987 there should be a new assembly in existence. By now therefore there ought already to be talks about 'political progress', which is the codename of the operation. A note of hysteria is beginning to be heard. John Hume wants talks; the *Belfast Telegraph* wants talks; bishops and moderators and what not want talks; HM Ambassador in Dublin wants talks.

What a bad moment for the Irish engine to stall, just when the scales are starting to drop from the eyes of the British public after thirty years and cracks are appearing in the axioms that have held sway so long. American goings-on in Central America were not too savoury perhaps; but after all that is America's backyard, is it not? What sort of show is it however when President Reagan is caught double-crossing his closest allies? What are the stakes for which officials and ministers on this side of the Atlantic as well as the other practise 'economy of truth' to their own people? When a Prime Minister frames a member of her own Cabinet and then employs the Cabinet Secretary to wangle her into the clear, what kind of games are being played in secret under cover of confidentiality and the national interest?

The sleeping dog of British opinion has got one eye open and one ear cocked. Presently it will get up, yawn, stretch and set about wondering whether after all, and why, it is so essential for the United Kingdom to comply with every fantasy of the United States that it must perjure itself and betray its own people in the process.

TO THE ANNUAL GENERAL MEETING OF THE SOUTH DOWN UNIONIST ASSOCIATION

Newcastle, Co. Down, 26 January 1990

What is the connection between Northern Ireland and Panama? It sounds like one of those bad riddles out of a Christmas cracker. In fact it is a sober and practical enquiry.

When the United States recently invaded Panama, a sovereign independent state, with the object amongst others of kidnapping one of its citizens, the world was aghast at so blatant an act of aggression and of contempt for international law. But astonishment followed astonishment. Hardly had the first bulletins been broadcast, when the Prime Minister of the United Kingdom made haste to heap praise upon the United States and its President and to assure them of Britain's support and approval. This is the same Britain and the same Prime Minister who, when a similar act of aggression was committed by the Argentine against the Falkland Islands, despatched a military expedition to the South Atlantic and took them back.

So why did the Prime Minister have to pipe up all alone and cheer President Bush on? There is no doubt about the answer. She considered the interest of Britain to be served by doing so. That is a warning to you and me, and a warning to the people of Ulster. Four years ago, defending herself in the House of Commons for having allowed the United States to use bases in Britain for an act of aggression against Libya, she said: 'The United States is our greatest ally. . . . In defence of liberty, our liberty as well as its own, the United States maintains in Europe 330,000 servicemen. That is more than the whole of Britain's regular forces.'

Some of us had been thinking that the events of the last two years must have altered that perspective by now. We had supposed that even the Americans could no longer believe it. We had allowed ourselves to imagine that the supreme guideline of English statecraft was no longer: 'do what the Americans tell you'. We were wrong. Her Majesty's Government had seen nothing, heard nothing, learnt nothing. So we in Northern Ireland must grin and bear it, and go on holding our ground as if nothing had altered. The American thumb is still on the buzzer. The British Government is still in the business of obeying the demand of the United States that Ulster be handed over to an all-Ireland state as the price at which (allegedly) Irish neutrality can be bought out and the whole island of Ireland drawn into NATO.

If the Prime Minister has to kowtow, why be surprised at Peter Brooke, why be surprised at the Northern Ireland Office? Well, you should never be surprised at the Northern Ireland Office. They exist for nothing else but to sell out Northern Ireland: it is their job in life, and has been so since they were created. They really ought to be called the Belfast Tramway Company. They have one battered old tram, derailed in 1974, which never ran and never will; but over and over again they try to hoist it back on to the rails, so that the Americans can see and be told that they are 'making progress'.

If we imagined they would give up now, we were mistaken. The Secretary of State knows as well as you or I that his Bangor initiative is not a starter. The Prime Minister knows – she told Jim Molyneaux and Ian Paisley as much to their faces – that it is not a starter. So why is the Northern Ireland Office trying it on again?

There is an answer to that, too. They are absolutely desperate to crank up their old bribery and corruption machine and get it working again before too late. One can almost sympathise with them. There are the Americans, losing interest by the week in NATO, the Eastern Atlantic and all its works. There is the Anglo-Irish Agreement, with the devolution trap built into it and the piece of cheese on the trigger going stale. There is the Irish Republic, sick to death of the whole operation and dying to find a way out of a responsibility for something they call 'the North', which causes them nothing but impotent embarrassment. There are the Unionists, immovable as a rock, explaining that part of the United Kingdom Ulster intends to stay and to be treated like any other part. Well, I ask you, if *you* were the NIO and *your* entire career consisted of getting rid of Northern Ireland, wouldn't *you* be desperate? And wouldn't you give thanks to God for a Secretary of State pliable enough to trot out your old rigmarole just one time more?

I hope I have not been exhibiting unseemly jocularity. There is a serious point to it all – Panama, the Belfast Tramway Company and the rest. The moral is that when your enemy is desperate, you have him licked: don't give him an inch, stand your ground, don't let him catch you off your guard when he is nearly beaten.

THE CONSERVATIVE PARTY

POWELL: Oh, no, no, no. I'm firmly in the framework of the Tory Party. I'm a Tory – I prefer that to Conservative – I'm a Tory for keeps.

'This Week: the World of Enoch Powell',
Rediffusion TV, 4 July 1968

The trouble about the Conservative Party is that nobody can still suppose there will be any resemblance between what they say before an election and what they do afterwards if they win it.

Daily Mail, 4 October 1976

'INFLUENCES THAT SHAPE PARTY PROGRAMMES'

Birmingham Post, 26 October 1950

The study of politics resembles the study of natural history much more than most people imagine. The policy of a political party, the way it changes and develops, is not unlike the evolution of a species. The processes are just as complex and just as difficult to trace and explain.

In theory the policy of the Socialist Party is laid down by their party conference. In theory the policy of the Tory Party is laid down by their leader. But these are only theories – however significant each may be for the mentality of the respective parties. The reality is different.

The 300 Socialists or Tories in Parliament are each a wide selection of human beings, so diverse that they might have been deliberately picked for their variety. The range of ideas and aims within each of these groups is naturally enormous, though obviously there are certain broad, very broad, principles – or should I say prejudices? – common to all the members of each group. This variety is more than reproduced in the millions of electors who voted Tory (or Socialist, as the case may be) last February and sent those 300 to Parliament.

These great masses of human beings which we call parties are themselves not stationary in a vacuum. They are marching on through time, living, suffering, learning, thinking, against the background of an ever-changing environment. Just as rays of the sun are focused through a lens to a single point, so from time to time all the elements of these complex and ever varying masses of thought and feeling are focused in a point which we call a party policy. The 'rays' pass first through the medium of the two parties in Parliament and then through the executive (however named) of each party, till they issue as *The Right Road* or *Labour Believes*.

The physical process of the burning-glass is a simple one. The focusing of political thought and feeling is infinitely complicated and gradual, but all the more fascinating to study. How best, then, study it and understand what is going on? Neither, I suggest, at one extreme – in the electorate at large – nor at the other – in the ultimate focus of the official policy. If you look at the electorate, you have to rely on the over-simplified direct questions of the Gallup poll. If you wait for official policies, you find them cold, cautious, impersonal and once again over-simplified.

The best place to stand is where you can watch the parliamentary parties – at the Tattenham Corner of politics. There the strands of thought which are spun from the mass of the electorate and will eventually be twisted into the single cord of official policy are still separately visible.

Herein lies the chief interest and value of those unofficial policies ('unauthorised programmes' Joseph Chamberlain would have called them) which come from time to time from small groups of MPs within parties. Such was the 'Keep Left' group in the Labour Party, or the 'Tory Reform' group in the wartime Parliament. *One Nation*, published a month ago by nine Tory MPs of whom I was one, is a document of the same kind.

We nine are in no sense a 'cave' of Adullamites nor a 'Fourth Party', but loyal rank-and-filers of the Tory benches. Lecturer, metallurgist, chemist, banker, solicitor, journalist, scholar, advertiser – beyond being all Tory, all university graduates (five Cambridge, four Oxford), all middle-aged (between thirty-three and forty-eight) and all in our first Parliament, it would be difficult to find more than one characteristic which we have in common. But that is the one which brought us together. It is the belief that true Tory social policy is not a pale version, nor even an improved version of Socialist policy or Liberal policy, but fundamentally different. Our book is an attempt to illustrate that fundamental difference in working practice.

The Socialist aims at equality (sometimes disguised as equality of opportunity) and sets no limit to the sphere of government. He therefore uses the social services as a deliberate means of equalisation and fearlessly entrusts to the state the responsibility for fulfilling all the individual's needs. The Tory believes that inequality is not only natural and inevitable, but within the framework of a sound society is of infinite value. He sets definite limits to the sphere of government and the responsibilities of the state, and would preserve and strengthen those of the individual and the family.

The touchstone of all policy is in the application. Which of these opposing theories, applied to our society, will give the better life not merely to some – for the nation is 'one nation' – but to all?

We have set ourselves to show that in health, in relief, in education, in housing, in the countryside, the *avoidable* evils of the present can be traced to the Socialist theory of the nation, and would be remedied by a policy based on the Tory theory. We argue, for instance, that Socialist 'fair shares' in housing have in practice meant fewer houses and worse conditions all round, and that real housing need would be better catered for if those who could help themselves were allowed to do so. It is of the essence of our view that the social services can and must be paid for without impoverishing the nation or penalising the individual thrift and effort upon which all prosperity ultimately depends. That is why our book includes a specimen calculation of the financing of a Tory social policy.

In writing our book, for which all take responsibility for all parts, we had many a hot debate with one another. As in all parties, so even in our little group there was a right wing and a left – 'no names, no pack-drill'. But whether we are out on a limb by ourselves or have given voice to a definite body of opinion in the party and the electorate, and if so, how large that body of opinion is, remains to be seen in the coming months.

At the Blackpool conference, *One Nation*, being unofficial, could not officially be discussed. But the Conservative Party possesses in its political education movement, called the CPC (Conservative Political Centre), an instrument of unofficial discussion; and *One Nation* has been adopted as one of its texts for the coming winter sessions throughout the country. Here in Birmingham, next Saturday, at a CPC conference, the chairman of the One Nation Group, Iain Macleod, MP for Enfield West, and another of its members, will be standing up to be shot at, and an outside (though we hope not entirely hostile) critic has been called in the person of Dr Charles Hill, MP for Luton, the 'Radio Doctor'.

One Nation, and the discussion of it, will be one factor, important or unimportant as may be, among the many which will form the Conservative policy of 1951 and the years after. Democracy is not restricted only, nor perhaps even chiefly, to the ballot-box. Public opinion inspires, shapes and dictates the very issues upon which it also decides.

'THIS WEEK: THE WORLD OF ENOCH POWELL'

Rediffusion TV, 4 July 1968

ALASTAIR BURNET: You do not regard yourself as challenging for his leadership?

ENOCH POWELL: Of course not. I've said and I've set my hand to it that I not only believe he will be Prime Minister but that I will support him.

BURNET: Do you represent a stratum in British life which is so dissatisfied with existing parties and institutions and would you like to lead that stratum into some other kind of constitution and some other kind of political life?

POWELL: Oh, no, no, no. I'm firmly in the framework of the Tory Party. I'm a Tory – I prefer that to Conservative – I'm a Tory for keeps. And I can only imagine political activity within the framework of this political party to which I belong, and I must say at the expense of being accused of being a Conservative with a small c, in the framework of the House of Commons roughly as I know it. You talked about earlier the attraction of the possibility of one day occupying a foremost position. Do you know, I believe there's an even greater attraction to many men in English politics, and that's being members of the House of Commons. And I'll tell you an experience I've had – you've referred to two or three of the occasions, when I wasn't in. The same things happened to me on every one of them and on one or two more that you didn't mention. But on the first occasion afterwards of going back into the House of Commons I've had an overwhelming sensation of warmth and comfort and what a wonderful thing it is to be here. And I remember just in April this year when I slipped into my place on the fourth bench above the gangway through the back door out of the Lobby in the first debate after Easter. I hadn't sat down for thirty seconds before I was looking round and thinking, by Jove, this is a wonderful place to be, how could one ever not be here? So within the framework of the constitution above all of the House of Commons, of government by debate, for that is what I believe is the essence of our government, and within the framework of the Tory Party which I love. Yes.

BURNET: You did not make your speech on race relations to the House of Commons, you chose a platform far away from it.

POWELL: Well, it's not usual for members of the Shadow Cabinet to make speeches in the House on subjects other than their own subject. So obviously, except on one's own subject which is defence, speeches on other subjects are made by all front-benchers of necessity in the country. After all, I suppose we make, all of us, what? five, ten speeches, more than that, fifteen, twenty speeches in the country to one in the House of Commons. And it was a very natural thing, the weekend before the House of Commons was going to resume for a division on a three-line Whip, four speakers, not only me, many other speakers, to explain why this was going to be and why it was right.

BURNET: To make a speech which had you thrown out of the Shadow Cabinet.

POWELL: To make a speech on that subject.

'VOTE TORY', ELECTION ADDRESS

Wolverhampton, 16 June 1970

For twenty years a majority of the people of this constituency have given to me the most precious privilege that a man can seek in a free country, the opportunity to be heard; to be heard in Parliament, but also, because of the unique nature and prestige of Parliament, to be heard outside. In recent years the voice which you have given me has carried further and further, until, without office or any other position or assistance except what you gave me, I have been able to be heard by my fellow countrymen from one end of the country to the other, and the response and echo has returned to me from hundreds of thousands of homes.

Tonight I mean to use that voice to say one thing and one thing only; but it is the one thing which most concerns the future of this nation and the well-being, not merely material, of all its inhabitants. In forty-eight hours they have one word to say, 'Yea' or 'Nay'; but in that word and its consequences are embraced all that they would wish for their tomorrow. There is, it seems to me, too great a danger that the gravity and (in some respects) the finality of that decision may not everywhere be realised, and that indifference or heedlessness or distraction could obscure it. We must regain, before the die is cast, the view of those great simplicities in the light of which the nation's decision ought to be taken.

In saying to you, and through you to the country: 'Vote, and vote Tory', I have at least one accidental advantage. It is not such as anyone would go looking for; but having it, I claim the right to use it. I have no personal gain to expect from the outcome, other than that of any other citizen. I am not among those candidates at this election who can look forward with assurance, or at least with hope, to retaining or to achieving political office under the Crown according as the result of the election inclines one way or the other. Whatever might have been obscure or undefined about the policies of the Conservative Party, this at least has been made crystal clear, over and over again, by the leader of the party, that if there is a Conservative Government after Thursday, I shall not be a member of it. The place to which I ask the electors of Wolverhampton South West to return me is that place, somewhere about the middle of the third bench above the gangway, which I have customarily occupied during more than half my twenty years in Parliament. The most I can hope is to be sitting there again – on one side of the House or the other. Nor have I received in the recent past from men who will form a Conservative Cabinet even the ordinary loyalties and courtesies that prevail generally between colleagues in the same cause. Not for them to repudiate attacks upon me which were unfounded, and which they knew to be unfounded. Not for them to place upon my words and arguments the more favourable, or the most obvious, construction, or even to accept my own assertion of my own meaning. Not for them to protest when in the House of Commons language has been used about me, and insults have been cast, the obscenity of which has lowered the dignity of Parliament itself.

No wonder that, by word and letter, from all parts of the country, a tide, which rose and fell but never ceased, of encouragement and reassurance has flowed in to me from strangers, from the general public, from the ordinary people of this country; for the instinct of fairness is one of the deep and characteristic instincts of this nation. No wonder that when this election came, electors have been writing to me, and have been saying to Conservative candidates in the constituencies, that they would not be voting Conservative 'because Enoch Powell would not be in a Conservative Government' or 'because of the way Enoch Powell has been treated'.

It is precisely because of all this that I claim the right at this moment to say to these people; to say to all those who, silently or vocally, have approved and supported what I have had to say and do in my public life; to say, indeed, to the whole electorate: 'Don't be fooled; don't fool yourselves, and don't let anyone else fool you. This election is not about me, not about Enoch Powell, not about any other named variety. This election is about you and your future and your children's future and your country's future.' Not surprisingly, considering the level of triviality at which most of this election has been spent, a great part of the electorate have been drugged into supposing that it is no more than a presidential contest of personalities, and that they are just being invited to decide if they prefer the country and the economy, which will be much the same anyhow, to be presided over by a man with a pipe or a man with a boat. But this is not a presidential election. This is not a pop contest. This is a decision not between two individuals but between two futures for Britain, futures irrevocably, irreversibly different.

If a socialist majority is returned on Thursday, then before another three or four years are over, the ownership and control of the state will have been extended, by one means or another, over the greater part of British industry and business. Even in the outgoing months of the old Parliament, even during the very election campaign itself, public money has been used to buy ownership and control in one major industry after another: in machine tools, in Rolls-Royce, in Cammell Laird, in British Leyland, in the exploration and exploitation of petroleum in the seas around these islands after private enterprise and risk had first revealed and brought to use that unexpected asset.

Anyone who supposes this 'take-over' will stop must be deaf and blind. Give this Socialist Government the opportunity, and the process will be speeded up and pushed forward with a ruthlessness that will accelerate as the parts of British industry where the bureaucrat does not yet have the upper hand diminish. The point is eventually reached when the remaining elements of free enterprise, realising that they are in the power of the state-controlled undertakings from which they buy and to which they sell, give up the unequal struggle and succumb. This is what socialism is about. This is the 'capture of the commanding heights' in the old-fashioned language of the pioneers. This is what another three or four years of Labour Government is intended to accomplish.

Another process will be going on at the same time. The young, the enterprising, the independent in mind and spirit, will be able to read the signs. In increasing numbers they will conclude that a socialist Britain is no place in which to lead their own lives, to bring up their children, and to foresee their descendants' future. At this moment about 130,000 British-born men, women and children emigrate yearly from this country. I would be guilty of my besetting fault of understatement if I described that as 'a trickle'; but however you care to describe it, the flow would broaden into a flood as more people saw the writing on the wall and understood what their future would be in a socialist Britain.

I am not just talking about freedom and enterprise in economic terms. I am talking also of individual liberty. Already in the last four years socialism has been forming up to withdraw the fundamental freedoms of personal and family decision; for it is not only the economy but society itself that these men intend to bring under the power and management of the state. In another four years who dare be sure that parents will be allowed to choose and to buy the education for their children that they think best? to choose and to buy the care in health and in sickness that they think best? to make provision and to save in the manner that they think best for their retirement and their families? All these freedoms have already been under attack in the Parliament which is ended. In the new Parliament, if it contains a socialist majority, the assault will be carried forward. I say again that there is a point where the best of the nation in all walks of life would give up the unequal struggle and either acquiesce in the managed uniformity of a socialist state or go where they will be free.

Listen, then; for there comes a time when it is too late to listen. On Thursday let none delude you that you are choosing between individuals, or that the questions you decide will come up again in the same form, the same circumstances, a few years ahead, should you dislike the outcome now. On Thursday your vote is about a Britain that, with all its faults and failings, is still free, and great because it is free. On Thursday your vote decides whether that freedom shall survive or not. You dare not entrust it to any Government but a Conservative Government.

'VOTE LABOUR', ELECTION ADDRESS

Birmingham, 23 February 1974

Not being a candidate in the present election, I have not thought it proper to put forward once again my views on the immediate circumstances in which the election was called or the issues on which those who called it hoped that the outcome would exclusively turn. I will only observe that nothing has transpired in the last fifteen days to rescue from the charge of fraud an appeal to the public in terms of 'who governs the country?', when neither the law has been broken nor the lawful administration defied and when the Government's embarrassments are the direct consequence of policies adopted in contravention of its own philosophy and promises.

I do not see however why my self-denying ordinance need extend to a subject which the Conservative Party is endeavouring to withhold from the electorate as sedulously at this election as it did in 1970. I feel the less inhibited because it is a subject which I have made no secret of believing to be of overriding importance for the future of the British Parliament and people. At the last general election I left my own electors in no doubt where I personally stood on the issue of Britain and the EEC. During the Parliament just ended I devoted to it more of my attention, inside the House of Commons and outside, in this country and on the continent, than to all others put together. It is for me supremely that kind of question on which, if there be a conflict between the call of country and that of party, the call of country must come first.

Curiously, it so happens that the question 'Who governs Britain?' which at the moment is being frivolously posed, might be taken, in real earnest, as the title of what I have to say.

This the first and last election at which the British people will be given the opportunity to decide whether their country is to remain a democratic nation, governed by the will of its own electorate expressed in its own Parliament, or whether it will become one province in a new European superstate under institutions which know nothing of the political rights and liberties that we have so long taken for granted. Eighteen months ago at the Paris summit conference this country was committed by the Prime Minister to 'economic and monetary union by 1980' with the rest of the European Economic Community. That means that, so far as this Conservative Government is concerned, the lifetime of the next Parliament will see the governance of Britain, throughout the whole range of monetary and economic affairs, transferred from Whitehall and Westminster to European authorities, whose decisions will take uniform effect throughout the territory of the present nine states. If 'economic and monetary union by 1980' means anything at all, that is what it means. There can be no doubt or quibble.

In fulfilling this commitment to 'economic and monetary union by 1980', not the slightest regard will be had to the House of Commons or to the wishes of the electorate.

The House of Commons was never given a hint that any such commitment was going to be undertaken, nor afterwards was it ever invited to debate or, still less, to approve it. If a commitment so far-reaching was undertaken without even a 'by-your-leave' to the body which it would strip of all economic authority, it is unlikely this Government will be very sensitive to parliamentary opinion in carrying the commitment out.

As for the electorate, the cynical contempt shown for it is more remarkable still. The Conservative Party's manifesto at this election – not the abbreviated one, which contrives to avoid mentioning the Common Market altogether, but the full version – has a passage of 750 words about the EEC. That long passage contains not one sentence with mentions or even suggests that Britain has been committed to European 'economic and monetary union by 1980'.

No one reading the document would suspect any such thing. So here we have the most far-reaching and revolutionary act of policy that can be imagined – and the Conservative Party does not think it necessary to tell the electorate, let alone seek the electorate's approval.

Why do you think this happened? Did somebody in Central Office, caught off balance by the snap election, forget to put that little bit in? Did the Prime Minister himself, in checking the draft manifesto, overlook the omission of his own personal, Parisian exploit? Or was he seized by a sudden impulse of modesty and decided to let others blow his trumpet, if they must, for having promised that by 1980 the British Parliament and people should have relinquished all control over Britain's economy? I must not tempt you to over-exert your imaginations. There is one reason and one reason alone why the most important fact about Britain and the Common Market was suppressed in the Conservative Party's appeal to the electors. It was suppressed because everybody knew that the electors would detest it if they were allowed to know about it. Bad enough that a large majority of the electors are hostile to British membership of the Common Market even as it stands at present. 'For Heaven's sake, Prime Minister,' says Lord Carrington, 'don't tell them what you have committed them to by 1980!' So it was left out. There's 'open government' for you!

We have no reason to be surprised. The whole story of Britain and the Common Market to date has been one long epic of deception.

At the 1970 election the electors were told they were not then being invited to take a decision about Britain and the EEC. Those were the famous deprecatory words, 'our sole commitment is to negotiate: no more, no less'. The electors *were* told, however, what would be the background to the negotiation: the Conservative Party's policies, so the manifesto stated, 'will strengthen Britain so that we can negotiate with the European Community confident in the knowledge that we can stand on our own if the price is too high'. So we had – the electorate was assured in 1970 – the whiphand: this was not to be for us a case of Hobson's choice. No wonder the manifesto went on to declare that 'there is a price we would not be prepared to pay. Only when we negotiate will it be possible to determine whether the balance is a fair one and in the interests of Britain.'

Nobody who read or heard what was said in 1970 could have guessed that the negotiation was to be concerned purely with transition – not with the terms on which we were to be members, but simply with how fast we were to become members – in other words, that our negotiators would accept the Community *in toto* exactly as it stood.

Even so, if any anxiety had crept into the mind of some elector, wondering whether to approve the Conservative 'commitment to negotiate, no more, no less', he would have been fully reassured by Mr Heath's eloquent declaration at the time of the election that British membership would be unthinkable 'without the full-hearted consent of Parliament and people': this overwhelmingly momentous step would be taken – nay, it could be taken – only with correspondingly overwhelming parliamentary and popular enthusiasm. If that assurance had been fulfilled, all would have been well. The Government would have stood on the firm ground that an act which in every one of the other states required an express declaration of electoral opinion would not be taken by Britain, with her much deeper-rooted democratic institutions at stake, unless the people themselves had sanctioned it in the most explicit and unmistakable manner.

As it is, there has been no moment when the keenest enthusiast for British membership could have claimed a bare majority in favour of it among the electorate, however often and however variously opinion has been tested. In Parliament, the House of Commons, having registered a vote of seven to five in favour of the White Paper, found itself faced with the Bill – in both senses of the word 'bill'! The bill or, as the election manifesto had called it, the 'price' turned out to be a comprehensive renunciation by the House of Commons of its control over the laws of the land, over the taxes of the people, and over the policies of the executive.

So great was the repugnance of the House of Commons – and remember: this was a House with a Government majority so subservient as not to waver when reversing one after another of the other policies on which they had all been elected – that the Bill could only be carried by one-figure majorities under the imminent threat of a dissolution. Even then it required the use of the guillotine procedure, which those Paladins of freedom and parliamentary liberties, the so-called Liberal Party, alone enabled the Government to obtain. Never was 'the full-hearted consent of Parliament and people' more conspicuously non-existent than when Britain was hijacked into the EEC.

But this was only to be the start. When the ink was barely dry on the Royal Assent to the Bill, the Prime Minister at the Paris summit of October 1972 proceeded to commit Britain to 'economic and monetary union' – a thing which, during all those previous months of argument and debate, had been treated as a remote and visionary contingency. He did it, as I have said, with not even a resolution or a debate to back it. Full-hearted consent to 'economic and monetary union by 1980' was not even mentioned, let alone sought. And now at a general election in 1974 Mr Heath gives us to understand that Europe is not a subject he wants to talk about; he hopes that, as in 1970, it will not be an issue – then it was only a 'commitment to negotiate', now it is to be a *fait accompli* – and just to avoid any awkward questions, he omits all reference to 'economic and monetary union by 1980' from his manifesto.

This is the party leader who, on the basis of a few defaulting town councillors at Clay Cross and some foolish utterance by a union official, is heard accusing his political opponents of lacking respect for Parliament and the law. It is a savage irony, and not the less so for being unconscious, that these taunts come from the first Prime Minister in three hundred years who entertained, let alone executed, the intention of depriving Parliament of its sole right to make the laws and impose the taxes of this country, and who then, without either electoral or parliamentary authority, took it upon himself to commit this country to economic and monetary unification with eight other nations of Western Europe before the lifetime of the forthcoming Parliament is out.

It is understandable that Mr Heath does not want the electors to take this issue with them into the polling booths. He does not want the British people to decide at the ballot-box the most momentous transformation in their history. He does not think they are to be trusted with anything so important. After all, they might reach the opposite conclusion to himself; and that would never do. The question is: can they now be prevented from taking back into their own hands the decision about their identity and their form of government which truly was theirs all along?

I do not believe they can be prevented: for they are now, at a general election, provided with a clear, definite and practicable alternative, namely, a fundamental renegotiation directed to regain free access to world food markets and recover or retain the powers of Parliament, a renegotiation to be followed in any event by a specific submission of the outcome to the electorate, a renegotiation protected by an immediate moratorium or stop on all further integration of the UK into the Community. This alternative is offered, as such an alternative must be in our parliamentary democracy, by a political party capable of securing a majority in the House of Commons and sustaining a Government.

In the last fortnight many hundreds of people have written to me, nearly always kindly and generously and sometimes movingly, about my decision that I could not seek re-election next Thursday as the Conservative candidate for my old seat in Wolverhampton. A great number of them have included the plea, sometimes almost the demand, that I should stand nevertheless as an independent candidate – a candidate of no party – or that I should manufacture my own party and stand for that. There is here a profound and dangerous misconception, which I want to do my best to dispel, not on my own account but because otherwise a considerable fraction of the electorate could fail of attaining their aim through a misunderstanding.

Politics and parliament in this country are about party. Without party neither responsible government nor responsible democracy is possible. If the electors went to the polls to select 635 good men and true, there would be no correspondence between government and electorate, no means of calling the executive to account, no means of intimating the direction in which public opinion was moving, no means of maintaining intelligent and realistic political debate in the interval between one election and the next. For parliamentary government, as for every other good thing, there is a price to be paid; and that price is party. The elector votes not for a person, but a party; and not for a party in the abstract, but for a party majority in the House of Commons. He is not at liberty, like some electoral Pygmalion, to fashion an eclectic party of his own, with none of the warts and all of the virtues, in order that he may have the luxury of voting for it. He must decide what it is that matters most to him, and then he must help to give a majority to the party which has that to offer.

Sometimes it happens that the thing which matters most will not be available from any party. In that event those who care enough about it can only hope and work to see it eventually find its place among the aims and policies of one party or another. However, at this general election that is not the predicament of the large element of the electorate – how large precisely, no one can say – which finds it impossible, as I do, to accept that Britain can be embodied in a European superstate without her people's willing assent openly given, or that any advantage can compensate for accepting Community membership on terms which deprive this country of its free self-governing institutions.

If that for us is the overriding issue – and how it could be less, I do not understand – then we have a clear national duty to help to decide it in the only way of which parliamentary representation admits. We shall be deceiving ourselves, and running away from what we know to be our country's cause, if we try to find some excuse or subterfuge to sacrifice the greater good for the lesser, or the lasting for the transitory.

'THE DEVIL WAS SICK, THE DEVIL A MONK WOULD BE.'

Daily Mail, 4 October 1976

The trouble about the Conservative Party is that nobody can still suppose there will be any resemblance between what they say before an election and what they do afterwards if they win it. All Governments are from time to time blown by the events of office out of the course on which they set off and on which their supporters look to them to persist; but the systematic inversion by the Heath Government between 1970 and 1974 of every pledge and principle on which it came to power was something of a quite different order. Harold Wilson in comparison could be mistaken for a ramrod.

That is why Thatcher and her colleagues, whatever they say now, can inspire no conviction. It is no help to them that, with the single exception of British (provisional) membership of the EEC, the acts of the administration to which they belonged have already been so demolished that not one stone remains upon another. Gladly would they let all that be forgotten. 'Listen to what we are saying now,' they plead. It is of no avail. The electors remember that these are the same people who said it all before, in the 'glad, confident' days of opposition in the 1960s, and the same people who proceeded to do the opposite as soon almost as they were in office.

If there had been so much as one Cabinet resignation – just one – in all those twists and turns through which Edward Heath led them, there might be some redemption; but there was none. Without exception, whatever happened, they put their cars and their chauffeurs, their salaries and their positions before their principles and promises; and Thatcher, whatever she secretly thought then or openly says now, did no different from the rest. For all the efforts to make her look brand new, she remains irretrievably shop-soiled. She too said it all before 1970 and then turned with the best of them 'when daddy turned'.

Hence the aching void in British politics on the opposite side to socialism – a void where there ought to have been a Conservative Party. Oppose nationalization? Who produced and supported the Industry Bill of 1972, which bequeathed to this Labour Government all the powers they wanted, so that the NEC is only for window-dressing? Cut public expenditure? Restrict money supply? Who was it that created in 1972 an unprecedented Budget deficit with the knowledge and the intention that it would swell the money supply and boost inflation? Promise tight control of immigration? Who was it that came into office six years ago – perhaps would not otherwise have got into office – on the promise of no further large-scale immigration and of assistance for all who wanted to return home? Ridicule price and wage controls and the 'social contract'? Who was it that wooed the TUC for week after week in 1972 and then came forward with the most strict and detailed system of statutory controls (including dividend control) that had ever been thought of in peacetime? No, there is nothing there for any Conservative – for any elector, even – to pin his rational hopes upon.

I will not forget Ulster. Who was it that came into office promising no change in Ulster's status 'without the consent of the Northern Ireland Parliament' and then, less than two years later, wiped that Parliament out of existence in forty-eight hours? Not much there to give confidence to the staunchest allies the Conservative Party ever had!

One trick the Conservative Party firmly believes it has got away with. They are mistaken. Of all their liabilities it is the most damaging. The electors who were told in 1970 that, on the Common Market, the Conservative Party's commitment was 'to negotiate, no less, no more' were deliberately deceived: on no other interpretation do those crucial words make the slightest sense. Having then carried EEC membership through that Parliament thanks only to the Liberals and the guillotine, and having opposed and scoffed at Lord Home's favourite device of a referendum, the Conservative Party now tells the electorate that the matter is settled for good and that the sooner our 'obsolete' nation is fully merged in the new European state the better. I repeat: they are mistaken. The old adage that 'the Conservatice Party is a national party or it is nothing' is as true as ever. A Conservative Party which denies the nation itself and wants nothing better for this country than to be a European province is already nothing.

What is wrong with the Conservative Party today is that it is morally bankrupt. Alas, there is no IMF to which they can resort for a loan to replace the credibility which the Heath Government squandered. That can only be won back, if at all, through the years – and by men and women not tainted by the guilt of 1970 to 1974.

'OFFICE BEFORE HONOUR'

The Spectator, 15 October 1977

I was (I confess it) one of those who, in the far-off days on either side of 1960, accused Harold Macmillan of having 'debauched' the Conservative Party. We meant that he had cunningly nudged it towards vote-buying by inflation and had inoculated it with mild strains of socialist virus, such as life peerages, 'indicative' economic planning, Concorde, consumer subsidies, etc. Mercifully the future at that time veiled from our vision the wholesale rape that was to be perpetrated by Edward Heath between 1972 and 1974 on a submissive Cabinet and a prostrate Conservative Party.

In the space of those two years the Chief Whip turned Prime Minister forced them to trample on every promise and principle on which they had been elected.

The party which proclaimed on entering office that it 'utterly rejected the philosophy of compulsory wage control' introduced – and destroyed itself in the attempt to enforce – a more comprehensive system of compulsory wage and price control than was ever imagined before or after. The party which had repudiated the control and absorption of industry by the state put on to the statute book an industry Act which rendered subsequent socialist legislation so superfluous that Labour's National Enterprise Board was little more than perfunctory window-dressing. The party which promised the electors – and would not have won the election without doing so – that it would put an end to large-scale immigration and promote repatriation presided over a continuing inflow little below the peak of the late 1960s. The party which assured Ulster there would be no charge in its status without the consent of its Parliament, made a mockery of the promise by destroying the Parliament itself – and that, without the first idea of what was to replace it. Finally, and above all, the party which studiously withheld from the electorate the question of the European Community by the formula of a 'commitment to negotiate, no less, no more', proceeded under two years later to destroy the legislative and fiscal supremacy of the United Kingdom Parliament and the political independence of Britain by a Bill which passed second reading by a majority of eight.

Those whom Edward Heath compelled to be his accomplices in all this knew quite well that they were going back on the essentials of what the party had stood for. Many of them, faintly to their credit, were ashamed of themselves and loathed the draught the Prime Minister was forcing them to swallow. But if they did not exactly 'relax and enjoy it', they submitted. Even among those decorated with the Resistance Medal, John Biffen voted for the price and wage freeze, and Nicholas Ridley was dropped from office before he had got his resignation in. Indeed, there were no resignations – at least, no Cabinet resignations, for I must not be forgetful of one or two who resigned junior or very junior offices over the Common Market, only in order to vote *for* it subsequently along with all the rest. Office before honour was the password of Conservative government.

I do not write these things for recrimination's sake, but because without recalling them it is impossible to understand the predicament of the Conservative Party now and why those who lead it are incapable of resolving that predicament. It is because they are the men and women in 1972 to 1974, the same to a man (or woman) who were 'consenting unto' the reversal and inversion of their own pledges: and now the same troupe of ham actors ask to be given parts next season in a revival. If, when they would fain be thought new Tories, with a fresh-minted gospel of freedom and self-reliance, patriotism and self-confidence, honesty and justice, they carry little conviction, there is no reason for them or anyone else to be surprised.

The opposition of today cannot atone for the Government of 1970 to 1974: they are the same men and women. No forensic skill on the part of the Conservative shadow Chancellor could prevent economic debates from being opposition catastrophes. Having himself, when in office, condemned compulsory wage control one month and introduced it the next, there is no question of policy on wages or inflation which he or the Conservative Party can confidently answer. Whatever they say, their own past words and deeds rise up to refute them. Neither on trade-union law, nor on subsidies, nor on the nationalised industries, nor on state intervention can the opposition turn in any direction without the ghost of its past barring the way.

Their fumblings and contradictions on such subjects arise from a deeper and less remediable cause than incompetence. Their declarations, however forthright, their calls, however clarion, would always echo hollow in the public car. Those who run away once will run away twice. Those who turned at the drop of a hat before and abandoned all that they had said will do the same again. Those who stuck to office in 1972 through every twist and tergiversation will not behave differently another time. Neither the penitential white sheet nor the cardboard coat of shining armour will now disguise the sort of people who are wearing them or restore the faith of a nation in the words of those who broke them before. It simply will not wash.

The conclusion to be drawn from all this is bleak. There are times in the life history of a party, as of a society, when a generation of leaders that has been hopelessly compromised has to disappear and when this necessity is in no way to be avoided. Circumstances can retard or accelerate the process. The Conservative Party of today suffers from the misfortune that no serious kernel of internal opposition survived the regime of 1970 to 1974 and the February debacle. The unexpected can sometimes come to the rescue; but soberly it is hard to see how the Conservative Party's predicament can be resolved without the interposition of another electoral defeat.

THE EEC

Direct elections to the European Assembly, so far from introducing democracy and democratic control, will strengthen the arbitrary and bureaucratic nature of the Community by giving a fallacious garb of elective authority to the exercise of supranational powers by institutions and persons who are – in the literal, but not the abusive, sense of the word – irresponsible.

Public Meeting at The Dome, Brighton, 24 October 1977

ELECTION ADDRESS

Tamworth, 15 June 1970

For many electors this is a most frustrating general election. They find, in a way that perhaps has never happened before, that they cannot use their vote to express their wishes on what seem to them the most important political questions. They can vote as between socialism and private enterprise, more nationalisation or less, and all the rest of that ilk; but on decisions, national decisions, which could be more important still, the electors find themselves confronted with a virtual unanimity between the official parties and often between the respective candidates in their own constituencies. The party system seems no longer to do its work of offering a choice between policies and it is not surprising to hear so many demanding that the parliamentary system itself should be short-circuited, and the people offered the direct opportunity to say Yes or No by referendum.

Of all the subjects on which this demand is heard, and this frustration felt, the most widespread is that of the Common Market, and not surprisingly, for the question of joining the Common Market is the most fundamental of all. It is the question not merely what *sort* of a nation are we to be, but *what* nation are we to be?

I say at once that I am no supporter of a referendum, least of all on this sort of subject. Out of many reasons I mention only two. First, it is inconsistent with the responsibility of Government to Parliament and to the electorate. If, on a subject of this importance, the Government were to propose one course and a referendum choose the other, then, unless the Government promptly resigned, they would be able thereafter to say, whatever happened: 'Well, don't blame us, it is no fault of ours; we wanted to do one thing, but you decided to do the other; so, ladies and gentlemen, you have only yourselves to blame.' The result of that would be, quite literally, irresponsible government.

Secondly, there are many people who believe – though I am not one of them, as I shall presently show – that the decision about Britain entering the Common Market ought to depend on what are called the 'terms' which can be negotiated. Obviously, from this point of view it is not possible to have a decision, yes or no, in advance. On the other hand, once the 'terms' had been negotiated and worked out in detail, then, as with a treaty or any other international instrument, they could not be rejected unless the Government itself were defeated. Only close and continuous debate, in Parliament and the country, during the progress of the negotiations could ensure that the 'terms' which were accepted were such as to satisfy opinion.

However, just because a referendum will not answer, it does not follow that the issue of the Common Market ought to be kept under wraps at a general election. On the contrary, in my opinion it is a duty which the electorate ought to exact from every candidate, to 'come clean' on this question. If his support of entry is unconditional, well and good, let him make that plain and the electors know where they stand. If he believes that the case for or against depends on the conditions, then let him indicate – not of course in detail but in broad outline – what the conditions are on which he would support entry. It is no use just saying: 'We will negotiate and see what terms can be had.' You are entitled to know what sort of terms are in mind, and how they will be judged. Are the terms to do with transitional arrangements, or are they permanent? Are they economic, or are they also political? If they are economic, are they concerned with agriculture or with currency or with taxation, and how high a price, broadly, would be regarded as acceptable?

There is, however, a third category of candidate, whose opposition to entry into the Common Market is unconditional and based on the nature of the Common Market itself: he too ought to declare his position.

This is the right way for public opinion on such a subject to find expression: the electorate ought to know, if they elect a candidate, where he will range himself on this issue. And let no one say that Members are mere lobby-fodder, and that a Government will get its way, no matter. It is only a year or so since, on a subject where public opinion was much less deeply exercised – the future of the second chamber – a major Government measure, to which the official opposition was at worst benevolently neutral, was destroyed by the determined action of private Members on both sides of the House. I would not care to put much money on entry to the Common Market coming about if a substantial minority of Members on the Government side were pledged to oppose it. In any case the maximum ventilation of the whole issue is something to which the Conservative Party is committed. Mr Heath never spoke truer words than when he said that 'the greatest possible mistake would be for the British people to go into this without themselves realising the full implications'.

What the 'full implications' are, becomes clearer on the side of the Economic Community with almost every week that passes. I myself believe that those implications are already firm enough for many people to make up their minds where they stand.

What has emerged with startling rapidity in the recent past is how profoundly political, how far-reaching and how imminent those implications are. Six months ago, I quoted the then head of the EEC Commission when he predicted that the Community would have a common currency and a common Parliament elected on universal suffrage before 1980. Yet even as recently as six months ago, people were inclined to treat such a prediction as the personal pipe-dream of an enthusiast. That is no longer possible. In the last fortnight the countries of the Six have not only adopted the target of a common currency before 1980 but have agreed that as from now 'whatever the International Monetary Fund may decide on greater flexibility for exchange rates, the Six will not accept any widening of the present permitted margins of fluctuation in dealings between their own currencies'. This was rightly described as 'the first step towards creating a common currency'.

I am aware that this may all sound very technical and financial. Indeed, it is not. On the contrary, it affects everyone directly. This election to a large extent is about prices, about wages, about inflation, even about balance of payments. If Britain were a member of a Common Market with a common currency, a British general election would have as little to do with those subjects as the municipal elections, and the British Parliament would have as little control over them as the Staffordshire County Council has today. Money is managed by governments, and the management of money determines wages, prices, employment and the whole economy. What else have we been arguing about for the last three weeks – or the last six years, for that matter? A single currency means a single government, and that single government would be the government whose policies determined every aspect of economic life. In the Common Market that government would not be a British government; it would be a continental government, and the British electorate would be a comparatively small minority of the electorate to which that government was responsible.

Remember, we are not talking about a remote future. We are thinking, let us say, of the next general election but one. At that election, if the Economic Community survives and develops – presumably there is no point in this whole debate unless we assume that will happen – and if Britain is part of the Community, then my fellow candidates and I, even if we are candidates for the European and not the British Parliament, will have a very different tale to tell you. Prices (let us imagine) have been going up by five or six per cent a year, and you the electors are justifiably angry. You want to turn out of office those responsible for this, much as you are going to turn out the present Labour Government later this week. But we, my fellow candidates and I, will say to you: 'Sorry; these are the results of the policy followed by the European Government, which controls the European currency. We have done, and we shall do, our best; but this is how the majority in the Community insist on having it.'

You will agree that it would be a tremendous step for this country to transfer to a unit in which it will be a permanent minority the control of its economic life – from unemployment to taxation, from prices to development policy. Yet even this does not exhaust the 'full implications' of entry into the Common Market. The twin argument which is urged in favour of entry is that, especially with the prospective reduction of American forces and commitment, it would give the countries of Western Europe a defensive capability which mere alliance does not. As the German ex-Minister, Herr Strauss, put it recently, 'Europe must become a political unit with a stronger defence capability'; for the continental politician often does not duck the realities, as too many British politicians do. The condition of a stronger defence capability is a common government, a common government which will decide for the whole of Western Europe how much of its resources are to be applied to defence and how those resources are to be used. Now, we in this country can take different views, as the Labour and Conservative parties do, of the relative priorities of education and defence; we may argue about whether defence should absorb 10 or 7 or 5 per cent of our national income. What I cannot believe is that the people of the United Kingdom ought to submit, or would submit, to these questions being decided, and to themselves being taxed and conscripted – and how can conscription not be involved? – by the government of a political unit in which they were a minority. Even less, if possible, do I believe that they should or would surrender the keys of the ultimate defence of these islands to a sovereign authority of continental character, continental location and continental outlook.

TO THE CROYDON SOUTH YOUNG CONSERVATIVES ANNUAL CONFERENCE

Salisbury, 10 November 1973

The idea is often hawked around that the dummy Parliament of the EEC could be galvanised into real parliamentary life by supplying it with the electric current of direct elections. Anyone who can entertain that proposition for an instant has never understood the first essentials of a free, sovereign Parliament.

Those essentials are power and party, not as separate ingredients but as interdependent.

A representative assembly cannot itself exercise executive power. Even in the tiny city-states of ancient Greece, attempts to combine the executive and the representative functions invariably and speedily foundered. The sovereignty of a representative body consists in its power to checkmate the executive, and the ultimate sovereignty of those represented, of the electorate, consists in turn in their power to change the composition of the body which holds the power to checkmate.

This sovereignty, however – the sovereignty of the assembly, which is ultimately the sovereignty of the electorate – cannot be exercised except by means of party. An assembly which could simply checkmate the executive would speedily reduce government to chaos. There would be nothing to prevent it from taking self-contradictory decisions – for example, by disapproving means while approving ends. There are only two methods of preventing this self-defeating result. One is to render the executive itself directly dependent on the electorate – in other words representative – and endow it with executive power independent (within limits) of the assembly altogether.

This is the method of the American constitution and of the French Fifth Republic. They are not parliamentary constitutions enshrining the supremacy and sovereignty of the representative assembly, but presidential constitutions, where the chief executive is endowed with power direct by popular vote.

The other method is that on which the English – and I mean the

English – stumbled in the seventeenth century, namely, to recruit the executive from the assembly itself, of which the executive remains an integral part. This method, the sole means known to man of maintaining sovereign parliamentary government, necessitates party, for the executive must belong to, and command, a working majority in the assembly, and this cannot just be a chance majority, here today and gone tomorrow, but one sufficiently durable to support a consistent policy. There have been periods, before the enlargement of the franchise, when the self-interest of members of the assembly itself was a sufficient basis for party: they were the days of the borough-mongers, the placemen, the potwallopers and the Secret Service money. Yet even under the most adverse circumstances, the fact that the representative assembly was periodically renewed by those whom it represented ensured that party was more than a synonym for faction or jobbery. The control of the electorate over the elected, the ultimate sovereignty of the people, cannot consist in substituting Mr B for Mr A and Sir Y for Sir X. The control is exercised when B is substituted for A, and Y for X, not as individuals but as members of their respective parties, with known, declared and (subject to the ordinary limitations of scepticism) believed and accepted policies and rules of action.

It is party which ennobles politics. It is also party which enables parliaments to exercise sovereign power. It is party which renders government responsible to Parliament, and Parliament responsible to the people.

The direct election of the assembly of the EEC would neither confer power nor create party. That assembly cannot be a sovereign Parliament unless and until by its vote, derived from the party composition which the electorate has given to it, it can substitute the government of one party for the government of another party. Nothing short of that could make it a real Parliament for nothing short of that could endow it with real power.

The question may be asked: 'But might not this thing be?' To answer that question we must lift our eyes from Parliament to the people whom Parliament represents. An electorate is not an assemblage in a particular geographical area of so-and-so many adults, equipped with ballot papers and pencils. The electorate of a real Parliament must be politically homogeneous, and for a reason of absolute necessity: since a real Parliament implies party government, the electorate underlying a real Parliament must be such as not only to accept party government but to be capable of substituting the government of one party for that of another. In other words, it must have a homogeneity of political loyalty which can effortlessly hold party differences in solution. This is to say more even than the electorate of a true Parliament must be a nation; for there are many undoubted nations in the world, accepting a common sovereignty as against the rest of mankind, which do not possess the homogeneity to sustain parliamentary government.

To transform the assembly of the EEC into a true Parliament and the government of the EEC into parliamentary government, would require more than constitutional reforms, amendments and devices. It would require the transformation of the inhabitants of Western Europe including the British Isles into a single politically homogeneous electorate, sustaining party governments by overall majority, irrespective of the party balance, let alone sectional interest, in any of its parts, however large. Each must form his own judgement of how miraculous such a transformation would be. What is certain is that whoever envisages the EEC in terms of political union without either confidently anticipating that transformation or alternatively renouncing what we in Britain know as parliamentary democracy is misleading himself and helping to mislead others.

SOVEREIGNTY

from *Freedom and Stability in World Economy*, 1976

The word 'sovereignty' has an old-fashioned, imperialistic sort of sound which for many people is repellent and to most is not conducive to clear thinking. It would probably be more enlightening if words such as 'independent' or 'self-governing' were used instead.

One very simple but widespread misunderstanding needs to be cleared out of the way, once for all, at the outset of any discussion of political independence. Independence is not the same as omnipotence. There is no nation in the world, not even Soviet Russia or the United States, which can do whatever it chooses to do: the policy of Soviet Russia has been blocked in the Middle East, and that of America frustrated in South East Asia. Yet nobody would dream of denying that Russia and the United States are independent, self-governing states. Every nation in the world depends both for its defence and for its livelihood upon some degree of intercourse and co-operation with others. This is so, and always has been so, but nobody has ever thought that the fact was inconsistent with the reality of political independence and self-government. This is as true of the pygmies as of the giants. Russia and America believe they need allies and go to great lengths to get and keep them; and the events of recent years and even months has reminded us how dependent they both are on imports, despite their huge size and strength. Switzerland and Iceland are undeniably politically independent and self-governed; yet they depend on trade for their very existence, and upon an external balance of power for their safety.

It is often said that nations have become more interdependent economically than they were in the past. This is probably true, though it is not self-evident; but however true it is, the fact has no relevance to political independence and self-government. When a score of independent nations in Africa were being carved out of the European colonial empire, nobody got up and said that this was nonsense and would have to stop, because the new states would depend on world trade, international investment and maybe mutual defence. It was taken for granted that they would have the wish and the right to govern themselves and to live under their own laws and policies, as separate and independent nations: it occurred to no one to argue that this would be inconsistent with the satisfaction of their needs for trade, investment and defence. It would be amusing to hear the protests, and where they would come from, if such an idea were suggested.

Having established then that economic interpendence and the constraints which the facts of the outside world impose upon any nation's freedom of action have nothing to do with political independence and self-government, it is time to define what independence and self-government are. They are easier to define in the negative. An independent nation is a nation whose laws are made by no one but itself, whose citizens are governed by no government but their own. The existence of self-government does not depend on the *form* of government. Opinions may differ as to whether the Soviet Union or the Republic of Uganda are democracies, and indeed about what democracy is, but they are both indubitably no less self-governed than Switzerland or the United States, because no external authority makes the laws or exercises the government within their territories. However, the principle of democratic government has far-reaching consequences for the extent and limits of the territories and populations that can form a self-governing independent nation.

Before coming to these, I must clear out of the way another prevalent and widely quoted fallacy. This is to assert that whenever a nation enters into a treaty, under which it undertakes to do certain things or abstain from certain other things, it loses to that extent its independence and self-government, its 'sovereignty'; and that therefore, by implication, there is no absolute difference between dependence and independence and a nation which has signed a treaty may as well, so far as the principle goes, sign away its independence altogether.

This is patently absurd. A man who has made a contract to deliver a sack of coals is still a freeman and not a slave. Because he has bound himself, under penalty, to do a specific thing, known in advance, he has not agreed that the man to whom he delivers the coals may order him to do any thing, whatever that may be, lawful or unlawful, whether he likes it or not. A nation which, in its own discretion, promises not to impose tariffs on the goods of another nation remains independent. Not so the nation which relinquishes permanently to another authority the power to take all decisions, whatever they may be, respecting its trade. The essence of the loss of independence is to bind oneself *in advance* to do whatever others may decide. The latter is the nature of the Treaties of Rome and Brussels, which require of the parties not specific performance but compliance 'for an indefinite period' (Rome Treaty) with decisions of the Community which will be binding upon the members. There is no parallel to such a contract in any other sort of treaty. The contract is incompatible with independence and self-government, and it is intended to be so.

It is therefore irrelevant to appeal to the analogy of defence treaties, such as the North Atlantic Treaty, which are not only expressly terminable but are implemented by the sovereign contracting parties, or to Charters, such as that of the United Nations, or Agreements, such as the General Agreement on Tariffs and Trade, to which effect can only be given by the domestic legislatures or the respective governments.

I have referred to decisions by 'others' – to being obliged in advance to comply with decisions taken by others. This raises the fundamental questions: who are 'we'? and therefore who, in relation to 'us', are 'others'?

There has been much use of the metaphor of 'pooling' sovereignty, in aid of the proposition that when sovereignty is 'pooled', it is not lost but enhanced. Partly this is the same fallacy as confusing independence with power. No doubt the Roman Empire was more powerful, in defence or aggression, than the states and nations which were absorbed into it; but this did not alter the fact that those states and nations no longer existed as such – their peoples were none the less for that no longer self-governed, or independent, or sovereign.

Apart from this confusion over independence and power, there is an inherent contradiction in the idea of 'pooling' sovereignty. The self-government of X is lost, if it is governed by XY or by XYZ. The only exception is if XY or XYZ are so constituted that X always prevails over Y and Z, in which case, of course, X is still governed by X, i.e. is still self-governed. It is no objection to say that X may sometimes or often persuade Y and Z to agree with it. So, in a single state such as Britain, may the representatives of a part, such as London or Cornwall, persuade the rest to take their point of view. This does not make London or Cornwall independent or self-governing. Those who admit this sometimes argue that nevertheless X, by agreeing to accept in advance the decisions of XYZ, may be better treated by Y and Z than it otherwise would have been. This may or may not be the case; but it has as little to do with the issue of independence and self-government as the fact that servants or slaves are often well treated has to do with individual freedom. Though XYZ may be formed from a combination of X and Y and Z, it is not the same as any of those three and none of them enjoys independence or possesses sovereignty if it accepts the overriding authority of XYZ: they are governed not by themselves but by 'others'.

So we come back to 'we' and 'they', to the question who is the 'self' about whose self-government we speak, or the 'we' who will fight to the death for 'our' freedom.

The simplest answer is that 'we' are those who all accept one government and no other authority external or additional to it. This is a tautology, an answer in a circle, because there is no *a priori* indication, no objective criterion, of a self-governing people: a visitor from Mars, presented with all the data he might request about the population of Europe, Asia, North America or South America except their political boundaries, would not be able to tell you whether each of these continents contained one self-governing people, or ten, or fifty.

However the definition is by no means so empty as it at first sight appears. I have used the word 'accept' – 'accept one government' – and that verb covers a wide range of meanings. I mentioned the Roman Empire just now. There is no doubt that all its inhabitants accepted Rome's *imperium*, some more willingly, some less so; but no one would consider the Roman Empire a self-governing, independent people. Charles V was the undoubted sovereign of the Netherlands, Burgundy, Austria and Spain; but that did not make the Spaniards and the Austrians into one 'we'. The alchemy lies in a different order of consent from that by which the myriads of the Roman Empire accepted the Eternal City or the subjects of Charles V acknowledged him as duke, king, emperor or whatever. Self-government and independence externally are the counterparts of self-government and free consent internally. Whenever that free consent is expressed, as we can alone imagine it, through representative institutions and responsible government, the outer limits of 'we' are the boundaries of those who will freely accept the decisions of a representative majority.

This is the key to all the discussions about 'nations' which are 'states' and 'nations' which are not 'states': the essence consists in the nature of the consent and the means by which it is secured. The Roman Empire was a state but not a nation. The United Kingdom is a nation, but so long and only to the extent that all significant parts of it consent to the authority of a representative majority. If that consent is withdrawn, for whatever cause, the boundary of the nation is correspondingly redrawn, and sooner or later the boundary of the state must conform. So we arrive at another but more significant tautology; 'we' are those who accept one and the same majority rule through a representative institution and the things about us which make us accept that rule and enable us to accept it are what constitutes our nationhood.

The importance of all this, applied to the European Community, is crucial. Nine 'we's' do not become one 'we' by dint of their governments undertaking the obligations of the Treaty of Rome or the Treaty of Brussels. The facile theory, so often heard earlier, that this would happen by force of habit, from 'working together', is now

---

rarely voiced. The juxtaposition of nine nations under a common authority does not create a new 'we', any more than those dynastic inheritances which made Charles master of half the world. In the absence of a new 'we', self-government, independence, sovereignty are surrendered without anything to take their place except bureaucracy or the irresponsibility of national governments exercising collective authority.

In this quandary a spurious solution is propounded. Since the active consent of self-governing nations is expressed through representative institutions, the idea is proposed that if the Community were provided with a parliament directly elected by the population of the entire Community, the self-government which the member nations have lost would be restored at the higher level. It is of course a fallacy. A representative assembly does not create a self-governing nation. Self-government through a representative assembly depends upon the will of all the component parts to accept majority rule through that assembly; but that is the very essence of the 'we' which is missing. It is the essential starting-point, not the end-product.

Those who seek or offer reassurance by asserting that the countries of the original Common Market, like France or Germany, have not lost, and have no intention of losing, their national identity, are not, as they suppose, proving that a nation can be part of the Community without forfeiting its independence. They are pointing to a very different consequence. If the component peoples in fact do not and will not so identify themselves as one that they are ready to accept self-government through the majority in a representative assembly, that does not mean that they will remain independent: already they are governed and legislated for by the institutions of the Community and on a scale which continually increases. It means that the institutions of government cannot be representative or – if the term is preferred – democratic. It is self-government that is forfeited as well as independence.

This is the sense in which it is true to say that the other countries can be reconciled to membership of the Community with less reluctance and loss than Britain; namely, because in Britain self-government and independence are uniquely identified with the untrammelled authority of a representative assembly, Parliament.

An understanding of the relationship between independence, self-government and self-identification ('we'-ness) is the antidote to the prevalent but unfounded belief that there is some sort of irresistible trend to the amalgamation of nations into larger and larger units, and that we had better resign ourselves therefore to our own share in this trend by surrendering independence and self-government in the European Economic Community.

At its crudest this belief is an example of the *non sequitur* which Bentley once attributed to Boyle: 'because Milo could carry an ox, therefore he could carry a brace of elephants!' Because the United Kingdom has been formed by merging under one sovereignty the component peoples of the British Isles, English, Scots, Welsh, Irish, not to mention the kingdoms of the Saxon heptarchy, therefore a new nation not only can but ought to be formed – and it is in the natural course of things that it should be – by merging the United Kingdom itself with the other nation states of Western Europe. So runs the fallacy. It is not so much that its historical substructure is defective: of all the components of Britain, Scotland at most can in any way be placed in the category of a nation state. The assertion is just a plain *non sequitur*. There is no reason to suppose that because the inhabitants of the British Isles can – or could? – combine to form a self-governing independent nation, therefore the peoples of Western Europe can combine to form one. There is no reason to suppose that because Britain comprises 55 millions and the United States comprises 210 millions, therefore Britain is destined to become part of a 200-million-inhabitant state. There is no reason to suppose that because America is a self-governing democracy, therefore Western Europe can be one or ought to be one.

Below the mere logical error of such ideas lies the deeper misconception of what that 'we'-ness is which makes self-governing independence possible – of how it comes into being and grows, of what are its natural limits, none the less real for not being precise. It cannot be blown up like a balloon, nor extended like a Meccano set, nor does it grow and grow like an amoeba. As Malthus observed, no cabbage is so large that a larger could not be produced, but we all know a cabbage cannot be as big as a house. Nation states are not artefacts, though, significantly, of all the original member states of the Common Market, France alone is not of comparatively recent and enforced creation – another fact which places the forfeiture of self-government and independence in a different perspective as viewed from Brussels and from Britain.

There is, however, no correspondence between the observed facts of the real world and the theory of a general and irreversible trend towards giant states. On the contrary there is a marked divergence. The salient feature of this century both in Europe and in the world at large has been the break-up of former giant states and imperial structures into smaller and sometimes very small self-governing and independent units. Modern Europe itself is the product of this process. The experiment of the dying British colonial empire with quite modest schemes of federation proved an almost total failure, from Africa to the Caribbean. Even under the iron pressure of Russian communist imperialism the separate nation states in their different ways, from Yugoslavia to Romania, have pertinaciously reasserted and maintained themselves.

Paradoxically, everywhere except in Western Europe, and in relation to almost every state except Britain itself, the urge to assert or maintain national self-government and independence is viewed not merely with toleration but approval. Scotland and Ireland in the British Isles can count on widespread, if ignorant, sympathy for such aspirations. It was not the mere desire to see the Warsaw Pact dented which imprinted Hungary and Czechoslovakia in 1956 and 1968 upon Western consciences. As for Africa and Asia, I have observed already that there is no limit to the fissiparous states that are sure of a welcome to the ever-widening ranks of the United Nations. By a cruel irony the people of one of the oldest nation states in the world, who themselves have played the liberators to so many other nations, are berated for the anachronism of desiring to retain their parliamentary self-governing independence.

In the end, the issue of sovereignty is not a matter of argument. Misunderstanding and fallacies can be disposed of, but finally it is the will and determination of a people to be independent and self-governed which, now as ever, is the only proof that they ought to be so or that they deserve to be so. That is the reason why, in this matter, the instinct and judgement of one citizen is worth as much as that of another.

PUBLIC MEETING AT THE DOME

Brighton, 24 October 1977

The impending battle in the coming session to prevent the direct election of representatives from this country to the Assembly of the EEC will be the most significant since the referendum. I would be prepared to go further and say that it will be the most significant since the great parliamentary struggle of 1972, in which the House of Commons by a margin of votes that could be counted on two hands consented to surrender its authority to an external institution and thus to abrogate the political independence and self-government of Britain itself. If anyone thinks I exaggerate – not that I ever exaggerate – he has only to listen to the alarm and anger being expressed on the Continent at the mere idea that the House of Commons might jib at creating a master over it in its own image. They know, and do not conceal their knowledge, that, once provide it with a directly elected Parliament, and the permanence of the new West European state will be entrenched and its evolution guaranteed. Denied that asset, they understand that its reversion to a mere manifestation of the 'Europe of Nations' must sooner or later occur. A battle which your enemy thinks will be decisive is a decisive battle.

As on all occasions when a nation is to be brought to renounce its independence, the most effective resource of the aggressors – far more effective than force – is deception. The deception in turn is most effective when it can be attached to a familiar and favourite notion. The British are deeply attached to representative institutions; they have a strong affection for elective government. Their directly elected Parliament – is it not the creative achievement of a thousand years of their history? Tell them that they are only being advised to apply and enlarge that achievement – to carry into the European community the very mechanism which they have been taught to regard as the guarantee of their individual and national rights – and you will have the best chance that they may listen to the voice of the tempter and leap before they look. That is the deceitful suggestion that a thousand glozing voices and columns – not all of them by any means unmotivated by self-interest – will be pouring into the public ear during the coming months. It is essential that the public be forewarned and forearmed against this trick, so that whenever in the coming months the sleight-of-hand of equating direct elections to the European Assembly with democracy is attempted it will be recognised for what it is.

Direct elections to the European Assembly are not democracy; they are the opposite of democracy. Direct elections to the European Assembly are not an extension of parliamentary self-government; they are the negation of parliamentary self-government. Direct elections to the European Assembly are not representation of the people; they are a denial of representation.

Something much more is involved here than the simple fact, important though it is, that the elected representatives of the United Kingdom would be in a permanent small minority – a minority that would become smaller still after the addition of elected representatives from Portugal, Spain and Greece, if the present pantomine goes on. The contrast between being a permanent minority in the existing Assembly of delegates from national parliaments and being a permanent minority in a directly elected Assembly is as great as the contrast between light and dark. As long as the Assembly consists of delegates, the ultimate authority remains with the national Parliaments and with the national Governments as members of the Council of Ministers. A majority vote in the Assembly of delegates has little significance. Once, however, the Assembly is directly elected, that position is totally changed. What appeal can there be beyond the representatives of the peoples, directly elected for that very purpose? The very fact of direct election implies the validity and binding nature of a majority: this is the meaning of directly elected assemblies the world over. From that moment the Council of Ministers and the national veto – so far as that actually exists – lose their logic; for their authority is then no greater than that of the national, or local, Parliaments, whose representative function in respect of European matters has been superseded by that of the directly elected European MPs.

So one effect of direct election must be to put the UK in a permanent minority in a body designed in its very nature to exercise decisive authority by majority decision. It is no answer to say that the same would apply to every other nation in the Community. Our responsibility is for our own future and our own democracy. It would be a novel argument to inform the British that because other nations were – actually or allegedly – willing to relinquish their national independence and self-government, we need no longer bother about ours. I wonder where that argument would have taken us in the past?

However, I return to the quite separate and fundamental fact that direct representation in the European Assembly would be neither parliamentary nor democratic in any sense in which we understand those terms in Britain, so that to use them to commend European direct elections is the most dangerous deception, whether those who do so are unscrupulous or merely unreflecting. The essence of parliamentary democracy as our constitution enshrines it is to render the executive and the legislature amenable to the people, through the answerability of each elected representative to his electors and their periodic opportunity to elect someone else. This whole process is dependent upon one indispensable ingredient. That ingredient is party – party programme, party membership, party whip, party government. Without party the electorate choosing between John Doe and Richard Roe would be choosing between a thin man with fair hair and a fat man with dark hair: they would exercise no voice in the manner of their government and possess no sanction over the non-fulfilment of their wishes. Only when John Doe belongs to one party with one policy and Richard Roe to another party with a different policy can the electors choose by a majority which policy they prefer or visit their displeasure at broken pledges or pronounce judgement on the outcome. Without party, elections are meaningless democratically. They become nothing but a periodic exercise of patronage to instal a number of individuals in a situation of influence without responsibility.

This is the exact description of the consequences of converting the European Assembly into a directly elected body. Consider the electorate of one of the eighty-one UK constituencies which are proposed. I will not labour the absurdity of constituencies averaging about half a million electors, nor the patronage and skulduggery which would attend upon the assignment of domestic political labels – Conservative, Labour, Liberal, etc. – to the respective candidates. But they would be elected not because they promised to take the whip of a right-wing, Christian Democrat or what-have-you grouping in the European Assembly, nor because of the contents of its manifesto (if it had one), nor contrariwise because of ditto for a left-wing European Socialist bloc. In fact they would probably spend much of their time disclaiming responsibility for any such document and dissociating themselves from any such outlandish companions. No, they would be elected – either straightforwardly by simple majority or crazily by proportional representation – as a result of the composition in terms of UK politics of the electorate in their particular slab of Britain.

What happens then when majorities in the directly elected European Assembly take decisions, or approve policies, or vote budgets which are regarded by the British electorate or by the electorate of some of the mammoth constituencies as highly offensive and prejudicial to their interests? What do the European MPs say to their constituents? They say: 'Don't blame me; I had no say, nor did I and my Labour (or Conservative) colleagues, have any say in the framing of these policies.' He will then either add: 'Anyhow, I voted against'; or alternatively he will add: 'And don't misunderstand if I voted for this along with my German, French and Italian pals, because if I don't help to roll their logs, I shall never get them to roll any of mine.' What these pseudo-MPs will not be able to say is what any MP in a democracy must be able to say, namely, either: 'I voted against this, and if the majority of my party are elected next time, we will put it right,' or alternatively: 'I supported this because it is part of the policy and programme for which a majority in this constituency and in the country voted at the last election and which we shall be proud to defend at the next election.'

Direct elections to the European Assembly, so far from introducing democracy and democratic control, will strengthen the arbitrary and bureaucratic nature of the Community by giving a fallacious garb of elective authority to the exercise of supranational powers by institutions and persons who are – in the literal, not the abusive, sense of the word – irresponsible. I cannot refrain from quoting once again the penetrating observations of the senior European correspondent of a British newspaper: 'Much as Canning called in the new world to redress the old, so Mr Jenkins, as President of the Commission, calls in the Parliament to redress the nationalism of the Council. Mr Jenkins and his Brussels colleagues look forward to direct elections so that the Commission can ally itself with a Parliament possessing a clear mandate.'

ULSTER UNIONIST

I am a lucky man. I represent in the House of Commons one of the most beautiful, if not the most beautiful, constituencies in the United Kingdom.

'Northern Ireland', from *Britain*, 1986

TO THE SOUTH BUCKINGHAMSHIRE CONSERVATIVE WOMEN'S ANNUAL LUNCHEON

Beaconsfield, 19 March 1971

For eighteen months a part of the United Kingdom has been under attack from an external enemy assisted by detachments operating inside. In Buckinghamshire you have neither seen nor heard: it requires an effort both of understanding and of imagination to realise the fact. Yet it is a fact which concerns Buckinghamshire as it concerns Cornwall or Aberdeenshire or County Down. For when one part of a nation is under attack, the whole is under attack. In this case the fact is not only concealed by distance and detachment; it is concealed still more by vocabulary, and vocabulary is one of the principal weapons in the enemy's armoury. The campaign in which the British Army is engaged, and in which the integrity of this country and the life and liberty of our fellow citizens are at stake, is obligatorily described, reported and discussed in terms designed to deny its real character.

The object is to persuade the people of Great Britain that the inhabitants of Ulster are quarrelling among themselves and, unable to refrain from sectarian and internecine violence, are involving in yet another of their everlasting broils the innocent British forces which are simply attempting to keep the peace between the contending sides and protect them from irreparably damaging themselves. The British public are intended in due course to exclaim: 'If they want to fight, let us leave them to it; Britain never had anything but trouble out of Ireland.' It is the sort of foolish, misguided talk and thought which does the enemy's work for him. The first thing necessary is to translate the nonsense language into straight English.

One of the most dangerous words is 'extremist'. A person who commits acts of violence is not an 'extremist'; he is a criminal. If he commits those acts of violence with the object of detaching part of the territory of the United Kingdom and attaching it to a foreign country, he is an enemy under arms. There is the world of difference between a citizen who commits a crime, in the belief, however mistaken, that he is thereby helping to preserve the integrity of his country and his right to remain a subject of his sovereign, and a person, be he citizen or alien, who commits a crime with the intention of destroying that integrity and rendering impossible that allegiance. The former breaches the peace; the latter is executing an act of war. To use the word 'extremist' of either or both conveys a dangerous untruth: it implies that both hold acceptable opinions and seek permissible ends, only that they carry them to 'extremes'. Not so: the one is a lawbreaker; the other is an enemy.

The same purpose, that of rendering friend and foe indistinguishable, is achieved by references to the 'impartiality' of the British troops and to their function as 'keeping the peace'. The British forces are in Northern Ireland because an avowed enemy is using force of arms to break down lawful authority in the province and thereby seize control. The army cannot be 'impartial' towards an enemy, nor between the aggressor and the aggressed: they are not glorified policemen, restraining two sets of citizens who might otherwise do one another harm, and duty bound to show no 'partiality' towards one lawbreaker rather than another. They are engaged in defeating an armed attack upon the state. Once again, the terminology is designed to obliterate the vital difference between friend and enemy, loyal and disloyal.

Then there are the 'no-go' areas which have existed for the past eighteen months. It would be incredible, if it had not actually happened, that for a year and half there should be areas in the United Kingdom where the Queen's writ does not run and where the citizen is protected, if protected at all, by persons and powers unknown to the law. If these areas were described as what they are – namely, pockets of territory occupied by the enemy, as surely as if they had been captured and held by parachute troops – then perhaps it would be realised how preposterous is the situation. In fact the policy of refraining from the re-establishment of civil government in these areas is as wise as it would be to leave enemy posts undisturbed behind one's lines.

Overshadowing all the other misconceptions sedulously propagated by skilful choice of language is that of 'grievance', 'reform', 'discrimination', 'civil rights'. These terms, which have passed into the orthodox Westminster vocabulary, have turned reality on its head first by reinterpreting deliberate acts of war as violence provoked by injustice, and then by importing ready-made the whole paraphernalia of the 'oppressed minority'. Thus has been built up in the public imagination on this side of St George's Channel the picture of a large and growing (which it is not) oppressed (which it is not) disloyal (which it is not) religious minority in Northern Ireland, whose existence is evidenced by the campaign of violence and thus brings down a deserved retribution of the majority. The propaganda success of the enemy has been brilliant: he has actually succeeded in getting his victims to broadcast and disseminate it for him, by putting his vocabulary into their mouths.

He is powerfully assisted by the presumption that it is wrong and dangerous and inflammatory to go around talking about Northern Ireland, and irresponsible, especially for English politicians in England, to lift up their voices about the affairs of that part of the United Kingdom. Naturally, the enemy prefers that no one should draw attention to his existence or his proceedings, and will call on all men of goodwill to help hush them up. An enemy does not, however, disappear because you ignore his existence or mistake him for something else. The danger in Northern Ireland lies not in the enemy being talked about but in the enemy not being talked about.

Given the disparity of physical force, he can only succeed by the method which has brought him increasing success so far, as the months have gone by: that is, by fostering the conviction that the Government never will treat the enemy as what he is, never will restore civil authority throughout the province, never will protect the law-abiding and uphold the loyal. There is scarcely any limit to the dangers people will face or the risks they will accept to defend themselves against attack from within or without, so long as they do not doubt that in the end they will prevail; but from the moment doubt starts to spread, authority and determination crumble, and men begin to look about them and take thought how they shall fare under some other dispensation. That critical point is coming nearer in Northern Ireland. It is coming nearer not because of speeches that are made, but because of speeches that are not made. A war cannot be waged, let alone won, when it is held necessary to assume that the enemy does not exist.

STATEMENT
10 July 1972

We have now reached the point in the affairs of Northern Ireland where not only those who support the policies of the Secretary of State but those who do not publicly dissociate themselves from them cannot escape responsibility for the consequences.

It is not even sufficient to have voted against those policies, as represented by the Temporary Provisions Act in March, explicitly on the grounds that they would prove disastrous. It is necessary to point again to the root cause of the violence and bloodshed. They stem from the fear on one side and the hope on the other that the British Government are not determined before all things to maintain the integrity of the United Kingdom, and that a way may yet be found to override the will of the majority in Northern Ireland. That fear and that hope have been and are being fostered by the attitudes and action of HMG, including most recently that of Mr Whitelaw in meeting IRA representatives and undertaking to consider their propositions. The only policy which can restore peace and reconcile all but the irreconcilable is one which proves to the world that Britain's object for the foreseeable future is to maintain the status of Northern Ireland as part of the UK.

TO THE CO. ARMAGH UNIONIST ASSOCIATION

Loughgall, 28 July 1972

Mr William Whitelaw, the Secretary of State for Northern Ireland, is much given to expressing astonishment and distress, in equal proportions, at the discovery that his assurances to the people of this province are not believed. He repeats frequently and emphatically the time-hallowed formulae about the people of Northern Ireland not being handed over without their consent. What more, he asks, can they want? Why do they not trust me?

I intend this evening to try to help Mr Whitelaw to understand, not so much because it is one's duty at all times to offer counsel and enlightenment to a colleague but because it is the incomprehension of basic reality which the British Government manifests in the person of the Secretary of State that is claiming a rising toll of death and suffering and is hurrying this province and its people towards the bourne from which there would be no return.

The reason why Mr Whitelaw and the Government are disbelieved is not that people think they are deliberately telling untruths and intending to deceive. The reason is simply this: their actions and their behaviour contradict their words. It is not possible both to assure the people of Northern Ireland that their place in the United Kingdom will be maintained, and at the same time to have parleyed with the IRA, face to face, in the capital of the kingdom; or at the same time to bask in the adulation of an opposition whose leader has been publicly complimented by the Government for proposals designed to produce a united Ireland in the measurable future; or at the same time to proclaim the intention of finding a 'political solution' to which no avenue will be treated as barred and to which the agreement is sought of those who are fundamentally committed against Ulster being part of the United Kingdom; or at the same time to seek what, before Stormont was suspended, used to be called 'tripartite' understanding on Northern Ireland with the Republic, whose very constitution asserts that Northern Ireland belongs to it already.

When those within and without, friend and enemy alike, observe the actions and reactions of Her Majesty's Government, they think to themselves: 'The British Government want out. They do not mean what they say. Otherwise, why would they talk about reconciliation with those who are irreconcilable? and why would they so scrupulously refrain from any act or attitude which would commit them to maintain the status quo against all comers?'

I will tell you of a little experience of my own. Last month I made a speech in County Down. It was a speech in which I warned the loyal majority, in clear and solemn terms, against taking the law into their own hands; and it was delivered before those actions of the UDA which we all remember. By chance, it came to my attention that, behind my back, in a letter to a constituent, one of Her Majesty's Defence Ministers, a Mr Kirk, had described the speech as 'bordering on incitement to subversion'. I concluded that he could not have seen what I actually said, and I sent him the text. To my astonishment he not only persisted in his accusation but cited verbatim in support of it the following sentence: 'All the more doggedly, therefore,' this is what I said to the Unionists assembled at Banbridge, 'must you fortify and entrench yourselves behind the plain uncomplicated things for which you stand.' And what were those 'plain, uncomplicated things'? I will read on: 'The answer is: loyalty to the United Kingdom of Great Britain and Northern Ireland; and union, meaning the union of all its parts, including this one'.

So things have come to this pass, that when a Member of Parliament exhorts his fellow citizens in Northern Ireland to remain peaceably loyal to the union of the kingdom, his words appear to one of Her Majesty's Ministers for Defence – for defence (mind you!), not social services or technological research – to be 'bordering on incitement to subversion'. When such is the mentality which prevails about Northern Ireland in the ranks of the Government itself, need Mr Whitelaw be so surprised if his assurances ring less than credible? After all, what do people think that the famous 'initiative' itself was all about, into which the Government talked themselves backwards in March, and in which we are assured, in the intervals between the detonation of bombs and the rattle of musketry, that they still persist? Was the purpose of the initiative to give the majority of this people a reassurance which they had hitherto lacked? to be able to grapple this province to the rest of the kingdom with tighter hoops of steel? to demonstrate more firmly still to whomsoever it might concern anywhere in the world that no threats or violence or assaults would prevail to prise Britain loose from her purpose? Did it look like that then? Does it look like that now?

No, Mr Whitelaw need not go far to find the answer to his puzzlement.

If Northern Ireland is to be saved from civil war and incalculable disaster, the policy of the Government must be radically altered.

When I say 'radically', I mean 'radically'. A week ago I asked Mr Whitelaw in the House of Commons how many more lives would be fruitlessly sacrificed before he came to realise that the political policy on which he is engaged will have to be altered. The grim answer – still, alas, incomplete – was given by the carnage of the three following days. Certain military steps were thereupon taken which, if they were possible and necessary then, had been possible and necessary two weeks, two months, before and ought to have been taken two weeks, two months before. But let no one make the mistake of concluding that thereby the fatal political contradiction of the British Government's policy has been eliminated. Within twenty-four hours Mr Whitelaw was heard inviting all and sundry to write to him with their ideas about how Northern Ireland should be governed – like a competition in *Tit-Bits* or *Home Chat* – and promising himself an interesting postbag. Within forty-eight hours his Minister of State, Mr Paul Channon, was inviting Miss Devlin to 'come forward with some constructive way in which we can achieve a political solution'.

I repeat: the policy must be radically altered; it must be so altered as to place beyond doubt what is disbelieved in words: that the integrity of this province as part of the kingdom will be upheld, come what may. This is not a doctrine of bloodshed and brute force; it is the reverse. The soil in which violence grows and flourishes is doubt of Britain's purpose. Until that doubt is removed, the results of military action – whether, in the hideous jargon, 'low-profile' or 'high-profile' – are written in water.

I have indicated over and over again what the main requirements are, and I will repeat them now.

First, recognise the fact, which Britain has denied for fifty years and the Republic has asserted for fifty years, that the United Kingdom and the Republic are two countries, two nations, and not one; and draw the consequences from that fact in the normal manner which prevails throughout the world. Implement the law which enables movement between the two countries to be policed and migration for employment or settlement to be controlled. Desist from regarding as citizens, for the purpose of voting and other rights of citizenship, those who have pertinaciously declared themselves to be aliens.

Secondly, and as a corollary, institute strict control over all transit of persons by land, sea or air, between the Republic and the United Kingdom; and for the duration of the emergency prohibit and prevent all vehicular traffic across the land frontier, except by a small number of routes. These are the measures which anywhere else in the world would be taken as a matter of course when enemy forces were based in the territory of a neighbouring country.

Thirdly, increase the police forces, including the police reserves, to the point at which they are capable of enforcing the law throughout the province and make arms available to them wherever necessary for this purpose. The troops are in Northern Ireland as an emergency backing and support to the police and the civil power, and not as an external, neutral arbiter or army of occupation. The Government must cease to connive at, or tolerate, the exclusion or replacement of the lawful civil power in any part of the province.

If there was one error more potent than another in bringing the present series of catastrophes upon the people of this province, it was the deliberate and almost gleeful supersession of the police in 1969, by a British Government which treated them with thinly veiled hostility. There can be no peace and no civilised life where law and order are the responsibility of the military and not the civil power. The business of the army is to defend the frontier, to destroy the enemy under arms within, and to support civil authority when it might otherwise be overwhelmed by superior force; but the Queen's peace and the laws can only be restored and enforced by a strong and confident police.

Finally, stop all the fiddle-faddle about conferences and constitutions and fancy franchises. We happen to have a constitution in the United Kingdom, and in Northern Ireland, and we have no need to invent new ones to amuse or appease those who want no Northern Ireland and no United Kingdom. If the Government will not give Northern Ireland democratic government from Westminster like the rest of the kingdom, let the democratic government which Westminster took away from Northern Ireland be restored.

There almost seems no limit to Westminster's appetite for self-deception over the affairs of Northern Ireland. For months and even years now, every pause or intermission in the advancing success of the war against this province has been hailed as evidence that 'we are getting on top of the gunmen', or, more recently, that 'the initiative is succeeding'. On the occasion of the recent so-called 'truce' it required wilful blindness of a supreme order not to perceive that the truce itself, far from being a sign of defeat or exhaustion on the part of the IRA, was a demonstration of their confident ability to switch from one tactic to another, a demonstration deliberately and (one would have thought) unmistakably underlined by the planned operations immediately preceding and following the period while the truce lasted.

To watch the events and listen to the accompanying Westminster commentary is like witnessing a gigantic and horrible cat-and-mouse performance. Like a nightmare, it seems as if it could go on for ever, one hideous episode following another. But the time is approaching when there has to be an end. Government cannot indefinitely fail to fulfil the most elementary duty of any government – to defend the citizen – without ceasing to be government at all. If that time were to come, it would not be Mr Whitelaw who would go. It would be Mr Heath himself; for on him is bound to rest the final responsibility for the successive phases of policy which have brought mounting disaster in the last two years.

A week ago we read that the Prime Minister had told an audience at the Royal Commonwealth Society that 'the British Government and people have a right to ask the people of Northern Ireland to assert themselves against the men of violence'. One would scarcely credit that such an exhortation could be addressed to unarmed men and women by a Government which is conspicuously and increasingly failing to provide them with the basic security and physical protection, let alone enjoyment of their lawful rights in peace, which it is the obligation of government to furnish. It is hard to say whether the lack of imagination or the lack of comprehension is the more dangerous: lack of imagination to realise how such language and such attitudes must strike the inhabitants of Belfast and Londonderry, Strabane or Portadown; or lack of comprehension to understand that the essential ingredient missing is that which the Government have themselves removed – conviction that the cause of Northern Ireland as part of the United Kingdom is the cause of the British Government and of the British nation.

TO A MEETING IN THE ULSTER HALL

Belfast, 18 April 1974

Whatever else the recent general election did, it transformed the outlook for the loyal majority in Northern Ireland. For the first time in years they now have a visible hope and a practical prospect of making good the proud but simple claim which they have always asserted – the right to live at peace in their own part of their own country, the United Kingdom. As one who has all along believed and asserted that this claim was binding upon the Government, Parliament and people of the United Kingdom, I hope I may be allowed to rejoice with you over this dramatic instalment and earnest of full success hereafter.

It is a remarkable example of the importance in politics, as in life generally, of dogged persistence in asserting what one knows to be right. When I recall the little remnant of faithful Unionist Members, and one or two others with them, a handful often down to half a dozen or less, who plodded through the lobbies at Westminster, under ridicule, contempt and hostility, to go on record against one device after another for depriving the people of this province of their rights, the transformation seems almost too good to be real. However, in history it is always by the few that nations are saved in the hour of extremity; and in future Ulster will remember with gratitude the names of those few sons of hers who refused to give up when the odds against them seemed impossible.

The electorate of Ulster have now done their part; and they have done it in a way which leaves no room for misunderstanding. Let me note briefly the major consequences.

On that day the Ulster Unionists declared an end of that alliance with the Conservative Party in Britain which in years gone by had been supposed the one sure guarantee of the union but which more recently had turned into Ulster's most insidious peril. For too long the traditional assumption held sway that a Conservative Government at Westminster was essential to Ulster's interests, and that no price was too high for Ulster to pay in order to sustain a Conservative administration and keep the imagined friendship of the Conservative Party. In the end it proved a snare and a delusion. The last

Conservative Government did more damage to the cause of Ulster in three years than any Government of any party had ever done. They were able to do it with impunity just because they were a Conservative Government; no other would have dared to or been able to.

Look at the record. In the Conservative manifesto of 1970, amongst the other debris of broken pledges and inverted policies, we read this about Northern Ireland: 'We reaffirm that no change will be made in the constitutional status of Northern Ireland without the free consent of the Parliament of Northern Ireland.' The Conservative Government's method of fulfilling that particular pledge was to abolish the Parliament of Northern Ireland altogether, and to abolish it in twenty-four hours flat – 'at a stroke', if I may coin a phrase – without ever consulting that Parliament, let alone obtaining its 'free consent'. Could cynicism be carried further? The answer is, yes perhaps, when one remembers the treatment which the Conservative Government meted out to one Ulster Premier after another, stringing them along with promises and half-promises, nods and winks, and then dashing them down with a diktat, like the luckless Brian Faulkner, summoned to London in March 1972 to be told that his Government and Parliament were both to be suspended and that he could like it or lump it.

All along it was not Ulster, a part of the United Kingdom, that the Conservative Government was thinking about, but Europe. Northern Ireland in its eyes was a squalid and untimely nuisance, always threatening to upset relationships at Brussels and Dublin and destined anyhow to be eaten up in the grand design of European economic and political union. What patience had the Conservative Party with a few hundred thousand people who insisted on saying they were British and meant to remain so? Fob them off with a constitution, and try not to look!

Talking about a faked constitution brings me to 'power-sharing', and to the second great assertion which the electorate of Northern Ireland made on 28 February – namely, that they would have none of it. The constitution forced on Northern Ireland in 1973 against the votes and voices of the representatives of the majority in this province is an absurdity. It is, as some of us said in the House of Commons at the time, an outrage upon the principles of responsible democratic government which no other part of the United Kingdom would tolerate, or be expected to tolerate, for an instant. Its absurdity guaranteed that it would be unworkable and rejected; yet the absurdity was not the result of mere stupidity or inadvertence. This monstrosity was framed in the attempt – albeit vain, as such attempts invariably are – to give satisfaction to those who are opposed to Northern Ireland being part of the United Kingdom at all. It was a constitutional contradiction in terms, behind which lay the barely concealed impatience of the Government at Westminster to see Northern Ireland glide or slide or slither into union with the Republic. To this chimera the electors of Northern Ireland have put paid, by decisively withdrawing from it all claim to represent them. It still exists in theory, but henceforward it is a dummy, a wreck, a waterlogged hulk. There is no life, or possibility of life, in it. Whatever the Government at Westminster or the men representing nobody who form the Executive may assert, the 1973 Constitution is dead and will soon have to be tidied away into the limbo where such abortions belong. Every day that it continues its charade of existence, the more harm it does – but more of that anon.

For the moment let us note another fact of 28 February. That day it confirmed, what Unionists and their friends here and elsewhere have tirelessly proclaimed amid mockery and contradiction – that the unequivocal assertion of the permanence of the Union is the key to the peace of this province and would command the overwhelming support of the population. The election did nothing to support the dangerous myth of a large Roman Catholic minority irreconcilable to the Union; on the contrary the figures in many seats are quite unintelligible unless really substantial numbers of Roman Catholics voted for the Union and against power-sharing, and not only that, but for the very men whom the press and the other media have been belabouring as 'extremists'. In the privacy of the polling-booth many of our Roman Catholic fellow subjects gave the lie to the press and the media on a scale which leaves no room for doubt as to where their hopes for peace and good government lie.

So I turn to the future and to how those hopes, which are the hopes of all but a small minority in this land, ought to be fulfilled.

For four and a half years now this province has been racked by murder and guerrilla war on a scale which is a scandal and disgrace to the Parliament and Government of the United Kingdom, who not only have always acknowledged the ultimate responsibility but have seized the direct responsibility. Under successive Parliaments, successive Governments have applied one expedient after another. There has been a distressingly uniform pattern. As each expedient was applied, it was enthusiastically proclaimed to have opened a new era. Downing Street declaration, direct rule, power-sharing, the rest, they all contained the hope-for magical ingredient – until they were tried; and then the same consequences followed, with the only difference that each time they were a little worse than the time before and the pessimism returned the more profound for repetition. On each occasion a handful of members at Westminster told a House of Commons which did not wish to hear, that only bloodshed would follow and that the promise of improvement was fallacious. They did so, and were always proved right, not because they were exceptionally lucky at a guessing game but because each successive act of policy contained the same, inevitably fatal element, by which it was predictably foredoomed.

That element was ambiguity. Go back to 1969, and trace from there, phase by phase the words and actions of the United Kingdom Government. Ask yourselves, as you come to each of them: 'Is this policy intended to strengthen the Union? Are these the words and actions of men who mean to give assurance that the Union is permanent?' In every instance the answer is: 'No: the opposite.' Whatever traditional formulae were repeated by those in official positions, nobody listening and watching could doubt which way the book lay. No doubt the majority in Ulster were for the Union, but always there was the fatal 'but'. Always the result was to convey to those who wished to see the Union destroyed that violence was pushing the British Government step by step in the direction which the violent desired. The violence did pay off.

Those who say that the fundamental remedy for the war in Northern Ireland is political are right, but not in the sense in which they have usually meant it. It is not the construction of constitutions and agreements which mean all things to all men and attempt to reconcile the irreconcilable that will bring peace to this province; for the violence feeds upon ambiguity. Ambiguity gives the green light to murder, while at the same time it conveys to those who wish to uphold law and order the message that sooner or later they may expect to be left in the lurch. This is why for year after year, not to their liking, I told the British House of Commons that the bloodshed in Ulster was upon their heads; for they it was who approved, nay insisted upon, the very course of double-talk and double-think which fuelled the guerrilla fire.

The political remedy, which has stared us in the face all these years, is to make it clear beyond peradventure that the present status of Northern Ireland as part of the United Kingdom is not going to be altered, and that since the Parliament of Northern Ireland is now no more, that affirmation is taken over by the only Parliament there is – the Parliament of the United Kingdom. The political remedy is to remove the ambiguity of the past and make it clear by deeds, not formulae, that the Union is beyond the reach of violence, however brutal, however persistent. Thereby violence is deprived of its hope; and hope is the food on which violence is nourished. Cut off the food: the violence will die. Men risk their lives and their immortal souls in a cause which has some possibility and prospect of success:

they will not throw them away for what is not there to be had. How then is certainty to be given?

There is one step which more than anything else would seal the status of Northern Ireland as being as near as humanly possible irrevocable in the eyes of the United Kingdom and the world. It is moreover a step which in common justice cannot be denied or argued against. And it is a step upon which fate has delivered into the hands of the Ulster Unionists the power to insist. If Northern Ireland, as all assert, is part of the United Kingdom, then Northern Ireland has an indefeasible and indisputable claim to be represented in the Parliament of the United Kingdon as amply as any other part. While Stormont existed, with a Parliament of its own and a Government of its own, the deliberate under-representation of the six counties of Ulster was at least superficiably arguable, though not logical. Now that Stormont is no more, even that argument is gone. It cannot be defended that these counties, which in any other similar part of the realm would be represented by twenty seats, or at the least eighteen, have only twelve.

How vital is the removal of this injustice becomes instantly clear when one listens to the excuses by which it is defended. Let us wait, say the apologists, to see how the new-fangled constitution will develop, in case that development should be inconsistent with full representation at Westminster. The White Paper of the late Government was even more revealing: 'integration' (that is, full representation at Westminster) 'would be unacceptable to the Republic of Ireland and would make co-operation [whose?] with the Republic more difficult'. There you have it. A part of the United Kingdom is to remain under-represented in Parliament to please a foreign country which happens to claim that part as its own territory. The maintenance of the unjust treatment of the Ulster electorate is the plain signal to the Republic and the republicans that the door to what they desire and the majority of Ulster people reject is being unlocked. Hence the temptation to push and kick that door open, or (should I say?) to blast it open with explosive. The connection between Westminster representation and death on the streets in Northern Ireland is direct and unequivocal.

Irrespective, therefore, of whatever may be the future form of the local administration of this province, I submit, as I have done consistently from the outset, that the foremost and unequivocal demand of the people of Northern Ireland must be for their full representation in the Parliament of their own United Kingdom. It is not a demand which the British House of Commons can refuse without self-contradiction. It is not a demand to which either of the two great parties in the state can without disgrace remain deaf: far though the Conservative Party has fallen in the recent past from the meaning and the idea of 'one nation', I fail to see how it can persist in denying to any part of a United Kingdom equality of treatment with the rest; and as for the Labour Party, heirs to the radical programme of equal constituencies and equal voting power, how can they reconcile their political conscience to the grotesque inequality imposed on those who live in Ulster?

The acceptance of this act of simple justice to the people of Ulster would not be divisive but healing. It is a truism, with which none but the tiniest minority in these counties would quarrel, that we wish to see our Roman Catholic fellow subjects take no less ample a part in the political life of this nation than any others; and I referred earlier to the significant and wholesome fact that thousand upon thousands of them had declared their will to do so in a United Kingdom at the ballet-boxes on 28 Febuary. It is a further truism, that we wish to see political life and work and thought concerned no less in this province than elsewhere with the great issues that confront the whole nation, with the entire sweep of economic, social and international policy. For many years, but of late to a degree intolerable and disastrous, these manifest desires of the people of Northern Ireland have been frustrated by the claustrophobia imposed upon them by a series of constitutional expedients and contradictions, as a result of which they have been held up to the world in the distorting mirror of caricature and slander as a people bigoted and parochial, quarrelling over past grievances with their backs to the outside world.

Everybody who knows the individual Ulster man or woman in the life and work of the United Kingdom and far beyond its shores, knows what a lie and calumny that picture is; but it is a mould that must decisively be broken. The full representation of Ulster in Parliament would be the unmistakable declaration that the years of quaratine for Ulster were over. Of course, 'the border' – that strange euphemism for Ulster's right to be and to remain part of the United Kingdom – cannot be 'taken out of politics' (as the sickly phrase runs), because it is supremely a political question – indeed, the supreme political question. But it is a political question of the United Kingdom as a whole. Those who thought or hoped that it could be otherwise were sharply undeceived in March 1972. The illusion that it could be left on the doorstep of Stormont bedevilled this province in the late 1960s; and its agony in the early 1970s had been increased and prolonged by successive attempts – Sunningdale and the paper constitution of 1973 are the latest – to imprison the people of Northern Ireland within it once more. So long as it remained so, and so long it does remain so, politics in Ulster – against its will and against its interest – will remain sectarian, divisive and violent.

As long as the Union endures, the politics of Northern Ireland are a part of the politics of the United Kingdom. Let the people of Northern Ireland be given at last their fair part, and no more than their fair part, in those politics – let them be treated no worse, and also no better, than the people of any other province of the realm – and we shall soon begin to see the nightmare of their years of exclusion and ostracism dissolve.

I will make a confession to you, a confession it is no shame for a parliamentarian to make. I believe in magic, in the magic of the free Parliament of a united nation. Whatever may be true of other countries, it is Parliament, the undivided sovereign Parliament of this Kingdom, upon which the unity of the nation depends. Ulster cannot share in that unity except by sharing, without qualification or diminution, in the undivided sovereignty of that Parliament. Hitherto the people of Northern Ireland have been provincial in nothing but their politics. Now their politics too, through the transformation that the general election brought about, must cease to be provincial. Henceforward no horizon need be too wide. I look forward to the day when the constituencies of Ulster will see those who represent them chosen among the rest, without regard to creed or class, to govern and to lead the British nation.

'NORTHERN IRELAND'

from *Britain*, 1986

The Government and Parliament of Northern Ireland which were created in 1919 and lasted until 1972 were modelled upon the constitution of a dominion, commonly called 'the Westminster model', of which the essentials are a cabinet government collectively responsible in effect to an elected chamber, taking decisions by majority vote. This majority in the elected chamber is liable in Great Britain to alter according to changes in circumstances and in the opinions of the electorate. Where the majority is for practical purposes unalterable, the system becomes unacceptable and arguably oppressive to a political minority. The circumstances of Northern Ireland from 1919 to 1972 were, from this point of view, peculiar in two respects: the majority political opinion, which was essentially in favour of Ulster remaining part of Britain ('Unionist'), was not likely to change in any foreseeable future; and secondly, the main minority political opinion was not in favour of running the province on different policies but of removing the province from the Union altogether. Thus, Britain imposed upon Ulster a 'home rule' which was not only unwanted, but which would not be workable in the spirit of the British constitution itself. To use emotive terms, it was Britain that built the sense of injustice into Northern Ireland.

This was due to the foreseeable permanence of the majority and not to the fact that the principal minority was secessionist. After all, both in Wales and Scotland there are minority political parties which aim at an eventual (if visionary) majority for secession in their respective countries. Yet this does not make the Westminster system unworkable or unacceptable in Wales or Scotland: the electorate of these countries participate in the political process of the whole United Kingdom and devolution has not been forced upon them – indeed in 1979 they refused it when it was offered.

If there were an equation between 'Catholic' (which in Ulster means Roman Catholic) and anti-Union and between 'Protestant' (which in Ulster means anything except Roman Catholic) and pro-Union, then that would again imply a fixity of minority and majority which would be self-evidently incompatible with the spirit of the 'Westminster system'. That is no doubt one reason why the equations are so popular, apart from the journalistic convenience of typecasting;

but the reality does not conform, refuses to conform, with the stereo-type. The religious question which in Ulster is included optionally in the census does not produce absolutely hard results, because of the considerable proportion – 18.5 per cent in 1981 – where no religious affiliation is declared; but the ratio of Roman Catholic to other denominations (28 to 53.5 per cent) would be generally accepted as broadly correct. It does not, however, translate directly into political terms, because there is cross-voting, negligible in the case of non-Roman Catholics voting for anti-Union candidates, but really substantial in the case of Roman Catholics voting for pro-Union candidates. An opinion survey in 1979, promoted (ironically) by the Government of the Irish Republic, which showed the Union as the preferred option of half the Roman Catholic voters in Ulster, agrees with the necessarily impressionistic view of Unionist parliamentary candidates that in marginal seats they benefit significantly by Roman Catholic votes – and abstentions.

If, however, the politico-religious equation is fallacious that does not mean that the religious factor is unimportant in the total picture of Ulster. On the contrary, the culture of the province has a religious dimension totally strange to the tolerant and slipshod self-identification with a national church which the unique form taken by the Reformation in England left as its legacy. In Ulster that relationship between church and state is simply not understood. The Act of Union of 1800 created, logically, a United Church of England and Ireland, but the disestablishment of 1869 and the political secession of 1921 left the Church of Ireland a vigorous and active, though not the largest, Protestant denomination in Ulster. It is rather the largest of the Protestant denominations, the Presbyterian Church of Ireland, which is most typical of Ulster ways of thought. It inherits the essentially convenanting notion of a compact between church and state, whereby the latter in return for civil obedience guarantees freedom of religion and the independent self-government of the Church.

This relationship is the key to understanding the political role of the Orange Institution, with its quasi-military ceremonial so misleading to the casual observer. It is a role which derives logically from the perceived function of the state as guarantor and the consequent need for the guarantee to be jealously policed and supervised. For its members, who have a prescribed obligation 'ever to abstain from all uncharitable words, actions or sentiments towards their Roman Catholic brethren', undertake 'to support and defend the rightful sovereign, the Protestant religion, the laws of the realm and the succession to the throne in the House of Windsor, *being Protestant*'. It could be said that what the reformation settlement and toleration are in England is represented in Ulster by the Bill of Rights and the

Act of Succession. When Ulster celebrates in July the Williamite revolution, it is wiser than the onlookers and many of the participants perhaps understand: for that was the phase of the evolution of the United Kingdom with which the Ulster Protestant's philosophy is most at home.

Since 1969, and explicitly since 1972, the Government and Parliament of the United Kingdom have exercised directly the authority over Northern Ireland which had always been implicit in its continued recognition as part of the Union. This explicit assumption of responsibility might appear an event as plain and decisive as the secession of the Irish Free State recognised in 1921. It might also seem the only possible resolution of the constitutional impasse which the enforced 'home rule' of 1921 had created, dissolving in the larger political unity the antitheses insoluble in a purely local context – the same idea indeed which had inspired the Union of 1800.

Parliament itself has been bewildered by the sequel. Every government since 1972 has attempted to reintroduce 'home rule', while in the interim renewing from year to year the power to legislate for Northern Ireland on 'home rule' subjects by ministerial Order in Council and preserving intact the structures of a 'home rule' government, such as a separate financial system and a separate Consolidated Fund. In the attempt, however, to eliminate the drawbacks, demonstrated by experience, of a fixed party majority, a series of 'fancy constitutions' were proposed embodying contrivances designed to put an electoral minority on an equal footing with an electoral majority. Since they were incompatible with the Westminster principles of a government resting on the support of an elected assembly, they either collapsed as soon as they were attempted – as, in 1974, the so-called 'power-sharing executive' – or were laughed out of court as soon as they were proposed.

Side by side with these attempts to square the circle ran the attempt to put back the machinery which the 1919 Act had contained for a gradual coalescence between Ulster and the Irish Republic. That was the 'Council of Ireland', of which acceptance at a conference held at Sunningdale in December 1973 was made the condition precedent to establishing the 'power-sharing executive'. Since then the name Sunningdale has been a by-word and a term of derision in Ulster politics.

The British state, it gradually became clear, had still not relinquished its cherished ambition of reversing the verdict of history and moving Ulster into an all-Ireland state; but it was clear that to succeed it would need to use more refined and subtle methods than heretofore.

The account of these methods will bring our story down to the present day. In 1981, the Council of Ireland was established in a camouflaged form as the Anglo-Irish Council, which would have three tiers, ministerial, official and parliamentary, the last being left temporarily in abeyance. Then in 1982 there was instituted an elected Northern Ireland Assembly, which avoided the 'home rule' conundrum by being destitute of all legislative and executive functions whatsoever, but even so did not escape being shunned by its anti-Union members. The crowning act of the wizard's wand would be to give the assembly real powers on condition that it provided the Ulster component for the missing Anglo-Irish parliamentary tier. At the time of writing that event had been deferred, if not aborted, by prime ministerial intervention; but play continues.

So what, ask the electorate and parliamentary representatives of the rest of the United Kingdom, is the 'solution'? The 'problem' of Northern Ireland, they complain, is too 'complex'. The 'problem' and the 'complexity' have consisted in perpetual and deliberate ignoring of the facts, the facts of Ulster and the facts of Ireland, such as this brief view has tried to display them. The 'solution', if the use of the word 'problem' makes it unavoidable to use the term all politicians should eschew, is to stop ignoring these facts, and to accept as historically and politically valid the continuing massive plebiscite of the Ulster electorate for membership of the United Kingdom, the Parliament of which is proud enough to believe that it can accord justice and a role even to the most intractable of minorities.

'FACE THE PRESS'
Channel 4 TV, 2 March 1986

JULIA LANGDON: Can I ask the same question, again, another way? As a politician, do you think that your party is doing the right thing in calling this strike?

ENOCH POWELL: In fact technically the Ulster Unionist Party didn't call the strike, the strike was to a large extent organised spontaneously, but as I've just made clear to you, it was very natural that the Ulster Unionist Party, which after all is the prime political representation of Ulster Unionism, should associate itself with this expression – just as it was associated with the expression when 200,000 people gathered together in Belfast, it was stated to be only 100,000, but the police said there were 200,000 – when 200,000 people gathered together in Belfast to say no, shortly after the agreement. It seems to me a perfectly natural form of expression.

LANGDON: But is it politically advisable – you, you're not answering the question Mr Powell?

POWELL: I think it is politically advisable in the sense that it brings home to those concerned, and I'm not sure that the Prime Minister has yet fully grasped it, the sense of distress and horror at this form of treatment which is felt by people in Northern Ireland, as it would be felt in the corresponding circumstances by the people of Yorkshire or any other part of the United Kingdom which was treated in that way.

GILLIAN REYNOLDS: You, you've plainly grasped it, because you're giving it eloquent voice now, but in that case, why aren't you there?

POWELL: I'm not there because I have a job to do, I'm Monday anchorman for the Ulster Unionist Party, indeed in a sense I'm London anchorman for the Ulster Unionist Party – and I was in touch this morning with the party leader about the business next week in the House of Commons and we were discussing how I would play a part in it, at the parliamentary end.

EDWARD MOLONEY: Well the organisers of this strike are making no secret – or some of the organisers of this strike are making no secret of the fact that this is a dry run for a full-fledged indefinite strike later this summer. We also know that there is paramilitary involvement in the organisation and co-ordination of the strike tomorrow – how can you as a constitutionalist justify and support that sort of action?

POWELL: I don't justify or support anything which is in contravention of the law, and certainly nothing which, so far as I know, is being proposed for tomorrow is unlawful, in the law of the United Kingdom as it applies in Northern Ireland. Now I think one would have to consider very carefully an attempt to use a strike for the purposes for which it proved successful in 1974; after all in 1974 there was a specific local objective. There was an executive set up which did not enjoy the support of the electorate, which had been imposed against the will of a majority of the electorate, and by what happened at the strike in 1974 it was made clear to that executive that it didn't enjoy sufficient support to carry on. Now, one would be mad to suppose that a strike in Northern Ireland will show the United Kingdom Government that the United Kingdom Government has to resign – that's absurd. So it's not an instrument – what is going to happen tomorrow is not an instrument to bring down an administration, as it proved to be in 1974.

REYNOLDS: How much effect do you think will Mrs Thatcher's appeal to, directly to the people of Northern Ireland have – she's been trying to talk above the heads of the Unionists?

POWELL: They won't listen, because they don't hear in her voice, yet, a comprehension of the outrage which she has committed upon that part of the United Kingdom, just as the people of Yorkshire, if she addressed them in the same way would say, but you don't seem to understand what you've done to us.

REYNOLDS: Do you fear violence tomorrow?

POWELL: There's the risk of it, as there must be wherever there are large crowds and wherever there is strong feeling and excitement. But violence which is inherently unlawful is something with which no politician in my opinion – no constitutional politician can be associated, but he can't say that because certain manifestations which are lawful can be the occasion of violence, therefore those manifestations oughtn't to take place, otherwise we shall have politicians in Great Britain saying there shouldn't be protests against unemployment, there shouldn't be protests against other government policies, in case there is fringe violence associated with them.

MOLONEY: Are you saying that tomorrow's strike should be a one-off affair and that you should –

POWELL: It is, it is organised as a one-off affair – that is what it is.

MOLONEY: – and that should be the end of that –

POWELL: And I am saying that before someone proposes that you should use a strike in order to enforce certain specific demands or propositions upon the Government of the United Kingdom, you will have to think very carefully indeed.[. . .]

REYNOLDS: What makes you say that Mrs Thatcher has succumbed to blackmail and bribery in signing this agreement?

POWELL: Because she did not believe the professed reasons for the agreement. The professed reasons for the agreement were to secure the co-operation of the Government of the Irish Republic in putting down the IRA in Northern Ireland, and to produce reconciliation between the Nationalist majority and the Unionist majority. Now, Mrs Thatcher is both too well-informed and too intelligent to believe either of those explanations, and even if that were not the case, as I believe it to be, she has been expressly advised by the security forces, as we know, that that was not the case. Let us take the two propositions – first of all, here is the Government of the Irish Republic. The Government of the Irish Republic which finds itself in the position of making that kind of agreement with the Government of the United Kingdom because of the existence and continuance of terrorism in Northern Ireland. That being professed as one of the reasons, is it conceivable that even if it was in their power to do so, which is very doubtful, the Government of the Irish Republic would be seen by its own electors to be helping the Brits to put down the IRA in part of the island of Ireland? The answer to that is no, and the Prime Minister knows that the answer of that, to that is no. And secondly, let's consider the matter of reconciliation. Do you reconcile quarrelling members of a family by bringing somebody in from outside and saying: Now you're on the side of a minority. You will be listened to. You're representing the minority. What would happen in Yorkshire if the minority in Yorkshire were told that in future they were going to be represented by an external power? Does that reconcile people? To be told that an external party is going to be the representative of one of the parties to a dispute?

REYNOLDS: Where does the blackmail come in?

POWELL: The blackmail is the blackmail which is exerted upon a Prime Minister to do something which is repugnant to her unionist belief – to her unionist instincts – knowing what the consequences will be.

REYNOLDS: Who's blackmailing her?

POWELL: The blackmail is blackmail of the United States, which has always wanted the price to be paid for bringing Ireland within the North Atlantic Treaty Organisation.

MOLONEY: Mr Powell, do you have any evidence for this? I mean, you've said this many times but . . .

POWELL: Well, attentive readers of the Irish press, and I dare say you are an attentive reader of the Irish press – indeed you are an active writer in the Irish press – are well aware that this belief is widely held in the Irish Republic itself, and this prospect is widely resented in the Irish Republic and is regarded as one of the motives of Fitzgerald in entering into this agreement.

REYNOLDS: What, just to get some money? I mean, being widely held is no evidence, is it?

POWELL: No. A *quid pro quo* – a *quid pro quo* which is politically attractive.

REYNOLDS: *Quids* for your *pro quo*?

POWELL: The *quid* is to be seen to be on the way to creating a united Ireland and the *quo* is to bring the island of Ireland, or the Irish Republic within the ambit of the North Atlantic Treaty, which has been a long-standing objective of the strategists of the North Atlantic Treaty.

REYNOLDS: And do you think that Mrs Thatcher has come under American pressure?

POWELL: Yes. As she came under American pressure in the film which was playing. No, I'm not referring to 'Yes, Prime Minister'. The film which was playing during the by-election, and a very convenient film it was to have playing, namely the Westland episode, where the Prime Minister was under so much pressure to ensure that the American deal went through, which she took the risk, the risk to herself personally, and the risk to her credibility of making it happen. And that's the risk which she has taken in the case of Northern Ireland. To make it happen. But unfortunately for her she attempted something which can't be made to happen, and my business as a politician – as a constitutional politician – is to indicate to the Government of the United Kingdom, the only way in which Northern Ireland can be governed and that is as what they say it is, an integral part of the United Kingdom.

SOCIAL POLICIES

This business of compulsion is not something theoretical or peripheral; it is of the essence of a right, because there is no point in declaring a right to what everyone is going to have anyhow. The whole object of declaring a right is to justify or commend the use of compulsion to alter the existing relationship between individuals in a society.

'Human Rights', Journal of Medical Ethics, 3, 1977

'HOUSING'

from *One Nation*, 1950

The first parliamentary Acts concerning housing in the nineteenth century were Public Health Acts, which laid down requirements as regards sanitation and public safety. Detailed regulations for the construction of new buildings were laid down in a great variety of Acts and bye-laws. In 1868 and 1879 the two 'Torrens Acts' made the owner of a house responsible for keeping it in a habitable condition, and gave powers of compulsion to the local authority. Further steps forward were taken in 1875 and 1879 when the 'Cross Acts' were passed. These empowered local authorities to clear and reconstruct unhealthy areas, with powers to purchase compulsorily and to limit compensation. The Housing of the Working Classes Act, 1890, unified previous housing legislation and remained the principal Housing Act until the consolidating Act of 1925. This Act of 1890 incorporated the 'Cross' and the 'Torrens' provisions, and empowered urban sanitary authorities to erect workers' dwellings independently of clearance schemes. Its powers were extended by the Housing Acts of 1894, 1900 and 1903, and also by the Housing and Town Planning Act of 1909, the first major housing measure not introduced by Conservatives. These early Acts stemmed very largely from sanitary powers, and did not provide any financial assistance beyond powers of borrowing money.

In tackling the grave problem of dilapidated and overcrowded property by reconditioning old houses and building new ones at low rents, the way was led, as it has so often been, by private individuals and voluntary associations. Pioneers such as Octavia Hill showed what could be done in altering and repairing sub-standard property and in new methods of housing management and rent collection. Others such as George Cadbury, who initiated Bournville Village in 1897, and Joseph Rowntree who started New Earswick Village, York, in 1904, experimented in creating model communities of houses built at prices which would enable them to be let at rents within the reach of working-class incomes. It was an important principle that these housing schemes should pay their way. In Joseph Rowntree's words, this ensured 'that residents should not be placed in the position of being recipients of a bounty'. Octavia Hill, too, adopted the principle that her housing ventures must be self-supporting, and that the tenants should pay an economic rent; she maintained that rate-aided housing might be a danger to poorer tenants, who would be in the position of having to contribute through the rates to council housing, when they could scarcely afford the rent for their own inferior accommodation.

Bournville and New Earswick were followed by other estates put up by Industrial Housing Associations such as Lever Brothers at Port Sunlight, and many more recent ones, to the present number of about fifty-four. The Housing Associations or Public Utility Societies took many forms and have prospered to this day. There are the Old People's Associations, about 100 of them, which do not pay dividends and, therefore, function as charitable institutions; also counted as charities are the Housing Trusts, such as the Peabody, Astor, Guinness, Lewis and Sutton Trusts, which started to build large blocks of flats in industrial areas at an early date. Then there were the Garden City Trusts, such as Welwyn, Hampstead and Letchworth. These pay a limited dividend and provide a variety of dwellings. The various types of Housing Associations continued to grow after the 1914–18 war, and under the Acts of 1930, 1936 and 1949 they became eligible for subsidies under certain conditions.

The Inter-war Years

After the 1914 war the building industry was completely run down and the nation's building capacity was almost non-existent. When Lord Addison was made Minister of Health he concentrated entirely on methods of financing council housing, and under the ill-conceived Housing and Town Planning Act of 1919 he guaranteed local authorities all losses over that covered by a penny rate. The money was raised on long term, mainly for forty years, and carried a high rate of interest. The annual payments in 1934 were about £6¾ millions. But the worst effect of this Act was its inflationary tendency. The local authorities had little encouragement to economise, and housing costs rose steeply. In August, 1920, the average cost of a local authority house was £930, about two and a half times as much as before the war.

Mr Neville Chamberlain, in his Housing Act of 1923, changed the subsidy arrangement to one by which the Government undertook to give a definite and limited contribution of £6 per annum per house for a period of twenty years. The grants applied to houses both for letting and selling, and the local authorities were empowered also to give help to private builders. The Chamberlain Act also provided for subsidising slum clearance schemes.

The Acts passed by Labour Governments, the Wheatley Act (1924) and the Greenwood Act (1930) to assist local authorities, were both used very extensively by subsequent Conservative and National Governments. The National Government's Housing (Financial Provisions) Act, 1933, by confining subsidies to those for slum clearance, provided the local authorities with an increased stimulus to clear away the slums. For the first time a mathematical definition of overcrowding was given by the National Government in their Act of 1935, and a determined attack was made on this evil. As a result the average number of people in a house, which was 4.0 in 1931, was reduced to 3.5 by 1939.

The basic Conservative policy between the wars was to encourage the speedy building of houses at low cost by every means and through every agency. The building of houses was not put into the hands of any one authority or any one agency. Local authorities, housing societies, private builders, all were encouraged to build or convert property, either to let or to sell. By encouraging the private builder to build houses at low cost to be let or sold, houses were provided at the least cost to the community. These operations were largely financed by the building societies, at a very low rate of interest. Modernisation and repair of rural cottages were also made possible by grants. As a result of the stimulus given by Governments, mostly Conservative, to the building of small houses, and the free play of competition in the building industry, costs fell greatly, till the average cost of a council house in 1939 was £380, instead of £930 in 1920. The results of this policy were remarkable. Ninety per cent of the houses built in the inter-war period were of low rateable value, not exceeding £26 (£35 in Greater London). During 1938 and 1939 slum-dwellers were being rehoused at the rate of 1,000 a day. In the five years 1934–8 an average total of 335,000 houses was built each year in Great Britain. In 1938 the total was over 360,000.

The Present

We do not condone the bad quality and deplorable appearance of some of the speculative building between the wars, nor the lack of physical planning and the wasteful development of land (often good farming land); we shall have more to say about this later in the chapter. But Mr Bevan's ranting polemics on the subject would perhaps sound better in the mouth of a Minister of Health who was getting enough houses built. We must now examine his record.

In the five years up to the end of April, 1950, the post-war housing programme had provided 686,018 permanent houses and flats in Great Britain. To this must be added the 157,000 temporary houses (the provision of temporary houses has now come to an end), the repair of war-damaged property, and the use of huts and service camps. For the month of April, 1950, the output of permanent houses and flats was under fifteen thousand.

In his Budget speech in April, 1950, the Chancellor of the Exchequer announced that 'for the three years 1950–2 we have decided that the programme for Great Britain should be at the completion rate of 200,000 houses a year'. It so happens that this rate is exactly the output of the building industry, averaged over the previous three years. In fact the 'decision' is not a decision at all, but an acceptance of things as they are.

Output of New Houses

The building industry has today an appreciably larger number of men at work than in the years immediately before 1939, though probably rather a smaller percentage of the total are building new houses. Yet the output is little over half what it was in the last five years before 1939.

Even when allowance is made for a certain diversion of effort from new house-building to repair, and for the possibility that the average size of the houses built in 1947–9 is slightly above that of those built in 1934–8, the contrast remains startling. If the production of houses could regain the level of the 1930s, the rate at which overcrowding, sharing, and sub-standard houses could be eliminated would clearly be greatly accelerated. The important work of slum clearance has been virtually at a standstill since 1939, only individual houses having been demolished, apart from an area in London intended as a showpiece for the Festival of Britain. Although there is no survey which would give the extent of overcrowding and involuntary sharing, the evidence of the local authority waiting lists and of everyone's personal experience shows it to be very great.

These conditions touch on many aspects of our national life: health threatened by overcrowded and insanitary homes; education retarded when children have no room in which to do homework, or arrive tired at school after sleeping in a room with several others; marriages broken up through the strain of sharing a home or making do in cramped and uncomfortable quarters; Borstal institutions, remand homes and approved schools filled by the products of an unhappy home life. A home of the right size and in the right place and at the right rent is everybody's first need. Less would need to be spent on the other social services if housing conditions were drastically improved.

Nothing short of absolute impossibility ought to prevent those measures from being taken which will as soon as possible restore the pre-war productivity of the building industry in new houses. There is no such impossibility.

Alleged Limiting Factors

At various times three different factors have been alleged to justify the limitation of the production of houses: the 'capital investment programme'; labour; and materials, especially timber. None will withstand logical examination.

The capital investment programme is, or rather purports to be, a plan for the employment of available resources of manpower and materials. If more output is obtained from the same manpower – which it is here contended could and should happen – then the allocation of resources so far as manpower is concerned will be unaffected. There remains, therefore, only the factor of materials.

Home-produced building materials, such as bricks and other refractories, adjust themselves to the prospective demand indicated by the numbers of houses contracted for and begun. Capital equipment (except in expanding lines like cement*) and, to a large extent, labour employed, remain constant whether or not producing at full capacity. Generally speaking, the home materials industry could support a greatly expanded building programme without an appreciable increase of labour or capital. A commentary on the effect of Government planning in the last few years is found in the recent report of the Working Party on the Building Industry: 'The producers of building materials . . . found that their assessment of the demand for their goods was liable to be upset by sudden changes of policy which they could not possibly foresee.'

There remain finally the imported materials, of which timber alone is alleged to be a real limitation. The price at which timber for building is bought has been higher than it need be and the amount

*The chairman of the Cement Makers' Federation (*Manchester Guardian*, 14 July 1950): 'Before the war no shortage ever occurred because the industry had been able to plan production and build new factories when and where required. In those days it took less than eighteen months to build a new cement factory. Now it takes over four years, because of the numerous public and official inquiries under the Town and Country Planning Act, Government policy and changes of policy on the location of industry and capital expenditure, the number of building licences required, the failure to co-ordinate them with raw-material authorisations and supplies, and, above all the delays and vacillations about steel authorisations.' In 1945 the industry had submitted plans to the Ministry of Works for the construction of three new factories and the reconstruction or enlargement of six others . . . the whole programme being designed to produce an additional 1,570,000 tons of cement a year. 'If we could have built them as quickly as before the war,' said Lord Selborne, 'they would have been in operation in 1947. But now at the end of five years, of this 1,570,000 tons a year new capacity, only some 300,000 tons a year are in operation.'

much smaller for two reasons: Government buying* and Government decisions. Both must be changed at once. With an average of nine months' notice, the timber trade – buying on its own responsibility – could procure, at a lower average price per standard than is being paid at present, enough timber for all the houses that the building industry can build. As long as import licensing continues, the requisite permits to import from dollar sources (Canada) should, if necessary, be given. It is not generally realised what a tiny percentage of our current dollar bill would be sufficient to buy another 100,000 houses' worth of dollar timber. Dollar expenditure on tobacco alone is at present ten times that on timber.

Mass Production

All turns, therefore, upon restoring the output of the house-building industry as soon as possible to at least its pre-war productivity. How is this to be done?

The answer lies in a comparison between the conditions under which it worked before the war and works now. Now, nearly the whole output of houses is built under contract to local authorities and the remainder – between a tenth and a fifth of the whole – are built by licence to individual order. Before the war the preponderant output was produced in mass for a prospective demand. At the ruling prices fixed in a market determined by competition to meet this demand, the local authorities placed their contracts for estates to be built for slum clearance and relief of overcrowding.

The contrast, as nearly as the character of the house-building industry admits of the comparison, is that between mass-production and individual work, and shows itself alike in cost and output. Under 'mass-production' conditions the industry was obliged to keep its labour-teams steadily employed, moving in a planned succession from one undertaking to another, and progressively brought down its costs to reach an ever-widening circle of demand for homes to buy or rent at economic figures. Council building reaped the benefit of the price set by private enterprise. The building materials industry geared itself to meet the steady predictable demand of the house-building industry, thus eliminating one of the chief impediments to the output of houses.†

*The Working Party Report says: 'When the materials concerned are in short supply, bulk buying tends to accentuate the shortage.'
†Thus Mr A. E. Marples, MP, states (*Manchester Guardian*, 1 July 1950) that in his experience bricklayers who have been temporarily thrown out of work owing to a shortage of bricks, on their next job spread out the work. 'The bricklayer is not going to work himself out of a job, and I don't blame him.'

If the conditions of the 1930s can be reproduced, the same effects will follow from the same causes. Our task is to bring back the mass-production element into the house-building industry, which can be done only by enabling it largely to work on its own authority for a prospective demand – by 'letting the dog see the rabbit'.

Two main changes are indispensable to this end: the complete or virtually complete abolition of the licensing system, and a drastic alteration of the principles of the Town and Country Planning Act, 1947.

Licensing

As long as the volume of work undertaken by house-building firms is dependent either upon local authority contracts or upon the doling out at yearly or half-yearly intervals of a meagre number of individual licences, so long will increased productivity, and the gearing to it of the output of the building materials industry, be impossible.

It is a mistake to suppose that abolition of the licensing system would now mean an excessive number of houses started, or a soaring of prices, or the cessation of council house building. The builder will not start more houses than he can reasonably be sure of completing in an economically short period of time, nor at a price at which he will be unable to dispose of them. So far from sending prices up, the abolition of licensing would immediately bring down the market price of existing houses and would in a short time begin to make an impression on the costs of new ones; for the pressure of demand for new houses at a cost of nearly £2,000 apiece for a council-type is, in our opinion, very limited. There is no objection to retaining an upper limit on size, though in practice people desiring large houses would either purchase old ones or wait until building costs fall. Nor, again, would local authorities be prevented from continuing to build at something like the present rate – though (as will presently be shown) for different purposes. The contractors who mainly tender for local authority contracts would continue to do so, just as in the 1930s, when private building was unrestricted, they built close on 100,000 council houses annually. The local authorities would, on the other hand, be able to take increasing advantage in their contracts of the competitive prices established in the private sector of house-building.

Town and Country Planning

The Town and Country Planning Act, 1947, in its present form offers an insuperable obstacle to competitive private building for a prospective demand. By nationalising the right to use land for a new purpose – in this case, to build houses on it – the Act has placed on all building land a value which is both high (because monopolistic) and arbitrary (because determined not by the market but by the individual, unappealable decisions of the Central Land Board in assessing 'development charge').

Somehow or other, a competitive market value for land for development must be restored. Only thus will land be made available at minimum instead of monopoly prices, and only thus will the would-be developer be enabled to foresee his commitments and calculate his risks – both essential conditions of 'mass production' in house-building.

The central idea of the Town and Country Planning Act was to make possible the control of development without incurring charges for compensation, by the device of nationalising all development rights in advance. We regard nationalisation of the land for all but its existing use (which is what nationalisation of development rights means) as a long step towards the nationalisation of the land itself. It may or may not be true that *positive* control of development, the compelling of development to conform to a particular plan determined by the state, is unattainable without nationalisation. But we do not want planning in this sense. We want rather to see the state intervene only to *prevent* such use of land as is clearly anti-social or wasteful, while otherwise development is guided and determined by choice and by economic forces.

Planning in this latter sense is, in our opinion, perfectly attainable without either nationalisation or an insoluble compensation problem. Briefly, we would prescribe certain categories of development which were prohibitable without compensation, while allowing others to be prohibited subject to full or partial compensation. Whether, or what, compensation accrued would be determined by impartial tribunals, judicial and expert. This method would mean prevention of development which was definitely unsound upon recognised objective standards, and the community would still be able to engage in amenity planning under the salutary control of paying for any economic value destroyed. It would be associated with exclusive powers to planning authorities to buy, redevelop and resell areas of 'obsolete or unsatisfactory development'.

We believe that a Town and Country Planning measure on the lines indicated would give planning authorities all the scope which they need and which the 1932 Act failed to give them.

Private Building

The re-creation of a large and expanding sector for private house-building, in the manner outlined above, would yield valuable by-products.

There are, no doubt, many modern methods of construction, including far-reaching standardisation and various forms of prefabrication, which, developed and applied over years, would produce permanent and substantial economies. The building industry, given an open field, competing for purchasers and paying a competitive price for its materials, will automatically be stimulated to invest in developing these modern methods, knowing that the reward of successful enterprise will in due course be reaped. Government assistance is not only unnecessary, but positively harmful.

Again, those elements of the house-building industry, both firms and individuals, which are at present to an alarming extent drifting into jobbing and repair work on account of the difficulty of obtaining licences, will find their way back into the housing field, and the existing danger of skilled house-building teams being broken up and not replaced will be avoided. When a considerable proportion of the industry is working competitively for the market, the inducement to employees and employers to introduce and operate incentive schemes will be greatly strengthened. Experience in the past two and a half years has shown both the general effectiveness of such schemes and the need for a much wider extension of them.

Finally, in location, size and amenities, the private builder (including to a large degree the housing association) necessarily builds to suit his customers and thus provides an index of demand. The distortions which occur under a system of all but exclusively local authority house-building – the tendency to conform to the past rather than the future location of population (with consequent immobilisation of labour), the wrong proportion of houses of different sizes, and the provision of more amenities than those for which tenants are prepared to pay the economic price – these will naturally correct themselves when private building is restored.

To combat the opposite extreme of jerry-building, we would make membership of the Housebuilders' Registration Council's register compulsory upon all contractors for local authority houses, with a view to rendering the building industry eventually an industry subject throughout to publicly-approved standards.

Social Policy

So far from disabling local authorities from pursuing a social policy and achieving the two great purposes of subsidised housing,

(a) the abatement of overcrowding or undesirable sharing, when associated with economic need; and
(b) the clearance of slum areas,

the abolition of licensing and the restoration of private building would again set them free to perform these tasks.

At present, local authorities are building not for the poorest, nor for the slum-dweller, but mainly for those better off. While the really poor live in privately-owned, deteriorating homes – and about 90 per cent of the houses in Britain are still privately-owned – the new council houses are occupied by those who will pay up to twice or three times as much in rent, even after allowing for a subsidy of at least 8s. 6d. a week, and often far more, out of the general rates and taxes.

The vast waiting lists of the local authorities,* as well as the existing local authority houses, contain large numbers of families who, with private enterprise building again at the rate and real cost of the 1930s, would be both able and willing to accommodate themselves at economic rents or prices. There is no need to apply a means test to applicants for council houses when the building industry has been freed: the lists and the tenancies will 'sort themselves out'.

At the earliest moment, local authorities should be required to submit a building programme for five or ten years to come, based upon a systematic plan to deal with slums and with acute overcrowding. As the volume of private building increases over the two or three years following the proposed changes of policy, local authority housing must as soon as possible be restricted to these objects. This is the logical consequence of bringing the building industry to full productivity; otherwise, the absurd situation is reached that housing, unlike any other normal necessity of life, is something with which a substantial proportion of the population can never be provided at a decent standard without subsidy. The conclusion of the policy being pursued at present is that eventually everybody will be subsidising nearly everybody's housing.

It would be wrong not to draw attention to the grave problem which is being created for the future by the production of large

---

*A waiting list of 51,878 in Birmingham will take over forty years to dispose of, if building there continues at the 1949 level of 1,271 houses and flats. Glasgow has a waiting list of 84,000, Liverpool one of 42,000, Sheffield of 26,537, and Manchester of 26,234 (*Financial Times*, 22 April 1950).

numbers of council houses at such rents that, if a fall occurs in building cost, difficulty will be experienced in letting them, despite the subsidy. It seems that when this crisis breaks, drastic policies of rent-pooling and of sale may be necessary to extricate local authorities from their financial difficulties.

Rent Policy

We have referred to council rents, but, of course, these are the only ones which are not frozen by the Rent Restrictions Acts. No housing policy can be sound which does not deal courageously with rent restriction as a whole. In its present form, rent restriction is causing an appalling wastage of existing accommodation and condemning millions of families to ever-worsening conditions, by restricting rents to levels which render the repair and maintenance of premises impossible.

The general lines of reform must be to permit increases on pre-war standard rents which will cover maintenance costs with a certain allowance for arrears; but these costs should be certified by the relevant local authority and only collectable upon that authority's certificate that the appropriate standard of maintenance has been attained. As soon as possible afterwards, the existing legal obligations on landlords in regard to repair and maintenance should be put into full force again.

The system of rent tribunals for furnished and post-1939 unfurnished houses is in our opinion a disgrace to British justice. A Court of Appeal from their decisions must be immediately provided. The whole arbitrary system itself, which was a temporary measure of protection for tenants in a period of acute post-war scarcity, should be dispensed with as soon as the output of the house-building industry has regained a satisfactory level.

This measure of reform in rent restriction will save hundreds of thousands of homes from becoming slums. By bringing restricted, council and 'free' rents closer together, it will also facilitate exchanges. This will liberate an undoubtedly large reservoir of housing space at present withheld from full use by sitting tenants whom rent restriction prevents from moving.

Conclusion

It is abundantly clear that the homeless have nothing to hope for from the socialist Government, which promised them so much in 1945 and so little in 1950. In the intervening five years the socialists have allowed the national stock of houses to deteriorate gravely, have allowed the building industry to drift into an inefficient and wholly artificial pattern, and have done their best to disorganise the building materials industries. They have created slums, not cleared them.

We believe that a Conservative Government, putting the provision of homes above the sanctity of unpractical doctrines, could stimulate a rate of building which would rise rapidly year by year. But we recognise that, in addition to a much higher rate of new building, additional emergency measures are needed to reduce the tragic number of homeless people. For example, it cannot be right that the Government should retain as offices private houses and blocks of flats while homeless families are dossed down in imperfectly converted workhouses, or forced to 'squat' in Nissen huts. Similarly, it would seem that an excessive amount of expensive building work is being put into palatial Government offices all over the country. We are as anxious as anyone to provide good working conditions for public servants; but would the public servants themselves honestly contend that working conditions during eight hours of the day should, in the present emergency, take priority over the living conditions of mothers and children for the whole twenty-four hours? We can scarcely believe it. At present, too many of the sacrifices are being borne by those who, for the sake of posterity, should least be called upon to make them.

'THE WELFARE STATE'

Speech, Brighton, 12 October 1961

The Roman poet says, '*dulce est desipere in loco*', 'an opportunity for indiscretion is sometimes pleasant'. If the doctrine of collective responsibility can never quite be forgotten or discarded, at least it weighs most lightly on the wearer in the bracing, not to say rarefied, intellectual atmosphere of the CPC. Therefore I do not see why tonight I might not occasionally, if the argument should lead that way, be guilty of saying in office some of the things which I have said out of office.

The Plowden Report on *Control of Public Expenditure* contained, amongst other nuggets of wisdom, the following sentence which I should like to take as my starting-point: 'The social changes of the last fifteen years have altered the incidence of hardship, so that there now may well be excessive social services for some purposes and inadequate ones for others.'

I should have thought that, in the abstract, no one was likely to quarrel with that statement. Indeed, the reference to 'the social changes of the last *fifteen* years' makes it an understatement: for there is not a single social service today which was not framed more than fifteen years ago. The conception of all of them, in more or less their present form, dates from the social revolution of 1942 to 1944. Yes, you heard me correctly: I said 1942 to 1944. The general election of 1945 was in some ways only a consequential recognition of the revolution which took place under, and inside, the Coalition Government at the height of World War II, and was announced to the outside world by a cloud of White Papers – on planning, social insurance, employment, a national health service – much as the election of a new Pope is first evinced by the smoke from the burning ballot papers.

But not only does the framing of the existing social services date back twenty years already. The conditions in the light of which those services were then framed were the conditions of the inter-war years – the only available peacetime background for the wartime revolutionaries to use. If the Plowden Committee had referred therefore to 'the social changes of the last *thirty* years' instead of fifteen, they would have been guilty of no inaccuracy. Those thirty years span some of the sharpest changes of trend in modern history, from persistent deflation, for instance, to persistent inflation, or from unemployment averaging 10 per cent to unemployment averaging 2 per cent, as well as a rise of at least one-third in national income per head.

It is therefore wildly unlikely that the Plowden Committee's assertion should not be well founded, that 'there now may well be excessive social services for some purposes'. It is also quite likely that there is truth in the other half of their assertion, which sounds as though it were consequential, but really is a quite unconnected proposition, namely, that there now may well be inadequate social services for other purposes. However, without for the moment looking at the two halves separately, I imagine everyone would be prepared to accept the proposition *in theory*. In theory, too, the Plowden Committee left it. They did not – and it was admittedly no part of their business to do so – inform us for *which* purposes the existing social services are 'excessive'; and it may be observed that other commentators, political and non-political, though they are frequently willing to indicate social services which in their opinion are 'inadequate', are extremely taciturn when it comes to illustrating the more obvious half of the truism with specific examples. Admittedly the CPC itself, in its 1958 symposium on *The Future of the Welfare State*, and more recently the Bow Group too have ventured to step upon the tail of this coat. But these are exceptions which prove the rule.

Inertia and Institutionalisation

Acceptance of a proposition in principle and rejection of it in practice is a perfectly normal human attitude, as common outside politics as inside. It is, I suppose, one manifestation of man's indomitable urge to 'have it both ways at once'. None the less an examination of the special reasons why the Plowden proposition is accepted as a truism in general but treated as an abominable heresy in particular may be worthwhile.

The most obvious of these reasons are political ones, in the pure, party, vote-catching sense of that term. In politics it is more blessed not to take than to give. The termination of a benefit or a payment or a service is a sharp, specific assault upon identifiable individuals; it gives political opponents something solid to talk about; they can actually produce the bodies and point to the wounds. By contrast, the failure to introduce new benefits, payments or services is a much blunter grievance: political opponents have only something hypothetical to discuss; individual electors do not easily identify themselves with the deprived. As Pericles told the Athenians in the Funeral Speech: 'It is not the lack of what we have never experienced, but the deprivation of what we are accustomed to, that we feel and regret.' Ministers of Health would have incurred little or no extra criticism if they had failed to provide the services which the £25 million yielded by the prescription charges have made possible; what criticism there was, would have been diffused over a hundred objects and none of it would have made a distinct impression on the mind of the electorate. Yet the utility of those services to the public is out of all proportion greater than the continuation of prescriptions free or at one shilling each would have been.

Moreover, while the *minus* is always identifiable and indisputable, the *plus* is often not identifiable separately or not identifiable as a consequence of the *minus*. No one, for example, can take hold of twenty-five million pounds' worth of health services and say that these, and these precisely, are owed to the fact of a prescription charge: you cannot point to the beds, the treatments, the nurses and demonstrate that these would not individually have been provided, however undeniable the fact may be in general. Even if the equation could be established, the beneficiaries are not the same or do not see themselves as the same: the patients paying two shillings for their bottles of medicine do not identify themselves with the patients admitted to hospital sooner or treated more efficiently. Similarly the citizen as a taxpayer does not identify himself – and indeed is only partially identical in fact – with the citizen as a recipient of tax-financed benefits.

Finally, there is the fact of human nature summed up in the saying, 'There's no gratitude in politics.' Even if there were equal numbers of equally identifiable gainers and losers, the political resentment of the losers would outweigh the political gratitude of the gainers. When an addition is made to the system of state-provided services, it is only made because there is a general opinion that the time is ripe for it and that such provision is 'only right'. The beneficiaries thus regard themselves as having received no more than their due, to which they were entitled anyhow, while those whose benefits are discontinued regard themselves as cheated of what they had a right to and had been encouraged to expect.

Politically, therefore, the inducements to continue what the Plowden Committee call 'excessive social services' are much stronger than the inducements to discontinue them or to supplement any which may happen to be 'inadequate'. But it would be a cynical mistake to limit the forces of inertia to these narrowly political ones.

It is the characteristic of social services that they become rapidly and strongly institutionalised. True, all acts of government policy create a presumption that they will remain in force and are an invitation to the citizen to adapt his private behaviour accordingly; but the tendency of decisions in the social service field to create vested interests is of a quite peculiar order. Take, by way of comparison, the fiscal system: even here, as in all human affairs, it is easier to leave things alone than to alter them. But look at the effective freedom which a Chancellor of the Exchequer possesses to make major alterations over a comparatively short span of time in the methods by which a given amount of revenue is raised. Surtax, profits tax, fuel tax – none of them, not even Schedule A of the income tax, has achieved the independent existence and power of survival which belongs to an institution.

The institutionalisation of the social services is an interesting study in its own right, especially for Tories, who are the connoisseurs of institutions, and I should like to offer some case histories.

Subsidised Housing

I will begin with what I always think is the queerest of the social services, and the one with the strangest story – subsidised housing. This was the social service which happened by accident. The story is well known, but always worth retelling. At the end of the First World War it was confidently and almost universally assumed that after a short time money would be back to its pre-war value and market prices (including market rents) to their pre-war levels. Meanwhile, as a very temporary measure, wartime rent restriction was retained and, equally as a very temporary measure, since new houses would not be built to let commercially in these circumstances, a subsidy was introduced to bridge the gap – between pre-war and post-war rents.

We know the sequel. Pre-war values never did come back; rent restriction never did cease to be considered necessary, even after the building of three or four million new houses; subsidies never were discontinued. Instead, they became an institution, and a vested interest. Mankind has a powerful desire to rationalise its actions; and when people found themselves ten, twenty years after the First World War still paying housing subsidies, this desire to rationalise, and perhaps a natural sense of shame, forbade them to recognise that they were doing so merely out of unwillingness to recognise that 1914 prices and money values had gone for ever. So it began to be asserted that this was a social service, and that there was something inherently reasonable and even laudable about subsidising the price of rented house-room – though how it could be reasonable or laudable to reduce by arbitrary and locally varying amounts the rents of an arbitrarily selected minority of families who have no common economic or other characteristic, is something which no one to this day has attempted to explain. It is as if we were to pay family allowances to every third family on a different scale in each place.

The natural history of the upas tree of housing as a social service, growing from the twin roots of rent restriction and indiscriminate subsidy, would be a fascinating subject for a long book. At each stage the vested interests – of protected tenants, of council tenants, and of local and national politicians – in the system, grew stronger and more complex, so that the wonder is not that it lived so long but that two men were found at last, in Duncan Sandys and Henry Brooke, of sufficient courage and determination to lay the axe to the roots and start hewing a way back to sanity.

If anyone thinks my language exaggerated or highly coloured – and such there might well be, considering that no one here under pensionable age can have any recollection of a world without rent restriction or subsidised rents – let him recall another upas tree which we only managed to cut down in the nick of time ten years ago. It was growing from the twin roots of controlled food prices and food subsidies. Perhaps you have forgotten about the food subsidies? Sir Stafford Cripps in 1950 pegged them at £410 million. (But after all he also pegged the cost of the National Health Service at £400 million!) If the incoming Conservative Government had not swept them away at once it would today seem no less difficult to abolish the 'social service' of subsidised food than the 'social service' of subsidised housing.

Luckily we killed it before it became a full-blown institution and today no one seriously expects that food, or clothing, or even that overriding necessity, a television set, should be subsidised for all consumers, still less for a minority. Otherwise, in the production and distribution of food we should have all the corresponding phenomena to those we actually have in housing: ten million family budgets based on artificially low rents; the machinery of house production divided sharply into two, councils building to rent, companies building to sell; the price of rented house-room a voting issue in local and parliamentary elections. In short, the ration book would have become a national institution like the council house.

As I said, housing is perhaps the extreme instance of irrationality among all the social services; each has its own peculiar form of institutionalisation.

Health Service and Education

The National Health Service was created by nationalising the hospitals and placing comprehensive state contracts for medical, dental and ophthalmic services. The new structure replaced the previously existing variety of organisations through which medical care had been financed: national health insurance, a multiplicity of forms of private insurance, local government finance, private contracts and payments, charity and endowment in all manner of guises. Comparison with other advanced countries, where medical care is financed in different ways, and with the trends in this country before the National Health Service, suggests that if the forms of organisation which the National Health Service replaced had continued and developed, the quantity, quality and distribution of medical care here today would not be very substantially different from what it is under the National Health Service. This does not mean, however, that it is practicable to switch out of this system again. The old channels through which the relevant resources flowed have dried up or been dug up. Without underestimating the possibility that we may still witness some increase of private medical insurance, it would not be realistic to pretend that one can see how an alternative system could now grow up beside, or be substituted for, the channelling of this £1,000 million of the national income through government agencies.

Indeed, this institution is self-perpetuating positively, and not only negatively – not only through inertia, but through activity. When the responsibility for providing medical care is focused and vested in a department of government, all the aspirations to improvement are bound to strengthen the institution. In the hospitals, for example, a Minister of Health who is trying to do his duty must aim at increasing the corporate sense, morale and public esteem of the service, because he knows that this will be one of the ways of raising standards. In proportion as he succeeds, the institution itself will be that much more deeply rooted. In this respect the National Health Service is unique among the social services: it is the only instance where the great majority of a specific service is the direct responsibility of an organ of the central government.

This makes it very different from education, where only the supervisory responsibility is central, while direct responsibility rests with between one and two hundred executive bodies, deriving their authority from a local electorate. Nor is the public education system historically the product of an act of nationalisation: it is the slow outcome of the fostering of voluntary, as well as the planting of state, establishments. Moreover, the commitment of the state to provide education is still quantitatively controlled, in a sense in which the commitment of the National Health Service to provide medical care is not: for example, the state fixes a compulsory period of school attendance, defines the standards of provision in schools within the system, and indicates the stages and branches in which further commitments will be accepted. It should perhaps be added that, although neither the National Health Service nor the education system is exclusive in the sense of prohibiting private provision, the prestige and importance of independent provision is immensely greater in the field of education than in that of health.

Pension Expectations

An interesting example of a different type of social service institution is that concerned with the provision of livelihood for those unable to earn by reason of sickness, disablement, lack of work, or above all, age. Provision for the subsistence of those no longer working has always been made by the community. It is the organisation for collecting and distributing that provision which changes. The history of state insurance and assistance from the early years of this century is one in which social and demographic changes intertwine strangely with political theories and motives. Socially and demographically the period has been dominated by two factors – the fall in the size of families and the increase in the expectation of survival to retirement, the effects of which are still far from having exhausted themselves. These changes stimulated the search for some substitute for the individual proof of need or 'means test'. In very broad outline, the first stage (1908) was to pay, subject to means, a pension well below subsistence which would supplement income from other sources. The next stage (1925) was to increase the pension but make it conditional on having paid certain contributions, which were compulsory below a given income. The third stage (1946) was to increase the pension to what was intended to be subsistence level, but render it conditional on retirement and make contribution compulsory for virtually all.

Thus, leaving the graduated scheme out of account for a moment, the position we have reached today is that the state pays to all retired persons, without regard to means, a pension roughly of subsistence value. It finances these pensions from a flat-rate weekly poll tax, called a contribution, and a levy on employers per head of employee, with some supplement from general taxation. The amount of the pension is not related actuarial to the sums which each recipient has actually paid in contribution; but the right to receive it is treated as flowing from the possession of a contribution record, and indeed the pension rates are represented as related to the contribution rates, assuming contribution over a full working life.

In this social service, therefore, the institutional element consists not in the great organisation over which John Boyd-Carpenter presides, with its large and efficient staff and its famous calculating machine at Newcastle. It consists in the expectation on the part of the whole population that they will receive from the state on retirement a pension sufficient for subsistence, whatever their income. They have been indoctrinated for nearly forty years with the belief that their right to this pension does not arise simply out of a public decision to pay it but is a right vested in the individual by virtue of certain payments made by him, and analogous to what would be his entitlement under a contract with an insurance company. This expectation has rather been confirmed than otherwise by the superimposition in the last two years of an element of graduation in the contribution, the additional yield of which for many years to come will mainly help to finance the standard pension but which creates a right to additions to it which will gradually build up over the next forty years on an actuarial basis.

Meanwhile, assisted and deliberately encouraged by various tax remissions, an increasing number of people are covered, to an increasing extent, by non-state pension schemes, many of which provide benefits well above subsistence. A priori it might have seemed logical that as these increase and spread, they would render the state pension superfluous and enable the system of compulsory redistribution which finances it to be discontinued progressively. In practice, the state scheme contributions pre-empt a slice of incomes which would otherwise be available for saving through pension schemes, and thus to that extent would be expected to slow down the growth of non-state provision. The great obstacle, however, to a withering away of the state pension is the fact that, although in economic reality current pensions are paid from current contributions and other taxes, the state pension scheme has been institutionalised as a structure of vested rights or expectations stretching forward over half a century.

Compared with the social services we have been examining, the residue present the institutional problem only in a comparatively mild form. Even the family allowances, though based in their present form upon the experience and conditions of the inter-war years – when Seebohm Rowntree's surveys in York suggested that one male in four earned less than was necessary to maintain a man, wife and two children above the poverty line – consist of a simple system of payments and enter into budgetary habits and expectations no more and no less than the fiscal allowances, of which I once suggested to a CPC conference they might be regarded as an extension.

Coping with Crime

So let us turn from the obstacles to applying in practice the theoretical truism in the first proposition of the Plowden Committee – that 'there may now well be excessive social services for some purposes' – and consider the second proposition – that there may now well be 'inadequate ones for others'. If we have blind spots, in what sectors will they lie? What social services ought this generation to be constructing which the next or next but one will erect when the need for them is already yielding place to others? Can we catch up, by a little clairvoyance, on the persistent tendency of state provision to come thirty years late? I will offer two guesses, in as many words – crime and age.

Ten years ago I remember I used to think that it was our mental hospitals which later generations would regard as the most staggering and incomprehensible blind spot of our time, on which they would look back as we do upon the generations which burnt witches or tried by ordeal. Thanks mainly to two or three key discoveries in the field of medical science, we now have it in our power and, I hope and believe, in our will, to expunge this blind spot. Treatment of the delinquent claims today the place which treatment of the lunatic but lately occupied, as a gross example of society's inadequacy to cope with its members.

I am not referring to the debate on methods: the disagreements of the floggers and anti-floggers are dwarfed by the appalling facts of prison provision and the deficiencies of our penal system. It may not be a popular view, but I would dare to say that prisons are our most important, and also our most deficient, social service. Here, whatever else is obscure, the need for a much greater commitment of resources is indisputable: without, for example, a massive renewal and expansion of physical provision, men and methods will not avail, though men are the essence of the service and methods cry out for more and more exploration.

New methods will come, no doubt, with the fruition of that research which the Home Secretary has urged and supported; but we cannot even claim to be using existing methods, when 7,550 prisoners are sleeping tonight three in a cell, and when policies which, but for the war, would have been on the statute book in 1939, and have already been on the statute book for half a generation, have hardly begun to be carried into effect for lack of premises.

Responsibility for the Old

If the maintenance of law and the management of delinquency are fundamental to any ordered society, responsibility for the old is scarcely less so.

It seems as certain as anything can be that the absolute numbers of the old, and for a long time also their number relative to the whole population, will be far higher in future than anything experienced in the past. This large and increasing number of old, and very old, people will contain a high proportion of individuals who have either no family setting and connections, or at any rate none that is of practical relevance to their way of life. The altered structure of society – the small family size, the small dwelling unit, the substitution of mechanical aids for domestic service – has contributed as much as the mere increased expectation of survival to this striking phenomenon of a large and increasing number of aged and isolated individuals. The problem which it presents is not primarily a financial one, but a physical one. It is not a problem which is solved, or even touched, by another 10s. or £1, or £2, on the pension. It is the problem of how the necessary support, in a physical and environmental sense, which in different circumstances the old would obtain in the setting of a family or a closely-knit village community, can be available to these millions of ageing individuals isolated in a modern industrial society.

I mean no disrespect to the geriatric branch of the hospital service nor to the domiciliary services or the rapidly increasing old people's houses and homes provided by local housing, health and welfare authorities when I say that I believe we are still groping and fumbling with this problem – all of us, social scientists and politicians alike. I also believe that the size of it and the rate at which it is growing indicates the use of the central organising function of the state (which is one characteristic of a social service). At the same time I doubt whether the state alone can solve it. Of course, the problem can be expressed in economic terms – the maintenance of a given number of aged people in the conditions of modern society is relatively more costly than in the past: in accommodation, in service, and in attention – but, as I say, money benefits and subsidies are not the heart of the matter. The heart of the matter is the provision of a physical and social environment through which the members of society may gradually withdraw from it as securely and as worthily as they enter it through the environment of home and education. It is in this form that I would express the challenge of the social and medical revolution which has given rise to the modern problem of old age.

I question whether we have yet found the secret. The more I see of provision for the old, the more irresistibly a thought rises in my mind, which, however hesitantly, I will try to express. It seems to me that it lacks somehow a soul or a purpose. As more and more survive and are kept alive beyond the utmost limit of working life, the economic or social function of the individual provides less and less of a motive or framework for his survival; and when we ask Why? we find ourselves thrown back upon purpose in a sense which is neither economic nor social nor even secular. We are brought face to face with the question, 'What is the purpose of human life itself?' The monastic rule of the Middle Ages expressed an answer to this question. 'The purpose of man,' it declared, 'is to praise God, and this, man's proper work, remains when all else is past or put aside.' The rule was a framework within which this answer to the question could be lived. I am conscious that I speak in parable; but all that vast organisation and provision which must be made for the old in the coming generation will bring disappointment unless the purpose at the heart of it is one that satisfies.

Principles and Practice

But I am straying from my theme. Enough if I have shown that if we care to do so, we can illustrate the second as well as the first half of what I may call the Plowden proposition. We see a range of existing social services, entrenched to varying degrees in institutional form, reflecting to varying degrees needs and economic conditions which have passed or are passing away. We see new needs, born of newer economic and social conditions, which call to be met. We recognise that logically this demands a transfer of resources and effort from the former to the latter, that in the words I have so often quoted, some social services are 'excessive' and others 'inadequate' – that it was bound to be so and that it is so.

The question for us, for the Conservative Party, is whether, having seen this, we put the file into the 'Too Difficult' tray and 'pass by on the other side'. I can see the expediency of that course; I can see the expediency of ministers not making addresses which explore this kind of territory and arrive at this kind of conclusion – except, of course, to the CPC, which is a living protest against the politics of expediency. However, I confess that I do not believe a party, any more than the society which it serves, can fail to suffer if it knowingly allows institutions to fall more and more out of correspondence with contemporary needs. In Britain of the 1960s this challenge of the Welfare State is not isolated: it is but one aspect of the challenge which confronts us throughout the whole political field. The world wants to know if Britain can adjust to the facts of life or will allow old fears, old habits, old prejudices, old prides to weigh down its vitality and eat up its resources. Dare I say, as a once member of One Nation, that the world wants to know if Britain dare make Change its Ally? I don't know the answer, for only the people can give it; but I do know that it is our duty to ask them.

The question falls to be posed in different terms in the different fields of policy. Here in the social services, which, in volume of resources involved, represent between one-third and one-half of the activities of the state, the question, it seems to me, cannot be posed by disconnected, spasmodic *pluses* and *minuses* but by presenting a broad and large conception of the manner in which resources ought to be redeployed to meet modern realities, and this will not be done without soberly assessing but boldly facing the in-built obstacles to that redeployment. This evening I have attempted a contribution to the work by taking the Plowden propositions and suggesting that if they are true in theory they demand recognition in practice. Perhaps in this operation the CPC can give a lead to the party and the Government. It would not be the first time that it had done so.

'A VIEW ON EDUCATION'

14 December 1963

I rise to return thanks on behalf of my fellow guests and myself for the honour you have done us, and the pleasure you have given us, by asking us to share in this, your annual occasion. As my own thank-offering I would like to try briefly to express some thoughts on education by which I have long been troubled and to which no place, for reasons which I will show, could be more appropriate than this.

One of the great moments in the literature of the world is a passage near the end of the second part of Dante's *Divine Comedy*. It is, in a sense, the climax of the whole work. The poet has ascended through all the regions of Hell and Purgatory, and now at last, on the threshold of Paradise, comes to his long-expected reunion with Beatrice. Her greeting to him is a speech of rebuke so savage that at first he stands dumb, then bursts into tears, and finally falls insensible.

What was the fault that had deserved this punishment? What was the error from which he could only be saved by the apocalyptic vision of the future world itself? It was no more and no less than this: he had deserted the only proper employment of the human mind, theology, to go a-whoring after other studies and other learning.

The reproof of Beatrice is not, I conceive, as remote as it might seem from our own world. On the contrary, it reasserts a central truth about education which ever and again we are tempted to forget or ignore, but a truth which we neglect at peril of our immortal soul: that it does matter infinitely what we teach and learn. The silliest and the most sinful of the many heresies of pseudo-democracy is to pretend that all studies and all learning are 'created equal'. They are not. It matters just as much to a person's education what he learns and is taught as it matters to his salvation what he believes. True education does not consist in being taught just anything, any more than true religion consists in believing just anything.

This, like most truths, is 'a hard saying'. It does not indeed oblige us to assert that in 1963, unlike 1300, theology is education and all else vanity. It does not even oblige us to assert that nothing but classics, or philosophy, or mathematics, or PPE is education. It does prevent us from assuming that students are being educated because they are at a university, irrespective of what their studies are. It does prevent us from daring to say that a subject becomes part of education because you teach it in a school, or at a CAT or in a university.

There are two aspects to education: one is the content, the subject matter itself; the other is the manner in which, and the purpose with which it is studied. 'All men,' said Aristotle, 'by nature desire to know.' The pursuit of truth, the effort to comprehend, arrange, interpret some aspect or other of the universe we perceive is an activity of humanity which justifies, rewards and motivates itself. The study of something for its own sake, for the sake of knowing, understanding, grasping it and for nothing else, is an essential characteristic of education, lower or higher, though more obviously of higher education. The content of education must therefore be that which men would wish to know for its own sake.

The knowledge which men desire for its own sake is never mere information, mere acquisition of separate isolated facts, like trains in a timetable, or careers in *Who's Who?* It is knowledge of a kind which relates facts to one another and illuminates, however faintly, a part of the great scene of life. It must therefore be acquired and taught in a way which gives it general significance.

These are the tests which determine what is education and what is not. There are some things which no one would wish to know for their own sake, some subjects which have no possibility of being endowed with general significance. In the words of the Robbins Report, 'it is this that furnishes the criterion of what institutions of higher education may properly teach'.

Education is not the whole of life and there is much information that men must acquire and many skills they must learn which are no part of education. No doubt people must learn hairdressing; but until the subject crosses into physiology – and ceases therefore to be hairdressing – it is not education. No doubt people must study management or business; but until they cross the boundaries of the social or economic sciences – until the knowledge becomes such as is sought for its own sake and organised to illuminate human life and history – management and business studies are not education; and then they are management and business studies no longer. We can apply the test to the technical and technological subjects, and not only those, but the professional subjects also; and the boundary line will run now on this side, now on that; but the things that it divides are different in kind, and only on one side of that line lies what we ought to allow to be education.

True, education is often also useful in its results – useful in the sense of promoting the creation of material wealth. It is probably this incidental side-effect of education which has given currency to another widespread heresy of our times: that education is desirable because it promotes economic growth. The facility with which not only politicians but people who should know better argue for education in the name of economic growth is frightening. Only a day or two ago in *The Times*, a high academic figure was complaining that 'the nature of the demand for education, at least over the next few years, seems unlikely to correspond with any precision to the national need for more scientists and technologists'. Why on earth should it? 'Considered,' say the Robbins Committee, 'as an investment, there seems a strong presumption in favour of a substantially increased expenditure on higher education,' and they argue that there is a relationship of cause and effect between the education and the productivity of a community.

Simply as a proposition this is open to grave doubt. If the citizens of modern London are more productive in a material, measurable sense than those of ancient Athens, it is not because more of them are educated or because they are better educated. The times and places of striking advance in productivity have by no means generally been times and places of educational advance; nor, where they have been, is it clear whether this is cause and effect or, if so, which is cause and which effect. But even if the proposition be true, it could not be the case for more and better education because of the nature of education itself. Education is a good in its own right, something which men desire because they are men, and which they will therefore spend their effort and their riches to procure for themselves and to bestow upon others. Being a good in itself, to provide it is a work of charity, an *opus caritatis*, which individuals and churches, cities and nations, may vie with one another to do, as they build hospitals or raise temples. If they are rich, they can spend more on it, and will; but there is no calculus which can tell us the optimum amount that we ought to spend on education, any more than on the relief of suffering and the cure of the sick, or on the arts. These things are absolutes and incommensurable.

The people who founded the Working Men's College understood all this very well. The working men for whom this institution was created had a thirst for education in a way we can scarcely any longer imagine today. It was not to pass examinations and qualify for better wages, not to raise themselves into a higher social class – though these are respectable ambitions and no doubt many of those early students felt them – but to get at knowledge for its own sake because without it their existence would be less worth to them, that the working classes demanded education and got it. This was part of the good life, and they were not to be denied it. To read and write, to borrow books and debate, to study the sciences and learn a foreign tongue – all these were so many steps not of economic advancement but of human dignity.

All that vast enlargement of educational opportunity which has happened in the century since then and continues to accelerate has not robbed their vision of its truth nor their example of its value. It may serve today as a living protest against the cheapening, the misunderstanding, the betrayal of education which programmes of expansion and popular education policies can so easily conceal. The Working Men's College says today, as it said a hundred years ago: 'We seek no greater good than education; we scorn to justify it save by itself.'

'THE IRRESISTIBLE MARKET'

New Society, 6 February 1964

Neddy meets again next week. It last met on the 8th of this month. You may remember that on that occasion the employers took the initiative in tabling a number of remarkable propositions about prices and profits. I would like to examine them with you this evening, because they appear to me to contain much more than the permissible percentage of nonsense.

A little nonsense now and then is not a bad thing. Where would we politicians be if we were not allowed to talk it sometimes? But nonsense in massive doses, solemnly swallowed by large and representative bodies of men, and commended, without the flicker of an eyelid, to the nation at large, is very dangerous indeed. It soon becomes respectable. Before long no one who aspires to be taken seriously can dare to question it in public. A conspiracy not to 'let on' is tacitly formed among those who know better, and those who do not take their cue from them.

Unfortunately nonsense remains, however many people accept or pretend to accept it; and it has a nasty habit of exploding in a nation's face with effects which can be as devastating as those of a nuclear weapon. It is high time, therefore, to promote a test ban on this particular brand before dissemination has gone too far to be reversed.

It is indeed high time. Already on the day following Neddy's pronouncement the industrial correspondent of *The Times*, whom I take as a representative of respectable opinion, was ecstatic with metaphors. The employers' initiative had 'opened the door for a new and fruitful phase in the council's activities'; the unions must now decide 'whether to keep the door open, let it swing, or slam it shut'; the employers' action was 'momentous in itself for British industry', it was 'nothing less than a confrontation' – the word had become indispensable for all of us, from French planners to Indonesian terrorists.

Let us look then at the propositions which earned these encomia. They are as follows:

The employers acknowledged that management should accept responsibility for doing everything possible to keep prices stable or reduce them.

The employers acknowledged that, in addition to the force of public opinion, another way to curb prices would be to establish a body (probably a prices commission) to examine particular prices and report on them publicly.

The employers acknowledged that if over a period profits should rise more than incomes, the balance should be redressed by taxation policy. This last was expressed in other words as willingness 'to see the ratio between profits and incomes preserved at a reasonable level by a tax which would become operative upon all industry when a certain figure was exceeded by profits as a whole'.

Now, when you find management – the representatives of enterprise and risk capital – standing up in public and saying that they have a responsibility to keep prices stable, or lower them, that individual prices ought to be reported on by a commission, and that profits ought to attract special tax penalties if they exceed a certain level, then it is a sign that either the millennium has arrived or else something is going very seriously wrong indeed. I am afraid it is the latter rather than the former. Let me now take the propositions in order, examine them individually, and then indicate how, in my opinion, the employers came to be talking this kind of tripe.

First then the proposition that management should accept a responsibility for doing everything possible to keep prices stable or to reduce them. Management has no business to accept any such responsibility; or rather, since 'management' is merely a collective abstract expression, managements have no business to accept any such responsibility. The duty of every management is to conduct the business, including the price policy of the business, in the way which in the opinion of the management is likely to maximise the return on the capital invested in the business. A management which does not do this betrays more than the shareholders in the business; it betrays the employees and the nation as a whole. The national interest lies in all the nation's resources being put to the most advantageous use possible. Anywhere outside a Communist state – and perhaps the time looks like coming when even that qualification will be superfluous – this is done by seeking to secure the largest possible return on capital.

To maximise profits is for management not an optional exercise or a work of supererogation: it is management's basic duty. If private enterprise in a capitalist society is not trying to do that, there is no point in private enterprise – nor, for that matter, in a capitalist society.

In some circumstances returns will be maximised by keeping prices stable or by reducing them. But in other circumstances returns will be maximised by raising prices. Wherever that is so, it is the responsibility and duty of the management concerned to raise its prices, whether in the home or in the export market. There neither is, nor can be, any *general* responsibility in managements not to alter prices, or if they alter them, only to lower them.

Of course, if prices generally do rise, the value of money falls with all sorts of unpleasant consequences for the classes who cannot raise their money incomes as fast as others, and, in the case of Britain particularly, for the national balance of payments. But this is a general proposition, which cannot be translated into a practical guide for individual action by declaring it to be the responsibility of each and every management never to raise prices and if possible to lower them. Indeed, stability of prices generally is perfectly consistent with the increase of some prices, provided others are reduced. But then again, how is the individual management to know if it happens to be one of those which ought to acknowledge a responsibility to maintain or lower prices, or whether it is one of the lucky ones which can be let off that responsibility?

This brings us to the *second proposition*, which was evidently begotten of inability to answer that difficult, because inherently unanswerable, question.

Let us go, says the second proposition, and find somebody else, some wise man who will be able to answer the unanswerable, who can tell us which are the sheep who can properly raise their prices, and which the goats who ought to keep their prices stable or lower them; and then, when he tells us, we will all go and scream blue murder at the goats and make them thoroughly ashamed and sorry for themselves.

This is the meaning of the proposition that 'another way to curb prices would be to establish a body (probably a prices commission) to examine particular prices and report upon them publicly'. Anyone who has got as far as saying this, has already thrown the first proposition overboard, because if it is 'the responsibility of management to do everything possible to keep prices stable or reduce prices', then we would not need a commission to tell us that managements which raise prices are falling down on their responsibility. All we would need to do would be to chop off the head of the price raisers. But everyone sees that this is absurd. One could imagine a 'price pause' for a limited time; but after that – is there something familiar about all this? – one would have to start discovering which prices ought to rise and which ought to fall to offset them, and this is just what we want a commission to do for us because we pretend that we don't know how to do it for ourselves. (Actually we do know, perfectly well. The apparatus is there all the time. But for certain reasons, which I will mention presently, we don't want to use it; so we pretend that it does not exist and hope that no one will be guilty of such bad taste as to refer to it.)

However, more of this later. Meanwhile, may I enquire how the commission would go about its task?

Management A has raised its prices.

'Why?' asks the commission.

'Please, sir,' answers the management, 'my suppliers of components have raised *their* prices, and unless I raise mine too I shall make a loss and have to sack my employees.' (A telling point, that; handkerchiefs at the ready!)

'Oh, very well,' says the commission, 'you can maintain your margin as before – but not a penny more, mind.' (At this point there is a disturbance at the back, while a small boy who shouted out 'Why?' is bundled into the street.) 'And remember,' continues the commission, 'if you ever find yourself here again, you will be most severely dealt with.'

Exit Management A, concealing a grin of triumph. Enter Management B.

'Please, sir,' says Management B, 'I haven't really raised my prices; I have actually produced what is a new and better article, so much better than those of my competitors that, although my price is much above theirs, I have full order books and the retailers tell me they are accumulating waiting lists.'

'Have your profits gone up?' asks the commission.

'Well, yes, I must admit,' replies management, 'that I am making a good thing out of this, the best break we have had for years – you see, my methods of production are so cheap and efficient.'

'Wicked management,' thunders the commission. 'Have you not read that restraint of profits is just as important as wage restraint? What would happen to us all if everyone were to behave like you? We shall be obliged to animadvert most severely upon you in our report.'

'May I ask just one question?' says management. 'If I cut my profits and prices to whatever lower level you prescribe – for I assume I shall have your guidance on what that should be – will you advise me about the basis on which I should ration the consumers of my article? Ought I to restrict supplies to certain retailers only, or release them only on the certificate of a doctor or justice of the peace, or simply rely on those who can afford to pay getting them on the black market?'

'These,' replies the commission, in a state of much irritation, 'are not questions for us. We have no intention of interfering with the conduct of your business.'

Management B leaves the court wearing an expression like Joan of Arc at Rouen.

I will bore you with no more such little scenes. They could be, and would be, multiplied indefinitely. The commission has no criterion, because it *can* have no criterion, to decide which prices ought to go up and by how much, or *vice versa*. As long as the public is not prevented from choosing one thing in preference to another, people will express their choice by what they are prepared to pay for the one compared with the other. Every change in the preferences of the public at home or abroad, every alteration in supply and demand – those dreadful archaic words had to be pronounced sooner or later – will express itself in a change of prices. But the only way to find out *which* prices and *how much* change is to 'suck it and see'. Either the commission intuitively knows how supply and demand will change – in which case the commission is miraculous but unnecessary – or else the commission is applying some other unspecified standards and judgements of its own – in which case the commission will be a tyrant if it can impose its decisions and a laughing stock if it cannot.

Better try something else, then; and here it is, in the shape of the *third proposition*: 'if over a period profits should rise more than incomes, the balance should be redressed by taxation policy'. We accept then that, responsibility or no responsibility, commission or no commission, prices may behave in such a way that profits rise faster than a certain rate, that rate being the rate at which incomes other than profits – or perhaps incomes including profits? – are increasing. Now, I leave entirely on one side the question why on earth the present ratio between profits and incomes generally is so supremely right that for all time it ought to be preserved, or at any rate allowed only to diminish, regardless of anything else that happens, such as the growth of savings and accumulation of capital. I leave entirely on one side all the difficult questions which are concealed by that little phrase 'over a period'. I address myself wholly and simply to the proposal that there should be some form of excess profits tax – that profits above a certain level should be taxed away.

The first question to be asked is: would this tax be imposed business by business, or overall? For example, if incomes were rising at 4 per cent, would any individual business whose profits rose more than 4 per cent have the excess taxed away? Or does it mean that if total incomes rise by 4 per cent and total profits by 5 per cent, all profits are subject to a levy of one-fifth of their increase over the previous period? This is a very obvious question. Someone must have asked the employers which they meant, and so they had to plump. They said it meant the latter; they said they were 'prepared to see the ratio between profits and incomes preserved at a reasonable level by a tax which would become operative upon all industry when a certain figure was exceeded by profits as a whole'.

This is very difficult, however. Because some people are making large profits, and raising the total of profits by so doing, it is proposed to come down on the 'innocent' businesses, whose profits may actually have gone down, who have been being 'responsible' and not increasing their prices; and their taxes will be put up – all because of the other bounders, who meanwhile are laughing their heads off. And how, pray, will this affect the attitude of the 'innocent' who are made to suffer for the 'sins' of the 'guilty'? The best thing for them to do would be likewise to get their profits up as far as possible above the datum line. They have gained nothing by 'restraint'; in fact, they have lost by it. So no more restraint for them!

This is so stupid that you might wonder why the employers did not plump for the other alternative – until you come to look at it! I dare say some of the employers remembered EPL and EPT and reminded their colleagues of them. That alternative means taking a datum line for each business and limiting the rise of its profits above that datum line to a certain rate. But unless the relative profitability of different enterprises on 1 April 1964, or whatever date you like to choose, is sacrosanct and uniquely right, it must be wrong to freeze that pattern in perpetuity.

'SHOULD WE HAVE AN INCOMES POLICY?'

Inflation, 1968

The subject 'Should we have an incomes policy' is in fact yours rather than mine. My first shot was 'Incomes policy and exchange rates' which rather reveals perhaps the track upon which I find my own mind has been running in recent months if not years. Still, any stick is good enough to beat with. I think we ought to start by definition. Failure to define, at any rate in politics, is the principal factor which keeps us in employment. If we could succeed in defining accurately and agreeing upon the meaning of the terms which we are employing, then I am afraid the House of Commons would be very largely deserted.

By an incomes policy I take it that, for the purposes of our discussion, we mean an attempt to influence the value of money by operating directly upon specific prices; and price of course includes earnings, i.e. the price of a quantity of labour in a particular application. I do emphasise this definition, which relies upon the influence upon the value of money being direct, being exercised upon particular prices; for of course all economic policies have an effect upon the value of money and thus upon prices, including incomes. It is therefore possible to say that any economic policy is an incomes policy, and in particular that any economic policy designed to prevent or reduce the rate of inflation is an incomes policy. It is in this latter sense that very often it is claimed that the Conservative Party is advocating an incomes policy, by which is simply meant that the policies which we advocate would, we believe, have as a result the stability of money values and thus have the effect that increases in earnings were real and not merely monetary.

So that is the sense, in which I am proceeding to consider incomes policy. Its object is concerned with inflation, with preventing or restraining a general fall in the value of money, as seen in a general rise in prices – however difficult it may be to attach a precise concept to a 'general rise' in prices. So far as I know, one cause of a general fall in the value of money is not open to dispute, either as theoretically possible or as practically instanced within our own experience: that is the monetisation of debt, in other words, the process whereby part of the expenditure of public authorities is financed by the creation of additional spending power. You are as familiar as I am with the processes of monetisation of debt and of the part which the money market in the City plays in the operation of that mechanism. So far as I know, no one has denied that inflation can be, and in fact often within our experience is, caused by the Government financing part of its expenditure by the creation of additional spending power which it then exerts.

I do not believe it is disputed that this factor has been powerfully in operation recently. If that were not so, there would be little meaning in the Budget of last month. The whole significance of that Budget was that it was designed to eliminate the need for, or the risk of, the monetisation of debt as a result of the level of Government expenditure in relation to the level of the national product. If one looks at the figures presented at Budget time for the previous financial year, for the financial year 1967/1968, it is pretty clear in broad terms on what scale the process had been in operation. The excess of Government expenditure in that year over the yield of taxation was forecast to be £1 billion and actually turned out to be just over £1½ billion. Since there was little or no lending to the Government during the year 1967/68, it follows that that billion and a half of expenditure was financed from one of two sources. One was the inflow of pounds into the Exchange Equalisation Account as the counterpart of the loss of reserves. The other – necessarily, by elimination – was the monetisation of debt. Now, I don't think we know what was the exact Sterling equivalent of the fall in our reserves during the last financial year, but it can only have been a minority of that total of £1½ billion of public expenditure which was met neither by the product of taxation nor by borrowing from the public. We are accordingly reaping, and have been reaping, the effects of monetisation of debt during the last twelve months on that sort of scale. But for the alteration in taxation in the Budget and also the minor alterations in projected expenditure which preceded it, we should have been facing 1968/69 with the identical prospect of a further creation of additional purchasing power.

I come now to what will be the first of many simplicities which I shall offer to you this afternoon; for I am sure you already realise from what you know of my speakings and writings – and it will be all the more painfully obvious in half an hour's time – that I am incurably simpliste. This is partly due to my experiences as a politician, because I know as a politician that when you are doing something naughty, nothing is more effective than to muddy the waters with complication. What you fear most is an opponent who will point to a few simple but undeniable facts, and this is why the economists, and above all that wonderful race of men the economic journalists great and small, are such indispensable allies to the politician: they enable the politician to fog up what he is doing, so as to escape the blame and often even criticism for his actions. So I am encouraged in my perhaps natural naïveté, I am encouraged to be simpliste, by my knowledge of the value of complication in fogging up the real issues in politics.

My first simpliste proposition is this. The natural deduction from what I have said so far would be for Governments to end the necessity of monetising debt and make sure that they don't put themselves in the position of monetising debt – at any rate in circumstances where there is not a substantial deficiency of demand for labour and where therefore the monetisation of debt would not be counterbalanced by an increase in real production.

Now see what has happened! Here we have an undoubted theoretical cause, and also the undoubted fact that this cause has been in operation on a massive scale. The natural reaction to that situation would be to say: 'Well, let's take the cause which is admitted to be in operation, and stop it, and then see if things are all right afterwards. If we find that when we have stopped it, either things are just as bad (which is improbable) or that they are still fairly bad, then indeed it will be easier, scientifically easier, to detect any other causes which may be at work.'

You may ask me then: 'Why don't we do just that? why has there been this passionate search for some other method of preventing the fall in the value of money or controlling the fall in the value of money, if a cause and perhaps the major cause is undisputed, assessable and obvious?' The answer is of course a political answer. The answer is that we politicians exist to enable the public to have its cake and eat it. This is a yearning which mankind insists shall be fulfilled and it has a specialised organ for doing this. That organ is the politician. The politician is the organ of society for having its cake and eating it, for escaping, if only for a moment, if only through a form of art – art is, after all, a means of escape – from the grimness of reality, from this grim fact that you can't have the cake and eat it, that you can't have public expenditure increased in excess of the rate of increase of the national product, unless private claims are correspondingly surrendered.

Now the most painful way to call upon the public to sacrifice its claims is by taxing. That is the last recourse to which any politician comes. Having read his Burke, he knows the aphorism which I will not insult you by quoting about taxation. Naturally, if he can borrow he borrows; but that is a lark that hasn't been 'on' in this country, taking one year with another, for the last ten years or more.

Borrowing from the public is more or less finished, perhaps it is finished for our lifetime, but at any rate it has been finished for the last ten years or so; you may get in a bit one year but you lose it again the next year. Therefore, if the Government can finance its expenditure without taxation by some other method, namely through inflation, by creating the additional spending power and infusing it into the economy, that is an ideal solution to an insoluble problem – how to increase public expenditure faster than the rate of increase of the national income without the rest of the community having to surrender any claims or expectations. You do it of course by deceiving them. It is a method of deceiving the public. It is a method of fulfilling a deep desire of the public to be deceived by the politician into thinking that public expenditure can be increased faster than the national income is increased without their noticing any diminution of their own rate of increase in purchasing power and standard of living.

So, the answer is that the strongest motives restrain Governments from limiting the rate of growth of public expenditure to that rate which they could be sure of meeting within the growth of the national product and thus without any substantial increase in taxation but also without relying upon borrowing and without monetisation of debt. It's a dangerous operation to set out on.

You might think the only safe course is straightforward, sound, economic government and you might wonder therefore why so rarely in recent years Governments have practised it, except when they have been hit over the head by external forces and events that they couldn't resist. However, you know, there is a powerful law which operates in politics, the law of the Dutch auction.

Let us suppose that a Government, a party, observing that the rate of increase of the national income has been as high as 3 per cent in real terms over the last few years, were to decide to make plans which involve the growth of public expenditure at the rate of 2½ per cent, so as to be a little within the recent happy experience. Just imagine the abuse with which they would be showered by people who would tell them: 'Since it is easily possible for the economy to grow at 4, 5, 6 per cent or any other figure you like, the public are being cheated of the growth of public expenditure which they have a right to enjoy by this niggardly Government which is only counting on being able safely to increase public expenditure at a rate of 2 to 2½ per cent.' When the late Conservative administration did its sums at the end of 1963 it found that its future programme worked out at an annual rate of increase of 4.1 per cent. As this was higher than the average rate over such a period that had been experienced at any historical time, something had to be done. There were two things that could be done. One was, in the year before an election, to say:

'Well, in that case the programme has to be scaled down; otherwise you will have higher taxation or inflation.' That was one course. The other course was to say: 'It will be all right, boys, because we are going to grow faster, we gotta growth plan.' Accordingly the Conservative Government – a non-planning party, mind you – announced that. Of course, they only started by 'examining the implications' of growing at 4 per cent; but presently they were *planning* to grow at 4 per cent, and soon they were *promising* to grow at 4 per cent. This is the other way: you fix the expenditure first, and you hope afterwards; and if it doesn't come off (which it is unlikely to, if you are gambling on an improbability), then the result is the monetisation of debt with the consequences which we know.

So there is the psychological explanation. We therefore have: 1) the malady if it is a malady; at any rate it is assumed to be a malady by the proponents of incomes policy; 2) a theoretical cause of the malady, which is not disputed; 3) the practical demonstration that this cause has been in operation; and 4) the psychological explanation why that cause is desired, fomented and sustained by Governments.

'What need we more?' the scribes and Pharisees said. Nothing more, according to me. That's why I am so simpliste. In other words, so far as I am concerned, unless and until we are prepared to deal with this demonstrated cause of inflation and want to do so, we are wasting our time; and as soon as we want to do so, there is no reason to suppose that there will be any problem or therefore any reason for an incomes policy as defined.

I apprehend however that it would be disappointing to you – I can't think why – if I were to stop at this point. I therefore pass to examine further – still in an entirely simplistic frame of mind – other theories which have been advanced to account for inflation. Remember the strong vested interest of politicians in alleging other causes of inflation, because if they can persuade the public that other causes than their own behaviour are really at work, then they will be able to transfer the responsibility from themselves to other people. In fact the principal political significance of incomes policy is as a device for transferring responsibility from the Government to others, something which politicians are expert at doing – which indeed is necessary for their survival. Since the politician is blamed for what is not his fault, he couldn't survive unless he devised methods of blaming other people for what *is* his fault. Hence the elaboration and the perfection of explanations for inflation which have nothing to do with Government is something in which you naturally find politicians of all schools, but particularly of the public expenditure school, joining with good will. It is sufficient motivation.

Well, there is the theory of spontaneous generation – like worms in Lucretius. Lucretius believed that worms were spontaneously generated in mud. There is for instance the theory that inflation is spontaneously generated by trade unions. This is very popular in the country because upon the whole trade unions are unpopular, and therefore, if you can attach the consequences of your own actions (for which you desire to transfer the blame to other people) to somebody who is unpopular already and attribute it to him, you are almost certain to be home and dry.

The 'worms in Lucretius' explanation of inflation works as follows: a trade union, because of its bargaining strength with monopoly powers, secures an increase in the remuneration of its members, say, 5, 10, 15 per cent – what they call 'excessive' or 'unjustified'. Then, says the theory, this naturally causes all the other wages and prices to go up too. Now, the beauty of this sort of explanation, where you have everybody on your side, when you are dealing with somebody who is unpopular, when you are all desperately anxious to find a scapegoat, is that your argument is unlikely to be at all jealously scrutinised. As Professor Housman used to say, 'Stand on a barrel in the streets of Baghdad and say twice two are four and ginger is hot in the mouth and therefore Mohammed is the prophet of God, and it is unlikely that anyone would question your reasoning; but if he should be bold enough to do so, you could easily silence him by calling him a Christian dog.' So it is, say I in my simplistic fashion, that the plain, screaming absurdity of the statement that trade-union action causes a general rise in wages and prices escapes scrutiny. Of course I realise that the fallacy is so crude that it would be below the dignity of any academic economist to soil himself with such much. I mean he has to take it seriously and occupy himself the effluvium which rises from it. But it is absurd.

'ENVY'

The Spectator, 12 March 1970

It is time that envy was reinstated in its rightful place, as one of the basic data of individual and social psychology. Treated by theology as one of the deadly sins and recognised and discussed without inhibition by philosophers, poets, psychologists and other observers of the human scene until the present century, it has all but disappeared from view in our own time and reference to its existence, let alone study of its function, has been sedulously avoided. Helmut Schoeck, the professor of sociology at Mainz, explains the reasons why in a comprehensive analysis* which restores the phenomenon of envy to a central place in social motivation. His book is not particularly well arranged, and tends to heaviness and repetition. One suspects that the language was no more beautiful in the German original than the English translation. But it provides a powerful aid to the understanding of some of the more baffling political manifestations of our time.

Envy, the thesis runs, is universal and ubiquitous in human beings. It is not dependent on any particular cause, so that, if that cause were removed, envy would disappear. There are no circumstances, and no society, where envy does not find the material it needs to feed on. In all societies, from the most primitive to the most advanced, envy and its counterpart, the fear of being envied, give rise to a whole series of often elaborate systems of behaviour.

Envy would not be so strong and indefeasible an instinct, unless it had an important function in the evolution and survival of human society, and therefore of mankind itself. Like other such instincts, however, envy is both preservative and destructive. Those societies survive and flourish which have discovered how to exploit its preservative effects while containing the destructive ones. Envy-management, in short, can be life or death for a society.

The negative social effects of envy (including, once for all, the fear of being envied) may be to stultify and prevent all progress, by making variation between individuals and manifestation of individual superiority too dangerous to be persisted in. This is characteristic of many primitive, taboo-ridden societies, and may be one of the explanations of economic backwardness. Moreover, if the validity of

Envy: a Theory of Social Behaviour by Helmut Schoeck

the envy motive is once accepted by a society, there is no limit to the sheer self-destruction which is possible, since no divestment of authority or privilege or difference is capable of neutralising envy: for instance, 'it does not need an exceptionally vivid imagination to realise the extent to which people of different ages would become obsessed by the discrepancies arising in a society in which age was the only distinguishing feature'. We are not far here from an insight into the deeper causes of current anarchical unrest.

On the other hand, it seems likely that a positive function in the evolution of human society has been exercised by envy in that it maintained variations of individual behaviour within tolerable bounds and maintained a mutual bond, policed by envy and the fear of envy, between all the differentiated members of a society. Success or failure have thus depended on the devices by which a balance could be maintained between the preservative and the destructive effects of envy.

The notion of luck is one of the simplest of these devices. Unknown to many primitive societies, it provides a lightning-conductor for envy, as may be seen from the readiness with which gains of pure chance are left outside an otherwise highly egalitarian ('envious') system of taxation. The notion is the very opposite to that widespread but typically Greek attribution of envy to the universe itself, as divinely personified by the envy of the gods, who lie in wait to punish the good fortune or prominence of mortals.

Professor Schoeck identifies the counteracting of envy and of the fear of envy by Christianity as one of the decisive factors in Western progress. Not only was the deity rendered benevolent (unenvious) towards men, but Christianity offered an interpretation of human life in which envy and the fear of envy became irrelevant. When St Paul declared that in Christ there is neither rich nor poor, bond nor free, man nor woman, he was precisely *not* advocating egalitarian taxation, equal rights or the abolition of slavery. That the Christian message is today thus misinterpreted – so as to destroy its envy-neutralising effect – is significant for the modern predicament.

Any policy which aims at exorcising envy and the concomitant sense of guilt – the reason why so many intellectually eminent individuals are attracted to levelling doctrines, because they aspire to purge the sense of guilt to which eminence itself is prone – by measures of social or economic equalisation is foredoomed to failure, because it rests on the false presumption that envy and envy-guilt exist only because they are 'justified', because the materials exist on which they feed. It is not possible, because of human nature itself, so to reorganise economic or social life that by that means envy and resentment cease to exist. The utopias which those most sensitive to envy and guilt have devised throughout the ages for their own relief remain literally utopian: the question is not how envy is removed, but how it is lived with. In a deliberately egalitarian policy it becomes actually less manageable, because envy fastens most upon the smallest, not the largest, inequalities and upon those who are nearest to ourselves, not furthest away. Perhaps in the command to 'love thy neighbour as thyself', the word 'neighbour' is after all meant in the most precise and narrow sense.

One of the areas which the social psychology of envy illuminates best is the modern craze for policies of international aid. One aspect after another yields to the open sesame of the envy theory. The exorcising of guilt and envy at a distance – as between people and peoples, who have no knowledge of one another – is a recognisable method of evading the problem posed by neighbour envy: hence the often observed fact that international and long-range do-gooders are commonly highly uncharitable at close quarters. The policies of international aid, which defy rational justification on either economic or strategic grounds, are at once intelligible when viewed as a collective purgation of the fear of envy, to which the 'affluent society' – itself an envy-guilt coinage – is especially prone and which is more vivid to the donors than the imagined envy is to the recipients. The result, of exacerbating both the fear and guilt of the affluent countries and the envy and hatred of the recipient countries, was perfectly predictable. The fact that the receiver of a gift hates the giver is commonplace: the gift does nothing to remove the material for envy; on the contrary, the act of giving becomes both a justification for the envy and an additional ground for feeling it.

The parallel with policies inside multi-racial societies for banishing or reducing racial 'discrimination' or for exorcising by economic and social reorganisation the mutual envy and fear of envy between the races, does not need to be laboured.

When so large a part of modern politics, above all in America, is concerned with policies which an insight into the psychology of envy would reveal to be inherently futile, it is perhaps not surprising that the study of that psychology has been instinctively or deliberately neglected.

'HANGING, LOGIC AND THE PUBLIC'

Daily Telegraph, 1973

Few, if any, Members of Parliament who voted, as I did more than once, for the abolition of the death penalty, can have failed to revolve in their minds many times since then both the reasons for their vote and what cause there might be to repent of it or to vote otherwise on a future occasion.

Perhaps the only person who finds his course clear is someone with an absolute objection, moral or religious, to society taking the life of any of its members. This has never been my own position. I am ready to acknowledge that there can be circumstances in which the taking of human life is, humanly speaking, the lesser evil. I have never been disturbed by the apparent anomaly that the death sentence remains in our law as the penalty for treason: I see no parallel or analogy between the punishment of crime within a society and the self-defence of a society against its enemies.

For me, therefore, the issue of the death penalty is primarily – though not, as I shall admit, wholly – a practical one. If I were reasonably satisfied that, other things being equal, substantially fewer persons would be murdered if the death penalty were available than if it were not, I should have opposed its abolition and would support its restoration.

The words 'reasonably satisfied' and 'substantially fewer' are selected deliberately; for the alternative is so grave that the choice ought not to be made on only a narrow margin of evidence or probability. It is so grave, because, on any view, the putting to death of a human being by the society to which he belongs is an appalling act, calculated in itself rather to familiarise that society with the taking of life than to heighten the sense of life being held sacred. The onus of proof must therefore lie heavily upon the advocacy of the capital penalty: the counterbalancing benefit must be clear and considerable. It will not do to say, 'If the death penalty will save a single life, it is justified.'

This brings me at once to what I have always found the most impressive fact about the evidence on this subject: its ambiguity, not to say its neutrality.

If the death penalty did deter, then so distinctive and so dramatic is the sanction that its effect ought also to be too marked to overlook or dispute. We might expect to find difficulty in relating, for example, the average length of prison sentences to the incidence of the crimes for which they are imposed; but to be at a loss to trace any clear connection between the prospects of being executed for murder and the prevalence of the crime of murder is startling and impressive.

The Royal Commission on Capital Punishment which reported in 1953 (Cmnd. 8932) examined the experience of countries throughout the world where the death penalty has been abolished, restored, abolished again or where it existed in some parts and not in others. The outcome of the analysis of this mass of evidence was indecisive as the Commission reported:

> This is an issue on which it is extraordinarily difficult to find conclusive arguments either way . . . The general conclusion which we have reached is that there is no clear evidence in any of the figures we have examined that the abolition of capital punishment has led to an increase in the homicide rate, or that its reintroduction has led to a fall. We also reviewed such evidence as has been submitted to us about the possible relation between the number of executions in particular years and the incidence of murder in succeeding years. It is sufficient to say that we are satisfied that no such relationship can be established.

It was natural, but not logical, that when the capital penalty in Britain was first restricted (in 1957), and then abolished, the sequel was scrutinised in the expectation of finding confirmation or refutation. By an irony of fate, abolition coincided with a period of rising crime, both violent and non-violent, in which Britain shared with most other countries on both sides of the Atlantic. It is a period which has not yet manifestly reached its climax; and in the more recent past it has been characterised in Britain, as elsewhere, by a marked increase in the use of firearms. To complicate matters further, substantial changes in criminal and penal law were made by the Criminal Justice Act, 1967.

In these circumstances facile and fallacious deductions about the consequences of having abolished the death penalty were bound to be rife. There was, however, one perfectly clear and simple condition which had to be fulfilled if any rational deduction was to be drawn as to the effect of abolition. That was that the crime of murder should behave distinctively. If murders, however defined, followed no more unfavourable a pattern than other violent crimes or crime generally, then at the very least a verdict of 'Not proven' must be returned. It would be mere superstition to attribute the increase in murders to the change of penalty and the increase in the rest of crime to some other cause or causes.

I realise that no series chosen to test this proposition can be free from some criticism or objection; but this fact is less serious when no such series has, so far as I know, been constructed which fulfils the condition of a uniquely unfavourable pattern for murder. With that caveat I offer one table out of many, which illustrates the negative outcome.

England and Wales

Murder, excluding 'insane, suicides and not cleared up'*		All violence against the person†	Fraud †
1965	62	15,501	5,802
1966	66	16,036	6,181
1967	72	17,076	6,775
1968	79	18,338	8,722
1969	76	20,855	11,451
1970	95	23,443	12,306
1971	94	26,266	13,107

*Hansard, 13 July 1972, Written Answers, 408.
†Annual Abstract, 1972. Table 82. There is some discontinuity between 1968 and 1969.

Thus, in 1973, we are no wiser than we were in 1948: the experience of twenty-five years has shed no more light upon the question, does the death penalty deter? than was available at the beginning – except perhaps that the neutrality of the evidence, which I have explained I find so logically impressive, has been reinforced. But has anything else that has changed in those twenty-five years – or, for that matter, in the years since abolition – been such that it ought to influence the mind of a Member who is unable to convince himself that capital punishment deters? The questions and the answers are bafflingly subjective.

The most recent perhaps is the emergence of terrorism, and not only in, or connected with, Northern Ireland (where incidentally capital punishment is available). I confess I do not find much relevance in this to the death penalty. The terrorist is normally a person who, as such, risks death either by his own weapons or in the commission of his act, and is at least as likely to court what he might regard as a martyr's or patriot's death as to be deterred by it.

Much more difficult is the general fact of rising lawlessness itself, whether violent or non-violent; for, though I feel obliged to consider the death penalty primarily by the test of deterrence, I recognise that the interrelation of crime, punishment and the opinion and behaviour of a society is something far more subtle and profound. Without plunging into the moral and intellectual 'deep end' of the arguments about retribution, I suspect there is a relationship of cause and effect between the state of opinion and the incidence of crime, and further, that the state of opinion and the penalties of the law are interrelated – at least to this extent, that, other things being the same, milder penalties generally imply less reprobation. An increase in severity may betoken – even, more arguably, may occasion – a salutary change in the climate of opinion. For this reason I am not averse from seeing a sharpening of sentencing policy within the present law.

Last and most impalpable of all is public sentiment. It also presents the most difficult problem for those who, like myself, are convinced on practical grounds that a sufficient case cannot be made out for the restoration of capital punishment.

I should be the last to imply that a Member of Parliament ought to subordinate his judgement of what is wise or right to even the most overwhelming majority of opinion. If he believes a thing harmful, he must not support it; if he thinks it unjust he must denounce it. In those judgements the opinion of those he represents has no claim over him. But capital punishment is not for me in that category: it is not self-evidently harmful, not self-evidently unjust. I cannot therefore deny that in this context a settled and preponderant public demand ought to be taken into account or that at a certain point it would have to prevail.

I do not believe that point has been reached; but it would be disingenuous for me to deny that it could exist.

'THE ROLE OF THE INDIVIDUAL'

Address to 'The Challenge of Crime', Police Federation Seminar, Cambridge, April 1976

Since I knew that I was to have the privilege of addressing this seminar, I have studied with great textual care the document issued by the federation under the title *Dear Fellow Citizen* because it appeared to me that it was 'the brief' for what I was to say to you. I have done so with the earnest endeavour to be able to speak to that brief, but I have to start by declaring failure and announcing that the results have been negative. So perhaps, if I spent my time explaining how and why I found difficulty, that must be some sort of substitute.

I take as typical of my difficulty a sentence from item six in your summary of your campaign: 'The need for the silent majority to assert itself in order that politicians and judges fully understand the true feelings of the public.' I have to tell you that this is a contradiction in terms. It contains an inherent fallacy: you are expecting the silent majority to speak. I am not joking. I have really nothing else to say, except to draw attention to the inherently contradictory nature of that for which you appear to be asking. For the silent majority will always be silent. It can never become the vocal majority. The majority never does speak. It is always the minority, the specialised organs of a society, that do the speaking. This is a similar fallacy to that of those in my profession who are constantly aspiring to bring everybody up to the average. You can't do that, because unless everyone is identical, the average will always be somewhere around the middle. For similar reasons, the majority will always be silent, and by definition, will not, at any rate by speaking in an overt way, assert themselves.

There is perhaps only one situation in which one can envisage the majority speaking, and it is not a voice which one wants to hear. When the majority does speak, it becomes a mob. The function of the majority in any society, like the function of the average, is to be silent or average.

That brings me to my next proposition. In all society, and as a condition of the survival of society, there is a balance between human characteristics. Particularly there is a balance between courage and cowardice and the average between the two. The average between courage and cowardice is the normal state of human beings and the characteristic of the silent majority.

I have the gratification, if such it be, that people not infrequently come up to me and say, 'Mr Powell, I wish all politicians were like you,' to which I reply, 'God help you, the place would be a mad-house.' Society would be ungovernable, Parliament would be unmanageable, if the majority of the Members had my courage and independence of thought and expression. Society would be inconceivable under those terms. It would be equally inconceivable that any army should be composed as to the majority of cowards, of gun-shy. It is neither composed of VC holders or aspirants nor of those who in earlier days would have been shot for cowardice. It consists principally of the in-betweens. For the survival of a society you have to have a certain number at one extreme and, therefore, a certain number at the other extreme, for without cowards there are no VCs.

It is the same with the notion that you can bring everybody up to the average. You can't, for if you are to have those who are above the average, you must have those who are below the average. And if you are to have those who are far above the average, you must have those who are far below the average. Some kind of mysterious balance of good and evil, of extreme good and extreme evil, is of the nature of human society and necessary to it.

Though I do not desire to stray into fields where others here are expert, I must point out that according to the first chapter of Genesis the world was so constituted from the beginning that good and evil were created together in it, and also that the knowledge of them existed before mankind. I will go further, and say that crime itself has to be viewed from the same aspect of society as a balance – a balance that can be lost, like the physiological or chemical balance in an organism, in which cases the organism is destroyed, but a balance which is always there, whether being gained, maintained or lost.

Crime is part of society. Delinquency is an indispensable part of society. You can't have a human society without crime. You can't have law and order without lawlessness and disorder, just as you can't have light without darkness. A certain element of delinquency, like a certain element of altruism, is essential to the life and health of any society. We need evil that there may be good.

I do not want to go too far into the philosophical or even the physiological aspects of the matter. My object at this stage is simply to depose the concept of society as an organism in which, far more subtly than we can measure or identify (it is only recently that we have begun to identify the chemical balance of the human organism of society), a certain balance between tendencies and elements, many in themselves dangerous, destructive and evil, has to be maintained as a condition of survival, but a balance which can be endangered, or lost, reversibly or irrevocably.

I notice that the federation talks about crime, about law and order and the breakdown of law and order as if they were single things. Crime to me is not one. The more I observe, the more different categories I think I discover, with different characteristics. Consequently, if law and order are the opposites to the breach of the law and the creation of disorder, then law and order are also not one thing, but a great complexity of things. I find it impossible to begin to think about the phenomena which are giving you anxiety and which, I assure you, are giving me anxiety, without some elementary attempt to classify those phenomena. I am going to attempt such a classification not with the belief that it is either scientific – this University has a Department of Criminology, and I am sure that my attempts would be regarded as very crude in those august circles – nor with the idea that the classification will be exhaustive, but by way of illustration of my essential point that different criminal phenomena, or anti-law-and-order phenomena, require different types of reaction on the part of the rest of society and imply different prognoses.

Let me start with the case which you mention first, the growth of mugging. Although there are aspects of mugging which are continuous, permanent, old-fashioned, the new word is describing a typically new thing. That new thing, as is recently being admitted, is connected with the change in the composition of the population of certain of our great cities. To use a crude but efficient word for it, it is racial. Its prevalence is due to the fact that an implant into our society has changed a community that was previously homogeneous into a community which is no longer homogeneous and self-identifying. I am fascinated to notice that your profession has at last started not merely to say that, but to criticise those who refuse to allow so manifest a fact to be stated in order that it may be examined. I was delighted with the terminology of the Metropolitan Police report to the Select Committee on Race Relations and Immigration, a fortnight ago. No politician could have bettered it: 'Experience has taught us the fallibility of the assertion that crime rates amongst those of West Indian origin are no higher than those of the population at large.'

Splendidly expressed! Beautifully expressed! I don't think even the most jealous Committee of Privileges could do anything with such a sentence, but its meaning is clear enough. Indeed the same evidence has been tendered, the same facts had been brought to the attention of the same Committee in 1972; but the Committee had reported to

Parliament in the opposite sense, stating the opposite to the evidence they had actually received from those who were competent to tender it. Still, we have to this extent moved on, that not merely are we, in the context of this phenomenon, allowed to refer to the facts but we are actually now allowed to criticise those who suppress the facts. This, I suppose, must be regarded as some sort of progress.

Here then is a criminal phenomenon that is associated with social disintegration – the fact that a society, the inhabitants of these areas of the great cities, who once regarded themselves as one, now no longer regard themselves as one, are not one, were one in the past but are not one now, and are still growing apart. What is the prognosis? What is the relevance to that public concern which you wish to stimulate here? It is that there is no community to appeal to; for the phenomenon itself is the evidence that there is more than one community, or a divided community. Consequently, the reaction of the host society to a growing imbalance, a growing injection of this particular form of crime, is not the natural reaction by way of the formation of antibodies, as it were. Society is increasingly helpless to deal with it because it has ceased to be society. No silent majority *there* to appeal to! Indeed, it is because there is no silent majority, no single entity which is being attacked by a hostile element, that this form is increasing.

My prognosis is extremely grave and follows from the diagnosis, that these are consequences of a divided society. There are those who believe that out of a divided society you can create a unitary section. I do not see. I see not the slightest prospect with the scale of introduction of these alien wedges into the population of our cities, of a community attitude growing up in the future. On the contrary it seems to be that, as the respective numbers become closer together, or even tend to overbalance in the opposite direction, alienation is bound to progress. So this is an area where no sort of remedy is obtainable from the attempt to invoke or elicit the natural response of a community to an attack upon its health. If you are asking me where the remedy lies, my answer is that I have told you before and I shall go on telling you, and you know perfectly well what it is, though everybody thinks that it is too difficult and that therefore there must be a different remedy.

I leave my first category, therefore, and come to one where the prognosis is less gloomy. You describe it in your notes as hooliganism, and you give the example of our national pastime (one with which I have never sympathised!) of watching football in large crowds. There is no doubt that a form of parasitic violence has battened upon this pastime and flourished to such an extent that it has almost killed the host institution.

The phenomenon seems to me to be different in kind from the first. I suggest – this is merely an illustrative explanation – that we are here dealing with a cyclical phenomenon. The propensity to hooliganism is inherent in every society. Historically we can establish that there have always been these waves of hooliganism in particular form. You can read in *The Spectator* of two hundred and sixty years ago that the streets of London were not safe at night because of the Mohawks, gangs who terrorised London and beat up the Watch, who tarred and feathered innocent citizens. It came and it went. It did not go of its own accord. Society reacted to it, the organs of law reacted to it and eventually but not as a result of direct cause and effect – it is something more subtle than that – it went out of fashion.

So here is an endemic form of crime and disorder, which becomes epidemic periodically under different forms and taking advantage of different fashions, such as the excursion train and the large football arena. I would have thought it is very dangerous to get football hooliganism mixed up with mugging. My suggestion to you is that the only connection between them is basic human nature itself, namely that the heart of man is incurably evil. For your professional purposes, and mine as a politician, we have to keep them as far apart as we can – providing of course that my analysis is sound.

Exploiting further this notion of that which is endemic becoming epidemic, there is the phenomenon of the increased use of firearms. This seems to me to illustrate what I would call the 'Breakthrough Phenomenon': the sudden discovery that something which has been assumed to be out of the question is not out of the question at all. Unless my recollection is at fault, it seems to be that two generations ago it accepted in our society that we did not use firearms. There was no more objective reason why firearms should not have been used in burglaries and bank hold-ups thirty or sixty years ago than today; but it 'wasn't done' – until it was discovered that it *was* done, that you *could* do it. There was never any problem in getting hold of the firearms; but nobody wanted to get hold of them, because it was 'not done' to use firearms. Then, after a bit, it becomes not something unacceptable, but something accepted or at least something which is demonstrated to be not out of the question. So you have the sudden appearance of a Breakthrough Phenomenon. After all, people have always wanted to do violence to those who stood in their way when they were attempting to commit robberies; but they have been bound by certain conventions of which they were unaware. They have assumed that certain methods were not available to them. Then something happened to destroy their former assumptions, and you have the phenomenon of the breakthrough. Here again, I don't see why the prognosis is particularly gloomy; for self-adaption to changing methods and circumstances is of the nature of a continuing society. So again I exhort you to isolate yet another category of what you generalise as the deterioration of law and order.

As an extreme example of the Breakthrough Phenomenon, the scourge of hi-jacking is quite fascinating. It presents the appearance of a contagious epidemic. It is one of those forms of crime which appear to be 'catching', as a disease is communicated from one country to another and one continent to another, like the importation of smallpox from India into London. What is happening is the discovery that a new method has made its appearance. 'Wheresoever the carcase is, there shall the eagles be gathered together.' When it is discovered that the combination of certain proportions of charcoal, sulphur and saltpetre produces disagreeable results, then there is no reason why the benefits of gunpowder should be restricted to China. You can make it in the kitchen. The ingredients are common. They have always been there. But someone discovered in China that you could put them together and it went off with a bang. That seems to be the story of hi-jacking. You only have to show that this act works for there to be takers everywhere. It can be applied to all kinds of objective situations or none at all. I am coming later to the 'none-at-all' which is one of the more emphatic observations that I have to make, namely that one must not assume there is necessarily a rational purpose, or even a felonious purpose, in the breach of law and order and the commission of crime. However, staying for a moment with hi-jacking, here we have a specialised form of the Breakthrough Phenomenon, which until the antidote is produced or produces itself, has quite startling pyrotechnic results, but collapses again as the antidote is devised. Is is rather like warfare, the seesaw of offensive and defensive, of tank armour and the high-velocity penetrating bullet. In fact I think it possible that in the context of hi-jacking we *are* developing the anti-tank weapon – one which is largely a moral weapon and lies mainly in the hands of political authority.

This is my pivot on which to turn to the last, and I think most important category of what you call the breakdown of law and order, because it leads us to concentrate our attention not on the silent majority but on another point in society. This last category is the thing that started, at least to the naked eye, in Berkeley, California about 1964, and swept around the world reaching its zenith about 1969–70 – just five years flat. You can plot its movement on a map of the world and date the times of arrival of the outbreaks. For instance, it arrived in Cambridge in November 1967: that can be dated almost to the day.

What is this thing? I used to have a file, but I found that, as with so many files one opens, I was putting so much in it that it ceased to be useful. It was called, 'The Thing'. I used to tell my secretary: 'That can go in "The Thing".' It did not have to have a name. It was the thing that started in Berkeley. It took various forms: university disorder; civil rights movements; anti-apartheid activities; race and immigration protests.

The essense of 'The Thing' is that violence is used in order to subjugate the will of the majority by destroying its good conscience. Let me take the university manifestation as perhaps the simplest. Quite suddenly, students at universities begin to behave outrageously. They break the rules, they break the things, they make life intolerable and impossible. But this is done in such a way that it creates the presumption that the university and its authorities, the institution, are at fault. It creates the presumption of grievance, of remediable grievance, and instantly shifts the onus of guilt from the wrongdoer to the institution which is under attack. 'The Thing' learnt how to make authority apologetic. It is one of the great discoveries of mankind. It will be looked back upon by history as one of the remarkable achievements of the human spirit to have discovered how a very little violence can destroy the good conscience of the major institutions of society, and interchange the positions of sense and nonsense, right or wrong.

Once the action and reaction grievance–violence–remedy of grievance has been set up, it goes on of its own accord. For the remedy which is sought to be applied, the removal of grievance is not a remedy at all, because the grievance is not the case, on the contrary it is an aggravation, it is dynamic.

Another of the characteristics of 'The Thing' is that it doesn't have a rational cause. It is not revolutionary in the old-fashioned sense of the term. It is not the attempt of the *sans-culottes* to get some *culottes*. It is not the revolt of the hungry against those who are hoarding food. It is not the revolt of those who are denied the franchise against those who are monopolising the franchise. It does not have a purpose in that sense of purpose. Its purpose is to destroy. This was stated in total emphatic form by the anonymous French student who retorted when General de Gaulle returned in haste from Romania and said: 'La réforme, oui. Le *shie-on-lit*, non'; the student said, 'No, you have it wrong; Le *shie-on-lit*, oui. La réforme, non.' That is the essential motto of 'The Thing'.

There is another secondary effect besides this establishment of the destructive spiral of violence–grievance–attempted remedy. It is not merely the passivity but the subjugation of opinion. Opinion, certainly overt opinion, has been on the side of the university disorder. University opinion has been on the side of it, and public opinion has been on the side of it. The teaching body in the university, so far as it has not joined 'The Thing', has always preferred to accept the philosophy of 'The Thing' rather than reassert what it well knew was the requisite of any academic society. Universities are now governed on the principle that it is right and natural for the management of a university to respond to the opinion of the students – a thing which is manifestly absurd. It is an illustration of the way in which 'The Thing' works by substituting nonsense for sense, so that presently everybody is talking nonsense, and nobody can talk sense any more. Nobody can draw attention, for instance, to the rational scholastic relationship between professor and student, without being considered a candidate for a mental institution. I remember that in 1970 I was actually called deranged because I drew attention to the various forms of manifest nonsense on which 'The Thing' was battening.

The civil rights movement in Northern Ireland in 1968–70 was a classic example of 'The Thing'. It applied the methods of Kent campus to imaginary grievances in a divided, or divisible, community in Northern Ireland. There were no grievances, and everybody knew there were no grievances. But immediately the violence started, everybody said: 'There must be grievances. Authority must be at fault. Therefore authority must remedy the grievances.' When authority had remedied the imaginary grievances and the violence still went on, and got worse and worse, then people said, 'Authority must be disposed of, because clearly it is evilly intentioned.' (Maybe you think that is a partisan statement of the circumstances in Northern Ireland? It is no more partisan than my description of what has happened in the universities.)

In Northern Ireland 'The Thing' eventually unchained some of the other phenomena that we have been discussing here, which are inherently separate: endemic hooliganism; the breakthrough of the use of the firearm; and the infinite potential for blocking the formation of antibodies, for blocking the natural reaction of a society to violence, which exists in a divided community. The forms of criminal or lawless activity which have followed the civil rights movement which came and went in 1969–71 will disappear as and when there is a general conviction that there is going to be one society and one particular sort of society in Northern Ireland – that is to say, one state, one particular sort of state, and no other.

I will not go on to examine by the same criteria the other manifestations of 'The Thing', such as the anti-apartheid demonstrations, in which open breach of the law was widely condoned and encouraged by the organs of public opinion. I need not even mention the agitation surrounding race and racialism and immigration in the unique circumstances of the last twenty years in the United Kingdom. In all these cases the reaction of society as a whole in the face of 'The Thing' is like that of an organism attacked by a parasite, or a specialised aggressor: it behaves in exactly the way which renders the aggression successful. There is a general passivity, a loss of good conscience – 'they must have been doing something very wrong there'; 'we must have been wrong'; 'I suppose these new ideas must be right'; 'I suppose we have got to get used to them', etcetera, etcetera. The overt expression of that passivity and self-condemnation is that a whole range of the voices of public opinion are on the side of what you and I call the criminals. They are on the side of this new engine for society-breaking.

That has brought us back again to the conundrum which you posed to me and in the face of which I had to express my helplessness – namely, how do we make the silent majority unsilent since that is by definition impossible? How does any society protect itself against this kind of comprehensive assault, which does not even need the charcoal, sulphur and saltpetre to make the gunpowder but can find the materials for the application of its marvellous discovery anywhere in the world and in any circumstances?

I will offer the best consolation I can.

I put to myself the question: 'How then, does it come right?' My first reply to that is: 'It doesn't have to come right. Societies do not have to survive. There is no law of nature which says that human societies are bound to survive so that we could say "Cheer up, chaps!" Indeed, history proves the opposite. There may be no answer, in the sense that there may be no available cure which will work.'

I am therefore reduced to asking: 'If there were one, what would it be?' In doing so I am rather like the doctor by the patient's bedside, who knows – although of course he does not tell the patient – that the outcome of the disease will depend upon something in the constitution of that patient which he cannot control nor further influence and which he cannot even ascertain, except by the event. I have often thought that one of the most interesting things for doctors about their patients is to see whether they survive or not.

So we are referred to the chemistry of the reaction of society; and here we are involved inescapably in a circularity of reasoning. If it is the sort of society that survives, it will react like this. If it does not react like this, it is not one of the sorts of society that survive. Not much consolation in that! But at least one can attempt to say what form the reaction is going to take. What one needs and has to have is a reaction. What we are looking for is the politics of reaction. I do not mean being reactionary, simply going back to a past state of affairs, I mean reaction as the antithesis of action. That will not, by definition, come from the silent majority. It must come from the minority of one. Anything in this world which is any good comes from a minority – above all, the minority of one. If you doubt that, read the Old Testament. I do not believe that reaction occurs except through individual resistance in the first place. This, therefore, is not the business of the silent majority which you have presented as your target. That's escapism. That's an excuse. You are really saying, 'We must find a way to do the impossible.' You are saying that the answer is to do that which is inherently contradictory, to make the silent majority speak, to make the average the exception and so on.

Reaction against the weapons of 'The Thing' – I take that now, in concluding, as typical of some, though not all, of the classifications into which I have exhorted you to divide the breaches of law and order – reaction against its contradictions, its absurdities, its defiance of known, established, healthy reality, can only come from individual persons – and from individual persons who speak. You will not find those individual persons amongst the majority, because by definition the majority is composed of individuals who do not speak. You therefore need people in the minority who will speak, the heretics, not to say martyrs. Indeed, martyrdoms you must have; for martyrdoms are a sign that the next generation will be orthodox. Generation One you burn at the stake; Generation Two you decorate with the CBE.

Unless people go out into the open, the reaction cannot take place. You ask, how do we set about organising that? You can't. There either are such people in sufficient quantities or there are not. There either is room for them in this society, and an eventual hearing (whether pre- or post-martyrdom), or there isn't. You cannot do anything about it. Or can you? That question is not addressed to an association or a federation. Federations don't do these things. Only individuals do them. I don't know – perhaps it might be *you*. But the *you*, remember, is in the singular.

'HUMAN RIGHTS'

Journal of Medical Ethics, 3, 1977

What are human rights? In this article Enoch Powell, MP (a former Conservative Minister of Health), approaches this question through a critical discussion of Article 25 (1) of the United Nations Universal Declaration of Human Rights.

Article 25 (1) of the United Nations Universal Declaration of Human Rights, subscribed by the United Kingdom in December 1948, runs as follows: 'Everyone has a right to a standard of living adequate for the health and wellbeing of himself and of his family, including medical care.'

The Declaration was – not surprisingly – unaccompanied by any mechanism for the enforcement of the rights which it declared. In that respect it differed from the European Convention of Human Rights, to which the United Kingdom adhered in November 1950 under the auspices of the Council of Europe and which came into force in September 1953. The Convention established a European Court of Human Rights, to which the signatory states accorded supranational powers, and before which at this moment Britain awaits judgment in respect of acts committed in Northern Ireland in 1971. Significantly, there is no provision (yet) in the European Convention corresponding to Article 25 of the UN Declaration.

However it would be unwise to conclude that, just because it has no enforcement mechanism, the Universal Declaration is as harmless as it is futile. Nonsense can never be talked with impunity by anyone; and when governments solemnly talk nonsense in the name of nations, harm is certain to come of it sooner or later. Most of the contents of the Universal Declaration are not merely nonsense but pernicious nonsense; and Article 25 is in this respect typical, not least in being both nonsensical and pernicious in several different ways at the same time.

A right is a claim which is, or ought to be, enforceable against others. An individual, apart from society, cannot be conceived as having rights – or if he does, they are rights as against God, which is blasphemy. Robinson Crusoe on a desert island may experience good luck or bad luck; but he can have no rights. The concept of enforcement involves – as the word implies – the use of force, compulsion: one man's right is enforced by others being compelled to do what they would not have done of their own free will. This is true even of immaterial rights: a right to free speech is a claim to say to others what they do not want to hear, and to do so, if necessary, thanks to the exercise of force against those who would like to interfere. But the compulsion becomes specially evident when the right is a claim to something material, because what one has another must go without: a right to free travel is a claim to compel others to transport me at their expense; a right to a pension is a claim to compel others to transfer part of their income to me.

This business of compulsion is not something theoretical or peripheral; it is of the essence of a right, because there is no point in declaring a right to what everyone is going to have anyhow. The whole object of declaring a right is to justify or commend the use of compulsion to alter the existing relationship between individuals in a society. An existing right is a claim which the society already enforces. A proposed right is a claim which the proposer would like the society to enforce. In fact a statement of human rights is either a description of a society or a critique of a society.

The compulsion with which rights are concerned will be either arbitrary or lawful depending on whether the compulsion is exerted in known and foreseeable circumstances by known and foreseeable process. For the compulsion to be lawful, the right must be 'justiciable'; that is, it must be definable, so that it can be uniformly and predictably applied, upon known principles. A right not stated in justiciable terms is tantamount to a claim to exert arbitrary compulsion. Article 25 is exactly of this character. The terms 'adequate' and 'wellbeing', not to mention 'standard of living' and even 'medical care', are purely subjective: to prescribe a 'standard adequate for wellbeing' is not to interpret a rule; it is to make an arbitrary decision, and an arbitrary decision about the compulsion to be exerted upon the members of a society. The definition will be not the ruling of a judge but the manifesto of a revolutionary junta. A 'standard adequate for wellbeing' is potentially unrestricted – 'the sky's the limit' – and therefore the actual limit imposed and the performance exacted are necessarily arbitrary, the decisions of brute force.

The arbitrary implications of undefinable rights are particularly evident where the right claimed is by its nature not capable of being satisfied by any degree of compulsion exercised within the relevant society. However vague may be the concept of 'medical care adequate for health', the right clearly cannot be realised if there are no doctors.

However subjective the 'standard of living adequate for health and wellbeing', it obviously cannot be achieved if population is outstripping subsistence. Unless therefore the right asserted is tautologous and meaningless – unless 'adequate' means simply whatever is available in the given circumstances – its assertion is a threat not merely of arbitrary compulsion but of unlimited and inherently futile compulsion: it is a programme of nihilistic aggression.

This is precisely the purpose with which it was framed by its authors in the United Nations. The society implicit in any statement of a right is not, in the context of the United Nations, a national society. The society intended is international – the so-called community of nations, or world society. The compulsion to be exercised in the attempt to satisfy the claim of right is not purely or mainly internal to particular societies: it is compulsion to be exercised by some societies against other societies, coercion to be brought to bear upon an international scale. The statement 'everyone has a right to medical care adequate to his health and well-being' is, in the Universal Declaration, tantamount to the highwayman's 'stand and deliver': if this right is not realisable within a society, it must be realised by compulsory redistribution and reorganisation as between societies, and if it is still impracticable even by compulsion on an international scale, so much the worse for the international community! The implicit nihilism and aggression are global.

It is not accidental that the assertion of 'the rights of man' has been characteristic of revolutionary regimes which aspired to interfere with and overturn the systems of law and society of their neighbours; and there could be no more striking evidence of the antagonism of Soviet Russia to Trotskyism than that 'human rights' have to be forced down its throat at Helsinki or Belgrade like spoonfuls of brimstone.

On the other hand it is possible to differentiate the nature and effects of the human rights 'declared' by the United Nations from those asserted as the basis of the American state in the second section of the Declaration of Independence. A right to 'life' may be philosophically opaque; and right to 'liberty' may mean anything or nothing; but a right to the 'pursuit of happiness' is unmistakably individualist, a claim upon society for the absence or minimum of restraint upon oneself, counterbalanced by the renunciation of restraint upon others. The right to the 'pursuit of happiness' and the right to an 'adequate standard of living' are dead opposites, as opposite as the right to pursue something and the right to be given something, as opposite as the demand for minimum compulsion in society and the demand for maximum compulsion. What a strange freak of human history it is that the Declaration of Independence should be among the lineal ancestors of the Universal Declaration of Human Rights!

It is a paradox upon which a Tory may perhaps be permitted one parting reflexion. The attempt to understand or to construct society starting from the individual is foredoomed to failure, if not to worse. The initial word 'everyone' in Article 25 (and in most of the other Articles) – however illogically linked with 'his family' – contains the same fallacy as 'all men' in the Declaration of 1776: 'rights' are not an attribute of individuals but a description of societies. Those who, wittingly or not, use the concept of 'human rights' to attack societies from within or without find in the end that the result is neither health nor well-being.

'GIVING AWAY THE ROD'

The Spectator, 21 January 1978

I am opposed to judicial corporal punishment, always have been and, so far as I can see, always shall be. I am even more opposed to the question of that penalty in the United Kingdom being submitted to a tribunal outside this country and to the decision of that tribunal being treated as binding. Assuredly the verdict of the Fool upon King Lear has come home to us:

> When thou gavest them the rod and
> puttest down thine own breeches,
> Then they for sudden joy did weep
> And I for sorrow sung,
> That such a king should play bo-peep
> And go the fools among.

Indeed we have 'given the rod' to nations which have been better acquainted than ourselves with tyranny and inhumanity. It was no good the Prime Minister telling the Bangladeshis last week that the making and administration of the laws of this country is our own business. He had evidently suffered a fit of amnesia, and overlooked not only the European Communities Act, 1972, which tore a great hole in this country's legislative independence, but that much earlier aberration, the signature of the European Convention of Human Rights in 1950.

At least the European Communities Act, if I remember rightly, had been the subject of a debate or two. The Convention of Human Rights did not even rate a half-hour adjournment. The Attorney General of the day (one Shawcross), informed an inquiring MP that 'it is not contemplated that any legislation will be necessary to give effect to the terms of this Convention' because 'I think we are entitled to say that the law of this country has always been in advance of the laws of most other countries in regard to human rights'.

All humbug is punished sooner or later; but Nemesis is notoriously slow, and it was a quarter of a century before she struck and the United Kingdom found itself, to the malicious glee of her neighbours, the first signatory state to the Convention to be found guilty of a breach of its terms, in Ulster in 1971. And now we have come up before the beak for a second wigging, because on the application of one of our own citizens we are accused of 'degrading treatment or punishment' inflicted in the Isle of Man.

It is impossible to exaggerate the revolutionary significance of the recognition of a binding judicial tribunal external to the realm. There is no similarity between this and international arbitration, where a state voluntarily agrees in a particular case to accept the judgment of a tribunal, as two individuals might freely agree to accept the adjudication of an arbitrator. International arbitration is no more a transfer of sovereignty than private arbitration is an ousting of the jurisdiction of the courts. The European Convention is different in kind, and the British signatories of it, worthy predecessors to the signatories of the Treaty of Brussels in 1972, put an end to a period of more than four centuries during which no causes have been carried out of this realm. It is a thousand pities that the writ of *Praemunire* which Henry VIII used against Wolsey etc. was no longer available to prevent them; for despite the fair-seeming terminology of Human Rights, the result is incompatible with the elementary principles of justice and of democracy as we understand them.

The consequences strike at the right of the people of this country to live under the laws made and altered by their representatives in Parliament. This ceases to be possible where a document accepted as binding is bindingly interpreted by an external court. In order to arrive at its findings, the European Commission does what no court in this country can do, namely sit in judgment upon the policy and justification of an Act of Parliament. What is more, and equally incompatible with our conception of parliamentary democracy, the judicial interpretation of the terms of such a document as the Convention is not susceptible to statutory control or modification. In the system to which the European Convention belongs, the judiciary are the legislators, and their powers as such are the more sweeping because of the necessarily vague and general terms in which the so-called human rights are defined.

There is a further twist of the knife in the birching case: it calls into question our right to maintain the peculiar forms of connection which exist between the United Kingdom on the one hand and the 'Islands', *viz.* Man and the Channel Islands, on the other hand. By accepting the jurisdiction of an external authority in domestic matters, the UK in effect converted her responsibility for the external relations of the Isle of Man into a total responsibility for its internal affairs, and abrogated by a sidewind the semi-independence of the Islands, which are under the Crown but not part of the United Kingdom. I wonder if the Manxmen and the Channel Islanders understood *that* in 1950!

However, if we do not like being judged by an external tribunal, if we do not like our citizens being interrogated by foreign judges about acts committed in the United Kingdom, if we do not like our Acts of Parliament and our internal administration being scrupulously picked over by a European Commission, if we do not like the relations between the Crown and its possessions being altered over our heads, the remedy is in our own hands. Do we really believe that the rights we enjoy under our laws compare favourably with those in other societies? Then let us tell the world so. If not, let us put our own house in order and not wait for others to do it for us. In either case, let us call off our participation in the dangerous humbug of international conventions of so-called 'human rights'. I don't expect we shall – not yet. But one day, if the long sickness of self-abnegation and denigration is ever over, we shall have to do it.

LETTER IN ANSWER TO SOLZHENITSYN'S HARVARD STATEMENT

21 June 1978

I am one of what must be an increasing number who find the portentous moralisings of A. Solzhenitsyn a bore and an irritation. Scarcely any aspect of life in the countries where he passes his voluntary exile has failed to incur his pessimistic censure. Coming from Russia, where freedom of the press has been not so much unknown as uncomprehended since long before the Revolution, he is shocked to discover that a free press disseminated all kinds of false, partial and invented information and that journalists contradict themselves from one day to the next without shame and without apology. Only a Russian would find all that surprising, or fail to understand that freedom which is not misused is not freedom at all.

Like all travellers he misunderstands what he observes. It simply is not true that 'within the Western countries the press has become more powerful than the legislative power, the executive and the judiciary'. The British electorate regularly disprove this by electing governments in the teeth of the hostility and mispresentation of virtually the whole of the press. Our modern Munchhausen has, however, found a more remarkable mare's nest still: he has discovered the 'false slogan, characteristic of a false era, that everyone is entitled to know everything'. Excited by this discovery he announces a novel and profound moral principle, a new addendum to the catalogue of human rights. 'People,' he says, 'have a right not to know, and it is a more valuable one.' Not merely morality but theology illuminates the theme: people have, say Solzhenitsyn, 'the right not to have their divine souls' burdened with 'the excessive flow of information'.

Just so. Whatever may be the case in Russia, we in the degenerate West can switch off the radio or television, or not buy a newspaper, or not read such parts of it as we do not wish to. I can assure Solzhenitsyn that the method works admirably, 'right' or 'no right'. I know, because I have applied it with complete success to his own speeches and writings.

'SOCIAL SERVICES'

The Times Health Supplement, 13 November 1981

The old Minister of Health, 1949–64, was responsible to Parliament directly for the hospital services, being almost wholly provided by the taxpayer, and indirectly for the health and welfare services provided partly out of the rates and partly out of taxes by local authorities. He also answered for the general practitioner, dental and pharmaceutical services.

There is nothing in common between all this, which consists in 'real' services, and the fixing and payment of money benefits, financed in great part by one special tax called 'contributions' – at least there is nothing common to these two functions which justifies demands for their being the province of one minister.

Maybe deficiency of income affects health; but so do housing and the environment, and so do conditions of employment. The unity of the consumer creates no presumption in favour of the unity of the supplier.

Unfortunately nowadays every departmental minister has to be a secretary of state, just as every unimportant diplomatic station has to be an embassy. This, and the multiplication of that half-breed known as ministers of state, is a product of a political inflation which even the present Government has not attempted to control.

No longer therefore, apparently, can we have one minister for health services and one minister for social payments; but that would be more sensible, all the same.

So I must restate the question as 'What would my priorities be if I were now what the Minister of Health was then?' 'Then' in 1960–3, eighteen years ago; and in the meantime, apart from summarising my reflections and discoveries before they passed from my memory in a slim volume entitled *Medicine and Politics*, I have done what most ex-ministers do when they have a left most departments – given the subject a wide berth. There is a good reason for this: with any luck, they will never be back *there* again, unless it was one of the great departments like the Treasury, Defence and the Foreign Office.

Your career politician is a generalist and eschews becoming 'typed'. In the case of Health, there is the special relief at having escaped from those incessant wrangles over money with income-orientated professions, whose members are taken by the general public for altruistic servants of humanity, if not for angelic comforters. Any past Minister of Health who wanted to be Minister of Health again would have very peculiar tastes.

So, 'What would my priorities be if the bad dream came true, and I were Minister of Health now?' If by 'priorities' is meant ambitions for changing the pattern and content of the service, I should be very reluctant to form any priorities. That pattern changes gradually as medical practice and fashions change and as public demand changes.

The plant – hospitals, equipment, surgeries – being state-owned and state-administered, those changes do not come about by a gradual process made up of an infinite number of individual decisions: they happen in lurches, of which the most visible form is not the provision of new plant but the discontinuance of old plant.

It is the nature of this process that it is always being overtaken by further changes in medical practice and fashion and public demand. One never, as a result, can get it right.

My mind goes back to the original fifteen-year Hospital Plan, published in January 1962. It was based, because in the then state of medical opinion it could not be otherwise, upon the concept of the district general hospital, with the full range of specialities. It was consequently characterised by the supersession of large numbers of small local hospitals, including those survivals from a byegone age, the 'cottage hospitals'. If rumour speaks true, the pattern on which the plan was based was obsolescent before the second five-year phase of the plan was far advanced. Opinion and fashion had changed: to talk of the 'district general hospital' now stamped the speaker as a Rip Van Winkle.

In the flush of enthusiasm, if not youthful, at least inexperienced, I set myself in 1960 two major objectives: one was the development of extramural services – 'community care' was the jargon – which would reduce the incidence of hospital care and counteract the institutionalism of long-stay hospitals; and the other, not unconnected, was to break down the huge mental hospitals inherited from the nineteenth century.

It is, as I noted at the time, a peculiar fact that most laymen who have had responsibility for the health service have interested themselves personally to a preponderant extent in the case of the mentally afflicted, both the mentally ill and the mentally handicapped. I attribute that fact, rightly or wrongly, to the realisation of everyone who occupies that position that, while in every other direction insistent and vocal public and professional demand keeps up a constant pressure for expansion and improvement, it is frequently only his own influence and authority which will be exerted to redress the balance.

I shall return presently to this matter of the popularity or unpopularity of different aspects of the health service. Meanwhile a sad reflection dawns upon the well-intentioned occupant of the ministerial chair. Contrary to common assumption, community care is far more costly than institutional care. Indeed, one of the reasons why it is superior is the much higher ratio of carers to cared-for, not forgetting the greater administrative cost of organising the one than the other.

It is vain to think that more of the load will be shouldered by voluntary effort. Every health minister gets put into his mouth in his early months an ambitious and laudatory summons to voluntary effort. In fact, the limits within which voluntary resources can be effectively used are narrow; and they can only be effectively used even within those limits if professional full-paid effort is put into making it happen.

Voluntary effort is not an easy option or a cheap supplement. The only naturally efficient form of community care is the family – but that is quite another story. Institutional care, therefore, especially of the long-term patient, is, however unattractive from some points of view, by far the most efficient in terms of manpower per patient.

Thus the endeavour to replace as much as possible of institutional with community care is a Sisyphean labour, which encounters the maximum obstacles, financial and organisational, quite apart from the fact that the responsibility for developing community care is fragmented and isolated through residing, in large part, with local health authorities and thus falling within a different system of finance and budgeting.

I would therefore be much more modest in my expectations and ambitions and would bear in mind one of the fundamental demand factors operating in the health service. This is the law that demand increases proportionately to the improvement and increased acceptability of the service offered.

Demand that had been suppressed or masked by what the old Poor Law debates used to call 'ineligibility' emerges as effective demand in proportion as, for example, custodial and institutional care is replaced by community care. The substitution is thus not only inherently costly, but it evokes increased demand or, if you like, creates increased need. Nevertheless, I should be wanting, as twenty years ago, to lean with all my weight in that direction.

I should, again as twenty years ago, be the Chancellor of the Exchequer's best friend. Let me hasten to explain what I mean. The total volume of resources applied by the health services is essentially an arbitrary figure. If it were 20 per cent greater, there would be no less dissatisfaction and unfulfilled demand at the margin; if it were 20 per cent less – I do not mean if it were reduced by 20 per cent but if it were now 20 per cent less than it actually is, nobody would be the wiser. It is not a cumulative figure obtained by adding up the cost of treating a given volume of specific diseases and of restoring to health, or transferring to a better world, a given number of patients.

All the same, I would expect and (I anticipate) receive agreement from the Chancellor to two propositions: first, I would wish the 'real' budget to be maintained, though I would not argue for any test of 'reality' other than the rough and ready conventional scale used for measuring inflation; and secondly, I would seek to agree a modest and gradual increase in that 'real' budget.

Let me be clear about the reason. This country has a static but ageing population and will continue to have one for some considerable time ahead even if the birthrate kicks upward again. Such a population, especially if the average size of a family continues to diminish, calls for more looking after, medically and physically, than an equal population of lower average age: it does not die so cheaply and it does not, medically speaking, survive so cheaply.

Consequently, to maintain a constant level of satisfaction – or, what is the same thing, of dissatisfaction – with the health services, expenditure upon them ought relatively to increase somewhat in real terms. The 'somewhat' is quite unquantifiable. That is why I said I would 'seek to agree' with the Chancellor: there is little by way of logical leverage that I could bring to bear upon them.

Within that slowly changing real total, major changes of pattern will, as I have already said, take place under the pressure of changes in medical practice and changes in medical fashion, as well as more subtle social and environmental changes. These changes of pattern take place by a process which bears much more resemblance to that in areas outside public provision and within the scope of market forces than is commonly supposed.

The new items of treatment or care are not superimposed as net additions upon what exists; they are, as it were, 'shoe-horned in' by the increased pressure of professional and public demand for them confronting types of provision of which the relative popularity and fashionableness is diminishing.

In this welter, such deliberate pressures as the responsible minister may himself exert are included and absorbed; but the less he purports or believes himself to be determining the outcome, the better. This is where lies the virtue, in the organisation of the NHS, of a certain institutionalised paradox.

Although the minister is uniquely and personally responsible to Parliament for everything – everything, that is, outside clinical decisions – which is done or left undone in the health service, he administers it through a hierarchy of non-elective bodies on which the professions are strongly represented and are influential more than in proportion to their numbers. This enables him to preside over the process which I have described with the minimum of overt interference, the constriction of the budgetary limits performing much the same role as the balance of supply and demand in a market system.

Before I was Minister of Health, I was inclined to be sceptical of the utility of this hierarchy, especially of the tier interposed between the minister and the direct administration of the hospitals. Reflection and experience changed that opinion.

I made it my practice, not without some official misgivings, to work through the chairmen of the regional boards as a collective body, behaving, though they were my appointees, as no more than their *primus inter pares*. I would do so again, believing that that relationship corresponds best with the reality of the processes which determine the composition and content of care within the NHS.

TO THE MIDDLE COMMON ROOM BANQUET

Magdalene College, Cambridge, 12 June 1991

Her Majesty's Government, by the mouth of the Queen's chief minister, has announced that no distinction is henceforward to be made between universities and other places in which students of similar age and attainments seek instruction and qualifications. This is grievous news, grievous not only for this and other universities but for the nation; for it is a grave national misfortune to be governed by those who do not know what a university is and what distinguishes it from other institutions of learning and study, not to mention training. The difference has been essential to European culture and civilisation since the Renaissance at least. It would be shameful and alarming if the United Kingdom professed a deliberate intention to contract out of recognising that difference.

A university, as Western civilisation has known a university, is an institution which is peculiar in a precise and definable way. It is a place where there live side by side in mutual intercourse persons whose life is dedicated to the pursuit of knowledge for its own sake, regardless of the consequences or applications of the knowledge thus acquired. The definition however does not end there; it has another essential element. It is a place to which resort, during the formative years of early adult life, those desirous and capable of learning how people engaged in the pursuit of knowledge for its own sake go about their business.

A university is a place where there is research, teaching and learning; but not just any research, any teaching and any learning. At a university the meaning of those terms is crucially qualified. A university is a society – a society of those engaged in similar endeavour and for similar reasons. They do their life-work the more successfully and enjoyably because, living together, they encourage, support and cross-fertilise each other. It is possible to pursue knowledge for its own sake in isolation, in a hermit existence; but the outcome is impoverished and the happiness is diminished thereby.

I have already used several interchangeable terms for happiness. Man is endowed with an insatiable curiosity about himself and about the world around him, in his perception of which his own nature finds its reflection. The attempt to satisfy that curiosity, because it obeys a deep and strong instinct, produces, especially in certain personalities, uniquely powerful sensations of pleasure. In the last resort the only satisfactory answer to the question, 'Why do you devote yourself to the attempt to understand?' is, 'Because I derive so strong a satisfaction from doing so.' Joy is the note and the reward of all learning.

A university congregates together that type of personality and places it at the disposal of the succeeding generation. The decision to make this process possible by the foundation of colleges or universities and the financial maintenance of students has been taken, down through the ages, by the sources of munificence in each succeeding period, until in our own day the lion's share is produced through public funds voted by central government and local authorities. It has at all times been an act of faith and a declaration of belief, the faith and the belief that a society and a nation will fare best, in this world and the next, where the most promising of its youth are withdrawn at a critical period of their development to spend several years in close and intimate proximity with one another and with those whose talent and delight is the pursuit of knowledge of all kinds for its own sake and the communication of that talent and delight to their successors. Like all acts of faith, it is not capable of mathematical or logical demonstration and can therefore be disavowed by those who do not share it. To our sorrow we know now that it is disavowed by the spokesmen of this nation today, who publicly and proudly profess not to share it.

No doubt they are also the victims of a gross and barbarous fallacy. The astonishing achievements of Western civilisation in controlling and exploring the resources of the world, and the consequent increase in material wealth and standards of living, would not have taken place if the procurement of knowledge for its own sake had not mapped out the paths of which technology and investment for profit thereafter took advantage. If thought and study had been restricted to whatever held out the visible prospect of material advantage, that explosive corruscation of human achievement which is European civilisation would never have occurred. Those who created nuclear physics were as innocent of ulterior motivation as those who distilled a knowledge of the administration and society of ancient Egypt and Assyria from cuneiform inscriptions or Greek papyri. The fatal fallacy is to try to turn the world inside-out and make economic progress the criterion of the pursuit of knowledge. That way lies futility and the strangulation of the human spirit.

It is easy to be misled. Human physiology and biochemistry are no less appropriate subjects for understanding in their own right and for university study and research because they have become the tools of the lucrative and utilitarian profession of medicine. Jurisprudence is no less an exploration of society and human nature because the practice of a solicitor requires acquaintance with statutory codes and court procedures. The philosophical implications of the physical universe are no less challenging to the human intellect because aero-engines and production lines function in obedience to the laws of physics. The same subjects – at any rate, the same subjects nominally – can be part of a university education and of a course in technology. That does not equate universities with polytechnic colleges nor university education with technical training, nor can any overlap between the two negate the essential difference in kind between them.

There is something about a university which is naturally antipathetic to the state. That is its autonomy. Those whose business is the pursuit of knowledge for its own sake recognise their fellows: there is a community between them which they acknowledge because their mutual cross-fertilisation depends upon the underlying unity of human inquisitiveness in all its manifestations. 'Show me the results in advance,' says the barbarian state, 'and then I will give you money. Provide me with a calculus of benefit, and I will justify distributing it.' 'Not so,' replies the university; 'give if you will; withhold if you must but understand if you can what nature of community we are and do not deprive us of our fredom, the freedom to pursue, and to teach others to pursue, knowledge for its own sake in whatever guise it presents itself to us; for that is of our very essence.'

THE EMPIRE AND COMMONWEALTH

HOWARD: . . . you used to believe in the British Empire. What caused you to change your mind?

POWELL: After the war . . . I thought that it was still possible for there to be a political link between the United Kingdom and India. I realised that that was an absurdity . . . after the evidence that India could not be part of the same political system, I still believed for a short time that an Empire of positions – that is to say the possession of points of communication around the globe – gave a significance to this country and a tenable and lasting position. That too was wrong and my lesson was learnt.

'Face the Press', Channel 4 TV, 9 October 1983

'THE MYTH OF EMPIRE'

Round Table 1910–1917

It is a solemn experience to sit in 1970 and watch the British people, seventy years before, being taught to 'think Imperially'. What is impressive is that the failure of all that was so busily constructed, attempted and imagined, was not merely predictable but predicted. We are not being wise after the event in pointing to the reasons why Imperial consolidation was foredoomed. They were known to our predecessors at the time and were expounded by them as clearly then as we can demonstrate them now; for the reasons were implicit in the facts of the world in 1900. It therefore required no feat of prophecy to assert that long before the twentieth century was out, the United Kingdom would be a country without empire and not in the front rank in size and power, and yet that this would not be synonymous with disaster, dishonour or extinction.

Watching the spectacle, one has the weird sensation that the actors really knew all the time that their professions were illusory, and that there was a kind of gigantic tacit conspiracy to pretend. Otherwise, one wonders, how could there constantly be those 'asides', which seem to reveal that the participants were actually aware the game was up or rather perhaps had never started?

One of the lessons to be drawn from the study of early-twentieth-century imperialism is the extraordinary durability of policies and programmes which lack all possibility of being realised. The remarkable thing about political houses built on sand, or castles in the air, is how long they often take to collapse; and this very time-lag becomes an argument in their favour and a supposed refutation of those who draw attention to the absence of foundations. 'There must be a foundation somewhere,' says the populace; 'for look, the building continues to stand up.'

There is yet one further stage of insight – and of pessimism – which awaits the student. In studying a period and a phase in which what could be proved at the time to be shadows were so determinedly pursued, is he after all studying not an aberration, not a deviation from the normal, but the common behaviour of mankind? Will it not be found that the political activity of societies consists ordinarily, perhaps invariably, in filling sieves and making sand ropes – sieves which those who fill them half know to be sieves, sand which those who weave it into ropes suspect to be sand after all? And the final reflection which suggests itself is that if this pattern of behaviour should prove to be normal, it should be assumed – at least until the contrary is demonstrated – that it is beneficial and has been evolved by trial and error as a preservative device or mechanism. Nations, and perhaps humanity itself, would then be seen to owe their survival to their follies, or at least to an appropriate dilution of rationality with pretence and self-deception.

South Africa, for example.* A united South Africa within the British Empire was the purpose for which, almost from the beginning of the Boer War, Lord Milner laboured and assembled the galaxy of British talent soon to be known as his kindergarten. In 1899 he was writing: 'The ultimate end is a self-governing white community . . . from Cape Town to Zambesi. There must be one flag, the Union Jack, but under it equality of races [i.e. British and Boer] and languages . . . but not before a loyal majority is assured'; or again, 'if ten years hence there are three men of British race to two of Dutch, the country will be safe and prosperous; if there are three of Dutch to two of British, we shall have perpetual difficulty'. He was as good as his word. By 1908, when he saw that his stipulation was ruled out by the failure of British immigrants and the Liberal acceleration of colonial self-government – soon to be followed by South African union – he unhesitatingly drew the correct conclusion:

> The policy to which we devoted years of labour must be regarded as a thing of the past. The S. African British are entirely relieved from any obligations to the mother country. They should devote themselves wholly to the problem of making life in South Africa, regarded as more or less a foreign country, bearable for self-respecting British men and women.

Mere logic and abstinence from wishful thinking had enabled Milner to summarise the story of the next sixty years. Significantly, his kindergarten would not see – or would not look. So they devoted themselves to promoting political movements which they could imagine would still reach the Milnerian goal. 'Both races hope for prosperity, prosperity means expansion, expansion means immigration, immigration means British'; the syllogism was false, in logic and experience, but it was good enough for those who did not want to go where logic and experience pointed.

One is not prepared, however, for the discovery that Milner, so realist and clear-sighted about South Africa, was himself at the very same time an illusionist on a world scale. In 1917 he could refer Garvin to a speech made in 1905 where he stated his ideal for the

---

Milner's Young Men: the Kindergarten in Edwardian Imperial Affairs, by Walter Nimocks, Hodder & Stoughton

British Empire: 'we think of a group of states, all independent in their own local concerns, but all united for the defence of their common interests and the defence of a common civilisation, united not in an alliance – for alliances can be made and unmade – but in a *permanent organic union*'. That anyone of Milner's mental power and insight could envisage a course of events which ran contrary both to the logic and experience of the actual British Empire over a hundred and fifty years is a staggering fact. He retained, however, sufficient contact with reality to know, and privately to say, that such a development was incompatible with the British parliamentary system. That given, the Burkian thesis must work itself out inexorably to the separation and independence not only of the great colonies (in the original sense of that word) but of every island and speck of rock on the globe: where there could not be representation in a common sovereign assembly, 'unity' would only be *de facto* and on sufferance, and thus diminishing with the passage of time – *organic* it could never be. Significantly the dream of an Imperial organic entity perished on the very battlefields of Flanders where the self-governing Dominions did apparently fight 'for their common interests':

> The more realistic minds in the [Round Table] movement quickly saw that the sacrifices made by Dominion troops and the concurrent growth in Dominion nationalism were harbingers of a new imperial relationship unlike anything they had proposed (Nimocks).

And even that sombre assessment understated the inevitabilities.

Still, after all, Milner was a man who stood aside from politics and despised them, and his kindergarten were defiantly administrators, not politicians. The power of the Imperial illusion is only properly appreciated when we watch the last phase in the career of a politician's politician of the first rank, Joseph Chamberlain.*

He built out of that illusion a political cause which stirred the British electorate as it had not been stirred for decades and which has left its imprint on the Conservative Party and on British trade policy down to the present. The story of how the Birmingham radical, turned 'unionist' in the United Kingdom context, became Colonial Secretary in a Tory administration is well remembered. It is not so commonly remembered that for him too it was the South African experience of the Boer War and its aftermath from which he emerged 'unionist' in the Imperial context. The sudden chill of isolation which Britain felt in a hostile world, and the thrill of Dominion contingents serving alongside troops from 'home', raised in new form what had long been a nagging conundrum – that the outlying parts of the

*The Life of Joseph Chamberlain, by Julian Amery, Vols. 5 and 6, *J. C. and the Tariff Reform Campaign* (1969), Macmillan

Empire which Britain defended bore no appreciable share of the burden, precisely because of the fundamental political syllogism: no taxation without representation; no representation without common responsibility; no common responsibility without sacrifice of separate independence. Over and over again initiatives towards 'Imperial union' had broken into spray against the rock. Was there perhaps some route by which it could be circumvented?

When Chamberlain returned from his post-war African tour to a hero's welcome in March 1903, he found to his hand a request from the Dominions themselves which, though it had nothing to do with Imperial unity, and indeed was rather symptomatic of growing independence, he seized upon and elevated into the first step towards 'consolidation of the Empire'. (It is a standard procedure of politicians, when embarking upon a course which lacks logical coherence, to disarm critics and criticism by describing what they do or commend as 'only a first step'; for who can demand logic from 'a first step'?)

Unlike the mother-country and its dependencies, above all India, the self-governing colonies were protectionist; but they were now prepared, and indeed in some cases were anxious, to afford the mother-country preferential treatment within their tariff system if the mother-country would reciprocate. In order to do this, however, Britain must herself become in some degree protectionist and place tariffs on foreign imports of at least the things which the Dominions had to sell to her – above all, food, if not also raw materials. It was thus a revolution in British fiscal policy which Chamberlain advocated in the name of Empire; and from his Birmingham speech in May 1903 until he was struck down three years later his advocacy of tariff reform and his Imperial theme dominated British policies. Yet the Imperial side of the argument – whatever view may be taken of the fiscal, economic and domestic – would not stand up to examination. If the Empire was to be welded into an economic unit, the parts of which would be interdependent economically because they were parts of the Empire, and if this unity was to stand in default or in anticipation of political unity, then what was necessary was Imperial free trade, a genuine *Zollverein*. Yet this was the last thing the Dominions would contemplate. They meant to build up their own industries behind their tariff barriers, and not to remain the permanent primary producers for the industrial United Kingdom; and when Chamberlain once incautiously disclosed this logical implication of his policy, he was forced to beat an instant retreat. Nor could Chamberlain ever show how a preference within the low tariffs, which were the most that Britain would conceivably tolerate upon her food or raw materials, could make the difference, as he constantly reiterated, between Imperial consolidation and Imperial dissolution.

Nevertheless, the magic worked, and the narrowness and unsoundness of the practical basis did not prevent the most glorious imaginary structures being reared upon it. Like the kindergarten, Chamberlain did not hesitate to invoke as a parallel the formation of the United States, transposing Alexander Hamilton's 'Learn to think Continentally' into 'Learn to think Imperially'.

How can the blowing of such a bubble, and, once it was inflated and released, its durability, be accounted for? The answer, in principle, is the same as for all political illusions which are successfully propagated – that vast numbers of people want to entertain them, that they fulfil a need. And some of the needs which sustained Chamberlainite and Milnerian imperialism are not far to seek.

One was the need for reassurance in a world of visibly consolidating Great Powers – from the United States in the West to the Teutonic and Slav empires in Europe and the East. The *Recessional* of 1897 was not the hymn of a nation strong in its own security.

> In the 1890s the atmosphere was not of that settled calm with which it was credited by later and even more anxious generations. However confident the mass of the population may have felt in the durability of Britain's world role, those who ruled in Britain knew full well the kind of dangers the country faced and the need to take steps to meet them . . . It would need a profound belief in providence to make one refrain from wondering why a group of foggy islands off Europe's north-western shores, populated beyond the means of subsistence that the islands could provide, endowed with no great natural assets outside the coalfields, should have become both the centre of a world empire and a possible arbiter of European rivalries. It might seem that so artificial a superiority was certain to prove as transient as the hegemonies that it had replaced, although those in whose hands power lay were for the most part undaunted by the new challenges to Britain's position that they sensed . . . They took it for granted that the international world was one of competing powers and that their duty was to make the most of whatever assets were available to them.*

I doubt, however, if it is right to limit these anxieties to 'those who ruled Britain'. The audiences of working men who acclaimed Joseph Chamberlain were not just afraid for their jobs, though the fear of German competition was real enough – the three men, in a speech of Chamberlain's, unloading trucks containing German wire, who remarked 'this is rather hard: we used to make this'. They also believed that other countries were overtaking Britain in every way; and of course, as in the 1950s and 1960s, the fallacy of a 'declining share' of world trade etc. was easy to convey and difficult to expose.

Imperial Sunset by Max Beloff, Vol. 1. *Britain's Liberal Empire 1897–1921* (1969), Methuen

Britain wanted to feel safe. Strategically, the alliance with Japan and the *entente* with France were expressions of this instinct; economically, it released the yearning for a closed area within which Britain could be commercially safe, even if perhaps less well-off than if she could have outfaced her rivals in open competition. But *need* she be less well-off? The wish was father to the thought. Could not imperialism go hand-in-hand with prosperity for the working man?

Here was the genesis of the myth, destined to lead to so many follies and disasters, that Britain was rich, as well as powerful, *because* of her Empire. The close links between the Fabians and Milner's kindergarten on the one hand, and the personal link in Chamberlain's own career between radical reform and tariff imperialism – he wanted the Conservative Party to hypothecate the financial yield of the preferential tariff to providing old age pensions – are reminders that at the beginning of the century 'social imperialism' did not sound the paradox it does today, and that the forefathers of modern British Socialism are to be found in larger numbers in the ranks of the imperialists than of the Little Englanders.*

Milner in 1907 was writing: 'there can be no adequate prosperity for the forty or fifty million people in these islands without the Empire and all that it provides'. It was the same idea of the Empire as a patrimony, or an estate, the source of a livelihood for the mother-country, to which Chamberlain had appealed: 'I know how our forefathers . . . bore themselves bravely in the titanic strife with Napoleon and came out victorious. What is our task to theirs? It is a mere trifle; it is only for us *to keep the fruits* of the victory that they have won' (Liverpool, 1903). Weirdly, but by a traceable line of descent through Unionism and Socialism, almost the same accents recur after thirty years: 'With the vast imperial resources which are the heritage of this country, the problems of poverty and want can easily be solved by a government empowered by the people to carry out their will. While democratic governments are giving away the Empire which our fathers won, our people are abandoned to poverty and unemployment. Yet the Empire belongs to you, the people of Britain.' The voice is that of Sir Oswald Mosley in October 1936. So easily did the rational fear of not being able to exchange their products so advantageously merge, for a whole generation, into the absurdity of supposing that they could somehow have access to a source of wealth other than their own production. It was not for that generation to complain if the inhabitants of India and of the dependent colonies took them at their word, albeit a mistaken word: the myth of an Empire exploited by the United Kingdom was a plant

*Imperialism and Social Reform by Bernard Semmel (1960), Allen and Unwin

which grew in the same soil as the myth of an Empire that alone secured 'adequate prosperity' to the forty or fifty million inhabitants of the United Kingdom.

Curzon was wont to complain, and with justice, that Chamberlain 'forgot all about India when he launched his scheme', and whimsically mused on 'what would have become of him and us if he had ever visited India . . . The Colonies would have been dwarfed and forgotten, and the pivot of the Empire would have been Calcutta.' The remark goes deep. It was not only Chamberlain but all the Imperial consolidators and Milnerites and Empire Traders who 'forgot India' – and with good season: they needs must. The Empire which would be bound together by reciprocal preferences, freely accorded, and which would thence ascend, perchance, to the unity of common counsels and common institutions, was an Empire of independent 'kith and kin' – 'the conception of the people of these islands as a great family bound by indissoluble ties to *kindred* families in other parts of the world' (Milner). Yet the Empire which the British Navy defended, and which made Britain an Asiatic power, or a world power, or indeed a power at all, was not the few million kith and kin living in North America or in Australasia or mingling with the Dutch in South Africa. It was overwhelmingly the empire of India. But with India there could be no 'consolidation'; its hundreds of millions were, necessarily, left out of the cosy computations of the Imperialists; and its membership of a community of independent yet united states was beyond the power of imagination to conceive.

Yet it was not beyond the power of reason and foresight to know that the days of the Indian Empire were numbered, if not in years, still in decades: the best and the wisest of the British in India had known and said it from the beginning. Nevertheless, a whole generation and more succeeded in forgetting or ignoring it, in order to live with the imperial illusion – 'ideal' was the kinder word – which they seemed to need.

'A WEEK IN POLITICS'

Channel 4 TV, 29 January 1983

ANTHONY KING: I would like to bring in, ah, Enoch Powell (really?) who, who has ah, – very much . . .

ENOCH POWELL: I do enjoy listening to other people talk. I'm quite used to it in the House of Commons. . . .

DENIS HEALEY: I've never noticed you enjoying it, Enoch.

POWELL: Oh yes, I enjoyed your speech the other day.

HEALEY: I'm so glad. Yes, well you should.

KING: Mr Powell, what do you conclude from all this; you once described the Foreign Office as a nest of vipers. Does listening to this conversation lead you to reinforce that conclusion?

POWELL: That – that nursery of traitors and nest of vipers. (*clears throat*) A phrase which has become classic if not an actual thing. The authorised description for that Department since then. What we've been shown in the Report, and what has, ah, emerged from this discussion, is that for some fifteen years, we engaged in a game of blind man's buff. We engaged in the game of looking for something which did not exist. Looking for something between sovereignty and not sovereignty. Something which as the Argentines were in no circumstances, ah, going to settle for, ah, and anybody could have told them that, and anybody knew that. There is nothing between sovereignty and not sovereignty.

But we hoped that something could be found. You know, you go on looking for a solution to this difficult problem. That's the formula by way – way – by which you get yourself nearer to disaster. And in addition to that, as governments knew that the House of Commons would not be agreeable, ah, the ah, polite phrase is 'had not been educated up to', ah, the acceptance of a transfer of sovereignty of the islands, an additional ingredient was thrown in. That this wouldn't happen, except it had the consent, sometimes – and I fear Nick Ridley fell into this – it wobbled over except aft – into – after consultation.

HEALEY: Even Mr Pym made the same wobble, yes.

POWELL: Yes, it's, it's a very dangerous wobble . . . (Interest and wishes . . .) And it helped to make the House of Commons very anxious and very angry.

KING: Are you saying in effect . . .

POWELL: Ah, ah, I, I am saying in addition that that either meant that the thing was going to be vetoed anyhow by the Falkland Islanders, and that therefore even if Britain wanted to get rid of, of sovereignty, she wasn't going to get rid of it in terms of her own statement; or that the Falkland Islanders were going to be put under so much pressure, ah – we needn't go into the details of what is meant in those connections, by pressure; I'm sure the Foreign Office will supply the details if requested – ah, would be put under so much pressure that eventually they would collapse and give way. Now that was what we were doing. We were playing a silly game, which had not a tragic outcome – it had, thanks to the mercy of providence, a fortunate outcome – but it had an outcome which is not one which ah statecraft should either aim at or be proud of having achieved.

KING: Simon Jenkins, you're the – you're the author of, ah, of the *Battle for the Falklands*, or the co-author. Ah, you probably know more about this than just about anybody outside government. Do you think that the Foreign Office, successive British governments, were playing a silly game?

SIMON JENKINS: No, I disagree with Enoch Powell on that. Ah, I think the Foreign Office was trying to pursue the only sensible policy as it perceived it at the time, right through the entire period, um, since 1965. And it . . .

POWELL: But it did exist.

'COMMONWEALTH MORNING AFTER THE IMPERIAL NIGHT BEFORE'

Daily Telegraph, 22 November 1983

With an impish glint of mischief in her eye the Muse of History looked down and watched the American Marines assault Grenada. Grenada was the last tiny but bitter dreg in the constitutional cup which the United Kingdom has drained in the past thirty-five years; and bravely, though not without a grimace of disgust, did we swallow it.

Anybody who supposes that the events of 1983 in the Caribbean have left the humbug of the Commonwealth unscathed is as self-deceived as those who imagine that the humbug of the United Nations has been unscathed by the events of 1982 in the South Atlantic.

After World War II the Crown in Parliament of the United Kingdom well understood that it could no longer govern the King Emperor's non-British, any more than his British subjects who were not represented, and could not be represented, in Parliament. With admirable diligence it worked away, renouncing its authority over one territory after another.

Thereby, in the eyes not only of the United Kingdom but of the world, each of these territories became a sovereign independent state, alias a nation. As such it was duly added to the membership roll of the contraption known as the United Nations, which asserts that all nations are equal (albeit some more so than others), with one vote each, just as if they were individual human beings in a right-little tight-little democratic State.

We disposed of the big fish first, not even so without difficulty; for while some, like Ceylon and Jamaica, were islands, which was a good enough demarcation for rough and ready purposes, others, like the Indians or Nigerians, were not so unmistakable and quarrelled violently over who they were. At times this caused quite a scuffle, especially when we tried to insist on lumping several together and pretending that the result was a nation, albeit a federal one – rather in the same way as the parliamentary managers of the eighteenth century used to bribe Scottish peers by the batch, half a dozen or a dozen at a time.

It was partly because these artificial agglomerations soon broke up that we were left at the finish with a lot of little scraps, which nobody, when not talking through the back of his head, could mistake for potential nations. What to do? We swallowed hard, stiffened our upper lip, and decided to 'see it through' by shutting our eyes and applying the same old formula regardless – a constitution, a mace, a copy of Erskine May, a Speaker's chair and national independence. By 1982 we had swept up all but a handful of awkward items whose inhabitants, for varying reasons, didn't want to be or couldn't be 'nationalised' – which was very untidy and inconvenient of them.

So, as I say, the Muse of History laughed when Britain, which had risen almost as one man to take the Falklands from the Argentine, then quite logically watched, passive and embarrassed, while the United States occupied the independent sovereign state of Grenada. Shall I say what the Muse is waiting for now? It is to see whether, when someone pinches Rockall, we shall sail to replant the Union flag upon it, exclaiming 'Rejoice, rejoice,' as when we repossessed the likewise uninhabited South Georgia.

The Grenada story is delicious on another account. It exposes on a minuscule scale a widely misunderstood but tiresome fact which Australia, Canada and other nations spawned by Britain have learned and taught on a larger scale. It is the fact that when people and territory previously ruled by the Crown in Parliament become a separate and independent state, we do not, because we cannot, endow it with a statehood like our own.

Britain is a prescriptive monarchy. The sovereign power inherent in the British Crown, as exercised through Council and through Parliament, derives not from a treaty or document or compact, but from prescription, from the fact that it has been so from time immemorial – that it is immanent in the nation itself.

When we create a new nation, however, we cannot transfer to it this prescriptive authority which is the essence of our own state. We can only pass an Act of Parliament and give it to them with a slap on the back and a 'best of British luck': 'Here's your constitution,' we say, 'now do what you like with it; you can because you are now independent.'

Before 1948 we used to pretend that all such countries were just copies of the United Kingdom, except that, in place of the monarch, they had a Governor-General, who, we assured ourselves and them, represented the monarch. We purported to atomise the person of the Sovereign, so that she was Queen of Canada, Queen of Australia, etc., and eventually, in the pantomime season, Queen of Grenada.

She was not, and she is not: the reference to 'her realms' (plural) in the Royal Titles is spurious. The Queen is the prescriptive sovereign of one realm only, the United Kingdom: elsewhere neither she nor her so-called representatives the governors-general possess an ounce of prescriptive sovereignty.

The proceedings of Sir Paul Scoon after the American invasion were just as revolutionary – meaning validated by force not law – as had been the proceedings of the superseded military regime. Putting the same point another way, Australia and Canada are as truly republics as are India, Pakistan and Bangladesh.

There was a time, no doubt – it must have been before 1948, when the United Kingdom itself abolished allegiance as the basis of citizenship – when the pretence of daughter monarchies around the globe was harmless and even arguably beneficial. People wanted to believe it, and no practical reality came into conflict with it. Now the signals are flying everywhere that that time has gone. The prescriptive monarchy of the United Kingdom stands constitutionally isolated in a world where some forty independent republics, large and minuscule, trace their historical origin from a period of rule under the British Crown in Parliament. That common accident endows them with nothing else in common – nothing else in their own eyes, nothing else in the face of the world, nothing else in verifiable fact, nothing else except a fiction British-made for British consumption.

How long can we healthily continue the diet of delusion? Not long, I think, now that internal revolution, disruption and secession, external interference, aggression and absorption are likely to be more and more the fate of these often unstable and highly artificial British ex-dominions. Zimbabwe, Grenada, Cyprus – they are so many flares that mark the outline of a new path. Their fates concern us in reality no more than those of other independent states which were never British dominions.

Our danger is to be beguiled by our own fiction into imagining otherwise. Some time there will have to be an end to this make-believe. Some day the Queen's ministers will have to stop advising her to undertake another and yet another journey through the phantasmagoria of cheering crowds and empty ceremonies which mock the memory of a power that was but is no longer.

'WHAT COMMONWEALTH?'

The Times, 26 January 1984

In a speech at Leicester last Friday I stated what I took to be a constitutional axiom: 'All the public utterances of the sovereign,' I said, 'are covered by the advice of ministers.' Immediately it was announced on behalf of the Prime Minister that there is an exception to this principle, namely, when the sovereign is addressing 'the Commonwealth'.

The consequences of that assertion, if it is valid, are peculiar and alarming; but fortunately I can examine it without criticising the sovereign or impugning her judgement, because ministerial advice that ministerial advice is not requisite is also ministerial advice, for which ministers must take responsibility and stand question.

If the alleged exception is valid, it must be valid whenever and wherever the sovereign speaks 'to the Commonwealth': it must apply equally on the Feast of Stephen and on Holy Innocents Day; it must apply whether she addressed 'the Commonwealth' from London or Ottawa or Delhi.

Now, it has long been understood that the public utterances of the sovereign to the people of a realm overseas, be it Australia or Grenada, are covered by the advice of her ministers in that realm. This proposition, admittedly, is not without its difficulties when the sovereign is the same person in two or more realms where her ministers may tender divergent or opposing advice on the same subject; but so far the possibilities involved in these different capacities of the sovereign have not caused embarrassment in practice.

The same principle however is scarcely thinkable in those countries of the Commonwealth which are republics and where therefore there are no sovereign or ministers. In what capacity does the sovereign address the citizens of India? As Queen of the United Kingdom, visiting India as she might visit France or Israel? If so, her utterances are covered by the advice of her UK ministers, notably the Foreign and Commonwealth Secretary. Or is it as Head of the Commonwealth? If so, there are no responsible ministers by whom she can be advised, because the Commonwealth as such has no government and no ministers, and she must be speaking therefore without responsible advice.

The difficulty is magnified when the sovereign is conceived as

602 Powell the Politician

addressing 'the Commonwealth' comprising some countries which she rules on the advice of the respective ministers and other countries over which she does not reign at all. This is not merely a curious conundrum. It is a situation which poses an insoluble problem for the Monarch, since there is by definition no common organ of consent and consequently no responsible ministerial advice on which she can constitutionally act. Expressed in other terms, 'the Commonwealth' is not a political entity, or indeed an entity at all except in make-believe.

The title 'Head of the Commonwealth', against which from the government benches I registered a lone protest upon the second reading of the Royal Titles Bill in March 1953, enshrines a paradox which thirty years ago two countries in particular conspired for their own purposes to ignore: India, in order to become a republic while forfeiting none of the privileges which allegiance had conferred, and Britain, in order to feed its delusion that the Empire was being transformed into something brighter and better still. The way had been paved, also deliberately, by the disastrous British Nationality Act of 1948, which purported to recognise a common citizenship based not upon common loyalty but upon adding together the citizenships defined by an ever-increasing number of independent states.

It was, incidentally, this severance of citizenship from political realities which made technically possible a huge and unintended settlement in Britain of Asian, African and Caribbean populations. It is the same severance which has placed the monarch in a situation constitutionally inexplicable and indefensible.

There is no doubt where the blame lies. It was upon the advice of the Crown's United Kingdom ministers that the chimera of the Commonwealth was invented and installed. Without the legislation, the UK legislation, of a series of British governments, the paraphernalia of a Commonwealth comprising eighteen kingdoms, five other monarchies of which the Queen is not the monarch, and twenty-six republics, with our sovereign as its purported 'head', could never have come into existence. There is equally little room for doubt who is responsible for its continuance and who alone could end the constitutional contradiction in which the sovereign has been caught up. It is Her Majesty's ministers in the United Kingdom – who else?

'END THIS FICTION'

The Times, 17 July 1986

Certain Cabinet ministers told the press on Tuesday they feared a head-on constitutional clash between the Prime Minister and the Queen over sanctions on South Africa. They did what they oughtn't. The sovereign is under a constitutional duty to accept the advice of her ministers tendered through her chief minister so long as they command her confidence – so long, that is, as they command a majority in Parliament. That being so, it is a gross breach of a privy councillor's duty to attribute to the sovereign personal opinions at variance with the advice of her prime minister or, worse still, to suggest that the sovereign might not accept that advice constitutionally offered.

The situation is in no way affected by the title 'Head of the Commonwealth', which, against my protest, was attached by Parliament in 1953 to the Crown of the United Kingdom. There is no function corresponding to that title which the monarch can constitutionally perform, for one very simple and conclusive reason. There is no constitutional source of advice to the sovereign as 'Head of the Commonwealth', because as such she has no responsible ministers on whose advice to act.

In those Commonwealth countries of which she is the sovereign, she or her representative acts in respect of those countries on the advice of their ministers. In the republics or a country like Malaysia, which has its own monarch, she has by definition no function and receives no constitutional advice.

The Queen, I am sure, understands the constitutional position fully and would not contemplate acting other than constitutionally. We have wronged her, and ourselves, by constructing the pretence of a political entity, the Commonwealth, and acting as if it really existed.

No amount of talk and pretence will make it reality. Unfortunately, in the course of talking and pretending, the sovereign states can harm themselves in the real exercise of real power. That is the nature of the self-punishment which Britain inflicted on itself by maintaining in its law the assertion that citizens of other countries, wholly independent and acknowledging a different head of state, were nevertheless in every respect members of the single category of 'British subjects', possessing within the United Kingdom the rights that attach to that category.

The consequences of that monumental humbug belong in this country to the realm of reality. Thirty years of contention and legislation have been powerless to prevent or reverse them.

What we can still do is to escape at long last from the constitutional fiction which we once grasped to ease our transition from the capital of a worldwide empire to a nation state alongside other nation states, but which, having produced so much havoc here at home, has turned into an instrument for external duress to be brought to bear on our own political institutions.

Above all, I do not believe the people of Britain want to see our constitutional monarchy, the 'eternal jewel' with which our political liberties are bound up, brought into danger or contention by the deceptive device once adopted so ill-advisedly so many years ago for a purpose that is past.

'THE CAUSES OF SUEZ'

The Spectator, 26 July 1986

After thirty years the memory which abides with me of the Suez episode that began with Egypt's nationalisation of the Canal on 26 July 1956 is of complete bewilderment and the sense of watching an unintelligible drama. It was not surprise that Egypt had appropriated the Canal. It was astonishment that anybody could have expected anything else and consequently at the paroxysms of indignation which Government and opposition, press and public, exhibited.

What did they think was going to happen after the last British troops evacuated the Canal Zone on 13 June 1956? I had been one of the twenty-eight (twenty-six plus two tellers) Conservative Members who voted on 29 July 1954 against the conclusion of the treaty with Egypt under which that evacuation took place. But I had done so not in the belief that indefinite British occupation of the Zone was practicable but in protest against a treaty which purported to give Britain rights of reoccupation and a policy which proclaimed that Cyprus, Jordan and Kenya afforded adequate geographical alternatives.

The frisson of angry surprise and the instant impulse to prepare for a resort to arms which greeted the inevitable puncturing of those myths were therefore emotions I could neither share nor understand. Hunched in a remote and subordinate cranny of government – devising a rent bill at the Ministry of Housing and Local Government, as a matter of fact – I was not disposed to go overboard when our armed forces were launched into the attack in November; but what on earth was intended to come out of it and how an occupation found untenable could be tenably restored and sustained by force was beyond the comprehension of this unmoved spectator.

How did it happen, and what did it mean? And what if anything does it mean still? William Clark, who was press adviser to Anthony Eden during his premiership, wrote, while under sentence of death from the cancer of which he died last year, a book of *mémoires d'outre tombe* in the unconventional yet quite literal sense of that description.* In them he included his diary entries of the days from Nasser's announcement to his own resignation on 6 November when

From Three Worlds by William Clark, Sidgwick and Jackson

the ill-fated invasion was ignominiously terminated by a ceasefire. As usual with any major historical event, the causes can be perceived at alternative levels, and as usual all are – partially – true. In the situation which he occupied William Clark's eye-level was necessarily that of personalities, above all the personality of the Prime Minister, who combined the propensity to violently emotional reactions with deep anxiety about his alleged indecision. The Prime Minister's wife, Clarissa, appears in the story as an aggravating factor: 'He [the PM] rang up Clarissa, who is becoming his unofficial and wholly bad press adviser, and asked her advice.' At this level of causation the outcome with a different personality at No. 10 would have been different; but is that historical reality? 'The fact is,' wrote Clark himself on 15 August, 'that if we lose out in the Middle East, we shall be immediately destroyed.'

The entry on stage of the French is equally significant. 'The French have been pressing Anglo-French union again [11 September]. We feel it is impossible *at present* because of the Commonwealth.' Indeed, in the very thick of the Suez preparations (14 September) 'the Cabinet was about Plan G – the current plan for Britain going in *with European federation*'; and then (18 September) 'the Cabinet held its second meeting on Plan G for British association with the Messina powers in Europe. Clearly the general view is that it will be *very dangerous for us to stay out* because we risk a German-dominated Europe.'

The Suez event was a parting of many ways; but justice is not done to their complexity by perceiving it as merely the last spasm of an Empire-orientated Britain, a Britain conditioned to regard 'losing out in the Middle East' as immediate destruction. Nor does the crude coincidence of the Suez episode with the run-up to an American presidential election tell all about the changes in Anglo-American relations which flowed from 1956. The assumptions of total British dependence on the USA with which the Clark memoirs show successive British Governments operating in the aftermath of World War II and which were pleaded as necessitating the climb-down in November 1956 were already undergoing an examination which 1956 only accelerated. The pattern of the 1970s and the 1980s was already beginning to be woven on the warp of America and the woof of the European continent. 'A pleasant, cheerful FO character said [30 October]: "It's rather fun to be at No. 10 the night we smashed the Anglo-American alliance." '

William Clark put his resignation in on the day of the ceasefire. It is not altogether clear why. 'I must go, clearly, because I cannot defend a policy I candidly dislike,' he wrote on 4 November, having already told Sir Walter Monckton, the Paymaster General, on 1 November that 'I felt I might have to resign as I thought the policy bad and disastrous.' Yet Clark had known all along of the military preparations 'Musketeer I' and 'Musketeer II' and had been dismayed when Dulles seemed to have aborted them with his Suez Canal Users Club; and after the Anglo-French meeting in London in September he had put out 'a dull communiqué, and no one has the least idea *of what big things were abroad*'. The operative straw seems to have been his exclusion from the inner circle during the twenty-four hours of the joint Anglo-French ultimatum, though back in August Clark had recorded quite dispassionately that 'a good deal of effort is going into trying to find a proper pretext for taking military action. This is because we need to justify our action, though its real basis is *salus populi suprema lex*.' So in the end what was wrong was the pretext.

Professionally that is understandable enough. To the lay reader the revelation of Clark's memoirs is the complete self-assurance with which the effective influence of No. 10 over what does and does not appear in the national media is assumed, whatever slips may occur between cup and lip. There reigned at No. 10 – and reigns no doubt to this day – the conviction that the press relations people can 'fix it' the way they are instructed to. Yet the two professions remain deliciously distinct.

> I do find the habit of ministers of being bloody when things go wrong a trying feature of this job. Success is theirs, failure is ours. I see now why civil servants get so desiccated. Perhaps the secret of all these people at the top is that they have vertigo but out of a feeling of 'the show must go on' they smile in public and are sick off stage.

Not all of them, I think.

'THE UK AND COMMONWEALTH'

Sydney University, 7 September 1988

There is no experience so uncomfortable for a nation as to run head-on unawares into an axiom. So unpleasant is the experience that nations adopt a variety of devices for coping with it. The simplest device is simply to deny the axiom altogether; but that is by definition foredoomed to failure. The alternatives are various kinds of pretence or self-deception.

The rebellion of the American colonies in the eighteenth century confronted the British with an axiom which, for reasons which are capable of being understood, they found so unpleasant that more than two centuries later they have still not ceased attempting to wish it out of existence. It is a scene of national psychopathology that has its humorous moments as well as its deplorable aspects.

By the middle of the eighteenth century the Parliament of England first and then Great Britain had established *de facto* control over all aspects of government. The people of Great Britain were governed, however tortuous and artificial the modalities, upon the authority of an elective institution which for historical and other reasons they were content to regard as representing them. The axiom with which America confronted them was that a government so controlled could not govern any population not represented in that Parliament.

In front of a consequence so stark the deepest political thinkers recoiled. In the noble eloquence of his plea for conciliation with the colonists, Burke, who based his case on the proposition that they had not been represented at Westminster, drew a strange and illogical conclusion. His own argument involved the admission that no common government, no common state, comprising both Great Britain and the colonies could subsist. Yet he proceeded to declare that by refraining from exercising in America the power of the executive which it controlled in Great Britain, Parliament would preserve the unity of the Empire:

> The more ardently they love liberty, the more perfect will be their obedience. Slavery they can have anywhere. It is a weed that grows in every soil. They may have it from Spain, they may have it from Prussia. But . . .

freedom they can have from none but you . . . Deny them this participation of freedom, and you break that sole bond which originally made,
and must still preserve, the unity of the empire.

It was magnificent; but it was nonsense, and self-contradictory nonsense. The dying Pitt, rejoicing in the House of Lords that the grave
had not closed over him before he could protest against 'the dismem-
berment of this noble empire', was a tragic figure; but the tragedy
was in the absurdity of the protest. After a few years the axiom had
taken upon itself the shape of practical reality. There was a new
independent nation in the world, and its ambassador, striped waist-
coat and all, was presenting his credentials to King George III.

The British forthwith addressed themselves to attempting to cope
with the axiom nearer home. Gloriously but illogically they rode off
to tilt at another windmill. Their trick this time was to pretend that
Parliament was really only a legislature and not also in consequence
the effective controller of executive government. On that basis the
Irish Parliament, whose legislative powers had since the fifteenth
century been subject to the sanction of the executive in London, had
that limitation removed from it and became a 'free Parliament', but
a Parliament on which no executive, not even the local Irish executive, was dependent.

It was an ingenious idea; but the war with revolutionary France
soon destroyed the fiction that there could be two Parliaments with
but a single executive. The defence of the British Isles was, and only
could be, conducted by the Government in London. The deduction
was drawn that Ireland and Great Britain, like England and Scotland
after 1707, must therefore have one single Parliament.

The Union of 1800 was a blamelessly logical acknowledgement of
the deadly axiom. It was not however for geographical reasons an
acknowledgement that could have been applied across the Atlantic;
and subsequent history in the British Isles emphasised a rider or
refinement without which the axiom itself is not complete. The axiom
states that a population not represented in a parliament cannot share
a government which that parliament controls. However, 'not
represented' must be understood to include 'not *willing* to be
represented', as well as 'not *able* to be represented' – a qualification
without which the very essence of parliamentary representation itself
is denied. From the mid-nineteenth century onwards it turned out
that not the whole population of Ireland was willing to be represented
at Westminster but only a portion, the portion namely in which
sixteen out of seventeen constituencies still choose to send Members
to Westminster today.

Meanwhile across the Atlantic Ocean an event had taken place which was destined to have the most far-reaching consequences. It was essentially a new attempt to revive the Burkeian fallacy of empire through freedom, obedience through liberty. Its surname is Canada; and its christian name is Durham. The immediate impulse was the prospect which arose in the 1830s that Canada might go the same way of rebellion as the American colonies. 'We know better now,' said the British. 'We lost the American colonies because the colonial governments were not in all things answerable to the local parliaments but to the Parliament at Westminster. So all we have to do is to tell the Governor-General of Canada to behave in relation to his local Parliament exactly as our monarch at home behaves in relation to her Parliament of the United Kingdom.'

Such was Britain's brave attempt to evade the dreaded axiom. The fatal, fateful thing was that for a century the device appeared to work: Canada felt and behaved as if it was still part of the empire. The impression which was made upon the British by what came to be known as the Canadian model was correspondingly deep and powerful. They were highly self-congratulatory. They had found the answer to the American conundrum, and they assured themselves that no other people on earth would have had the qualities necessary to do so. In fact, they exhibited all the satisfaction of someone who has hit upon a method for causing water to flow uphill.

Of course they had not. They were overlooking two facts. As neighbours of the enormously powerful and expansionist United States, the Canadians had a direct and abiding interest in maintaining for their part the fiction that they belonged to the same political entity of the rich and powerful United Kingdom. The fiction seemed a low insurance premium to pay for diplomatic and naval protection, the more desirable in a world where other predatory powers besides the United States were arising. The premium and the insurance however gradually came to look less and less desirable; and when the nexus between them was finally broken in the Second World War, the fiction would be abandoned. Meanwhile – and it was a long meanwhile – the British were delighted with themselves and with their statecraft.

The other fact which they had overlooked was of a different character but no less important in the long run. The Governor-General had not, by acting like the sovereign on the advice of the spokesmen of a majority in an elected assembly, become the same thing as the sovereign. He had become the president of a republic, exercising a defined formal and ceremonial function, and no amount of royal visits and royal Governors-General could alter the fact. The British monarchy is the seedbed in which parliamentary authority germinated in the soil of England. It is unexportable, because prescription, the inherent authority of that which has always been so, is a writ which runs only where it has always been so and amongst those amongst whom it has always been so. The British were mistaken in supposing that they continued to have the same sovereign and therefore the same national identity *vis-à-vis* the outside world as the Canadians. They did not: the Canadians had one sort of sovereign, and the British had another sort.

The person who sits on the dais in Ottawa or Canberra and goes through the motions of opening a Parliament is not and can not be the same being at all as the person who does these things and has done them from time immemorial at Westminster. The difference is subtle, but the difference is fundamental, even though for a hundred years the British managed not to realise it, because they desperately wanted not to. The point is not, as sometimes supposed, that the sovereign had been made divisible. That could be met by the division of the spheres in which the divided sovereign acted upon different collective advice. The point is that by its nature the British parliamentary monarchy exists only in Britain.

However as the nineteenth century proceeded, even the division of the spheres of government – the separation of internal and external policy – became increasingly difficult to maintain. If there was to be a common external policy, economic and strategic, which appeared more and more desirable, as between the parliamentarily self-governing populations around the world that were deemed all to be parts of one empire, the logical but crazy conclusion must be to defy the impracticability that had been so clear in the eighteenth century and to envisage an imperial parliament. Sure enough, Joseph Chamberlain and others proceeded to do just that; and sure enough, it was the Canadians who patiently but persistently explained that they would have none of it. A parliament is an institution which implies the common governability of those represented in it. That was where lay the inherent strength of the axiom which the British imagined they had defeated. A common desire and willingness to be subordinate to it is the essential pre-condition of a parliamentary state. In their futile endeavour Joseph Chamberlain and his contemporaries were only re-enacting in modern dress the plot of the mid-eighteenth-century drama, by proceeding as if a common will and desire to be subordinate existed when it did not.

The Canadian model has a curious corollary, which was to have an unhappy future, extending almost down to the present day. I refer to the federal corollary. In Canada the British not only deluded themselves that they had defeated the axiom; they also imagined it was the federal ingredient that had enabled them to do the trick. For the Canadian model to work, a unitary electorate analogous to that of the UK is required. Where populations, therefore, are incapable of sustaining a single parliamentary representation through their internal differences, the prescription runs: in that case, create a federation, give the federation a parliament, and you have solved your problem. It is of course cheating. But if cheating is necessary, you can commonly get away with it for a time. So everybody had to go federal – Canada, Australia, South Africa and later on Central Africa and the Caribbean, where it all came unstuck.

I have run ahead of chronology however and in particular of the First World War, which the peoples that had entered it as parts of the Empire ended as free-standing independent nations. Britain in 1918 was deeply impressed with the strategic and military contribution made by those nations to victory in Europe and assumed it to be proof of the success of the Canadian model, to which the second Labour Government in 1931 gave statutory form, rather like catching moonbeams, by declaring in the Statute of Westminster preamble that the common identity of the sovereign was of the essence.

The end of the First World War was accompanied by unmistakable evidence that the population of the greater part of Ireland had no intention of remaining within the United Kingdom; and when the attempt to force a home rule constitution upon them provoked a rebellion, Britain had to recognise defeat, but insisted upon the Irish Free State accepting what was called Canadian status by recognising the King Emperor as its representative for external purposes. Thereby it remained, in Britain's eyes though not in its own, a part of the Empire, which was beginning about that time to be called the Commonwealth, and its citizens remained British subjects. Crazy logic had reached the ultimate apogee of absurdity – or perhaps not quite.

The British in India had from the beginning of the nineteenth century seen clearly that so unnatural a phenomenon as the government of that teeming subcontinent by the parliamentary electorate of the British Isles could not be destined to be permanent. What they did not profess to understand was how it could be terminated. However, as the nineteenth century proceeded, two developments took place. Britain became obsessed with the conviction that its very existence as a great power hinged upon the possession of India, to the extent that all major policies – Britain's activities in Africa, for example, or in the Mediterranean, and even its alignments in Europe – were deduced from the supposed requirements of the Indian Empire and the Route to India. The other concurrent development was the growing and irrepressible conviction that the inhabitants of India would claim and must sooner or later obtain responsibility for their own government.

Fantastic though it may seem, in retrospect, the British proceeded to apply to India the Canadian model, complete with its Burkeian fallacy, that liberty equals empire, and with its federalist corollary. An Indian federation would continue part of a transformed Empire by dint of becoming a self-governed nation. It is doubtful whether a more impressive specimen of mass self-delusion can be produced from any era of recorded history. The final shattering of the delusion did not take place until the 1940s; but when it did occur, it prompted not the abandonment of the system of the delusion itself but a further and almost incredible elaboration of it.

The architects and future leaders of the Indian successor state were determined utterly to obliterate any trace or relic of former dependence on Britain and at the same time to maintain that political unity of the subcontinent which British rule had produced. History sometimes exhibits weird symmetries between events distant from one another in place and time. There is such a symmetry between the impossibility of a Canadian-style India and the impossibility of a Canadian-style Ireland. In each case the Canadian fiction of a supposedly identical sovereign was repudiated; and in each case the continuance of a unity which had been due only to the former British connection was made a prior condition for even pretending to play the Canadian game. However, 1948 was not 1921; and India, it may be added, was not Ireland. In order to maintain the illusion that the Indian Union, though a republic in form as well as in reality, remained nevertheless part of the same political entity as the United Kingdom, the British in effect abolished their monarchy itself. That may be an arresting statement, but it is hardly an exaggerated description of what they did. In 1948 they abolished allegiance as the basis of the status of British subjects. Henceforward British subjects were to be the sum total of the citizens of those territories – some independent and some not independent as yet – which had formerly been within the allegiance as dominions of the Crown.

This alteration in the basis of national status was to have devastating consequences for the present and future population of the United Kingdom. With those consequences I am not in this lecture concerned. More immediately, it meant that, as a matter of self-respect, nearly all the remaining territories of the former empire, as they successively became independent, were bound to become independent as republics.

In order that the element of farce might not be missing, it was recognised that the old trick with the Irish Free State and the King Emperor was now obsolete. Rather however than acknowledge that the Irish state, which refused any longer to play the Commonwealth game and declared itself a republic, was therefore a foreign country, Britain proceeded to divide the world not as hitherto into two portions

– British subjects and aliens – but into three – British subjects, aliens
and Irish. By a crowning touch of irony, the last-mentioned were
still to be treated in the United Kingdom as equivalent to British
subjects.

The unitary monarchy, though itself (as I have argued) fictitious,
on which the Statute of Westminster had insisted in 1931, had now
vanished. The reality that an independent nation could pick any
sovereign it liked had to be recognised. Still a device was invented
to cover up the disappearance of an old landmark; and at the
accession of Her present gracious Majesty, she was unlawfully proclaimed by a new title 'Head of the Commonwealth', subsequently legalised by the Royal Titles Act 1953, against which I am
proud to recall that I protested in my place in the House of Commons.

I would not wish to underestimate the capabilities of my fellow
countrymen for self-deception; but it is difficult to believe that there
can be further instalments of the saga which began for the people of
Great Britain with the successful revolt of the American colonies. It
is an amazing web of delusion which has been woven continuously
from Burke in 1775 to, let us say, Fiji in 1987. I am not able, as
others may be, to find an aesthetic pleasure in admiring the pattern
as it unfolded; for the spectacle is not to an Englishman a reassuring
one. Today the United Kingdom is the only prescriptive monarchy
which remains on the face of the globe. In it alone, from the Reformation Parliament of 1529 to the European Communities Act of 1972,
the prescriptive and therefore undefined and unlimited authority of
the monarch has been exercised through an equally unique representative institution.

It is an institution which until recently my fellow countrymen valued
so highly as willingly to pay any price needful for its preservation.
Whether, as one generation succeeds another, that valuation remains
intact, I have no means of judging; but there is a counterpart to the
uniqueness of that inheritance. The counterpart is that by its nature
it cannot be shared with those who by disposition or location are
incapable of being represented in the Parliament of the United Kingdom. If parliamentary self-government is the essence of British liberty, the condition upon which we enjoy it is that the United Kingdom
is politically distinct and separate. It is easy to understand how irk-
some that condition has been felt to be and how strong has been the
temptation to try to tamper with it. There is something in the British
character which predisposes us to push to the limit, and beyond, the
resources of self-deception to create the illusion that we can enjoy
incompatible advantages simultaneously and secure a prize without
paying the price for it. In this process the danger is that we destroy

the inner reality of that which we appear to be preserving. To this anxious and not impartial observer, the United Kingdom today looks perilously near to destroying the inner reality of its inherited parliamentary liberty.

DEFENCE

Q: May I ask Mr Powell whether by 'we' he means anybody resident in the British Isles, excluding Ireland, or would he include people of our blood, such as the Australians and New Zealanders?

A: If we are to defend people of our blood, we shall be defending a good deal of the United States as well. A nation is a political not a genealogical entity and defence and defence policies are concerned with nations.

'Britain's Military Role in the 1970s', RUSI, 18 September 1968

'THE ATOM BOMB MAY NOT BE USED'

Newcastle Journal, 30 July 1949

A Coventry alderman complained recently that 'we are just toying with the problem of civil defence'.

Coventry's experience of high-explosive bombs in 1940 was appalling enough, but how many times worse would be the casualties and devastation of atomic war!

Probably most people are thinking more or less what the alderman said.

If they are right, and if preparations which are essential and practicable too are being neglected, then indeed the sooner public outcry stirs the Government to action the better. But a little straight thinking starts doubts.

There are two sorts of air defence – active and passive. Theoretically either can be carried to a point where it is absolutely effective by itself.

If a country's air forces could dominate the air so completely that not one hostile aircraft penetrated to its target, there would be no need for passive defence.

On the other hand, if the entire population and economy could be buried or camouflaged or sheltered or dispersed, an air force would be – for defensive purposes, at least – a luxury.

In practice, of course, every nation uses both methods. The real problem is to devote each extra man-hour of effort and each extra £ of expense to just that kind of defence which will give the greatest return in security.

Now, every man enlisted in the civil defence services is a man less for industry (which, directly or indirectly, means war industry) or for the forces (which includes the air forces). Every ton of cement and steel used for blast-proofing is a ton less for economic uses or for airfields and anti-aircraft guns.

The question to be answered is not whether more men and materials would strengthen civil defence, that is obvious. But whether we ought to use more on civil defence and less on other things, including active defence.

The present policy is broadly to have a voluntary skeleton

organisation for rescue, fire-fighting, and casualties based on the police, the fire services, and the National Health Service, and planned and supervised by the local authorities.

In war this would be expanded compulsorily, and aid from the Army at home was only counted on in extreme straits.

The more useful and less inconvenient of the old shelters and defences are being maintained; but, so far as the public has been told, new construction is not in train.

We have to decide if this is 'toying' or common sensè.

Take the atom bomb first. No doubt, if we made up our minds that nothing mattered but passive defence against atomic attack, we could make a fair job of it.

Our cities could be compulsorily dispersed, our junctions and ports put underground or sheathed with material proof against rays and blast, our factories and installations tunnelled into hillsides, and our population drilled in the use of free-issue protective devices.

If we did this, then, at the cost of disrupting our whole social and economic life, we could perhaps achieve partial – but only partial – immunity from the consequences of atomic attack.

Is it worth it and is it necessary? It will be some years before any nation likely to be our enemy is ready to wage war with atomic bombs. Some experts even put the period at twenty years; none probably would reduce it below five.

Later on, when atom bombs are a stock line in the principal arsenals of the world, the absolute certainty of reprisals reduces the likelihood of their being used, though it cannot, of course, eliminate the possibility.

Nevertheless, the atom bomb in World War III may be like poison gas in World War II – a constant potential menace, but never an actual one.

Preparations for passive defence against atomic warfare are therefore against a contingency which is certainly not immediate and which may well not, after all, be a feature of warfare in future.

What of our old friends, the high-explosive bomb and its effective companion, the incendiary? The bombers which delivered them here in 1940 and 1941, when our Civil Defence Services took and held the strain, were infantile by comparison with the forces which pounded Germany in 1943–5.

It was because Germany lost command of the air that her cities were flattened; her hollow-mountain factories, her concrete bunkers, her dispersal industrial zones could do little to delay paralysis.

It was because we dominated the British skies that our population and industries enjoyed relative immunity in 1943 and 1944.

Then the rocket and its variations. Before the last war ended, active defence was beginning to draw ahead of this new menace.

If ranges and accuracy of rocket projectiles are increased, it will only be by effective measures to locate and destroy both the projectiles in flight and the launching-sites from which they come that we shall obtain tolerable security for our cities, our factories, and our communications.

With these prospects and these uncertainties, the sensible course is to take no action which might put a brake on our industrial efficiency or divert men and resources from building up our air forces and strengthening their economic and technical foundations.

By all means let us not cast away anything from the last war which might still be useful in the future, neither the structures nor, what is far more valuable, the morale, tradition, and *esprit de corps* of the civil defence forces.

But let us not launch out into vast new schemes under the influence of fears and conjectures.

War, and the preparation for war, is always a balancing of chances. There is no good reason to think that our present policy is weighting that balance unduly against civil defence.

'THE SUEZ CRISIS'

Letter to *New Commonwealth*, 4 January 1954

Sir, – May I offer a few remarks on your 'Commentary' on the negotiations with Egypt, as I feel readers might gain from it a somewhat misleading impression as to what is at issue.

It has never been denied that the Government contemplate an agreement under which, within eighteen months, all British forces would leave the Zone and within seven years the 4,000 technicians remaining would be reduced to nil, while the cost of the base remained to be borne by Britain. As you mention, the only two outstanding items are the questions of uniform and side arms for the technicians and of re-entry to the base if Turkey, as well as some member of the Arab League, is attacked.

Unless the attitude and behaviour of Egypt changes with miraculous completeness and suddenness, this amounts to an agreement for unconditional evacuation; for to imagine that 4,000 technicians will fare better than 80,000 troops or that Egypt will be less ready to repudiate her new agreements than her old, argues an optimism which has no place in foreign relations.

You say that the supporters of such an agreement 'argue that Suez is a commitment which should be maintained on an international basis'. If so, the argument has nothing to do with the case. There is no international agreement in prospect, nor are the present negotiations in any way related to earlier proposals (now apparently dropped) for a Middle East Defence Organisation. The argument for 'removing a major obstacle to the improvement of Anglo-Arab relations' is one that has been heard before. Its validity depends on whether one thinks that goodwill is gained by negotiating under duress with a party whose ill faith one is simultaneously condemning. To say that 'the Suez Canal has lost much of its strategic importance' may be an argument for quitting the Zone; it is not an argument for transferring to Egypt a base which the military experts assure us is, if not absolutely indispensable, at any rate ideal.

Finally, the advantage of 'a drastic redeployment of our Middle East forces' depends entirely on the repercussions of the agreement with Egypt. If they are such as to encourage our new hosts to give us a dose of the Egyptian medicine, the balance will be on the debit side.

However, with one sentiment in your Commentary I do warmly agree. You refer to 'the failure of Australia and New Zealand to feel any increased need to come to the aid of the Commonwealth as a whole'. No doubt if an agreement is concluded with Egypt on the lines which many at home deplore, the Government will tell us that Australia and New Zealand were 'kept informed'. This is not enough. Australia and New Zealand ought not to leave it to the Government and political parties in this country to take fateful decisions alone and unaided about matters which equally concern them. We have a right to know what the Australians and New Zealanders think about the future of areas where their forces have fought side by side with our own in two great wars.

Will they back us if we stay? Will they share the ignominy if we 'scuttle'?

TO THE BRIGHTON CONFERENCE

October 1965

I am happy and proud to be called this morning to answer this motion – happy because it is a number of years since I have had the opportunity to address this Conference on any subject more important than the supply of wigs and teeth to foreigners under the NHS; proud because to carry the responsibility, although it is only for the present 'shadow' responsibility, for the defence of this country is the fulfilment of an almost lifelong ambition.

The nub of this motion is in its concluding words: the defence of our national interests. To defend this nation's existence and its continuity is the one object which a Tory places unconditionally above all others. That is easily said. But before the determination can be turned into policy, we have to ask, and to answer, a number of crucial questions.

In the first place, what do we mean by 'the nation'? I will say what I believe we mean. We mean the United Kingdom. Whatever other meanings the words 'the British nation' can have and do have, this is the sense in which we use them when Her Majesty's Government in the United Kingdom and the Parliament of the United Kingdom take measures for security and defence. Whatever obligations and commitments we have besides, the ultimate reason and the ultimate justification for those commitments is that we hold them to be necessary or advantageous for the defence of the United Kingdom.

The United Kingdom is a European power. True, it has characteristics, profoundly relevant to defence, which make it different from any other European power. But if the rest of Europe succumbed to an enemy, the safety of these islands would be even more precarious in the future than when that event has threatened or occurred in the past. Therefore, an alliance which can successfully defend Western Europe against attack from the East – the only present direction from which danger is apprehended – is central to our defence policy. Forces and materials which are needed for the purposes of that alliance have an overriding claim on the resources which we can devote to our defence – overriding with only one proviso, that no commitment be entered into which would irrevocably deny us all possibility of

independent action, to deter an enemy or to maintain our own existence, however unforeseeable the circumstances may now be in which
that might be necessary.

This means, among other things: that our right to control the use
of our own strategic nuclear weapon must be retained to the limit of
our ability, at least until military and political circumstances are
profoundly different from what they are today. It is the merest casu-
istry to argue that if the weapon and the means of using it are
purchased in part, or even altogether, from another nation, therefore
the independent right to use it has no reality. With a weapon so
catastrophic, it is possession and the right to use which count.

On the other hand, we could not, without forfeiting the possibility
of ultimate self-defence, allow ourselves to be dependent on foreign
supply for the requirements of a whole arm of our services. That is
why we condemn policies, as this motion condemns them and as
even the solitary speaker against the motion condemned them, which
would leave British industry destitute of the capacity to produce by
itself and to co-operate with other European countries in producing
modern military aircraft, or whatever may be destined to replace
them, in the third dimension of warfare in the future.

As a European power, we have also to insure against the hazard
that hostile operations on the Continent might be so extensive and
successful as to prejudice the safety of the United Kingdom without
the nuclear curtain being rung down upon the scene. Here, again, it
is speculation, perhaps idle speculation, to try to describe circumstances in which war might be waged in Europe without the strategic
nuclear weapon being invoked almost instantly. But any British
Government might shudder before the responsibility of resting the
safety and the existence of this nation on the blind assumption that
no such war which could endanger them would ever happen. He, for
instance, who would risk destroying our Territorial Army as a force
capable of training men and units for major war, or who would
contemplate leaving this country without home defence, must be
surer than I would dare to be that he himself knows exactly what
such a war will, and will not, be like. And so we insert, I assume,
wholeheartedly and determinedly the amendment which refers to the
Territorial Army into the motion.

So far I have spoken about the supreme national interest, the
defence of this realm. What are the other national interests which,
though still secondary to that, might claim to share the resources we
allocate to defence? One that is often mentioned is trade and access
to raw materials. The freedom to buy and sell, to import and export,
is indeed an obvious and vital interest of this nation, as it is of others
– not least, of other European nations. It may be that in the past

'trade followed the flag' as the phrase went. But whether that be so or not – and my own reading of history would incline me to turn the maxim the other way round – it has no validity today. Nations, competitors of ours, which depend equally or more on trade, have outstripped our own performance without any military presence either in the areas from which their raw materials are derived or in those where their principal markets are situated. Indeed, a military presence has more than once proved rather an obstacle than a safeguard to the development of trade, and hindered instead of promoting that recognition of mutual material interest which is the only sure basis of all trade. I do not think a defence requirement for this country could easily be founded on our economic or commercial interests in themselves.

Often, however, these are seen as merging in another interest, that of assigning limits to the extension, outside Europe, of the thing we call communism. We do not, of course, mean communism literally: for communism is an abstract theory, and you do not shoot theories with bullets. We mean the Russian empire and, in the second place, the Chinese empire, both which we apprehend might threaten Europe and thus ourselves by commanding the adjacent continents of Asia and Africa.

This generation which now is has twice narrowly escaped destruction at the hands of a military empire which possessed only a private, nationalistic creed. We cannot take lightly the danger of military empires armed with an ideology that claims to appeal to all mankind. It is in the solemn presence of that danger that the British Government and people have nevertheless to weigh two great propositions with the utmost candour. One proposition is this. Assuming that Western military power could limit, or be a factor in limiting, the extension of the Russian and Chinese influence in Asia and Africa, we should still have to measure the practical effect of British military effort against the size of the resources it demands and the consequences of diverting them from other pressing uses – defensive as well as economic.

The other proposition is this. However much we may do to safeguard and reassure the new independent countries in Asia and Africa, the eventual limits of Russian and Chinese advance in those directions will be fixed by a balance of forces which will itself be Asiatic and African. The two communist empires are already in a state of mutual antagonism; but every advance or threat of advance by one or the other calls into existence countervailing forces, sometimes nationalist in character, sometimes expansionist, which will ultimately check it. We have to reckon with the harsh fact that the attainment of this eventual equilibrium of forces may at some point be delayed rather than hastened by Western military presence.

These are the great issues in Europe and in the world which any defence policy worth the name must weigh. Without prejudice to the requirements of diplomacy or of military security, the nation must be told simply and firmly what are the assumptions on which its preparations for defence are based.

The present Government have undertaken to review all these matters. What is, or will be, the outcome of that review, we have as yet been given no inkling; yet decisions have been taken and announced in detail and are being implemented, which are bound to prejudice the major answers. The Government's proposals on the Territorial Army are typical. A policy for reserves must, in logic, be the last link, not the first, in the chain of military reasoning: we must know what are to be our objectives, our methods and the nature of our regular and wartime forces, before we can proceed to deduce what reserves we require. But everything has been the other way round. The Government started with an arbitrary financial limit, threw out a series of unconnected economies and told us what arms and armies they proposed to dispense with. We are still waiting to know what commitments are accepted and what wars we expect to fight. And what a criminal absurdity it was to put out those proposals about the Territorial Army, with their inevitable effect upon the morale and the future of our reserve forces for as far ahead as one likes to look, without even inquiring whether they were practicable at all, let alone wise.

When eventually the Government's answers are forthcoming, it will be for the Conservative Opposition to consider and debate them, remorselessly and also dispassionately. The demands which duty lays on a man or a party in time of peace, though less obvious or simple than in time of war, are perhaps not less exacting. Year by year we commemorate the Few who saved us in 1940. The memory was evoked in the very first words of this debate. But without decisions, the right decisions, taken long years before, their gallantry would have gone for nothing. In time of war it is life and possessions that we offer in the cause of our sovereign and our country. The service required from us in peace is the deepest insight, the clearest and most unprejudiced thinking, and the most resolute decision that the minds of men with a common purpose can achieve.

'NUCLEAR WEAPONS AND WORLD POWER'

Listener, 17 February 1966

The period of twenty years which has elapsed since the atomic bombs fell on Japan has not been unique in its freedom from wars and violent conflicts in various parts of the world. In some of these conflicts neither of the parties has possessed nuclear weapons; in some of them one party has possessed them; in some, again, the friends or allies or co-ideologists of both parties have possessed them. One such conflict, that in Vietnam, is being waged at this moment with an intensity – at least on the side which itself possesses the nuclear weapon – which brings it within the category of a major war. Certainly the Vietnamese war today bulks as large for the American people as, let us say, the Crimean war did for England or Russia 111 years ago.

I admit that in each individual case it is possible by special pleading to explain why the existence of nuclear weapons neither prevented the conflict from breaking into violence nor yet caused it to escalate into the nuclear dimension. Nevertheless, looking at the picture as a whole, it becomes increasingly difficult to sustain with any conviction certain propositions which have been widely, if not dogmatically, held to be self-evident at various times during the last twenty years. There was the proposition, for instance, so memorably enshrined in the opening words of the British defence White Paper of 1958, that 'the world today is poised between the hope of total peace and the fear of total war', in other words that there could be no war which was not total, that is, nuclear. There was the belief that as long as the United States and Britain alone possessed nuclear weapons it was this which prevented Soviet Russia from piercing the boundaries of the North Atlantic Alliance and engulfing Western Europe, as she had mediatised Eastern Europe up to Bohemia inclusive. There was the subsequent belief that the possession of nuclear weapons in large numbers and high potential both by the United States and by Russia ensured, or could be made to ensure, that any attempt by one hegemony to entrench upon the other would provoke the nuclear catastrophe, and that consequently the political division of the world had frozen rigid.

For any observer who is ready to undergo the hardship of giving up a convincing simplification, these propositions stand discredited today. Even in Europe, the principle of the 'trip-wire' – the frontier guard which automatically sets off nuclear war rather as a burglar trap rings an alarm bell – has been abandoned in the official thinking of the North Atlantic Alliance, or at any rate it has been replaced by the less grotesque idea of substantial forces which have to be driven in before nuclear escalation is deliberately set in train. Perhaps after all in 1949–50 the Alliance halted Russian penetration of Western Europe simply because the Russians then concluded that further forcible advance involved the risk of war with the United States and Britain and did not sufficiently like the look of it.

We know now that the major powers, nuclear and non-nuclear, are still able as in the past to carry on military operations, including military operations designed to improve their position at each other's expense or to prevent that attempt from succeeding. In fact in the nuclear age as we call it, nation continues to lift up sword against nation – non-nuclear sword, at any rate. We have not stumbled upon an implement which frightens us all into peaceableness.

In retrospect, it is not difficult to see why. In the present state of the offensive and defensive techniques, resort to nuclear warfare between major nuclear powers spells near-destruction for both. The only gain worth purchasing at the price of near-destruction is the avoidance of complete destruction, or at least of what a nation regards as complete destruction. But, as Adam Smith remarked in a different context, 'there is a deal of ruin in a nation'. That is, a nation can lose or forfeit or risk a great deal before a point is reached anywhere near equivalent to complete destruction. There is even more ruin in a nation's allies, and yet more ruin still in interests which are peripheral or remote. It follows that those remote or peripheral interests can be forcibly disturbed – indeed more, that very great inroads can be made into a nuclear nation's allies or even a nuclear nation's own integrity – before the time comes when the balance tips over in favour of the choice of near-destruction. This is why big operations of war and violent disturbances of the balance of power can and do and will take place, even when the interests of major nuclear powers are at stake. It is implicit in the playing of this game that in those operations of war the major nuclear powers not only do not employ nuclear force, but leave a wide *cordon sanitaire*, a manifest gap in potential, between what they use and anything that could conceivably be mistaken as a signal for nuclear exchanges.

The logic is different for other powers. That which is peripheral to one may be vital to another. It is possible, though only just possible, to imagine that the point of balance where nuclear self-defence becomes acceptable could be reached in the case of such a power as I am describing by the word 'peripheral' in relation to the interests of major nuclear powers. At that moment, however, the interests which were so vital for the smaller nation would still be far below the level of nuclear equivalence for its enemy as well as for its ally or potential ally. It is from this consideration that there arises the desire of nations other than the major nuclear powers to acquire nuclear weapons or to retain them once they have them: 'One day,' these nations think, 'that moment might come for us when the risk of doing a Samson act and pulling down the temple on our own heads by nuclear assault on an enemy about to destroy us, might be our only safety in a world where other powers, however friendly, were unwilling to commit *hara-kiri* for the sake of our beautiful eyes.'

This is a line of reasoning which in theory any nation might follow to the point of providing itself with nuclear weapons – in theory, but not of course in practice. With all armament for all nations a limit is prescribed by sheer ability: what they are able or willing to devote to the purpose. There might be excellent reasons for Norway to possess a fleet of hunter-killer submarines equivalent to the Russian; but they do not, because they cannot – at least, in the sense that at the cost involved they do not want to. Likewise there is a fairly narrow limit to the number of powers which will find it practicable or desirable to provide themselves with a nuclear armoury: more, one would guess, than the three or four now in, or entering, the field, but perhaps only a few more.

Admittedly this reasoning would be undermined if a nuclear armoury ever became cheap, so that countries could pick up a set – 'kit' would perhaps be the precise word – at a price which many could easily afford. One ought, I suppose, not to exclude such a possibility as wholly inconceivable; but there are good grounds for regarding it as at least remote. In order that the logic which leads a power to equip itself with nuclear armament should be satisfied, it is necessary to have the power to inflict severe, though not necessarily utter, havoc upon an opponent when one is oneself in an unfavourable, not to say disastrous, military situation. It follows that just an odd warhead or two will not do: there must not only be the means to inflict large-scale devastation, but reasonable assurance that the means of penetration and delivery can be kept intact. In terms of present techniques, these requirements involve maintaining what it is fashionable to call 'highly sophisticated' methods of delivery and protection for the launching equipment, which will be beyond the capacity of most nations at least for a considerable time to come.

All this seems to afford little prospect for the idea of securing 'non-dissemination' or 'non-proliferation' by treaties of mutual guarantee.

The thought is that all powers except two would renounce or abandon nuclear armament on the understanding that one or other of the nuclear powers guaranteed them against aggression. However, the same logic which tells us that interests which may be vital to one ally need not be sufficiently overwhelming in the eyes of another ally to ensure that the latter would initiate the nuclear duel if those interests were infringed, applies with equal if not greater force to a treaty of guarantee, where the degree of common interest between the parties would normally be less than in an alliance. It would simply not appear credible that the giant states should undertake to destroy one another if one small state somewhere in the world were threatened with extinction by another. To say this is no more to impugn the good faith of a guarantor than the sincerity of an ally: it is simply to recognise the inevitable calculus of life and death. Not that there are not other grave weaknesses in the theory. One is that it must bind the non-nuclear powers hand-and-foot to the nuclear, since it would be impossible to demand a guarantee of this absolute character without at the same time surrendering absolute control over the policy which might result in the guarantee being invoked. It is bad enough at the best of times to have to commit national suicide because someone else is in a scrape, but out of the question if the scrape was of his making, not yours.

Where, in any case, does China fit into this? The reasoning which impels China to develop a nuclear armament may not be solely or mainly that logic of self-defence which we have been exploring. It is at least as likely that China aspires to enter the Russo-American class of great powers with virtually the capability to destroy one another. The greater the population, physical resources, and industrial power of a state, the stronger the incentive to match the destructive capability of the other colossi. It would be a more daunting prospect for a major nuclear power to give non-nuclear nations an unconditional guarantee if it had two rivals in the world to contend with, and not just one.

Is then the prospect of two or three major nuclear powers, plus a somewhat larger number of minor but significant nuclear powers, a prospect which need necessarily lead us to conclude that the world is on its way to total destruction unless we find the means speedily to extinguish the nation state or, in the words which Lord Chalfont used at the outset of the first of his talks, 'to devise a system of international politics from which war and the threat of war have been eliminated'?

One common ground of apprehension ought, I believe, to be excluded from our calculations at the outset. This is what is called the madman's act, sometimes referred to as 'accident' or 'miscalculation'. It is necessary here to be clear whether the terms are being used literally or metaphorically. If they are used in the literal sense, then, while an act of pure insanity or mischance which discharges a nuclear weapon cannot be ruled out, the consequences of the act would be limited by its very nature, and it would be in the interests of all concerned to demonstrate that the act was in fact insane or accidental. If, on the other hand, the terms are being used metaphorically, in the sense in which one might call Hitler insane or say that Napoleon miscalculated when he invaded Russia, then the present state of nuclear armament is exceedingly unpropitious to the use of nuclear power by a state which exaggerates its strength or miscalculates. On the contrary, for similar reasons to those which we have been examining, such a power will be intent on achieving its aims with the maximum *cordon sanitaire* between the methods it uses and the invocation of nuclear war. Incidentally, a miscalculation of nuclear power or of the state of the nuclear equation – if that be what is in mind – is scarcely attributable, even in theory, to any but the major unclear states, rather than the other powers at which non-dissemination is aimed.

So we are compelled to contemplate as probable the very thing which both political and military thought during the last twenty years has strenuously attempted – not to say, conspired – to regard as improbable, namely, the prospect of non-nuclear warfare between all sorts and conditions of powers. Indeed, as I have pointed out, our actual experience has verified this. Military conquest (as of Goa by India), military assault (as by France, Britain, and Israel on Egypt), military occupation (as of Hungary by Russia), frontier wars (as between China and India, or Malaysia and Indonesia) continue as merrily in our own nuclear age as ever they did before 1914. When it is said, and said with reason, that a large-scale conventional war in Europe is not a practical prospect, this is no more than to say that the conditions for a major war in Europe are not considered to exist or to be in sight. But there have been many previous periods of equal length, though not in the lifetime of any but the very old, when the same could have been said for similar reasons.

What it can be more plausibly argued has been changed by the existence of nuclear weapons on a grand scale is not so much the possibility as the character of non-nuclear warfare between major powers. In the Second World War we saw attack upon the home bases of industry and economic strength and upon the civilian popu-lation carried to a pitch which, as an operation of war, had probably not been known to mankind previously; for this was different from the consequences of defeat – pillage, enslavement, massacre – which were apt in earlier ages to follow the loss of a battle, a campaign, or a war. The ability to strike at the enemy's homeland with indiscriminate destruction 'escalated' – though in those days we did not then know the word in this sense – from Coventry to Dresden and thence to Hiroshima and Nagasaki. In future such operations as these may well fall within that ambiguous zone where they could be taken for the early stages of a nuclear escalation; indeed, in a world where nations possess megaton warheads, the '1,000-bomber-raid' would be as senseless as perilous. We may therefore find that the boundary line of military forces, operations, and objectives is more firmly and narrowly drawn in the future than it has been since the advent of the zeppelin and the military aircraft in the First World War. A non-nuclear conflict might prove to be limited and slow-burning simply because it was non-nuclear and everyone was determined that it should remain so.

Thus – and this is where I think I principally differ from Lord Chalfont – the world is not in a fundamentally new situation, but in one where the old arguments about disarmament, world government, and prevention of war continue to apply without basic change. I see no reason to agree with him that nuclear weapons 'have brought about a comprehensive change in the relationship between political and military power'. What has happened is rather that a further octave has been added to the scale of human conflict, without however eliminating any that existed before. The fact remains, after the nuclear weapon as before, that a world authority wielding sole military power implies a sovereignty or empire which, unless and until it was felt as morally binding and inwardly compulsive by all beneath its sway, would only be an exertion of tyranny. None of the theoretical or practical difficulties of discovering how such a sovereignty could be created has been removed by the advent of nuclear weapons. The fact remains, after the nuclear weapon as before, that progressive reduction of armaments by agreement is a desirable and rational object of policy, but one which reflects rather than produces a lessened expectation of hostilities, and which cannot pass beyond certain limits as long as separate sovereignties, national or collective, exist.

The statesman, it appears to me, has still to apply his mind to securing that the changes which must occur in the relationship between the infinitely various human societies on this planet are accompanied with the minimum of avoidable violence. He may be not less but more successful in this if he is not also seeking the philosopher's stone of a compulsorily peaceful globe. The nuclear weapon, at any rate, is not that stone.

'EAST OF SUEZ'

The Australian, 8 June 1966

A speech on defence which I made at the Conservative Party conference at Brighton last year attracted a degree of attention – in Australia, among other places – which was more remarkable than anything that I said in the speech.

Efforts were made in certain quarters to represent me as having
been speaking only for myself, or as having been thinking aloud.

In fact, the text of my speech was concerted and agreed in detail
beforehand with the colleagues most concerned, and what I said has
been said before and has been said since by others without attracting
the same notoriety.

Notably, for instance, in almost the same words by Sir Alec
Douglas-Home in the most recent foreign affairs and defence debate
in our House of Commons on 27 April.

There were really two propositions relevant to Australian defence.
One was this: 'Assuming that Western military power could limit, or
be a factor in limiting, the extension of Russian or Chinese influence
in Asia and Africa, we should still have to measure the practical
effect of British military effort against the size of the resources it
demands and the consequences of diverting them from other pressing
uses.'

The other proposition was this: 'However much we may do to
safeguard and reassure the new independent countries of Asia and
Africa, the eventual limits of Russian and Chinese advance in those
directions will be fixed by a balance of forces which will itself be
Asian and African.

'The two communist empires are already in a state of mutual
antagonism.

'But every advance by the one or the other calls into existence
countervailing forces, sometimes nationalist in character, sometimes
expansionist, which will ultimately check it.

'We have to reckon with the harsh fact that the attainment of this
eventual equilibrium of forces may at some point be delayed rather
than hastened by Western military presence.'

I confess that in prospect as well as in retrospect these two propositions seemed to me to be so obvious as to verge upon the platitudinous.

But I could not have guessed that they would start so soon to be illustrated on a grand scale.

The end of confrontation between Malaysia and Indonesia (if that actually has happened) tends to restore and reveal the natural and underlying alignment of forces in South East Asia which has been masked for a time by the curious post-colonial episode which had found 55,000 British and Gurkha troops involved in a local quarrel between two powers naturally antagonistic to China and apprehensive of aggression from that quarter.

Whatever form the new and, as I have suggested, natural alignment takes, it is predictable that a Western military presence purporting to guarantee it will be found increasingly embarrassing.

In the days immediately before the recent British general election I secured from the Labour Government an absolute undertaking for the future that there was no question of any British armed forces being sent to Vietnam.

And I see that President Johnson has just reassured Mr Heath that this is accepted by the United States.

There remains Singapore, and a defensive treaty deemed to carry over from that with Malaysia in its old form (before the secession of Singapore), which links Britain with one part only of Maphilindo or whatever constellation is to emerge.

Now, it is nice, even for so affluent a state as Singapore, to have a lot of British about, spending a lot of money – other things being equal.

But how long will other things stay equal?

As Mr Healey, the British Secretary of State for Defence, put it in reference to that maddeningly silly phrase 'east of Suez':

'The question is not whether we stay east of Suez, but in what strength and for what purpose and for how long' (7 March 1966).

Life is full of the unexpected, not to say the impossible.

But the chance that the Singapore base, now almost a unique vestige in the whole world of the vanished British Empire, will long survive agreement between the anti-Chinese powers of South East Asia, must surely be assigned to the first, if not to the second, of those categories.

Such an agreement could have the most far-reaching repercussions, both on American and on Australian defence policy.

To the United States, it might afford at last the possibility of extricating themselves from the Vietnamese impasse.

If the rigour of the so-called 'domino theory' ('if South Vietnam goes, Laos goes, Thailand goes, Malaysia goes, everybody goes'), could be relaxed, then it might be possible for the United States to find the disproportion between effort and results in Vietnam as grotesque as it seems to much of the rest of the world.

For Australia, the long-term implications might be larger still.

The kangaroo pattern – if a mere pommy may dare to use that metaphor to describe the universal tendency to be friendly with one's next neighbour but one – would be altered.

At present it has been Malaysia and Singapore which were 'the other side' of the assumed threat from Indonesia.

But what would be 'the other side' of Maphilindo? Japan? or perhaps (who knows) China? Strange, yet not the strangest *renversement des alliances* which the world has ever seen.

What is involved is a change from forces which were conceived as those of a colonial empire to the forces appropriate to a European maritime power.

'BRITAIN'S MILITARY ROLE IN THE 1970s'

RUSI, 18 September 1968

It is in no carping, hypercritical spirit that I draw attention to the title given by our institution to this lecture which it has done me the honour to invite me to deliver. The wording of it, which must appear ordinary or even trite to any British person hearing or reading it, is to me highly significant. Indeed, the fact that such an extraordinary title seems natural goes to the heart of our predicament and of the principal issues of our defence policy.

With the possible exception, and that perhaps more apparent than real, of the United States, no other country keeps asking itself what its military role is. Discussion and policy start effortlessly from the axiom that a country's military role is its own defence, and proceed immediately to consider how that defence is best to be secured by military means. For us it is not so. We are not even agreed on who we are. The assertion, which I now make, that Britain's military role is the defence of the United Kingdom, so far from being dismissed as wasting a sentence on stating the obvious, becomes at once the subject of an acrimonious debate, in which choice epithets like 'little Englander' and 'post-imperialism' fly to and fro.

The truth is that, for Britain, 'who we are' has changed radically in our lifetime and we encounter a natural difficulty in adjusting our habits of thought, our instincts and our emotions to the new reality. But failure to conform to reality is biologically dangerous, and history is full of the fate of nations which perished because their thinking continued to conform to circumstances that had changed. Until a quarter of a century ago the 'we' in question was not the United Kingdom; it was the British Empire, of which India was still, as it had been for 150 years, the centre of gravity. The Empire was a political entity: and its integrity and, since it was worldwide, its internal connection and communications were therefore the object of defence. For 150 years our habits of thought about defence, about our military role, had conformed with that object. No wonder if we find them hard to alter now.

Within the last quarter of a century or so, the British Empire has ceased to exist: there is no longer a 'we' which corresponds to it.

Objectively, of course, we all recognise this; but instead of identifying and accepting the consequences of the new 'us' for our military role, we tend to take the course of psychological least resistance; we retain the old pattern of thought and behaviour, but attempt to rationalise it with motives which would never have occurred to us if 'we' had always been who 'we' are today. Once perceive that this is what is going on, and one has the key to explain actions and policies which otherwise would seem to demand the psychiatrist rather than the psychologist.

Take the Persian Gulf – sorry, 'the Gulf'. You know its history. This was one of the tiresome little sideshows which were run from India, both militarily and politically. If we had not been in India, we would not have been in the Gulf, where we (the old 'we') took up our position long before petroleum was dreamt of. Much later, in our own time, the Gulf became more than a sideshow: it became part of the Route to India, that great object of defence policy, from the real or supposed requirements of which every British post or possession east or south of Gibraltar can be shown to have directly or indirectly arisen, and which explains why still today, when there is no India and no Route, the report of Russian warships in the Mediterranean sets all the alarm-bells ringing in our subconscious, though really it is no more remarkable and no more alarming than the appearance of Russian warships in the Skaggerak. However, there in the Persian Gulf 'we' still are, this different 'we', and so have to find a reason why. The answers come tumbling out: it is to preserve stability; it is to prevent the sterling balances being shifted; it is to keep our oil supplies; it is to keep our oil investments; it is to deny the oil to the Russians; it is to hold that part of the 'front against communism'. The difficulty of dealing with assertions such as these is like that of convincing a patient at the Maudsley that he is not Napoleon Bonaparte. If you say that our oil supplies have actually been switched off, in 1951 and 1967, and the sterling balances moved out, but we neither used nor thought that we could use force to prevent it, you are told that that was different. If you point out that neither the oil companies nor the other nations who buy the oil betray the slightest desire for us to remain militarily in the Gulf, the answer is 'Ah, they rely on the British "umbrella" and think they needn't worry.' If you suggest that the nation which has been driven by force or the threat of force out of every other position in the Middle East neither is, nor will be thought to be, able to preserve stability or hold a front against anybody, in this, its last residual toehold, you are told 'Ah, but the sheikhs there love it, and everybody wants us to stay.'

On the old Indian Empire's other flank is another residual toehold – the scene of what Churchill called 'the greatest disaster to British arms which our history records' – and round it the same delusions cluster thick. 'The stability of South East Asia is for us a vital interest': on this proposition has been rested the recent announcement by HM Opposition that British forces ought to be retained by agreement on the mainland of South East Asia 'to help to maintain stability'.

In order rationally to examine such a proposition, it is necessary to offer some definition of 'stability'. I take it, then, to mean a situation such that the government of a country is not overthrown by internal subversion or external force. It is, for example, the condition which the United States has been attempting, with colossal exertion, but so far with conspicuous lack of success, to produce in South Vietnam. Now, the assertion that it is a vital interest, a matter of life and death, for the United Kingdom that there is stability in South East Asia is patently absurd. There is no reason to suppose that such a condition is attainable at all anyhow – and human history so far in the East and in the West is a commentary on the opposite. But suppose that stability conceivably were attainable, in what sense is stability in South East Asia a matter of life and death to the United Kingdom?

Every political alteration anywhere in the world has or may have *economic* implications for the United Kingdom; but from this it cannot be deduced that those implications, if they could be foreseen, would be worth while exerting the military effort necessary to prevent political change or to guide it in the desired direction. Of course, if a large and certain economic advantage could be purchased by a small and limited military effort, it would be a rational policy; but it is in supposing precisely this that the delusion lies. How can the object-lesson of the United States in Vietnam be resisted? As the evidence mounts that the USA must extricate itself regardless of eventual stability, two arguments are put forward to differentiate that case and render its implications irrelevant for British policy. One is that the British in Malaysia were successful both against the communists and against confrontation, and that therefore they can do the same or a similar thing again and again if necessary. This is a prevalent but erroneous deduction from what – in lucky instances – was possible during colonial rule and at the moment of its termination to what is possible afterwards. Success with small forces in such contexts depends on who is expected to stick it out. It was because the British were assumed a permanent feature of the scene that in colonial days small forces could produce such disproportionate results, and the opinion carried on by inertia for some time after – we are not alone in experiencing the inertia of ideas. But the opinion of Western presence in South East Asia is a rapidly dwindling asset, and the American ill-success will soon have bankrupted it altogether.

The other contention is that in any case only small British forces could or would be committed; and it appears that the prospect of our continued presence on the mainland of South East Asia may sagely be made conditional on the continued presence of Australia and New Zealand also. However, the argument is self-defeating. The reason why a small force is effective, by deterrence or by actual intervention, is the knowledge that the power deploying it is ready and able, if need be, to reinforce to any extent necessary to secure victory. That is why three battalions hold West Berlin: they are a token that certain acts would mean war on a literally unlimited scale. That is why the lone gunboat in the past could conduct 'gunboat diplomacy': behind it lay the Royal Navy and a power which, however tardily and clumsily, would be exerted to win, sooner or later. But a small force whose owners declare, if that were not self-evident anyhow, that there will be no more to come, is a laughing-stock, to be tolerated as long as convenient, and then to be brushed aside. A long experience of colonial soldiering – too long for our present good – has deeply infected our thinking, and especially our professional thinking, with indifference to the fact that war is about winning, and winning is about superiority of force.

The notion, then, that economic ends can be served by a deployment of forces to maintain stability in remote regions is a mirage. We are by no means so much dependent as a number of other nations on overseas trade and investments for our standard of living; but we are the only one that dreams of protecting them with garrisons.

I turn to the other sense in which stability in South East Asia is sometimes argued to be our vital interest, namely, defence: the proposition that a disturbance of the political status quo at the other end of Asia increases the risk of the United Kingdom being successfully attacked. One might have thought it suspicious that none of our continental neighbours thinks so. If the British Isles are to be attacked, something pretty unpleasant will have happened before that to most of the other countries of Western Europe. They are more vulnerable than we. Yet it no more occurs to them to exert themselves militarily for the stability of South East Asia than of South America or Central Africa. Of course, the historian may *ex post facto* trace a connection between events and movements distant in time and place. There could conceivably be a long and complex chain of causation between the political alignment of North Borneo and a future threat to the United Kingdom, just as there may have been between the detachment of Korea from China in 1894 and the German invasion of Belgium in 1914. But one could not on that account attempt to defend the Channel Ports by operations in the China Sea; for even if one had been able to influence the outcome of the Sino-Japanese

War, one would not have known which of the possible outcomes would be favourable or otherwise in its ultimate repercussion at the other end of the Old World land mass. A military presence in South East Asia is an exorbitant premium against a risk so remote and hypothetical that it cannot be identified. Once again, our imperial experience has tricked us into ignoring another axiom, the inverse relationship between military power and distance. So much of the power of the former British Empire, and particularly that relevant to South East Asia, was centred on the possession and resources of India. We have forgotten this, and behave as if the distances had been measured from London. The political situation immediately to the south east of the frontiers of the Indian Empire (including Burma) was of direct or at least measurable relevance to the security of that Empire. Its relevance to that of the British Isles is to the last degree remote and speculative.

If 'we' then are now the nation whose home is the British Isles (or rather the British Isles less the Irish Republic), and if we identify and eliminate the habitual modes of thought and behaviour which relate to a 'we' that no longer exists, the military role of Britain in the 1970s is the defence of the British Isles.

At this point it would, until quite recently, have been necessary for me to insert a long passage to dispose of a fundamental objection – namely, that the British Isles do not need to be defended militarily, because either they are defended by the nuclear deterrent or, alternatively, in its absence they are indefensible. The long vogue of this contention is easily explicable amongst Treasury Ministers and other politicians; for if you can really take it seriously, it relieves the budget enormously – the cheapest of all defence policies is the nuclear deterrent, plus its logical corollary of no other defence at all. What is much more remarkable and instructive is that the services themselves have tolerated and even embraced a proposition which renders their profession virtually superfluous.

Partly no doubt the explanation was the same ghost of the old 'we' that I have been laying. If there was no reason for employment at home, this made it easier to find and accept excuses for pottering about on the other side of the world – the role of preserving stability in the Far East from an undefended, because indefensible, base in the North Atlantic looked all right. To this extent the theory was one more narcotic to help the dreamer to keep on dreaming. I believe, however, that there was another psychological explanation, which it is important to identify and expose, because it calls for long and difficult remedial action. The professional armed forces of this country, partly because they *are* long-service professional forces and partly because of their 150-year-long imperial background, have a profound aversion from European warfare, and consequently grasp instinctively at any theory which enables them to turn their back on the beastly conditions of the North Atlantic and on the even more beastly conditions of continental warfare, where one is mixed up with great masses of foreigners – I don't mean tribesmen, Indians, Arabs or nice people of that sort – and also with great masses of civilians who are serving 'for the duration'. It is hard to say which are the worse.

No wonder the central military problem that has engaged for years and still engages the best brains of a nation which twice in our lifetime was all but overwhelmed by a military power located 200 miles away, has been how to stage the opposed landing of a brigade group in the Far East. The nuclear hypothesis has provided an escapist mechanism, which enabled the professional services to hold at bay the dreaded realisation that they now exist to defend the United Kingdom and that in this context they will be profoundly different in motivation, philosophy, organisation and armament from the services which garrisoned and policed a worldwide Indo-British empire.

For convenience I will date the moment of truth about the beginning of this year when the Defense Secretary of the United States, from the very Vatican of nuclear theology, stated that his country contemplated a long sea war against a major antagonist and land operations of indefinite duration, because, in his words, 'the threat of an inconceivable act is not a credible deterrent'. And so we have come home at last. The threat of an incredible act is a deterrent to the threat of an incredible act: the 'second strike' can be the answer to nuclear blackmail. Against the divisions, the missiles and the submarines of an aggressor it affords no security except that of suicide. No less than at any previous time, the defence of the United Kingdome requires the fulfilment of two conditions: (1) that the minimum external communications of the British Isles essential in war be secured; and (2) that the adjacent continent be denied to an enemy so far as he might use it to attack the British Isles, or, in the worst case, that such an attack be repelled.

My subject this afternoon is the role, the object rather than the methods; but I must carry both these conditions at any rate to the next stage of definition. If you are blockading a city, you do not try to destroy all the possible sources from which supplies for it might originate, nor to intercept them at or near those sources. You sit down as near to the city as possible, since all supplies and routes relevant to your purpose must converge there. The only area where enemy superiority could be decisive against the essential communications of these islands is where they approach these islands – namely, in the North Atlantic. I am not, of course, dogmatising about the relevant definition of that wide term, nor ignoring the natural ubiquity of some – not by any means all – forms of maritime force: but I am warning against that vision of the *Emden* burning its heart out on the beach at Cocos which could spirit us away back to the dream-world of the old 'we'. Even in World War I the decisive maritime struggle, so barely won by a world-policing two-power-standard Royal Navy, was in the North Atlantic.

I must not shirk the supplementary question: 'What allies, if any, are to be assumed for this purpose?' Everyone who has produced intelligence appreciations knows it is always possible to construct an insuperable 'worst case'. I do not believe we should assume more than one major maritime power as an enemy, nor that such an enemy would have no other calls upon his offensive maritime strength. Further, I believe we are entitled to assume that a continental enemy would attach the first priority to success in land operations and that consequently his maximum threat to our command of the North Atlantic would emerge more or less gradually, and that some allied support of our maritime forces could be allowed for. Finally, I would point out that we would have the advantages of concentration, shorter range and inner lines. Having prefaced my answer thus, I am obliged to give it as follows: 'A Britain which did not aim at being able to fulfil the maritime condition of her survival with her own resources would have no real political independence, and would not appear to other nations a sufficiently significant military power for her to fulfil the second, or landward, condition, to which I now come.'

The economical and practical method of fulfilling this second, or landward, condition of the defence of the British Isles has always been to maintain or restore such balance of power in Europe as would prevent an enemy from using the adjacent mainland to invade us. At any rate since the supersession of mercenary armies, the only way for Britain to influence this balance was to offer the prospect that she was not only able to secure her own maritime defence but also ready and able to participate in continental warfare on a sufficient scale to make it probable that the combination she joined would eventually prove victorious. This means two things. It means that Britain must be seen to have available at the outset of hostilities a European field army, with air component, which is of substantial size and (if I may be permitted a self-quote) 'equal in philosophy, training and armament' to any other. It also means that she must be seen to have the means of expanding and maintaining that army for as long as the conflict might have to be prolonged.

Of these two requirements we possess one already, thanks to the course of events in the last twenty years which has left Britain, for the first time in her history, with a first-class European field army in time of peace. It is the second requisite which at present is decisively lacking, having long been excluded even from consideration by the nuclear hypothesis of a brief war or no war at all. To satisfy it we must have a cadre army and a training army as well as a field army, and we must re-form a volunteer reserve on new lines to provide the framework both for initial reinforcement and for subsequent expansion. If I had to indicate what I believe ought to be the principal preoccupation of our landward forces in the next decade, I would point without hesitation to the reserves. In terms both of material and of manpower, the theory and the methods of expansion ought to dominate our concern, if the ravages of recent neglect are to be made good.

But I have already strayed well beyond 'role' (which is largely politician's business) into 'method' (which is largely not). On looking back, my assessment of Britain's military role in the 1970s seems to have been a statement of the obvious. But often the obvious is the most controversial and the hardest to achieve.

'FACE THE PRESS'

Channel 4 TV, 9 October 1983

FRANK JOHNSON: Well, do you think that we should be a member of this [NATO] alliance?

ENOCH POWELL: I think there are great advantages. Even now. And certainly there were a decade or two ago in Britain being part of a continental alliance. Advantages for Britain for the maintenance of her defence forces and her defence preparations. The besetting problem, defence problem, over the generations, for Britain, is that we could not accustom ourselves to the notion that the ultimate purpose of our army was to participate in continental warfare. We therefore found ourselves, at the outset of both world wars, with an essentially colonial army and had painfully to learn the implications of participating in the grand drama of continental warfare. Now, I want to see a British Army – not in size, but I think I've said, in philosophy, in training and in outlook, which is on a parity with the great armies of the Continent – not in size, it doesn't need it – but I do not want the British Army to drift away ever again into the notion that we're an imperial or an army of the oceans, because in the end eh, when the ultimate, mortal threat is offered to this country it will be the European enemy with whom we would have to contend.

ANTHONY HOWARD: When did you change you mind about that? Because you used to believe in the British Empire. What caused you to change your mind?

POWELL: After the war, I thought it possible, for a year or two, and I suppose it was the experience of India which most consciously brought me into politics – I thought that it was still possible for there to be a political link between the United Kingdom and India. I realised that that was an absurdity. But to one brought up on a diet of Curzon perhaps that's intelligible if not forgiveable. After that, after the evidence that India could not be part of the same political system, I still believed for a short time that an Empire of positions – that is to say the possession of points of communication around the globe – gave a significance to this country and a tenable and lasting position. That too was wrong and my lesson was learnt. Not at the invasion of Suez but previously, when I opposed the making of the Suez Treaty which was based upon the assumption

that we could reoccupy the Suez Canal at will. It seemed to me
clear that we were leaving the Suez Canal Zone because we
couldn't maintain ourselves there and I argued, well, if we can't
maintain ourselves in that position the notion of a worldwide power
based upon positions has to be abandoned and I had abandoned
it before we invaded Suez.

HOWARD: Can I, just before we go on to Northern Ireland, which we
must do, ask one other question? When did you come to your
present position on the bomb? It seems to me that you are almost,
now, a closet unilateralist. You cannot have been that when you
were Mr Heath's defence spokesman in 1965–9.

POWELL: Well, whether Mr Heath read the Hansards regularly, I
don't know, but I did take the opportunity of a debate – I think it
was on the army estimates, it may have been the air estimates –
in 1967, to put on record, without dissent from my party or my
fellow junior spokesmen on defence, the reasoned argument for
the nuclear hypothesis on which the possession of a British nuclear
weapon was based, being unsustainable. And that's '67. But I could
certainly trace my inability to account for the nuclear – to accept
the nuclear hypothesis, a long way before that.

HOWARD: John?

JOHN WHALE: You said that, in this whole strategic area, part of your
interest was a Northern Ireland interest. What is that?

POWELL: Because I am sure that it is the potential strategic value of
the island of Ireland, and specifically of the Irish Republic, to the
American alliance, which has been the driving force in the last two
decades, let us say, in an intensification of the effort on the part
of – now this is difficult – on the part of an element in British
Government to being about, somehow, the detachment of Ulster
from the United Kingdom and, somehow, the appearance if not
the reality of an all-Ireland state. [. . .]

'WHY I DON'T BELIEVE WE NEED TO KEEP THE BOMB'

Today on Sunday, 30 November 1986

Peace has reigned in Europe for forty years. In 1948, admittedly, the Soviet Union was foiled by the allied airlift in its attempt to force Berlin by blockade into the communist alliance; and, in 1956 and 1968 respectively, Russia used military force to make sure that Hungary and Czechoslovakia remained within that alliance.

Otherwise, nothing has happened to disturb or threaten the relative positions of the Soviet Union and its former wartime Western allies as at the moment of the German capitulation in 1945.

Why? One undeviating answer to that question has been taken for granted and repeated like an incantation in the countries of the North Atlantic Alliance over all the years between.

Russia, it says, is afraid of the Alliance's arsenal of nuclear weapons.

That is why the bear has put not so much as a paw across the line. If the nuclear arsenal had not existed, superior Soviet forces would have swept across Europe long ago and obliterated the parliamentary democracies of Western Germany, of France and of Britain.

Since almost the whole of that nuclear arsenal is American, it is assumed – the Prime Minister and her colleagues repeat this incessantly – that our safety and that of the other countries of Western Europe depends on the American alliance and American armament.

Notwithstanding this, Britain and France also maintain their own comparatively insignificant nuclear armaments – the so-called 'independent nuclear deterrent' – but only for use in what, without further description or explanation, is called 'the last resort'.

These mini-arsenals have, of course, to be kept up to date: we in Britain do so by replacing them, when they grow obsolete, with the latest commodity we can buy from the United States. That's what Trident is.

I don't believe a word of the whole story. I don't believe that if nuclear weapons had never been invented, the Soviets would have gone to war to occupy and subjugate West Germany, France and Britain even if they had wanted to.

That they do want to seems to me wildly improbable, considering the inconvenience of attempting to digest and amalgamate into the Soviet state systems 160 million Germans and Frenchmen and Britons. It's bad enough for the Russians to have to manage the Poles, the East Germans, the Czechs, the Hungarians and the Rumanians, without taking on that other shower on top.

However, even if they had wanted to, they wouldn't have dared, for one simple overwhelming reason: it would have meant a war they couldn't expect to win. Alliance or no alliance the United States would be dragged into it, as in World War One and Two, and a long war of attrition, fought across the world against the greatest industrial and economic power on earth, is not what the Kremlin is looking for.

While Russia piles up her continental and naval forces to the detriment of her economy, a balance of fear that has nothing to do with nuclear weapons holds the ring in Europe. The Russians may, from our point of view, be pretty nasty people. Mad they are not: and for Russia to provoke a war in the West with all that involves would be the midsummer of madness.

That is the real deterrent. The nuclear deterrent, about which we hear so much, is a pretend deterrent, in which nobody seriously believes. The theory behind it is that if the Soviet Union invaded Western Europe and won a battle or two the United States would initiate an exchange of nuclear attacks at first perhaps limited to Europe (which includes Russia) but soon developing on to an intercontinental scale.

What is incredible about this is the assumption that the United States would choose the devastating consequences to itself of that action in preference to continuing a war which it was likely to win anyhow.

The evidence that this scenario is incredible to the three European nations primarily at risk – West Germany, France and Britain – is to be found in their actual behaviour.

If the West Germans believed it, they would move heaven and earth to put themselves into a position to win rather than lose the opening battles.

The nation of von Moltke and of Ludendorff would not be prevented, at whatever economic cost, from acquiring the forces for the early victory that would alone ransom it from nuclear devastation. As for France and Britain, what is that 'last resort' for which they profess to regard a nuclear weapon of their own as indispensable? What else can it be except the event in which the United States proved reluctant to blow out its own brains?

In providing these independent nuclear deterrents, France and Britain fall victims to their own reasoning. They calculate that in certain circumstances of dire danger to them the United States might decline, when the crunch came, to oblige them by accepting horrific damage to itself.

What they fail to do is to apply the same logic to their own scenario of 'last resort'.

Since our Government has resolutely declined to provide any explanation of what it means by 'last resort', we are left to our own devices to construct it. But it would surely not be unreasonable to assume that an enemy has occupied the continent of Western Europe and stands poised, as Hitler was in the early autumn of 1940, to invade this island.

The question, which no Government spokesman has yet been willing to answer, is whether in these circumstances, with the invasion barges, let us suppose, actually under way – any British government would initiate a nuclear exchange in which the population might be expected to come off second best.

To my belief, the answer would be: 'No, let us fight it out as best we can. If we lose, at least we shall not have destroyed the basis of our future resurgence.'

The same scenario is also helpful for exploring the theory that possession of the nuclear weapon is not meant for use but as a defence against blackmail.

On this theory the enemy high command sends an ultimatum: 'Surrender or else.' Secure in his possession of vastly superior conventional force, the enemy is at liberty to bluff or not to bluff as he chooses.

Suppose, however, that the ultimatum is rejected and the enemy proceeds to inflict a deliberately limited nuclear strike as a specimen of what he can do. The victim, if it has the means of retaliation ('the independent nuclear deterrent' – Trident, let us say), will then face the unacceptable option of preferring unlimited devastation following a subsequent nuclear exchange to the consequences of capitulation after a single nuclear strike.

The Labour Party has resolved to renounce the British 'independent nuclear deterrent' and to require NATO's nuclear deterrent to be no longer based on Britain.

The Labour Party and – if it listens to the Labour Party – the whole country, will find that they cannot stop there. The theory of the nuclear deterrent will have to be re-examined from top to bottom.

I hold that there is good reason to think such a re-examination would lead to its rejection. If it goes much else goes with it. We should not be far from a wholesale reappraisal of Britain's defence and foreign policy and of the nature of the Western Alliance itself.

INDEX

This index is designed to provide a selective guide to the 'Reflections': for example, although *George Wigg* appears in the main text as one of the participants in an 'Any Questions' programme, it has not been thought necessary to provide him with an index entry nor for a passing reference to *Byzantium* in the Inaugural Lecture; but there is, however, an entry for *deterrence*, *death penalty* and one for *Crown in Parliament*.

The lists of selections at the beginning of the sections are printed as the main indications of the nature of the matter that follows.